The Study of Anglicanism

30-50
427-495

9/22 176-187
9/29 249-350 ~~364-377~~

Uniform with this volume:

The Study of Liturgy
SPCK, revised edition 1992

The Study of Spirituality
SPCK, 1986

The Anglican Tradition
Fortress Press, 1991

Documents of the English Reformation
Fortress Press, 1995

The Study of Anglicanism

Edited by
Stephen Sykes, John Booty and Jonathan Knight

Revised Edition

SPCK / FORTRESS PRESS

First published in Great Britain 1988
SPCK
Holy Trinity Church
Marylebone Road
London NW1 4DU

First published in North America 1988
Fortress Press
Box 1209
Minneapolis
Minnesota 55440

Revised edition 1998
Second impression 1999

British Library Cataloguing in Publication Data
A catalogue record for this book is available from the British Library

ISBN 0-281-05175-5

Cataloguing in Publication Data for this book
is available from the Library of Congress

ISBN 0-8006-3151-X

Typeset by David Gregson Associates, Beccles, Suffolk
Printed in Great Britain by Arrowsmiths, Bristol

CONTENTS

Contributors · viii
Preface to the First Edition · x
Preface to the Second Edition · xv
Abbreviations · xvi

PART I *The History of Anglicanism*
1. From the Reformation to the Eighteenth Century · 3
   WILLIAM P. HAUGAARD
2. From the Early Eighteenth Century to the Present Day · 30
   PERRY BUTLER

PART II *The Gospel in Anglicanism* · 55
   LOUIS WEIL

PART III *Authority and Method*
1. Scripture · 87
   REGINALD H. FULLER
2. Tradition, Fathers and Councils · 100
   HENRY CHADWICK
3. Reason · 115
   A. S. MCGRADE

PART IV *Anglican Standards*
1. Prayer Books · 131
   MARION J. HATCHETT
2. The Articles and Homilies · 144
   PETER TOON
3. Ordinals · 155
   PAUL F. BRADSHAW
4. Catechisms · 165
   JAMES HARTIN, revised by JONATHAN KNIGHT
5. Standard Divines · 176
   JOHN E. BOOTY

6. Lex Orandi—Lex Credendi   187
W. TAYLOR STEVENSON
7. Councils, Conferences and Synods   202
FREDERICK H. SHRIVER
8. Canon Law   216
DANIEL B. STEVICK

PART V *Church, Sacraments and Ministry*
1. Doctrine of the Church   249
PHILIP H. E. THOMAS
2. The Fundamentals of Christianity   262
STEPHEN W. SYKES
3. The Laity   277
FREDRICA HARRIS THOMPSETT
4. Initiation   293
DAVID R. HOLETON
5. Holy Communion   308
WILLIAM R. CROCKETT
6. Ministry and Priesthood   321
JOHN WEBSTER
7. Episcopacy   333
RICHARD A. NORRIS

PART VI *Anglicanism in Practice*
1. Anglican Spirituality   351
A. M. ALLCHIN
2. Anglican Morality   364
PAUL ELMEN
3. Anglican Pastoral Tradition   378
O. C. EDWARDS JR
4. Church–State Relations   392
PETER HINCHLIFF
5. Sociology of Anglicanism   405
W. S. F. PICKERING, revised by PETER BRIERLEY AND GRACE DAVIE

PART VII *Prospects*
1. The Ecumenical Future   427
MARY TANNER
2. Non-Anglo-Saxon Anglicanism   446
JOHN S. POBEE
3. What is 'Anglicanism'?   459
PAUL AVIS

4. Anglicanism, *Ecclesia Anglicana*, and Anglican:
   An Essay on Terminology   477
   J. ROBERT WRIGHT
5. Anglicans and Mission   483
   T. E. YATES

Glossary   497
Index   507

CONTRIBUTORS

Stephen Sykes is Bishop of Ely, UK.

John E. Booty is Professor Emeritus of Anglican Studies, School of Theology, University of the South, Tennessee, USA, and Historiographer of the Episcopal Church, USA.

Jonathan Knight is Research Assistant to Stephen Sykes.

William P. Haugaard is Diocese of Chicago Professor Emeritus of Church History, Seabury Western Theological Seminary, Illinois, USA.

Perry Butler is Priest-in-Charge of St George's, Bloomsbury, London and a Fellow of the Royal Historical Society, UK.

Reginald H. Fuller is retired Professor of New Testament at the Protestant Episcopal Theological Seminary, Virginia, USA.

Sir Henry Chadwick is the retired Master of Peterhouse, Cambridge, and formerly Regius Professor of Divinity in the University of Cambridge, UK.

A. S. McGrade is retired Professor of Philosophy at the University of Connecticut, USA.

Marion J. Hatchett is Professor of Liturgics, University of the South, Tennessee, USA.

Peter Toon is President of the Prayer Book Society of the Episcopal Church and a Priest of the Diocese of Quincy, Illinois, USA.

Paul F. Bradshaw is Professor of Theology at the University of Notre Dame, Indiana, USA.

James Hartin (deceased) was Professor of Pastoral Theology and Lecturer in Church History at Trinity College, Dublin, Republic of Ireland.

W. Taylor Stevenson (deceased) was Professor of Theology at Seabury Western Theological Seminary, Illinois, USA.

Frederick H. Shriver is retired Professor of Church History, The General Theological Seminary, New York, USA.

Daniel B. Stevick is Professor Emeritus of Liturgics and Homiletics, Episcopal Divinity School, Cambridge MA, USA.

Philip H. E. Thomas is Vicar of Heighington, County Durham. He held the St. Augustine (Stephen Bayne) Fellowship at Oxford University, 1995–96, UK.

Fredrica Harris Thompsett is Academic Dean and Mary Wolfe Professor of Historical Theology, Episcopal Divinity School, Cambridge MA, USA.

David R. Holeton is Professor of Liturgics at the Charles University, Prague, Czech Republic.

William R. Crockett is Professor of Systematic Theology, Vancouver School of Theology, British Columbia, Canada.

John B. Webster is Lady Margaret Professor of Divinity in the University of Oxford, UK.

Richard A. Norris is Professor Emeritus of Church History, Union Theological Seminary, New York, USA.

A. M. Allchin is Honorary Canon of Canterbury Cathedral, and Honorary Professor in The University of Wales, Bangor, UK.

Paul Elmen is retired Professor of Christian Ethics at Seabury Western Theological Seminary, Illinois, USA.

O. C. Edwards Jr. is retired President and Dean, Seabury Western Theological Seminary, Illinois, USA.

Peter Hinchliff (deceased) was Regius Professor of Ecclesiastical History in the University of Oxford, UK.

W. S. F. Pickering is retired Senior Lecturer in Sociology at the University of Newcastle-upon-Tyne, UK.

Mary Tanner is General Secretary of the Council for Christian Unity, Church of England, London, UK.

John S. Pobee is head of the Department of Ecumenical Theological Education of the World Council of Churches, Geneva, Switzerland.

Paul Avis is Vicar of Stoke Canon, Poltimore with Huxham and Rewe with Netherexe in the Diocese of Exeter; Sub Dean of Exeter Cathedral; and Director of the Centre for the Study of the Christian Church, UK.

J. Robert Wright is St. Mark's-in-the-Bowery Professor of Ecclesiastical History, General Theological Seminary, New York, USA.

T. E. Yates is an Honorary Canon of Derby Cathedral, UK.

PREFACE TO THE FIRST EDITION

The purpose of this collection of essays is to provide the reader with an introduction to the history and ethos of the Churches which constitute the Anglican Communion. This is at once a difficult and controversial undertaking. It is difficult because of the sheer number and variety of aspects which ought to be taken into account; and it is controversial because of the well-known breadth of conviction which Anglicanism has traditionally embraced.

In planning this work, the editors tried to cover as much of the substance of Anglicanism as can be reasonably contained in the pages of one volume. A glance at the table of contents will quickly show the reader what has been included, and what has had to be left on one side. The book begins with a survey of Anglican history from the Reformation onwards—a starting-point which is admittedly controversial and is discussed below. After the two historical chapters, a long contribution, the longest in the volume, considers the way in which the Churches of the Anglican Communion have understood and borne witness to the Gospel which Christ has entrusted to his Church. These two Parts together are foundational for all that follows. First, in Part Three, comes the consideration of Scripture, Tradition and Reason as traditionally constitutive of the Anglican understanding of authority and theological method. These chapters are succeeded by a section which deals with specific Anglican standards (Part Four). Here we treat not merely Prayer Books, The Thirty-nine Articles, and the Ordinals of Anglicanism, but also standard divines—those whom experience has shown to be eloquent interpreters of the faith—councils, conferences and synods, and canon law. Here too we find place for a theological treatment of a theme of great importance to Anglicans, the relation between prayer and belief.

The Churches of the Anglican communion teach and embody both a theory and a practice, which are examined in Parts Five and Six of the book. The doctrines of the Church, the sacraments and the ministry include in their perspective the whole people of God in their vocation and ministry, and the doctrine of the fundamentals of Christianity, beloved of Anglicans, as well as the equally foundational sacraments of baptism and Eucharist and the specific questions of priesthood and the episcopate. The section on

Anglicanism in practice (not that what precedes it is 'mere theory') deals with spirituality, moral teaching, the pastoral tradition and Church-State relations. It is also eminently part of the practice of Anglicanism that its contemporary configuration is subjected to sociological scrutiny. The final section of the book, Part Seven, deals with some prospective issues, ecumenism, the growth of Anglicanism in its newer dioceses, the complex matter of Anglican coherence, and, finally, its attitude to mission.

From this outline it will be apparent that we have not attempted to offer a description of the contemporary Anglican Communion, Province by Province. This has been done in the past,[1] and Bishop John Howe has provided an illuminating picture of aspects of contemporary world Anglicanism;[2] but a general survey of the whole Communion would have been another undertaking altogether and has not been attempted in this volume.

The focus of this work is, rather, upon the sort of 'ism' which Anglicanism constitutes; and that is nothing if not controversial, for a number of obvious reasons. It is notorious that general terms for complex movements in human history (terms like Platonism, Buddhism, Existentialism and so forth) tend to suggest to the reader that a definition is going to be offered which will place the phenomenon in some secure location on the map of human thought. This is always an illusion, and it is one of the advantages of a collected work from many hands that it cannot be presented as though it offered a single perspective on a complex phenomenon. Any bias in our choice of authors, who, we believe, amount to a reasonable cross-section of current Anglican opinion, will have been unconscious.

At the same time it will be obvious that all of us have written from contexts in which there is the leisure to pursue the demanding task of historical enquiry, and these are mostly coterminous with those places in which what is sometimes called 'classic Anglicanism' has taken shape and has flourished.[3] But this sort of account of, and apology for, Anglicanism is unquestionably English in character, accent and idiom. Constructed in seventeenth-century England and strongly revived in the nineteenth century by the Tractarians, it was disseminated throughout the world by the rapid growth of the Anglican Communion. 'Classic Anglicanism' is what many people believe Anglicanism to be; and in giving an account of that phenomenon, we plainly run the risk of lending weight to its ossification, of freezing Anglicanism in its Anglo-Saxon past, or at least of assuming its normativeness.[4]

No one, however, who has considered the massive shifts taking place in world Christianity today, especially the numerical shift from the predominance of the Churches of the northern hemisphere to those of the south, can fail to ask whether the days of 'classic Anglicanism' are not numbered. This, indeed, was one of the questions faced by the Inter-Anglican

Theological and Doctrinal Commission (of which three of our authors were members), and the mature and sensitive clarification of the issue in their first report is relevant to what we have attempted here.[5] They argue that for centuries Anglicanism has been marked by two characteristics; a readiness to be 'located' in a particular culture, place and time, and an acceptance of internal pluralism. They conclude:

> It is natural and appropriate, therefore, that the Anglican communion today should take the form of a fellowship that encourages local and regional initiative and nourishes styles of church life which fit—and address—particular societies and cultures.

This book is compiled in the same conviction. It is intended to assist, not to frustrate, that process of 'location' or 'relocation', by making it easier for Anglicans in all parts of the world to understand how they came to be where they are.

We should not overlook the fact that adaptation of 'classical Anglicanism' has already been taking place in such places as North America, the West Indies and Australasia. Here much of the Englishness of Anglicanism has been qualified by cultures which are in important respects unlike those of the British Isles. But even in those parts of the world experience shows that it is a matter of some difficulty to distinguish between what is Christianly essential and what is accidental, or merely cultural colouring. If the future of the Anglican Communion is to contain still more pluralism than we have already experienced, we are going to have to be equipped and prepared for a lot of frank and informed argument with one another. It is the editors' hope that this book may contribute usefully to that discussion.

But why start a historical account of Anglicanism at the Reformation? Is this not to rule out by editorial fiat any consideration of an issue which many Anglican writers have insisted is central to the identity of Anglicanism, namely its claim to continuity with the whole history of the Church and its special fidelity to the early Church? Did not the see of Canterbury come into existence in the sixth, not the sixteenth century?[6]

In order to do some justice to the issue which is at stake we have to distinguish between claims and observations. It is indeed true that the Anglican reformers of the sixteenth century and the apologists of the seventeenth went to great lengths to *claim* that the Church of England lived in continuity with the undivided Church of the early centuries. It is also the case that many modern Anglicans *claim* that their Church does not constitute or cultivate a separate denominational identity. Despite these claims, one is bound to *observe* that the *de facto* distinctness of Anglicanism begins in the sixteenth century, and that the seventeenth-century apologists devoted the most strenuous efforts to distinguish their Church from both Roman Catholicism and non-conformist Churches.

What we have tried to do as editors is not to prejudge a verdict on the claim, and to ensure that the views of those inclined to stress the continuities are represented together with the opinions of those who affirm the importance of the reforms. At the same time we are keen to embody another proposal, namely that as an 'ism' Anglicanism looks to the future, precisely because it has not decided the question whether the Church must always be what it was in the sixteenth or in the fourth centuries. We agree that Anglicanism, even if we could successfully define it, could not be a definitive form of Christianity. While in the providence of God the Churches of the Anglican Communion may at present still have a witness to bear among the Churches of the Christian world, we can be certain that they must continue to reform themselves in the future, as they have repeatedly done in the past. In that sense we do not have to insist on the perpetuation of 'classic Anglicanism' of the sixteenth, seventeenth or any other century. We are provisional Churches; and in asserting that we do not find ourselves to be distinctive in world Christianity.[7]

The last word, however, must concern a trend which we believe we detect in some Anglican writing of the recent past. This has to do with an apparent willingness to allow Anglicanism to be isolated from the central traditions of world Christianity. It seems as if Anglicans have become rather unwilling to expose their understanding of the Church to the comment of other Christians; and it would be in complete contradiction to the intention of this volume were the result of it to be increased self-satisfaction and isolation.

The book was planned because we perceived a need to bring together in a single volume authoritative essays on the many aspects of the history and ethos of Anglicanism. We were conscious that teachers who prepare students for ministry in the Anglican Church cannot presume on much familiarity with Anglican traditions. We realized too that nowadays many Anglicans find themselves in ecumenical contexts in which they are under pressure to supply explanations for their de facto distinctiveness.

A sense of all these pressures has sustained the editors during the not inconsiderable labour of assembling and editing the volume. But we acknowledge a danger in its outcome, namely a further encouragement to the already detrimental isolation of Anglicanism. As editors we would by no means deplore the existence of courses (and even chairs!) in Anglican studies, but they need to be integrated with all other aspects of the study of the Christian tradition. A careful reader of the footnotes of 'classical' Anglican writers will discover to what an extent those authors were engaged in dialogue with the Fathers of the early Church, with the scholastics of the

Middle Ages, with the leading Protestant Reformers on the continent, and with contemporaries, both Roman Catholic and Protestant, from many countries. It would be a complete negation of the catholicity of that tradition were we now to content ourselves with knowledge of our own great writers, or with the celebration of our own modes of thought in isolation from the concerns of contemporary theology.

What Anglicanism has become in the twentieth century needs to be submitted to the friendly appraisal of many other Christians. Our sense of living in a 'single communion and fellowship' of Christ's religion requires that we give an account of our stewardship of the nurture of those fifty million of today's disciples who live their Christian lives enriched, or impoverished, by our structures and disciplines.

It is in that spirit that we offer this collection of studies to friends in our own and in other traditions, with a prayer

for the good estate of the Catholic Church; that it may be so guided and governed by [God's] good Spirit, that all who profess and call themselves Christians may be led into the way of truth, and hold the faith in unity of spirit, in the bond of peace, and righteousness of life.

(From The 1662 Book of Common Prayer)[8]

STEPHEN SYKES
JOHN BOOTY
November 1987

NOTES TO PREFACE

1 See J. W. C. Wand, *The Anglican Communion: A Survey* (OUP 1948), and G. F. S. Gray, *The Anglican Communion: A Brief Sketch* (SPCK 1958).

2 In *Highways and Hedges: Anglicanism and the Universal Church* (London, CIO Publishing, 1985).

3 The implicit claim to classical status is contained in the well-known work edited by P. E. More and F. L. Cross entitled *Anglicanism: The Thought and Practice of the Church of England, Illustrated from the Religious Literature of the Seventeenth Century* (first published SPCK 1935).

4 In his contribution to this volume Professor John Pobee discusses what he calls 'the Anglo-Saxon captivity of the Anglican Church'; see below, pp. 450–1.

5 See *For the Sake of the Kingdom: God's Church and the New Creation* (published for the Anglican Consultative Council, London 1986).

6 See the discussion of the origins of the term 'Anglican' by Professor Robert Wright, below, pp. 477–81.

7 See, for example, the argument of Christian Duquoc OP, in *Des Églises Provisoires* (Paris, Éditions du Cerf 1985); ET, *Provisional Churches* (SCM 1986).

8 The collect is thought to have been drafted by a former Regius Professor of Divinity (from 1661) and Master of St John's College Cambridge, Peter Gunning, later Bishop of Ely.

PREFACE TO THE SECOND EDITION

The publication of a second edition offers a welcome opportunity to review and improve on the articles in the first edition, especially by updating the bibliography sections in each chapter. The contributors have revisited their own work and most have revisited the work of another. In one case an entirely new article has been written.

The editors note with regret that three of the contributors have died since the last edition. These are James Hartin, Peter Hinchliff and W. Taylor Stephenson. We have looked at their work ourselves and where necessary made minor amendments.

The usefulness of *The Study of Anglicanism* has established itself in the last ten years. The same decade has, however, sharpened the question of how the churches of the Anglican Communion are to develop in response the new conditions and new challenges. One of those challenges is undoubtedly the tendency to drift into an indefinite pluralism of options. Another is the ecumenical challenge to consider, or reconsider, our attitude towards the papacy. Both concern the issue of unity in multiplicity; and one may just as well admit, with all the major confessional families of Christendom, that a convincing model for the resolution of this matter eludes us.

Nothing, however, is gained by ignorance of our traditions, the rock from whence we were hewn. We, therefore, represent these essays, which focus largely on classical Anglicanism, and pray that our church may continue to be, under God, an agent in the reconciliation of divisions in God's church.

STEPHEN SYKES
JOHN BOOTY
JONATHAN KNIGHT
May 1998

ABBREVIATIONS

AB	Anchor Bible
AC	Alcuin Club
ACC	Anglican Consultative Council
ARCIC	Anglican–Roman Catholic International Commission
ASB	Alternative Service Book
BAS	Book of Alternative Services (Canada)
BCP	Book of Common Prayer
BEM	World Council of Churches, Faith and Order Commission, *Baptism, Eucharist, and Ministry*, 1982
CHP	Church House Publishing
CIO	Church Information Office
CMS	Church Mission Society
COPEC	Conference on Politics, Economy, and Citizenship (1924)
CTS	Catholic Truth Society
CUP	Cambridge University Press
DLT	Darton, Longman & Todd
ET	English translation
FE	The Folger Library Edition of the Works of Richard Hooker. Cambridge, MA, 1977–81.
GB	Grove Books. Bramcote
GLS	Grove Liturgical Studies. Bramcote
IATDC	Inter-Anglican Theological and Doctrinal Commission
JTS	*Journal of Theological Studies*, vols. 1–50, new series vol. 1–. Oxford and New York.
LCC	Library of Christian Classics. Philadelphia and London 1953–66
OED	Oxford English Dictionary, Oxford, 1884–1928
OSB	Order of St Benedict
OUP	Oxford University Press
(P)ECUSA	(Protestant) Episcopal Church of the United States of America
PEER	R. C. D. Jasper and G. J. Cuming (eds.), *Prayers of the Eucharist: Early and Reformed.* 2nd edn., New York 1980.

SBT	Society for Biblical Theology
SCM	Student Christian Movement
SL	*Studia Liturgica*. Rotterdam 1962–
SPCK	The Society for Promoting Christian Knowledge
SPG	Society for the Propagation of the Gospel
USPG	United Society for the Propagation of the Gospel
WA	Weimar Ausgabe
WCC	World Council of Churches

PART ONE

The History of Anglicanism

1 From the Reformation to the Eighteenth Century

WILLIAM P. HAUGAARD

THE FIRST AND FORMATIVE CENTURY OF ANGLICANISM: 1509 TO 1611

The Church of England emerged from its first century as an autonomously governed body with a developing character that distinguished it from other European churches. 'Anglicanism', as a term for a particular way of understanding and practising Christianity (see pp. 460f., 477–81), appeared only in the nineteenth century, but a distinctive trajectory of faith and practice was launched 300 years earlier. Anglicanism began to evolve as English people shared in those movements of reformation and counter-reformation which divided the Church of Western Christendom into denominational divisions that have persisted to our own day.

THE ENGLISH CHURCH IN THE FIRST YEARS OF HENRY VIII

Religion in England at the beginning of the sixteenth century was typical of the Christian West. Foreign visitors observing well-attended churches commented favourably on English piety, and this impression was echoed in the popularity of both Latin and English devotional books that flowed from the newly invented printing presses. Deficiencies in religious life which were to evoke drastic change in the Western Church were endemic in England as elsewhere: inadequate instruction of most lay persons, the related low level of the education of most clergy, prevalent satisfaction with minimal conformity and with mechanical participation in liturgical and sacramental life, failure to emphasize the principal themes of Christian faith, widespread sub-Christian superstition especially in the cult of the saints, preoccupation with manipulation of conditions of life after death to ensure a graceful passage through purgatory, and relative decline in the spiritual quality of life in most monastic and other religious orders. Many laity resented the political power of the clergy when they held civil offices, their judicial power in church courts, and, above all, their economic power in managing a significant portion of national wealth in the properties that provided income for clergy and the religious orders.

Two Movements of Protest: Lollardy and Renaissance Humanism

Before the thunder of the continental Reformation began to resound on English shores, prevailing religion was called in question by two movements: one local, covert, and comprised largely of humble men and women; the

3

other international, manifest, and patronized by the highest levels of ecclesiastical and lay society. Lollardy, owing its origin to the fourteenth-century John Wyclif, embraced scattered loosely related coteries of sectarian believers in English towns who read their Bible in English from forbidden manuscripts and denied the priestly authority of the clergy. Such groups were to provide ready seedbeds for Reformation teachings from Saxony and Switzerland that would differ much in substance from that of the Lollards, but would share a common concern for Bible reading, preaching, and a repudiation of much of medieval theology. Renaissance humanism had struck as deep roots in English as in any European soil. Before the turn of the century, John Colet, soon to be Dean of St Paul's in London, returned from studies in Italy with a zeal for biblical studies which he shared with the young lawyer Thomas More and his Dutch visitor Desiderius Erasmus. At the invitation of the newly crowned Henry VIII, Erasmus returned to England where he prepared the text for his influential Greek New Testament. Court and the universities had their circles of scholars and dilettantes who discussed the 'new learning' and its implications for introducing reforms in the teaching and life of the Church. Lollardy and humanism both fostered dissatisfaction with the religious *status quo* in England.

England as a Part of Western Christendom
Geography has often encouraged ambivalence in the relations of England with the rest of Europe, an ambivalence reflected in the life of the English church. When Henry VIII ascended the throne in 1509, England was immersed—as it had been since the Norman conquest—in European secular and ecclesiastical politics; even though English continental territories, once half of France, had been reduced to a tiny enclave around Calais. In spite of growing nationalism and the ineffectiveness of the unifying role of the Western Empire, the medieval ideal of Christendom or the *corpus Christianorum*, comprising western and central Europe and most effectively symbolized by the papal office, persisted: one society, politically and religiously united, ruled by dual hierarchies of civil and ecclesiastical governments. The hierarchies could meld with one another; Thomas Wolsey was unique only in the extent of his power when, in Henry's second decade, he combined the highest offices of Church and state, serving as Lord Chancellor as well as Archbishop of York and special papal legate. As elsewhere, royal and priestly authorities had often clashed, and neither in conflicting theories nor pragmatic resolutions had England differed substantially from continental nations. In part motivated by a pervasive lay anti-clericalism, England's Parliament had been, among nascent European legislatures, uniquely active in championing the royal cause against a church hierarchy

4

whose upper reaches belonged to a foreign papacy. Strains had appeared periodically between the ideal of a united Western Christendom and that of the English kingdom whose identity was effectually expressed when ecclesiastics, nobility and commons joined the sovereign to form the governing 'King-in-Parliament', the corporation of the English nation. The strains might have been contained, had not increasing discontent with prevailing religion provided the impetus for writing the medieval ideal small within the confines of one nation (see pp. 392–405).

English Responses to the Opening of the Continental Reformation

At the beginning of the second decade of Henry's reign, Pope Leo X excommunicated Martin Luther who, in turn, publicly burnt not only the offensive papal bull, but also a copy of the canon law that united the Western Church under papal leadership. Gutenberg's movable type, still only three-quarters of a century old, made possible the flow of Lutheran literature throughout Europe, and some inevitably found its way across the North Sea. Before the end of the decade, these Reformation publications were augmented by the works emanating from Zurich and Basle where a 'Reformed' theology, distinctive from Lutheranism, was developing. The audacious challenges to established religious authority were read with mixtures of relish and horror by those authorities, by university circles, and by literate persons either drawn to reforming convictions or merely intellectually curious. English merchants and reform-minded clerics living and travelling abroad drank the heady wine of the new teachings. In 1524, a young scholarly priest, William Tyndale, sought the freedom of the Continent expressly in order to prepare a vernacular English Bible. The trumpet calls of the continental Reformers evoked scattered but augural resounding chords among English Christians in the second decade of Henry's reign. Lollards, as they became aware of these new religious currents, judged they had found powerful religious allies. Humanists divided: between those like More—and Erasmus—who read in their Bibles a message of Christian unity and opposed the sundering of the Western Church, and those convinced that scriptural teachings demanded reform even at the cost of Western unity.

The initial official responses of the church hierarchy to the rumblings of the continental Reformation were all negative. The Bishop of London publicly burned Tyndale's New Testament when copies appeared in England, and the Archbishop of Canterbury made a futile attempt to buy all surviving copies. Charges of heresy were pressed against those suspected of propagating the new continental teachings, which, in officials' judgements, merged with native Lollardy. The anti-Lutheran work *Assertio Septem Sacramentorum* bore Henry's name as author, and, in appreciation, Leo X granted Henry and his successors the title 'Defender of the Faith'. Thomas More, who had risen in royal service while Wolsey was Henry's chief minister and had aided the King in composing the book, took an increasingly active role in suppressing the continental 'heresies'. He insisted that Tyndale had translated the New Testament in accordance with 'the heresies that himself teacheth and abideth by'.[1] The first two priests to die in England for their Reformation convictions, one primarily as a consequence of More's initiative, went to the stake at the very time More's own conscience was struggling with Henry's anticipated break with Rome.

CONTINUITY AND CHANGE IN CHURCH LIFE FROM 1529 TO 1611

In a thirty-year period from the latter portion of Henry's reign to the opening years of Elizabeth's, no less than six varieties of Christian faith and practice successively prevailed in the English Church. Under Elizabeth and James, pressures for further alterations were to be contained by official policies that would brook no major modification in the norms established. In Anglicanism's formative century, the two periods, one of fluctuating change and the other of tension-laden stability, provided the successive crucibles from which a recognizably distinctive form of Christianity emerged.

Ecclesiastical Independence: Henry VIII

Although concern for religious reform and national interests underlay the motivations for an independent English church, it was Henry's well-known desire to shed Catherine of Aragon in order to marry Ann Boleyn that precipitated the break with Rome. The Pope's canonical doubts about a possible annulment were strengthened by the presence in Rome of the soldiers of Catherine's nephew. The papal predicament, Henry's infatuation with Anne, his rationalized troubled conscience, and national concern for a male heir all combined to motivate the King to press for an exclusively English solution.

 Thomas Wolsey had shown Henry how ecclesiastical and civil authority might be effectively combined. From Wolsey's protégé, Thomas Cromwell, Henry learned to manipulate Parliament to achieve royal goals. A four-year series of parliamentary Acts culminated in 1534 with the declaration that England's king is 'the only supreme head in earth of the Church of England, called *Anglicana Ecclesia*'. The concurrent clerical convocations affirmed that, according to the Scriptures, the Bishop of Rome had no 'greater jurisdiction in England than any other foreign bishop'. In some English eyes, the Church had returned to its ancient pristine condition when it had been 'sufficient and meet of itself, without the intermeddling of any exterior person' to manage its own affairs.[2] The judgement of others, that

6

England had betrayed the unity of Christendom, was reflected in the witness of Thomas More and the respected Bishop John Fisher who were executed for their refusals to acquiesce in the implementation of the parliamentary decisions.

Parliament expressly declared that ecclesiastical independence did not imply any intention 'to decline or vary from [. . .] Christ's Church' concerning 'the Catholic faith of Christendom'.[3] Yet Henry designated Thomas Cranmer to be Archbishop of Canterbury, a priest touched by Lutheranism through his reading at Cambridge and his experience in Germany where he had married a niece of Andreas Osiander a prominent reformer at Nuremberg. By 1540 English monasteries, fixtures of society since the sixth century, disappeared, their wealth to be employed for the public good as the King might define it. If the dissolution of the monasteries was the most significant direct social consequence of the break with Rome, the provision of the vernacular 'Great Bible' which first appeared in 1539 was the most significant religious consequence. Other changes in church life were minor, and official stances on Christian faith and practice remained much as they had been when Henry came to the throne.

Programme of Coherent Protestant Reform: Edward VI
When the nine-year-old Edward VI ascended the throne in 1547, the ruling Privy Council designated by Henry included a majority who favoured reformation. The new king's uncle, the soon-to-be Earl of Somerset, successfully gained control of the Council, and in tandem with Archbishop Cranmer and other fellow councillors began to encourage policies for religious change. Two and a half years later, Somerset was replaced by the less scrupled Earl of Northumberland, and the pace of reforming measures accelerated until they were abruptly halted by Edward's death in 1553.

Initially the Council prescribed homilies and ordered a greater use of English in parish worship. By abolishing chantries for requiem Masses and other church endowments, Parliament transferred a second block of properties into royal and private treasuries. Within two years, Parliament authorized the fully-fledged English liturgy of the 1549 Book of Common Prayer. Three years later, just as the country was becoming accustomed to the new vernacular forms, they were replaced by those of a second Prayer Book, more markedly identifiable with the continental Reformation. Convocation and Parliament formally sanctioned clerical marriage. Reform-minded bishops were appointed to replace those unwilling to support the changing norms. A new doctrinal stance was underscored in 1553 by forty-two *Articles of Religion* (see pp. 144–54) and an accompanying catechism (see pp. 167–71). In six years the Church of England had moved from traditional patterns through two sequential stages of religious reform.

7

Return to Roman Obedience: Mary
Mary Tudor interpreted the widespread rejoicing that greeted her accession to the throne, and the consequent fall of the unpopular Northumberland, as a mandate to return to the 'old religion' which 'God and the world' knew she had 'ever professed from her infancy'.[4] Within a year and a half, successive Parliaments repealed in stages the legislation of Edward and Henry, and Cardinal Reginald Pole absolved the nation from its sin of schism from the Roman see.

Married clergy, the Prayer Book, 'heretical' teachings, even the vernacular Bibles disappeared from public view, and only the largely untouched transfers of property remained of the reforms of the two preceding reigns. The revival of heresy laws brought nearly 300 martyrs to the stake. Other English men and women practised their religion in secret as Lollards had once done, and some 800 fled abroad to Protestant havens. Outwardly, Mary's five-year reign restored the forms of the English church to those of the earlier years of her father's reign. Contrary to Mary's deepest hopes, however, many came to identify the Roman obedience with the stench of burning flesh, with her unpopular marriage to Philip of Spain, and, near the end of the reign, with the loss of Calais. When she died in 1558 Mary, like her brother, had not reigned long enough to stabilize the 'old religion' she would have replanted in English society and in English hearts.

A Stable Settlement of Religion: Elizabeth I
Six months after Mary's death, Paul IV received a report that Elizabeth was torn in religious matters between 'her pernicious learning on the one hand and her fear of losing the State on the other'.[5] The 'pernicious learning' from the reigns of her father and brother had already carried the day, for, from her first week as Queen, the records evidence a consistent determination to repudiate papal authority once again. After the Queen's death, Francis Bacon commented that 'within the compass of one year she did so establish and settle all matters belonging to the church, as she departed not one hair's breadth from them to the end of her life'.[6] Parliament passed legislation that recognized the sovereign as 'supreme governor' of the church and prescribed a third Prayer Book largely based on Edward's second book. Elizabeth issued a set of injunctions governing various details of church life, and these, together with the 1559 Prayer Book (see pp. 138–9) and royal supremacy, undergirded religious policy throughout her reign.

The Council of Trent held its final sessions during the first decade of Elizabeth's reign, and Roman Catholicism, fortified by the vigour of Counter-Reformation spirituality, proved a formidable opponent to the established Church of England. However, English men and women who clung to the 'old ways', and priests who attempted to minister to them, were caught in the dilemma posed by international politics. When in 1570 Pius V excommunicated and formally deposed Elizabeth, he identified English papal adherents as potential traitors. Fanatics who sought to force a return to Roman obedience by foreign invasion or by the assassination of Elizabeth never gained popular support among their coreligionists. Their plots, nevertheless, brought the savage forms of torture and execution reserved for traitors down upon missionary priests who sought, for the cause of religion, to maintain and expand the Roman Catholic community in England.

Even in Elizabeth's first year, it became clear that there were, among reform-minded lay persons and clerics, determined militants who viewed the 1559 Settlement as an interim measure, leading to fuller reform modelled by the continental churches that some of them had known in exile. Militants looked forward hopefully to the 1563 clerical Convocations, but all that emerged was a conservative revision of the Edwardian *Articles of Religion*. Disputes initially centred upon vestments and outward clerical dress. But from 1572 on, a well-organized minority among those who became known as 'Puritans' worked to replace the established episcopal ministry with presbyterian structures in order to implement the discipline and godly order in behaviour and worship that they professed to find in the New Testament. Failing in Convocations, Puritans turned to Parliament where, although they could muster significant support, the Queen repeatedly frustrated their proposals. Elizabeth's death in 1603 left an English church whose character had been both shaped by the 1559 Settlement, by the external struggle with Roman Catholics, and by the internal tensions between supporters of that Settlement and those who judged the Reformation still unfinished in England.

Continued Struggle and Collaboration: First Years of James I

As James VI of Scotland travelled south to assume additional responsibilities as James I of England, he was met by Puritan representatives who hoped that he, raised in the Reformed Scottish Kirk, would bring in the 'due and godly reformation' that Elizabeth had so often blocked. Implementing his initial genial response, James brought bishops and Puritan divines together for a conference in Hampton Court Palace that concluded with the King's ringing support of the bishops and led to the promulgation of the 1604 Prayer Book (see p. 139), which included only minor concessions to Puritan consciences. From the ensuing Convocation, a *Book of Canons* (see p. 221) emerged which largely reaffirmed established norms and left little legal room for Puritan nonconformity.

The conference produced one major fruit: a new translation of the Scriptures. Marian exiles had prepared the 1560 Genevan Bible, and the Elizabethan bishops had produced their own revision in 1568. The bishops

9

and James objected to doctrinally biased explanatory notes in the Genevan work, and Puritans protested inaccuracies in the authorized Bishops' Bible. When Puritans spontaneously broached the idea of a new translation, James enthusiastically entrusted the project to Bishop Richard Bancroft, soon named to the see of Canterbury. Bancroft organized a series of scholarly committees to undertake the work, and staunch upholders of the establishment worked hand in hand with fellow churchmen who longed for further reformation. In 1611, the Authorized or 'King James' Bible appeared, to become *the* Bible for three and a half centuries for all English-speaking Christians except Roman Catholics—perhaps a unique instance in human history in which a committee has produced a literary masterpiece.

The century from Henry VIII's accession to the publication of the King James Bible had been formative in shaping the outlines of a distinctive way of believing and practising the Christian faith.

WORSHIP AND TEACHING IN THE ENGLISH CHURCH

Although Anglicanism has never been easily defined, the weight of most descriptions rests upon the historical ancestry of Anglican Churches through the English Reformation. This merely shifts the question: how can the English Reformation be interpreted? No single dominating personality, no single coherent theological principle, no single developed theological system, no single distinctive vision of community discipline predominated in directing the course of events in England. The English Reformation may be best understood as a *political* occurrence—provided that 'political' be understood to refer not only to civil matters, but to wider human relations as they reflect the varied aspects of community life, including religious practices, convictions and church structures. Continental Reformations were also political in this sense. But the political processes for Lutherans, Reformed and Anabaptists were subordinated to, and/or rationalized by, more clearly articulated and more sharply focused religious grounds that carried wide acceptance by members of these particular church communities. In continental terms, the English process (but not the content) was most akin to that of the Roman Catholic 'Counter-Reformation'.

The two sixteenth-century English leaders with the greatest influence on the eventual character of Anglicanism were the martyred cleric Thomas Cranmer, the primary architect of the Book of Common Prayer, and his goddaughter, the royal laywoman Elizabeth Tudor, whose consistent policies during her long reign allowed the Settlement to shape religious attitudes and convictions. Neither expressly laid out for contemporaries—nor for later scholars—full expositions of their understandings of Christian faith and practice. Whereas, in continental Reformation communities, the theological giants of the respective traditions appeared as the communities were

10

initially formed, the sixteenth-century English theologian most widely read in succeeding centuries was Richard Hooker, who did not publish until the 1590s (see pp. 177–8, 357–9). Hooker, born in Mary's reign, grew to maturity within the Elizabethan church, and he wrote to defend and to explain the church in which he had experienced the gospel and had learned theology. An articulation of the theological stance of the English church came toward the end, rather than at the beginning, of its reformation.

Foundations of New Religious Understandings: Bible and Prayer Book
When Henry VIII in 1538 ordered the English Bible to be placed in parish churches where 'parishioners may most commodiously resort to the same and read it', the theologically conservative monarch supplied the foundation for doctrinal change and a new piety. Initial royal injunctions of Edward's reign built on the foundation by ordering English lections to be read at certain Latin rites and by instructing clergy not to discourage private reading, but to 'exhort every person to read [the Bible] as the very lively word of God' that Christians must 'embrace, believe, and follow, if they look to be saved'.[7] In two years vernacular Prayer Books included English eucharistic lessons and a lectionary for daily offices in which most of the Old Testament was read once, and most of the New three times, yearly. Editions of English Bibles appeared in increasing numbers, and, by the time the King James version (the Authorized Version) was undertaken, the vernacular Scriptures had secured a dominant place in the cultural, educational and political, as well as the religious, life of the nation (see pp. 279–82).

The new ordination rites required priests to teach nothing as 'required of necessity to external salvation', but that which might be 'proved by the scripture'.[8] In Elizabeth's reign, disagreement concerning the application of biblical authority to those things not 'required' for external salvation underlay the conflict between reformers pressing for further change and upholders of the Settlement. The Cambridge Puritan William Perkins expressed the conviction of English militants and continental Reformed that Scripture 'must be our rule and square whereby we are to frame and fashion all our actions'.[9] Like Lutherans who judged that the Bible permitted what it did not expressly prohibit, Hooker argued that 'it is no more disgrace for scripture to have left a number of ... things free to be ordered at the discretion of the Church, than for nature to have left it unto the wit of man to devise his own attire'.[10]

With the exception of a 1544 English Litany, Latin rites remained in place under Henry, but Thomas Cranmer's genius for vernacular liturgy immediately found free reign under Henry's son's government. Royal injunctions and orders accompanying a parliamentary Act for communion in

11

two kinds inserted English sections and devotions in the Latin services, including a general confession which encouraged communions by circumventing preparatory private confession. The Uniformity Act authorizing the 1549 Prayer Book replaced Latin services entirely with English rites allowing fuller congregational participation, reducing the eight monastic offices to public Morning and Evening Prayer, and reforming the eucharistic rite to emphasize communion and to minimize the sacrificial character of the Mass (see pp. 321–7).

Critiques of continental Reformers Martin Bucer and Peter Martyr Vermigli from English university posts, the example of John à Lasco's London strangers' church and conservative interpretations of the new services combined to encourage reformers to see further change. When the 1552 Prayer Book emerged, its rubrics confirmed the replacement of altars with a wooden holy table in the midst of choir or nave, eliminated traditional vestments except for the surplice and the bishops' choir dress, added a penitential tone to the daily offices, and severely reformed the Eucharist, leaving a drastically shorn, but still precatory, canon of consecration (see pp. 308–11).

After the eclipse of liturgical reform under Mary, the 1559 Prayer Book and Elizabeth's orders in the first years of her reign established norms of worship slightly more traditional than those of Edward's final year. Puritan consciences were offended by 'popish' remnants still present in Prayer Book rites: the required vestments, now including the cope; clerical street dress; the draped holy table placed, out of communion, as an altar; unleavened communion bread; crossing of the forehead in baptism; and the ring in marriage. Conscientious nonconformity was common and led to bitter battles in church courts and pamphlet polemics. Puritan-endowed lectureships in some towns provided additional sermons, but, in spite of the dramatic increase of educated preaching clergy from 1559 to 1611, militant reformers continued to bewail clerical 'dumb dogs' who could only read homilies. Congregational reluctance to depart from the customary medieval yearly communion meant that Eucharists were commonly celebrated only quarterly or monthly. Lengthy liturgies of Morning Prayer, Litany, Antecommunion, and sermon or read homily comprised the normal Sunday worship of English congregations. By 1611, a third generation of English men and women were learning and practising their religion within the context of the Prayer Book which, together with the Bible, provided the foundation of religious teachings and piety.

Doctrinal Definitions and Postures

Church authorities under Henry alternately entertained and rejected Protestant teachings, and the reign ended with doctrinal norms encapsulated in

the 1539 Six Articles Act and the 1543 *King's Book*, which affi
slightly modified medieval teachings. At the beginning of Edwaι
Parliament voided the two conservative standards, and the Counc   ⌐ued
the *Homilies* (see pp. 148–9) which were to be read by non-preaching clergy
and included Cranmer's unequivocal assertion of justification by grace
through faith (see pp. 69–77). The Prayer Book reflected these new emphases, and also confirmed traditional doctrine in the use of the Apostles',
Nicene and Athanasian Creeds and in a brief children's catechism. The
forty-two *Articles of Religion* with an appended catechism, published just
before Edward's death, reflected common protestant convictions. Although
echoing many phrases from Lutheran formularies, in understandings of
predestination and the eucharistic presence, the *Articles* were closer to
the Reformed Churches.

John Jewel published in Latin *An Apology of the Church of England* in
1562, seating the church firmly with continental Lutherans and Reformed
in opposition to both Roman Catholic and Anabaptist. Dean Nowell of St
Paul's produced a catechism more heavily indebted to Calvin's Genevan
catechism than to the 1553 English catechism. Although militants failed to
gain confessional status for it in the 1563 Convocation, the bishops later
authorized schoolmasters to employ the catechism in both Latin and English to instruct their charges. The same Convocation remoulded the 1553
Articles into the durable Thirty-Nine Articles, to which clergy were to be
required to subscribe at times of vocational transitions. The new version
emphasized rejection of current Roman Catholicism, weakened the article
on predestination, and, in concert with Prayer Book changes, strengthened
the affirmation of eucharistic presence. Many Calvinists, increasingly concerned to emphasize the decrees of double predestination, found the revised
article too ambiguous. The Articles excluded both transubstantiation and a
minimalist Zwinglianism. Capable of interpretations compatible with eucharistic teachings ranging from those of Bullinger to those of Melanchthon, rigid Lutheranism represented by the 1577 Formula of Concord would
have judged them inadequate. Parliament's 1571 act requiring clerical subscription was claimed by some Puritans to apply 'only' to doctrinal Articles,
excusing them from those concerning polity and order. The unambiguous
canons of the bishops, unratified yet enforced, insisted on the full thirty-
nine.

The latitude of English theological standards was well established during
the half-century after the Settlement. William Perkins developed a well-
formed 'Calvinist' theological system that was influential throughout the
Reformed world. At the same time in the same Church Richard Hooker
provided a theological framework that eschewed systems and grounded its

13

judgments in the authority of Scripture and reason illumined by tradition (see Part Three).

An Articulated Anglicanism: Ecumenical Implications of a Non-Confessional Church

The political and social processes of the formative century of Anglicanism established a national church unique in the Reformation era. Incorporating the fundamental insights of the continental Reformers, the Church of England grounded its religious unity, not in a confessional statement, but in (1) the supremacy of Scripture in matters of external salvation, and (2) an agreed liturgy which, with many *implicit* theological perspectives, contained as *explicit* doctrinal standards only the ancient creeds and a brief children's catechism. The Articles provided teaching standards for the clergy. Laity were directly exposed to the Book of Common Prayer and its scriptural sections; only indirectly did official doctrinal standards touch them as they listened to the official Homilies or to preachers expected to conform to the Articles.

The medieval emphasis on 'sacrament' over 'word' shifted radically in the Reformation. Understanding 'word' to include sermon, all English Reformers regretted—and militants violently condemned—non-preaching priests. Archbishop Grindal, who shared many Puritan concerns, termed sermons the 'ordinary mean and instrument of the salvation of mankind'.[11] Yet Richard Hooker, who could warmly commend sermons as 'Keys to the kingdom of heaven', insisted that scriptural readings, catechetical exercises, and the homilies also qualified as 'preaching'. Hooker wedged his discussion of preaching in between discussions of church buildings and liturgical minutiae; when he turned to the sacraments, he drew back to discuss fundamental christological doctrines:

> It seemeth requisite that we first consider how God is in Christ, then how Christ is in us, and how the sacraments do serve to make us partakers of Christ. ... They which by baptism have laid the foundation and attained the first beginning of a new life have [in the Eucharist] their nourishment and food prescribed for continuance of [that] life in them.[12]

Hooker's balance of word and sacrament is quite different from Grindals's. In spite of the infrequency of eucharistic celebrations in the Elizabethan church and sacramental doctrinal standards held in common with English Puritans, Hooker's understanding of the *role* of sacraments in the Christian life is far closer to their place in traditional Catholicism.

In a period in which most Western churches were narrowing standards of orthodox belief and practice, the official policies of the Church of England remained remarkably open to wider understandings. The devout and the indifferent, traditionalists and Puritans, learned and illiterate, lived out their faith within one framework. Both Roman Catholics without and militants within the communion of the national church might dissent, but increasing numbers of English clerics and lay persons had become convinced that, in words Elizabeth had written to Emperor Ferdinand, they followed 'no novel and strange religions, but that very religion which is ordained by Christ, sanctioned by the primitive and Catholic Church and approved by the consentient mind and voice of the most early Fathers'.[13] In this context, Richard Hooker could suggest that the bloodshed and waste of the divisions of 'Christendom' might induce churches 'on all sides' to enter into 'such consultation as may tend to the best reestablishment of the whole Church of Jesus Christ'. He was confident that the 'calm and moderate' course of the English Reformation would 'serve as a profitable direction' for that ecumenical endeavour.[14]

VISIONS OF A UNITIVE SOCIETY: TEMPORAL AND SPIRITUAL GOVERNMENT

The medieval vision of a unitive society continued in various forms among the established separated churches of Western Christendom. With political theories grounded in theology, various configurations of coercive authority linked the spiritual and the temporal within societies that constituted both political and religious units. The distinctive English configuration was characterized by royal supremacy and traditional episcopal church government.

Royal Supremacy and Parliament

Parliament established royal supremacy in English statute law even though, in theory, the legislators had only recognized what they believed 'justly and rightfully is and ought to be'.[15] English legislative authority lay with the vaguely defined 'King-in-Parliament', and although bishops already represented the spiritual estate in the House of Lords, some judged the clerical Convocations to be adjuncts to Parliament. According to Hooker, ' the very essence of all government' depended upon Parliament 'together with the Convocation annexed', a body consisting of the king and all his subjects, present either in person or by representation. The Henrician laws provided the king with the same legislative initiative and veto over canons of Convocation that he held over statutory legislation in Parliament. Hooker denied that 'the clergy alone' ought to be able to legislate laws for laity; rather the Crown and the temporal lords and commons, together with the spiritual estate, were required to provide the 'general consent' of the whole church necessary 'to define [its] regiment' in coercive law[16] (see pp. 393–5).

Parliamentary statutes introduced the major structural changes of the English Reformation. Historians are still debating how the balance con-

15

tained in the phrase 'King-in-Parliament' changed in favour of the representatives in the course of the sixteenth and seventeenth centuries. The degree of an actual power shift in Elizabethan days was probably minimal, but, on occasion, Protestant militants in the Commons under Elizabeth acted as though their right of free speech included a right *to initiate* religious legislation. Even privy councillors at times encouraged legislative proposals that would have modified the religious settlement. As the causes of Puritanism and parliamentary democracy began to converge, the Queen repeatedly employed her royal prerogative to block consideration of such Puritan proposals.[17] Elizabeth, forbidding Parliament to modify the terms of the 1559 Settlement, looked to Convocation as the proper arena for religious initiatives.

Royal Supremacy: Limits and Exercise

In spite of centuries of royal direction of church affairs and theories of imperial authority stretching back to Constantine, when the king was declared 'supreme head', no clear precedent dictated either the limits of royal supremacy or the means by which it might be exercised. The reigns of Henry and Edward produced experimental models, but only in the long rule of Elizabeth did a workable pattern emerge that was, with diminishing degrees of skill, exercised by her Stuart successors.

Henry VIII's insatiable vanity encouraged grandiose images of royal supremacy that lacked definition of limits. The exercise of supremacy by Edward's Council and its theoretical repudiation by Mary made extravagant claims less tenable. When Elizabeth substituted 'governor' for 'head', she cleared the title of implications stemming from its Pauline imagery. Her Injunctions repudiated any claim to 'the authority and power of ministry of divine offices', and the Supremacy Act denied the Crown's right to define any heresy but that determined by plain scriptural words or the first four ecumenical councils, assigning more subtle doctrinal definitions to lay and clerical orders in Parliament and Convocation. What the Queen held was, as the *Articles* put it, 'the chief government of all estates', ecclesiastical and civil.[18] Whereas continental Lutheran and Reformed deprecated what they judged an erroneous sacerdotalism in the distinction between estates spiritual and temporal, English royal supremacy was based on that distinction. Throughout Europe, religion was expected to be enforced by police powers; in England, as Hooker described it, the monarch exercised that coercive authority 'over all both persons and causes', but she did so by law whose 'bounds and limits' were known.[19] The limits might be fuzzier than Hooker's statement suggests, but the fact of limits was clearly acknowledged.

Until Henry executed Thomas Cromwell, he delegated his new authority to his chief minister. Appropriating the monasteries, issuing royal injunctions, or supervising the English Bible, Cromwell acted as a lay 'vicegerent' for the king's jurisdiction ecclesiastical. In Edward's reign, the Privy Council wielded royal supremacy on the boy's behalf, making day-to-day decisions on church matters alongside other business. Cranmer held a key voice in religious affairs, but the net effect tended to reduce the church to a governmental ministry of religion. Elizabeth avoided the indiscriminate mingling of ecclesiastical and civil affairs by exercising her supreme governorship primarily through commissions authorized by the 1559 Act. Her chief instrument was the central Ecclesiastical Commission at London, which always included the Archbishop of Canterbury, the Bishop of London, other higher clerics, and a clutch of prominent lay persons. The governmental instruments of the church maintained their own identity which was not erased by the many conjunctures at national and local levels. Archbishop Whitgift might serve on the Council and privy councillors on church commissions as 'convenient and meet' interlocking directorates but when the Queen formally exercised her governorship of the church, the channels she employed remained distinct from those of the state.[20]

Structures of Church Ministry and Government

Those Puritans who looked to Geneva sought 'an equality of ministers' instead of 'an archbishop or lord bishop', a 'godly Signor' in every congregation instead of 'chancellors, archdeacons, officials, commissaries, proctors, summoners, church wardens, and such like'; and a 'deaconship' which was not 'confounded with the ministry'.[21] Puritan dismay at the structures of their national church eloquently testifies to the continuity of medieval forms of ministry and government through the English Reformation. The organizational life of provinces, dioceses, cathedrals and parishes with their varied officials, courts and procedures remained as it had been before 1534. Canon law, although drastically modified by repudiation of the papacy, remained in force except as cancelled by specific statutory and canonical legislation or by exercise of royal supremacy.

The medieval system of patronage prevailed. The dissolution of monasteries significantly increased the proportion of lay patrons as parish livings passed to them from the Crown. Crown, nobility, bishops, various collegian bodies and local gentry appointed clergy to posts whose income often bore little relation to the responsibilities of the cure. The Crown continued to name the candidates whom cathedral chapters were expected to elect to the episcopates, but no longer could appeals to Rome frustrate the royal will. Edwardian legislation, by which the monarch named bishops by simple letters patent, proved short-lived, and the Elizabethan laws returned to the traditional procedures.

The English church, in dropping the subdiaconate and minor orders, gave prominence to the threefold ministry of bishops, priests and deacons. The Ordinal insisted that a diligent reading of 'holy scripture and ancient authors' would testify to the continuity of these orders from the Apostles' times, but neither it nor the relevant Articles defined the degree to which such continuity might be essential to the Catholic integrity of the church.[22] Initial responses to presbyterian militants argued only that episcopal polity was permissible; towards the end of the century, an increasing number of voices insisted that episcopacy had a clearer scriptural as well as a traditional mandate. Hooker regarded episcopal ordination as 'the ordinary institution of God', but acknowledged that examples of occasional 'exigence of necessity' made it impossible to urge that 'without exception' ordinations required 'a lineal descent of power from the Apostles by continued succession of Bishops'[23] (see pp. 333–47).

The Vision of Coherent Christian Faith and Practice in a Unitive Society

Non-confessional teaching and prescribed liturgical practice, with their implications for future ecumenical outreach, were contained within an intensely national church community which did not easily separate loyal citizenship from communicant membership in the Church of England. Significant numbers of committed clerical and lay persons who sought tighter doctrinal and disciplinary standards and looser liturgical strictures, nonetheless, urged their reforms from within. Only a handful of Protestant separatists and a somewhat larger scattered Roman Catholic community attempted loyally to support their sovereign while they rejected the communion of the national church.

Royal supremacy provided the capstone of interlinking structures of civil government and traditional Catholic order. Crown and Parliament provided a means for laity to participate in religious decisions bearing upon the whole church. The future constitutional struggle between Crown and Parliament, deeply involving religion, had begun to emerge in the initial formative century of Anglicanism. The momentum of Elizabeth's skilful use of royal supremacy and handling of parliamentary dissent carried over into James' reign. A coherent Anglicanism, centered on Bible and Prayer Book, had emerged within the national church. The King James Bible, reflecting scriptural authority, royal patronage, national cultural achievement, wide collaborative execution, and episcopal leadership symbolizes the evanescent vision of coherent Christian faith and practice capturing the wholehearted allegiance of a people in a unitive society.

MAINTENANCE OF AN ARTICULATED FAITH AS THE VISION FADES IN THE SECOND CENTURY OF ANGLICANISM: 1611–1738

Both on the Continent of Europe and in Britain, seventeenth-century wars under religious banners and the dawning 'Enlightenment' generated increasing religious scepticism and the increasing tendency to move religious issues to the periphery of political life. When the Evangelical Revival, marked by John Wesley's conversion experience in 1738, emerged, this most powerful religious movement in and out of the established church evolved without the participation of civil authority (see pp. 33–5). In 1611, however, the vision of the unitive society still dominated the understanding of religion in English minds and hearts.

CONTINUITY AND CHANGE IN CHURCH LIFE FROM 1611 TO 1738

The struggle between militant reformers and supporters of the establishment dominated English religious history from the middle of the reign of James I until the 1689 Toleration Act. Religion provided the focus for the constitutional struggles and civil war between King and Parliament, dramatically marked by the execution of Charles I, Oliver Cromwell's Commonwealth, the Restoration, and the Glorious Revolution that brought William and Mary to share England's throne. Gentry and mercantile classes, growing in political and economic strength, were changing the social texture of the nation. From Queen Anne's 1702 accession and under her Hanover successors, party politics dominated an ascendant Parliament. Deism of the 'Age of Reason' informed and challenged theologians, the Industrial Revolution began to channel the national economy and demography, and religious pluralism, although neither warmly embraced nor justly implemented, became a legalized reality in the national scene.

Increasing Polarization: James I (Later Years) and Charles I

James I, until his death in 1625, maintained the alliance of crown and mitre firmly forged at the opening of his reign. Clashes between the royal will and the endemically Puritan House of Commons occurred sporadically in matters of conscience, most notably over James' opposition to sabbatarian prohibitions of 'lawful recreations and honest exercises' on Sunday.[24] His intermittent easing of penalties against Roman Catholics also aroused militant anger, which peaked as he negotiated to marry Prince Charles to continental Catholic princesses. In his first years Charles I sought to quell an inherited theological dispute with a declaration, subsequently prefixed to the *Articles of Religion*, ordering that they be taken 'in the literal and grammatical sense', prohibiting any public claim which insisted that

19

one's 'own sense' constituted their meaning.[25] Three months later a Commons committee endorsed a strict Calvinist interpretation of predestination to be *the* 'orthodox doctrine of our Church'. In response to this and other signs of parliament's independence, Charles determined to rule without the legislative assembly.

He avoided assembling Parliament until 1640, when his attempt to impose an Anglican-like liturgy on Scotland had led to war requiring taxes that only legislators could authorize. Bonds that had made 'King-in-Parliament' a workable governing principal were stretched too far, and within two years civil war engulfed the land. From the beginning of Charles' reign, William Laud had been his principal ecclesiastical adviser and, from 1633, Archbishop of Canterbury. Puritans bitterly resented Laud and the increasingly dominant faction of clerics who, in Puritan eyes, promoted 'popish' doctrines and ceremonies and enforced conformity with relentless severity. Gentry, resentful of government strictures on land enclosures for grazing, and common lawyers, protesting the civil law procedures of prerogative courts, proved significant allies of Puritans and parliamentarians who together struggled against 'tyranny' in church and state.

Anglicanism Disestablished and Restored

The executions of Laud in 1645 and of the King four years later punctuated the successive religious changes imposed by new authorities. By Laud's death, episcopacy, the Book of Common Prayer, and the *Articles of Religion* had been replaced under parliamentary ordinances by a presbyterian ministry, a reformed *Directory of Public Worship*, and the majestic Calvinist *Westminster Confession of Faith*. By Charles' death, the dedicated General Oliver Cromwell had repudiated the rigid imposition of presbyterianism in favour of the policies of the 'Independents'. In Cromwell's Commonwealth, congregations might determine their forms of Christian teaching and worship, provided that 'this liberty be not extended to popery or prelacy', to neither Roman Catholicism nor Anglicanism.[26]

Continental observers might conclude that Anglicanism no longer existed. Prayer Book religion, however, lived on both openly at the exile court of Charles II and more furtively in England as approximately a quarter of beneficed English clerics refused to conform. Some wrote in its defence, and many served as tutors or chaplains in royalist households. They and conforming sympathizers employed Prayer Book forms wherever they might elude governmental zeal.

The Convention Parliament which recalled Charles II in 1660 was dominated by Presbyterians disillusioned by the religious and political chaos of the Commonwealth, but the new 'Cavalier' Commons, elected the following year, contained a solid majority nurtured by Anglican loyalists. Together with solidly Anglican Convocations, the legislators followed the lead of Lord Clarendon, architect of Charles' return, and passed laws to assure that both Prayer Book liturgies and episcopal leadership and ordination would be restored to the Church. Effectively separating many conscientious Puritans from the national church, the statutes provided severe penalties for public nonconforming worship and ministry.

The Church of England in a Pluralistic Society

Charles II's 1685 deathbed reception into the Roman Church and, much more, his brother James II's open espousal of Roman Catholicism alarmed all English Protestants. Although James promised that his private religion would not compromise his duties as 'supreme governor', increasingly Romanizing measures reached a pinnacle in 1688 when he ordered the clergy to read a declaration suspending 'all manner of penal laws' against Roman Catholics and other Nonconformists.[27] The defiance of Archbishop Sancroft and six other bishops won them imprisonment in the Tower of London and overwhelming popular support. Their acquittal led inexorably to the flight of James and the welcoming of his daughter Mary and her Dutch husband William. Parliament declared them joint monarchs; the legislature had won senior status in the corporate sovereignty of England's 'King-in-Parliament'.

As an ironic consequence of the Glorious Revolution, some 400 clergy, including Archbishop Sancroft and four other bishops who had defied James in the Tower, were separated from the ministry of the national church. These 'Nonjurors', regarding their earlier oaths to James as a personal obligation, refused to swear allegiance to the new sovereigns. Schism was perpetuated with the consecration of new bishops, and the Nonjuring clerics, with a tiny group of lay adherents, continued for a hundred years as a curious non-established Anglican aberration.

The substantial national consensus against James' policies, together with William's Reformed allegiance, created a favourable climate for the Toleration Act granting freedom of worship to all dissenting Trinitarians except Roman Catholics. As England moved into the eighteenth century, religious issues no longer remained central concerns of national politics. Mary's sister Anne, who acceded to the throne in 1702, was consistently solicitous of the Church, but her succeeding Hanover cousins, the Lutherans George I and George II, fulfilled their church responsibilities in a more perfunctory manner. The civil rights of dissenters to hold public office were still restricted, but the English 'constitution' now incorporated religious toleration, increasingly extended de facto to Roman Catholics and nascent Unitarians. The Church of England remained uniquely established, but in an acknowledged religiously pluralistic society.

21

Beginnings of Anglicanism outside England

Anglicanism was present in the rest of the British Isles and some overseas territories. Although the four Welsh dioceses were integrally part of the English Province of Canterbury, Welsh translations of the Bible and Prayer Book and Elizabeth's appointment of Welsh-speaking bishops had helped to preserve a cultural identity which subsequent sovereigns failed to nurture.

The episcopal office had not been totally eliminated from the Reformed Church of Scotland until Charles I's anglicizing policy firmly linked nationalism and Presbyterian discipline. Charles II reintroduced bishops into Scottish polity, all of whom became Nonjurors in 1689, separated from the national church with a small band of followers. Links forged with English Nonjurors encouraged the development of a recognizable Anglicanism in the Episcopal Church of Scotland.

Ireland's subservient Parliaments in the sixteenth century dutifully followed English Reformation precedents, but local struggles against England firmly linked the Reformation 'Church of Ireland' with foreign rule. A Gaelic Bible and Prayer Book were not forthcoming until the seventeenth century. Retaining all the ancient churches and foundations, the Church of Ireland retained only a small minority of Irish people, augmented by Protestant immigrants given land in the wake of the ruthless suppression of Irish support for James II in 1690.

As English explorers, traders and colonists travelled abroad from the sixteenth century onwards, they carried their church with them. By the early eighteenth century, Church of England congregations were dotted around the Caribbean islands and the north Atlantic coast from Newfoundland to Georgia, and were formed in territories of the East India Company on that subcontinent of Asia. The Bishop of London, with nominal jurisdiction over these congregations, exercised little supervision. A beginning of support and oversight was made through the societies for 'the Promotion of Christian Knowledge' and 'the Propagation of the Gospel', founded about 1700 by Thomas Bray, who had briefly served as bishop's commissary in Maryland. The royal charters of both mentioned evangelization of the inhabitants of the far-flung regions; but, apart from sporadic beginnings of missions to native Americans and African slaves in the Western hemisphere and support of the Royal Danish Lutheran missions in southern India, most of the efforts of the societies were directed toward settling 'the state of religion ... among our own people' abroad.[28] Anglicanism was still almost exclusively British.

WORSHIP AND TEACHING IN THE ENGLISH CHURCH

Throughout the turbulence of the second century of Anglicanism, the King James Bible and the Prayer Book remained the foundations of worship and doctrine in the English Church, and the Thirty-Nine Articles provided the clergy with teaching guidelines. Church leaders under Charles I continued to block Puritan attempts to 'complete' the Reformation, and militants, noting what they judged fresh doses of 'popery', redoubled their efforts to reshape the national church. Their short-lived victory only exacerbated tensions within the restored church. In addition to depriving it of dedicated clergy and laity, the subsequent departure of many Puritans to form dissenting denominations ended efforts to conform the Church of England to continental Reformed patterns. The doctrinal breadth of the English formularies, however, continued to encourage theological variety within the national church, as Anglicans entered the eighteenth century as the established—but not exclusive—representative of the Church of Jesus Christ in England.

Varieties of Prayer Book Worship

Although the Prayer Book rites fixed the words of worship and specified some of its ceremonial, its setting and performance could vary considerably. In the early seventeenth century, elaboration of ceremonial became more common. Laud first encouraged and then ordered Holy Tables to be left for Communion in the traditional place of the altar, fenced off by rails. The use of candles and incense, care for existing crucifixes and paintings and refurbishment with new ones, more elaborate vocal music and organs, bowing towards the altar and clergy vested in richly ornamented copes more frequently characterized Anglican worship, to the dismay of Puritans. The Eucharist became celebrated not only more solemnly, but more frequently as 'the principal office of God's service', as one scholarly priest put it.[29]

Two opposing liturgical patterns of Prayer Book revision were urged at the Restoration. Charles II sponsored a conference to attempt to design a Prayer Book acceptable to both Presbyterians and Anglicans, while an ad-hoc Catholic-minded group prepared a liturgy which looked something like the first 1549 Prayer Book. A few modest revisions in both directions were granted, but these and the many uncontroversial minor changes left the 1662 Prayer Book solidly in the Elizabethan tradition, 'the mean between two extremes' as the preface put it.

The 1661 ad-hoc proposal, more fully reflecting pre-Reformation patterns, drew from the 1637 liturgy that Charles I had attempted to impose on the Scots. Nonjurors, both in Scotland and England, employed these and other sources in scholarly liturgical experimentation. In the established church, eighteenth-century worship would be judged 'dull' by most moderns. A small minority of clerics, known as 'High Church', kept up weekly Eucharists and public daily Morning and Evening Prayer, but ceremonial enrichments of like-minded predecessors a century earlier had ceased to distinguish them from other clerics. In most English parishes, the Eucharist was celebrated quarterly, and parishioners continued to attend lengthy Sunday morning services of Morning Prayer, Litany, Antecommunion, and sermon.

Doctrinal Debate and Latitude

Official doctrinal formularies, grounded in Scripture and the agreed liturgy, remained unchanged. Clergy and others with teaching responsibilities subscribed to the Thirty-Nine Articles, and, in spite of Puritan demands, Charles I's insistence on the 'literal and grammatical sense', with its implications for interpretive flexibility, eventually carried the day.

As clerical educational norms rose, Puritans no longer protested the 'dumb dogs' without the ability to preach, but those who would 'vent what errors they will and neglect preaching at their pleasures'.[30] Such 'errors' often touched predestination, which had become increasingly important to the international Reformed community. The 1618 Dutch Synod of Dort condemned 'Arminians' who sought to modify the developed Calvinist doctrine of election, and Puritans used the heretical label to mark English clerics who strayed from Calvinist orthodoxy and whose liturgies smacked of 'popery'. 'Caroline Divines' has come to designate seventeenth-century English church leaders, who might adhere or not to much of Calvin's theology, but who would have agreed with Laud that an *unqualified* doctrine of eternal reprobation makes 'the God of all mercies to be the most fierce and unreasonable tyrant in the world'.[31] Like Cranmer, Jewel and Hooker before them, in the interpretation of Scripture the Carolines gave special, but not unqualified authority to the writers of early Christian centuries, and cited them more frequently than most continental Protestant theologians (see pp. 110–13).

Fifteen centuries of Catholic tradition and sixteenth-century Reformation emphases were both easily identifiable strains in early seventeenth-century English theology, but the third strain, reason, historically related to the Renaissance, became increasingly visible (see pp. 115–17).

Great Tew, an estate near Oxford, was the scene of informal discussions in pre-Civil War years by a group of intellectually acute clerics and lay persons, some of whom became leaders in the Restoration church. Repudiating Calvinist dogmatism, members of the circle also distanced themselves in varying degrees from Laud's ecclesiastical policies. During and after the Civil War, reason found other champions in a group of Cambridge dons who, nurtured in Puritan colleges, had found the doctrine of the decrees of election 'the most mischievous' news ever 'communicated to the world'.[32] Deeply attached to Neoplatonic philosophy and mysticism, these 'Cambridge Platonists', repelled by whatever they judged superstition or unreasoned dogmatism, insisted that 'in the use of reason and the exercise of virtue, we enjoy God'.[33]

Increasingly attractive to men and women wearied by killing and strife in the name of the Prince of Peace, these 'Latitudinarian' teachings drew many younger clerics in the Restoration Church. When Nonjuring consciences cleared the episcopal bench of its most stalwartly Catholic-minded bishops, William filled the gap with Latitudinarians. The Church of England entered the eighteenth century with a leadership sympathetic to the intellectual climate of the 'Age of Reason'. Deism challenged traditional Christianity, arguing for a God known only through creation, not by revelation. Bishop Joseph Butler, in his *Analogy of Religion, Natural and Revealed* (1736), turned the deists' weapons against them by arguing the fundamental reasonableness of Christian claims, an apologetic *tour de force* unsurpassed in the European scene of the times.

Comprehension and Its Limits

Key decisions made in Anglicanism's second century included its reaffirmation of the Prayer Book and its consistent refusal to become a 'confessional' church by narrowing doctrinal boundaries. Until the heightened bitterness under Charles I, the English Church kept most Protestants within its communion including many unhappy with much of its official stance. In these protesters' eyes, insistence on Catholic traditions embedded in the liturgy and form of ministry caused the schismatic separations. Yet these very elements helped to preserve possibilities of ecumenical outreach in other directions. In the bitterness of Catholic/Protestant relations of these centuries, when Puritans identified Rome with 'Antichrist', Hooker and the Carolines maintained that although not a 'right' church in all her teaching and practice, the Roman Church was nonetheless a part of the 'true' Catholic church. As the limits of comprehension, drawn tighter by the complex strains in English society, were reached, the Church of England lost an important and vigorous sector of its constituency, but its trajectory for the future was firmly established in the direction on which the Elizabethan Settlement had launched it and for which Hooker had provided a theological foundation.

FALTERING VISIONS OF A UNITIVE SOCIETY

The unitive society assumed by sixteenth-century Reformers proved to be illusory in the second century of Anglicanism. The vision, however, did not easily fade, and the church which had embraced the vision groped toward a foundation resting instead on its understanding and practices of Christianity. Even though committed Anglicans linked religion with hopes for royal restoration during the Commonwealth, they practised Anglicanism apart from the structures of national government. Nonjurors, in spite of their schismatic status, provided a later example of non-established Anglicanism. As constitutional and societal changes took place, Anglicans began to develop an understanding of their religious identity no longer dependent upon their cultural and national identity.

Royal Supremacy and Parliament

By 1738, English sovereignty had shifted from the Crown's side of the 'King-in-Parliament' to the legislators', marking a process which would eventually lead to the investment of Parliament with almost all real power. Royal supremacy could not remain as it had been theoretically envisaged and practically exercised under Elizabeth. With the most recent supreme governors a Roman Catholic, a Dutch Calvinist, and two German Lutherans, thoughtful Anglicans could not but judge a relatively modest role appropriate for royal supremacy in the life of the church. The central Ecclesiastical Commission of Elizabeth's reign had increasingly functioned as a judicial body known as the 'Court of High Commission' whose reputation for penal severity reached its apex under Charles I. This agency of royal supremacy was not revived at the Restoration. The staunchly Anglican Cavalier Parliament, in fact, effectively sheared the supremacy of much of its authority by placing most of the enforcement of religious legislation in the hands of government authorities.

The monarch's need to convoke the Convocations at the times of Parliament evaporated when, by tacit agreement in the wake of the Restoration, clergy began to pay ordinary parliamentary taxes in place of the Convocation subsidies. After rancorous disputes between a lower house dominated by 'High Church' clerics and Latitudinarian bishops, George I, in 1717, ended the meetings of Convocations, effectively silencing the clerical appendage to Parliament envisaged in Tudor theory (see p. 15). Bishops continued to sit in the House of Lords, still an equal partner of Commons, and with the advent of organized parties of Whigs and Tories in effective control of Parliament and the Crown's ministries, the episcopal block of votes became increasingly crucial. Not only were bishops absent from their dioceses for longer periods at frequent parliamentary sessions, but party advice increasingly determined royal choices for the episcopal bench. With royal supremacy reduced, Convocations dormant, and bishops immersed in party politics, the machinery of church government was more subservient that at any other time to the established civil government.

Structures of Church Government and Ministry

The medieval systems of church courts, patronage, and provincial and diocesan organization maintained their place in English church life.

26

Queen Anne directed clerical taxes, transferred by Henry from papacy to Crown, to her 'Bounty', a fund to alleviate the grosser inequities in the inherited medieval system of clerical incomes. The eclipse of the Convocations eliminated effective clerical consideration of church needs in a time of the turbulent economic and social changes of the Industrial Revolution.

Episcopal polity was rapidly reasserted at the Restoration, and, in spite of presbyterian expectations and royal promises, there was no compromise on the requirement of episcopal ordination. With the departure of Protestant dissenters, protests against episcopal government within the church ceased. However, in spite of confident assertions of the importance of 'apostolic succession' in the episcopal office, nearly all seventeenth-century Anglicans qualified their claims for episcopacy, as Hooker had done, by a recognition that circumstantial necessity might dictate another course. One such writer did so by distinguishing 'the true nature and essence of the Church' which non-episcopal Churches might claim, and 'the integrity or perfection of a Church' which demanded traditional Catholic order.[34] Many Latitudinarians, while thoroughly supporting episcopacy, would have rated it of much less importance for the 'integrity' of a Christian community.

Coherent Faith and Practice in an Increasingly Pluralistic Society

Religion and church life shared in the radical changes that touched human life on this globe in the years between the appearance of the King James Bible and the conversion of John Wesley. Not only was the vision of an all-inclusive national Church shattered, but public repudiation of Christian faith became a viable possibility for educated English as for other Europeans. Historians may debate whether the survival of a distinctively recognizable Anglicanism through this period better testifies to the integrity of its Christianity or to the tenacious persistence of entrenched institutions, but Anglicanism's adaptation to its changing environment evoked courage and searchings of heart from many committed to its appropriation of the Christian gospel. The Anglicanism shaped in its first century continued on its trajectory through times of social and political change in the seventeenth and early eighteenth centuries. Its adherents faced adaptations of even more momentous proportions in the years ahead.

BIBLIOGRAPHY

Booty, J., *John Jewel as Apologist of the Church of England*. SPCK, London, 1963.

Collinson, P., *Archbishop Grindal: The Struggle for a Reformed Church*. Jonathan Cape, London, 1979.

Collinson, P., *The Religion of Protestants: The Church in English Society 1559–1625*. Clarendon Press, Oxford, 1982.

Cragg, G. L., *Freedom and Authority: A Study of English Thought in the Early Seventeenth Century*. Westminster Press, Philadelphia, 1975.

Davies, Julian, The Caroline Captivity of the Church: Charles I and the Remoulding of Anglicanism, 1625–1641. Clarendon Press, Oxford, 1992.

Dickens, A. G., The English Reformation. Batsford, London, 2nd ed., 1989.

Doran, Susan and Durston, Christopher, Prince, Pastors, and People: the Church and Religion in England, 1529–1689. Routledge, London, 1991.

Duffy, E., The Stripping of the Altars: Traditional Religion in England 1400–1580. Yale, New Haven CT and London, 1992.

Green, I., The Reestablishment of the Church of England 1660–1663. OUP 1978.

Haugaard, W. P., Elizabeth and the English Reformation. CUP 1968.

Haigh, C. (ed.), The English Reformation Revised. CUP 1987.

Haigh, C., English Reformations: Religion, Politics, and Society under the Tudors. Clarendon, Oxford, 1993.

Higham, F., Catholic and Reformed. A Study of the Anglican Church 1559–1662. SPCK, London, 1962.

Jones, N. L., Faith by Statute. Parliament and the Settlement of Religion. Royal Historical Society, London, 1982.

Lake, P., Moderate Puritans and the Elizabethan Church. CUP 1982.

Lake, P., Anglicans and Puritans? Presbyterianism and English Conformist Thought from Whitgift to Hooker. Allen & Unwin, London, 1988.

McAdoo, H. R., The Spirit of Anglicanism: A Survey of Anglican Theological Method in the Seventeenth Century. A. & C. Black, London, 1965.

MacCulloch, D., Thomas Cranmer: A Life. Yale, New Haven CT and London, 1966.

Scarisbrick, J. J., The Reformation and the English People. Blackwell, Oxford, 1984.

Spurr, John, The Restoration Church of England, 1646–1689. Yale, New Haven CT, 1991.

Tyacke, N., The Anti-Calvinists: the Rise of English Arminianism, c. 1590–1640. Clarendon, Oxford, 1990

NOTES

1 The Complete Works of St. Thomas More (Yale University Press, New Haven CT, 1963), Vol. 8. i, p. 177. The spelling of all quotations in this chapter has been modernized.

2 These quotations come from the 1534 Act of Supremacy (26 Henry VIII, cap. 1), the 1534 meeting of the Convocation of York (register of Archbishop Lee), and the 1533 Act in Restraint of Appeals (24 Henry VIII, cap. 12). Most of the relevant legislation is reproduced in H. Gee and W. J. Hardy, Documents Illustrative of English Church History (Kraus, New York, 1966), pp. 145–256.

3 From the 1533 Act in Restraint of Appeals (24 Henry VIII, cap. 12).

4 From Mary's initial proclamation of 6 July 1553; Gee and Hardy, Documents, pp. 373–6.

5 An observer, Canobio, in Brussels with reports from the Spanish ambassador in England to Paul IV, 10 May 1559; J. M. Riggs (ed.), Calendar of State Papers, Relating to English Affairs, Preserved Principally at Rome, Vol. i (London 1916), p. 10.

6 Basil Montagu (ed.), The Works of Francis Bacon, Lord Chancellor of England (London 1825–1834), Vol iii, p. 477.

7 The second Injunction of 1538 and the seventh of 1547; Walter Howard Frere and William McClure Kennedy, Visitation Articles and Injunctions of the Period of the Reformation, 3 vols. (AC, London, 1910), Vol ii, pp. 35–66, 118.

8 The First and Second Books of Edward VI (E.P. Dutton, New York, 1949), pp. 309, 455.

9 I. Breward (ed.), *The Works of William Perkins* (Sutton Courtenay Press, Appleford, 1970), p. 454.
10 *Of the Lawes of Eclesiasticall Politie*, III. iv. 1; FE Vol. i, p. 213.
11 Edmund Grindal's December 1576 letter to Elizabeth refusing to obey her order to suppress the 'exercises' and to limit preaching licences, in William Nicholson (ed.), *The Remains of Edmund Grindal* (Cambridge 1843), pp. 376–90.
12 Hooker, *Lawes*, V. xxii.1 (FE, Vol. ii p. 87); V. xviii.1 (Vol. ii, p. 65); V. xviii–xxii (Vol. ii, pp. 65–110); V. li–lvii (Vol. ii, pp. 209–48); V. l. 3 (Vol. ii, pp. 208–9); and V, lxvi. 1 (Vol. ii, pp. 330–1).
13 Rigg, *Calendar of State Papers*, Vol. i, (London 1916) pp. 154–5.
14 *Lawes*, IV. xiv. 6 (FE Vol. i, p. 342).
15 The Supremacy Act, 26 Henry VIII, cap. 1; Gee and Hardy, *Documents*, p. 243.
16 *Lawes*, VIII. vi. 7 [Keble: 8] and 11 (FE Vol. iii, pp. 393–4, 401–4).
17 John E. Neale, *Elizabeth I and her Parliaments*, 2 vols. (London 1953–7), Vol. ii, p. 435. However subsequent work may modify Neale's ground-breaking studies, both volumes document the many instances of Elizabeth's consistent interference in Puritan parliamentary plans. See J. R. Elton, *The Parliament of England: 1559–1581* (CUP 1986).
18 W. H. Frere and W. McC. Kennedy, *Visitation Articles and Injunctions of the Period of the Reformation* (AC 1910), Vol. iii, pp. 8–29; this statement is among the provisions added after the numbered injunctions; Article 37; *Statutes of the Realm*, Vol. iv (London 1819), p. 350, 1° Elizabeth, cap. I.
19 Hooker, *Lawes*, VIII. vi. 1, viii. 9 (FE Vol. iii, pp. 357, 434).
20 Hooker describes the 'conjunction of power ecclesiastical and civil' in one person as 'convenient and meet' in the circumstances of his day; *Lawes*, VII. xv. 14 (FE Vol. iii, p. 240).
21 The 1572 *Admonition to the Parliament* (2nd edn) as included in W. H. Frere and C. E. Douglas, *Puritan Manifestoes* (SPCK, London, 1907), p. 16.
22 Preface to the 1550 and subsequent English Ordinals; *The First and Second Prayer Books of Edward VI* (J. M. Dent, London, 1949), pp. 292, 438.
23 *Lawes*, VII. xiv. 11 (FE Vol. iii, p. 227); see also III. ii. 16 (Vol. I, p. 264) and VII. v. 10 (Vol. iii, p. 170).
24 From the 'Book of Sports', issued by James in 1618 and reissued by Charles in 1633; Gee and Hardy, *Documents*, p. 529.
25 November 1528; Gee and Hardy, *Documents*, p. 520.
26 From the 1653 Instrument of Government defining the powers of the 'Lord Protector'; Gee and Hardy, *Documents*, p. 576.
27 First issued by James in 1687, the King revived the Declaration of Indulgence with the order to announce it from pulpits of the national Church in April 1688; Gee and Hardy, *Documents*, p. 641.
28 First anniversary sermon of the SPG, 1702; C. F. Pascoe, *Two Hundred Years of the Society for the Propagation of the Gospel* (London 1901), p. 7.
29 Isaac Barrow in a treatise published posthumously in 1681; Paul Elmer More and Frank Leslie Cross, *Anglicanism* (SPCK, London, 1951), p. 504.
30 From the Root and Branch Petition of 1640, item 6; Gee and Hardy, *Documents*, p. 539.
31 William Laud, *Works*, Library of Anglo-Catholic Theology (Oxford 1847–60), Vol. vi, p. 133.
32 Henry More, *Immortality of the Soul* (London 1659).
33 Benjamin Whichcote, *Moral and Religious Aphorisms* (London 1753), No. 40.

34 John Bramhall in a 1660 writing, summarizing the views of Lancelot Andrewes, *A Vindication of Himself and the Episcopal Clergy from the Presbyterian Charge of Popery*, in his *Works* (Oxford 1842–5), Vol. iii, p. 518.

2 From the Early Eighteenth Century to the Present Day

PERRY BUTLER

INTRODUCTION

Since the early eighteenth century, Anglicanism has undergone a remarkable transformation. The national Churches of England and Ireland, together with the disestablished Episcopal remnant in Scotland, have become the 'mother' of a worldwide family of self-governing churches in communion with the see of Canterbury. This expansion has largely paralleled the expansion of British interests and Anglicans are mostly found in countries of the British Commonwealth and the United States. However there has been significant growth in areas like francophone Africa, Latin America and the Pacific and the modern Anglican Communion displays an increasing cultural diversity. Numerically (at least in terms of a committed membership) its centre is now in Africa.

The development of the Anglican Communion has, therefore, been shaped more by historical circumstance than by deliberate design. While this has contributed to its particular ethos, it creates difficulties when locating it among the various groupings of Christendom.

The Anglican Communion is not a federation, nor in the strict sense a confessional family. It is held together more by common loyalties than organizational structures, and by the participation of its bishops in the Lambeth Conference, convened by the Archbishop of Canterbury and held at roughly ten-year intervals since 1867. Indeed, being in communion with the see of Canterbury has become the touchstone of Anglican identity.

Movements within the Church of England and the internal conflict they have aroused also make a definition of Anglicanism problematic. The Evangelical Revival in the eighteenth century gave an important stimulus to the Reformation tradition. The Oxford Movement in the nineteenth century, with its stress on the historic continuity of the church signified by the apostolic succession of the bishops and its sacramental doctrine, effectively distanced Anglicanism from the Reformation, emphasizing its Catholic rather than Protestant heritage. Latitudinarian churchmanship in the eighteenth century, and the impact of biblical criticism and theological liberalism

30

since the nineteenth century, have raised fundamental questions regarding the nature of belief and the traditional understanding of authority. To the outsider the development of this tri-party conflict between Evangelical, Catholic and Liberal and the resulting 'comprehensiveness' of Anglicanism might seem its most important characteristic.

Anglicanism has also experienced a profound liturgical transformation resulting mainly from the Oxford Movement. Public worship has greatly altered in style and ceremonial. To the lay person this would probably seem the most significant change since the early eighteenth century. In the twentieth century especially, liturgical change has included Prayer Book revision. This has had theological consequences, since changes have modified doctrinal emphases and may thereby have, unwittingly, weakened the cohesion of the Anglican Communion which owed so much to a shared liturgical tradition.

In one area, however, modern Anglicanism has changed less than may have been anticipated. At his enthronement in 1942 Archbishop William Temple described the Ecumenical Movement as 'the great new fact of our era'. The Anglican Churches have played an important role in that movement from the beginning, not least in providing leadership. Some have seen Anglican Churches as the ecumenical churches *par excellence*, comprehending both Catholic and Protestant elements. Yet despite developments in the Indian subcontinent, there have been fewer successful attempts at forming united churches including Anglicans than seemed likely. The Anglican Communion has not disappeared, in fact the last thirty years have seen the development of more Anglican self-consciousness in parts of the Communion and a desire for greater centralization which has partly been fulfilled.

THE EIGHTEENTH-CENTURY CHURCH IN ENGLAND AND WALES

The eighteenth-century church was once a byword for pastoral neglect and worldliness. Modern historians, less partisan than their nineteenth-century predecessors, have taken a kinder view. Perhaps its chief faults sprang from a too easy accommodation to the temper of the age, an undue Erastianism and, in the later part of the century, immobility in the face of unprecedented social change.

After the religious upheavals of the preceding century the prevailing desire was for stability. There was a distrust of 'enthusiasm'. The church stood for moderation. Morality was exalted above dogma, a sober practical piety over mysticism or emotion. This was exemplified in the sermons of

Archbishop John Tillotson (1630–94) which became the model for much eighteenth-century preaching.

Acute controversy arose when the mostly Tory lower clergy attempted to condemn the Bishop of Bangor for a sermon in which he denied that the visible Church had any divinely bestowed authority (the 'Bangorian Controversy'). To stop political bickering Convocation was silenced by the King in 1717. Preferment went to bishops who were sound Whigs—a necessity because in the House of Lords the bishops provided a bloc of votes crucial for successive administrations. Episcopal appointments were managed by Walpole's 'Pope', Edmund Gibson (1669–1718), Bishop of London. In 1736 the Walpole–Gibson pact collapsed and for the next thirty years appointments were in the hands of the Duke of Newcastle. Much lower patronage, however, remained in the hands of Tory squires.

Benjamin Hoadly (1676–1761), successively Bishop of Bangor, Hereford, Salisbury and Winchester, is often taken as the archetype of the ambitious Low Church Whig. His notoriously Erastian views provoked 'the Bangorian Controversy'. Most of the bench, however, were conscientious and orthodox and strove to do their duty in large ramshackle dioceses, with poor communications and pastoral work restricted to the months Parliament was not sitting.

The publication of journals and diaries, notably James Woodforde's *Diary of a Country Parson*, has allowed a rehabilitation of the lower clergy. If unheroic, they too were dutiful and benevolent. As the majority of parishes were rural and poor, pluralism and non-residence were almost a necessity. As a result of the Enclosure movement towards the end of the century, however, the social and economic position of the clergy improved. New rectories were built, many clergy became magistrates and took their place in county society. It was the age of the 'Squarson', a clerical cast which was both squire and parson. Nor should lay piety be undervalued simply because it was usually unobtrusive. There was a remarkable growth in the sale of religious books throughout the century. Dr Samuel Johnson (1709–84) is a good example of an earnest and convinced churchman.

Yet as an institution the church remained antiquated and cumbrous, and this hindered its effectiveness. Whatever latent strengths it possessed, it was simply unprepared for the changes that were being unleashed on English society. Faced with the growth and shift of population, urbanization and the onset of the Industrial Revolution, it could not respond.

Eighteenth-century Anglicanism was not without theological achievement, however, despite the strongly rationalist tone of intellectual life. Perhaps its greatest was the response to the Deist challenge.

Deism's roots lay in the seventeenth century, but it enjoyed considerable vogue in the early eighteenth. It was an attempt to produce a purely rational religion, reducing Christianity to a code of moral precepts. The shrewd 'pin-prick' attacks by Deists nevertheless unsettled many orthodox believers. Belief in God was accepted, but all possibility of special revelation rejected. Miracles, the Trinity and the incarnation were ridiculed, the inconsistencies and apparent immorality of Scripture, especially the Old Testament, were highlighted. One of the ablest and most influential Deist works was Matthew Tindal's *Christianity as Old as Creation* (1730).

The challenge was met most effectively by the Nonjuror William Law (1686–1761) and the future Bishop of Durham Joseph Butler (1692–1752). Law, better known as the author of *A Serious Call to a Devout and Holy Life* (1729), was an able controversialist. His reply to Tindal, *The Case of Reason* (1731), was followed in 1736 by Butler's *Analogy of Religion*. Butler's *Analogy* considered natural and revealed religion analogically to the world and argued for probability as the basis of action. It became one of the seminal works of Anglican divinity (see p. 120).

Another outstanding exponent of classical orthodoxy was Daniel Waterland (1683–1740). A prolific theologian, his writings on the Eucharist, notably *A Review of the Doctrine of the Eucharist* (1737), were particularly influential.

THE EVANGELICAL REVIVAL

The spiritual deficiencies of the Hanoverian church left a vacuum that was largely filled by the Evangelical Revival. An international phenomenon embracing German Pietism and the American 'Great Awakening', in England it had three strands: Arminian Methodists following John Wesley, Calvinistic Methodist groupings inspired by George Whitefield, and those who remained within the Church of England. Anglican Evangelicalism was, therefore, no 'off-shoot' as has often been asserted. With its own origins, doctrinal emphases and methods it was a parallel movement. Its leaders looked neither to Wesley nor Whitefield, and were often critical of them.

Although preceded by an awakening in Wales associated with Howell Harris (1714–73) and Daniel Rowland (1713–90), its English origins can be traced to those 'gospel' or 'awakened' clergy who, between 1730 and 1760 underwent a conversion experience. This drew them together in common cause to revitalize the church and evangelize the nation. At first unorganized and thinly spread, they tended to coalesce notably in Cornwall and Yorkshire. Pioneers included Samuel Walker (1719–60) of Truro (Cornwall), Thomas Adam (1701–81) of Winteringham (Lincolnshire), William Grimshaw (1708–63) of Haworth (Yorkshire), John Berridge (1716–93) of Everton (Bedfordshire) and John Fletcher (1729–85) of Madeley (Shropshire).

33

The Evangelical Revival recovered the Protestant emphases on conversion, the supremacy of Scripture, and gospel preaching in reaction to the prevailing rationalism. Anglican, in common with other Evangelicals, sought to revive the Augustinian strain in theology and reassert the doctrine of justification by faith. Their emphasis, however, was on justification as a felt experience that became the badge of authenticity of saving faith, not quite what the sixteenth-century Reformers taught.

While they appealed to experience rather than to the intellect, Anglican Evangelicals did nevertheless possess a simple and practical theology usually called 'moderate Calvinism'. Its foundation was the doctrine of total depravity, from which followed the necessity of conversion, justification by saving faith, the centrality of the atonement and sanctification by the Holy Spirit. Most refused to make predestination a central tenet or to teach predestined reprobation. Grace was for all, a view which fuelled their intense evangelistic endeavour. For the source of their doctrine they looked to Scripture and the Anglican formularies rather than the less accommodating logic of Calvin's *Institutes*.

Anglican Evangelicals differed from Wesley on a number of theological issues, notably his doctrine of Christian perfection and his understanding of assurance, which they regarded as too subjective. Many were uneasy about his stress on instantaneous conversion. Church order, however, provided the main stumbling block. Some early Evangelicals like Berridge had practised itinerant preaching. Walker, Adam and other 'regulars' vigorously attacked this undermining of the parochial system as an unwarranted attack on clerical authority.

Adherence to church order was fundamental if Evangelicals were to gain a firm foothold within the established church. As it was, their views provoked hostility: bishops were disinclined to ordain them and livings were difficult to procure. For mutual support they banded together in clerical societies such as the Elland Society in Yorkshire.

By the late eighteenth century, the situation was changing. Evangelicals could be found in Oxford and Cambridge colleges and in the metropolis, and had sufficiently increased in numbers to make their presence felt. By the turn of the century they had become a definite and confident church party, perhaps 300 to 500 strong and growing rapidly.

The first three decades of the nineteenth century were the Evangelicals' 'golden age'. Vital religion began to permeate the upper middle classes. William Wilberforce (1759–1833) was converted in 1786 and in 1797 published his influential A *Practical View*, contrasting the conventional religion of the time with committed Christianity. Dedicated to the abolition of the slave trade and the reformation of morals, Wilberforce was at the centre of the 'Clapham Sect', a group of wealthy Evangelical laymen.

Wilberforce also coordinated an Evangelical lobby in Parliament whose members were nicknamed 'the Saints'.

The Christian Observer (founded 1802) became the official organ of the party, and Evangelical causes were advanced by voluntary societies—some interdenominational like the Religious Tract Society and some not, like the Church Missionary Society (see pp. 485–7). To secure adequate patronage for Evangelicals, the Simeon Trustees were established in 1836 and advowsons (the right of presenting a clergyman to a particular parish, subject to the bishop's consent) purchased. The Trust was named after Charles Simeon (1759–1836), the foremost Evangelical clergyman of his age. For forty-four years he was Vicar of Holy Trinity Cambridge, where he had enormous influence on generations of undergraduates, and exercised a remarkable preaching ministry.

The progress of the Oxford Movement from the late 1830s pushed Evangelicals on to the defensive. Continuing to be a significant force within the Victorian church, they tended to become part of a wider undenominational Evangelicalism hostile to popery and ritualism. Lord Shaftesbury (1801–85) was a prominent leader and, while Palmerston was Prime Minister (1855–65), exercised considerable influence over ecclesiastical patronage.

HIGH CHURCHMANSHIP AND THE OXFORD MOVEMENT

High Churchmanship was subdued for much of the eighteenth century. With the Whig ascendancy it ceased to be an influential church party, and as a religious tradition it survived largely among individual clergy and laity. Broadly speaking, High Churchmen stressed the apostolic order and authority of the visible Church and valued obedience to its ordinances and liturgy. As the century progressed, many High Churchmen tended to become stiff and unemotional, hence the description 'high and dry' applied to them by the Tractarians.

Significant eighteenth-century High Churchmen included George Horne (1730–92), Bishop of Norwich, his biographer William Jones 'of Nayland' (1726–1800) and Jones' biographer William Stevens (1732–1807). Stevens was a devout London businessman and treasurer of Queen Anne's Bounty. 'Nobody's Friends', the club that perpetuated his memory, became the centre for the later revival of the High Church party.

High Churchmanship gathered momentum from the time of the American Revolution and was given further impetus by the French Revolution. Confronted with the threat of radicalism and irreligion, there was renewed emphasis on order and authority. Samuel Horsley (1733–1806), successively

Bishop of St David's, Rochester and St Asaph, was an able champion of High Church views.

The real leadership increasingly lay with the 'Hackney Phalanx'. Stevens' protégé Joshua Watson, a wealthy London wine merchant, retired to Hackney where his elder brother Archdeacon Watson was rector and H. H. Norris a neighbouring incumbent. In 1811 they founded the National Society for the Education of the Poor in the Principles of the Established Church (which promoted church schools among the poor), and in 1812 acquired the *British Critic* as a platform for their views. Associated with the group were Archdeacon Charles Daubeny (1745–1827), whose *A Guide to the Church* (1798) put their case in its most definite form, Thomas Sikes of Guilsborough (1757–1834) and a future Bishop of Durham, William Van Mildert (1765–1836). During Lord Liverpool's administration (1812–27) the 'Phalanx' exercised considerable influence on ecclesiastical appointments, and in 1818 secured the Church Building Act which provided £1,000,000 for church extension.

Mention should also be made of the strong native traditions of High Churchmanship in Scotland, Ireland and the United States. Henry Hobart, Bishop of New York (1816–30, coadjutor from 1811), provided strong leadership under the banner of 'Evangelical Truth and Apostolic Order', shaping a kind of High Churchmanship that in its fervour was rather different from the English sort.

Although High Churchmanship was reviving in the early nineteenth century, it was transformed by the Oxford Movement. This originated as a response to the weakening of the church-state relationship through the constitutional revolution of 1828–32. Catholic Emancipation in 1829 alarmed churchmen; and when the Whig government suppressed ten Irish bishoprics, John Keble (1792–1866), the Oxford Professor of Poetry, described it as 'National Apostasy' in the Assize Sermon of 14 July 1833.

Keble's disciples included the Vicar of the University Church, John Henry Newman (1801–90) and Richard Hurrell Froude (1803–36). Their views were disseminated in a series of Tracts. In 1835 the Tractarians, as they were called, gained intellectual prestige when they were joined by the Regius Professor of Hebrew, Edward Bouverie Pusey (1800–82).

The movement was at its height in 1839, but in that year Newman began to experience doubts regarding the validity of the Anglican position. The hostile reaction to his *Tract* XC and the attempt to establish a joint Anglican-Lutheran bishopric in Jerusalem added to his anxieties. In 1843 he resigned his living. Further difficulties arose from the development of an aggressively pro-Roman faction within the movement associated with W. G. Ward (1812–82) and F. Oakeley (1802–80). Ward's *Ideal of a Christian Church* was condemned at Oxford in February 1845. Ward and others were received into the Roman Catholic Church, and Newman followed in 1845. His loss marked the end of the Oxford Movement in the narrower sense, but the Catholic revival continued as those who had been influenced by it went into the parishes.

After 1845 it seemed possible that the leadership would fall to Henry Edward Manning (1808–92); but he also seceded to Rome in 1851, after the Gorham Judgement on baptismal regeneration which symbolized for many the intrinsic Erastianism of the Church of England. Pusey, therefore, became the effective leader of the Catholic Movement until his death in 1882.

The Tractarians reasserted the spiritual independence of the Church of England at a time when it was under attack from the reforming tendencies of liberalism in church and state. They took their stand on episcopacy in historic succession as the *esse* of the Church. Where they differed from most of their High Church predecessors was in using this to 'unchurch' other Protestants and their explicit downgrading of the Reformation. Froude's vilification of the Reformers in his *Remains* is notorious. The Tractarians judged the Reformation by the primitive Church in preference to accepting the Reformation Settlement as the norm for Anglican belief and practice. This provoked a sharp cleavage between them and other High Churchmen like William Palmer 'of Worcester' (1803–85), and W. F. Hook (1798–1875) who remained loyal to the older tradition and its hostility to Roman Catholicism.

The ramifications of the Catholic Revival within Anglicanism have been enormous. From it have come the restoration of liturgical practices and sacramental teaching associated with Roman Catholicism, the revival of the religious life, greater emphasis on the priestly office and a deepening of devotion. This was not without conflict, which was especially bitter in the ritual controversies of the second half of the nineteenth century.

In the longer term the Catholic Revival opened Anglicanism to a wider understanding of catholicity and sacramental spirituality with profound ecumenical implications for its relationship with the Orthodox and Roman Catholics, but its doctrine of the ministry has proved a stumbling block in reunion with non-episcopal churches.

LATITUDINARIANISM AND LIBERAL THEOLOGY

The term 'Latitudinarian' was coined in the mid-seventeenth century to describe those who favoured latitude of opinion in religious matters and an end to religious controversy. Forms of church government, liturgy and controversial doctrines were regarded as 'things indifferent'. John Locke's *The Reasonableness of Christianity* (1695) popularized the view that Christianity

37

consisted of a few simple fundamental truths accessible to reason (see pp. 115–28).

In the eighteenth century Latitudinarianism sometimes veered towards anti-Trinitarianism as well as to Deism. Samuel Clark (1675–1729) publicly espoused a position akin to Arianism, as did Bishop Clayton of Clogher. The desire for a liturgy broad enough to accommodate these views led to attacks on the Athanasian and Nicene Creeds.

In the 1750s an Anti-Subscription Movement developed under the leadership of Archdeacon Blackburne. In 1771 he and his supporters drew up the 'Feathers Tavern Petition' requesting Parliament to abolish clerical subscription to the Articles and Liturgy. Some 250 names were attached, but it was rejected by the House of Commons.

The conservative reaction to the French Revolution checked the progress of liberal theology. Mention should be made, however, of William Paley (1743–1805) whose *Evidences of Christianity* (1794) had remarkable success as a work of popular apologetics, not least as a set text in the universities.

In the early nineteenth century the most distinguished group of liberal Churchmen were the 'Noetics' of Oriel College Oxford. Edward Copleston (1776–1849), Provost of the College from 1827, Richard Whately (1787–1863), later Archbishop of Dublin, and Thomas Arnold (1795–1842) later Headmaster of Rugby, were prominent in this group. All were staunch supporters of the union of church and state, and Arnold's *Principles of Church Reform* (1833) was an influential plea to Christianize the nation by comprehending all Christians (except Quakers and Roman Catholics) into one national church.

Although Arnold was an historian, the 'Noetics' were mainly interested in Aristotelian logic and political economy. Their views on church and society may have had some influence on the Whig government in the 1830s. Cambridge liberal theology tended to have a more historical and literary cast, and to be influenced by Plato. Connop Thirlwall (1797–1875), afterwards Bishop of St David's, translated Schleiermacher's *Treatise on St Luke* and with Julius Hare (1795–1855) translated Niebuhr's *History of Rome*. Both were Fellows of Trinity. Attempts to open the universities to dissenters were made by liberal churchmen in the 1830s but proved abortive. University reform was delayed until the 1850s.

The term 'Broad Church' came into use around 1850. It is found in an article in the *Edinburgh Review* of that year by A. P. Stanley, later Dean of Westminster. The biographer of Arnold, Stanley was the archetypal Victorian Broad Churchman who gloried in the Church of England as an expression of national Christianity and opposed all efforts to narrow its comprehensiveness.

S. T. Coleridge (1772–1834) and F. D. Maurice (1805–72) are often discussed in the context of liberal theology, but both drew on the earlier tradition of the Greek Fathers and seventeenth-century Platonism. Coleridge was one of the seminal minds of the nineteenth century, not least in his repudiation of the determinist mechanistic philosophy of Locke with its reductionist implications concerning human understanding. Lacking the application to produce a *magnus opus*, he nevertheless pointed to new directions in such works as *Aids to Reflection* (1825), exploring the relationship of reason and understanding, *Confessions of an Enquiring Spirit* (published posthumously in 1840), dealing with the question of biblical inspiration, and his *Constitution of the Church and State* (1829).

F. D. Maurice, the son of a Unitarian minister, was baptized into the Church of England in 1831. His greatest work, *The Kingdom of Christ* (1838), saw the denominational identities of English Christianity as polarities held together in a church which witnessed to the Divine Order grounded in the Trinity. He understood this to be the particular vocation of the Church of England.

The publication of *Essays and Reviews* in 1860 was a landmark in Anglican liberal theology. It provoked an acrimonious controversy in which its seven authors were described as *septem contra Christum*. Benjamin Jowett's essay *On the Interpretation of Scripture* attracted the greatest criticism for its wholehearted acceptance of biblical criticism and its rejection of traditional views of the authority and inspiration of Scripture. Although the controversy died down, it showed that liberal theology was firmly rooted in the Church of England. This liberal theology differed from earlier Latitudinarianism, however, for by extending the critical method to the Bible and Creeds liberal churchmen made more difficult the continued acceptance of the distinction between fundamental and non-essential doctrines which the original Latitudinarians had held, and so weakened a hitherto essential element in classical Anglicanism (see pp. 473–5).

THE EXPANSION OF ANGLICANISM

The initial expansion of Anglicanism was prompted by English commercial interests. Church of England parishes were established in North America (beginning with Jamestown, Virginia in 1607) and in the Caribbean. Chaplaincies were established in European ports and further afield as the Levant and East India Companies flourished. From the time of Laud, Anglicans abroad were under the theoretical jurisdiction of the Bishop of London.

With the foundation, respectively in 1698 and 1701, of the Society for the Promotion of Christian Knowledge (SPCK) and the Society for the Propagation of the Gospel (SPG) a new era opened. Initially SPCK funded Danish missionaries in South India, but eventually appointed its own. SPG was concerned mainly with North America. Both societies owed much to the creative energy of Thomas Bray (1656–1730), commissary for the Bishop of London for the American colonies; and although they were voluntary organizations, each was incorporated by royal charter (see pp. 485–7).

The creation of an overseas episcopate was impeded; an Act of Parliament was required to create a new bishopric, and new bishops had to be consecrated in London under royal mandate. Schemes for a bishop in the American colonies came to nothing, though this was as much the result of American fears of prelacy as political difficulties in England.

American Independence created further problems but also opportunities. In 1783 the clergy of Connecticut chose Samuel Seabury (1729–96) and sent him to London for consecration. Law forbade the Archbishop of Canterbury to consecrate a 'foreigner', so Seabury turned to the bishops of the disestablished Episcopal Church in Scotland. He was consecrated there in 1784 and returned to America promising to adopt the distinctive Scottish Communion Office in his church. Constitutionally the American Church was to break significant new ground: synodical government by bishops, clergy, *and laity*. This provided an alternative model of ecclesiastical organization for colonial churches within the British Empire.

In 1786 an Act was passed allowing the Archbishop to consecrate those not subject to the Crown. In the following year two other Americans were consecrated at Lambeth. In that year also, Charles Inglis was consecrated for Nova Scotia and in 1793 Jacob Mountain became Bishop of Quebec. Calcutta received a bishop in 1814. In 1824 two bishops were appointed for the West Indies, and in 1836 a bishop was consecrated for Australia.

In 1841, the Colonial Bishoprics Fund was created, inspired by Charles James Blomfield (1776–1857), Bishop of London. This greatly speeded the expansion of the overseas episcopate, so that by the first Lambeth Conference in 1867 there were nearly fifty bishops in the British colonies and thirty-five dioceses in the USA. Three years earlier Samuel Adjar Crowther (1806–91) had become the first African bishop, consecrated for Nigeria.

Anglicanism could exist independently of a state connection, as the Episcopal Church in Scotland and the United States showed. But the relationship between the church in the colonies and the mother church was complicated by establishment. As at home, dissenters in the colonies were hostile to the pretensions of an established church, and it proved very difficult to make establishment abroad effective. The legal difficulties were complex and came to a head in the so-called 'Eton college case' when it was judged that the *established* Church of England could not exist in those colonies where there was a local legislature (see p. 401).

Colonial churches were already beginning to evolve forms of synodical government (see pp. 208–10). G. A. Selwyn (1809–78), the first Bishop of New Zealand, summoned an informal synod of his clergy in 1844. The granting of a measure of self-government to New Zealand in 1852 was followed five years later by a Constitution of the Church of New Zealand. This became the model for many subsequent constitutions. The Constitution of the Province of South Africa was adopted in 1876. The West Indies province promulgated its first canons in 1883. In 1893 the General Synod of the Canadian Church was formed. The organization of the Australian Church dates from the early twentieth century.

The missionary impulse was an important feature of nineteenth-century Anglicanism. For instance, the CMS arrived in Sierra Leone in 1804 to bring the gospel to the freed slaves of the colony, and in 1858 the Universities' Mission to Central Africa, the most Anglo-Catholic of the missionary societies, answered David Livingstone's call to evangelize up the Zambezi. An interesting aspect of UMCA strategy was the use of the bishop as missionary pioneer, an idea sparked off by Archdeacon Grant's Bampton lectures of 1843. C. F. Mackenzie (1825–62) was consecrated in Cape Town in 1861 to lead a missionary party to Lake Nyasa.

Subsequent missionary expansion has increasingly owed its impetus to the efforts of indigenous Anglicans. The twentieth century saw the Anglican Communion rooted in all continents. No longer is its membership perceived as culturally British. Especially since World War II there has been a rapid movement towards provincial autonomy, beginning with West Africa in 1951. Bishops and clergy are mostly natives of their country, worship is in local languages and reflects local cultural styles.

THE LAMBETH CONFERENCE AND THE LAMBETH QUADRILATERAL

The growth of the Anglican Communion (the term first appeared in 1851) stimulated a desire for closer links between its parts. From the 1850s a growing Pan-Anglican consciousness was becoming apparent. American bishops shared in the celebrations for the 150th Anniversary of SPG. The 1866 Church Congress at York was the first to include colonial and American bishops.

The attempt by Archbishop Gray of Cape Town to depose Bishop Colenso for heresy, and the latter's subsequent appeal to the Privy Council, raised questions as to the relationship between colonial churches and the Crown. The revival of Convocation in the Church of England in 1852 raised the further question of whether its actions had any bearing on the overseas churches which, in any case, were developing their own synods. There was

41

anxiety about *Essays and Reviews* (see p. 122). To some the time seemed ripe for an Anglican gathering.

Inspired by Bishop Lewis of Ontario, the Provincial Synod of the Canadian Church formally requested that members of the Anglican Communion meet in a 'General Council of her members gathered from every land'. In a letter to Archbishop Charles Longley (1794–1868) in 1865, it asked that he convene a Synod of bishops from home and abroad (see p. 210).

Such was the origin of the first Lambeth Conference. Longley was sympathetic to the request but cautious. Some English bishops doubted the wisdom or even the legality of such a gathering and before invitations were sent Longley made it clear that the proposed meeting could neither enact canons nor make any decision binding the church. Invitations were extended to 150 bishops; 67 attended, though the Archbishop of York, hostile from the first, refused. The gathering, therefore, was not a Synod and attempts to make it one were resisted. It met from 24 to 27 September 1867 and considered intercommunion between the Anglican Churches, the colonial Church, and co-operation in mission. An encyclical was issued.

Ten years later a second conference was held; subsequent conferences have taken place at roughly ten-year intervals with increasing episcopal participation. They have become, in Bishop G. K. A. Bell's words, 'a special opportunity for knitting the various provinces and dioceses of the Anglican Church together in mutual counsel'. The Lambeth Conference has remained a deliberative body convened solely at the invitation of the Archbishop of Canterbury. Whatever the respect accorded to its deliberations, it has no canonical nor constitutional status. It has, however, enhanced the Archbishop's primacy within the Communion.

At the 1888 Conference what has become known as the Chicago–Lambeth Quadrilateral was adopted (see pp. 249–50). This had its origins in 1870 in *The Church Idea, An Essay toward Unity* by William Reed Huntington (1838–1909), an American Episcopalian priest. The term Quadrilateral derived from the Lombard Quadrilateral, the four key fortresses by which Austria held north Italy prior to Italy's unification in 1870. The Lambeth form contained four elements held to be 'a basis on which approach may be by God's blessing, made toward Home Reunion': the holy Scriptures as containing all things necessary for salvation; the Creeds as the sufficient statement of the Christian faith; the sacraments of baptism and holy communion; and the 'Historic Episcopate, locally adapted in the methods of its administration to the varying needs of the nations and peoples called of God, into the Unity of His Church'. The precise implications of this last element, which was deliberately used to embrace the differing interpretations of episcopacy within Anglicanism, have consumed much Anglican theological energy. In twentieth-century ecumenical discussion the Quadrilateral has played an important role, its originally somewhat defensive ring acquiring a different colouring: the four things Anglicans think should emerge as the distinctive features of the coming ecumenical Church.

ANGLICAN THEOLOGY FROM THE LATER NINETEENTH CENTURY

The later nineteenth century was a period of theological reconstruction as the church painfully adjusted to the new scientific and historical discoveries. The 'Cambridge Triumvirate' of J. B. Lightfoot (1829–89), B. F. Westcott (1825–1901) and F. J. A. Hort (1828–92) showed that critical study of the New Testament need not result in the scepticism of earlier critics, thereby giving biblical criticism greater respectability within the church. Lightfoot became Bishop of Durham, and Westcott succeeded him in 1890. Hort's Hulsean lectures *The Way, the Truth and the Life* remain an impressive example of the Anglican theological temper.

The publication in 1889 of *Lux Mundi: A Series of Studies in the Religion of the Incarnation* inaugurated a new era in Anglican theology. The book was by a group of young Oxford scholars who aimed to unite the theology of the Tractarians with modern critical scholarship. Significant elements in the *Lux Mundi* synthesis were the stress on God's immanence, the use of evolutionary ideas, a critical attitude to the Old Testament and acceptance of some limitation of our Lord's knowledge by way of a 'Kenotic' Christology. To older Tractarians like H. P. Liddon (1829–90), the book represented a capitulation to German rationalism.

Charles Gore (1853–1932), the group's leader, described his incarnational theology as 'Liberal Catholicism', arguing that its combination of Catholic doctrine and devotion, critical method and social concern represented the authentic Anglican vocation. It is often seen as the fusion of the Tractarian inheritance with the theology of F. D. Maurice. 'Liberal Catholicism' had an important influence on the church during the archiepiscopate of Randall Davidson (1903–28), since three of the book's contributors, including Gore, became bishops.

But Gore found himself at odds with a new generation of Liberal Catholics more influenced by the theology of experience of some Roman Catholic Modernists and prepared to allow a critical approach to the creed. *Essays Catholic and Critical*, edited by E. G. Selwyn in 1926, was the manifesto of this later school.

Anglican Modernism flourished in the 1920s. Heir to the 'Broad Church' tradition and influenced by continental liberal Protestantism, their forum was the Modern Churchmen's Union under H. D. A Major. At their conference in Girton College Cambridge in 1921, some speakers appeared to deny Christ's divinity. The ensuing controversy led to the appointment of an Archbishops' Commission on Christian Doctrine in 1922.

The Commission's Report, *Doctrine in the Church of England*, was eventually published in 1938. Since it surveyed rather than defined the doctrine of the church it did little to delineate the permitted limits of theological diversity. The recognition it accorded liberal interpretations of credal statements was ambiguous and the church never officially accepted it. The Commission's Chairman, William Temple, Archbishop of York, later of Canterbury (1942–4), commented in his introduction that were the Commission to begin again it would make the theology of redemption central. The era of incarnational theology begun with *Lux Mundi* had reached its end.

This theological shift was evident in the return to 'biblical orthodoxy' in many quarters. It had been foreshadowed in the work of E. C. Hoskyns (1884–1937). He had translated Karl Barth's commentary on *Romans* in 1933 and had been a contributor to *Essays Catholic and Critical*. Other Anglican exponents of 'Biblical Theology' such as A. G. Hebert and Lionel Thornton also had a Liberal Catholic background.

'Biblical Theology' was not a revival of fundamentalism; however, it emphasized the unity of the Bible and the distinctiveness of biblical revelation. Its weakness lay in occasionally over-simplifying critical issues and concentrating on the biblical revelation to the exclusion of God's wider activity in the world.

The 1960s saw an extraordinary explosion of 'radical theology'. Two contributions by Anglicans were the American Paul Van Buren's *The Secular Meaning of the Gospel* and J. A. T. Robinson's *Honest to God*, both published in 1963. Robinson's views, being those of a bishop, provoked particular controversy. Both wrote with an avowedly missionary purpose, attempting to make Christianity more accessible to 'modern man'. Robinson drew heavily on continental Protestant theologians like Bultmann, Tillich and Bonhoeffer, combining them in a not always justified synthesis.

In reaction, presumably, recent theological trends show a resurgence of conservatism, most clearly manifest in the revival of Conservative Evangelicalism within the Church of England and elsewhere. This newer Evangelicalism is, however, more sacramental and scholarly than its late-nineteenth-century equivalent and often displays a stronger commitment to social theology. Radical theology has not been eclipsed. Bishop David Jenkins in England and Bishop John Spong in the United States have attracted notoriety, and the existence of Anglican theologians who seem explicitly to repudiate the incarnation, or, in the case of Don Cupitt and the

'Sea of Faith' network, objective theism, bewilders those in churches with firmer ecclesiastical discipline.

LITURGICAL DEVELOPMENTS

The eighteenth century was not a period of liturgical innovation except among a few Nonjurors. Sunday worship in the Church of England consisted of a morning service comprising Matins, Litany and Ante-communion read from the pulpit with the responses led by the parish clerk. Metrical psalms were sometimes sung, accompanied by a village band. Holy Communion was celebrated at the north end of the altar, but its frequency tended to decline during the century. In country districts quarterly celebrations were usual with a monthly celebration in towns. The Evangelical Revival, however, prompted more frequent communion and more extensive hymn singing.

The Romantic Movement had an important effect on religious sensibility with its emphases on 'feeling' and its idealization of the Middle Ages. In architecture Neo-classical gave way to Gothic Revival. The Cambridge Camden Society, later known as the Ecclesiological Society, of which J. M. Neale (1818–86) was a leading member, promoted the cause of Gothic and had enormous influence on church buildings and fittings. Neale also translated many patristic and medieval hymns, thus communicating their sacramental doctrine to ordinary congregations.

Ritualism formed no part of the original Tractarian programme, though the Tractarians did promote daily services, weekly communion and the keeping of the liturgical year. Ritualism became an important element in the 1850s and 1860s as Tractarianism became Anglo-Catholicism. It attempted to teach the Tractarian understanding of sacraments and priesthood through the eye by the introduction of the eastward position, candles, eucharistic vestments and even incense. Some priests in slum areas saw it as a way of evangelizing the unlettered. It did, however, destroy liturgical uniformity within the church and met with open hostility from Protestant-minded Anglicans.

A Royal Commission on Ritual reported inconclusively in 1867 and the Public Worship Regulation Act of 1874 aimed to destroy what Disraeli the Prime Minister called the 'Mass in masquerade'. But the subsequent imprisonment of five ritualist priests helped change opinion, and in the late 1880s the trial of the saintly Bishop Edward King of Lincoln for ritual irregularities added to public disquiet. Another Royal Commission reported in 1906 that the 'law of public worship is too narrow for the religious life of the present generation'.

Ritualism provoked similar strife in other parts of the Anglican Communion but it flourished where traditional High Churchmanship provided a welcoming environment, e.g. in Scotland and parts of the United States, and in missionary areas under Catholic influence, notably Southern Africa and the West Indies. Disestablishment in 1869 allowed the Church of Ireland to introduce canons expressly forbidding ritual innovation. In England the interpretation of the Prayer Book ornaments rubric was always the source of much legal wrangling, and episcopal injunctions were largely ignored.

Unofficial amplification of the Prayer Book and reservation of the sacrament which had started in the 1860s became more common in the early twentieth century. While some other Anglican Churches worked towards official liturgical revisions, a revision of the English Prayer Book was attempted in 1928 to contain these developments. Most factions found it unsatisfactory and its provisions stirred the latent Protestantism of the House of Commons who rejected it.

The influence of the Liturgical Movement enabled subsequent liturgical reform to be undertaken for its own sake, rather than as a means of curbing Anglo-Catholic lawlessness. Originating in continental Roman Catholicism, its ideas were mediated to Anglicans in two seminal works; A. G. Hebert's *Liturgy and Society* (1935) and the symposium Hebert edited entitled *The Parish Communion* (1937). The latter gave theological underpinning to the growing practice of making the Eucharist the main Sunday service. The idea was enthusiastically promoted after the Second World War by the 'Parish and People' movement in England and the 'Associated Parishes' in the United States. In *The Shape of Liturgy* (1945) Dom Gregory Dix presented the scholarly case for liturgical revision; his subsequent influence, especially on the structure of the eucharistic rite, has been enormous (see pp. 316–19).

In the last twenty years there has been a proliferation of revised liturgical texts in modern Anglicanism, as elsewhere. This process has involved considerable experiment and ecumenical cross-fertilization, particularly in regard to common modern language liturgical texts.

A new prayer book was produced by ECUSA in 1979 and many provinces have followed suit. In England the established Church could only venture on the path of liturgical reform with Parliamentary approval. The 1662 Book of Common Prayer remains normative and the book produced in 1980 is therefore called *The Alternative Service Book 1980*. Unlike other Provinces of the Anglican Communion (e.g. Ireland, Canada and the USA), the Church of England has never had an official hymn book.

ANGLICANISM AND ECUMENISM

Many Anglicans have felt a concern for Christian unity, and in modern times an ecumenical vocation has become part of Anglican self-understanding.

Cranmer and James I both had ecumenical ideals of a sort. In the early eighteenth century Archbishop William Wake (1651–1737) corresponded on Christian unity with Reformed theologians such as Jablonski and Turrentini as well as with Roman Catholic Gallicans such as Du Pin and Girardin. The Anglican claim to continuity in faith and order with the primitive Church and the distinction between fundamentals and non-essential matters of faith were seen as possible bases for fruitful ecumenical endeavour (see pp. 262–77).

The Oxford Movement's understanding of the Church led its followers to seek reunion with other episcopal churches. The Association for the Promotion of the Unity of Christendom was founded in 1857 by the Roman Catholic Ambrose Phillipps de Lisle and the Anglican F. G. Lee but the venture ended with condemnation by Rome in 1864. The Eastern Churches Association was founded in 1863. Pusey published three *Eirenicons* between 1865 and 1870 appealing for unity, and Anglicans took a sympathetic interest in the Old Catholic Congresses of the 1870s.

The beginning of modern ecumenism is usually traced to the 1910 Edinburgh Missionary Conference. Charles Henry Brent (1863–1929), Canadian-born Bishop of the Philippines, returned from Edinburgh with the vision of an international conference at which doctrinal issues would be faced squarely. Delayed by the war, the first World Conference on Faith and Order was held at Lausanne in 1927. For seventeen years this movement was led and funded largely by American Episcopalians. A second conference at Edinburgh in 1937 revealed Archbishop William Temple as a leading ecumenical figure. It fell to Temple's successor, Geoffrey Fisher, to inaugurate the World Council of Churches in Amsterdam in 1948. Another noted Anglican ecumenist, Bishop G. K. A. Bell (1883–1958), was the first chairman of the Central and Executive Committees. Every Anglican Province has joined the WCC.

The Anglican commitment to visible unity was expressed most prophetically in the 'Appeal to all Christian People' issued by the 1920 Lambeth Conference. A moving plea for organic union, it reaffirmed the Lambeth Quadrilateral as the basis for such a united Church. A key figure in this initiative was A. C. Headlam (1862–1947), later Bishop of Gloucester, whose *Doctrine of the Church and Reunion* (1920) was published just before the Conference.

Some practical results followed. Anglican–Orthodox relations became more cordial, a measure of intercommunion was established with the Church of Sweden and, perhaps most significantly, full intercommunion

47

was attained with the Old Catholic Churches as a result of the Bonn Agreement (1931).

Reunion between Anglicans and non-episcopal churches has proved more intractable. After twenty-six years of negotiations the Church of South India came into being in 1946. This union between Anglicans, Methodists and Reformed, on the basis of future episcopal ordination but not reordination of non-episcopal ministers, was regarded by some Anglicans as a betrayal of fundamental principles; full acceptance of the United Church by the Anglican Communion has taken time. The Churches of North India and Pakistan were formed in 1970 avoiding difficulties over ministry by a service of incorporation.

In England Archbishop Fisher's Cambridge Sermon (1946) suggesting the Free Churches might 'take Episcopacy into their system' met with a promising response from Methodists. But the scheme for Methodist–Anglican unity foundered in both 1969 and 1972 because it failed to win sufficient support among Anglicans. A new initiative involving the United Reformed Church, 'Covenanting for Unity', foundered in the same way in 1982. However, despite these setbacks informal conversations continue and progress is being made at the local level in local ecumenical projects (LEPs).

One reason for the failure of these national schemes was the changing stance of the Roman Catholic Church since Vatican II, and fears that concessions to 'Protestants' might jeopardize rapprochement with Rome. The friendship between Viscount Halifax and the French priest Abbé F. Portal had led to an initiative that was blighted by the condemnation of Anglican orders in 1896. The Malines Conversations in the 1920s, again involving Halifax, came to nothing though the ecumenical ideal proposed by Dom Lambert Beauduin of a church 'united but not absorbed' remains important. In 1966, however, the visit of Archbishop Michael Ramsey to Pope Paul VI resulted in a Common Declaration and the setting up in 1970 of an Anglican–Roman Catholic International Commission (ARCIC I) which published its Final Report in 1982. This was received positively by the 1988 Lambeth Conference but the Vatican Official Response published in 1991 asked for classifications. A commission with a revised membership (ARCIC II) has met since 1983 and has contributed significantly with regard to justification and the meaning of communion. Sadly the ordination of women within Anglicanism, together with the Vatican call for clarifications, has complicated matters and provoked a cooling of enthusiasm in some quarters.

Schemes for regional united churches (e.g. in England, Nigeria, Sri Lanka, New Zealand and the Consultation on Church Union on the USA) have rather lost impetus. The Anglican Communion, however, is a participant in six international bilateral dialogues. In addition to the one with Rome there are discussions with the Orthodox, Oriental Orthodox, Lutheran, Reformed and Methodist. Interim eucharistic fellowship has been achieved in the United States by Episcopalians and some Lutherans since 1976 and proposals for 'full communion' are being evaluated. In Europe the Church of England has entered into the Meissen Agreement with Lutheran, Reformed and United Churches in Germany and in 1994/5 the Episcopal Church of Scotland agreed to enter into communion with the Nordic and Baltic Lutheran Churches, the Churches of England and Ireland, and the Church in Wales.

At present the ecumenical future is far from clear. Anglicans remain officially committed to ecumenical dialogue, but the achievement of visible unity has proved more elusive than many hoped forty or so years ago. Anglicanism's doctrinal divisions have hindered its effectiveness as a so-called 'bridge church' and this has put a question mark against its claim to a special ecumenical vocation.

RECENT DEVELOPMENT OF THE ANGLICAN COMMUNION

The 1930 Lambeth Conference described the Anglican Communion as 'a federation without a federal government'. With the formation of many new autonomous Provinces the problems this presents have become acute. The last forty years have, therefore, seen efforts to strengthen communication and consultation within the Communion.

The appointment of the American Bishop Stephen Bayne (1908–74) as first Executive Officer of the Anglican Communion in 1960 following a recommendation from the 1958 Lambeth Conference was the first significant step in this direction. Pan-Anglican Congresses were held in Minneapolis in 1954 and Toronto in 1963. An Anglican Centre was established in Rome in 1966.

The Anglican Consultative Council was created after the 1968 Lambeth Conference and the Executive Officer replaced by a Secretary-General appointed by and responsible to the Council. The ACC is unique in that it is the only international Anglican body with a legal and constitutional position, since it was set up by a series of decisions taken by the synodical bodies of the various provinces. It provides a continuity of consultation and guidance on policy which the Anglican Communion has hitherto lacked. Each province appoints one to three members, and the total membership of sixty-two includes clergy and lay people. Three members are nominated by the united Churches of South and North India and Pakistan. There is a permanent Secretariat based in London, and meetings are held in different parts of the world at two- to three-year intervals. The first was held at

Limuru, Kenya, in 1971. One of its recommendations resulted in the creation of an Inter-Anglican Theological Commission in 1980.

To further advance cohesion, a Primates' Meeting has been held regularly since November 1979, though this is in no sense a 'higher Synod'.
Such developments have nonetheless affected the role of the Archbishop of
Canterbury. He has become a more significant focus of unity within the
Communion and is expected to travel extensively within it. This international role fits uneasily with his position as Primate of a national and
established church.

A further problem that faces modern Anglicanism is uncertainty surrounding its doctrinal basis and the acceptable limits of doctrinal variation.
New Prayer Books, the effective 'demoting' of the Thirty-Nine Articles and
theological liberalism have weakened the appeal to the classic sources of
Anglican doctrine (see pp. 150–3).

The ordination of women to the priesthood in an increasing number of
Anglican provinces has also created difficulties. Women were ordained in
Hong Kong in 1971 and in Canada in 1976. In the USA the first canonical
ordinations took place in 1977. Other provinces have followed and in 1994
women priests were ordained in the Church of England. Women have been
consecrated to the episcopate in the USA (1989), New Zealand (1990), and
Canada (1994). Whether such ordinations are ecumenically prudent or
indeed theologically acceptable continues to be debated. The 1978 Lambeth Conference was unable to do more than accept variety of practice while
affirming its commitment to the preservation of Anglican unity.

Modern Anglicanism is therefore being forced both by its inner tensions
and its position within Christendom to explore its peculiar vocation. Certainly a fellowship embracing Evangelicals, Catholics and Liberals within a
Communion of autonomous churches and provinces needs to evaluate
afresh its distinctive understanding of 'Reformed Catholicism' and 'dispersed
authority' if it is to share its gifts with Christians of other traditions in the
common search for unity (see pp. 459–75). In this task it will be able to
draw upon a rich and remarkable historical experience.

BIBLIOGRAPHY
Avis, P., Anglicanism and the Christian Church: Theological Resources in Historical
   Perspective. T. & T. Clark, Edinburgh/Fortress-Augsburg, Philadelphia PA, 1989.
Bradley, I. B., The Call to Seriousness. Jonathan Cape, London, 1976.
Brilioth, Y., The Anglican Revival: Studies in the Oxford Movement. Longmans, Green
   & Co., London, 1933.
Chadwick, O., The Spirit of the Oxford Movement: Tractarian Essays. CUP 1992.
Cragg, G. R., Reason and Authority in the Eighteenth Century, CUP 1964.
Davies, H., Worship and Theology in England, Vols. iii, iv, v. OUP 1961.

Howe, J., *Highways and Hedges: Anglicanism and the Universal Church*. CIO Publishing for Anglican Consultative Council, London, 1985.

Jacob, W. M., *The Making of the Anglican Church Worldwide*. SPCK, London, 1997.

Nockles, P. B., *The Oxford Movement in Context: Anglican High Churchmanship 1760–1857*. CUP 1994.

Page, R. J., *New Directions in Anglican Theology: A Survey from Temple to Robinson*. Mowbrays, London and Oxford, 1967.

Ramsey, A. M., *From Gore to Temple: The Development of Anglican Theology between Lux Mundi and the Second World War 1889–1939*. Longmans, London, 1960.

Ramsey, A. M., *The Gospel and the Catholic Church*. Longmans, Green & Co., London, 1936, 1955; SPCK, London, 1990.

Reardon, B. M. G., *From Coleridge to Gore: A Century of Religious Thought in Britain*. Longmans, London, 1971; reprinted as *Religious Thought in the Victorian Age: a survey from Coleridge to Gore*, Longmans, London, 1995.

Rowell, G., *The Vision Glorious: Themes and Personalities of the Catholic Revival in Anglicanism*. OUP 1991.

Sachs, W. L., *The Transformation of Anglicanism: From State Church to Global Communion*. CUP 1993.

Stephenson, A. M. G., *Anglicanism and the Lambeth Conferences*. SPCK, London, 1978.

Walsh, J., Haydon, C. and Taylor, S., *The Church of England, c. 1689–c. 1833 From Toleration to Tractarianism*. CUP 1993.

PART TWO

The Gospel in Anglicanism

The Gospel in Anglicanism

LOUIS WEIL

One of the most notable fruits of ecumenical dialogue in recent decades has been the emergence of growing evidence of convergence among separated Christians. This convergence touches fundamental areas of theological dispute which have been the apparently insuperable basis of alienation for several centuries. This convergence is multilateral, as the Lima Statement *Baptism, Eucharist and Ministry* testifies,[1] but it has been most dramatic in the particular encounters between two traditions where there have been long-standing areas of dispute. The Roman Catholic dialogue with Lutherans, for example, has demonstrated remarkable convergence on the issue of justification by faith.[2] Between Anglicans and Roman Catholics, the ARCIC statements on the Eucharist and on the ordained ministry have revealed convergence on two theological issues which have been the source of deep-rooted hostilities in the past, and some advance on the difficult issue of authority.[3]

Convergence does not, however, equate with reunion. The Lima Statement, for example, demonstrates what are for many of the participating churches theological views now held by only a minority of members; a theological élite perhaps, but one which in recent decades has represented a growing common ground among Christians of different traditions. The New Testament teaching that there is 'one Lord, one faith, one baptism, one God and Father of all' seems to be creating a deeper imperative for that unity to come into a practical realization in Christian experience. Although that goal will not be reached in the near future, the awareness of convergence on basic questions has inevitably affected Christian consciousness, whatever the tradition, of the significant areas of common faith which Christians share (see pp. 427–45).

An essay on the gospel in Anglicanism which is written in the last years of the twentieth century is thus written in an atmosphere which is quite different from that which dominated, for example, a century ago, and even into comparatively recent times. Even today, many laity and clergy of churches which are officially committed to ecumenical dialogue find this movement threatening to their own sense of identity not merely as one denomination among others, but rather as members of the Church as Jesus Christ intended it to be. Life within a particular religious tradition has a powerful formative impact upon believers, shaping their expectations of religious faith and practice in quite profound ways.

So the gospel is both a fundamental which Anglicans share with other Christian communions, and also a particular—that is, the gospel as it has been understood and practised within the Anglican tradition. What sharply distinguishes our situation today from that of a century ago is that the evidence of convergence is readily available to those who are disposed to see it. Our discussion of the gospel in Anglicanism thus involves an awareness that the fundamental tenets of the gospel are also present in the foundations of faith in other Christian traditions (see pp. 262–77).

What then, for Anglicans, is distinctive about the way the gospel is understood and lived? What particular facet of the infinitely rich gospel of God has most influenced Anglican thinking and experience? Anglicanism has never been disposed to unchurch other Christian traditions, that is, to insist that one aspect or another of its own self-understanding, if missing, would invalidate the right of another tradition to be called Christian. By way of example we might mention the episcopate. Certainly from the time of the Reformation, Anglicans have adhered to what is called 'the historic episcopate', that is, to the succession of bishops as the sign of the ordered transmission of pastoral authority in the Church from generation to generation (see pp. 333–47). In its debate with the Puritans from the time of Queen Elizabeth I, the episcopate emerged as a fundamental characteristic of the Anglican understanding of the Church. Yet Anglican reflection on the episcopate has not defined the nature of that ministry in sharply exclusive terms, and our participation in recent ecumenical dialogue has indicated an attitude toward the episcopate as a gift to be shared for the building up of the Church's unity, rather than as a basis for the exclusion of non-episcopal traditions from fellowship with us. This fellowship has extended even to the sharing of the eucharistic gifts which are the fundamental expression of our unity in Christ.

In Anglicanism, then, what is distinctive is not necessarily divisive. What is distinctive in Anglican faith and practice is seen rather in terms of gift, particular gifts of God which are part of a treasured heritage, and which Anglicans are called to bring to the shared vision of the Church which is truly one and which will encompass all the diverse gifts which the Holy Spirit has given Christians at all times and in all places.

Those diverse gifts include the particular history which each religious tradition carries, the unfolding of its experience as a people of faith in encounter with God. These particular histories, prior to the twentieth century, were often lived in comparative isolation from each other. This made it possible to be complacent about divisions within the Church because contact was so limited; in practice, it made it easy to understand the Church in terms of the particular characteristics of one's own history. The radical changes in social structures and in human mobility that have developed in this century have brought Christians of different traditions into direct and substantial contact. This new situation has opened the door to mutual awareness and dialogue, and an awakening to the integrity of forms of the Christian life in other traditions. This has led to a recognition that differences in theological formulations of ministerial structures, or differences of forms of worship or spirituality, do not necessarily embody irreconcilable traditions among the churches. Such differences may be seen rather as complementary, as expressive of the diversity which characterizes the Church in history, taking root in all the varied cultures of the world.

So the understanding of the gospel in Anglicanism would not claim to define all that might be said, much less all that might be experienced, of the good news that God is the creator of all that exists and that he has entered into and shared our human life in Jesus Christ so that the whole creation might come to its fulfilment. The words, images and rites used to proclaim this good news in the Christian traditions vary, and that diversity of articulation reflects the impact of history and culture spoken of above. Yet this wealth of language which has emerged within each tradition always points to the central and mysterious reality, that 'God was in Christ, reconciling the world to himself'. This is the gospel which Christianity knows as the paschal mystery. This central theme of the doctrine of redemption has been proclaimed within the Anglican liturgical tradition with dramatic power, in the anthem which Archbishop Cranmer appointed for use on Easter Day in the Prayer Book of 1552 and which has continued in use since that time. The anthem is made up of texts from St Paul, and is known by the opening words of the form it has had since the Book of 1662, 'Christ our Passover is sacrificed for us'. The focus of the text theologically is found in the second part of the anthem, where Cranmer's version began, with these words from the Epistle to the Romans:

Christ being raised from the dead dieth no more;
  death hath no more dominion over him.
For in that he died, he died unto sin once:
  but in that he liveth, he liveth unto God.
Likewise reckon ye also yourselves to be dead indeed unto sin,
  but alive unto God through Jesus Christ our Lord.

This is the heart of the paschal mystery, that death has been conquered by the dying and rising of Christ, and that the members of his Body share that victory.

During the recent decades of liturgical renewal and the revision of liturgical texts which has been common to all the major Christian communions, there has been a recovery of the identification which was recognized during the patristic period between faith in the paschal mystery and its ritual celebration in the liturgies of Holy Week and in Eastertide, the 'great fifty days' between Easter Day and Pentecost. Cranmer's association of Paul's paschal theology with the Church's celebration of Easter demonstrates his remarkable liturgical intuition at a time when early texts of the Holy Week rites were not available for study.

Cranmer's Easter anthem finds a rich complementarity to a medieval text which was associated with the Easter Vigil of Holy Saturday night. In that text, known as the *Exsultet*, Christ is proclaimed as 'the true Paschal Lamb, who at the feast of the Passover paid for us the debt of Adam's sin, and by his blood delivered your faithful people'.[4] Although it is a poetic elaboration of the biblical faith, the close relation of this to the verses selected by Cranmer is obvious:

> For since by man came death,
> by man came also the resurrection of the dead.
> For as in Adam all die,
> even so in Christ shall all be made alive.

The use of such texts in the celebration of the Easter rites offers a pastoral opportunity to renew in the awareness of the people gathered a lively sense of the gospel, not merely in words but in an experience of the celebration of that gospel which draws into the liturgical action both the story and the signs of redemption.

This emphasis on liturgical experience offers us a key to a significant aspect of the Anglican understanding of the gospel, namely, the importance of our experience of God's present action as the way in which God's work in Christ touches and is effective in successive generations of believers. For this reason, the doctrine of the Church as a visible society in history plays a major role in the way Anglicanism has understood the consequences of faith (see pp. 249–62). Faith is not seen as a private matter between God and the believer. Faith is corporate: it is the common faith of the Church into which new members are baptized and come to participate in the power of the paschal mystery. The individual enters into a dying and rising with Christ which is understood as the common experience of all the baptized, so that the Church itself is seen as an article of faith, the fellowship of all those who share a common identity in Christ. Our unity in Christ is nourished by the sharing of the Eucharist, not as an act of private piety but as the celebration of that common identity which baptism has created. The Church's outward rites, its sacraments and all those signs which give external expression of God's inward activity, are thus fundamentally related to the Anglican understanding of the gospel. The whole structuring of the Church's common life is an instrument for God's saving action, as it signifies the abiding grace and power of the paschal mystery in the lives of those who believe.

It is in this perspective that we see why the Book of Common Prayer has played so fundamental a role (see pp. 131–42). In no other Christian tradition does the authorized liturgy take on so great a significance. The Prayer Book is first of all the basis for *corporate* prayer. In other words, the book itself supports the dimension of common experience spoken of above. In addition to this essential role, and as a kind of natural overflow from it, the Prayer Book is also a formative element in the private prayer of Anglicans. Even in solitude, the use of the collects or psalms, or the texts of the various rites, link the individual Anglican at prayer with the common prayer of the larger fellowship. Again, the Prayer Book is also turned to as a source for the teaching of the Church. Anglicanism gives forceful expression to the ancient adage, *Lex orandi legem statuat credendi*, 'the law of prayer establishes the law of faith'[5] (see pp. 187–201).

LITURGY AND DOCTRINE

If Christian worship and the doctrines of Christian faith are so closely related, what is the nature of that relationship? How is their implied mutuality realized in practice? Wherever there is a tendency to understand faith as an intellectual activity, there has been a consequent denigration of the role of worship and sacraments in the Christian life. The Enlightenment, with its exaltation of human reason, had such an effect upon the worship of seventeenth-century Anglicanism. If rites were to be tolerated at all, the rationalist would see them only as a means by which Christian truths might be taught. The purpose of liturgical rites was thus essentially didactic. Yet this is not adequate to the Church's experience of encounter with God in the liturgical action.

It was suggested earlier that Anglicanism has understood the gospel, God's work of redemption, as present to the experience of believers in every generation. That experience is not primarily a mental activity but rather one in which the whole person is involved. Authentic liturgical worship draws all that is human into its frame of reference. Reason is not put aside, but neither should it dominate. Faith in God involves the mind but it is not desiccated intellectual activity. In faith the mind is illuminated by the heart. Understanding does not precede belief, but is one of its fruits.

The implications of this for the liturgy are far reaching. Fundamentally it means that liturgical rites are not ceremonial clothing for doctrinal teaching. Rather than *teaching* the faith, in the usual sense of that word, the liturgy *celebrates* the faith. It lifts it up through words and signs in a corporate experience which expresses the faith which has summoned the people to gather. Yet it also nourishes that faith, and sends the people forth to live it in their daily lives. It is a transforming experience in which the people themselves are renewed as signs of the mystery which they have assembled to celebrate.

Because of the deep mutuality between what the Church believes and what it prays, the revision of the liturgical rites has serious doctrinal implications. It is not merely a question of modernization of language or clarification of ritual. Our language of corporate prayer—both word and action—is expressive of our experience of God. For a people of faith, rituals hallowed through years of use in public prayer participate in our encounter with the Holy One: they are the instruments of that encounter. Since the sixteenth century, Anglicanism has acknowledged in its liturgical documents the need for revision from time to time. In the Preface to the Book of Common Prayer in 1549, the liturgy is seen as one of the human aspects of the Church which may, for appropriate and serious reasons, undergo change or correction so that it may serve its true purpose. If such revision is not undertaken, the liturgy eventually becomes alienated from the lives of Christians as an encapsulated divine activity which ultimately betrays its roots in the incarnation. Liturgy must be experienced in its connectedness to the lives of worshippers.

Yet such changes do not remain only on the external level. The need for change is itself an indication that the context in which Christians are living their lives has changed, and with that, that our understanding of our relation with God has shifted to new ground. Worship is an articulation of faith. Liturgical change is thus an indication of underlying change both in the Church's self-understanding and in the way it understands the God who is the focus of its worship.

During recent decades, the major Christian churches have been involved in the official revision of their liturgical books. In each communion, and, indeed, in each national body of the various communions, the character of the work of revision has been shaped by a wide range of particular factors of history and culture which cannot be considered within the limitations of this essay. In spite of such differences, however, it is possible to assert that this extensive effort is itself the fruit of the Liturgical Movement whose origins may be discerned in the latter part of the nineteenth century (see pp. 45–6).

The liturgical changes of recent years bear a somewhat ironic relationship to the Romantic Movement and its idealization of the Middle Ages. The relationship is ironic because the impact of the neo-Gothic revival upon the churches (we might note in this regard the Anglican, Lutheran and Roman Catholic Churches in particular) was to hold up certain ideals of liturgy and doctrine, of architecture and sacred music based upon the supposed standards of the High Middle Ages.[6] This initial stage of the Liturgical Movement was at least an answer to the dry rationalism of the Enlightenment, but it also set up static models for the liturgy which were recognized, as the Church moved into the twentieth century, to be pastorally unsuited to a radically different cultural framework from that of medieval times. This awareness carried the Liturgical Movement from its early goal of restoring medieval norms into a recognition that new liturgical imperatives imposed new pastoral requirements upon the official books. In that perspective, it must be acknowledged that the various newly authorized books contain not merely refurbished old rites, but rather patterns for liturgical celebration based upon a profound recovery of a sense of liturgy as the whole Church's celebration of its shared faith. In this we are offered a particular insight into the relation of the gospel to the liturgy within the Anglican tradition, for the Prayer Book tradition is nothing less than the ordered means through which the community of the baptized participate in the redemption which those rites proclaim.

When the final stages of Prayer Book revision had been reached in the United States, organizations which favoured the preservation of the 1928 Book of Common Prayer published articles and tracts which criticized the 'new theology' of the proposed revision. Some of us who are professional liturgists responded defensively that although the rites had been revised, the Prayer Book faith remained the same. We soon realized that this response was naive to say the least, and perhaps even dishonest. The criticism was, in fact, correct, but in a positive sense. The new rites reflected significant theological changes, virtually all of them related to a recovery of a more biblical understanding of the nature of the Church as this touched such basic issues as Christian initiation, the Eucharist, and the role of the ordained ministry in relation to other ministries. In other words, the sacramental and liturgical study of the past several decades had gradually shaped a new mentality, and the eventual effect was to create pressure within the Church that its liturgical rites be more honestly expressive of the faith to which they witness.

To one degree or another, the entire Anglican Communion has been involved in this process. Provinces which are located in the so-called Third World are somewhat later in this development, because of their particular histories in regard to the nations from which they were evangelized. Nineteenth-century missionary attitudes involved not only the proclamation of Christ but generally the imposition of an alien cultural framework as well. In regard to liturgical norms, this led to an uncritical assumption that liturgical practice would quite simply conform to the models which the missionaries brought from home. These were accepted as a definitive standard with little idea that the local culture might bring its own unique gifts into the richness of the Church's liturgical prayer. At best, the Book of Common Prayer was translated, where the local language was not English, but in strict conformity to the model even if this produced anomalies in the second language.

Recent reflection on the theology of mission has brought a severe judgement upon the limited vision of this culture-biased view of liturgical worship. Deeper insight into the theology of symbol and of language, as well as a willingness to recognize the multicultural implications of the incarnation in Christian faith and practice, have placed all these issues in a much more open field in which fresh air is bringing new life to the traditional forms and images.

In other words, the revision of liturgical rites is not a concern restricted to a small group of liturgical specialists. The pastoral need for such revision from time to time has been recognized within the Anglican tradition from the beginning, and was given explicit articulation in the Preface to the first American Book of Common Prayer in 1789, where we read that rites 'may be altered, abridged, enlarged, amended, or otherwise disposed of, as may seem most convenient for the edification of the people'. The revision of the Book of Common Prayer has to do in its most fundamental purpose with the constant reclaiming of the gospel to which the Church is called. For Anglicans, that reclaiming inevitably bears a special and intense relationship to the way the Church prays, that is, to the ways in which the Church articulates its faith in corporate prayer. In the light of this, a revision of the Prayer Book is not limited to some changes in language.

It is interesting to note how often critics of one or another of the new versions have focused upon the question of language, to the virtual exclusion of the wider complex of other, often non-verbal, aspects of liturgical prayer.[7] The newly authorized versions are expressive of theological change, especially in regard to the recovery of a sense of the Church coming into self-realization in its liturgical celebrations. This suggests a greatly expanded theological horizon in which the Church is seen as the gathering place of all cultures and peoples whose languages and symbols merit an equal place within the framework of the Church's life. Such a theological expansion is deeply challenging to the prerogatives which the 'mother church' concept has engendered, and the full extent of this expansion is at this time far beyond our abilities to discern. It challenges us to recognize that the God to whom the traditional rites have been addressed is, if understood as the terminus of those rites, too small a God. Our rites have tended to domesticate God within the images of Western culture projected into the heavenly places. Liturgy is most authentic when it is experienced as awestruck praise, the creature standing at the threshold of the Holy. In praise God is recognized, acknowledged, and thus adored not as the *end* of our prayer but always as the One who moves beyond the grasp of our stuttered praises. The American writer Annie Dillard has summed up the point, saying, 'I often think of the set pieces of liturgy as certain words which people have successfully addressed to God without their getting killed.'[8] No 'God in a box' is at the heart of the gospel, but the Holy One who is consuming fire.

Liturgy must follow a difficult course if it is to permit the faithful to assemble before God 'without their getting killed' and at the same time not so tame the images of God that he becomes unworthy of authentic faith. At the centre of Christian liturgical prayer we find the doctrine of God, not as a series of credal statements but in the lifting up of images which are expressive of how God is understood through Christian faith. The collects, for example, offer a rich array of such images in a succinct form of corporate prayer.[9] In the collects, God is addressed especially in reference to his mercy, grace and love; for example,

Let thy merciful ears, O Lord, be open to the prayers of thy humble servants ...

or

O God, who declarest thy almighty power chiefly in showing mercy and pity, mercifully grant us such a measure of thy grace, that we, running the way of thy commandments, may obtain thy gracious promises, and be made partakers of thy heavenly treasure; through Jesus Christ our Lord.

This theme of the mercy of God occurs again and again, especially as it is manifest in his acceptance of the prayers of the Church or in the preserving of its members from harm.

The grace of God in the collects is often linked to God's forgiveness of sin or in God's enabling us to do good. The first, for example, is seen in the collect which Thomas Cranmer composed for the Book of Common Prayer of 1549 for use on the first Sunday of Advent:

Almighty God, give us grace that we may cast away the works of darkness, and put upon us the armour of light ...

The same theological perspective is expressed in yet another of the traditional collects:

Grant, we beseech thee, Almighty God, that we, who for our evil deeds do worthily deserve to be punished, by the comfort of thy grace may mercifully be relieved; through our Lord and Saviour Jesus Christ.

Here God's mercy and grace are brought together in the forgiveness of sinners. Grace as God's gift enabling us to do what is good is found in a very brief example of the form:

Lord, we pray thee that thy grace may always prevent and follow us, and

63

make us continually to be given to all good works; through Jesus Christ our Lord.

The grace of God as articulated in these examples is expressive of the divine power to touch human life to heal or to enable. The doctrine of God articulated here is not of a distant deity unconcerned with human pain, but of a God who is near at hand, attentive to prayers of his creatures.

The highest attribute of God is his love, as of a father or mother caring for beloved children. Here the liturgy brings us into direct encounter with the paschal mystery; since the love of God has been most clearly revealed in the sending of Jesus, through whose death and resurrection, and our participation in them through baptism, we have been made the children of God, now addressing God as Abba—'Father'. This aspect of the Christian doctrine of God is marvellously expressed in the familiar collect for Palm Sunday:

> Almighty and everlasting God, who, of thy tender love towards mankind hast sent thy Son, our Saviour Jesus Christ, to take upon him our flesh, and to suffer death upon the cross, that all mankind should follow the example of his great humility; Mercifully grant, that we may both follow the example of his patience, and also be made partakers of his resurrection; through the same Jesus Christ our Lord.

The theological significance of a text such as this as an expression of fundamental doctrine, and in this example of a distinctively Anglican character, becomes evident when we note the changes which Cranmer made from the Latin original of this collect. In adapting it for the 1549 Prayer Book, he added the phrase 'of thy tender love', thus indicating that it was God's love which was the motivating energy behind the incarnation of Jesus Christ. Further, with again a strong doctrinal concern, Cranmer removed the petition that we might 'merit to be partakers of his resurrection' and substituted the petition that we might 'follow' Christ's example. Here we see a characteristic concern of the Reformers that there be no question of grace earned through merit. In Cranmer's version, the grace and action of God are seen as the expression of God's love, not as rewards to be earned.[10]

Given these attributes of God which recur throughout the repertory of Anglican collects, the human response to these qualities finds its appropriate expression within the liturgical context, when the children of God gather on the basis of their common identity in Christ. That response is praise and thanksgiving, not only in the specific liturgical action of the Eucharist but in the whole of life as an offering of praise to God.[11] As expressed in the words of the General Thanksgiving, 'We, thine unworthy servants, do give thee most humble and hearty thanks for all thy goodness and loving-kindness to us, and to all men.' In words which have been used in Anglican worship since 1662, the prayer brings together every aspect of life as the ground of thanksgiving. At the centre is 'the redemption of the world by our Lord Jesus Christ', but the response of praise is to be 'not only with our lips, but in our lives, by giving up ourselves to thy service'. Here within the liturgical context the critical link is made between what we believe, what we pray and how we live.

Using the texts of the Prayer Book tradition, we might similarly explore the fundamental aspects of Christian faith as expressed and celebrated in the forms of Christian prayer. Although it is not possible to consider other examples here, it should already be evident why the Prayer Book plays such a fundamental role in Anglicanism as the basis of a shared faith. What is prayed is, as the adage affirms, what is believed. Although the *Articles of Religion* hold a significant place in Anglican history as a summary of Christian doctrine, and have special importance in showing how Anglicanism found a place to stand within the polarizing debates of the sixteenth century, it is not in such documents that the spirit of Anglicanism is to be found, but rather in its worship (see pp. 144–54).

Yet the liturgy does not articulate a static norm of faith. There is an extraordinary dynamic within the liturgical act which always holds up a 'beyond', at which the Church has not yet arrived. In this regard, there is always a proleptic, or anticipatory, dimension in the liturgy. One sees this, for example, in eschatological references such as are found in the Advent Collect quoted earlier where, after speaking of the humility of Christ's birth, the prayer continues, 'that in the last day, when he shall come again in his glorious majesty to judge both the quick and the dead, we may rise to the life immortal'. The liturgy thus holds before us not-yet-realized aspects of Christian faith. In this perspective, the liturgy always points us to God's future action, and thus works against attempts to fix the truth of the gospel in static formulas. To claim the gospel we are required to open to dimensions of it which have not yet been revealed, or which we have failed to discern. The Church's re-examination of its liturgical rites is thus a necessity if we are not to become complacent simply because the phrases have become so familiar. A kind of discontinuity becomes a pastoral necessity if we are to be jolted into hearing the eternally new call of God which lies behind the words and rituals.

It was to this fruitful discontinuity that I alluded earlier when I spoke of the reaction to the *new* theology of the recent versions of the Prayer Book. The theology is new precisely because it is the theology of the great tradition which must be reclaimed in terms of the life and culture of each generation of the Church's members. The eternal gospel is not preserved through a rigid adherence to the familiar rites and phrases, but rather in allowing it to speak from its centre, the experience of the paschal mystery in the lives of Christians today. In this way, the Prayer Book plays a dynamic role in shaping a new liturgical mentality in which the odd truths are seen afresh. Such a transition never takes place easily, because there seems to be a natural conservatism in worshippers in regard to the rituals through which faith has been articulated. An individual believer may have used certain forms of prayer for decades, and this matter must therefore be approached by the Church with great sensitivity. But at the same time, as we have seen, change must come so that we may be faithful to the gospel as it speaks to the real world in which we live. If the law of prayer establishes the law of faith, then new forms of prayer can challenge Christians to grow into a deeper understanding of the faith they profess.

There is evidence that the Book of 1979 has already begun to reshape the theological understanding of members of the Episcopal Church in the United States. Such reshaping, as we have observed, takes place slowly because theological attitudes which have been shaped through years of experience do not change easily, and for years to come there will be clergy as well as laity who will attempt to use the new Prayer Book upon the ground-plan which operated beneath the previous edition. This misuse restricts liturgy to its surface dimensions, so that what the rite is intended to say is undermined by the manner in which it is celebrated.

One example of this problem comes immediately to mind. The baptismal rite of the 1928 Book of Common Prayer took as its model the baptism of a child or infant. Adult candidates are a clearly secondary expectation. The rite further presumed that the baptism was a separate liturgical action, not connected to any important corporate celebration, such as the Sunday Eucharist. The baptismal liturgy of the 1979 Book of Common Prayer is quite different in its expectations, in regard not only to the above matters but in its whole ethos. It is not simply a matter of changes or adjustments of the texts, but more significantly, of the theology upon which Christian initiation is based (see pp. 293–307).

The new rite, for example, establishes that an adult is the normative candidate for baptism through the way the liturgy is structured: adults and older children are presented first, thus indicating a theological priority for those who can speak for themselves. Again, the way the rite is printed indicates that the normative pattern should be celebration of baptism in the context of the Eucharist, and this is supported by an introductory rubric to the rite. The new rite thus reverses the expectations upon which the former rite was based.

Such significant changes are not a matter of mere ritual updating, but are indicative of a major shift in the theological understanding of the rite. The new form breaks with the privatized model of baptism which had dominated in pastoral practice for centuries. We see in this shift the fruit of decades of study of the history and theology of Christian initiation as it bubbles forth at the level of pastoral practice. The rediscovered theology of initiation is directly related to the recovery of a biblical understanding of the Church as the people of God. The gospel of our participation in the paschal mystery through baptism is thus reclaimed by changes in the liturgical rite which support such a theology.

Further results have developed out of this fundamental theological change. The celebration of baptism within the Eucharist on Sunday has reawakened the Church's awareness of the essential link between the two sacraments, that baptism is entrance into the communion fellowship, and that the Eucharist is itself a sacrament of initiation, the fulfilment of the process of the making of a Christian. Yet this link has been obscured for centuries at the level of pastoral practice, which had separated Communion from the rite of baptism and attached it to a later rite associated with a certain level of intellectual understanding. Historical research in this area has again borne fruit at the pastoral level, by revealing the questionable influences which separated what had for centuries in Christian practice been understood as integrally related.[12]

These matters concerning baptism and related issues are but one example of a whole complex of critical areas in which the mutuality between liturgy and doctrine may be seen. It is not that the liturgy is a didactic tool, but rather that it inevitably articulates an underlying theology. When research leads to deepened knowledge, when historical facts turn out not to be what we thought they were, when theology has strayed from the strong lines of the great tradition, and when pastoral practice does not bear fruit in building up the common life of the Body of Christ, then ritual patterns must be critically revised so that they may more adequately fulfil their role as signs of the abiding action of God in the Church. Liturgical change is the response in the Church to the awareness of God's present imperatives within the community of faith.

The Book of Common Prayer is for Anglicans far more than a collection of rites. Within Anglicanism the Prayer Book is a living expression of the profound union between what we believe and what we pray; a doctrinal document, not because it may contain such didactic materials as a catechism, or historical materials of doctrinal significance, but because it is in corporate worship that Anglicans find the common ground for their profession of faith. In this sense, Anglicanism has never understood itself as a 'confessional church' in the way, for example, that Lutheranism has identified its faith with certain documents which are fundamental to its identity. Anglicanism has claimed no faith of its own, but only that faith which the Church at all times and in all places has celebrated in its corporate worship.

Although the Nicene Creed is a statement of faith issued by a general council of the Church and thus accepted as authoritative for Anglicanism, its significance as a doctrinal foundation among Anglicans is probably far more the result of its liturgical use than of a preoccupation with the authority of a council. This is but one example of the way in which corporate prayer has shaped belief through the impact of the Book of Common Prayer, not only in shaping Anglican piety but theology as well.

This experience of the reciprocity of liturgy and doctrine is reinforced as a normative relationship in a comment made by Aidan Kavanagh at a meeting of the North American Academy of Liturgy in 1983, when he noted that liturgical theology is

> the primary theological act of believing Christians, as distinct from, say, systematic theologies *about* the liturgy or whatever, which are secondary. I think that the liturgical act, so far from being related to secondary theological endeavor as matter has been said to be related to form, is in fact the primary and foundational theological act from which all subsequent theological activity arises. The liturgical assembly is a theological corporation.[13]

These words of Kavanagh are a remarkable and forceful confirmation of the Anglican experience: 'The liturgical act ... is in fact the primary and fundamental theological act'. The living God is present, known and adored by a people of faith: the liturgical action is the embodiment of the response of faith. This liturgical act, Kavanagh is saying, is the primary place at which the Church *does* theology. It is the fruitful awareness of God's presence and grace and thus both expresses faith and nourishes it. Systematic reflection upon this faith experience is what we usually call 'theology', but, Kavanagh tells us, this latter is theology in a derived sense. Primary theology is what the whole Church does in its liturgical prayer.

So it is that in the Anglican tradition, faith and praise are united. The fundamental energy which sustains the liturgical action is the faith of the gathered people. That faith may be illuminated by a high level of study and reflection: theologians also go to church and share in the common prayer. But standing beside those whose vocation it is to think about the faith, there are others who are no less fully members of the family of God. They offer prayer together. The liturgy is not concerned about distinctions of intellect, but calls all the members of the Body into a common act of praise. Their presence in such an assembly is the fundamental expression of their participation in the paschal mystery of Jesus Christ through baptism, and of the continuing activity of the Holy Spirit in deepening the life of faith. That participation in the Trinity is the way the gospel is experienced through life in the Church. It is there that the saving work of God is proclaimed, believed and celebrated (see pp. 351–64).

JUSTIFICATION BY FAITH

The doctrine of justification stands above all other theological issues as the distinctive mark of the Reformation. Although the doctrine is most closely associated with Lutheranism, it is in fact a primary aspect of the Anglican tradition as well, and indeed of all the churches shaped out of the painful confrontation within the Church in the sixteenth century. The doctrine is concerned with God's free and gracious initiative for the salvation of the human race, an initiative revealed in human history in the paschal mystery of Jesus Christ. The fruit of God's initiative in Christ is transforming grace which liberates men and women from the burden of personal guilt and alienation from God. This act of God—*salvation*—is a free gift. It cannot be bought or earned. It can only be accepted or rejected. Its acceptance is the act of faith by which, in spite of the reality of sin, the free grace of God justifies us.

The term 'salvation' is understood in different ways in the various Christian traditions. For Anglicans, it involves not only the forgiveness of sins but also the call to a holy life. The fruit of God's gift is sanctification, that is, to live in the power of God's transforming grace. Anglicanism has traditionally emphasized the life of those who are justified, a life of sanctification and of service to mankind. This emphasis on holy living is a fundamental aspect of the Anglican interpretation of the doctrine of justification, and in regard to this essay, is an essential link with the role of the liturgy in the Christian life. In the worship of the Church, in the proclamation of Scripture and preaching, and in the celebration of the sacramental signs of faith, God's gift of grace through the death and resurrection of Jesus is articulated in word and act, that is, through the senses, as God continues to touch and transform the human situation. Although each individual person is called to accept this gift in faith, the individual can never be radically isolated from the corporate life of the community of faith. From the moment a person is baptized, the whole Church is engaged as the context in which God's gift is both proclaimed and received. This proclamation through word and sign is the most basic work of the Church, calling into and sustaining within its fellowship those who perceive in Christ the sacrament, the human and historical sign, of mankind's encounter with God.

In the *Articles of Religion*, the doctrine of justification is set forth in these words:

We are accounted righteous before God, only for the merit of our Lord

69

and Saviour Jesus Christ by Faith, and not for our own works or deservings. Wherefore, that we are justified by Faith only, is a most wholesome Doctrine, and very full of comfort, as more largely is expressed in the Homily of Justification.[14]

The essential concern in this passage is linked to the word *merit*: it is only 'for the merit of our Lord and Saviour Jesus Christ by Faith' that mankind is justified before God, 'not for our own works or deservings'. In the latter Middle Ages until the time immediately prior to the Reformation, the idea was linked to the principle that 'those who do what is in them' will not be denied the grace of God. We can see the importance of the human response to God's gift. As noted above, Anglicanism's concern with sanctification as the fruit of salvation indicates that the acceptance of God's grace is not just an internal mental activity but is visibly manifested in the transformation of the believer's life-style. This characteristic balance on so hotly debated an issue is reflected in the Article following the one on Justification, 'Of Good Works'. The text reads:

Albeit that Good Works, which are the fruits of Faith, and follow after Justification, cannot put away our sins, and endure the severity of God's judgment; yet are they pleasing and acceptable to God in Christ, and do spring out necessarily of a true and lively Faith; insomuch that by them a lively faith may be as evidently known as a tree discerned by the fruit.[15]

This latter Article was aimed at striking the Anglican *via media* between what was seen as the Roman overemphasis upon good works as a means of earning forgiveness and merit on the one hand, and the rejection of any significant role for good works in the life of faith, a view attributed to Luther.

The Reformation debate on justification grew out of what was generally viewed by the Reformers as the corrupt theological climate of the later medieval period. A concern had emerged about the role of human nature in the divine–human encounter which had led into a preoccupation with what it is that Christians are called to *do* in their daily lives. It was taught that if we do what is in us, God will not deny us the gift of grace. This principle flowed easily into a dangerous distortion of the gospel in which certain types of doing—good works—were seen to earn us the grace of God. It led, in pastoral practice, to clergy urging people to prove themselves worthy of acceptance by God through the doing of such good works. For the Reformers, this was a major theological error, but it was not only an intellectual concern for them. It was in the area of practical piety that the bitter fruit of the error was most evident: salvation had come to be generally viewed as something earned by such 'good works' as the fulfilment of an array of penitential disciplines, and through stipends paid for the intentions at Mass. The latter came to be identified especially with the system of requiem Masses which developed into ever more extended and elaborate patterns as the medieval period began to wane. This system was a major source of income for the church.

The attacks levelled by the Reformers against such practices were a threat to the entire clericalized power structure of the church, a threat which was immediately recognized by an often decadent clergy. The emphasis of the Reformers upon the doctrine of justification must be seen against this background. They were particularly concerned about countless numbers of the faithful who lived at the edge of despair because they were unable to buy or earn sufficient merit to be assured of salvation. It was to this situation that the the Reformers responded that it was 'not for our own works or deservings', but only through the grace of God which we accept in faith. The gospel was reclaimed that only through the death and resurrection of Jesus, that is, through what God has done and not anything on our own part, was salvation possible at all. This was the fundamental article of faith, that Jesus Christ 'was put to death for our trespasses and raised again for our justification'.[16]

Given the impact of the medieval merit system upon the piety of Christians, it cannot surprise us that the Reformers were deeply concerned about liturgical and sacramental matters. The corruptions associated with the stipend system left their taint upon the Eucharist itself. There was a desire for radical purification of the liturgical life of the Church as a whole, the removal of abuse and superstition, and the restoration of an authentically biblical piety. Within some of the Reformed traditions, memory of the corruptions led to disparagement of the medieval liturgical heritage. Simplification along the lines of what were believed to be the biblical standards became an imperative, and on the whole, most of the medieval tradition was swept away.

The reform did not take so radical a path in Anglicanism, however, and this seems to have been the result not only of a natural conservatism but perhaps most significantly because of the understanding of the relation of sanctification to justification: justification involves sanctification in the Christian life, and the instrumental means of that sanctification is found in the sacramental life of the Church. Behind this we see the importance of the incarnation for the Anglican understanding of both Church and sacraments. As we read in the Article 'Of the Sacraments':

> Sacraments ordained of Christ be not only badges or tokens of Christian men's profession, but rather they be certain sure witnesses, and effectual signs of grace, and God's good will towards us, by the which he doth

work invisibly in us, and doth not only quicken, but also strengthen and confirm our Faith in him.[17]

We see the incarnational principle here in the reference to 'effectual signs of grace'. The whole idea behind the sacraments for Anglicans is that God acts through persons, events and things. The physical, material world is not alien to God; it is his creation. That relation of the physical world to the will and purpose of the Creator is fully exemplified in the incarnation in which, through the instrumentality of the life of Jesus, God has brought redemption to the world.

The *Articles of Religion* thus offer a sensitively balanced treatment of this question within Anglicanism, clearly sympathetic to the emphasis placed upon the doctrine of justification as interpreted by continental Reformers, yet cutting its own path between the polarized positions on both sides. The first major exponent of the Anglican view was, of course, Richard Hooker. In a sermon preached while Hooker was Master of the Temple, and later published as 'A Learned Discourse of Justification', Hooker shows how faith and works do not exclude each other although justification is itself through faith alone. He writes,

> [Our adversaries] claim that we tread all Christian virtues under our feet, and require nothing in Christians but faith; because we teach that faith alone justifieth: whereas we by this speech never meant to exclude either hope and charity from being always joined as inseparable mates with faith in the man that is justified; or works from being added to necessary duties, required at the hands of every justified man.[18]

In this passage, Hooker refuses to isolate the doctrine of justification as though it may be esteemed in separation from the other dimensions of the Christian life, including good works as a requirement of those who have been justified.

It is in this perspective that we must consider the strong emphasis which Hooker places upon the sacraments as outward signs of God's justifying grace. In *The Laws of Ecclesiastical Polity*, Hooker speaks of the necessity of sacraments in the effecting of God's purposes:

> That saving grace which Christ originally is or hath for the general good of the whole Church, by sacraments he severally deriveth into every member thereof. Sacraments serve as the instruments of God to that end and purpose, moral instruments, the use whereof is in our hands, the effect in his [. . .] For we take not baptism nor the eucharist for bare *resemblances* or memorials of things absent, neither for *naked signs* and testimonies assuring us of grace received before, but (as they are indeed and in verity) for means effectual whereby God when we take the

sacraments delivereth into our hands that grace available unto eternal life, which grace the sacraments represent or signify.[19]

For Hooker, God's gift of justification is thus effectively signified in the sacramental signs which are truly, by God's purpose and effect, instruments of grace.

Does Hooker's teaching differ significantly from the other positions taken during the debate on justification? First, let us consider the teaching of the Augsburg Confession of 1530, since Article XII of the *Articles of Religion* was at least in part intended as a contradiction of 'solifidianism', the idea that we are saved by a bare faith. The first important question is whether this was indeed the Lutheran teaching. The Article on justification in the Augsburg Confession reads as follows:

> It is also taught among us that we cannot obtain forgiveness of sin and righteousness before God by our own merits, works, or satisfactions, but that we receive forgiveness of sin and become righteous before God by grace, for Christ's sake, through faith, when we believe that Christ suffered for us and that for his sake our sin is forgiven and righteousness and eternal life are given to us. For God will regard and reckon this faith as righteousness, as Paul says in Romans 3.21–26 and 4.5.[20]

The most interesting contrast between this statement and the Anglican Article on justification is the significant emphasis given here to the forgiveness of sin, which is not even mentioned in Anglican form. Although there is no major theological difference in the intention of the two versions, there is clearly a difference of ethos. A certain weight of responsibility for justification falls upon Christians to *believe* they are justified, an idea which also finds no place in the Anglican Article. Yet certainly the central point in both is that justification comes only through God's grace, and that the only merit involved is that of Jesus Christ.

What is the role of good works within the Lutheran system of thought? Article XX of the Confession deals with 'Faith and Good Works'. Its opening sentence is a direct response to the accusation of 'solifidianism': 'Our teachers have been falsely accused of forbidding good works.' Later in this rather long Article, the problem of the relation between faith and works is explored in detail. First, it affirms that our reconciliation with God happens only through faith, and that works cannot achieve this purpose. This view is supported with reference to St Paul's teaching in Ephesians 2.8–9: 'For by grace you have been saved through faith [. . .] not because of works.' Reference is also made to the teaching of St Augustine on this point.

The passage then continues with an aspect of the question which seems to have been of central concern to Luther, that is, the unrest of conscience suffered by many Christians who attempted to find salvation within the merit system: 'The conscience cannot come to rest and peace through works, but only through faith, that is, when it is assured and knows that for Christ's sake it has a gracious God.' Since clergy had failed to preach justification by faith, people had been driven to rely on their own efforts.

The final part of the Article addresses the question of good works:

It is also taught among us that good works should and must be done, not that we are to rely on them to earn grace but that we may do God's will and glorify him. It is always faith alone that apprehends grace and forgiveness of sin. When through faith the Holy Spirit is given, the heart is moved to do good works.[21]

There is obviously a tension in this passage which finds no comparable parallel in the Anglican Article of good works. One senses the depth of reaction against a piety of merit, nor is there place here for the idea that good works are 'pleasing and acceptable to God in Christ', as is found in the Anglican version. The Lutheran form takes a far more polarized view on the issue, and in this regard is more characteristic of the passion which supported this teaching in the heat of the Reformation.

Similarly, there is evident contrast between the Anglican article on the sacraments and that of the Augsburg Confession. The whole thrust of the statement in the Confession is the relationship of the sacraments to faith:

They are signs and testimonies of God's will toward us for the purpose of awakening and strengthening our faith. For this reason they require faith, and they are rightly used when they are received in faith and for the purpose of strengthening faith.[22]

None of this is contradicted in the Anglican Article, but in the latter we find a firm emphasis upon the instrumentality of the sacraments as 'effectual signs of grace [. . .] by the which he doth work invisibly in us'. The contrast suggests that underlying the Lutheran form is a conscious cautiousness resulting from abuses of pastoral practice of the sacraments, and hence a resulting hesitancy about any reference to objective grace being effected through them.

For Calvin, faith is the source of a double grace, first, 'that being reconciled to God through Christ's blamelessness, we may have in heaven instead of a Judge a gracious Father; and secondly, that sanctified by Christ's spirit we may cultivate blamelessness and purity of life'.[23] Thus, Calvin sees both justification and sanctification as the fruit of faith. The latter, sanctification, is seen by Calvin as inseparable from justification. The justified life of faith bears fruit in good works; faith and good works must cleave together. By faith, Calvin writes, we grasp Christ's righteousness, by which alone we are reconciled to God. Yet you could not grasp this without at the same time grasping sanctification also. [. . .] Therefore Christ justifies no one whom he does not at the same time sanctify. These benefits are joined together by an everlasting and indissoluble bond. [. . .] We are justified not without works yet not through works, since in our sharing in Christ, which justifies us, sanctification is just as much included as righteousness.[24]

Justification is itself God's free gift, in no sense a reward for good works. Those who are justified by faith are justified apart from any question of merit for works, but simply as a gift of God's mercy.

When we consider Calvin's teaching on the sacraments, it is immediately evident that abuses in sacramental theology and piety exert a powerful influence upon his views. Calvin sees the purpose of the sacraments as the confirmation of faith, not in their own right but as agents of the Holy Spirit. Their value is as God's instruments, since they do not, according to Calvin, impart grace of themselves. In his discussion of this issue, we find a high level of revulsion in Calvin against magical conceptions which had become attached to a certain type of sacramental piety. What is primary for Calvin is God's gift of justification and sanctification. In a reference to the teaching of Augustine, he rejects the idea of an objective instrumentality because 'there can be invisible sanctification without a visible sign, and on the other hand a visible sign without true sanctification'.[25] This is an important contrast to what we observed above in Article XXV of the Anglican *Articles of Religion* in which God's invisible work is effectively linked to the sacraments as outward signs of grace.

Finally we may consider how the Council of Trent dealt with the doctrine of justification. The Council reaffirmed the unique role of Christ whose passion is the source of grace for those reborn in him. Without this rebirth, a person cannot be justified before God. No one comes to justification through any personal merit, whether by faith or works. We come to be justified only by the grace of God.

It is important to note that the bishops at Trent insisted upon the primacy of faith in their description of justification: 'Faith is the beginning of human salvation, without which it is impossible to please God.' Yet faith does not stand alone but is vivified in relation to hope and charity. Thus, the bishops wrote,

In justification itself one receives through Christ, into whom one is engrafted, along with the forgiveness of sins, all these gifts infused at the same time: faith, hope and charity. For faith, unless hope and charity be added to it, neither unites one perfectly with Christ, nor makes one a living member of his body.[26]

The council then went on to speak of faith as co-operating with good works so that consequently God finally judges human beings 'not apart from' the merit which he gives them. Although Trent asserted that Christians should never trust in themselves, this approach to the merit attached to good works left the way open for what Reformers saw to be the undermining of the gospel that trust was to be placed in God alone. In its conclusion on the issue of justification, Trent says that the justified person 'by the good deeds which are done by him, through the grace of God, and the merit of Jesus Christ (of whom he is a living member) truly merits an increase of grace, eternal life, and the attainment of that eternal life (if indeed he die in grace), as well as an increase in glory'. Although Trent's reaffirmation of the primacy of grace in justification was an important response to the Pelagianism of much late medieval piety, in the end the council's approach to good works did not deal radically enough with the central concern of the Reformation.

This overview of the justification question reveals not only the unity of the various Reformed traditions in the rejection of any concept of merit as the source of the grace of justification, but also the distinctions of approach between Lutherans, Calvinists and Anglicans. While clearly within the Reformation tradition in its understanding of justification, Anglicanism distanced itself from both Calvin and Luther in ways which have been presented here. It is particularly with regard to the role of the sacraments as instruments of grace that Anglicanism maintained its own middle way: as Hooker wrote, 'Sacraments serve as the instruments of God.' They are thus God's actions toward mankind, occasions in which through participation in the outward forms, men and women are involved in an active response to the grace of God. In this perspective, Anglicanism pursued the *via media* which permitted the Prayer Book tradition to continue many of the forms of liturgical prayer which had been the Church's heritage from centuries past; and yet, at the same time, to take a firm stand on the Reformation principle that it is only by the gift of God's grace that we are saved. This reliance upon the grace of God as affirmed and celebrated within Anglicanism fostered that we might call a 'theology of confidence', which has set Anglican piety within an ethos clearly distinct from that of either Lutheranism or Calvinism in its emphasis upon the victory of Christ. It is thus that the image of Christ the High Priest has played so significant a role for Anglican devotion. It is a theology that underlies the world-affirming incarnational character expressed in Anglican worship, which draws its orientation from the great affirmation of the Epistle to the Hebrews:

Since we have a great high priest who has passed into the heavens, Jesus, the Son of God, let us with confidence draw near to the throne of grace, that we may receive mercy and find grace to help him in time of need.[27]

SACRAMENTAL WORSHIP AND THE GOSPEL

Our consideration of the doctrine of justification has shown, among the Churches shaped by Reformation principles, that Anglicanism has seen a special importance in the sacraments as visible means of God's grace. This high claim for the sacraments can be made because of the dynamic relation between sacraments and faith. The sacraments presume faith and yet are at the same time articulations of it. Without faith, the liturgical rites are merely external forms. This was Calvin's concern, as we noted earlier, when he asserted that 'there can be invisible sanctification without a visible sign, and on the other hand a visible sign without true sanctification'. What Calvin claims here is true, and it is a fact of the Church's life that it is possible for parishioners to participate in sacramental actions without (in so far as can be judged from the outside) the fruit of sanctification being evident. It is not a question of one standard model for a holy life by which this may be judged. What seems lacking in these instances is a making of connections, a recognition that what is proclaimed in the liturgy and professed by our lips is connected to how we go out from the liturgy to live our daily lives. It is, I think, what Hooker was referring to when he called the sacraments 'moral instruments' in that they must be linked to the inner core of a Christian's life.

The living out of the connections between worship and life takes place, for Christians, in the context of the Church. It is a major part of the Church's prophetic work—its speaking for God—to enable people to make those connections so that worship is not reduced to a pious Sunday morning routine. Through baptism, the members of the Church have been incorporated into God's saving work in Christ. It is around this work that the life of the Church is structured, not around the providing of religious rites which serve as a veneer to unconverted lives. The baptized community, through participation in the paschal mystery, is nurtured for maturity in the life of faith and is enabled to go forth to proclaim that saving mystery to the world. Through faith believers are given access to an intimate union with God, sharing in the divine energy which enlivens and nourishes the whole body. That union is created through baptism and in turn signified and deepened through the shared eucharistic meal. Yet this whole participation in the presence and grace of God springs from faith. Without faith, the sacraments are like a body without breath or blood.

Reflection on the sacraments has, on the whole, not focused adequately on their relation to faith. As we observed in Article XXV on the sacraments, they are instruments of God by which faith in him is quickened, strengthened and confirmed. Through their physicality the sacraments correspond to our physical nature, so that as the expression of love involves not just an interior attitude but the whole person, so is it also with faith: faith requires an enfleshing, a response in which the whole physical being is involved.

This is the principle upon which the idea of sacrament is founded. It is reflected in the words of Tertullian, 'The flesh is the hinge of salvation.'[28] The outward, physical aspects of the sacraments are the instrumental means by which faith articulates both God's gift of grace and the human acceptance of the gift. The gathering of the baptized on the Lord's Day to celebrate the Eucharist is a recapitulation of the whole meaning of incorporation into Christ's Body. The celebration of the paschal feast is the means by which the faithful enter into the paschal mystery into which they are baptized. The whole integrity of the act depends upon the active faith of the participants which connects its meaning with all the dimensions of human life. The gospel is seen to illuminate not just a religious segment of life, but life itself. The full meaning of the act is that of a life-bearing event which lifts the whole of life in thanksgiving to God. Surface rituals do not have such power. They tend to remain encapsulated in a private world of piety. But the sacraments link us to creation as God's first act of love toward mankind, and our participation in faith links us to God's redemptive purpose as it illuminates the whole of human history.

Every sacramental action is first of all an expression of God's initiative, and the context of our response is always shaped by the cultural and historical realities of the Church's life at a particular time and in a particular place. In our earlier discussion of liturgical change, we observed how strong the tendency seems to be to set the Church's liturgical practice in stone, as a static expression of God's changelessness. Yet the liturgical rites did not descend from heaven on a cloud. They are not divinely authored, but rather divinely imbued. As Hooker wrote: 'The use (of the sacraments)... is in our hands, the effect in his.' Our responsibility for their use as the Church expresses its faith in every time and place requires a sensitive ear to the voice of God speaking often in new ways as the act of creation goes on. The right use of the sacraments involves an intuitive insight into how the signs of faith may best express that faith in the ordinary materials of human life. The incarnation reveals God's action in the humility of the ordinary, within the common realities of human life.

Christian belief in the incarnation establishes a principle by which we may discern the signs of God's abiding presence in the whole of creation. God's grace is not limited to the sacraments, but the sacramental principle enables us to recognize God's presence and activity beyond the quite specific framework of liturgical rites. We are permitted to see the Christian sacramental system as rooted in the elements of our common humanity. To suggest that God's grace is effective only through the sacramental forms carries us into the realm of magic. That was Calvin's fear, and he was right. God is not limited to any set of forms and rituals. But to recognize in the Church's sacraments the signs of God's active gifts of grace is to discover their purpose as his instruments for building up the Body of Christ. The sacraments can never be a private means of grace, because they always unite us to the whole family of faith in a common offering of praise and thanksgiving. As Hooker taught, 'That saving grace which Christ originally is or hath for the general good of the whole Church, by sacraments he severally deriveth into every member thereof.'

PLURALISM AND THE GOSPEL

At the opening of this chapter, the question of the understanding of the gospel in Anglicanism was placed against the backdrop of the present ecumenical scene. The discussion of justification revealed how certain aspects of the Church's teaching can overlap between one tradition and another, and yet that complementarity was also paralleled by contradiction. Justification, a fundamental issue in the understanding of the gospel, was understood differently by the various participants in the Reformation debates. The identification of these various churches with certain geographical areas made it all too easy for each tradition to go its separate way. And so there evolved those particular constellations of factors, of worship and piety, of biblical interpretation and theological method, which came to characterize, for example, Anglicanism or Lutheranism or Roman Catholicism. Denominationalism was the result of a failure within the various traditions to deal with diversity. The hostilities of debate reinforced by geographical distance made it all too easy to live as though the other traditions scarcely existed.

We cannot look at questions of Christian faith and practice in this way any longer. No characteristic is narrowly defined by a denominational line. The Book of Common Prayer has over the centuries supplied liturgical materials for the use of other traditions. But in recent years, the influence is mutual as common ecumenical forms find a home in an increasing number of national versions of the Book of Common Prayer. We are no longer defined by what separates us from other Christians, or at least we may say that the number of Christians who are ill at ease with such a basis for religious identity is growing.

My point is that the gospel is fundamental to all Christians, and that although there are inevitable differences of ethos within each tradition, the

79

common ground is becoming ever more visible. The Lima Statement referred to at the beginning of this chapter is a powerful example of the remarkable degree of convergence which has already been achieved. If we cherish our particularity, this can no longer include a rejection of the commonality which Christians share by virtue of the one baptism.

In its document *For the Sake of the Kingdom*, the Inter-Anglican Theological and Doctrinal Commission speaks convincingly of the pluriformity of the Church. The Anglican tradition has encompassed 'differing styles of piety, differing idioms in theology, and differing agenda for Christian witness and action'. This diversity has been difficult for some Anglicans who have wanted to envision the Church in a single mould of their own design. But the document suggests that the pluralism which has characterized Anglicanism is in fact the reality in which the whole Church finds itself, and there is thus set before us a very different cultural situation from that in which denominational distinctions were nurtured. The document continues,

If the church, because it lives 'in Christ' by the grace and power of the Holy Spirit, is a sign and agent of God's Kingdom in and for the world, it is so—always and necessarily—in a radically 'located' fashion. The church exists in particular places and at particular times, and the truth which its life and action carry is conveyed only to the extent that it too is 'located'. This means, as we have seen, that Christians in a given place and time both will and must share the cultural idiom of their geographical and social locale. It also means that their life and witness both will and must address the issues, moral and political, with which historical circumstance confronts them in that locale. The church belongs to all its many places and times, and it is in this fact that its legitimate pluriformity is, in the end, rooted.[29]

Such pluralism is not simply a situation to be endured, but is rather a stimulus to a deeper penetration into God's purposes for the Church. It is an opportunity through which Christians may come to a fuller awareness of the scope of the Gospel.

To affirm pluralism, then, is to affirm not one but two things. On the one hand it means to assert that there is good in the existence and continuing integrity of a variety of traditions and ways of life; on the other hand, it means to assert that there is good in their interplay and dialogue. For Christians, moreover, such affirmation of pluralism has a special meaning. It embodies a recognition that every human culture has God's Kingdom as its horizon in creation and redemption. At the same time, it acknowledges that, in the dialogue between traditions, people's understanding of the meaning of God's Kingdom, and of the

Christ who bears it, may be enhanced. Pluralism, when understood in this way, is a stimulus to the repentance by which believers discern and turn to God's Kingdom.[30]

The gospel in Anglicanism is, then, one facet in a vast mosaic. In its essentials, it corresponds to the gospel as it has been proclaimed and believed all over the world. Yet it is also characterized by its particularity as an experience of God's saving work in particular cultures, and is shaped by the insights and limitations of persons who were themselves seeking to live the gospel within a particular context. In Anglicanism, the gospel tradition has been closely linked to a particular understanding of worship in the Christian life. In our dialogue with Christians of other traditions, that will be no small gift to offer.

BIBLIOGRAPHY
Anderson, H. G., Murphy, T. A. and Burgess, J. A., *Justification by Faith: Lutherans and Catholics in Dialogue VII*. Angsburg, Minneapolis, 1985.
Avis, Paul, *Ecumenical Theology and the Elusiveness of Doctrine*. SPCK, London, 1986.
Bull, George, 'On Justification' in P. E. More and F. L. Cross (eds), *Anglicanism: the thought and practice of the Church of England, illustrated from the religious literature of the seventeenth century*. SPCK, London, 1935, pp. 296–300.
Bunting, I. B. (ed.), *Celebrating the Anglican Way*. Hodder & Stoughton, London, 1996.
Chadwick, Henry, 'The Context of Faith and Theology in Anglicanism' in A. A. Vogel (ed.), *Theology in Anglicanism*. Morehouse-Barlow, Wilton CT 1984, pp. 11–31.
Doctrine Commission of the Church of England, *Believing in The Church: The Corporate Nature of Faith*. SPCK, London, 1981.
Doctrine Commission of the General Synod of the Church of England, *We Believe in God: A Report*. CHP, London, 1987.
Doctrine Commission of the General Synod of the Church of England, *We believe in the Holy Spirit: A Report*. CHP, London, 1991.
Doctrine Commission of the General Synod of the Church of England, *The Mystery of Salvation: The Story of God's Gift*. CHP, London, 1995.
Hardy, D. W. and Ford, D. F., *Jubilate: Theology in Praise*. DLT, London, 1984.
Hooker, Richard, 'A Learned Discourse of Justification, Works, and How the Foundation of Faith is Overthrown' in *Works*, vol. iii. Oxford 1841.
McGrath, A. E., *Iustitia Dei: A History of the Christian Doctrine of Justification*, 2 vols. CUP, 1986.
McGrath, A. E., *The Renewal of Anglicanism*. SPCK, London, 1993.
Ramsey, A. M., *The Gospel and the Catholic Church*. Longmans, Green & Co., London, 1936, 1955; SPCK, London, 1990.
Second Anglican–Roman Catholic International Commission, *Salvation and the Church: an agreed statement*. CHP, London, 1987.
Stevenson, K. and Spinks, B. (eds), *The Identity of Anglican Worship*. Mowbray, London, 1991.

Weil, Louis, *Gathered to Pray*. Cowley Publications/Forward Movement, Cambridge MA 1986.

NOTES

1 *Baptism, Eucharist and Ministry*. Faith and Order Paper No.3 (WCC, Geneva, 1982).

2 Anderson, Murphy and Burgess (eds), *Justification by Faith: Lutherans and Catholics in Dialogue VII*. Cf. *Anglican–Lutheran Dialogue: The Report of the European Commission* (SPCK, London, 1983), pp. 8–10; *Lutheran–Episcopal Dialogue: Report and Recommendations* (Forward Movement, Cincinnati, 1981), pp. 22–4.

3 Anglican–Roman Catholic International Commission, *The Final Report* (SPCK, London, 1982).

4 The Paschal Proclamation (*Exsultet*) from the Easter Vigil, *The Book of Common Prayer* (Church Hymnal Corp., New York, 1979), p. 287.

5 See Geoffrey Wainwright's discussion in *Doxology* (OUP, New York, 1980), pp. 218–83. Important related material by several authors may be found in *Worship* 57:4 (July 1983), pp. 309–32.

6 A thorough discussion of the impact of the Gothic Revival upon the liturgy is presented in *The Cambridge Movement* by James F. White (CUP 1962); the wider cultural context of these matters is analysed by Kenneth Clark in *The Gothic Revival*, 3rd edn (John Murray, London, 1995).

7 See Richard K. Fenn, *Liturgies and Trials: The Secularization of Religious Languages* (Blackwell, Oxford, 1982).

8 Annie Dillard, *Holy the Firm* (Harper Collins, New York 1977), p. 59.

9 See my study of the collect-form, *Gathered to Pray*.

10 An interesting discussion of doctrinal aspects of the Anglican collects is found in James A. Devereux SJ, 'Reformed Doctrine in the Collects of the First *Book of Common Prayer*', *The Harvard Theological Review* 58:1 (1965), pp. 49–68.

11 See Hardy and Ford, *Jubilate: Theology in Praise*, for a useful exposition of the role of praise in Christian life and faith.

12 The literature on this one subject alone is vast. See especially J. D. C. Fisher, *Christian Initiation: Baptism in the Medieval West: A Study in the Disintegration of the Primitive Rite of Initiation* (SPCK, London, 1985).

13 Aidan Kavanagh, 'Response: Primary Theology and Liturgical Act', *Worship* 57:4 (1983), pp. 321–2.

14 XI. Of the Justification of Man, *Articles of Religion*, BCP.

15 XII. Of Good Works, *Articles of Religion*, BCP.

16 Rom. 4.25.

17 XXV. Of the Sacraments, *Articles of Religion*, BCP.

18 'A Learned Discourse of Justification, Works and How the Foundation of Faith is Overthrown' in *Works* (Oxford 1841), Vol. iii, p. 530.

19 *The Laws of Ecclesiastical Polity*, V.lvii. 5 (FE Vol. ii, p. 258).

20 Article IV, *The Augsburg Confession* (Augsburg, Philadelphia, 1980) p. 11.

21 Article XX, *The Augsburg Confession*, pp. 19–22.

22 Article XIII, *The Augsburg Confession*, p. 15.

23 John Calvin, *Institutes of the Christian Religion*, ed. J. T. McNeill, trans. Ford Lewis Battles et al. (Westminster Press, Philadelphia, 1960), 3. xi. 1, p. 725.

24 Calvin, *Institutes*, 3. xvi. 1, p. 798.

25 Calvin, *Institutes*, 4. xiv. 7–17 *passim*, pp. 1281–94.

26 *Enchiridion Symbolorum*, 33rd edn (ed. H. Denzinger and A. Schönmetzer), nn. 1530–1. My discussion of Trent's view of justification is based upon material from nn. 1523–82 *passim*.

27 Hebrews 4.14, 16.

28 *On the Resurrection*, 8. In this passage, Tertullian shows the intimate relation between the internal and external aspects of Christian initiation, and thus epitomizes the sacramental principle.

29 Inter-Anglican Theological and Doctrinal Commission, *For the Sake of the Kingdom* (CHP, London, 1986), para 94, p. 58.

30 *For the Sake of the Kingdom*, para 98, p. 60.

PART THREE

Authority and Method

1 Scripture

REGINALD H. FULLER

THE BIBLE AS THE WORD OF GOD

In the new Anglican liturgies, the readers of the Old Testament and New Testament lessons are instructed to conclude their readings with the words: 'The Word [ASB: This is the Word] of the Lord.' Probably to many people this suggests that the Anglicans are fundamentalists who believe that the words of the Bible are the direct oracles of God. Such people would not be surprised by the eloquent utterance of the famous Dean Burgon in the last century:

> The Bible is none other than the voice of Him that sitteth upon the throne. Every book of it, every word of it, every syllable of it (where are we to stop?), every letter of it, is the direct utterance of the Most High. The Bible is none other than the Word of God, not some part of it more, some part of it less, but all alike utterances of Him Who sitteth upon the throne, faultless, unerring, supreme.[1]

In his day, Dean Burgon was a fine apologist for classical Anglicanism, but on the subject of Holy Scripture we can no longer follow him. There are many reasons for this. First, his claim for the inerrancy of Scripture was never made by the Church of England even at the time of the Reformation, where there was a strong emphasis on the Bible as the word of God. Article VII of the Thirty-Nine Articles pointed to knowledge of the saving work of Jesus Christ as the real point of the Bible: 'In both the Old and New Testament everlasting life is offered to Mankind in Christ.' Earlier, Article II had called the Son of God 'the Word of the Father', thus encouraging us to see the Word primarily in a person rather than in a book (see pp. 144–8).

There is a more modern reason for thinking that the Anglican Churches do not require us to hold that the Bible is the word of God in a literalist sense. This is the application to the Scriptures of the historical-critical method.[2] This method has shown that however much the Bible may contain the word of God in the sense that it speaks of Jesus Christ, it is nevertheless also a very human product, the work of many human authors over a period of a thousand years or more, and all of them conditioned by the cultural assumptions of their age. Biblical criticism has further shown that the Bible is a highly pluralistic work, containing the views and perspectives of many different writers, views that were shaped by the peculiar situations in which they were written. In sum, the word of God is conveyed to us through the words of human beings.

This is something we should gladly embrace, for it is wholly analogous to the doctrine of the incarnation. The eternal Word of the Father became incarnate as a first-century Jew, with all his limitations. It is also analogous to the sacraments. God uses the frail elements of water, bread and wine as the means of communicating the redemptive presence and action of his Word to us. It is also analogous to the Church, which likewise is a very human institution, constantly in need of reform ('where in anything it is amiss, reform it', American BCP, p. 816). All the way through, with the Bible as with all the other means God uses for our salvation, the same principle is at work: God in his wondrous condescension stoops to use human and earthly means to accomplish his saving purpose.

As the incarnate Word is the sacrament of God, as the bread and wine are sacraments of Christ's body and blood, as the Church is the sacrament of God's presence in the world, so the Bible is the sacrament of God's word, his offer of salvation through his eternal Son and Word. When we call the Bible as a whole or a single pericope the word of God, we are speaking sacramentally, as we do when we call the consecrated elements 'the body and blood of Christ'. In Hooker's language they are the instruments which convey what they signify, and may therefore be said to be what they convey, like a dollar bill or a pound note.

THE INSPIRATION OF SCRIPTURE

The Christian Church inherited from Judaism the belief that its Scriptures were inspired by God. This was interpreted in different ways. To some it meant that God guided the pens of the human writers or dictated his words to their minds. More indirectly, it was held to mean that God was the ultimate, not the immediate, cause behind the writing of Scripture. This more indirect view seems to be what Cranmer asserted in the traditional Collect of the Second Sunday in Advent (American BCP, Proper 27): 'who hast caused all holy Scriptures to be written for our learning'. It was human beings who wrote them, but God who was the primary cause of their writing.

Some contemporary Anglican theologians have argued that the doctrine of inspiration ought to be abandoned today.[3] This is because it is frequently associated with the concept of inerrancy (to be discussed below). But it ought to be retained for the following reasons. First, it is a doctrine found in our formularies. See for instance 'An Outline of the Faith, commonly called the Catechism' (American BCP, p. 853), which says that the Old and New Testaments were 'written [...] under the inspiration of the Holy Spirit'. Second, its abandonment would have serious implications for ecumenical dialogue with the Roman Catholic, Orthodox and Lutheran Churches, all of which affirm the inspiration of Scripture. Third, it need not necessarily imply the doctrine of inerrancy. The primary work of the Holy Spirit is not to guarantee inerrancy, but to produce an authentic witness to the salvation event in Jesus Christ.[4] A sacramental understanding of the Bible as the word of God would seem to require a doctrine of inspiration, not in the sense that the human words came directly from God and are therefore inerrant, but in the sense that the human words proclaim the Christ event with the power to evoke faith. To produce faith is precisely the work of the Holy Spirit.

The claim to inspiration covers both Old and New Testaments, as the 'Outline of Faith' (American BCP, p. 853) and Article VII assert. In both Testaments we are offered salvation through Christ. The historical criticism of the Bible would seem to have undermined that claim as far as the Old Testament is concerned. The Old Testament prophets, the critics tell us, were speaking of events in their own day. Isaiah 40, for example, refers to the return of the exiles from Babylon, not to the coming of Christ. This is true. However, after the return it became clear that this was not the full and final event of salvation that the prophets expected it to be. The prophecies still awaited their final fulfilment. And so Luke 3.4–6 can pick up Isaiah 40.3–5 and apply these verses to the appearance of John the Baptist and Jesus Christ.

The Old Testament texts lived on in the community of faith and eventually were seen to have a fuller meaning than originally intended by the authors. The whole of the Old Testament pointed forward to a future saving event, and thus came to rest in Jesus Christ. Hence Article VII's claim about the Old Testament can still stand, even in the light of biblical criticism.[5]

The inspiration of Scripture is not to be understood as a once-for-all accomplished event. When Scripture is read in the church, the Holy Spirit uses it ever anew to proclaim the living word of salvation. This proclamation requires the response of faith, and that too is the work of the Holy Spirit. The Collect about Scripture which we quoted above goes on to pray:

> Grant that we may in such wise hear them, read, mark, learn and inwardly digest them; that by patience and comfort of thy holy Word, we may embrace and ever hold fast the blessed hope of everlasting life which thou hast given us in our Saviour Jesus Christ.

The work of the Holy Spirit is not confined to the original writing which produced the authoritative witness.[6] The witness has to be constantly rekindled in the community of the faithful, particularly in the context of the liturgy. The word of God is not a static, dead document: it constantly recurs as event, and has to be apprehended through the Spirit.

If the Holy Spirit continues to inspire the reading and preaching of the word and the hearing that produces faith, in what sense is the Bible unique? Not apparently because it is inspired, whereas all other Christian writing and speech are not. Wherever Christ is proclaimed and believed in, there the Spirit is at work. But the Holy Spirit's inspiration of Scripture is unique because Scripture is the normative witness to which all later witness has to conform. There is no word without Spirit and no Spirit without word. This is expressed in the Collect written by Cranmer for the feast of Saints Simon and Jude (Proper 8, American BCP):

> O almighty God, who hast built thy Church upon the foundation of the apostles and prophets, Jesus himself being the chief cornerstone: Grant us so to be joined together in unity of Spirit by their doctrine, that we may be made an holy temple acceptable unto thee . . .

THE SUFFICIENCY OF SCRIPTURE

Article VI of the Thirty-Nine Articles is entitled, 'Of the Sufficiency of Holy Scripture for Salvation.' The body of the Article goes on to define sufficiency to mean that:

> Holy Scripture containeth all things necessary to salvation: so that whatever is not read therein, nor may be proved thereby [i.e. tested— the question of Scripture as norm will be discussed in the next section] is not to be required by any man, that it should be believed as an article of the Faith, or thought to be necessary or requisite to salvation.

In the traditional Ordinal (see BCP-USA 1928) the second question put to the candidate for ordination to the diaconate, priesthood and episcopate was: 'Are you persuaded that the Holy Scriptures contain all Doctrine required as necessary for eternal salvation through faith in Jesus Christ?' This question has been removed in the present American BCP, but the same point is made in the oath of conformity which is now printed in the beginning of the American Ordinals: 'I . . . solemnly declare that I do believe the Holy Scriptures of the Old and New Testaments to be the Word of God, and to contain all things necessary to salvation.' The corresponding question in the ASB reads: 'Do you accept the holy Scriptures as revealing all things necessary for eternal salvation through faith in Jesus Christ?' The Bible alone (in this sense the Anglican Churches accept the Reformation principle of *sola scriptura*) contains the primary authoritative witness of the mighty acts of God in salvation history (see pp. 144–8). No other book, however early or inspiring, can add anything to the witness of these acts of God, however much it may contribute to our understanding of them.[7] This is because the saving acts of God took place once-for-all, and with the events there is also a once-for-all authoritative witness. This witness is the work either of those who had themselves directly witnessed

90

those events (the eyewitnesses and ministers of the word, Luke 1.2), or of those who were in immediate contact with that witness, who, in Hoskyns' words were 'so completely created by apostolic witness and formed by apostolic obedience that they are veritably carried across into the company of the original disciples of Jesus and invested with the authority of their mission'.[8] It is true that there are some fuzzy areas here: some sub-apostolic texts such as *1 Clement* were not taken up into the canon, while others who according to modern criticism were seemingly at greater distance from the original witness, such as the author of 2 Peter,[9] were further away from it. Yet there remains a central core of apostolic writings in the strictest sense.

We may be thankful that the Anglican formularies never claim that all things in Holy Scripture are necessary to salvation. There is much in the biblical books—genealogies, primitive myths, legends and sagas, primitive religious concepts (Yahweh as a vengeful deity) and the like—which we can hardly accept when proposed to us as articles of faith. Once again, we are only concerned with what proclaims to us salvation in Jesus Christ.

We have laid considerable stress on the christological interpretation of the Old Testament. But this is not the sole reason for its use. The gospel asserts that God was acting in Christ. The original disciples did not meet God for the first time in Jesus Christ. Rather, they recognized God in him as a result of their nurture in the Old Testament-Jewish tradition. Therefore the Old Testament has to be read for its own sake, as well as for its christological significance. The God who was manifest in the Christ event was the God who also created heaven and earth, who called all nations into being, and who called Israel out of Egypt and gave it the law. Therefore the Old Testament's authority extends beyond its prefiguring of the Christ event.

THE PRIMACY OF SCRIPTURE

The primacy of Scripture means that Scripture is the norm of faith and the norm by which other norms (creeds, tradition, confessions of faith) are judged. In the past the Bible was frequently used as a proof text for doctrinal systems. Commentaries on the *Articles of Religion* often consisted of texts supporting each statement in the Articles, and that was the diet of theological education for candidates for the ordained ministry. Today we would question the validity of this procedure for a number of reasons. First, faith is primarily not the acceptance of a series of propositions, but the acceptance of the gospel as the good news of the mighty acts of God for us and our salvation. Theological propositions have only a secondary significance. They are the attempts of faith to understand itself—*fides quaerens intellectum.* There are already attempts in the Bible itself to produce an understanding of faith, to reflect upon the meaning of the kerygma. This is notably the case in the writings of St Paul, e.g. in his Letter to the Romans. Here Paul starts with the primary datum, the kerygma or apostolic message as his readers had received it, and proceeds to draw out its implications for controverted points of interpretation (Rom. 3.21—11.36). Another example is in 1 Corinthians 15, where Paul is dealing with the resurrection of the believers from the dead. Paul first sets out the kerygma of Christ's resurrection (1 Cor. 15.3–8) and then expounds the significance of that kerygma for the resurrection of the believers (1 Cor. 15.12–58). Paul's doctrinal conclusions are inevitably coloured and limited by the world-view of his time. The Bible as norm can no longer be thought of as prescribing to us a ready-made theology for our own day and age. What the Bible offers by way of norm is a model of procedure, whereby we too in our own day and age can move from the fundamental message or kerygma to our own problems and questions. The normative function of the Bible in matters of doctrine is therefore not rigidly prescriptive, but far more like a series of guidelines along which we may proceed in formulating doctrine. If it has any prescriptive character, this can only act negatively, ruling out certain doctrinal conclusions which are clearly incompatible with Scripture. Thus, for instance, any theology which asserted that Jesus was the revelation of God only for Westerners and not for the whole world (a view which is being proposed by some Christian theologians today) must be ruled out as contrary to the scriptural norm (Heb. 1.1–2).

The Bible, as well as being a norm for theology, is also a norm for ethical behaviour. Modern Anglicans do not regard it as a code-book of law. Rather, the specific ethical commands of the Bible are illustrations of the kind of behaviour God requires in specific situations. They are derived from what God has done for us in his saving acts. We have many situations to face today which are not covered by the specific demands of Scripture, and therefore we have to go beyond the confines of the canon. But always we have to ask, what kind of imperative does the indicative of the gospel (what God has done) imply (see pp. 364–78)?

The Old Testament has been a characteristic resource for Anglicans in the matter of ethics. For centuries it was regularly read at Morning Prayer, which was part of the main service on Sundays. From this, Anglicans have drawn the perception that politics and the state are a special arena where Christians have to work out their obedience to God (see pp. 392–405). In earlier days, this expressed itself in England through a loyal adherence to the monarchy. But as Anglicanism spread beyond the confines of England, especially after the American colonies became independent, Anglicans have had to work out a political ethic under other forms of government. On the one hand Anglicanism respects the state as the servant of God

(Rom. 13.4, 6), with a God-given task to promote the good of society. On the other hand Anglicans know that the state may sometimes forget that it is the servant of God and may become the instrument of injustice and tyranny. In such situations the Church has to adopt a prophetic critique of the state. This is what Hensley Henson did when as Canon of Westminster he denounced the Putumayo atrocities in 1912, or as a long line of archbishops did with regard to apartheid. There was no explicit command in the Bible forbidding apartheid in the ordering of secular society, but the indicative of the gospel led to this kind of imperative. The teaching of the prophets, such as Amos and Isaiah, has played a prominent role in Anglicanism as in other Churches. The concern for world hunger is another issue in which Anglicans have been to the fore. We may rightly claim that these concerns are biblically based.

CANON

Closely connected with the notion of Scripture as norm is the idea of the canon, the list of books recognized as belonging to the normative writings.

The canon of the New Testament was not a matter of controversy at the time of the Reformation. Article VI simply states that 'All the Books of the New Testament as they are commonly received we do receive, and account them as canonical'. With regard to the Old Testament, the situation was more complicated. Like the other Churches of the Reformation, the Church of England recognized the canonicity of those books which were contained in the Hebrew Bible. It relegated the 'other Books' (Article VI), i.e. the additional items in the Greek Bible which we call the Apocrypha, to an appendix of books 'read for example of life and instruction of manners'. The Article, however, continued: 'Yet doth it [the Church] not apply them to establish any doctrine'. Anglicans have always made some liturgical use of the apocryphal books, and twentieth-century lectionaries have extended that use. Modern scholarship has broken down the sharp division between the Old Testament and the Apocrypha, and it might be a good thing if Anglicans were to adopt the Roman Catholic designation of the apocryphal books as 'deutero-canonical'. We read them and value them, but they have a secondary position, being used only to reinforce the doctrines of the proto-canonical Old Testament books.

The shape of the New Testament canon is not often a matter of reflection on the part of Anglicans, but it deserves attention because it has, albeit unconsciously, shaped all Christian theology including our own. The New Testament canon has this structure: the four Gospels, Acts, the Epistolary writings, and Revelation. The fact that the four Gospels come first means that the incarnation together with the Trinity is, for Anglicanism, fundamental to the faith (and this of course involves faith to the God of the Old Testament, which precedes the New Testament in the canon). The structure of the Thirty-Nine Articles reflects this pattern, for the Articles begin with the Trinity and the incarnation (I–V) (see pp. 146–7).

The Pauline corpus, while presuming a high Christology, employs this Christology as a basis for soteriology. The Pauline writings proclaim the doctrine of redemption under various images, of which the most important are justification and reconciliation.[10] Some strands of Anglican theology have at times been tempted to overemphasize the doctrine of the incarnation and to treat it as though the incarnation were in itself salvific.[11] This has no sanction in Scripture or in the Thirty-Nine Articles, where Articles IX–XVII develop a doctrine of salvation through Christ.

The Pauline corpus contains not only Galatians and Romans, but also the deutero-Pauline Colossians and Ephesians. These letters place the doctrine of salvation in a corporate, ecclesial perspective. The Colossian-Ephesian doctrine of the Church as the Body of Christ of which he is the Head is of particular significance in Anglicanism.

On the fringe of the Pauline corpus stands the so-called Letter to the Hebrews. This book has played a long and important role in Anglican doctrine, particularly in the doctrine of the Eucharist. It was Hebrews' insistence on the once-for-all character of Christ's sacrifice that gave Cranmer the warrant for his exordium to the Prayer of Consecration in the Communion Service of 1549–1552: '. . . who made there (by his one oblation of himself once offered) a full, perfect, and sufficient sacrifice, oblation and satisfaction, for the sins of the whole world'. Article XXXI repeats this emphasis, placing it in the context of sixteenth-century polemic against the Romish doctrine of 'the sacrifices of Masses'. Classical Anglicanism in the seventeenth century and Tractarianism in the nineteenth sought to recover a more positive doctrine of the eucharistic sacrifice along patristic lines, but always worked within the parameters set by the finality of Christ's sacrifice as expressed in Hebrews. The same is true of Anglican attempts to formulate a doctrine of ministerial priesthood. Such a doctrine must not be allowed to compromise the finality of Christ's high priesthood. These doctrines based on Hebrews received quasi-official formulation in the archbishops' reply to the 1896 papal Bull condemning Anglican orders (see pp. 328–9).[12]

The Church, too, has a historical mission, as is indicated by the Acts of the Apostles, which forms a bridge between the two major parts of the canon, the Gospels and the Pauline corpus. This poses a challenge to contemporary Anglican theology. It has to be not just the theology of mission for the Church of England, but a theology of the worldwide Anglican Communion, in which South America, Africa, India, Asia and

Oceania have to make their contribution, as well as the British Isles and North America.

It has become increasingly clear to New Testament scholars that there is a third major stratum in the New Testament. Pre-critical Anglican theology was not able consciously to draw this distinction, but it should help Anglican theology today to clarify what had, albeit unconsciously, always been its position. This is the existence of a body of literature which belongs to the sub-apostolic age and is a witness to early Catholicism *(Frükatholizismus)*. It includes those institutional features of the second and third generation of the Christian Church which were devised to perpetuate apostolic faith and practice after the death of the original witnesses. The New Testament writings in this category include: the (deutero-Pauline) Pastoral Epistles, and some of the Catholic or General Epistles, perhaps James, 1 Peter and Jude, and certainly 2 Peter. Acts and Hebrews may exhibit a few traces of early Catholic concern, though this is highly debatable, while the Johannine appendix (John 21), produced in the same period, bears witness to the institutionalization of the Johannine churches.[13] The institutional features in question include: credal forms, an incipient canon of Christian writings (cf. 2 Peter) and an organized ministry with ordination and succession replacing the more spontaneous charismatic ministries of Paul's churches (Acts, Pastorals). Radical Protestantism has generally deplored these developments. In the pre-critical period they were thought to have been introduced after the New Testament era in such writings as *1 Clement* and the *Epistles of Ignatius*. But given a later dating for the New Testament writings in question, the initial development of early Catholic institutional features is now already discernible in the New Testament. As a result, radical Protestantism at this point invokes the principle of a 'canon within the canon'. Ernst Käsemann finds this inner canon in the Pauline-Lutheran 'message of the justification of the ungodly by faith alone apart from the works of the law'.[14] He regards early Catholicism as a denial of this central message, and would therefore relegate these writings to the periphery of the canon. Anglicans would react differently to this debate.[15] It is noteworthy, to begin with, that the early Catholic institutional features are precisely those elements which in a developed form are included in the Chicago–Lambeth Quadrilateral (see pp. 42–3). Accordingly, Anglicans may welcome the presence of early Catholicism in the New Testament. The canon itself sanctions the development of creeds, a canon of Scripture and a regularized ministry.

The gospel could not exist *in vacuo*. It required institutional forms to perpetuate it. The New Testament documents which attest to their initial growth are secondary to the four Gospels and the authentic Pauline Epistles; Anglicanism has perhaps been tempted at times to suppose that they are primary.[16] Rather, it is the gospel that is primary; the early Catholic institutions exist only to serve the gospel. Thus the understanding of the structure of the canon serves both to vindicate and to challenge traditional Anglican theology.

The canon of the New Testament concludes with the Book of Revelation. This can hardly be said to be a favourite book of Anglicans, and until recently it has not figured very much in the lectionaries. It is perhaps significant that those passages which have commanded most attention are those which deal with the worship of heaven (Rev. 4, 7, 21). Anglicans have always understood their liturgy to be more than just human activity initiated here on earth: it is a participation in the worship of heaven. The ultimate destiny of humanity is seen in participation in that worship.

SCRIPTURE AND TRADITION

The subject of tradition will be dealt with more fully in this volume by H. Chadwick. But a number of points about tradition in relation to Scripture need to be made here. We have already indicated that Anglicanism accepts the *sola scriptura* of the Reformation in the nuanced sense that only in Scripture do we find authoritative witness to the Christ event. We also noted that Scripture has its centre in that witness, but also that there are contingent applications of that witness to ongoing situations in the New Testament period. This resulted in developments in the understanding of the original witness, and consequently in doctrinal developments or trajectories.[17] A most noticeable example of this is in the field of Christology. The earliest Christologies were functional or agent Christologies. They describe the role played by Jesus in salvation history, and what God had done through him.[18] By the time the Johannine Prologue (John 1.1–18) was composed, Christology was becoming more concerned with the person of Jesus and his relation to God's being.[19] Jesus was now seen as the incarnation of the pre-existent *logos* of God, who was the agent of creation, of general revelation, and of the special revelation to Israel. It was this Johannine Christology (combined with the Matthaean-Lucan assertion of Jesus' virginal conception) which formed the basis for the Christology of Nicaea and Chalcedon. To this developed Christology Anglicanism has traditionally adhered. Recently, however, a number of Anglican exegetes and theologians, especially in England, have advocated a return to the agent types of Christology, leaving Nicaea and Chalcedon on one side.[20] Against this, other Anglican theologians have protested, maintaining that it would lead to a loss of Anglican identity.[21] Today Anglicanism cannot justify its adherence to the doctrines of the Trinity and incarnation unless it is prepared to accord an authority to the Church as

96

'witness and keeper of Holy Writ' (Article XX). It is on the authority of the Church of the early centuries, not of the Bible alone, that Anglicanism upholds them.[22]

Similar considerations apply to the ordained ministry. In earlier days Anglicans appealed directly to the New Testament for the institution of episcopacy.[23] Today it is commonly held by critical scholars that the Pastoral Epistles are deutero-Pauline and therefore cannot be used as evidence for the ministry in Paul's own lifetime. Rather, in Paul's churches the ministry seems to have been largely charismatic (1 Cor. 12.4–31; Rom. 12.6–8). By the time of the Pastorals, a ministry of bishop-presbyters and deacons was developing. Ignatius of Antioch (c. AD 110) is the earliest witness for 'mon-episcopacy', a single bishop in each local church presiding over a group of presbyters. Today Anglicans can justify adherence to episcopacy only by appealing to post-New Testament developments. It is noteworthy that as early as 1930 the Lambeth Fathers sought to legitimate episcopacy in terms of development:

> The Episcopate occupies a position which is, in point of historic development, analogous to that of the Canon of Scripture and of the Creeds. In the first days there was no Canon of New Testament Scripture, for the books afterwards included in it were still being written. So, too, the Apostles' Creed is the result of a process of growth which we can in large measure trace. If the Episcopate, as we find it established universally by the end of the second century, was the result of a like process . . . that would be no evidence that it lacked divine authority.[24]

Once again, we have here a trajectory from the New Testament to the patristic age (see pp. 333–47).

At present, Anglicanism is becoming more open—as indeed classical seventeenth-century Anglicanism was in theory open—to a Petrine trajectory which would justify a 'primacy of honour' for the Bishop of Rome.[25] At the same time Anglicanism would reject papal claims to universal jurisdiction and infallibility as a deviation from the trajectory of the Petrine office which begins in Scripture. In this way Scripture acts as a norm over subsequent developments.

CONCLUSION

Since the Reformation, Anglicanism has understood itself in terms of a reformed or scriptural Catholicism. The *modus operandi* of that appeal to Scripture has changed since the acceptance of the historical-critical method. Yet we may justly claim that the results of this change are broadly consistent with our historic formularies, the Book of Common Prayer, the

Articles of Religion and the Catechism, as well as with our standard divines from the Reformation to the present day.

BIBLIOGRAPHY

Barr, J., *The scope and authority of the Bible*, new edn. SCM, London, 1993.

Barton, J., *People of the Book? The Authority of the Bible in Christianity*, new edn. SPCK, London, 1993.

Beckwith, R. T., *The Old Testament Canon of the New Testament Church and Its Background in Early Judaism*. SPCK, London, 1985.

Borsch, F. A. (ed.), *Anglicanism and the Bible*. Morehouse-Barlow, Wilton CT, 1984.

Childs, B. S., *The New Testament as Canon: An Introduction*. SCM, London, 1984.

Fuller, R. H., 'The Authority of Scripture in Anglicanism' in *The Report of the Lutheran–Episcopal Dialogue*, Second Series 1976–1980. Forward Movement, Cincinnati OH, 1981, pp. 87–113.

Greenslade, S. L. (ed.), *The Cambridge History of the Bible*, Vol. iii, *The West from the Reformation to the Present Day*. CUP 1963, esp. pp.141–70 and 361–82.

Langford, T. A., *In Search of Foundations: English Theology 1900–1920*. Abingdon, Nashville TN, 1969, Ch. V, 'Authority, Anglicanism, the Bible and the Creeds'.

Meade, D. G., *Pseudonymity and Canon: An Investigation into the Relationship of Authorship and Authority in Jewish and Earliest Christian Tradition*. Eerdmans, Grand Rapids MI, 1987.

Metzger, B. M., *The Canon of the New Testament: Its Origin, Development and Significance*. Clarendon Press, Oxford, 1997.

Morgan, R., 'Non Angli Sed Angeli: Some Anglican Reactions to German Gospel Criticism' in S. W. Sykes and D. Holmes (eds), *New Studies in Theology*. Duckworth, London, 1980, pp. 1–30.

Neill, S., *The Interpretation of the New Testament, 1861–1988*, rev. edn by N. T. Wright. OUP 1988.

Reventlow, Henning Graf, *The Authority of the Bible and the Rise of the Modern World*. SCM, London, 1984.

NOTES

1 Cited by A. Richardson, *Preface to Bible Study* (Westminster, Philadelphia, 1944).

2 For a brief history of the rise and reception of the historical-critical method in Anglicanism see R. H. Fuller in F. Borsch (ed.), *Anglicanism and the Bible* (Morehouse-Barlow, Wilton CT, 1984), pp. 143–68.

3 R. P. C. Hanson recommended dropping the doctrine of inspiration in his inaugural lecture as Lightfoot Professor at Durham University in 1962. He has reiterated his position in a systematic theology written in collaboration with his twin brother, A. T. Hanson, *Reasonable Belief* (OUP 1980), pp. 40–2.

4 See e.g. Mark 13.11; Luke 12.12; John 15.26–7; Acts 1.8; 1 Cor. 12.3; 1 Thess. 1.5.

5 *Contra* J. Bowden, *Jesus: The Unanswered Question* (SCM, London, 1988).

6 Hence the inspiration of the Holy Spirit should be seen at each stage of the biblical tradition. In the Gospels the Holy Spirit inspired the original reception of the Jesus material by the first witnesses, its transmission in the oral tradition, its first writing and subsequent redactions, its transmission as part of the canon, its interpretation throughout Church History and finally its reception today.

7 It is often asked whether any newly discovered apostolic writings could be added to the canon. Aside from the difficulty of securing ecumenical consensus, such a writing would have to conform to the existing canon for its acceptance; thus the present canon would in practice remain the norm.

8 E. C. Hoskyns, *The Fourth Gospel*, ed. F. N. Davey (Faber, London, 1950), p. 92.

9 For an excellent discussion of the problem of 2 Peter see D. G. Meade, *Pseudonymity and Canon* (Eerdmans, Grand Rapids MI, 1987), pp. 183–6.

10 'Atonement' has long been used as a comprehensive soteriological term in Anglican theology. In the OT however it is used exclusively in cultic contexts to translate words from the *kpr* root, denoting 'to cover' and hence to cleanse. In the KJV (AV) 'atonement' occurs only at Rom. 5.11, where it translates quite a different term, *katallagē* (RSV 'reconciliation'), a concept derived from interpersonal or international relationships. It would be best to use 'soteriology' for the comprehensive term, to confine 'atonement' to OT cultic contexts, and to use 'reconciliation' for *katallagē* and its cognates. Thus 'atonement' in the sense of reconciliation should be dropped, despite its alleged etymological origin as 'at-one-ment'.

11 Such tendencies are discernible in F. D. Maurice, B. F. Westcott, the *Lux Mundi* School and William Temple. Hoskyns redressed the balance at this point. See A. M. Ramsey, *An Era in Anglican Theology: From Gore to Temple* (Scribner's, New York, 1960). Anglican Evangelicals have sometimes tended to stress soteriology to the neglect of the incarnation. See, however, a more balanced treatment by an older Evangelical, W. H. Wilmer, *The Episcopal Manual* (George, Philadelphia, 1841).

12 For the relation between the High Priesthood of Christ and ministerial priesthood see R. H. Fuller, 'Scripture, Tradition and Priesthood' in R. Bauckham and B. Drewery (eds), *Scripture, Tradition and Reason: Essays in Honour of Richard P. C. Hanson* (T. & T. Clark, Edinburgh, 1988), pp. 101–14.

13 See R. E. Brown, *The Community of the Beloved Disciple* (Paulist, New York/ Ramsey NJ, 1979), pp. 159–61; *The Epistles of John* (Anchor Bible 30; Doubleday, Garden City NY, 1982), pp. 106–15.

14 E. Käsemann, *Essays on New Testament Themes* (SBT 41; SCM, London, 1964), pp. 95–107.

15 See R. H. Fuller in R. Kahl (ed.), *Christ and Christianity: Studies in the Formation of Christology* (Trinity Press International, Valley Forge PA, 1994), pp. 139–50.

16 As manifested in the negative attitude of some Episcopalians to the interim eucharistic fellowship with the Evangelical Lutheran Church in America, a body which maintains the canon, creed and gospel sacraments, and a high doctrine of ordination, though without episcopal succession. The Porvoo agreement (1992) is meeting a similar reaction in the Church of England. The classical Anglican position was that episcopacy belongs to the perfection rather than to the being of the Church (Bramhall), to its *plene esse* rather than to its *esse*.

17 The concept of trajectories was introduced into biblical scholarship by J. M. Robinson and H. Koester, *Trajectories through Early Christianity* (Fortress, Philadelphia, 1971). I have discussed the implications of this concept for biblical authority in *Christ and Christianity*, pp.161–77.

18 See the Bampton Lectures of A. E. Harvey, *Jesus and Constraints of History* (Westminster, Philadelphia PA, 1982).

19 See R. H. Fuller and P. Perkins, *Who Is This Christ?* (Fortress, Philadelphia PA, 1983), pp. 43–9. Martin Hengel thinks that this development took place as early as 35–50 CE. See M. Hengel, *Between Jesus and Paul* (Fortress, Philadelphia PA, 1983), pp 30–47. J. D. G. Dunn, *Christology in the Making* (Westminster, Philadelphia PA, 1980) thinks that pre-existence Christology proper was not developed until the Johannine Prologue, i.e. after 90–100 CE. For a mediating position see R. E. Brown, *An Introduction to New Testament Christology* (Paulist, New York/Mahwah, 1994). In any case it cannot be denied that the formulae in Paul, Hebrews and John all exhibit a continuity of subject between the pre-existent Son and the earthly Jesus.

20 Examples are: G. W. H. Lampe in the Bampton Lectures for 1976, *God as Spirit* (Clarendon, Oxford, 1977); J. A. T. Robinson, *Twelve More New Testament Studies* (SCM, London, 1984), pp. 138–54, 171–80, and his Bampton Lectures for 1984, *The Priority of John* (SCM, London, 1986). The Hansons in *Reasonable Belief* (see above, n. 3) adopt a mediating position. While retaining a strong doctrine of the *logos* and the Trinity, they argue for dropping the Chalcedonian doctrine of the personal identity of Jesus with the *logos*. The human Jesus thus becomes the bearer or spokesperson of the *logos*. For a defence of pre-existence Christology see Fuller, *Christ and Christianity*, pp. 153–60.

21 See, e.g., S. W. Sykes, *The Integrity of Anglicanism* (Mowbrays, London, 1978); R. Morgan, 'Historical Criticism and Christology' in S. W. Sykes (ed.), *England and Germany* (Lang, Frankfurt am Main, 1982), pp. 80–112.

22 The tradition of the first five centuries (which means in effect four ecumenical councils through to Chalcedon) has always enjoyed a special authority in classical Anglicanism, which also appealed to the 'three Creeds' as a hermeneutical principle for the interpretation of Scripture.

23 Thus the traditional Preface to the Ordinal appeals both to Scripture and to 'ancient Authors' for the claim that 'from the Apostles' time there have been these orders of ministers in Christ's Church—Bishops, Priests, and Deacons'. American BCP (1928), p. 529. Today, in the light of historical criticism, we have to rely more heavily on the development attested by the 'ancient Authors'.

24 G. K. A. Bell, *Documents on Christian Unity*, Third Series, 1930–48 (OUP, London/New York, 1948), p. 7.

25 See Anglican–Roman Catholic International Commission, *The Final Report* (SPCK and CTS, London/Forward Movement, Cincinnati OH, 1982), pp. 57–8.

2 Tradition, Fathers and Councils

HENRY CHADWICK

Although as Christians we do not believe by proxy, faith is always a sharing. The baptized believer is incorporated in the family of God. To adhere to God's Word in Christ is also to adhere to the fellowship of the Spirit—to the gospel in Bible, preaching and sacraments. These are means of grace; the media entrusted to, and creative of, the community within which the Word of God is heard and the vision of his glory seen. In the life of the fellowship a special place is occupied by the sacred written records of the Bible transmitted to us by the community. Copied with varying degrees of accuracy by ancient and medieval Christian scribes, and translated (with similar variations) into many languages and even versions in the same language, this collection of books possesses a unique position in the tradition of the Church.

Since the invention of printing, Bibles have been relatively inexpensive and widely diffused. The historical-critical study of this book has greatly illuminated the circumstances within the community which produced both particular writings and the collection as a whole. It has brought out the way in which the early Christians appealed to Scripture as a witness and as a confirming illustration of what they already did and believed. The Word of God was in their hearts before it was put into books, and in any event the Graeco-Roman world into which the first missionaries went out contained a high proportion of illiterate people. Ability to read and write has never been a prerequisite for faith and baptism. In the mid-second century Papias of Hierapolis felt nearer to the authentic tradition when speaking with those who could recall the oral teaching of the apostolic and sub-apostolic age, than when reading books.

And yet—in defending the tradition of the community, the books were indispensable. In the Scriptures received or written by the apostolic generation, the ancient Church had its title-deeds, a unique witness to the revealed will of God for his people. The early Christian 'Fathers' (the term long used for orthodox writers of East and West of the first six or seven Christian centuries) claimed very much for their authority, and distinguished between Christian literature that might be read in the lectionary and books which were edifying but outside the canon. The process of forming the canon was gradual.

For the ancient and medieval Church no official document, not even a conciliar definition, was invested with authority in the same kind or degree as the original witness of Scripture. But the consensus and apostolic tradition of the Church in worship and doctrine was of profound importance. In the medieval period from at least the eleventh century in the West, disputes and controversies not only began to set reason and logic against the received doctrine of the community, but also mountingly stressed the literal meaning of the original text. Some writers over-simplified matters by setting the literal sense over against the allegorical (over-simplified, because often the intended sense of the original was allegorical), and then equating the allegorical interpretation with the ecclesiastical tradition. So diverse were the expositions that Alan of Lille remarked that the authority of the biblical text had 'a nose of wax'.

101

Furthermore, from about the eleventh century the Church, at least as represented by its higher officers, seemed to an increasing number of Christians (both clerical and lay) to be too involved in the secular business of property and power. Noble medieval cathedrals were not built on Hail Marys. It was not only heretics like polemical Waldensians and Lollards who contrasted the poverty and simplicity of the primitive Church with the great endowments and rent-lists of their own time.

Humanists of the fifteenth-century Renaissance were in reaction against the learning of the medieval universities and schools. There were complaints that people knew more about the logic of Boethius than about the Bible. One should return to the sources.

Against this background it becomes easy to understand that a contrast between Scripture and the contemporary practice of the Church was much in the air. Moreover, it was an axiom of the Augustinian tradition that all necessary doctrine for salvation is in the Bible. Augustine not infrequently enunciated the principle that a Bible given by God to disclose his will must be clear on anything really indispensable to salvation (or the divine will would be frustrated). He drew the conclusion that where Scripture is unclear, the doctrine taught may indeed be true, but must be less than utterly necessary. Augustine did not draw the conclusion that we need only this minimum found in Scripture alone, and can therefore dispense with the tradition of faith in the living community. That was the inference that Reformers of the sixteenth century wished to make.

The question of authority in belief was not new in the sixteenth century, but the debate was far sharper. The problem might appear simple if only one could say that 'Scripture alone' suffices, and could then decide to neglect any other medium of guidance. But mountainous difficulties arise. 'Scripture alone' is not, after all a principle that can be derived from Scripture alone. The formula is actually a tradition; the manner in which it is deployed determines whether it is used rightly or wrongly. It cannot work if the community and Scripture are conceived as if external to one another and capable of being set in strong antithesis to one another. If the Church has authority, that depends on the Lord's commission, not upon texts, even though the texts are historical witnesses to the Lord's intention for the Church. An anti-ecclesial employment of 'Scripture alone' confronts embarrassment in the Church's role in the formation of the New Testament canon. There are also important practices such as Sunday observance which are community tradition, rather than explicitly sanctioned by Scripture.

The tradition of the fellowship, in which Scripture is certainly the most substantial element, is also a sense which determines the Christian's discernment of what is central and what is peripheral not only in the Christian past but in Scripture itself. The consequence of stressing the author's intention, as was widespread in the later Middle Ages, produces the axiom that the biblical books were never better understood than by their original writers and first readers. To say that, or even something approximating to it, is to become aware of a great distance in time and culture between our modern world and that of the Bible. To avert mere arbitrariness and individualism in interpretation we need to formulate guidelines, and these hermeneutic rules will not be unrelated to the consensus of the community. One of the side-effects of the sixteenth-century Protestant stress on the Bible over against the Church was to give far greater practical authority to the learned professor skilled in ancient languages than to the pastors of the believing community, and so set up the deep tension between historical and dogmatic theology which has marked the history of the subject since the seventeenth century.

The question of authority in belief might appear simple if only one could say that in fact the decision about what is to be believed or done entirely rests with the individual's private judgement according to his or her best reason and conscience. That the individual reason and conscience play much more than a merely passive part seems clear. But there are problems when the individual is set up in judgement against the community and the tradition of its sacred texts. In some vehemently anti-Anglican Puritans of seventeenth-century England such as John Owen, appointed by Cromwell to be Dean of Christ Church and to purge that society of any attachment it might have to the Book of Common Prayer, the axiom of 'Scripture alone' is combined with the second axiom of private individual judgement by the believer; that is, God has given an infallibly inspired text, indeed the sole source of infallibility, but its interpretation is in no sense committed either to the community or to its pastors but is free for every believer to take in whatever way he feels to be right. The position was a kind of caricature of something St Augustine himself had said, namely, that Scripture, given by God for our illumination and therefore clear in essentials, nevertheless contained numerous obscurities and mysteries to exercise the thoughtful, and could have many justifiable interpretations. But Augustine located an ultimate control over these many interpretations in the Rule of Faith transmitted within the worshipping community, of which the bishops as proper pastors are the collective guardians.

In reality the community decisively forms (which is not to say that it wholly creates) the individual conscience, and provides the framework of principles within which and from which reason operates. Rational discourse is a communal activity, not a private soliloquy. For the believer, reason is never properly set in stark antithesis to authority as if the latter were always inscrutable and arbitrary. Reason is neither a subordinate handmaid always submissive to its dogmatic teacher, nor a dangerous harlot ready to seduce, but rather a great gift of God for the understanding of the faith and of the proportion and coherence of its various elements. Human minds suffer the weaknesses of incomplete knowledge, bleary vision, partial understanding of the relevant considerations and facts, often a partisan self-concern, and seldom have the time and leisure to think through a complicated question. The community with its past wisdom and experience acts as a check on partiality and idiosyncrasy.

There are acute problems, however, in talking too blandly about the authority of tradition in the Church, where the legacy of history has been division and contention taken to the point of suspending eucharistic communion. The resulting rancour turns every separated communion into a distinct body with defensive fortification against rivals. 'Tradition' as a proper norm of doctrine in the Church, derived from the interpretation of Scripture, needs to be distinguished from particular and rival traditions, reluctant to listen to one another, inclined to much caricature of the other's beliefs and practices, at some times in history ready to resort to physical violence against one another. Even in a more ecumenical age, each advocate tends to begin conversation with the assumption that disunity is conquerable only when everyone else comes to be converted to his own tradition in the narrower sense of that word. It cannot of course be denied that it is hard to assert absoluteness of one's own tradition when the particular group to which an individual happens to belong is often determined by where he was born, or by whose agency under God he came to be a believer, whether Boston Irish or Sydney Evangelical. Such differences make it more difficult for Christians to understand one another; and talk about 'our tradition' then becomes a formula for pointing up differences and ignoring the usually larger areas of agreement. Common experience shows how rare it is for, say, a Baptist, with the best will in the world, to give an account of the essentials of Roman Catholic belief which will seem accurate and balanced to a Roman Catholic listener, or a sympathetic Roman Catholic to delineate Anglican belief and practice in a way that Anglicans would recognize to be totally just and correct. The point has to be allowed, even when allowance is made for the fact that there are many diversities within each of these communions. On the other hand, there are also illusions in the self-portrait that each divided body nurses in regard to itself. Sixteenth-century Anglicanism, as we shall see, adopted a policy of wide formulas in the articulation of matters of faith, trying to leave legitimate options open, and of a narrow uniformity required in liturgy and devotional practice. It can surprise Anglicans of the late twentieth century to discover that despite their self-portrait of an Erasmian liberality and comprehensiveness they may look to most non-Anglicans a body quite remarkably intolerant in regard to devotional practice, and bordering on the incoherent in central matters of faith. Roman Catholics can also be astonished and embarrassed to discover that their self-portrait as a monolithic and unchanging body, without diversity of interpretation, is far from the actuality that friendly observers perceive. Within the Anglican Communion the accepted norms of authority are located first in the faith declared in Scripture, then in the safeguard of interpretation provided by the Catholic Creeds, and finally in the liturgical tradition of Prayer Book and Ordinal, both of which are in essentials rooted in ways of worship much older than their sixteenth-century origin. The partly controversial Thirty-Nine Articles of 1571 have a standing which varies in different provinces of the Anglican Communion, but have been influential on the historical shaping of Anglicanism in its middle path between Roman Catholicism and Protestantism.

In the Book of Common Prayer and the English Ordinal, Anglican theology has commonly found its most characteristic expression, seeking to include rather than to exclude. In the spectrum of Reformation service-books, they are conservative texts. Their principal author, Archbishop Thomas Cranmer, was by instinct and training a scholar, deeply read in the Greek and Latin Fathers and in the ancient church councils. He aspired to restore an ancient Catholic purity in prayer and spirituality, unencumbered by late medieval developments in theology and popular devotions, towards a number of which he was sharply critical. It was a matter of principle to him that Bible and liturgy must be in the vernacular as in the early Church; that clergy (as the holy Paphnutius had successfully urged at the Council of Nicaea in 325) should not be canonically required to be celibate; that, as had been the general practice until the later centuries of the Middle Ages, communion be offered in both kinds;[1] that the Eucharist should be a community act, not an isolated priest making a propitiatory offering on behalf of a passive non-communicating congregation (see pp. 131–9).

Most of these propositions (other than the non-obligation of celibacy) are self-evident to modern Roman Catholics, but did not seem so in 1550 when they were associated with the upheaval of the Reformation, in Catholic eyes a malicious rebellion against due authority disrupting the unity of Western Christianity. Cranmer, in practice, bequeathed a traditional pattern both of liturgy and ministerial authority. His preface to his first Prayer Book of 1549 (since 1662 printed under the title 'Concerning the Service of the Church') declared the purpose of restoring 'the godly and decent order of the ancient Fathers'. The preface to the Ordinal emphatically stated the intention of continuing the threefold ministry of bishop, priest and deacon, transmitted since the time the Apostles passed from the scene. The deliberate retention of the name 'priest' rather than minister, as a title for the second order of ministry, did not at the time or later seem to all Protestants to express a fully reformed view of the ministry, and it is certain that Cranmer was entirely

105

ready to accept that the presbyterate exercised a 'sacerdotal' function. Both the 1549 and 1552 Prayer Books granted only to bishops and priests the authority to absolve, bless and to preside at the Eucharist. That implied a strong adherence to patristic tradition. Moreover, the forms of absolution at the Eucharist and at the visitation of the sick are entirely traditional in both letter and spirit. Only there was a shift, of far-reaching consequence, in the fact that the penitent with grave sin on his conscience is invited, rather than obliged as a prerequisite for salvation, to make his confession to a discreet priest of his own choice. In the rite for the ordination of a priest, the main text, stressing the pastoral character of the ministry, was drawn from Martin Bucer's Strassburg model. But Cranmer, while omitting the commission of the medieval Latin pontifical to offer sacrifice for the living and the dead (and thereby giving conservative Catholic critics ground to assert that the distinctively priestly authority was lacking and even by implication denied),[2] abandoned Bucer at the critical point of the commission at the imposition of the bishop's hands, where the traditional words of the Latin rite in translation were kept intact (see pp. 155–64, 321–7).

The Thirty-Nine Articles were finally agreed after Pope Pius V had excommunicated Queen Elizabeth I and declared her government illegitimate (1570)—thereby identifying Catholicism with treason (an event most unwelcome to the English Roman Catholic community, which came to suffer so severely that slightly more lives were lost in the Catholic cause than had been lost in the Protestant cause under Mary Tudor). Most of the substance of the Articles may be labelled Reformed Catholicism. The rejection of transubstantiation in Article XXVIII was balanced by clauses intended to protect the real presence and causing offence to the Zwinglian party. In Article XXXI there is an apparent rejection of the notion that in the Eucharist the priest offers Christ to propitiate the Father on behalf of the living and the dead. On the other hand, the prayer of oblation in Cranmer's eucharistic liturgy includes an intercessory pleading of the merits of Christ's passion on behalf of the entire Church. There is no such positive statement in Article XXXI, but since the time of Bishop Lancelot Andrewes at the end of the sixteenth century it has been a question whether the concept of eucharistic sacrifice affirmed in the definition of the Council of Trent (1562–3) corresponds to that denied by Article XXXI. Andrewes thought not (see pp. 308–13).

The Articles contain several clauses which to Calvinistic Puritans were painful and even unacceptable. At first sight this is surprising. A rapid reading could leave the impression that so massive a stress is placed on the primacy of Scripture as to leave no room for any other authority. But on this point the wording is ambivalent and therefore hard to interpret decisively. Article VI declares that Scripture declares everything necessary to salvation, with the Augustinian inference that nothing should be prescribed as an article of faith, or necessary to salvation, which cannot be either 'read therein or proved thereby' (a phrase which has its own difficulties, notably in deciding what proof, or making explicit, would mean in this context). The lectionary was to retain readings from the books misleadingly called by St Jerome 'Apocrypha'; that is, those admitted to the canon of the Septuagint and the Bible of the early Gentile churches, but absent from the Hebrew. The two books of largely Protestant *Homilies* (1547, 1571) commended in the Articles contain many citations from these books. Since Carlstadt challenged their inspired status in 1521, the left wing of the Reformation had disliked them. Article VI offers a conciliatory traditional formula (echoing Cardinal Cajetan) that one should follow St Jerome, in reading them for moral but not for dogmatic guidance (see p. 93).

In Article VIII the Catholic Creeds are accepted because they can be 'proved' from the Scripture. This again echoes patristic language. In the mid-fourth century, Cyril of Jerusalem explained to his catechumens that each clause in their baptismal creed could be verified from Scripture. Some clauses in the Nicene and Athanasian Creeds would admittedly be hard to 'prove' in a 'mathematical' sense if one had nothing but the Bible to do it with. Article XX is bolder, with a clause that Puritans hated: 'The Church has authority in controversies of faith'—subject of course to consonance with Scripture.

This last sentence troubled Calvinists, and some printed texts of the Articles appeared in which the clause was omitted. The sentence raises the question of by what organs the Church exercises this authority. The traditional answer of Christian antiquity, from the late second century onwards, was the episcopal synod, at which the collective mind of the Church (e.g. on the date of Easter, on disciplinary procedures, then on doctrinal issues) was articulated by an assembly of bishops, each representing his diocesan family. In AD 325 controversy extending far beyond Egypt was raised by the teaching of the Alexandrian priest Arius, that the Son was not identical in his divine being with God the Father, and a worldwide council, with representatives of many Greek provinces and delegates from Rome, was summoned. The emperor Constantine the Great took it over, transferred it to the city of Nicaea near his residence, and enforced its decisions with the secular arm. Binding authority upon the entire Church, at least within the Roman Empire, thus came to be expressed through a series of 'ecumenical councils' at which both Greek East and Latin West were represented. The main decisions were ratified by the great patriarchates and by the emperor. The first seven (Nicaea 325, Constantinople 381, Ephesus 431, Chalcedon 451, Constantinople 553,

Constantinople 681, Nicaea 787) were all in the Greek East. The second and the seventh were not quickly acknowledged as ecumenical in the Latin West; and the fifth provoked temporary opposition as well.

The first four councils, which Pope Gregory the Great (living after the fifth council which he also acknowledged) hailed as a canon like the four Gospels, are treated in some Anglican texts of the sixteenth and seventeenth centuries as having special status (see pp. 203–8). This is notably so in the Act of Uniformity of 1559, where orthodoxy is defined by the Scriptures, 'the first four general councils or some other general council' (given biblical support), or (evidently with conscious exclusion of the Pope) as what may be defined by 'Parliament with the assent of the clergy in convocation'. In fact, the fifth and sixth councils gave definitions on the refinements of Christology which the Anglicans of the sixteenth and seventeenth centuries happily accepted. Their handling of the seventh council condemning iconoclasm needs special treatment (see p. 112).

The Thirty-Nine Articles affirm the doctrines of the Trinity and the incarnation in the language of the ancient ecumenical councils, thereby recognizing the standing of the councils responsible for the definitions. Nevertheless, the Articles are cautious about awarding absolute authority to any of the great patriarchates, including Rome, or even to general councils (XIX and XXI). They are far less reserved about the authority of princes (XXI and XXXVII), which is a reminder of the primary role played by Crown and government in the English Reformation. No English Reformer, recalling that all the ancient ecumenical councils were summoned by emperors, not by popes, would think that Rome had an exclusive right to summon councils, or that their authority depended essentially upon papal ratification. In any event, it was (and is) unclear that the Western councils entitled general or ecumenical, called by the popes after the eleventh century estrangement between East and West, possess the same status as the first seven. It did not pass unnoticed in sixteenth-century England that the Greek East had declined to receive the Council of Florence's affirmation of universal Roman authority throughout the Church.

There was nothing controversial in the observation that the co-operation of secular authorities is required if a general council can take place at all (though the framers of the Article may well have intended more than they actually said on this point). Nor would Cardinal Bellarmine have disagreed with the proposition that some assemblies claiming the title 'ecumenical' have made errors (classical examples cited in medieval discussions are Ariminum 359, and Ephesus 449). Their decisions were not received by due authority and by the faithful generally.[3]

On the other hand, the last sentence of Article XXI seems distinctly prickly and reserved when it says that the definitions of faith given by general councils have 'neither strength nor authority unless it may be declared that they be taken out of Holy Scripture'. Heretics condemned by ancient ecumenical councils plentifully appealed to Scripture, and the councils would not have been necessary if Scripture had been unequivocal on the matters under debate. The Councils of Nicaea (325) and Chalcedon (451) both found it indispensable to resort to terms not in Scripture, to fend off distortions of the community's faith in the divinity of Christ and the completeness of his humanity. In a broad sense, no doubt, the faith these councils defended was 'taken out' of Scripture. In practice, the Articles grant that it is only 'sometimes' that general councils have erred, and in Article VI the universal unquestioned consensus of the community is the ground for accepting the traditional biblical canon.

Article XXI, even in its last sentence, is correct if understood to be declaring that even general councils have no power to make arbitrary decisions on their own plenary authority; they always interpret dogma in obedience to a framework which is ultimately biblically based. The slightly exaggerated wording reflects Anglican reserve both towards the decree of the Council of Constance allowing communion in only one kind, and in relation to the Counter-Reformation Council at Trent (1545–63) in northern Italy, at which bishops attending were bound by oath to defend papal claims. Despite the mere handful of bishops attending Trent's early sessions, this council claimed ecumenical standing.[4] Sixteenth-century Protestants contended that Trent was no 'free' council because the pope was judge in his own cause, controlling the bishops through his legates who presided.

Nevertheless the Articles are surprisingly reticent about Roman authority. They say no more than the wholly non-controversial assertion that sometimes popes have made mistakes even on theological matters, and—much more sharply—that because of the royal supremacy over causes both ecclesiastical and civil, 'the Bishop of Rome hath no jurisdiction in this realm of England'. This reticence stands in contrast with the vehement words of the Presbyterian Westminster Confession of 1643 requiring assent not merely to the Calvinist doctrine of double predestination, but also to the proposition that by office the pope is Antichrist.[5] This totally negative view of the papacy found no place in the Articles or Prayer Book (except for a time in the form of a special service inserted by parliamentary authority to give thanks for the escape of James I and Parliament from 'Gunpowder Treason' on 5 November 1605—an alarming liturgical form that has long disappeared from all printed texts of the book). Yet it was a view which had a few Anglican supporters, including Cranmer himself, and became diffused in the seventeenth century by the exposition of the Apocalypse by Joseph Mede (1586–1638). The cabbalistic occultism of some Cambridge Platonists of that time produced in Henry More (1614–87)

109

some of the most luridly antipapal pages one can read. More was appalled by the exegesis of the moderate Protestant Grotius (1583–1645), denying that the prophecies of Daniel, 2 Thessalonians 2, and the Apocalypse referred to the papacy at all. The presbyterian Richard Baxter conceded that the biblical texts were very obscure, but remarked that if they did not refer to the Pope, he had 'ill luck to be so like Antichrist'.

An altogether more positive view of Roman Catholicism appeared, much to Puritan distress, in Richard Hooker. He 'gladly acknowledged' the Roman Catholics to be 'of the family of Jesus Christ' and to maintain the authentic fundamentals of the faith. Similarly his close friend Richard Field (*Of the Church*, 1606) affirmed Anglican piety and polity to be continuing the old Catholic conciliar tradition before Trent had turned school opinions into articles of necessary faith, and before the unchallengeable supremacy of popes over councils (and independence of them) came to be asserted (see pp. 254–6).

Anglicans of the generation before Field and Hooker were much divided about tradition, Fathers and councils. Heated controversy in the first stages of the English Reformation produced a negative appeal to antiquity against Roman 'innovations'. Jewel's Challenge Sermon of 1559 listed a catalogue of contemporary Roman Catholic doctrines and practices for which he defied anyone to find evidence during the first six centuries of the Church. This argument presupposed considerable researches in patristic texts; and for the argument to stand up it had to be selective. It was effective polemic to list the claims of Hildebrand, Boniface VIII and the medieval papacy; the technical language of substance and accidents to explain the eucharistic change; the (superstitious) veneration of images; Eucharists at which only the priest received communion; the withholding of the cup from the laity. It was more difficult altogether to suggest that there was no very ancient authority for commemorating the faithful departed, a practice which hard-line Protestants felt irreconcilable with justification exclusively through the imputation of Christ's merits rather than on the ground of anything given by grace in the believer's moral life. Nervousness on this last point may explain the deletion of a censure of prayer for the dead from the original text of Article XXII. In the 1570s, Whitgift and the Puritan Cartwright engaged in sharp exchanges over whether or not prayer for the faithful departed was implied in the Burial Service of the Prayer Book, in the petition 'that we with all those that are departed in the true faith of thy holy name may have our perfect consummation and bliss . . . '. Cartwright thought it was.

These and similar arguments evoked a positive evaluation of the early Fathers and ancient councils. The Thirty-Nine Articles frequently echo, and even directly cite, Augustine in the propositions concerning justification. In sixteenth-century controversies about e.g. the materiality of real presence and eucharistic sacrifice, about free will and predestination, about the unicity of the Church, both sides appealed on a huge scale to works by, or generally ascribed to, Augustine. Towards councils Augustine was always respectful, especially to Nicaea (325) in debate with Arians. He held a strongly conciliar doctrine of the presidency of the Roman see, the prime duty of which was to enforce the observance of conciliar canons. Augustine was aware that, for a Christian, authority does not have to be total and absolute to be real. Councils he saw to be an indispensable tool for co-ordinating policy, for keeping unity amid much natural diversity, and for defining the bishops' position in a controversial situation. He did not think a council's decisions could not be corrected or supplemented and balanced by later assemblies. On major questions, he did not think a provincial council had the authority to make its own decisions in disregard of other provinces.

This last point raised sensitive issues for the Anglicans. To what extent could the Church of England act unilaterally in making liturgical changes? Article XXXIV, 'Of the Traditions of the Church', adopts a fascinating zigzag course. It works from the implied axiom that what has been ordained by divine authority cannot be changed, but there is freedom in particular or national churches to change 'ceremonies or rites', subject to edification. Liturgical diversity between different countries, times and customs has always been the case. But the argument for freedom suddenly turns around to attack the Puritans challenging the liturgical uniformity imposed by queen and parliament. It is intolerable for anyone 'through his private judgment' deliberately to break the traditions and ceremonies approved by common authority. (Puritans hated the popish surplice and thought kneeling for communion implied transubstantiation.)

The Puritans objected to the preface to the Ordinal with its insistence that the episcopate is the providentially intended order for the continuity, unity and sacramental life of the Church through the ages. From the 1570s onwards, the Anglicans were confronting a Calvinist claim that presbyterianism is the only ministerial structure which has divine authority in the New Testament, and that 'antichristian' bishops obscure the Lordship of Christ over his Church. From the initial position that all matters of church order are in principle 'ceremonies and rites' left to the freedom of particular Churches, the Anglicans from the 1590s moved to the harder position that the episcopate is a gift of God to the Church for its unity and apostolic order, something no particular Church is actually free to change, though historical circumstances in some parts of Europe in the upheaval of the Reformation might have led to severe difficulties. The immensely learned James Ussher, Archbishop of Armagh, tried to commend a synodical concept of episcopacy, seeing the bishop as moderator of his presbyters and not making major decisions without their consent. But Hammond, Archbishop Bramhall and Herbert Thorndike argued for a more rigid view, with the bishops as the keystone of the arch, the guarantee of visible continuity and assured sacramental life in the Church (see pp. 333–47).

In this debate, patristic argument loomed large. Much seemed to hang upon the epistles of Ignatius of Antioch, the authenticity of which became a heated issue. The debate was in effect settled by Ussher (1644) with a masterly vindication of the seven letters of the so-called 'middle' recension. Two years after he wrote, Voss first printed the Greek text of a manuscript with the text Ussher had defended as authentic. The no less massive learning of John Pearson (*Vindiciae Ignatianae*) annihilated the contention of Jean Daillé (1666) that all Ignatius' letters are spurious in all recensions. In passing, it is noteworthy that Pearson applied first-rate patristic learning to demonstrating the very high probability that St Peter was martyred in Rome. He noticed how easy it became for Roman Catholic controversialists when Protestants were seduced by the short cut, taken in 1324 by Marsilius of Padua, that St Peter cannot be shown from Scripture to have gone to Rome at all.

The seventh in the list of ancient ecumenical councils, the second Council of Nicaea in 787, anathematized the dishonouring of images of saints, while simultaneously forbidding worship of them. The left wing of the Reformation was largely iconoclast, and deplored Luther's conservative defence of holy pictures and statues. English Lollards of the century before the Reformation hated images and pilgrimages to them. Article XXII rejects (peremptorily and without argument) 'the Romish doctrine concerning [...] worshipping and adoration as well of images as of relics, and also invocation of saints'. In fact both the seventh council and Trent distinguish the honouring of saints, as represented by their images, from the worship due only to God.

The very Protestant Homily on the Peril of Idolatry (1571) expressed fear of popular superstitions attaching to images, and painted a lurid picture of the persons and politics at the seventh council. The actual text of the council of 787 was carefully considered by Richard Field (1606). He observed that for an Anglican the Council's definition created no difficulty, and that there was no disagreement between Anglicans and Roman Catholics that risks of superstitious abuse must exist.

Archbishop Bramhall tersely observed, in regard to the decrees of the seven ecumenical councils: 'I know of none we need to fear'.

Seventeenth-century theological controversy was profound in both erudition and intellectual acuteness. But soon there came a weariness with researches in folio volumes, combined with alarm at the inhuman consequences of the religious zeal that was so large an ingredient in the Thirty

Years' War and the English Civil War. The disputes of scholars were acrimonious, and mutually deaf. The disagreements were in the sphere of revealed theology: could peace come by confining oneself to the fundamental truths of religion (see pp. 262–77)? Within Anglicanism, in 1650 a powerful plea for tolerance and reason came from Jeremy Taylor's book, *The Liberty of Prophesying*. He deplored excessive definition beyond the fundamentals of the Apostles' Creed, 'the unreasonableness of prescribing to other men's faith and the iniquity of persecuting differing opinions'. Learned himself in the writings of the Fathers and decrees of councils, he did not believe they could provide an absolute certainty where Scripture itself was unclear. From the wisdom of the past the living tradition draws guidance, but Fathers and councils do not present a unanimous witness with an authority before which reason can only bow in submission. Taylor had no doubt of divine assistance to synods of good bishops, like Nicaea, enabling them to articulate not indeed new doctrines, but the faith of Scripture, sound reason and tradition.

The voice of reason and liberality also came (through William Chillingworth) to the philosopher John Locke. By 1689 patristic studies were under a cloud, though still vigorously defended by George Bull (1634–1710). Bull engaged in controversy with the French Jesuit Denys Petau, who deployed vast learning (1644–50) to argue that the 'orthodox' writers before the Council of Nicaea of 325 were in fact Arian in their opinions. Not that Petau thought Nicaea in any way mistaken. He was turning the flank of the Protestant argument that the Church of the ancient Fathers provided a model by comparison with which modern Roman Catholicism was shown to have made gross innovations. Petau proved that doctrine was not immutable, and inferred that therefore to decide between diverse developments a living teaching authority is required. Bull's *Defence of the Nicene Faith* was no less learned and acute than Petau, and delighted Bossuet in France. He was convinced that by patient historical study, one can elicit a consensus among the Fathers which is a sign of unchanging continuity.

Eighteenth-century Anglicanism was little interested in tradition, councils and Church Fathers. Disillusionment with old dogmatic controversies either led into reasoned philosophical arguments (Joseph Butler against the Deists) or into the piety of feeling—often with the minimum of intellectual content, as in the case of the Evangelical Revival, but in William Law finding an exponent of mystical piety combined with a strong sense of tradition as an indispensable lifeline in Anglican spirituality.

The revival of appeal to tradition came with Keble and the Tractarians. In their eyes it was disastrous to rest the authority of the Church of England on its national character, or that of bishops on their nomination by the Crown, or that of the Prayer Book on its authorization by a secular

113

Parliament. Bishops must derive authority only from their consecration in the apostolic succession, not from the secular power. Liturgy and spirituality should be fed from study of the Fathers. 'The Library of the Fathers' and volumes of 'Lives of the Saints' were to provide for this need.

The study of the Fathers on the assumptions of Bull or Bossuet about unchanging revelation makes it easier for Anglicans or Gallicans to ignore Petau's thesis that there has been development in the Church like a living organism, and therefore an organ of authority is needed to adjudicate between valid and invalid developments. J. H. Newman in effect abandoned Bull for Petau, and thereby converted himself to Roman Catholicism with the argument that development in doctrine is inevitable and good, and that, while no modern Christian communion now corresponds exactly to the ancient Church, at least the Roman Catholic Church has changed less than others.

In modern Anglican theology, as in modern Roman Catholicism or Orthodoxy, the appeal to the Fathers remains a living force. It is significant that Augustine is quoted more often than any other writer in the texts of Vatican II, and the discerning reader of the Final Report of ARCIC I (1982) will notice many echoes of patristic tradition.

BIBLIOGRAPHY
Chadwick, H., 'The Status of Ecumenical Councils in Anglican Thought' in D. Nieman and M. Schatkin (eds), *The Heritage of the Early Church*. Festschrift Florovsky, Orientalia Christiana Analecta 195, Rome 1973, pp. 393–408.
Greenslade, S. L., 'The Authority of the Tradition of the Early Church in Early Anglican Thought'; G. V. Bennett, 'Patristic Tradition in Anglican Thought, 1660–1900'; and M. F. Wiles, 'The Consequences of Modern Theories of Reality for the Relevance and Authority of the Early Church in our Time' in *Tradition im Luthertum und Anglikanismus. Oecumenica* (1971/72), pp. 9–33, 72–87, 130–45.
Lampe, G. W. H., 'The Early Church' in F. W. Dillistone et al., *Scripture and Tradition*. SCM, London, 1955, pp. 21–52.
Parker, T. M., 'The Rediscovery of the Fathers in the Seventeenth-Century Anglican Tradition' in J. Coulson and A. M. Allchin (eds), *The Rediscovery of Newman: An Oxford Symposium* (SPCK, London/Sheed & Ward, Melbourne, 1967).

NOTES
1 Cranmer's 1549 Prayer Book affirms that under each kind the whole Christ is received.
2 The modern Roman Catholic rite for ordaining a priest lacks any such commission. The bearing of this point on the papal Bull *Apostolicae Curae* (1896) has as yet been unconsidered.
3 Reception is a major theme in regard to the decrees of councils or popes, but one of peculiar complexity. It would be absurd to think that a council's decrees derive no authority from their framers or from the reasonableness and evidently biblical

base for their decision, but entirely from the approval of posterity. If the faithful community has received a decree as true, then we believe it was not made true by that reception, but was received because it was true. The receiving is a manifestation of its truth. The reception process also takes time. Both Nicaea and Chalcedon had long struggles to gain acceptance. In the Roman Catholic Church the Council of Trent was not accepted until the seventeenth century, after long and hard argument. Moreover, the receiving process is not merely passive, but is an active interpreting and assimilation by the community.

4 In the seventeenth century the Anglican view of Trent was largely determined by the brilliant but cool history by Paolo Sarpi, the Venetian.

5 Today in the Church of Scotland presbyterian ministers accept the Confession with freedom of conscience except in matters affecting 'the substance of the Gospel'.

3 Reason

A. S. MCGRADE

No Church claims irrationality as an identifying mark, nor do Anglicans claim that they alone are reasonable. What, then, can be distinctive about 'reason' in Anglicanism? A simple if negative answer is to be found in reason's relation to the other bases of authority and method presented in this chapter, Scripture and tradition. Reason has served Anglicans, and has often been explicitly invoked by them, as a counterpoise to unthinking biblicism or unthinking conformity to historical precedent. The Reformation principle that 'Scripture containeth all things necessary to salvation' did not prevent bitter controversy under Elizabeth I about Scripture's meaning and the Church's discretionary authority in matters of liturgy and governance. In the culminating contribution to this debate, Richard Hooker's *Of the Laws of Ecclesiastical Polity*, reason is defended as not only presupposed for an accurate understanding of Scripture but as competent to determine a broad range of issues not explicitly covered in Scripture. Indeed, Hooker held that the Church could reasonably prescribe contrary to a biblical precept, if the purpose of the precept in its historical context could be understood and could be understood to be irrelevant in current circumstances (*Laws* II–III). Hooker's unwillingness to have the Bible used as a source of ahistorical, unambiguous proof texts for dogmatic solutions to all problems is typical of later Anglican thought.[1] Thus, Locke, although he leaned heavily on the Bible in expounding a 'reasonable' Christianity free of unnecessary obscurities, sought to approach revelation itself in a reasonable way. He objected to the slicing up of Scripture into separate verses, which led so easily to citation out of context for sectarian dogmatic purposes, and to the disparagement of reason in favour of revelation: he argued that taking away reason to make way for revelation was like persuading a man to put out his eyes to receive the remote light of an invisible star by telescope.

England was not in the forefront of modern scientific criticism of the Bible. Benjamin Jowett's essay 'On the Interpretation of Scripture', which had as its first principle that Scripture should be interpreted 'like any other book', shocked many when it appeared in 1860; yet there was good precedent in earlier Anglicanism for some aspects of the new approach—and there is good precedent for the respectful wariness of contemporary Anglicans towards the exclusively revelation-oriented theology of Karl Barth. The rational exegesis of Scripture in Anglicanism—the faithful acceptance of Scripture as normative witness to what is needed for salvation—has seldom purported to be simply a spelling out of truths accessible to faith alone. From Hooker onwards, human or natural reason has also been allowed to contribute (see pp. 112–14).

With regard to tradition, too, Anglicans have felt a need for reasonable discretion to temper a positive basic attitude. Ever since Bishop Jewel's undertaking to defend the *ecclesia Anglicana* against Rome on the basis of the Fathers, there has been a strong although not unopposed tendency in Anglicanism to follow tradition unless specific reason could be given for departing from it—but the possibility that there might be such reason has generally been recognized. Thus Jeremy Taylor in 1647, arguing that reason, proceeding upon best grounds, is the best judge:

It is a good argument for us to follow such an opinion, because it is made sacred by the authority of councils and ecclesiastical traditions, and sometimes it is the best reason we have in a question [. . .] but there may also be, at other times, a reason greater than it that speaks against it, and then the authority must not carry it.

Today, when some Anglican theologians propose substantial revisions in traditional credal formulations, this is not done from lack of sympathy with the patristic making of doctrine, but from a sense that the project of intelligibly articulating Christian faith must continue: 'The tradition criticizes us, but we have also to criticize the tradition, drawing upon the best intellectual and moral insights of our own day' (Maurice Wiles in *Christian Believing*).

If Anglican reason can be characterized negatively as a counterpoise to unreasoning biblicism or traditionalism, what can be said of it positively? For better or worse, no single specific account can be given. This is partly because Anglicans have disagreed among themselves about what counts as reason, partly because of historical change in what counts as reason in the world at large. A good example of both these sources of variation is the controversy between Locke and Bishop Stillingfleet over the purported anti-Trinitarian implications of passages in Locke's *Essay Concerning Human Understanding*. The Bishop's views concerning such metaphysical notions as nature, essence and person have been thought to resemble those of the great scholastic, Duns Scotus. Locke found them unintelligible. Stillingfleet, in return, had difficulty comprehending Lockes's 'new way of ideas', which was to set the course of British philosophy for more than a century. (Lest this dispute be taken as a sign of lay-clerical antipathy in Anglicanism, we may note that the next major figure after Locke in the empiricist tradition was an Anglican bishop, George Berkeley.)

The best access to the essence—or varieties—of Anglican reason is through the works of Anglican reasoners. Besides the separate works of major writers such as those already mentioned, Bishop Butler, the Tractarians, F. D. Maurice, Frederick and William Temple (father and son Archbishops of Canterbury), Charles Gore and several more recent authors, much is to learned from a number of collaborative volumes representing different, often conflicting viewpoints within Anglicanism but close to one another in their concern to address reasonably the conditions of their time: *Essays and Reviews* (1860), *Lux Mundi* (1889), *Foundations* (1913), *Essays Catholic and Critical* (1926), *Soundings* (1963), *Christ, Faith and History* (1972), and *Christian Believing* (1976). Some important figures in English literature have been Anglican clerics: Donne, Herbert, Swift and Sterne (the last two are significant critics of their rationalist era); and Anglican lay poets and critics such as Coleridge, T. S. Eliot and C. S. Lewis have had great influence in their treatment of religious themes. The present survey must be drastically selective and will be limited almost entirely to developments in England. Nevertheless, both the range and the problems of Anglican reason can be suggested.

COSMIC AND CORPORATE REASON: RICHARD HOOKER

Hooker based his insistence on the role of reason in church polity on an idea of reasonable law, which he took to be manifest in the workings of God and the various orders of creation. This vision of a cosmos of many levels, at once mysterious and teleologically intelligible, combined the best insights of classical and medieval speculation and was presented in Book I of the *Laws* (1594) with the grace and power of the best Renaissance style. It has served as an ideal model for many later Anglicans, even when it has been largely discarded as an image of reality in the modern world generally. The polemical thrust of Hooker's work depended also, however, on reason in another sense. Hooker defended public or corporate reason—the collective wisdom of the whole body of the Church—as against the judgements of individuals who objected to the Elizabethan Settlement as not sufficiently reformed. The unfortunate textual history of Hooker's account of religious and political authority in the posthumously published concluding books of the *Laws* has obscured both its originality and its logical and moral coherence. But no matter how we construe Hooker's system, the fact remains that an important aim of his work was to show that in 'things indifferent'—matters not of the essence of Christianity—the English church corporate had coercive authority over all English Christians (see pp. 262–9). This claim was to be successfully contested not only in the battles of the civil War and its aftermath, but also in the next era of Anglican reason.

CONSCIENCE AND THE REASONABLENESS OF CHRISTIANITY

John Locke's first political essay appealed to Hooker to affirm the legitimacy of coercion in theologically indifferent religious matters, but Locke's later *Letter on Toleration* (1688) is a classic defence of voluntariness as essential to authentic religion. 'Whatsoever may be doubtful in religion, yet this at least is certain, that no religion, which I believe not to be true, can be either true or profitable unto me.' Locke held the mutual toleration of Christians in their different professions of religion to be 'the chief characteristical mark of the true church', and he withstood repeated critical onslaughts in trying to make it a mark of his own church, or at least of his country's law. Indeed in the legal sphere, although he held that atheists ought not to be tolerated, he argued for the religious freedom of non-Christians: 'Neither pagan, nor Mahometan, nor Jew, ought to be excluded from the civil rights of the commonwealth because of his religion.'

It is a great mistake to interpret Locke's advocacy of toleration as secular or unchristian in motive or intent. When he wrote the first letter on toleration, he had freshly before him the savage harrying of Protestants after the revocation of the Edict of Nantes. As he wrote later, 'The horrid cruelties that in all ages, and of late in our view, have been committed under the name, and upon the account of religion, give so just an offence and abhorrence to all who have any remains, not only of religion, but humanity left, that the world is ashamed to own it.' There was a challenge here to discover a Christianity which could cease being a moral and religious scandal on the face of the earth. It is his desire to meet this challenge which explains the doctrinal minimalism and moral earnestness of Locke's major theological work, *The Reasonableness of Christianity as Delivered in the Scriptures*: if what was necessary and sufficient to be believed to attain eternal life could be reasonably established on the basis of Scripture, Christians might differ in their further professions, but (besides tolerating adherents of other religions in their civil society) they would at least be able to recognize one another as Christians.

This is to say that Locke's aim, like Hooker's, was to achieve a basic Christian consensus which any reasonable person could accept. Hooker could take doctrinal agreement for granted and defend the national church's corporate reason as a basis for practical uniformity in things indifferent. Locke perforce (and perhaps by preference) argued for the acceptability of a plurality of Christian religious bodies within a single civil society, but employed reason in the form of common sense in seeking an overarching Christian peace and unity. As Mark Pattison put it in one of the less dated contributions to *Essays and Reviews*, This popular appeal to the common reason of men, which is one characteristic of the rationalist period, was a first effort of English theology to find a new basis for doctrine which should replace the foundations which had failed it.' First the Reformation and then the reaction against Laudianism had effectively destroyed the authority of the Church, but the radical alternative of individual inner illumination had led only to extravagance and discord under the Commonwealth:

> The re-action against individual religion led to this first attempt to base revealed truth on reason. And for the purpose for which reason was now wanted, the higher, or philosophic, reason was far less fitted than that universal understanding in which all men can claim a share. The 'inner light', which had made each man the dictator of his own creed, had exploded in ecclesiastical anarchy. The appeal from the frantic discord of the enthusiasts to reason must needs be, not to an arbitrary or particular reason in each man, but to a common sense, a natural discernment, a reason of universal obligation. As it was to be binding, it must be generally recognizable [...] Truth must be accessible to 'the bulk of mankind.' (*Essays and Reviews*, p. 291, with reference at the end to Locke, *Essay Concerning Human Understanding*, IV.19.3.).

In the beginning, then, the appeal to reason at the level of common sense had a vital religious motive.

Locke held that the existence of God could be strictly demonstrated, and that there were objective, rational grounds for accepting Jesus as the Messiah sent by God to lead those who would believe in him and obey his commandments to immortality and bliss. This positive side of Locke's sort of rationalism was pushed further by a number of eighteenth-century authors, reaching its height of confidence in Warburton, who had a proof of Christianity 'very little short of mathematical certainty, and to which nothing but a mere physical possibility of the contrary can be opposed', and its height of eloquence in William Paley, whose *View of the Evidences of Christianity* (1794) and *Natural Theology* (1802) long retained their popularity. Locke had also emphasized the limitations of human understanding, however, and had insisted on a sharp distinction between religious faith and scientific certainty. The limited scope of human knowledge in an empiricist scheme of things is maintained with great honesty in the work of Joseph Butler, successively Bishop of Bristol and Durham.

In his sermons preached at the Rolls Chapel (published in 1726), Butler challenged his age's tendency to equate rationality with egoism by arguing that self-interest and benevolence are fundamentally compatible, that the authority of reflective, impartial moral judgement is natural, and that virtue is therefore according to nature and vice unnatural. Disinterested love of God would thus be a rational and psychologically appropriate response to God's goodness. But how is God's goodness to be known? Butler considered that reason was 'the only thing we have wherewith to judge concerning any thing, even revelation itself', and that reason can and ought to judge, 'not only of the meaning, but also of the morality and the evidence, of revelation'. The distinctive thing about his own reasoning, however, is that it candidly moves on the level of probability. He is the first, in the introduction to *The Analogy of Religion Natural and Revealed to the Constitution and Course of Nature* (1736) to speak of probability as 'the great guide of life'. The analogy in the *Analogy* is between nature as a system imperfectly understood and religion as a system imperfectly understood. 'Christianity is a scheme quite beyond our comprehension', but then, too, 'every thing in nature shows us our ignorance in the constitution of nature'. Butler's conception of nature and religion as systems allowed him to adduce many features of the former as evidence for the latter—the marked differences in the life-stages of many creatures in nature, for example, lend plausibility to the idea that our earthly life is a stage on the way to an immortal afterlife—but all of this shows, not the 'reasonableness' of religion, but its credibility. The *Analogy* is conceded to be 'by no means satisfactory; very far indeed from it', but, 'The evidence of religion then being admitted real, those who object against it, as not satisfactory, i.e. as not being what they wish it, plainly forget the very condition of our being: for satisfaction, in this sense, does not belong to such a creature as man.'

Mark Pattison had high praise for Butler's integrity, in contrast with the more assertive apologists of the age (in whom he noted 'the astonishing want of candour in their reasoning, their blindness to real difficulty, the ill-concealed predetermination to find a particular verdict, the rise of their style in passion in the same proportion as their argument fails in strength'), but like many of his contemporaries he found this phase of rationalism unsatisfactory—not for its empirical uncertainty but for its flatness. It produced a theology 'which excludes on principle not only all that is poetical in life, but all that is sublime in religious speculation'. He agreed with a German reader's response to the *Analogy*: 'We weary of a long journey on foot, especially through deep sand.'

MYSTERY AND SCIENCE IN THE NINETEENTH CENTURY

Locke had argued that Christianity was reasonable despite what was mysterious in it. A recovery of the poetical in life and the sublime in religious speculation and a changed conception of reason are all evident in Coleridge's contention that Christianity was most reasonable precisely in its mysteries: 'The Christian faith is the perfection of human intelligence [. . .] There are indeed mysteries, in evidence of which no reasons can be brought. But it has been my endeavor to show, that the true solution of this problem is, that these mysteries are reason, reason in its highest form of self-affirmation.' Coleridge could attempt to show the rationality of articles of faith rightly classed as mysteries because of his appropriation of Kant's distinction between reason and understanding. Understanding (the reason of the empiricists) is a capacity for judging according to the senses. Reason, on the contrary, is 'the power of universal and necessary convictions, the source and substance of truths above sense and having their evidence in themselves'.

For Coleridge the relation between reason and understanding, which was mediated and focused by the creative imagination, was tense but mutually vivifying. In his most popular theological work, *Aids to Reflection* (1825), he urged upon his readers the exercise of their reasoning and reflecting powers as necessary to keep faith alive in the heart; conversely, he insisted that 'never yet did there exist a full faith in the divine Word [. . .] which did not multiply the aims and objects of the understanding'. Those who based their thinking about religious realities on the natural theology of earlier empiricism were subject to increasing pressures in the nineteenth century from the new theories of geology and evolutionary biology. Coleridge's theological position, not dependent on science for its rational foundation, had less to fear from religiously uncongenial scientific developments; but it could consistently take up religiously positive ones. The mistakes of scientific men, he held, had never injured Christianity, while every new truth discovered by them has either added to its evidence or prepared the mind for its reception.

Coleridge's most direct influence was on the Broad Church movement, but the shift in sensibility he helped to bring about also had effects in other quarters.[2] So far as reason is concerned all of the main positions in nineteenth-century English theology can usefully be viewed in relation to his.

The Oxford Movement was set in motion by a professor of poetry who acknowledged a profound spiritual debt to Coleridge's sometime collaborator, Wordsworth. In his own immensely popular cycle of poems,

121

The Christian Year, Keble set out to exhibit the 'soothing' quality of the Book of Common Prayer, and his programme for the Church of England was avowedly to make it more poetic. (Newman, after his conversion to Roman Catholicism, commented in reviewing a book of Keble's: 'Poetry is the refuge of those who have not the Catholic Church to flee to and repose upon, for the Church herself is the most sacred and august of poets.') Here we see a full development of the view that religion moves on a level above the empirical understanding, that it is concerned with truths which have their evidence in themselves. Thus liberated from the burden of proving their theology by an accumulation of natural evidences, the Tractarians were correspondingly undisturbed by the supposedly anti-religious results of modern science. They did not, however, take the further step of trying to place science itself in a positive theological light.

The liberal theologians represented in *Essays and Reviews* were like the Tractarians in locating religion and science in different, non-competing realms of meaning or truth. Instead of finding the mark of reason in the distinctive mysteries of traditional Christianity, however, they were inclined to equate spiritual truth with morality. Also unlike the Oxford Movement, liberalism took an enthusiastic positive interest in the course of science in its own area. As to the assignment of religion and science to separate domains, Baden Powell wrote: 'The more knowledge advances, the more it has been, and will be, acknowledged that Christianity, as a real religion, must be viewed apart from connexion with physical things.' In an advanced age recourse to miracles for proof of Christianity is counter-productive: 'If miracles were in the estimation of a former age among the chief supports of Christianity, they are at present among the main difficulties, and hindrances to its acceptance.' For all the disconnection between real religion and physical things in liberal theology, the attitude towards science is strongly positive. The entire range of inductive science is based upon, and invariably confirms, the 'grand truth' of the universal order and constancy of natural causes as 'a primary law of belief'. Darwin's *The Origin of Species* must soon bring about an entire revolution of opinion in favour of the 'grand principle' of the self-evolving powers of nature. All highly cultivated minds and duly advanced intellects have now in some measure learned to appreciate 'the grand foundation conception' of universal law. It is noteworthy, however, that liberal enthusiasm for science involved no attempt to show that science provided evidence for religion. The clearest indication of this in *Essays and Reviews* is C. W. Goodwin's detailed *refutation* of all attempts to reconcile the biblical account of creation with the findings of modern science.[3]

The contributors to *Lux Mundi*, like the Tractarians, saw the Church as properly 'standing firm in her old truths', but in some ways they were more

122

positively engaged with modern science than the *Essays and Reviews* liberals. Their ideal aim was to assimilate new material, 'to welcome and give its place to all new knowledge'. This project is in a sense frankly opportunistic. Christian faith is presented as 'an energy of basal self' which uses as materials the sum of all our faculties—hence, no one faculty, including reason, can fully vindicate an act of faith—and so 'it uses as its instrument every stage of science; but it is pledged to no one particular stage'. Christian dogmatism is itself 'devotion to truth for truth's sake', and the doctrine of the Trinity is 'an appeal to reason'. In this spirit, the theory of evolution could be explored for possible theological significance without its dictating that significance entirely on its own scientific terms. Thus Aubrey Moore argued that evolution restored 'the truth of the divine immanence', which Deism had denied—but this led to a pantheistic reaction. In relation to these extremes, orthodox theism could be presented as reasonable, as 'the safeguard of rational religion against deism and pantheism'. Another attempt to integrate evolutionary theory with previous Christian thought was made in this volume by J. R. Illingworth, who argued that 'the theory of evolution has recalled our minds to the "cosmical significance" of the Incarnation', which was a prominent thought in the early and the medieval Church. The tone here is different from that of natural theology à la Paley, but also different from that of *Essays and Reviews*. There is no insistence that scientific theory or empirical findings 'prove' Christianity, but neither is there an insistence that real Christianity must be viewed 'apart from connexion with physical things'.

TWENTIETH-CENTURY EXPERIENCES

Nineteenth-century Anglo-Catholicism and liberal Anglican theology both appealed to experience, although in ways different from one another and from the empiricism of Locke's era. The recovered experience of Catholic devotion and tradition and the liberated moral experience of a theology no longer competing with natural science both found points of contact with the mind-centred idealism of philosophers like T. H. Green. Along with the development of philosophical idealism in writers like William Temple, A. E. Taylor and R. G. Collingwood, there was from around the turn of the century also a rising consciousness that the existing human world was far from ideal. Frederick Temple's sweeping historical optimism about 'The Education of the World' at the beginning of *Essays and Reviews* in 1860 was replaced by a somewhat sombre assessment of 'The Modern Situation' in *Foundations* (1913), a collection to which William Temple was a chief contributor. F. D. Maurice's attempts to promote Christian Socialism in the mid-nineteenth century had failed, but the efforts of Temple and others between the wars were more successful, as faith in an assured human progress driven by science or a reason immanent in history vanished. Experience has continued to serve as a starting point for much Anglican theology, but it is often the experience of God as a source of hope and meaning in an existence which is otherwise radically problematic, only seldom the experience of a natural and divine cosmic harmony. Even in these conditions, refined philosophical debate about the meaning and truth of religious discourse has continued, influenced in England by the propinquity of theology faculties to philosophy faculties in the ancient universities. Austin Farrer, Ian T. Ramsey, Basil Mitchell and others have contributed ably to these discussions, with varying degrees of commitment to perennial philosophical positions and new trends of thought. A serious attempt to take account of the philosophy of Martin Heidegger is central in the theology of John Macquarrie, and an Anglican interest in non-Christian religions (present in Hooker, for example) has been maintained by such scholars as Ninian Smart. Farrer's work is a particularly attractive recent example of qualities we have encountered in earlier authors. The 'rational' theology of *Finite and Infinite* (1943) displays speculative vision, exact metaphysical analysis, and searching inquiry: the Thomistic analogy of being is affirmed, but the dialectic through which God's relation to creatures becomes evident is marked by incisive criticism of the traditional arguments at each stage. In *The Glass of Vision* (1948), poetry as well as metaphysics proves congenial to orthodox theology.

Something of the range of reason in more recent Anglican theology can be seen in the Anglican contributions to *Christ, Faith and History: Cambridge Studies in Christology* (1972). The first of these, by Maurice Wiles, approaches Christology as something which 'has never ceased to puzzle and perplex' the minds of Christians from earliest times, and applies a distinction between 'two different kinds of story', a scientific or human story and a mythological story, to suggest the positive lines of thought which might take the place of a (possibly mistaken) traditional Christology. The last essay in the volume, by D. M. MacKinnon, suggests in contrast that the Aristotelian metaphysical categories of substance and nature underlying the patristic *homoousion* are analytically respectable, perhaps inevitable; and that the *homoousion* itself may be theologically essential for riveting attention on the person of Christ and understanding and maintaining the Church's dependence on him (as against primary involvement in its own consciousness). Intervening essays make adroit use of philosophy in, for example, showing the poverty of a general scepticism about knowledge of the past and questioning the appeal to a supposedly interpretation-free modern experience as a foundation on which to criticize traditional theology.

MYTH, NARRATIVE AND REASON IN CONTEMPORARY ANGLICANISM

Christ, Faith and History includes in a single volume proposals for a remark-ably wide range of doctrinal positions, although the range is perhaps no wider than the gulf in spirit between *Tracts for the Times* and *Essays and Reviews*. A similar range of opinion is apparent in the two appendices and eight individual essays following the joint statement in the Doctrine Com-mission of the Church of England's *Christian Believing* (1976) and in sub-sequent controversy over the 'myth' or truth of the incarnation.[4] When one Anglican theologian says with ostensible generosity towards traditional belief that we must be 'frankly mythological' in some of our religious affirmations, another is apt to take this as an attack, to fear that the affirmations in question are being demoted or rejected, and the fear is all the greater when talk of myth is accompanied by an intense concern with logical economy and coherence in the non-mythological parts of theology, or by a paramount interest in removing the real but supposedly unnecessary obstacles to belief so widely felt in our materialistic modern culture. The truth of the incarnation, it may alternatively be thought, is in the persistent, historically coherent testimony of Christians to exactly those things wit-nessed by the first disciples, and the true adventure of Christian faith is not a struggle to reject anything that may come to seem inductively unlikely but a life of openness to something always beyond all natural possibilities. Recovering serious involvement in biblical narrative in its own strongly realistic terms may thus seem the most reasonable course.[5] But is not a renewed openness to revelation also open to old objections in the light of reason? Yes, but the light of modern, Enlightenment rationality is also open to critical scrutiny. The presupposition of a secular, non-sacred nature as the starting point for reason is not inevitable.[6]

What can reasonably be said of such dissension? Against the background of previous theological debate within Anglicanism, the present situation looks familiar in form, however radical it may seem in content. A fervent dogmatic minimalism has seemed both reasonable and Christian to many Anglicans in the past, while to many others the self-evidently highest rationality of Christian faith has been its adherence to a God mysterious alike in transcendence and in presence. The sharply differing values as-signed to terms such as 'mythological', 'poetic' and 'history-like' in recent discussions recall earlier attempts to make the Church's faith poetic or imaginative—attempts which must fail if they make the object of faith imaginary. All would no doubt agree in some sense with Coleridge's aphor-ism: 'He who begins by loving Christianity, better than truth, will proceed by loving his own sect or church better than Christianity, and end in loving himself better than all.' The difficulty is that while this can be taken in the spirit of absolutely unrestricted free inquiry—'to know God is to be bound to question everything' (David Jenkins, *The Contradiction of Christianity*)—it need not be so taken: 'Christian dogmatism is, after all, devotion to truth for truth's sake (R. C. Moberly in *Lux Mundi*). No one can identify equally with every candidate for reasonableness in the tradition we have surveyed, but the consideration of past diversity may lead to a clearer recognition of personal integrity and a concern for corporate integrity in those who presently take positions very different from one's own.

A reasonable Church takes account of reason in the world at large. That world today imposes no compelling decisions on current theological controversies, but it does offer resources for prosecuting the debate more thoughtfully. Much recent philosophical work tends to obliterate any hierarchical distinction in cognitive rank between science and literature. Sensitivity to the importance of creativity in science, to revolutionary shifts within science concerning its own criteria of objectivity, and to the dehumanizing potential of an essentially mythic commitment to science and technology as substitutes for religion all serve to diminish the antagonism between science and theology, even when theology proceeds on other than an empirical basis. In this atmosphere there is no loss of status in accepting H. E. Root's analogy in *Soundings*: 'Believers are in love, theologians write love-poems and metaphysicians—natural theologians—write criticisms of poetry.'

Yet other developments encourage the pursuit of natural theology along more traditional lines. A century of research has revealed the vitality and restored the intelligibility of much of medieval thought. Modern modal logic and possible worlds semantics have led to renewed interest in the ontological argument for God's existence. Cosmological speculation is no longer excluded on principle from having theological implications.[7] In this atmosphere it is not shocking to find John Macquarrie propounding a natural theology of 'dialectical theism' which has positive incarnational and Trinitarian implications and which claims as its antecedents some of the most daringly speculative thinkers of classical, medieval and modern times, including Plotinus, Pseudo-Dionysius, Scotus Eriugena and Nicholas of Cusa.[8] And an analytic philosophy not compelled to identify intelligence with scepticism can argue for the cognitive value of 'Christian mystical perceptual practice'.[9]

Anglican reason has been a dialogue of various endemic conceptions of reason with one another and with various and successive rationalisms in the world at large.[10] When integrity has been maintained—when dialogue has not collapsed into diatribe and separatism—this has not been due to the dominance of any one species of reason, but to the acceptance of comprehension as a condition of life. The acceptance has sometimes been grudging, sometimes highly idealized. In any case, it is the intellectual reflection of the same commitment to corporateness expressed in this communion's peculiar attention to common prayer. In eucharistic prayers modelled on the 1549 Prayer Book, Anglicans offer God 'our selves, our souls and our bodies, as a reasonable, holy, and lively sacrifice'. The suggestion here that so repeatedly plural a subject—'selves', 'souls', 'bodies'—may in worship become one—'a' sacrifice—and a one which is reasonable, holy and alive in devotion to God indicates a proper and concrete spiritual context for Anglican theology. It is in worship or with reference to worship that all sorts and conditions of reasoners can practise the way of handling dissension proposed by Jeremy Taylor as God's way, the way of love. (This is in contrast with various human ways, ranging from submission to an infallible guide, through compromise, to indifferentism.) 'Theology is rather a divine life than a divine knowledge. In heaven indeed we shall first see, and then love; but here on earth we must first love [. . .] and we shall then see and perceive and understand.'

BIBLIOGRAPHY

Alston, William P., *Perceiving God: The Epistemology of Religious Experience*. Cornell University Press, Ithaca, New York and London, 1991.

Butler, Joseph, *Works*, 2 Vols., ed. W. F. Gladstone. Oxford 1897.

Cosslett, Tess (ed.), *Science and Religion in the Nineteenth Century*. CUP 1984.

Farrer, Austin, *Finite and Infinite*, 2nd edn. Dacre Press, Westminster, 1964.

Frei, Hans, *The Eclipse of Biblical Narrative: A Study in Eighteenth and Nineteenth Century Hermeneutics*. Yale University Press, New Haven CT and London, 1974.

Hooker, Richard, *Works*, general ed. W. Speed Hill, 6 vols. Belknap Press of Harvard University, Cambridge MA; London; and Binghamton, New York, 1977–93.

Jenkins, D. E., *The Contradiction of Christianity*. SCM, London, 1976.

Locke, John, *Epistola de Tolerantia: A Letter on Toleration*, ed. Raymond Klibansky, tr. J. W. Gough. Clarendon Press, Oxford, 1968.

Macquarrie, John, *In Search of Deity: An Essay in Dialectical Theism*, The Gifford Lectures, 1983. SCM, London, 1984; The Crossroads Publishing Co., New York, 1985.

Milbank, John, *Theology and Social Theory: Beyond Secular Reason*. Blackwell, Oxford and Cambridge MA, 1990; reprinted 1993.

Peacocke, Arthur, *Intimations of Reality: Critical Realism in Science and Religion*. Published for De Pauw University, Greencastle, Indiana by University of Notre Dame Press, Notre Dame IN, 1983.

Prickett, Stephen, *Romanticism and Religion: The Tradition of Coleridge and Wordsworth in the Victorian Church*. CUP 1976.

Williams, Rowan, *Arius: Heresy and Tradition*. DLT, London, 1987.

NOTES

1 The question of just how typical of later Anglicanism Hooker is on this and on other matters is well worth discussing in the quest for Anglican identity. The detailed commentaries in the recently completed Folger edition of Hooker's works are a good point of departure for such discussion. See also A. S. McGrade (ed.), *Richard Hooker and the Construction of Christian Community* (Medieval and Renaissance Texts and Studies, Tempe AZ, 1997).

2 'Through Coleridge, and through the radical shift in religious sensibility that he helped to bring about, Maurice was able to create a vision of the English Church, at once spiritual and social, that Anglicans have yet to assimilate. Through Coleridge and Wordsworth the Oxford Movement was able to re-assert both the independence of the Church and its interdependence with society. Through Coleridge and Maurice, MacDonald was able to discover something in the Church wider and more spiritual than could be found among the Congregationalists of Arundel or the moral precepts of Arnold. Perhaps most ironic of all, through Newman, the Anglican tradition of Coleridge has become part of the heritage of the Roman Catholic Church itself.' Prickett, *Romanticism and Religion*, p. 267.

3 'The Mosaic Cosmogony', reprinted with other interesting documents and useful introductions in Cosslett (ed.), *Science and Religion in the Nineteenth Century.*

4 John Hick (ed.), *The Myth of God Incarnate* (SCM, London, 1977); Michael Green (ed.), *The Truth of God Incarnate* (Hodder and Stoughton, London, 1977). Also see Michael Goulder (ed.), *Incarnation and Myth: The Debate Continued* (Eerdmans, Grand Rapids, 1979), and Durstan R. McDonald (ed.), *The Myth/Truth of God Incarnate* (Morehouse-Barlow, Wilton CT, 1979).

5 See Frei, *The Eclipse of Biblical Narrative.*

6 See Milbank, *Theology and Social Theory.*

7 Stephen Toulmin, *The Return to Cosmology: Postmodern Science and the Theology of Nature* (Univ. of Calif. Press, Berkeley, 1982). Various misuses of science as a surrogate for religion receive appropriately devastating criticism in Mary Midgley's *Evolution as a Religion: Strange Hopes and Stranger Fears* (Methuen, London and New York, 1985). See also A. R. Peacocke (ed.), *The Sciences and Theology in the Twentieth Century* (University of Notre Dame Press, Notre Dame IN, 1981).

8 See Macquarrie, *In Search of Deity.*

9 See Alston, *Perceiving God.*

10 'The Holy Spirit, who guides us into all truth, may be present not so much exclusively on one side of a theological dispute as in the very encounter of diverse visions held by persons or groups of persons who share faithfulness and commitment to Christ and each other.' 'Pluralism and the Norms of Christian Judgement', in the Inter-Anglican Theological and Doctrinal Commission's *For the Sake of the Kingdom: God's Church and the New Creation* (Forward Movement Publications, Cincinnati OH, 1986), p. 48. For Rowan Williams in *Arius: Heresy and Tradition,* the success of orthodoxy depends on its taking adequate account of the sound impulses behind the doctrines it rejects.

PART FOUR

Anglican Standards

1 Prayer Books 131~17�6

MARION J. HATCHETT

To know what was generally believed in all Ages, the way is to consult the Liturgies, not any private Man's writing. As if you would know how the Church of *England* serves God, go to the Common-Prayer-Book, consult not this nor that Man.   John Seldon (1584–1654)[1]

In other branches of Christianity the decisions of certain councils (for example, Trent) or the writings of particular leaders (for example, Luther, Calvin or Wesley) or certain confessional statements (for example, the Book of Concord or the Westminster Confession) have possessed authority beyond that ever granted in Anglicanism to any council, individual, or confessional statement. A distinguishing mark of the Church of England at the Reformation was the establishment of one uniform liturgy. It was not long before apologists for the Church of England would use as an argument in its defence the fact that in the Book of Common Prayer it possessed a liturgy true to the Scriptures, consonant with the practice of the early Church, unifying to the Church, and edifying to the people. As lines began to be drawn between Anglicans and Puritans, the principle distinguishing mark of the Anglican was allegiance to the Book of Common Prayer. In sermons and in the writings of theologians and apologists, the primary standard as to what an Anglican believes and as to how an Anglican is to serve God would become the Book of Common Prayer. Though it has been revised over the years and adapted for various provinces of Anglicanism, more than anything else it is the Book of Common Prayer which is a principle bond among Anglicans throughout the world (see pp. 55–69).

A push for liturgical reform gained momentum soon after Henry's break with the papacy. 'Marshall's Primer', the Ten Articles, the Royal Injunctions, the Bishops' Book, the Thirteen Articles, Hilsey's Primer, the Six Articles, the King's Book, the Rationale of Ceremonial, the reform of the Sarum Breviary, Thomas Cranmer's drafts for Daily Offices, the English Litany, Henry's Primer, the Book of Homilies, the Edwardian Injunctions, the English editions of the *Consultation* prepared by Martin Bucer and Philip Melanchthon for Archbishop Hermann von Wied of Cologne, the *Order of the Communion*, and the 'Cranmer's Catechism' would each in one way or another help prepare the way for the Act of Uniformity which required exclusive use of the Book of Common Prayer by Whitsunday 1549.

THE 1549 BOOK OF COMMON PRAYER

Some have said that the 1549 Book of Common Prayer was simply the Sarum rite simplified. Others have suggested that it was simply another German Church Order. The book does not fit either category, but has an integrity of its own. The sources covered a broad spectrum: the early Church

131

Fathers, Eastern liturgies that had recently come into print in Latin, various uses of the medieval Roman rite, the Reformed Breviary of the Roman Cardinal Francisco Quiñones, various German Church Orders, especially the *Consultation*, various English Reformation formularies, and Cranmer's two earlier drafts for Daily Offices. Very few texts were retained from earlier sources without editing or without revision in the process of translation.

The title, *The Booke of the Common Prayer and Administracion of the Sacramentes, and Other Rites and Ceremonies of the Churche After the Use of the Churche of England*, indicates that in contrast to the various medieval uses there was to be one liturgical use throughout the realm. In place of the various books for the clergy (Missal, Breviary, Manuale, Pontifical, and Customary or 'Pie') one book, available at a reasonable price, was to serve both clergy and laity. The texts of the rites, in a language the people knew or were able to learn, were available to the laity for their instruction.

The Church year was simplified along lines common to German Church Orders. Morning and evening offices were provided for daily use; Wednesdays and Fridays were to be distinguished by the reading of the Litany and Antecommunion after Matins; and 'The Supper of the Lorde and the Holy Communion, commonly called the Masse' was to be celebrated on Sundays. The only holy days retained in the calendar, or for which propers were provided, were feasts of our Lord and the days of Apostles and Evangelists, St Stephen the protomartyr, the Holy Innocents, St Mary Magdalene, St Michael and All Angels, and All Saints.

From reading the Church Fathers, Cranmer surmised that the Daily Office of the early Church was grounded in reading 'all the whole Bible (or the greatest parte thereof)'. He eliminated non-scriptural readings. To assure that substantial portions of the Scriptures would not be omitted, he arranged the lectionary according to the civil calendar rather than the Church year. The New Testament, except for the Apocalypse, was to be read every four months, and the Old Testament every year, except for certain repetitive portions and 'certain bokes and Chapiters, which bee least edifying'. The whole Psalter was to be read every month. Clergy with cures were bound to say the Offices publicly rather than as private devotions. To simplify the offices for the people, many anthems and responses were omitted and the diet of canticles curtailed, principally to those retained in German Church Orders. The use of the Athanasian Creed was reduced to six times a year, on principal feasts.

The Litany, to be said after Matins on Wednesdays and Fridays, except for the omission of the invocation of saints, was that authorized in 1544, which was drawn largely from the Sarum Processional and from Luther's Litany.

Among the propers the Graduals, Alleluias, Sequences, Tracts, proper Offertory sentences and prayers, and proper Postcommunion sentences and prayers were all omitted. For the Introit, a short Psalm or a section of Psalm 119 was appointed, generally in course but sometimes related to the day. One collect of the day only was provided; many were fairly literal translations from the Latin, others were revised, and a number were new to the book, especially those for Saints' Days. The Epistles and Gospels were basically retained from the Sarum use.

Many of the changes in the eucharistic rite came from Cranmer's reading of the Church Fathers, others from his acquaintance with some Eastern rites and with German Church Orders (see pp. 308–9). All of the private prayers of the priest were eliminated except for the Lord's Prayer and the Collect for Purity which were to be said during the singing of the Introit. The Kyrie and Gloria in Excelsis were to be sung straight through, rather than in a farced or troped form. The Collect of the Day was to be followed by a Collect for the King. The Epistle was to be followed immediately by the Gospel and the Nicene Creed. A sermon or one of the authorized homilies, or a portion thereof, was required. An exhortation to worthy receiving of Communion, drawn largely from German sources, followed. At the Offertory the people were to place alms in the poor men's box and the bread and wine, which was to be furnished by the communicants in turn, was to be placed on the altar. The whole of the eucharistic prayer was to be said aloud. The 'Prayer for the whole state of Christ's Church' portion derived from both the Roman Canon and German Prayers of the People. The remainder of the prayer drew upon the Roman Canon, the Greek Liturgy of St Chrysostom (for the epiclesis), German and English Reformation formularies, and the writings of St Basil. The amplified Institution Narrative of the Roman rite was replaced by one which was a conflation but relied entirely on the scriptural accounts. The prayer is a careful theological statement about sacrifice: Christ on the cross offered once for all 'a full, perfect, and sufficient sacrifice, oblation, and satisfaction, for the sins of the whole world' and he commanded us to 'celebrate a perpetual memory of that his precious death'; we offer this 'our bounden duty and service', 'our sacrifice of praise and thanksgiving', and the 'reasonable, holy and lively sacrifice' of 'our self, our souls and bodies'. Since in the late medieval period eucharistic piety had come to centre on the elevation of the elements at the Institution Narrative, and Cranmer wished to recover a eucharistic piety centred on the receiving of the sacrament, the elevations which had been introduced at that point in the late thirteenth and fourteenth centuries were forbidden— the only ceremonial actions to be explicitly prohibited. Communion of priest and people was preceded by an invitation, general confession, absolution, 'comfortable words', and Prayer of Humble Access from the 1548 Order of the Communion, which was principally derived from Hermann's *Consultation*. This preparation for Communion form had precedents in the late medieval devotions which preceded receiving Communion outside the Mass from the reserved sacrament immediately after private confession. For the medieval form 'Behold the Lamb of God, who takes away the sins of the world' at the showing of the elements to the people prior to Communion, Cranmer pointedly substituted a new text: 'Christ our Paschal Lamb is offered up for us, once for all, when he bare our sins on his body upon the cross, for he is the very Lamb of God that taketh away the sins of the world; wherefore let us keep a joyful and holy feast with the Lord.' The 1549 book specified that wafers be 'without all manner of print, and something more larger and thicker' and that each 'be divided in two pieces, at the least', thereby recovering the symbolism of Christ's body broken and of bread shared. The people were to receive the cup as well as the bread. The Sentences of Administration were amplified from Lutheran sources ('given for thee', 'shed for thee'). Alternative Postcommunion sentences and a fixed Postcommunion prayer were followed by a blessing from the Lutheran tradition, beginning 'The peace of God which passeth all understanding . . .'

Cranmer dealt in analogous manner with the other rites. The baptismal rite is preceded by a rubric stressing that baptism is a public act, for the receiving of the child and as a reminder to the people of their baptismal profession (see pp. 293–5). The rite begins with an exhortation on the necessity and meaning of baptism, which, like the rubric, is dependent on German sources. This is followed by Luther's 'Flood Prayer', common to many German rites, and by a signation accompanied by a form which is related to Thomas Aquinas' definition of the meaning of the Western medieval rite of confirmation. A translation of a German revision of an ancient prayer preceded the exorcism. Following German precedents, Mark's account of the blessing of the children is substituted for Matthew's; and this is used not in connection with the exorcism but as scriptural precedent for the baptism of infants. The Creed and the Lord's Prayer— remnants of the ancient *redditio symboli*—follow, with a slightly modified version of a prayer first found in the *Consultation*. A series of prayers drawn from an ancient Gallican source replaces The Blessing of the Font of the Sarum rite. The threefold renunciation is not the traditional one of Satan, his works and his pomps, but of the world, the flesh and the devil. The threefold affirmation is followed by traditional questions concerning the desire to be baptized. The child, unless 'weak', is to be immersed three times. The Sarum postbaptismal anointing which preceded the vesting is omitted, but the giving of the remnant of the vesture is followed by an anointing associated with a form which uses a phrase, 'the unction of his Holy Spirit', common to medieval theologians in relation to the confirmation anointing, commonly considered the matter of that rite.

Having provided for the perpetuation of the medieval rite called 'confirmation' in the baptismal rite, the 1549 book set forth another rite called 'confirmation' which had precedents among the Bohemian Brethren and the German and Swiss Reformers (see pp. 294–5). This rite linked together catechetical instruction, ratification of baptismal promises, and admission to Communion. The Book of Common Prayer tied it more tightly to the bishop than its continental counterparts or even the medieval rite of 'confirmation'. The prayer for the gifts of the Spirit was revised. The ceremonial action was not an anointing as in the medieval rites, but a laying on of hands as in the German Church Orders. The imposition of hands was followed by the peace, a prayer derived from the *Consultation*, and a blessing. The order of the elements and portions of some texts resembled the medieval rite but the rationale was clearly that of the German Church Orders, though the rite could be performed only by a bishop.

The marriage rite was designed for celebration at a public Eucharist. It was drawn from the Sarum and York traditions, the *Consultation* and other German Church Orders, and the exposition of marriage in the King's Book. A homily was provided for use at the Eucharist, if the sermon did not expound upon the duties of husbands and wives. The couple was required to receive Communion on that day.

The Sarum form for the visitation, anointing and Communion of the sick had come to be used principally for the dying; that of the 1549 book is intended for use not just with the dying but with any who are seriously ill. The book provides for Communion from the reserved sacrament on the day of a public celebration or for a celebration in the sick person's home on other days. The provisions derive principally from the Sarum rite and from the Cologne and Brandenburg Church Orders. An exhortation in the eucharistic rite commended private confession for those who could not through private prayer or a general confession quiet their consciences, and the visitation rite included an absolution to be used in all private confessions.

The 1549 book provided a burial rite which had four parts: the procession to the church or to the grave, the burial, a brief Office, and the Eucharist. The sources included the Sarum Manuale, German Church Orders, and the Diriges of English Reformation Primers. Prayers contained petitions for the departed, but the rite is far less penitential and more hopeful than its Sarum ancestor.

The ordination rites were not published until 1550 (see pp. 155–63). No provision was made for minor orders, or even the subdiaconate. The medieval rites had become so lengthy and complicated that there was a debate as to what constituted the essential form and matter. The model and principal source of the ordination rites was a treatise *De ordinatione legitima* by Martin Bucer of Strassburg, which was modified by some rearrangement and by the inclusion of other material, principally from the Sarum Pontifical. The rites are preceded by a preface which asserts that the three orders of bishops, priests and deacons existed from apostolic times, that admission to these orders was by 'public prayer, with imposition of hands', that these orders were to be continued in the Church of England, and that no one not presently a bishop, priest or deacon should function as such in the Church of England without ordination according to these forms.

THE 1552 REVISION

From early in the seventeenth century it has been popular in some Anglican circles to idolize the 1549 book, but that book was not well received at the time. It was too radical for the Devonshire rebels and for such conservative bishops as Edmund Bonner, Thomas Thirlby and Stephen Gardiner, and for priests who continued to use the old service books or to 'counterfeit Masses'. But, on the other hand, its revisions were not radical enough for the Norfolk rebels, or for continental Reformers such as Martin Bucer and Peter Martyr who now occupied prominent positions in the universities, or for the Anabaptists, or for some of the clergy and bishops, such as John Hooper and John Knox.

Many have written about the protestantizing tendencies of the 1552 revision, and there were quite a few. A penitential introduction was appended to the Daily Offices. Psalms were included as alternatives to the Gospel canticles. The Introits for the eucharistic rite were omitted. The preparation of the table at the offertory was dropped, and the eucharistic prayer drastically abbreviated. Communion was required three times a year rather than once. Different Sentences of Administration were substituted, and the 'Black Rubric' which denied 'any real and essential presence' inserted, and the curate is to have what remains of the bread and wine 'to his own use'. The exorcism and the chrismation were dropped from the baptismal rite, and the signation from the rite of 'confirmation'. The anointing and provision for Communion from the reserved sacrament were dropped from the Visitation of the Sick. The burial rite was simplified, the eucharistic propers for burial dropped, and almost all petitions for the departed eliminated. References to the chasuble, the alb, the tunicle and the cope, and to candles on the altar, were deleted. In fact, use of the word 'altar' was totally eliminated. The giving of other instruments in addition to the Bible (cup and bread for priests, pastoral staff for bishops) was deleted from the ordination rites.

The 1552 revision certainly represented a move to make the book more acceptable to those more favourably inclined toward the continental Reformation, but it also brought back various medieval elements in an effort to reconcile conservatives. A few Black Letter Days, for example, were restored to the calendar, and a remnant of the octaves. The obligation to say the Daily Offices was laid on all clergy, not just those holding cures. The Athanasian Creed was to be said thirteen times a year rather than six. The late medieval custom of having the Epistle read by the priest rather than a clerk was restored. The stipulation that the bread and wine be furnished by the people in turn was dropped. The growing custom of the late medieval period, that people receive Communion kneeling, was made obligatory. (The 1549 book had not specified posture, and in some places priests had begun to administer to the people seated in their pews as in some of the continental Reformed Churches.) At various points the revisions of 1552 were reactionary rather than Protestant.

The Second Act of Uniformity, which enforced the use of this new book on and after All Saints' Day 1552, spoke of the old book as a 'godly order' that needed reform only because of misinterpretations and because of doubts as to the manner of ministration. That seems to be a pretty fair statement of the attitude of the revisers. Many of the changes were aimed at tightening rubrics and at stating explicitly what was implicit in the 1549 book.

For the first time several Occasional Prayers were provided. The Introits were dropped, and the propers for St Mary Magdalene. In 'The Order for the Administration of the Lord's Supper, or Holy Communion' the Lord's Prayer and the Collect for Purity were to be said aloud. Following precedents of medieval troped Kyries and of various Reformed rites, the Decalogue with the response 'Lord, have mercy upon us, and incline our hearts to keep this law' replaced the ninefold Kyrie. The Gloria in Excelsis was moved to the end of the rite. The sermon was followed by the collection of alms and the prayer for 'the whole state of Christ's Church militant here in earth', a revised form of the intercessions from the 1549 eucharistic prayer. Next came the exhortation, the invitation, general confession, absolution and 'comfortable words'. The Eucharistic Prayer itself was drastically revised (see pp. 308–9). The Sursum Corda, Preface, and Sanctus were retained but the Benedictus Qui Venit was reduced to one line, 'Glory be to thee, O Lord, most high'. This was followed by the Prayer of Humble Access, which had been a pre-Communion devotion in the 1549 book, and by a revised version of the paragraph which concluded with the Institution Narrative in the 1549 prayer. In it a petition for worthy reception replaced the epiclesis. Immediately after the Institution Narrative, Communion was administered to the people, who were directed to kneel to receive. Different Sentences of Administration, capable of a Zwinglian interpretation, replaced those of 1549. The administration was followed immediately by the Lord's Prayer and one of two Postcommunion prayers. The first of these was a truncated

137

version of the final paragraph of the 1549 eucharistic prayer, the second a revised form of the 1549 Postcommunion prayer. The act of receiving Communion thus occurred in the midst of the revised 1549 prayer at precisely the place occupied by the elevations in the medieval rite—a deliberate attempt to substitute a piety centred on receiving the sacrament for one based on adoration of the consecrated elements. The bread for the Eucharist may be 'such as is usual to be eaten at the table'.

The initial signation, the exorcism, the vesting and the anointing were all dropped from the baptismal rite. The renunciation, the affirmation, and the expression of desire for baptism were all framed as single questions, and only one immersion was required. Yet the rite incorporates a new bidding and thanksgiving which express more explicitly than any text in the 1549 rite the doctrine of baptismal regeneration. The anointing is gone but its place is taken by a signation on the forehead, the site of the medieval confirmation anointing (in contrast to the baptismal anointing on the crown of the head), accompanied by a text which echoes the medieval confirmation anointing form and is related to Thomas Aquinas' definition of the medieval rite called 'confirmation'. Changes in the 'confirmation' rite of the 1552 book only make more explicit the rationale behind the 1549 rite which had been spelled out in the writings of Cranmer and other Reformers.

The 1552 book in the Visitation of the Sick omitted the provisions for anointing and for Communion from the reserved sacrament or for abbreviating the eucharistic rite when celebrating for a sick person.

In the burial rites petitions for the departed were curtailed, and no special provisions were given for an Office or Eucharist, though accounts of burials down into the nineteenth century indicate that on occasion the body was carried into the church for a Daily Office and Eucharist before the burial.

The 1552 revision of the ordination rites eliminated directions concerning the vesture of the candidates, and did away with the delivery of any instruments other than the Bible.

THE 1559 REVISION

The 1552 Book of Common Prayer was in use for less than a year when Edward VI died and Mary ascended the throne. She restored the Sarum rite, but Elizabeth in 1559 brought back the 1552 book with some revisions. Most of the changes seem to have been aimed at conciliating those of more conservative leanings. The 'Black Rubric' was deleted. The 1552 Sentences of Administration were prefaced by those of 1549. An 'Ornaments Rubric' (subject to varying interpretations) restored the vestments of 'the Second Year of the Reign of King Edward the Sixth'. In 1561 a new calendar containing more than sixty Black Letter Days was issued. In 1562 a metrical version of the Psalter with a few hymns and metrical versions of certain Prayer Book texts was authorized for use before and after services and sermons—a concession to those enthralled with the metrical psalmody of continental Reformed Churches. During Elizabeth's reign, there was growing dissatisfaction with the Book of Common Prayer among those of Puritan persuasion.

THE 1604 REVISION

When James I came to the throne Puritans presented him with the 'Millenary Petition', which consisted largely of complaints about the 1559 book. The resultant Hampton Court Conference authorized a revision that made a few concessions to the Puritans—the chief one being the limiting of the ministration of private baptism to authorized ministers. On the other hand, Puritans were not altogether happy with the content of the addition to the catechism concerning the sacraments of baptism and the Lord's Supper, and were offended by certain other minor changes such as additional Black Letter Days.

THE 1637 SCOTTISH BOOK OF COMMON PRAYER

During the reign of James I, efforts were begun to bring Scottish practice more into line with the Book of Common Prayer. Finally, in 1637, an effort was made to impose a revision of the Book of Common Prayer on the Church of Scotland. This book, often referred to as 'Laud's Liturgy', is now known to have been principally the work of Scottish bishops John Maxwell and James Wedderburn. It incorporated a number of features valued by the Scots and missing from the 1604 Prayer Book, including a presentation of the elements, an epiclesis, a breaking of the bread, and the liturgical use of deacons. It downplayed the Apocrypha, substituted the word 'presbyter' for 'priest', used the King James Version rather than the Great Bible for scriptural passages, and incorporated other changes designed to make the book more acceptable to the Scots. But other features (for example, an increase in the number of Black Letter Days) were offensive, and it was still entitled 'Book of Common Prayer' and retained the basic format and contents of the 1604 book. Efforts to introduce this book brought a temporary end to episcopacy in Scotland.

THE 1662 REVISION

During the Interregnum the Book of Common Prayer was outlawed. At the time of the Restoration the Puritans presented their 'Exceptions' and

Baxter's alternative liturgy, but by that time people anxious to restore the Book of Common Prayer were in control both in Convocation and in Parliament. Cosin prepared a draft for revision—'The Durham Book'—which made some concessions to the Puritans but was largely based on notes he and Wren had made earlier. Relatively few changes were actually made. Some occasional prayers and thanksgivings and the 'Sea Forms' were added, and a few changes were made in texts, among which were inclusion of a petition for the blessing of baptismal water and a commemoration of the departed. The most important changes were in the rubrics rather than the texts. Many of these came from the Scottish book of 1637 and represented a heightening of eucharistic doctrine: the bread and wine were to be presented at the offertory, the eucharistic prayer was given the title 'Prayer of Consecration', a breaking of the bread was restored, a portion of the eucharistic prayer was to be repeated if additional elements were needed, and remaining consecrated elements were to be consumed by the communicants rather than being given to the curate for his own use. The ordination rites were tightened against presbyterian interpretation. On the other hand, the Black Rubric was restored, though in a form that denied not 'any real and essential presence' as in the 1552 book but 'any Corporal Presence of Christ's natural Flesh and Blood'. The 1662 revision is still the official Prayer Book of the Church of England.

REVISIONS FOR OTHER PROVINCES OF ANGLICANISM

The newly acquired independence of the United States of America made a revision of the Book of Common Prayer necessary. Developments since 1662 caused it to involve more accommodation to the changed political situation. Many of the Puritan and Laudian proposals had not died with the Act of Uniformity. Attempts at reconciliation were made through proposals for revision in 1668 and 1689. Some Anglicans published and used with small groups revisions based on Eastern liturgies, especially the Apostolic Constitutions. Additional rites were bound with Prayer Books printed for use in Ireland. English and Scottish Nonjurors revised certain rites. Latitudinarians published proposals for revision, as did the late-eighteenth-century 'Arians'. In 1784 John Wesley published a revision for American Methodists, and in 1785 King's Chapel, Boston, adopted a revision based on that of the 'Arian' Theophilus Lindsey. A number of people involved in the first American revision were familiar with and sympathetic to these various proposals and revisions.

The first American Book of Common Prayer of 1789 updated the language slightly, simplified rules on fasting, cut back on repetitions, abbreviated somewhat various pastoral offices, and allowed for a selective use of psalmody in the Daily Offices. It omitted the Athanasian Creed, allowed the Apostles' and Nicene Creeds to be used as alternatives, and allowed the omission of the phrase 'He descended into hell' or the substitution of 'He went into the place of departed spirits'. It deleted references to private confession from the Exhortation and the Visitation of the Sick, abridged the Benedictus Dominus Deus, and omitted the Magnificat and the Nunc Dimittis. The most important feature of this revision was the inclusion of a eucharistic prayer, modelled after that of the Scottish 'Wee Bookies', which was much closer in structure and content to the historic eucharistic prayers than was the prayer of the 1662 book.

The only Prayer Book revision in the nineteenth century, other than the 1892 American, was the 1877 revision for the newly disestablished Church of Ireland. This book made some concessions to Evangelicals and did some tightening against the growing 'ritualism' of the period and against certain 'advanced' interpretations of the rites. The only changes made officially in the nineteenth century related to the English Prayer Book were the withdrawal of the State Services in 1859, the new lectionary of 1871, and the 'Shortened Services' Act of 1872 (see pp. 45–6).

A committee on 'Prayer Book adaptation and enrichment' of the Fifth Lambeth Conference of 1908 adopted certain principles for Prayer Book revision: adaptation of rubrics to custom; reduction of repetitions and redundancies; provision for enrichment, alternatives and greater elasticity; substitutions for obscure or commonly misunderstood words; revision of Calendar and Tables prefixed to the book. The Prayer Book was soon revised in Scotland (1912 and again in 1929), Canada (1922), Ireland (1927), and the United States (1928). An English revision (1928) received the approval of Convocation but not of Parliament. In all these revisions, most of the changes were in the interest of flexibility and enrichment. The most controversial aspects had to do with prayer for the departed and with changes in the eucharistic rites (in the eucharistic prayer or in the order of the components) which were seen as affecting eucharistic doctrine. In the following decades, similar revisions were made in various other provinces of Anglicanism.

REVISIONS SINCE LAMBETH 1958

The Lambeth Conference 1958 acknowledged that the time for more drastic Prayer Book revisions had come and set forth certain guidelines which were more fully developed by the Anglican Congress 1963. Since that time, most provinces of Anglicanism have revised their Prayer Book or have authorized 'Alternative Services'. These revisions have been carried out with the aim of returning to the sources, the biblical and patristic heritage, incorporating the results of liturgical scholarship, and adapting to present conditions and missionary and pastoral needs. These revisions attempt to make the language more intelligible, to incorporate social concerns, and to allow for more flexibility to meet needs of particular worshipping communities. Various provinces have participated in ecumenical groups developing common translations of texts (International Consultation on English Texts, or its equivalent for other languages) and have adopted common lectionaries, based on either the post-Vatican II Roman lectionary or that developed by the Joint Liturgical Group.

The newer books in the Daily Offices allow more flexibility and provide a richer diet of canticles and lectionaries more closely related to the Church Year. Some of the new books provide proper liturgies for major days, such as Ash Wednesday, Palm Sunday, Maundy Thursday, Good Friday, Easter (including a vigil), and Pentecost. In the eucharistic rite the new books allow more flexibility in the entrance rite, provide for an Old Testament Lesson and Psalm as well as a New Testament Lesson and Gospel, and provide alternative forms for the Prayers of the People. The Peace is restored, and also the four-action shape of the Liturgy of the Table: preparation of the table, eucharistic thanksgiving, breaking of the Bread, and Communion of priest and people. The eucharistic prayers of the new books have recovered elements of ancient prayers, normally including thanksgiving for creation and the incarnation as well as redemption, an eschatological reference, an invocation of the Holy Spirit in some form, and a concluding doxology. The oblation and epiclesis obviously continue to be matters of controversy in some provinces.

The revised rites of initiation differ greatly, but indicate some common concerns: indiscriminate baptism, confirmation as a rite for a mature re-affirmation, admission to Communion not tied to confirmation, parents admitted as sponsors and making promises, and ceremonial enrichment, including in some cases the use of chrism.

In several of the new books a thanksgiving for the birth or adoption of a child replaces the old churching rite. Some of the new books provide a rite for the reconciliation of a penitent. Other pastoral rites are enriched and made more flexible.

Though the revisions that have followed Lambeth 1958 have been the most radical revisions in Prayer Book history, they have been based on the same principles that were said to underlie the first Book of Common Prayer of 1549: (1) 'grounded upon the holy Scriptures'; (2) 'agreeable to the order of the primitive Church'; (3) unifying to the Church; and (4) 'edifying' to the people.

BIBLIOGRAPHY

Booty, J. E., *The Book of Common Prayer 1559: The Elizabethan Prayer Book*. The University Press of Virginia, The Folger Shakespeare Library, Charlottesville, 1976.

Brightman, F. E., *The English Rite: Being a Synopsis of the Sources and Revisions of the Book of Common Prayer with an Introduction and an Appendix*, 2 vols. Rivingtons, London, 1915.

Buchanan, C. O., *Latest Anglican Liturgies 1976–1984*, Alcuin Club Collections, No. 66. SPCK, London, 1985.

Buchanan, C. O., *Latest Liturgical Revision in The Church of England 1978–1984*. Grove Books, Bramcote, 1984.

Buchanan, C. O., *ARCIC and Lima on Baptism and Eucharist, Including the Lima Eucharistic Liturgy*. Grove Books, Bramcote, 1983.

Cardwell, E., *A History of Conferences and Other Proceedings Connected with the Revision of the Book of Common Prayer; from the Year 1558 to the Year 1690*, 3rd edn. Oxford University Press 1849.

Clarke, W. K. L. (ed.), *Liturgy and Worship: A Companion to the Prayer Books of the Anglican Communion*. SPCK, London, 1932; reprinted 1981.

Couratin, A. H., *Reshaping The Liturgy: Invitation to a Parish Enquiry*, Church Information Office, 1964.

Cuming, G. J., *The Godly Order: Text and Studies Relating to the Book of Common Prayer*. Alcuin Club, London, 1983.

Cuming, G. J., *The Durham Book: Being the First Draft of the Revision of the Book of Common Prayer in 1661 Edited with an Introduction and Notes*. OUP 1961.

Cuming, G. J., *A History of Anglican Liturgy*, 2nd edn. Macmillan, London, 1982.

Dix, G., *The Shape of The Liturgy*. A & C Black, London, 1945; Seabury Press, New York, 1982.

Donaldson, G., *The Making of the Scottish Prayer Book of 1637*. Edinburgh University Press, 1954.

Hatchett, M. J., *Commentary on the American Prayer Book*. Seabury Press, New York, 1980.

Hatchett, M. J., *The Making of the First American Book of Common Prayer 1776–1789*. Seabury Press, New York, 1982.

McGarvey, W., *Liturgiae Americanae: or the Book of Common Prayer as Used in the United States of America Compared with the Proposed Book of 1786 and with the Prayer Book of the Church of England, and an Historical Account and Documents*. Philadelphia Church Publishing Company, Philadelphia, 1907.

Marshall, Paul D., *Prayer Book Parallels*, 3 vols. Church Hymnal Corporation, New York, 1989, 1990.

Milton, A., *Catholic and Reformed: The Roman and Protestant Churches in English Protestant Thought*. CUP, 1995.

Spinks, B. D. (ed.), *The Sacrifice of Praise: Studies on the Themes of Thanksgiving and Redemption in the Central Prayers of The Eucharistic and Baptismal Liturgies*. Rome, Centro Liturgico Vicenziano, 1981.

White, S. J., *Christian Worship and Technological Change*. Abingon Press, Nashville, 1994.

NOTES
1 *The Table-Talk of John Seldon Esq.: with a Biographical Preface and Notes by S. W. Singer Esq.* (William Pickering, London, 1847), p. 115.

2   The Articles and Homilies

PETER TOON

As part of the one, holy, Catholic and apostolic Church, the reformed Church of England proclaimed its doctrine and polity in relation to holy Scripture, the ancient creeds and certain contemporary theological questions and controversies in its Thirty-Nine Articles of 1563/1571. By doing so the Church also made it clear upon what theological principles it had already produced its Book of Common Prayer (see pp. 131–9). Thus the Articles and the Prayer Book belong together both in the Settlement of Elizabeth (1559) and the later one of Charles II (1660–62) (see pp. 8–21). To the Prayer Book and Articles must also be joined the Ordinal (which Article XXXVI authorizes (see pp. 155–63) and the First (1547) and Second (1571) Books of Homilies (which Articles XI and XXXV authorize). The two books (bound together from 1623) present a lively, sermonic declaration of Christianity in terms of salvation by grace and faith in the context of the vision of, and call for, a renewed Church in a just society.

It will be our task in this chapter to examine the origins and contents of the Articles and Homilies, to notice their teaching in the context of the sixteenth century, to comment upon the way in which they have been interpreted within Anglicanism, and to note their position and authority within the Anglican Communion of churches.

THE ARTICLES

ORIGINS[1]

To find the effective origins of the Thirty-Nine Articles, we must go back through the reign of Mary Tudor (1553–8) and the young Edward VI (1547–53) to the latter part of the reign of Henry VIII. After the break with Rome in 1534, three statements of faith appeared in order to identify where the Church of England was in the disputes of the time: they were the Ten Articles (1536), the Institution of a Christian Man (1537), which was known as the 'Bishops' Book', and A necessary Doctrine and Erudition for any Christian Man (1543), known as the 'King's Book'. These represent the way in which the Church of England was being pulled by the old and new religious forces in one way, then another, in the changing theological climate of western Europe. However, the Thirteen Articles (1538), which were never published at that time, represent a distinctly Protestant statement of faith in the theological agreement arrived at by Lutheran and English theologians.

144

They had met in England with the agreement of Henry VIII because it suited his foreign policy at that time to have a concord with Lutheran princes. What they produced, which owed much to the Lutheran Augsburg Confession (1530), may be seen as the first stage of the process which culminated in the Thirty-Nine Articles of thirty years later.[2]

Archbishop Cranmer had many contacts with Lutherans and he had been prominent in the agreement involving the Thirteen Articles. And he was also the major figure behind the next stage of the process, the drafting, authorizing and the publication of the Forty-Two Articles (1553). In between his original drafting and the production of the final version, they were examined by various bishops and advisers to the young king. Yet they had to wait for their appearance until other Protestant publications (for example, the Prayer Books and the *First Book of Homilies*) had appeared; and when they did appear, there was little time to enforce them, due to the death of Edward and the reign of the Roman Catholic Mary. There is some debate as to whether or not they were officially approved in Convocation; but they certainly appeared on 19 June 1553, accompanied by a Royal Mandate, requiring all clergy, schoolmasters and members of the universities taking their degrees, to subscribe to them.

The Forty-Two Articles are certainly Protestant, that is, Reformed Catholic, in their positive teaching concerning the orthodox doctrines of the Trinity, the person of Christ and human sinfulness and concerning their particularly Protestant emphasis upon justification by faith, the Scriptures and the two gospel sacraments. They safeguard this Reformed Catholicity by the rejection of a variety of views being propagated by the radical reformers ('Anabaptists') and by the Church of Rome and medieval, scholastic theology.[3]

With the accession of Queen Elizabeth I in 1558 and her Settlement of Religion (1559), the Church of England reverted to her Reformed Catholicity as a Protestant Church. The production of the Thirty-Nine Articles is to be attributed primarily to Archbishop Parker, a disciple and admirer of Cranmer. He made use of the recently published Lutheran Confession of Württemberg (which had been presented to the Council of Trent by the ambassadors of Württemberg in 1562) and account was taken of the Calvinist ('Reformed') views of the recently returned exiles from Switzerland and Germany.[4]

Essentially, the Thirty-Nine Articles are a revised form of the Forty-Two Articles and the former were approved, virtually in what became their final form, by the Convocation which met in 1562–63. When they appeared in print there were two changes from the manuscript copy agreed by the bishops in Convocation in February 1563. Article XXIX, 'Of the wicked who eat not the body of Christ', was omitted, and to Article XX was added the clause 'and authority in controversies of faith' to strengthen the teaching on the authority of the Church. The Queen and her Council were responsible for these changes made in the original Latin edition which came from the royal press. However, eight years later Article XXIX was replaced by Convocation and the clause on authority was also retained. Thus in 1571 the Thirty-Nine Articles in their final form were approved first by Convocation and then by Parliament. There appeared official versions in both Latin and English, and the Bill that went through Parliament required their use in English, to be signed by all candidates for ordination. The full title was *Articles Agreed upon by the Archbishops and Bishops of both Provinces, and the whole Clergy in the Convocation holden at London in the year 1562, for the avoiding of diversities of opinions and for the establishing of Consent touching true religion.* In 1628 Charles I added a preface to the *Articles*, in which he stated that they 'do contain the true doctrine of the Church of England agreeable to God's Word' and he as 'Defender of the Faith and Supreme Governor of the Church' required all his 'loving subjects to continue in the uniform profession thereof'.

DOCTRINE

In drawing up and imposing the Articles the purpose of Cranmer and his colleagues was fourfold. They wanted to ensure that the Church of England was an apostolic Church in the sense that it taught apostolic doctrine; they desired to ensure that the clergy would be sound in their teaching and thus not expose the laity to unorthodox (radical or Roman) teachings; they wanted to have genuine unity within the Church (as the full title of the *Article* suggests); and they wished to set the perimeters of a comprehensiveness based upon the gospel.

There are various ways of indicating the themes of the Articles, by breaking them down into groups. For example, it has been proposed that there are four principal groupings of Articles, as follows:

(i) the substance of faith (I–V);
(ii) the rule of faith (VI–VIII);
(iii) the life of faith, or personal religion (IX–XVIII);
(iv) the household of faith, or corporate religion (XIX–XXXIX).

Within the last section the subgroupings are also reasonably clear, as follows:

(a) the Church (XIX–XXII; though the consideration of purgatory seems out of place);
(b) the ministry (XXIII–XXIV);
(c) the sacraments (XXV–XXXI);

146

(d) church discipline (XXXII–XXXVI);
(e) church and state (XXXVII–XXXIX).[5]

We now see why, in the title of the Articles, it is claimed that they are 'for the avoiding of diversities of opinions and for the establishing of consent touching true religion'. In the effort to set forth Reformed Catholicity, the writers of the Articles set aside troublesome views being propagated by the active sectarians ('Anabaptists'), by the traditionalist Romanists and by the growing band of Puritans. But they also sought peace in their attempts to provide straightforward statements of such doctrines as predestination and the descent into hell. Therefore, from one viewpoint, they are *pacificatory*, while from another they are *denunciatory*.

The Articles are certainly not ambiguous (when interpreted historically and contextually) but they are minimal in their requirements, leaving many secondary questions open. Bishop John Pearson rightly claimed in 1660 that:

> The book [of Articles] [...] is not, nor is pretended to be, a complete body of divinity [...] but an enumeration of some truths, which upon, and since, the Reformation have been denied by some persons; who upon denial are thought unfit to have any cure of souls in this Church or realm ...[6]

The Articles only laid down, within the mid-sixteenth-century situation, as much as was necessary to secure Catholic faith and ordered life in the Church of England; and they do not seek to go past the minimum. On the central issues of the gospel they are full and exact. Yet they are as broad and comprehensive as was deemed to be consistent with theological safety.

Apart from being conscientiously minimal, the Articles are also conscientiously eclectic. As we have noted they make use of the teaching of the patristic period for doctrines of the Trinity, Christology and original sin; of the Augsburg and Württemberg Confessions for the teaching on the gospel and justification; and of the teaching from Geneva and Calvinism/Reformed theology for sacramental understanding (Articles XXV–XXIX). As a whole they present the Reformed Catholicity of the *ecclesia Anglicana* and are (in the title of the first commentary upon them) *The English Creede; consenting with the True, Auncient, Catholique and Apostolique Church in all the points and articles of Religion which everie Christian is to knowe and beleeve that would be saved* (1585, 1587 in two parts by Thomas Rogers).

Generally speaking, expositions of the Articles from the seventeenth to the twentieth century have fallen into four types—(1) Evangelical and Reformed (2) Broad Church and Latitudinarian (3) High Church and generally Arminian, and (4) Anglo-Catholic.[7] Of course some expositors

147

have had feet in two traditions of interpretations. That there have been different traditions of interpretation is generally acknowledged; it ought also to be generally accepted that, 'the Articles ought to be read in the light of the situation out of which they came, and to which they were addressed, and [...] their words must be taken in the context and the sense they bore at the time of writing, and their statements construed in the light of the known views, assumptions and intentions of their authors'.[8]

THE HOMILIES

ORIGINS[9]

As with the Thirty-Nine Articles, so with the Homilies: their origins are to be sought in the reign of Henry VIII and in the reforming zeal of Cranmer. Inspired perhaps by his knowledge of Luther's collection of sermons for reading in parish churches, the Archbishop had conceived the plan for a book of homilies as early as 1539. It must be remembered that the office of preaching was highly valued by the Reformers, for they saw it as the divinely appointed way of taking the truth of the gospel to the minds, hearts and wills of the people. And if the men who were supposed to preach were ignorant, then they had to be given something good to preach (read).

In the Convocation of 1542–3 Cranmer was busy explaining why a book of homilies was necessary, and inviting men to write sermons for it. Not only must the gospel be proclaimed in all parishes, but also the errors of the ignorant and heretical must be prevented from being disseminated. By the end of the Convocation some sermons were prepared but, due to the opposition of the King, the collection remained in manuscript form. It was not until 1547, following the death of Henry VIII and the beginning of the reign of Edward VI, that Cranmer was able to bring his plan to fruition by releasing what we have come to call the *First Book of Homilies* of 1547. This book contained at least a couple of sermons recently prepared, but it appears that the majority of the twelve had been produced in 1542/3. As a doctrinal statement, set against the doctrinal publications of Henry's reign (to which we referred above when discussing the Articles), the Homilies represent the first, coherent statement of the reformed doctrines of salvation to be set forth by official authority in England. In particular they present a clear, unambiguous, 'Lutheran' statement of justification by faith; and they replaced the 'King's Book' of 1543 as authoritative doctrine.

The Homilies were published with a preface by Edward VI, whose royal Injunctions of 31 July 1547 required every parish church in England to have a copy of the whole Bible in English, the Paraphrases on the Gospels and Acts by Erasmus (translated by Nicholas Udall) and the Homilies, and to use these three as the basis for reading, studying and preaching from the Bible. Thus the Homilies were part of a larger plan to bring the message of the word of God to the people of England.

They cover these topics: Reading Scriptures; the Sinfulness of mankind; Justification by faith; Apostasy; How to die well; Obeying magistrates, and Public and private morality. Apart from Archbishop Cranmer's contribution of four sermons, other writers included John Harpsfield (d. 1578), Bishop E. Bonner (d. 1569), Thomas Becon (d. 1567) and Bishop H. Latimer (d. 1555). The third homily on Justification is the most famous, since Article XI points to it for an authoritative exposition of the subject (see pp. 69–77).

DOCTRINE

It would be wrong to see these twelve sermons merely as teaching basic, biblical doctrine and morality. Taking various themes from the royal preface, Dr John N. Wall Jr has suggested that the contents of the Homilies

> are, quite specifically, to be read in order, 'as they stande in the boke'; in some sense, they form a unit, a collection specifically arranged to move in a progression of argument from a beginning toward a particular end. Second, they emerge as a way to meet specific needs—'the decays of religion' and 'the desire of subjects to be delivered from all errors'—and to achieve specific goals—'to honor GOD, and to serve their kynge and to behave them selfes'—by specific means; 'the true setting furth of GODS woorde'. The Preface also defines the ends of the work in terms of moving 'the people to honor and worshippe almightie GOD, and diligently to serve hym'. It described what this means in terms of honouring God, serving the king 'with all humilitie and subjeccion' and 'godly and honestly, [behaving] them selfes towarde all men'. What is being evoked here is the vision of the *respublica christiana*, the true Christian commonwealth, that humanist vision of national life, which goes beyond matters of religious ceremonial or devotional practice to embrace total reform of all aspects of human society.[10]

Obviously both the Christian humanist and the Lutheran soteriological roots of the Homilies need to be seen in order to capture their original intention.

After being widely used in the reign of Edward VI, the Homilies had no official sanction during the reign of Mary but were effectively reintroduced by the Act of Uniformity of April 1559, since the rubric in the Communion Service requiring them to be read was unaltered in the modestly revised Prayer Book. Therefore a new edition appeared in 1559 bearing the subtitle, 'By her Grace's advice perused and overseen, for the better understanding of the simple people' and with the Queen's title changed from

Supreme Head to Supreme Governor in the tenth homily. There was a further edition in 1562 whose Preface declared that her Majesty commanded and strictly charged the clergy to make right use of them.

In the Second Prayer Book of Edward VI of 1552, the following rubric is found after the Creed: 'After the Crede, if there be no sermon, shal follow one of the homelies already set forth, or hereafter to be set forth by commune authoritie'. The young king was at this time looking for the 'making of more Homelies'; regrettably he never lived to see them appear.

The Second Book of Homilies was approved by Convocation in early 1563 along with the Thirty-Nine Articles. However, the Queen and her advisers took a few months to review the twenty sermons (divided into thirty-eight parts) and some alterations were made. The book appeared in the summer of 1563 under the title: *The Second Tome of Homilies, of such matters as were promised and intituled in the former part of Homilies: sent out by the authority of the Queen's Majesty, and to be read in every Parish Church agreeably.*

Apparently Bishop John Jewel (1522–71), author of the important *Apologia Ecclesiae Anglicanae* (1562), was the editor of this volume of homilies. Some sermons were written solely by him while others were adapted by him from a variety of sources. Both the present and the next Archbishop of Canterbury, Parker and Grindal, made contributions. In 1571 a further 'Homily against Disobedience and wilful Rebellion' written by Archbishop Parker was added, following the rebellion in the north of England in late 1569.

The *Homilies* of 1563 provide sermons for all the major festivals as well as for the rogationtide services of an agriculturally based society (13–17). They teach a powerful doctrine of conversion to God (20), of personal spirituality (4, 7) and of moral standards for personal and family life (5, 6, 18, 19). They place great emphasis upon the need not only to attend but rightly to participate in the services of the parish church (8–9). The latter is to be truly a house of worship and prayer, suitably furnished for those who hear and live by the gospel (1–3). The 'Homily against the Peril of Idolatry' is exceptionally long, being about one quarter of the total before the addition of the further long sermon on rebellion in 1571. Even as Cranmer believed that justification by faith was the primary message that must be heard in 1547, Jewel held that in 1563 the primary message was the purity and right ordering of Christian worship—free from a medieval images cult. The Homilies are clearly Protestant, but they are not Puritan.

THE ARTICLES IN THE ANGLICAN COMMUNION

There have been, in the history of Anglicanism, three kinds of dispute about the Articles. In the first place the interpretation of the Articles was a central feature of the argument which raged between Calvinist and Arminian Anglicans. As late as the early nineteenth century, a distinguished theologian, Bishop Herbert Marsh of Peterborough (1757–1839), attempted rigorously to exclude from his diocese all clergy inclined to a Calvinistic interpretation. Secondly, throughout the eighteenth century there were disputes about the propriety of scholar-clergymen being tied by an oath of assent to doctrines which, on rational investigation, they might find to be untenable. In 1722 the Feathers Tavern Petition against clerical subscription attracted the signatures of about 200 liberal-minded supporters, and was debated, and defeated, in Parliament. Thirdly, associated with the Oxford Movement was a determination to interpret all merely Reformation standards in the light of the tradition of the undivided Church. Newman's effort along these lines in Tract XC (*Remarks on Certain Passages in the Thirty-Nine Articles*, 1841) provoked such a storm that it brought the series to an end.

The precise implications of subscription to the Articles, which has never been required of any but the clergy and, until the nineteenth century, members of the universities of Oxford and Cambridge, has received various accounts. Some have held the necessity of a very precise assent. Others, among them the seventeenth-century Archbishops Laud, Ussher and Bramhall, agreed in holding that clergy were not bound to agree at every point, merely to refrain from public dissent. At the end of the century the moderate scholar-Bishop Burnet of Salisbury (1643–1715) expounded the Articles as an expression of the comprehensiveness of the Church of England. In 1865 the form of assent for clergy of the Church of England was changed in line with these understandings. In 1975 a new Declaration of Assent accompanied by a Preface was produced in the Church of England and incorporated in Canon C15. It runs as follows:

PREFACE

The Church of England is part of the One, Holy, Catholic and Apostolic Church worshipping the one true God, Father, Son and Holy Spirit. She professes the faith uniquely revealed in the Holy Scriptures and set forth in the Catholic creeds, which faith the Church is called upon to proclaim afresh in each generation. Led by the Holy Spirit, she has borne witness to Christian truth in her historic formularies, the Thirty-Nine Articles of Religion, the Book of Common Prayer and the Ordering of Bishops, Priests and Deacons. In the declaration you are about to make will you affirm your loyalty to this inheritance of faith as your inspiration and guidance under God in bringing the grace and truth of Christ to this generation and making Him known to those in your care?

DECLARATION OF ASSENT

I, AB, do so affirm, and accordingly declare my belief in the faith which is revealed in the Holy Scriptures and set forth in the catholic creeds and to which the historic formularies of the Church of England bear witness; and in public prayer and administration of the sacraments, I will use only the forms of service which are authorised or allowed by Canon.

One of the points of this declaration, which was largely prepared by Bishop Ian Ramsey, though amended by the General Synod, is that it relieved clergy of the Church of England from even that relatively unspecific assent by which they had been bound since 1865. Despite this, the Articles remain one of the authorities mentioned in Canon A5 of the Church of England:

The doctrine of the Church of England is grounded in the holy Scriptures, and in such teachings of the Ancient Fathers and Councils of the Church as are agreeable to the said Scriptures. In particular such doctrine is to be found in the Thirty-nine Articles of Religion, the Book of Common Prayer, and the Ordinal.

It is in some degree a reflection of the foregoing history that the Articles do not have the same position in each of the Provinces of the Anglican Communion. The Churches of Ireland, Scotland, Wales, Australia, Canada and New Zealand, along with those of Uganda, Ruanda-Burundi-Zaire, Nigeria and West Africa have retained them. The Churches of Kenya and Tanzania make them an option an individual diocese may adopt. At least in their Constitutions the rest of the Churches do not specifically refer to the Articles. However, in some cases it is possible that there is an implicit reference to them when the claim is made that the same faith is shared with the mother Church of England.[11]

A deliberate attempt to demote the Articles can be seen at the Lambeth Conference of 1930, where the Report of a committee on the Anglican Communion defined the identity of the Communion in an ecclesiastical and doctrinal sense without reference to the Articles:

[...] the Anglican Communion includes [irrespective of geographical location, those] whose faith has been grounded in the doctrines and ideals for which the Church of England has always stood.

What are those doctrines? We hold the Catholic faith in its entirety: that is to say, the truth of Christ, contained in Holy Scripture; stated in the Apostles' and Nicene Creeds; expressed in the Sacraments of the Gospel and the rites of the Primitive Church as set forth in the Book of Common Prayer with its various local adaptations; and safeguarded by the historic threefold Order of the Ministry.[13]

A somewhat hasty decision along the same lines was taken in the closing hours of the 1968 Lambeth Conference, when, against the advice of Bishop Ian Ramsey, the Conference bishops voted strongly for the proposal that each Province of the Communion should (a) consider whether the Articles needed to be bound up with the Prayer Book; (b) no longer require assent to the Articles from its ordinands and (c) ensure that subscription to the Articles should only be given in the context of the full range of the inheritance of faith and within their historical context.[12]

It is evident that these decisions, whatever their authority (Lambeth Conferences have, of course, no legislative power), raise the question, whether Anglican Churches are to be thought of as 'confessional' bodies in the same sense as Lutherans (with the Augsburg Confession and other documents) or Presbyterians (with their confessions, e.g. the Westminster Confession). Certainly some Protestants in the sixteenth century thought so; hence the inclusion of the Articles in *A Harmony of the Confessions of Faith of the Orthodox and Reformed Churches* (Geneva, 1581)—and this despite the fact that the Articles do not cover all major aspects of doctrine (for example, eschatology is omitted).

However, in the developing Anglican tradition since the sixteenth century the (orthodox) tendency has been more to view the Articles as one strategic lens of a multi-lens telescope through which to view tradition and approach Scripture, than to treat them as the single doctrinal foundation of the Anglican Household of Faith. Therefore it was recommended in *Subscription and Assent to the 39 Articles* that the Articles be always printed in the same volume as the Book of Common Prayer and the Ordinal. The other important lens, on this way of stating their place, is the Catholic Creeds. Such an approach leaves open the possibility of a further 'lens' being produced by the Churches of today or tomorrow.

BIBLIOGRAPHY

Applegate, S. H., 'The Rise and Fall of the Thirty-Nine Articles: An Inquiry into the Identity of the Protestant Episcopal Church in the United States'. *The Historical Magazine of the Protestant Episcopal Church of the United States.* 1:4 (1981), pp. 409–21.

Archbishops' Commission on Christian Doctrine, *Subscription and Assent to the 39 Articles: Report of the Archbishops' Commission on Christian Doctrine.* SPCK, London, 1968.

Gibson, Edgar C. S., *The Thirty-Nine Articles of the Church of England,* 4th edn. Methuen & Co. 1904.

Griffith Thomas, W. H., *The Principles of Theology: an Introduction to the Thirty-Nine Articles.* Longmans, Green & Co., London, 1930.

Griffiths, John (ed.), *The Two Books of Homilies.* OUP 1858.
Hardwick, Charles, *A History of the Articles of Religion.* Cambridge 1859.
Kidd, B. J., *The Thirty-Nine Articles,* 5th edn. Rivingtons, London, 1911.
MacCulloch, D., *Thomas Cranmer: A Life.* Yale, New Haven CT and London, 1996.
O'Donovan, Oliver, *On the Thirty-Nine Articles: A Conversation with Tudor Christianity.* Paternoster Press, Exeter, 1986.
Packer, J. I. and Beckwith, R. T., *The Thirty-Nine Articles: Their Place and Use Today.* Latimer House, Oxford, 1984.
Turner, H. E. W. (with J. C. de Satgé, J. I. Packer, H. G. G. Herklots and G. W. H. Lampe), *The Articles of the Church of England.* Mowbray 1964.

NOTES

1 The best study of the origins and history of the development of the Articles is still Hardwick, *A History of the Articles.*
2 The text of the *Thirteen Articles* was found among the papers of Archbishop Cranmer and is printed both by Hardwick, *History,* pp. 259ff., and by Kidd, *The Thirty-Nine Articles,* pp. 22ff.
3 For the text of the *Forty-Two Articles* see Hardwick, *History,* pp. 275ff; and Gibson, *The Thirty-Nine Articles,* pp. 70ff., for the text in Latin and English.
4 The Württemberg Confession is printed in *Die Bekenntnisschriften der altprotestantischen Kirche Deutschlands,* ed. H. Heppe (Cassell 1855). For the Marian Exiles see C. H. Garrett, *The Marian Exiles* (CUP 1938).
5 In W. H. Griffith Thomas, *The Principles of Theology,* 2nd edn. Longmans, Green & Co., London 1930, pp. lix–lx.
6 J. Pearson, *Minor Theological Works,* ed. W. Churton (1844), Vol. ii, p. 215.
7 Examples would be the expositions by (1) W. H. Griffith Thomas and D. B. Knox (1967); (2) Bishop G. Burnet (1699); (3) Bishop W. Beveridge and (4) Bishop A. P. Forbes (1867–8).
8 *Subscription and Assent to the 39 Articles,* p. 13.
9 The most accessible studies of the origins of the Homilies are provided by John Griffiths in the Introduction to the *Two Books of Homilies* (1858) and by John N. Wall Jr in 'Godly and Fruitful Lessons: The English Bible, Erasmus' Paraphrases and the Book of Homilies' in *The Godly Kingdom of Tudor England,* ed. John E. Booty (Morehouse-Barlow, Wilton CT, 1981), chap. 2. I also had access to the MS on the Homilies by Canon John Tiller of Hereford Cathedral: regrettably this has not yet been published.
10 Wall, 'Godly and Fruitful Lessons', p. 91.
11 I am grateful to Miss Wild at the offices of the ACC in London for helping me to examine the constitutions.
12 *The Lambeth Conference 1968: Resolutions and Reports* (SPCK, London, and Seabury Press, New York, 1968), pp. 40–1. See also the Addendum on 'The 39 Articles and the Anglican Tradition' on pp. 82–3.
13 *The Lambeth Conferences, 1867–1930* (SPCK, London, 1948), p. 246. See also Resolutions 48 and 49 at p. 173f.

3 Ordinals

PAUL F. BRADSHAW

HISTORY OF THE ORDINAL

The first Anglican Ordinal was published at the beginning of March 1550 under the title, *The forme and maner of making and consecratyng of Archbishoppes, Bishoppes, Priestes and Deacons*. It is generally agreed that its primary source was an ordination service drawn up by the German Reformer Martin Bucer, who had come to England in 1549. In this Bucer had directed that, since there were three orders of ministers in the Church, changes should be made so that when a bishop was ordained it should be carried out 'more solemnly and at greater length' and when a deacon was ordained it should be simplified. This was in effect what was done in the three Anglican rites, that for bishops being also intended for use at the consecration of an archbishop. The variations between them were effected mainly by the addition of elements adapted from the medieval ordination rites.

With the publication of the second Book of Common Prayer in 1552 (see pp. 136–8), the Ordinal was bound up with the Prayer Book, although it retained its own title page. A number of changes were made to it at this revision. Whereas the first Ordinal had directed that candidates for the diaconate and the priesthood should be vested in a 'playne Albe', and candidates for the episcopate in a 'Surples and Cope', in 1552 all these directions were deleted in response to protests from extreme Protestants who regarded them as encouraging the perpetuation of a medieval concept of the nature of the ordained ministry. At the same time, and for the same reason, the delivery of the symbols of office within the rites was modified. The first Ordinal had taken from medieval practice the custom of handing over to the newly ordained something which symbolized their new role. Thus the medieval deacon had received a book containing the liturgical Gospels which he would read, the priest a chalice and paten, and the bishop, after having had the book of the Gospels laid on his neck during the imposition of hands, then received it along with the rest of the episcopal insignia (pastoral staff, mitre, ring and gloves). The 1550 Ordinal had provided for the New Testament to be given to deacons, the Bible along with the chalice and bread to priests, and for the Bible to be laid on a new bishop's neck after the imposition of hands and a pastoral staff to be given to him. In the 1552 revision, however, whilst deacons continued to receive the New Testament, both priests and bishops were given only the Bible.

At the 1661/2 revision of the Prayer Book, some, albeit vague, directions about vesture were restored to the Ordinal: candidates for the diaconate and

155

priesthood were to be 'decently habited', and a candidate for the episcopate was to be 'vested in his Rochet' and was to put on 'the rest of the Episcopal habit' during the rite, after the examination. Further alterations made at this time will be treated at appropriate points below.

REQUIREMENTS FOR ORDINATION

The rites were preceded by a Preface which, among other things, required candidates for the diaconate to be at least twenty-one years of age, those for the priesthood to be twenty-four years old, and those for the episcopate to be 'fully thirty years of age'. The minimum age for the diaconate was increased to twenty-three in 1575, although the text of the Preface was not amended to take account of this until 1662. Candidates for ordination were also required to be 'first called, tried, examined and known to have such qualities as were requisite'. Such a requirement was typical of the ordination practice of all mainstream Reformation Churches at this time, as they sought, on the one hand, to put an end to what they saw as the lax conditions of the Middle Ages when little had been demanded of ordinands, and on the other hand, to oppose the position taken by some extreme sects who denied the need for any formal admission to ministry at all. Thus, by 'called' was meant not the inner vocation of God, though that was always presupposed, but the outward mandate of the Church: no one 'by his own private authority' (to quote the 1550 Preface) might presume to execute the functions of the ordained ministry.

With regard to 'trial and examination' the Preface itself prescribes only that the candidate should be 'of virtuous conversation and without crime' and 'learned in the Latin tongue and sufficiently instructed in holy Scripture', though other regulations were subsequently made in canon law. Following earlier medieval practice, at the presentation of the candidates for the diaconate and priesthood (though not the episcopate) at the beginning of the rites, the archdeacon presenting the candidates affirms that he has examined them and thinks them to be suitable in their learning and 'Godly conversation', and an opportunity is given to the congregation present to allege any crime or impediment which would constitute a bar to their ordination. All three rites also include a series of questions addressed to the candidates concerning their beliefs and intentions, drawn from Bucer's service. Such public examinations were a universal feature of Reformed rites of ordination, and were modelled on similar questions which had been put to candidates for the episcopate in the medieval rites.

The Preface also directed that the diaconate was to be conferred on a Sunday or holy day, and that this was to be done 'in the face of the Church'—both these requirements being characteristic of all Reformed ordination rites and intended to restore ordination to the public event it had been in the early Church. Presumably these directions were also meant to apply to the conferring of the priesthood. No such instructions were needed in the case of the episcopate, since it was already the medieval custom for this to be restricted to those days, although at the 1661/2 revision an explicit note to this effect was appended to the title of the rite. At the same time the statement was added to the Preface that the diaconate was to be conferred 'at the times appointed in the Canon' (i.e. during the traditional Ember seasons) and only 'on urgent occasion' on another Sunday or holy day.

THE RITES

During the Middle Ages there had been considerable diversity of opinion among theologians as to what constituted the minimum essential features of an ordination rite. According to scholastic theology all sacraments were composed of two elements, 'matter' and 'form', categories derived from Aristotelian philosophy. In this context, by 'matter' was meant the material element used in the sacramental act and by 'form' the words which must necessarily accompany it. In the case of ordination, 'matter' and 'form' were not easy to define, not least because of the large number of ceremonies which had gradually been added to the medieval ordination rites, and as little was known at the time about the relative antiquity of many of them, some strange conclusions about the essential elements were often drawn. Some theologians believed that the matter and form for all the orders had been instituted by Christ himself, others that it had been left to the Church to determine what was appropriate in each case. Many believed that the ritual handing over of the symbols of office constituted the essential 'matter' of ordination, whilst others included the anointing or the laying on of hands. They usually designated as the 'form' the imperative formulae which accompanied these actions.

The Preface to the Ordinal cut through this confusion by turning to New Testament evidence and defining the essential ceremony of admission to office as 'public prayer, with imposition of hands', a conclusion which more recent scholarship has shown to concur with the practice of the early centuries of the Christian Church. There was, however, one significant difference. Whereas in the early Church the prayer had comprised both the petitions of the whole worshipping assembly (either in silence or in the form of a litany) and also a prayer for the candidate said while hands were laid on him, this was not the case in the Anglican rites. Its compilers appear to have understood the New Testament to be speaking only of congregational prayer preceding the act of ordination, and not of an ordination prayer for the candidate in close association with the laying on of hands. Thus in the rite for the diaconate prayer is made for the ordinands in the litany near the beginning of the service by means of a special suffrage and concluding collect, but then the ministry of the word and the examination of the candidates intervene before the imposition of hands itself, which is accompanied not by prayer but by an imperative formula, following the model of common medieval practice, although the form itself is a new composition: 'Take thou authority to execute the office of a Deacon in the Church of God committed unto thee: in the name of the Father, the Son, and the Holy Ghost. Amen.'

The rite for priesthood is similar, except that in this case there is a prayer immediately before the imposition of hands, taken from Bucer's rite, but it completely leaves out the central section of the original, which was a petition that the Holy Spirit might be poured out on the candidates, and so turns it into a general prayer for the congregation instead. The imposition of hands here is accompanied by an imperative formula based in part on John 20.22–3, which had been used in this way in some medieval rites: 'Receive the Holy Ghost, whose sins thou dost forgive, they are forgiven: and whose sins thou dost retain, they are retained, and be thou a faithful dispenser of the word of God and of his holy sacraments. In the name of the Father, and of the Son, and of the Holy Ghost. Amen.'

In the rite for the episcopate, the litany with its special suffrage and collect is preceded by a bidding which claims that in praying before 'we admit and send forth this person presented unto us', the congregation is following the example of Christ, who continued the whole night in prayer before he chose and sent forth the twelve apostles, and of the Christians at Antioch, who fasted and prayed before they 'laid hands upon, or sent forth Paul and Barnabas'. On the other hand, there is also in this case a prayer for the candidate immediately prior to the imposition of hands, formed by the fusion of the beginning of the prayer from Bucer's rite with a free translation of part of the medieval ordination prayers, although the imposition of hands itself is again accompanied by an imperative formula, this time using material from 2 Timothy 1.6–7: 'Take the Holy Ghost, and remember that thou stir up the grace of God, which is in thee, by imposition of hands: for God hath not given us the spirit of fear, but of power, and love, and of soberness.'

In spite of the statement concerning prayer in the Preface to the Ordinal, these imperative formulae accompanying the imposition of hands came to be thought of by many Anglicans as the essential 'form' of ordination, and in the seventeenth century those in the rites for the priesthood and episcopate came under heavy criticism from Roman Catholics for failing to name explicitly the particular order being conferred. At the revision of 1661/2, therefore, the words, 'for the office and work of a Priest/Bishop in the Church of God, now committed unto thee by the imposition of our hands', were inserted into them, in an attempt to remedy this alleged defect.

THE THREEFOLD MINISTRY: BISHOPS AND PRIESTS

In contrast to the medieval ordination rites, which had portrayed the priesthood primarily in cultic and sacrificial language, the Anglican service, although retaining the term 'priest', instead stresses the ministry of the word and of pastoral care (see pp. 321–4). Thus one of the Gospels appointed is John 10, with its reference to shepherding the sheep, and the exhortation addressed to the candidates by the bishop speaks of them as having been called to be 'the Messengers, the Watchmen, the Pastors, and Stewards of the Lord, to teach, to premonish, to feed, and to provide for the Lord's family, and seek for Christ's sheep'. The questions in the examination refer to teaching from the Scriptures, to ministering the doctrine and sacraments, and the discipline of Christ, to being diligent in prayer and study, to being an example to the flock of Christ, and to encouraging 'quietness, peace, and love' amongst those committed to their charge. Finally, after the imposition of hands, when the bishop hands a Bible to the newly ordained (together with the chalice and bread in the first Ordinal), he says: 'Take thou authority to preach the word of God, and to minister the holy sacraments . . . .'

The Ordinal describes the bishop as appointed to 'the government of the congregation of Christ', and modifies the questions in the examination of the candidate, which are derived from the rite for the priesthood, so as to emphasize the bishop's particular functions of maintaining the purity of doctrine, correcting and punishing the disobedient, and caring for the needy (see pp. 333–7). The prayer before the laying on of hands, using language taken from the medieval rites, speaks of him spreading abroad 'the glad tidings of reconcilement to God' and of using his authority for the good of God's family, and the formulae addressed to him after the imposition of hands refer to teaching and to shepherding.

Throughout the Middle Ages there had been a considerable theological debate concerning the relationship between the priesthood and the episcopate. Some regarded the two as distinct orders of ministry, but others held the view that the episcopate was simply a hierarchical rank or 'dignity' within the one order of priesthood, and preferred to speak of a bishop being 'consecrated' rather than 'ordained' to his office. Among the theologians of the Reformation it was widely accepted that the New Testament did not distinguish between bishops and priests, a belief shared by Thomas Cranmer, Archbishop of Canterbury at the time of the composition of the Ordinal and undoubtedly its chief architect.

Thus, although the Preface begins by affirming that 'it is evident unto all men, diligently reading holy Scripture, and ancient authors, that from the Apostles' time, there hath been these orders of Ministers in Christ's Church, Bishops, Priests, and Deacons', this does not necessarily mean that those responsible for framing the Ordinal were all agreed that bishops and priests constituted two separate orders. Just as the eucharistic rite of the 1549 Prayer Book seems to have been deliberately worded in a way which would encompass different understandings of the sacrament, so too certain features of the ordination rites appear to have been intended to permit the interpretation that those being appointed as bishops were not receiving a new order or new powers of the Holy Spirit, but merely the commission of the Church for a particular function.

Firstly, whilst the rites for the diaconate and the priesthood begin with 'an exhortation declaring the duty and office of such as come to be admitted Ministers, how necessary such Orders are in the Church of Christ', no such rubric appears in the rite for the episcopate. Secondly, whilst the titles of the rites for the diaconate and priesthood speak of 'ordering', that for the episcopate uses the word 'consecrating' instead. Thirdly, within the rite for the episcopate itself 'ordain' and 'order' are not used, and even 'office' occurs only once, but 'consecrate', 'work', and 'ministry of a bishop' are found instead. Fourthly, in the bidding preceding the litany, the prayer made by the Church at Antioch before the commissioning of Paul and Barnabas (Acts 13.3) is cited as a precedent for what the congregation is about to do. Fifthly, the identity of bishops and priests in New Testament times is further emphasized by the use of 1 Timothy 3, which speaks of the qualities required in a bishop, as the Epistle in the rite for the priesthood as well as the rite for the episcopate; and by the use of Acts 20.17–35 as the alternative Epistle in the rite for the priesthood, since in verse 28 it describes the elders of the congregation at Ephesus as 'overseers' who are to 'rule the Congregation of God'. Finally, whilst the imperative formula at the imposition of hands in the rite for the priesthood begins, 'Receive the Holy Spirit ...', that in the right for the episcopate has, 'Take the Holy Ghost, and remember that thou stir up the grace of God, which is in thee, by imposition of hands ...', which is at best ambiguous about whether a new gift is being conferred at this time or whether a gift received at a previous imposition of hands is being revived.

Puritans in the Church of England later fastened on many of these points to support their contention that a distinction ought not to be made between bishops and priests, but since by the seventeenth century the supporters of episcopacy did believe that bishops constituted a separate and distinct order, it is not surprising that some changes were made in the 1661/2 revision of the Ordinal. The words 'ordaining or' were inserted before 'consecrating' in the title of the rite for the episcopate, and 'ordained and' was inserted before 'consecrated' in the words used at the presentation of the candidate. Ephesians 4.7–13 was substituted for 1 Timothy 3 in the rite for the priesthood, and the reading from Acts 20 was transferred to the rite for the episcopate. Even two of the three alternative Gospels in the rite for the priesthood, Matthew 28.18–20 and John 20.19–23, both of which contained commissions to the Apostles, were transferred to the rite for the episcopate, presumably to show that bishops and not priests were the successors of the Apostles; and another Gospel, Matthew 9.36–8, was substituted in the rite for the priesthood.

Moreover, the word 'pastors' was deleted from that rite, so that the Puritans could no longer argue that the Church of England taught that priests as well as bishops were to rule over the flock of Christ: the word made an appearance instead in a new collect at the beginning of the rite for the episcopate, which also spoke of the bishop administering 'the godly discipline'. A reference to the bishop's 'well-governing' of the Church was added to the collect after the litany, and an additional question inserted in the examination now made explicit mention of his duty of ordaining. Finally, the imperative formula at the imposition of hands was also amended so that it now read: 'Receive the Holy Ghost, for the office and work of a Bishop in the Church of God, now committed unto thee by the imposition of our hands. In the name of the Father, and of the Son, and of the Holy Ghost. Amen. And remember that thou stir up the grace of God which is given thee by this imposition of our hands ... .'

THE THREEFOLD MINISTRY: DEACONS

The concluding collect and rubric in the rite for the diaconate expect that deacons will pass from 'this inferior office' to 'the higher ministries' of the Church after a minimum period of one year in which they are to become 'perfect and well expert in the things appertaining to the Ecclesiastical administration'. Nevertheless, the rite contains a number of other features which suggest that its compilers viewed the order as something rather different from the mere stepping-stone to the priesthood which it had become in the course of the Middle Ages and which unfortunately it would continue to be even after the composition of the Ordinal.

Firstly, there is no reference anywhere in the rite to the Holy Spirit being bestowed through it, as there is in the case of the priesthood. The hymn 'Come Holy Ghost' is not used in the service, though it is in the other two rites; the imperative formula at the imposition of hands does not mention the Holy Spirit, but merely 'authority to execute the office of a deacon'; and the concluding collect of the litany attributes the appointment of ministers

161

to 'divine providence' instead of to the 'Holy Spirit', which is the case in the equivalent collect in the rites for the priesthood and the episcopate. Indeed, the Holy Spirit is only mentioned once in the whole rite, and that is in the opening question of the examination of the candidates, which is not found in the other two services. This asks whether the candidates trust that they are 'inwardly moved by the Holy Ghost' to take upon themselves this office, a requirement almost certainly deriving from the account of the appointment of Stephen and his companions in Acts 6.2–7, used as one of the alternative Epistles in the rite, where the Apostles direct the people to choose men 'full of the Holy Ghost'. This suggests that the diaconate was here viewed as a creation of divine providence working through the Apostles, in which the authority of the Church to minister was given to men who had already received the Holy Spirit, in contrast to the priesthood in which the Holy Spirit was given to the candidates just as it had been bestowed upon the Apostles by Christ.

Secondly, the deacon is not portrayed as having merely liturgical functions, although those referred to in the medieval rites—assisting at the Eucharist, reading the Scriptures, baptizing and preaching—are still mentioned, but also as having the duty of searching out 'the sick, poor, and impotent people of the parish', a dimension which had disappeared from the office in the course of the history of the Church and which other Reformers had already suggested was of its essence. In response to Puritan criticism that baptizing was not a normal function of the diaconate, this was restricted to occasions 'in the absence of the priest' at the 1661/2 revision.

THE MINISTER OF ORDINATION

The Ordinal assumes that the presiding minister at all ordinations to both the priesthood and the diaconate in the Church of England will be a bishop, and makes no provision for any alternative. At the consecration of a bishop it directs that the presiding minister is to be the archbishop of the province 'or some other Bishop appointed'. In accordance with early medieval practice, other priests present at the ordination of a priest, and other bishops present at the consecration of a bishop, are to join in the imposition of hands on the candidate. Traditionally, at least three bishops were required to participate in the ordination of a bishop, and although the Ordinal does not specify any minimum number for this, two other bishops need to be there in order to present the candidate to the archbishop. In 1559, at the beginning of the reign of Elizabeth I, four bishops were charged with the duty of consecrating Matthew Parker as Archbishop of Canterbury, and the Scottish Ordinal of 1620 included a rubric directing that at least three bishops must consecrate a bishop, and four an archbishop. Subsequent consecrations have usually involved more than that number.

Nevertheless, this does not mean that the Church of England has always regarded this as the only method of ordination which was valid. The original intention in 1550 seems to have been to continue former practice because there was no compelling reason to change it. The evidence appears to suggest that in the sixteenth and seventeenth centuries the commonly held opinion among Anglicans was that where episcopal ordination was available, then it should be retained, but that in what were viewed as cases of necessity where this had not been possible, as for example in Reformation Churches elsewhere in Europe, then presbyteral ordination might suffice. An entirely different attitude was taken, however, towards those Puritans in England who had refused to accept ordination by a bishop and were ordained instead by presbyteries or by congregations, since no plea of necessity could be made in such cases. For this reason, when episcopacy was restored to the Church of England in 1660 after the period of the Commonwealth (see pp. 19–25), the bishops insisted on reordaining all ministers who had been ordained in some other way during that time.

It is hardly surprising, therefore, that when the Ordinal was revised in 1661/2, changes were made in it in order to require episcopal ordination as an absolute necessity for admission to the ministry of the Church of England. Whereas previously the Preface had simply stated that no one who was not already a bishop, priest, or deacon should be permitted to execute the office unless he were admitted 'according to the form hereafter following', it was now amended to read that no one would 'be accounted or taken to be a lawful Bishop, Priest, or Deacon' unless he were admitted 'according to the form hereafter following, or hath had formerly Episcopal Consecration or Ordination'. Since this requirement applied to ministers from all non-episcopal Churches, both in England and elsewhere, it thus effectively—even if unintentionally—resulted in the Church of England adopting a position which denied the sufficiency of non-episcopal ordination.

THE ANGLICAN ORDERS CONTROVERSY

From the sixteenth century onwards, Anglican orders were continually alleged to be invalid by Roman Catholic theologians. At first such attacks tended to centre on the claim that sufficient consecrating bishops could not be found when Matthew Parker had been appointed as Archbishop of Canterbury by Queen Elizabeth I, and that therefore both his consecration and those of all subsequent Anglican bishops were invalid. Fuel was added to the fire by the invention of the 'Nag's Head Fable' in 1604, which asserted that Parker had actually been consecrated in the Nag's Head Tavern, Cheapside, by a strange, illegal and invalid rite; the flames of controversy were later fanned by the discovery that there was no extant record of the consecration of William Barlow, Parker's chief consecrator. Anglicans attempted to answer these historical doubts and subsequently relatively little emphasis was placed on them in the polemic between members of the two denominations; but there still remained allegations that the Anglican rites themselves were defective in matter, form or intention, although there was considerable diversity of opinion as to what constituted the essential requirements of an ordination rite in these respects.

This long-running controversy finally culminated in the issue by Pope Leo XIII in 1896 of the Bull *Apostolicae Curae*, which declared that there had been defects of both form and intention in the 1550 rites for the priesthood and the episcopate: the imperative formula at the imposition of hands in the rite for the priesthood was not sufficient as the form because it did not definitely express the order of priesthood or its grace and power, nor were other prayers in the rite able to provide a valid form because they too were insufficient for a number of reasons, and especially because all references to the Catholic concept of sacrifice and priesthood had been deliberately removed from them. The same was true of the formula and prayers in the rite for the episcopate, and since their meaning could not change in the course of time, any alterations made in 1662 were in vain. Moreover, the substitution of a new rite for that approved by the Church with the manifest intention of rejecting what the Church did and what by the institution of Christ belonged to the nature of the sacrament clearly demonstrated that 'not only is the necessary intention wanting to the Sacrament, but that the intention is adverse to and destructive of the Sacrament'. The Bull concluded, therefore, that 'Ordinations carried out according to the Anglican rite have been and are absolutely null and utterly void'.

This did not finally settle the matter, and the debate continued, with Roman Catholics attempting to interpret and clarify the meaning of the Bull, and Anglicans challenging its reasoning. However, with the development of ecumenical dialogue and the emergence of a different approach to sacramental theology, the discussion about ordination and ministry between the two churches has now begun to be conducted on an entirely different basis. Perhaps the one positive lesson which emerges from this whole story is that the validity of orders can never be satisfactorily determined merely by appeal to technical issues concerning rites, intention, or episcopal succession, but is intimately related to the recognition of the sufficiency of the faith of the ecclesial body in which those ministries are exercised and the ordinations performed.

MORE RECENT DEVELOPMENTS

Other provinces of the Anglican Communion tended at first to adopt the 1662 Ordinal with only the minimum changes necessitated by their different circumstances, but after the appearance of the unsuccessful proposals for a revised Prayer Book in England in 1927–8, certain features of the Ordinal included in it influenced revisions taking place in other parts of the Anglican Communion, the most notable being the introduction of an ordination prayer immediately prior to the imposition of hands in the rite for the diaconate, the insertion of a petition for the candidates into the equivalent prayer in the rite for the priesthood, and a strengthening of the existing petition for the candidate in the prayer in the rite for the episcopate. It was, however, the rites of ordination drawn up for the Church of South India in 1958 which established a new pattern for Anglican practice. These dispensed with the imperative formulae at the imposition of hands and reverted to the primitive practice of an ordination prayer said while hands were laid on the candidate, and this has since become the standard arrangement in nearly all recent Anglican revisions, among them the 1979 Book of Common Prayer of the Episcopal Church in the USA, and the Church of England's *Alternative Service Book 1980*. The Province of Southern Africa (1988) is the sole exception.

BIBLIOGRAPHY
Bradshaw, P. F., *The Anglican Ordinal: Its History and Development from the Reformation to the Present Day*. AC 53. SPCK, London, 1971.
Brightman, F. E., *The English Rite*, Vol. ii. Rivingtons, London, 1915, pp. 928–1017.
Buchanan, Colin, *Modern Anglican Ordination Rites*. Grove Books, Nottingham, 1987.
Franklin, R. W. (ed.), *Anglican Orders: Essays on the Centenary of Apostolicae Curae 1896–1996*. Mowbrays, London, 1996.
Hill, C. and Yarrold, E. (eds), *Anglican Orders: The Documents in the Debate*. Canterbury Press, Norwich, 1997.
Hughes, John Jay, *Absolutely Null and Utterly Void*. Sheed and Ward, London/Corpus Books, Washington, 1968.
Hughes, John Jay, *Stewards of the Lord: A Reappraisal of Anglican Orders*. Sheed and Ward, London and Sydney, 1970.
Whitaker, E. C., *Martin Bucer and the Book of Common Prayer*. AC 55. Mayhew-McCrimmon, Great Wakering, 1974, pp. 176–83.

4 Catechisms

JAMES HARTIN, revised by
JONATHAN KNIGHT

In the Anglican Communion we have a continuous history of the use of catechism since 1536.[1] Even in the 1960s when many new questions were being asked about the ways of Christian education, most churches of the Anglican Communion took on the task of revising and enlarging the traditional catechism rather than making decisions to abandon its methods and basic content. A revised Catechism set out in 1961 in the report of the Archbishops' Commission to revise the Church Catechism is a good example of this process in the English scene. An earlier attempt at revision in 1887 had come to nothing. Other efforts had been made in 1926 and 1939. The English revised catechism was in 1971/2 taken up and used in the Church of Ireland with minor alterations. A similar process is seen at that time in the churches of North America—and in the Church of India, Pakistan, Burma and Ceylon (1960). It was a period of catechism revision and enlargement to meet new needs.

The continued presence of the catechism in Anglican Prayer Books or in documents associated with them emphasizes the strong and consistent Anglican conviction that the members of the church are to be encouraged to grow in personal understanding of the faith, in the devout practice of worship and in godly ways of life. We continue to witness to this hope by including a form of catechism alongside our liturgical documents. Certainly we have had wide-ranging criticism of the idea of 'catechism' as a learning by rote—but there is much evidence that the church intends the material to be used by the catechist in a personal and flexible way. The very idea of question-and-answer is capable of wide extension in practice, and suggests an effective learning experience going on between teacher and student. In the world of education, many lectures and classes lead to sessions of question-and-answer in which what has been set out earlier in principle and broad statement can be analysed in a more immediate way; and so the information is absorbed into personal understanding. The method of catechizing seems to offer a way of bringing together the church's double responsibility of teaching as clearly as possible basic tenets of Christian faith and life, and of doing so in a way which will awaken personal response in those who are taught. The ideal of catechizing suggests steady interchange between clergy and people in the Christian learning process. It implies also the use of the comparatively small local group. It also links the personal experience of learning in the local group with what is going on in the church as a whole, so that there is some sense of all the members of the church being formed in basic belief in much the same way. But of course in practice not all use of the catechism has gone on in these ways nor produced these results. George Herbert in the seventeenth century set out reasons for the country parson's use of the Catechism—'He useth and preferreth the ordinary Church Catechism partly for obedience to Authority, partly for uniformity sake, that the same common truths may be everywhere professed, especially since many remove from Parish to Parish, who like Christian soldiers are to give the word, and to satisfy the Congregation by their Catholic answers.'[2]

The term 'catechism' derives from various forms of a Greek word which means to repeat, like an echo. It may have been used to describe a teacher pronouncing a sentence to his pupils and then making them repeat it back to him. It seems to have been applied at first to elementary types of teaching and later to all kinds of instruction. An important element in its meaning was that of oral instruction by one person to another. Several of these nuances flow together in our use of the term 'catechism', with its particular emphasis on teaching by question-and-answer. The word catechism comes into use in this special sense in the early sixteenth century as part of the experience and process of Protestant Reformation. The use of the word is new in that period, but the emphasis on the need to teach the faith of the Church is not new.

The practice of instruction at times by question-and-answer was a regular feature of Jewish life. From that background it could pass easily into the life of the early Christian Church. Catechizing was the regular process of preparing catechumens for baptism—this form of instruction was not confined to a question-and-answer method. An important development of the whole concept of catechizing is seen in the famous catechetical school of Alexandria flourishing from the second to the fourth century. Here the work was basically that of theological education as teachers gave courses of lectures on the elements of the Christian faith—instruction going on at a different level from the regular preparation of people for baptism. We may assume that some of these lectures would be followed by the use of question-and-answer to ensure that the content of the lectures had been assimilated and understood, just as a lecture in the modern university context may turn into something more like a seminar when the lecturer tries to discover, by some careful questions, whether his class has followed some difficult argument. The term 'catechetics' and others associated with the basic concept had then, and continue to have now, the connotation of instruction carefully given on a personal basis with the aim of arousing personal understanding, acceptance and response in the hearers.

In AD 400 we find St Augustine writing to a young deacon on the subject of catechizing. His letter gives the deacon, Deogratias, some valuable practical hints about methods of teaching the basic elements of the Christian faith and life. In the preface Augustine writes:

> You have told me, brother Deogratias, that at Carthage where you are a deacon, persons are often brought to you to be instructed in the rudiments of the Christian faith, in consequence of your reputation for possessing great resource and power in catechizing, on account of your

knowledge of the faith, and your happy way of expressing yourself; but that you yourself always experience a painful difficulty in deciding how to set forth with profit to your hearers that very truth by believing that we are Christians.[3]

St Augustine's understanding of the process of catechizing included the need for conviction and understanding in the catechist and for effective gifts of communication. He expected that the catechist would be personally concerned to achieve a good response to his catechizing, so that the hearers would be set forward in their faith and life.

The specific task of 'catechizing' those preparing for baptism is set in new liturgical contexts in the medieval Church, but the responsibility of instructing the faithful continues to be emphasized. In England many manuals were available for use by the clergy and some 'primers' for the laity. Bishops and synods issued injunctions requiring the clergy to teach and explain the Creed, the Lord's Prayer and the Ten Commandments in English to the children and people for whom they had spiritual responsibility. In 740 Egbert, Archbishop of York, directs 'that every priest do with great exactness instil the Lord's Prayer and the Creed into the people committed to him, and shew them to endeavour after the knowledge of the whole of religion, and the practice of Christianity'. The emphasis here is on direct teaching by the clergy; there is no suggestion of a dialogue between clergy and people, such as the sixteenth-century term 'catechism' was to imply. The Council of Clovesho (747) provides that priests shall explain, in the regular tongue, the Creed, the Lord's Prayer and the meaning and words of administration of Baptism and Holy Communion.

In the sixteenth century the early days of reform created fresh efforts to teach the faithful. Henry VIII and Edward VI issued royal injunctions about the teaching of the Lord's Prayer, the Creed and the Ten Commandments in English—the clergy are to teach their parishioners and to exhort all parents and householders to teach their children and servants the same, as they are bound in conscience to do. This attempt to involve parents and householders in teaching the faith of the Church to the young is reflected in Marshall's Primer of 1534 which contained 'A Dialogue Between the Father and the Son' expounding the baptismal covenant with the Creed and Commandments.

It was natural therefore that when the new Book of Service was prepared, a Catechism should be placed in it, as in authoritative exposition of the profession and renunciation in Holy Baptism, and in connexion with the service of Confirmation, with directions for its use as the basis of a system of catechizing to be maintained on Sunday afternoons in each parish.[4]

The title 'catechism' is first used to describe a body or book of Christian teaching in the early sixteenth century. The Reformation emphasized religious instruction, and this emphasis led to the writing of many catechisms. Martin Luther issued his *Shorter Catechism* in 1529, set out as a dialogue between father and son—this was to be the most famous of the sixteenth-century catechisms and remains a Lutheran standard work. In the Calvinist traditions the *Heidelberg Catechism* (1563) was to be equally important. The shape of Anglican preparation for confirmation was to be set by the catechism in the 1549 Prayer Book. The Roman Catholic Church produced many catechisms, some of which are really doctrinal expositions.

John Bossy in his *Christianity in the West 1400–1700* regards this widespread carrying to the people of catechism versions of Christianity as having, in the long run, more considerable effects than any other innovation of the sixteenth century. In the very early stages of the use of catechism, there was the hope of parents teaching children in this way in the home—this ideal lay behind Luther's *Shorter Catechism*—but very soon the emphasis in both Protestant and Catholic Reformations was placed on the catechizing duties of the clergy.

Hence the Church of England hierarchy was not out of step with the general practice of reformed Churches in taking it for granted that catechism was a parochial activity and that parishes would be well edified if their children spent Sunday afternoons learning by rote the obligations which had been undertaken for them at their baptism. There was also no obstacle, in the state of alarm inspired by the success of Reformation catechizing, to Catholic borrowing of the outlines of Reformation catechisms as a guide to their own efforts in the field, as the Jesuits did on a large scale.

The sixteenth-century catechisms were of course intended for the instruction of children after baptism, so that they might come to a real knowledge of what baptism had meant for them and so be prepared to take religious responsibility on themselves as they approached confirmation. This was in great contrast with the practice of the early Church, where catechizing was the preparation for baptism. It reflects the effective medieval separation of the initiation rites of baptism and confirmation. John Bossy analyses the effects of the sixteenth-century catechism teaching:

Catechism was well designed to instil obedience and mark out boundaries, between versions of the Reformation as much as between Catholic and Protestant, and it could be the foundation of a reflective Christian life. It was less well adapted to inspiring a sense of the Church as a *communitas*, a feeling for the sacraments as social institutions, or simply the love of one's neighbour.

The use of catechism was becoming an effective medium of instruction about behaviour and deference to parents and civil authorities—there was in the process an element of the desire to impart 'Christian civility' as an ingredient in a quiet and well-ordered community.[5]

The Church Catechism with which we are familiar makes its first appearance in the first Prayer Book of Edward VI in 1549. This must not be confused with the Catechism of 1548, which proved to be a fiasco, and of which nothing was reused in the 1549 Prayer Book. We find there the service of 'Confirmation, wherein is contained a catechism for children' (see pp. 295–9). The direction given is that those who are to be confirmed must be able to say in their mother tongue the Articles of the faith, the Lord's Prayer and the Ten Commandments—they must also be able to answer 'to such questions of this short Catechism, as the Bishop shall by his discretion appose them in'. The parish clergy are directed that at least once in six weeks upon some Sunday or holy day, they shall instruct children in the Catechism for half an hour before evensong openly in the church. Parents, masters and dames are to cause their children, servants and apprentices who are not yet confirmed to come for this instruction. In the Elizabethan Prayer Book the clergy are to give this instruction diligently upon Sundays and holy days before evening prayer. The Church of England now had a definite form of instruction in the faith of the Church—available for general use in the shape of a catechism. This was an important part of the effort to create a system of Christian education for the young.

The Catechism of the 1549 Prayer Book 'was derived entirely from English official teaching materials of the previous decade, including Hilsey's 1539 Primer and the 1543 King's Book'.[6] MacCulloch notes that, by this time, Cranmer had crossed the Rubicon in terms of his eucharistic theology; and by then accepted the position that he would set out at length in the *Defence* and the *Answer* between 1550 and 1551. This is that the Eucharist embodied the 'spiritual presence' of Christ, as opposed to what he had maintained earlier, that it embodied a 'real or corporal' presence.

The Catechism of the sixteenth century was set out in four sections—the privileges and profession of a Christian, the Creed, the Commandments and the Lord's Prayer. In 1604 the section dealing with the sacraments was added. This section was prepared by Overall, Dean of St Paul's, and incorporated elements of the catechisms upon which Dean Nowell worked in the 1560s and 1570s. The later sixteenth century was a time of great interest in the work of religious education in England, interest created by the need to instruct the people of the Church of England in their distinctive religious attitudes in contrast to the continued claims of the papacy and the challenge of more extreme forms of Protestantism. Plans were made to produce catechisms for use with those who were already communicants and for use in schools. The developing schools provided further opportunities for instruction in the Teaching of the Church. In 1662 the Catechism was printed in the Prayer Book as a separate item between the services of Holy Baptism and Confirmation—the title is altered from that of 1549 to replace 'child' with person. Since 1662, the title in the Book of Common Prayer has been 'a catechism, that is to say an instruction to be learned of every person, before he be brought to be confirmed by the bishop'. The clergy are diligently to instruct and examine the children in this Catechism—upon Sundays and holy days after the Second Lesson at Evening Prayer he may do so openly in the church. Here would seem to be the possibility of drawing the congregation as a whole into the experience of the children.

The use of the word 'person' lies behind such statements as that of Bishop Ashton Oldham of Albany USA in his book *The Catechism Today* (1929)—'Just at the outset I wish to correct the very prevalent though erroneous impression that the Catechism is meant only for children. It is equally valuable and necessary for adults [...] The principles of the Catechism are essential for all who desire to make any progress in the Christian Faith.'[7] Through the centuries the Church has created a powerful tradition of teaching based on the Catechism, in the hope that this teaching of the young may become the foundation on which the adult Christian life can be built. The Catechism appears as we know it in the Prayer Book of the Church of England, but it has been adopted and used in variant forms through the Anglican Communion. In Canada and the United States a number of revisions have been made to update the use and content of the Catechism as a teaching medium for different age groups.

The ideal place of catechism in the work of a seventeenth-century priest is set out by George Herbert in his writing on *A Priest to the Temple, or, The Country Parson his Character, and Rule of Holy Life*. Herbert devotes a chapter to 'The parson catechizing' and concludes it all by insisting on the use in catechizing of homely dramatic illustrations to illuminate divine truth—'Doubtless the Holy Scripture intends this much, when it condescends to the naming of a plough, a hatchet, a bushel, leaven, boys piping and dancing; showing that things of ordinary use are not only to serve in the way of drudgery, but to be washed and cleansed, and serve for lights even of heavenly truths.' Herbert is very much aware of the need of a lively, personal and down to earth approach by the parson using the catechism; he has the material and the method, but he has to create the conditions of effective communication.

171

The Country Parson values catechizing highly [. . .] He exacts of all the Doctrine of the Catechism; of the younger sort, the very words; of the older, the substance [. . .] He requires all to be present at Catechizing [. . .] that those who are well grown in the knowledge of religion may examine their grounds, renew their vows, and by occasion of both, enlarge their meditations.

Herbert views the use of the catechism as a progressive process—different groups of the people in the parish are at different stages of religious understanding, and so require different treatment. His understanding of Christian education is clearly from the cradle to the grave, and his great source of teaching material was 'the Church catechism to which all divinity may easily be reduced'. Herbert encourages the parson in catechizing to learn to ask his own distinctive and supplementary questions:

Helping and cherishing the Answerer, by making the Question very plain with comparisons, and making much even of a word of truth from him [. . .] this is an admirable way of teaching wherein the Catechized will at length find delight, and by which the Catechizer, if he once get the skill of it, will draw out of ignorant and silly souls, even the deep and dark points of religion [. . .] At sermons and prayers men may sleep and wander; but when asked a question, he must discover what it is. This practice exceeds even sermons in teaching.[8]

In this century, many efforts have been made in revising and enlarging the Catechism in different Churches of the Anglican Communion. Efforts were made in England in 1926 and 1939.

In May 1956 the Convocations of Canterbury and York requested the Archbishop to appoint a Commission for the Revision of the Catechism. This was done in 1958, and the Commission reported with a proposed revised Catechism in 1962.[9] The statements of the members of this Commission give us a well-considered view of the place of the Catechism in the 1960s.

One of the first questions faced by the Commission was whether the catechetical form of instruction remained valid in the twentieth century [. . .] the weight of opinion was on the side of retention. The question and answer method emphasizes the moral responsibility of each person for his actions. Its increasing use in various forms of publicity indicates that it is not to be discarded because it is out of date.

The Commission would be reinforced in their approach by the present increasing popularity of many kinds of quiz programmes on radio and

172

television in which people create enormous interest among thinkers, as well as listeners and viewers, by long series of question-and-answer sessions.

The Commission decided against the suggestion of two catechisms, one for children and one for adults.

Behind the use of any Catechism stands the teaching Church. The catechist is a most important person. It is for him to select from the Catechism, or to enlarge and amplify it; bringing in, no doubt, much material which different people would have liked to see included in the new Catechism but for which there is no room [. . .] The Catechism is meant to be a tool in the hands of the teacher.

In producing the revised Catechism the Commission added considerably to the teaching given, and modernized the language. They gave attention to the changed social conditions of the day in which there is less distinction between social groups and strong resentment of any kind of paternalism. The revised Catechism added to the older form new material on church worship and the ordained ministry, on the sacraments and other means of grace, on the Bible, on Christian duty and Christian hope.

In the discussions which arose after the revised Catechism was published, two main sets of issues were clear. There is great difficulty in producing any form of catechism which will be able to meet the need to supply a brief but adequate statement of the faith of the Church and the responsibility asked of the Christian, and at the same time to set these out in a form which will meet the requirements of the teachers of the young in these days.

In *The Catechism and the Order of Confirmation* (1963), Canon Frank Colquhoun set out a pattern of preparation for confirmation based on the use of the Revised Catechism.[10] 'The value of the Church Catechism is that it is concise and comprehensive, simple and scriptural. It adheres firmly to the essential facts of the Christian religion and refuses to get side-tracked by secondary issues.' He quotes the famous statement of Archbishop Benson in 1891: 'I believe that there never has been in the hands of any Church any manual representing the doctrines, the true spirit of the Bible, to compare with the Catechism of the Church of England.'

There remains within the Anglican Communion a great affection and regard for the Catechism. It continues to represent our experience of re-formation in which we emphasized strongly the need for the people of the Church to be helped towards a personal understanding of the Christian faith. The method of the Catechism begins where people are, in their immediate human experience, and encourages them to think through their place in the Church, and to keep on discovering what membership means. At the present time we are examining again what baptism means and that is where the Catechism begins. To know ourselves as members of the Body of Christ requires us to move on to deeper examination of all the implications of discipleship—and that is the way set out in the Catechism. The simple direct questions raise many issues which have to be explored— what are our basic beliefs in an understanding of reality, what are the principles which should shape our human life in community, what .are the sources of guidance and strength as we face the tasks of humanity. The Catechism leads us into this exploration and analysis along the path of human experiment and growth in the framework of Christian belief. It is the way towards personal maturity, set at once in the worshipping life and fellowship of the Church and in the wider world of social reality where we need all possible encouragements in living by and witnessing to Christian principles of life.

A scrutiny of three recent Prayer Books of the Anglican Communion shows three different possibilities for the future of catechesis. *The Alternative Service Book 1980* of the Church of England makes no reference to catechizing in its confirmation services, and does not reproduce any version of the Catechism within its text. The *Australian Prayer Book* of 1978 includes a Catechism which is a modern-language version of the Catechism of 1662, with no alteration in sense whatever. The book has two forms of confirmation, the second of which makes no reference to the Catechism, while the first contains the words 'Our Church requires that all who are to be confirmed should know and understand the Creed, the Lord's Prayer, and the Ten Commandments, and be able to answer the other questions in the Church-Catechism.'

By contrast with both those books, the proposed Book of Common Prayer of ECUSA (1977) contains a document called 'An Outline of the Faith Commonly Called the Catechism'. This document partly reflects the common catechetical tradition, but in structure is a systematic work, beginning with the heading 'Human Nature', and working through sin, covenant, Scriptures, sacraments etc., to end at 'The Christian Hope'. The question-and-answer form is used throughout. The rubric states that the Outline is 'a point of departure for the teacher' and provides 'a brief summary of the Church's teaching for an inquiring stranger who picks up a Prayer Book'. The Outline is certainly an attempt to provide an alternative to adopting simply the contents of 1662, with the risk of its being ignored, or going the way of silence as in the Alternative Service Book.

The Catechism comes to us through our history and it carries within it distinctive sixteenth-century understandings. These understandings of Christian experience arose in a period of radical and complex change in almost every area of life. The framers of the Catechism in content and method aimed to give Christians a solid base of self-knowledge, personal understanding of basic Christian principles and high aspirations for Christian life in a confusing and demanding world. They hoped to teach the members of the Church to see the Christian life as human experience lived out fully in their own times and places, and to rely upon the work of grace being wrought in them by the divine initiative of God in Christ. Twentieth-century Anglicans find themselves in an equally confusing world with the constant pressure of rapidly changing situations. The basic concept and approach of the Catechism still point us to the authentic Christian responses to be made in our own kind of language in our contemporary situations in many forms of human society, where the greatest need is for some kind of consensus about the ultimate meaning of humanity. To think, to believe, to pray and to live in the Catechism way seems to be the essence of that elusive Christian experience which we describe as 'Anglicanism'.

BIBLIOGRAPHY

A Revised Catechism: Being the report of the Archbishops' Commission to revise the Church Catechism. SPCK, London, 1961.

A New Revised Catechism. CHP, London, 1990.

Green, I. M., The Christian's ABC: Catechisms and Catechizing in England c. 1530–1740. Clarendon Press, Oxford, 1996.

MacCulloch, D., Thomas Cranmer. Yale University Press, New Haven CT and London, 1996.

Siegenthaler, D., 'Religious Education for the Citizenship: Primer and Catechism' in J. Booty (ed.), The Godly Kingdom of Tudor England. Morehouse-Barlow, Wilton CT, 1981.

Thompsett, F. H., 'Godly Instruction in Reformation England: The Challenge of Religious Education in the Tudor Commonwealth' and Booty, J. E., 'The American Church Since the Reformation; An Emphasis on the American Experience' in A Faithful Church: Issues in the History of Catechesis, Morehouse-Barlow, Wilton CT, 1981.

Tudor, P. 'Religious Instruction for Children and Adolescents in the Early English Reformation', Journal of Ecclesiastical History 35 (1984), pp. 391–413.

Wilson, W. G., The Faith of an Anglican: A Companion to the Revised Catechism. SPCK, London, 1980.

NOTES

1 See Tudor, 'Religious Instruction'. For evidence of catechetical formulae dating from 1530, see Green, Christian's ABC, p. 702.

2 J. N. Wall (ed.), George Herbert: The Country Parson, the Temple (SPCK, London, 1981), p. 83.

3 Walker Gwynne, Primitive Worship and the Prayer Book (Longmans Green & Co. 1917), p. 296.

4 A New History of the Book of Common Prayer: On the Basis of the Work by Francis Proctor, Revised and Rewritten by W. H. Frere (Macmillan & Co., London, 1955), pp. 599, 600.

5 John Bossy, Christianity in the West 1400–1700 (OUP 1985), pp. 118–120.

6 MacCulloch, Cranmer, p. 391.

7 G. Ashton Oldham, The Catechism Today (Longmans Green & Co., London, 1929), p. 2.

8 Wall, *George Herbert*, p. 83f.

9 *A Revised Catechism: Being the Report of the Archbishops' Commission to Revise the Church Catechism* (SPCK, London, 1961).

10 F. Colquhoun, *The Catechism and the Order of Confirmation* (Hodder and Stoughton, London, 1963), p. 15.

5   Standard Divines

JOHN E. BOOTY

Although Anglicanism has no theologian comparable to Thomas Aquinas for the Roman Catholics, Luther for the Lutherans, or Calvin for the Calvinists, there have been certain theological writers whose works have been widely regarded as, in some sense, standards not only for faith and doctrine but also for public worship and personal spirituality. Such persons are defined here as 'Anglican divines'. There is no authoritative list of such divines, and different people of differing theological convictions would list different theologians. Nevertheless, there are some whose names would most likely be found on most lists, divines whose names appear in calendars of lesser feasts, those whose works are most often anthologized.

What constitutes an Anglican divine? Examining some of the most prominent in the sixteenth and seventeenth centuries, when modern Anglicanism was in process of development, we may begin by observing that an Anglican divine is a bishop or priest of the Church of England, a learned theologian who has bequeathed to posterity a body of writings. That corpus customarily includes a wide range of materials: theological treatises, polemical or apologetical tracts, catechetical works intended for the instruction of communicants, books and essays designed to counsel the faithful in making moral-ethical decisions, sermons, liturgical forms, prayers and meditations for personal devotions. The Anglican divines are persons committed to the faith as conveyed by Scripture and Creeds and embodied in the Book of Common Prayer; they therefore regard theology and prayer as a whole, after the example of the ancient Greek Fathers of the Church. Anglican divines are committed to the one, holy, Catholic, and Apostolic Church as embodied in the Church of England and defend that Church and its daughters and sons against its detractors to the right and to the left. Such persons adhere to a *via media* which is not a matter of compromise but a positive position, witnessing to the mystery and the universality of God and God's kingdom working through the fallible, earthly *ecclesia Anglicana*. Anglican divines on the whole regard Scripture interpreted through tradition and reason as authoritative in matters concerning salvation. They believe that Scripture presupposes the existence and activity of tradition and reason and

176

thus co-operation between God and nature, God and humanity, the sacred and the secular. Authority for doctrine and the Christian life is not interpreted narrowly, therefore, but rather as dispersed. The rigid doctrine of infallibility is rejected. The distinction between things essential to salvation and things not (adiaphora) is frequently made (see p. 296). There is a largeness in their understanding, a constant impulse to reach out to all people and all nature in the realization of God's universal rule, as Creator, Redeemer, and Sanctifier, the Alpha and Omega. A close investigation reveals a constant devotion to Christ, an emphasis upon the incarnation as viewed from the perspective of the crucifixion. Over and over again in their writings they emphasize the doctrine of sacrifice, of God's self-offering in Christ, inspiring Christians to offer themselves, their souls and bodies, as a living and a reasonable sacrifice. This profound theological doctrine is both rooted in Scripture and in the liturgy of the Prayer Book, and helps to emphasize the Eucharist, eucharistic devotion and eucharistic living, in the Church. Such are some of the elements in a definition of Anglican divines. There assuredly are others and there admittedly are other ways of defining the term.

Who were the Anglican divines? The names of Hooker, Andrewes and Taylor come to mind most readily, but when thinking of the formative period in modern Anglicanism many would add Hall, Laud, Ussher, Cosin and others. A case can also be made for including the metaphysical poets, especially Donne and Herbert. Richard Hooker (1554–1600) comes first. He acknowledged his debt to John Jewel and was deeply immersed in the Book of Common Prayer. By extension, many would include Cranmer and Jewel as prominent among the Anglican divines, but Hooker rightly comes first. He was pre-eminently a theologian; his major theological work, Of the Laws of Ecclesiastical Polity (1593 seq.), had very great influence on those who came after him, and was the theological writing most often consulted through the years by those scholars concerned to understand the nature of Anglican teaching.

The Laws is a defence of English church government over against those who sought to restructure that government after the example of Calvin's Geneva and that of the Book of Acts; but it was far more than that. Its first book is a philosophical treatise of considerable profundity, and its eighth book is a treatise on church and state widely noted in histories of law and of political theory. The much-debated sixth book contains a short treatise on repentance and church discipline that seemingly influenced the development of moral theology in England, as well as the Devotions upon Emergent Occasions and the 'Holy Sonnets' of John Donne. The fifth book is central to an understanding of this complex yet rationally constructed theological masterpiece. A casual perusal reveals that it is the first systematic commentary on, and defence of, the Book of Common Prayer, and contains a very important dissertation on the incarnation. But there is much more to it that that.

The fifth book is the theological heart of the *Laws*, its central chapter, 56, being linked to Hooker's *Discourse of Justification*. Taken together the two places cited indicate the intensity of Hooker's conviction that salvation comes through Jesus Christ, that it is unmerited, and that at the very moment of justification the gift of the Holy Spirit is received, and habitual sanctification begins to be actualized (see pp. 72–7). In Chapter 56 of Book V this teaching is related to the concept of participation, which further deepens and universalizes his doctrine of sanctification and prepares the way for an understanding of the sacraments in which both baptism and the Holy Communion are means of participation in Christ and thus in God, baptism being the sacrament of justification and the Eucharist the sacrament of sanctification. It is not surprising that Hooker elected to emphasize the ends and purposes for which the sacraments are given—personal and communal salvation—and disdained to discuss whether or not, and if so how, the bread and wine become the body and blood of Christ. For him as for many others the consecration was in the use, not in the magical transformation of the elements.

Doing theology was thus for Hooker far more than an academic occupation or intellectual game. Theology involved prayer and was concerned with ultimate issues. Nor was his theological focus alone on the individual yearning for salvation. He had a deep awareness of the unity of all in God and of the vital importance of the community and especially the worshipping community. He wrote, 'God hath created nothing simply for itself, but each thing in all things, and of every thing each part in other have such interest, that in the whole world nothing is found whereunto any thing created can say, "I need thee not"'. Here was the foundation for political and social action in years to come, as well as a basis for such interest in the natural world as that exhibited by John Ray (1625–1705), the priest and naturalist, author of *The Wisdom of God Manifested in the Works of Creation*. Finally, it should be noted that Hooker was a parish priest who ended his days in the country living of Bishopsbourne in Kent where he shepherded his flock, feeding his sheep the bread of life and the water of life. He represents a degree of humility often, but not always, found among Anglican divines.

Hooker provides a measure, a standard, by which to judge those who came after him. Lancelot Andrewes (1555–1626), who knew Hooker, ended his days as Bishop of Winchester. Andrewes wrote no *magnum opus* such as Hooker's *Laws*, but he left behind a much larger body of works than did Hooker. There are writings involved with controversy such as the *Tortura Torti* and the *Two Answers to Cardinal Perron*, defences of the Church of

178

England against its Roman Catholic detractors. He was best known for his *Ninety-Six Sermons* and his *Preces Privatae*, published posthumously. In these works the profound piety of this Anglican divine is most apparent, influencing many from his day to the present. In addition, there are catechetical works, such as his *A Pattern of Catechistical Doctrine* and his sermons on prayer and the Lord's Prayer. There are also liturgical contributions such as *A Form for Consecrating Church Plate*, and there is *A Manual of Directions for the Sick*. His fundamental theological position is best discovered in his sermons. Andrewes was united with Hooker in regarding the universe of grace, grace which does not destroy God's creation but perfects it. 'Nature, *qua natura*, is "good", yet imperfect', he said, 'and the Law in the rigour of it not possible, through the imperfection of it. Nature is not, the Law is not taken away—"good" both; but grace is added to both to perfect both.' Reason as a part of the created order is thus not a hindrance but an aid. Reason is the candle of the Lord and all who resist this light of nature are *rebelles lumini*. 'Howbeit this light hath caught a fall, as Mephibosheth did, and thereupon it halteth; notwithstanding, because it is of the blood royal, it is worthy to be made up.' And grace comes to do just that. Here was a fundamental teaching of Andrewes, one that remained central in his thought throughout his life.

His sermons were impressive not only for their doctrine, but also for the manner in which they conveyed God's word. T. S. Eliot, in writing his poem 'Ash Wednesday', was inspired by Andrewes' image of turning, in an Ash Wednesday sermon on Joel 2.12–13. In that sermon Andrewes dwelt on turning as the inspired dancer might turn: 'Now at this time is the turning of the year [. . .] Everything now turning, that we also would make our time to turn to God in.' His Good Friday sermon on Zechariah 12.10 was a meditation with Christ on the cross held high before his auditory, water and blood issuing from his pierced side. We pierce him by our sins; he pierces us by his love. And from his pierced side flow the water of baptism and the blood of the Eucharist. 'Mark it running out, and suffer it not to run waste, but receive it.' Receive the blood we shall, at the holy mysteries this day. 'There may be partakers of the flesh of the Morning Hart, as upon this day killed. There may we be partakers of "the cup of salvation", "the precious blood" "which was shed for the remission of our sins".'

R. W. Church in the nineteenth century honoured Hooker for his 'vindication on its behalf [of] the rights of Christian and religious *reason*, that reason which is a reflection of the mind of God'. He honoured Andrewes for his vindication 'on its behalf [of] the rights of Christian *history*'. Andrewes regarded the Church of England as belonging to the Church universal and its history beginning from Jerusalem. In his *Preces Privatae* he drew inspiration and much content from the Eastern as well as the

Western Church, and prayed for all churches ('catholic, eastern, western, British') as a member of the one Church to which all belonged. So long as Andrewes' influence was felt, Anglicanism would be neither ahistorical nor insular.

Jeremy Taylor (1613–67), fellow of All Souls College, Oxford, and Bishop of Down and Connor in Ireland, followed in the way of Hooker and Andrewes. In his voluminous works there are collections of sermons, and there is a manual of daily prayers called *The Golden Grove*, with its 'Credenda; or, What is to be believed', its 'Agenda; or, Things to be done', and its 'Postulanda; or, Things to be prayed for'. There is his great work of casuistry, *Doctor Dubitantium*, and there are the spiritual classics, *The Rule and Exercise of Holy Living* and *The Rule and Exercise of Holy Dying*. There are useful treatises such as *The Doctrine and Practice of Repentance* and *The Worthy Communicant*. There are edifying works such as his *Life of our Blessed Lord and Saviour Jesus Christ* and his *Discourse of Confirmation*. And there are apologetic works such as the *Dissuasive from Popery* and *An Apology for Authorized and Set Forms of Liturgy*. Taylor reminds us of the strong practical, ethical and moral thrust in Anglicanism, not only in the seventeenth century but throughout its history.

An avid concern for correct behaviour can pave the way for obscuring the truth in the doctrine of justification through the cultivation of Pelagian zeal. Taylor has been faulted for straying from Hooker's understanding of justification and sanctification, but if he did, it was in large part because he shared Joseph Hall's concern—expressed most strongly in *The Divine Arte of Meditation* (1606)—that intellect, or correct doctrine, was being emphasized while the affections, and thus the modification of human behaviour in the light of the truth, were being neglected or ignored. Hooker himself urged that attention be paid to the end or purpose of the divine law; and thus, looking at the Eucharist, he argued that grace was given to change lives, not material elements. Taylor was concerned for changed lives, for repentance, for holy living and holy dying.

Furthermore, in his *The Liberty of Prophesying* Taylor contributed to the discussion concerning the distinction between essentials or fundamentals and *adiaphora*. Hooker had outraged Calvinists by arguing that it is sufficient to believe in salvation by Christ alone in order to be saved (belief, of course, issuing in acts of love). Taylor agreed with Hooker, citing Romans 10.9, and concluded that persons may deduce other doctrine from this central one, but 'no such deduction is fit to be pressed on others as an article of faith'. Nor is the Church to be followed when it goes beyond the legitimate task of making 'belief more evident' to add to that essential belief, making it 'more large and comprehensive', but in effect, narrower and more exclusive, possibly even false and tyrannical. Then, too, Taylor maintained the same basic understanding of reason as that taught by Hooker. 'By reason', he said, 'I do not mean a distinct topic, but a transcendent that runs through all topics; for reason, like logic, is instrument of all things else; and when revelation and philosophy, and public experience, and all other grounds of probability or demonstration have supplied us with matter, then reason does but make use of them.' Such an understanding was losing ground in Taylor's day, the realm of reason being more and more limited to quasi-mathematical reasoning such as was necessitated by modern science. But the Hookerian view was to be perpetuated by the so-called Anglican divines.

The divines we have been considering were learned men, rightly designated in the saying: *clerus Angliae stupor mundi*; but they wrote no great summas or systems of theology. Rather they drew upon Scripture and tradition, especially the tradition of the early Church, its councils and doctors, and to a lesser but still important extent upon the great theologians of the Middle Ages and of their own times, interpreting in the light of God-given reason what they received from the past in order to explain the gospel, to defend the Church, to preach and teach, to counsel and advise, their intellects ranging through the cosmos, penetrating nature's mysteries, and yet regarding the ultimate with awe and acknowledging mystery and miracle.

Who were the successors of Hooker, Andrewes and Taylor? There were the rest of the Caroline divines, of course, and the Cambridge Platonists and their successors among the great Latitudinarians. In the eighteenth century there were the Wesleys and Whitefield. There were William Law and Joseph Butler—Law justly famous for *A Serious Call to a Devout and Serious Life*, and Butler for his sermons and his *Analogy of Religion*. Some critics will regret the omission of any discussion of learned churchmen such as Tillotson, Waterland and Warburton, but none of them have had the influence that Hooker, Andrewes and Taylor have had on subsequent generations.

As we approach the nineteenth century there emerge prominent Anglican Evangelicals, pre-eminently Charles Simeon (1759–1836), the author of many sermons, such as *The Offices of the Holy Spirit: Four Sermons Preached before the University of Cambridge*. A major work was Simeon's *Horae Homileticae: or, Discourses digested into one continued series, and forming a commentary upon every book of the Old and New Testament*. Simeon, along with William Romaine and others, was devoted to the Scriptures and taught the twin doctrines of the corruption of human nature through the fall and recovery through Jesus Christ by means of conversion. But while some of his fellow Evangelicals tended to slight the public worship of the Church of England as they promoted personal piety, Simeon was a defender of and an apologist for the church's liturgy. He taught that 'the scope and tendency of our Liturgy is to raise our minds to the holy and heavenly state, and to build

181

us up upon the Lord Jesus Christ as the only foundation of a sinner's hope.' He revered the Prayer Book in which 'truth, the whole truth, is brought forward without fear [. . .] but also without offence; all is temperate, all is candid; all is practical; all is peaceful and every word is spoken in love'. While Simeon did not display the range of scholarly work found in the earlier divines he was nevertheless, at least much of the time, in tune with them.

In the nineteenth-century Church of England there were many who at least to some degree followed in the tradition of Hooker, Andrewes and Taylor. Space is limited to naming but a few, and again I am concerned chiefly with persons who have served in some sense as 'standards'. There were, for instance, John Keble (1792–1866), Edward Bouverie Pusey (1800–82), and John Henry Newman while an Anglican (1801–45)—all men of influence. They had a wide range of interests and concerns from polemics, such as Keble's Assize Sermon and the *Tracts for the Times*, to homiletics (Newman's university and parochial sermons are still read and still merit attention); from theological works such as Pusey's *The Doctrine of the Real Presence* and his edition of St Augustine's *Confessions*, to devotional works such as John Keble's *The Christian Year* and Newman's edition of Andrewes' *Preces Privatae*. It was Keble who edited the first modern edition of the *Works* of Hooker. There are others amongst the leaders of the Oxford Movement who might be mentioned, such as Robert Isaac Wilberforce with his theological trilogy, crowned by his *The Doctrine of the Incarnation*; Richard Church, the historian of the movement and widely acknowledged preacher, historian and essayist; and in the background, hovering over all, Samuel Taylor Coleridge. But for widespread influence it would be difficult to equal men like Keble, Newman and Pusey.

Frederick Denison Maurice (1805–72), who served for years as Chaplain of Lincoln's Inn at the Inns of Court in London and died as professor of Moral Theology and Moral Philosophy at Cambridge, was a loyal priest, a founder of the Christian Socialist movement, and author of works ranging from the theological *magnum opus, The Kingdom of Christ*, to articles in the weekly *Politics for the People*. It is possible that his sermons were most influential, especially his *Lincoln's Inn Sermons*, but also the sermons published as *The Doctrine of Sacrifice* and *The Prayer Book ... and the Lord's Prayer*. With his doctrine of Christ as 'the head of everyman whether that fact is acknowledged or not', with his success in thus bridging the chasm developing between the sacred and the secular, with his view of reason as 'conversant with that which is universal as well as with that which is necessary', with his devotion to Scripture and the Church of the incarnate Lord, Maurice distinguished himself and took his place with the long procession of Anglican divines, and has influenced many since his own day.

Other names come to mind when contemplating the nineteenth century, such as Richard Whately (1787–1863) among the Noetics, Thomas Arnold (1795–1842) among the Liberals, and J. C. Ryle (1816–1900) among the Calvinist Evangelicals, but they cannot stand comparison with the Cambridge triumvirate of Lightfoot, Hort and Westcott. Joseph Barber Lightfoot (1828–89), Bishop of Durham, wrote commentaries on Paul's epistles, edited the works of the Apostolic Fathers, wrote on the Christian ministry and preached sermons subsequently collected in numerous volumes. F. J. A. Hort (1828–92), Cambridge don and priest, edited the Greek text of the New Testament with Westcott, wrote commentaries on New Testament epistles, edited the works of Clement of Alexandria, and published lectures on *The Christian Ecclesia*, on the creeds, and on *The Way, the Truth and The Life*. Brooke Foss Westcott (1825–1901), also Bishop of Durham, most clearly conforms to our early models, at least in his writings. He too was a biblical scholar, writing commentaries on New Testament epistles, publishing a survey of the history of the New Testament canon, of *The Bible in the Church*, and of the *English Bible*. He wrote major theological books such as *Christus Consummator* and *The Incarnation and Common Life*. He surveyed *The History of Religious Thought in the West* and lectured on the Apostles' Creed. He preached many sermons, subsequently published, and prepared *Common Prayer for Family Use*. In addition he applied his theological insights to the modern industrial world in books such as *Lessons from Work, Social Aspects of Christianity*, and *The Two Empires, the Church and the World*. As did Lightfoot and Hort, Westcott helped mediate the transition of Anglican thought as found in Hooker, Andrewes and Taylor to the modern world of historical, biblical criticism, natural science, and industrial progress. He did this while professing belief that all people live in Christ: 'Life which Christ is and which Christ communicates, the life which fills our whole being as we realize its capacities, is active fellowship with God.' Furthermore, 'The coming of Christ, the Incarnation, binds together two worlds, and makes the earthly with all its workings a sacrament, so to speak, of the heavenly.'

Bridging the nineteenth and twentieth centuries there is Charles Gore (1853–1932), Bishop of Oxford, whose writings range from theological dissertations such as *The Reconstruction of Belief* to sermons, such as those on *The Deity of Christ*; from instructive works such as *The Church and the Ministry* to works dealing with modern problems, such as *Christ and Society*. In the twentieth century there is William Temple (1881–1944), Archbishop of Canterbury, with his theological trilogy, *Mens Creatrix, Christus Veritas*, and *Nature, Man, and God*, his popular *Christian Faith and Life* and his *Readings in St John's Gospel*, his *Repton School Sermons* and his *Christianity and Social Order*. Temple was, and still is, a towering figure in Anglicanism with a spirituality that embraces the cosmos. For Temple the aim of the Christian life is fellowship with God, 'fellowship with Love—utter, self-forgetful and self-giving love'. Who else might be suggested for the twentieth century? Dare one suggest, amongst others, Austin Farrer, or Ian Ramsey, or Stephen Neill, or J. A. T. Robinson, perhaps? Only time will tell whether or not such men, prominent in their own time, will be remembered and remain persons of authority in time to come.

The designation 'Anglican divines' is not properly limited to Englishmen, however rooted it may be in the sixteenth- and seventeenth-century Church of England. Scotland may very well look back to Robert Leighton (1611–84), Professor of Divinity at Edinburgh University and Archbishop of Glasgow, author of commentaries and lectures on New Testament books, of theological and of expository lectures, of *An Exposition of the Creed, Lord's Prayer, and Ten Commandments* [...] *To which is annext a short catechism*, meditations, spiritual exercises, *Rules and Instructions for a Holy Life*, and many sermons. Leighton attempted to reconcile episcopacy with presbyterianism and thus heal the wounds dividing his country. In the process he wrote *A Modest Defence of Moderate Episcopacy*.

In colonial America there is Samuel Johnson (1696–1722), one time teacher at nascent Yale College, Connecticut priest and pastor, the first president of King's College (later named Columbia University). Johnson was a learned man, author of a brief *Encyclopedia of Philosophy*, and defender of the Church of England in *Three Letters to Dissenters* and *Letters Concerning the Sovereignty of God*. He produced *A Short Catechism*, preached carefully polished sermons, including *A Demonstration of the Reasonableness, Usefulness and Great Duty of Prayer* and *The Beauty of Holiness in the Worship of the Church of England*, and published *A Form of Morning and Evening Prayer*, and *Two Collects*, for private and family use. Johnson emphasized the incarnation as instrumental for our incorporation into Christ, 'so that by being united to our nature and dwelling in it, he is united to and dwells in us, and we in him. Thus dwelling in the tabernacle of his Body he has united himself and dwells in mankind.'

In the Protestant Episcopal Church of the United States of America there is William Porcher DuBose (1836–1918), a teacher at the University of the South in Tennessee. Widely recognized as the most original and creative thinker the American Church has produced, author of numerous works, including *The Reason of Life, The Gospel in the Gospels, The Soteriology of the New Testament*, and *High Priesthood and Sacrifice*, DuBose was assuredly a learned and devout churchman of wide-ranging sympathies and interests, but he is seldom read or referred to, save in passing, and as included in the American calendar. Others might be mentioned, including John Henry Hobart (1775–1830), Bishop of New York, William Meade (1789–1862),

Bishop of Virginia, and others who for their times and places were learned, wrote theological treatises, gained reputations as influential preachers, provided materials for public and private devotions and (to recall the name of one of Meade's works) provided *Reasons for Loving the Episcopal Church.* Two other bishops warrant attention. One was Phillips Brooks (1835–93), Bishop of Massachusetts, a great preacher whose chief legacy has been volumes of exemplary sermons, but who also published works on *Baptism and Confirmation,* on *Preaching,* on *Tolerance,* on *The Influence of Jesus,* and a collection of *Essays and Addresses, Religious, Literary, and Social.* As A. V. G. Allen has said, Brooks and others of Broad Church persuasion 'held with Hooker and Bishop Butler that the human reason was the God-given faculty for verifying the divine revelation'.

The second bishop worthy of note is Charles Henry Brent (1862–1929), Bishop of the Philippines and of Western New York. Brent was a Canadian born and bred, who served the Church in the distant Philippine Islands. An ecclesiastical statesman of consummate skill, Brent was also a thoughtful theologian, author of *The Commonwealth, its foundations and pillars,* *The Mount of Vision, being a study of life in terms of the whole,* and *Presence.* He was a deeply spiritual man, author of *Adventures in Prayer,* and concerned for the welfare of planet earth, as demonstrated in his *With God in the World.* And of course there are others, in the United States of America and elsewhere in the Anglican Communion. Amongst Canadians, in addition to Brent, who became a citizen of the United States, mention should be made of Philip Carrington (1892–1975), Archbishop of Quebec, author of a commentary on Mark, a history of the Church in Canada, a history of *The Early Christian Church,* and a treatise on *The Meaning of Revelation.*

Admittedly one could and perhaps should mention numerous others, prominent members of Anglican Churches around the world. But sufficient examples have been provided to point the way toward the identification of others. It should be added that the character of Anglican divinity is such that it allows for expansion and modification, as was required with the development of non-Anglo-Saxon Anglican Churches, especially in the southern hemisphere. Then too, it should be noted that this discussion of Anglican divines has been limited to men alone. With the ordination of women in member Churches of the Anglican Communion, this limitation will pass away. It is therefore appropriate to inquire who, among women in the past, future Anglican divines who happen to be women will be able to regard as predecessors.

There comes to mind Lady Ann Bacon, the translator of John Jewel's *Apology* (1564), one of the learned, devout Cooke sisters. And what of Queen Elizabeth I, her public utterances and her prayers? More seriously, there is the venerable Evangelical, Hannah More (1745–1833), with her

185

tracts and treatises, her writings on St Paul and on *Christian Morals*, her *Practical Piety* and her *Book of Private Devotions*. However, there would be those who would justly complain that she was not very learned; and it is doubtful that she influenced many very far beyond her own time. But Evelyn Underhill (1875–1941) was certainly learned and remains influential among many Anglicans. Her major works were the scholarly classics, *Mysticism* (1911) and *Worship* (1937). She also wrote more popular books such as *The Life of the Spirit and the Life of To-day* and *The Fruits of the Spirit*. In her understanding of adoration, communion and co-operation as representative of Trinitarian faith and life, Underhill summed up much that has been passed on and emphasized from the Anglican divines of the early genera- tions. Theology and prayer are one in her writings, and she laboured to overcome the bifurcation of the sacred and the secular, individuality and community, and similar divisions.

Although she has not had the influence of Evelyn Underhill, the marks of the Anglican divines can be seen in the writings of Vida Scudder (1861– 1954). Professor of English Literature at Wellesley College in the United States and an early member of the Society of the Companions of the Holy Cross, Scudder translated and edited the letters of Catherine of Siena and wrote a history of the Franciscans in their early years. She wrote fiction; a biography of James Huntington, the founder of the Order of the Holy Cross; *On Journey*, a spiritual autobiography; and the scholarly *The Life of the Spirit in Modern English Poets*. A socialist, she possessed a keen sense of the relevance of the Christian gospel to the social crises of her day, and wrote books on *Christian Citizenship*, *The Witness of Denial*, and *The Social Teachings of the Christian Year*. For Scudder as for Underhill and Maurice, Pusey and Simeon, for Hooker, Andrewes and Taylor, the concept of sacrifice was of central importance. 'Willingness to accept the death of God offered that we may live, to take the ever-renewed sacrifice into that ever-changing being which can otherwise not live at all, is the ultimate act of faith', wrote Scudder. 'It is the seal on the awful mystery of interdepen- dence, the lie forever to all attempts to live a self-sufficing life. Existence itself is a continual Communion, in which man feeds upon the universal God.'

In thinking of the expansion and modification of Anglican divinity it is important to note the prominence of certain laity, other than women, in the twentieth century. In England there are prominent, influential Angli- cans such as C. S. Lewis with works ranging from the Narnia series and other novels to *The Screwtape Letters* and essays in Christian apologetics. In relation to Lewis one should also mention the barrister, Owen Barfield; the immensely creative Charles Williams; and another woman, Dorothy L. Sayers, who wrote theology, such as *The Mind of the Maker*, translated Dante, and contributed other works that were largely apologetic. T. S.

Eliot, an American by birth but an Englishman by temperament, mediated Anglicanism to many people through his own devotion to and explanation of Andrewes and the metaphysical poets, as exemplary of that unified sensibility that he considered essential to the fullest humanity and found most fully in Prayer Book worship. In America during recent years there is William Stringfellow, praised by Karl Barth. Such Anglicans have exercised considerable influence, and have some claim to being considered in any list of standard divines; because, as local members of the Church and devout Christians, they have understood the coinherence of theology and devotion with personal and social life.

What is an Anglican divine? The answer to this question is to be found in the lives and theological writings of persons such as those mentioned in the course of this essay. There is no 'standard' or authoritative list of such theologians, there are only those people of learning and piety who have served the Church in the tradition identified with the *ecclesia Anglicana*, and who's influence has permeated the Anglican Communion in varying degrees down through the years.

BIBLIOGRAPHY

Hill, W. S. (ed.), *Studies in Richard Hooker*. Press of Case Western Reserve University, Cleveland and London, 1972.

McAdoo, H. R., *The Spirit of Anglicanism*. A. and C. Black, London, 1965.

More, P. E. and Cross, F. L. (eds), *Anglicanism: The Thought and Practice of the Church of England, Illustrated From the Religious Literature of the Seventeenth Century*. Milwaukee 1935; SPCK, London, 1935, 1962.

Neill, S. C., *Anglicanism*. Penguin, Harmondsworth, 1958.

Rowell, G. (ed.), *The English Religious Tradition and the Genius of Anglicanism*. IKON, Wantage, 1992.

Standing Liturgical Committee of the Protestant Episcopal Church in the United States of America, *Prayer Book Studies XVI. The Calendar and the Collects, Epistles, and Gospels for the Lesser Feasts and Fasts*. New York, 1963.

Sykes, Stephen W., *Unashamed Anglicanism*. DLT, London, 1995.

Wolf, W. J. (ed.), *Anglican Spirituality*. Morehouse-Barlow, Wilton CT, 1982.

Wolf, W. J. (ed.), *The Spirit of Anglicanism*. Morehouse-Barlow, Wilton CT, 1979; Edinburgh, 1981.

6 Lex Orandi—Lex Credendi

W. TAYLOR STEVENSON

In Anglicanism, the worship of the people of God plays a very distinctive role, being the principal arena not only of supplication and praise but also of theological experimentation and formulation (see pp. 55–81). This relationship of worship and belief is often discussed under the Latin tag, *lex orandi, lex credendi*—'the law of praying is the law of belief'.[1]

187

How did this distinctive situation emerge in Anglicanism, and what are its strengths and limitations? How is it possible to justify the process of having worship as the principal arena of theological experimentation and formulation? Are there ways in which this distinctive situation can be reappropriated, so that its strengths may be enhanced and its weaknesses diminished? If so, what difference would that make in relation to church, sacraments and ministry? It is the purpose of this essay to explore each of these questions in turn.

THE DISTINCTIVE ROLE OF WORSHIP IN ANGLICAN THEOLOGY AND SELF-UNDERSTANDING

There is not now, and there never has been, a distinctive Anglican theology. We have no Thomas or Luther, no Calvin or Zwingli. Nor is there any authority in Anglicanism which corresponds to the magisterium of the Roman Catholic Church or the theological themes which provided the touchstones of theological inquiry of the Protestant Reformation. The pre-eminent theologian who is identifiably Anglican is Richard Hooker, whose late sixteenth-century *Laws of Ecclesiastical Polity* is respected but has never been definitive nor influential in any systematic way. If there is any theology which has been pervasively influential for Anglican thought, it is the conflicted, ambiguous, and largely christologically-oriented patristic theology, which clusters around the first four ecumenical councils, culminating in Chalcedon (451) (see pp. 100–14). This theology, however, couched in the Hellenistic thought-forms foreign to the historical consciousness of the modern period, can only be one resource among many for Anglican theology.

What has been definitive for Anglicanism, from its inception in the sixteenth century until the present day, is the Book of Common Prayer in its successive editions (see pp. 131–42). The Prayer Book contains the daily offices of Morning and Evening Prayer, the forms for the administration of the Eucharist, Baptism, and the other sacraments; the litany; the Ordinal; the Psalter; and lesser rites and collections of prayers. Because the successive editions of the Prayer Book have been infrequent and conservative in spirit, it is fair to say that the first two Books of Common Prayer (1549 and 1552, respectively) together established the fundamental outline and spirit of Anglican theology and practice. The first made moderate changes in a Protestant direction; the second, reflecting the outgoing development within Anglican theology and practice during the period, continued those changes in a more thoroughgoing way. Hence, the contemporary concern to make Christian theology and Christian practice interdependent in a Christian 'praxis' was at least prefigured in the crucial liturgical experimentation which marked Anglicanism from its beginnings.

The formation of the Prayer Book 1549 was presided over, and marked by the genius of, Thomas Cranmer (1489–1553), who, over a period of years, gathered, edited, and himself contributed to the collection of texts which eventually resulted in the formation of the first Prayer Book. Consequently, if it can be said that anyone is the definitive Anglican theologian, then that person is Thomas Cranmer. Cranmer, however, was not a theologian in the sense of somebody who produced systematic reflections upon theological topics. He was, rather, a priest and pastor; and, as Archbishop of Canterbury, an administrator and politician. In addition, he was in effect what we would call today a liturgiologist. His theology is formulated (1) in terms of the selection, arrangement and composition of the prayers that are prayed constantly by Christian people, and (2) in terms of the rubrics which stipulate the permissible variations in the prayers and the ceremonial practice which accompanies them. In addition, the Prayer Book's 'Lectionary' stipulates, with some degree of latitude, which portions of Scripture are appropriate to be read in the worship of the church during each week of the church year. In these ways 'the law of worship is the law of belief': *lex orandi, lex credendi*. The texts which are heard and prayed, according to the Book of Common Prayer, inform profoundly the Christian self-understanding and systematic theological reflection of Anglicans. This situation prevailed in Anglicanism during the Reformation in the sixteenth century, and continues to prevail to the present day.

Two aspects of the formation of the Prayer Book of 1549 need to be stressed because they are essential to the subject of this essay.

First, Cranmer's Prayer Book was an arena both for theological formulation and for theological experimentation. In formulating the 1549 Prayer Book, Cranmer drew upon Latin, Greek Orthodox, Lutheran and other sources. During the decade prior to 1549, he had prepared certain major portions of the envisioned Prayer Book, and some of these were used experimentally in parishes in England. The theological and popular reactions to these experimental liturgies were taken into account in the formulation of the Prayer Book of 1549. The 1549 Prayer Book itself then became, in effect, the experimental text which was modified in the successive revisions of 1552, 1559, and (after a period of suspension of the use of the Prayer Book due to the ascendancy of the Puritans in England) 1662. In this process of liturgical formulation, experimentation and reformulation, the reforming of the Church in England was effected which established a distinctive form of Christianity which was both Reformed and Catholic. In England, the 1662 Prayer Book continues as the legal Prayer Book until today, alongside recently authorized revised liturgies.

189

A similar process of theological formulations and experimentation has prevailed as the other churches within the Anglican Communion have each proceeded to produce their own Prayer Book, including the first American Prayer Book (1789). Thus, the production of the American Prayer Book of 1979, the most comprehensive and theologically significant revision of any Prayer Book since 1662, was marked by this same process as successive 'trial' Prayer Books (or portions thereof) were formulated and then given to the church for experimental use within the context of the congregational life of the American Episcopal Church. The reactions of those who prayed these 'trial' liturgies, week in and week out, were taken into serious account in the final formulation of the 1979 Prayer Book. It is significant that the variety of liturgical options permitted by this Prayer Book far exceeds anything that could have been imagined in previous centuries, and this flexibility in prayer both reflects and reinforces the flexibility in belief to be found in the pluralistic church of the late twentieth century: *lex orandi, lex credendi.*

WHENCE COMETH ANGLICANISM? THE ENGLISH ETHOS

The Christian heritage of worship and theology available to the Church in England at the time of the Reformation was not substantially different from that available in many other areas of Western Europe. Why, therefore, did the distinctive approach to theological formulation and Christian self-understanding described above arise only in England? Historical questions of this scope do not have definitive or exhaustive answers because the issues involved are so complex. Nevertheless, there were political and social conditions present in England in the sixteenth century which were conducive to the unique way in which the process of *lex orandi, lex credendi* was manifested there. In addition, even a brief description of these conditions begins to uncover the strengths and weaknesses of this Anglican process.

These political and social conditions I will summarily denominate the 'English' or, more generally, 'Anglican' ethos. An ethos is made up of the predominant conditions and assumptions of an ethnic group; it is the underlying feelings which inform the beliefs and customs of that group. An ethos tends to be intractable because it consists of *underlying* assumptions and feelings, and because they are underlying they go unchallenged and thereby dominate the group. An ethos is a 'habit of the mind', but more importantly it is constituted by 'habits of the heart'—a way of being in the world. There are two aspects of the English ethos which are most important for the purposes of this essay, both well known. First, there is the assumption that consensus, comprehensiveness and contract is the normative mode for establishing and maintaining the order of society. The living-out of this assumption contributes to a prevailing absence of violent conflict, and reinforces the related assumption that the continuation of this condition is both desirable and feasible. Second, there is in the English ethos a certain pragmatism and lack of speculative interest in the approach to human affairs. These two fundamental aspects of the English ethos are interrelated and reinforce one another, and each needs some brief additional comment in order to clarify its pertinence to this essay.

CONSENSUS, COMPREHENSIVENESS, AND CONTRACT

At least since the time of the Magna Carta (1215) the English were engaged in a halting but persistent struggle to transform their hierarchical medieval society. The strength of medieval society was that it imposed some degree of order upon its diverse economic-political components. The weakness of such a society was that the order imposed was limited, fragile, and brought with it the conditions of almost constant limited warfare.

Theologically, and notwithstanding the many accommodations which the Church made with it, this medieval ordering of society in England as elsewhere in Europe was in tension with the Christian vision of human life. That tension was expressed in such specific ways as the Church's imposition of periodic truces in warfare and in the practice of 'sanctuary', and more generally and ambiguously in the centuries-long struggle between church and state which had, in England during the years 1162–74, reached a protracted, dramatic, and violent expression in the conflict between Archbishop of Canterbury Thomas Becket and Henry II. Pragmatically, this medieval ordering of society was less and less able to provide coherence and stability for a society in which there was the burgeoning of a sense of individual liberty (by the norms of the thirteenth century, not the twentieth), and in which self-contained local agriculture was being progressively modified by commerce and international trade.

PRAGMATISM

This was the context which enabled Magna Carta to be thinkable, and then to succeed. The 'Great Charter' is not only the first major document in the process of English constitutional development, but it also established the spirit of that development. The Great Charter was pragmatic. It established definite and practical remedies for temporary evils. There is very little in it which is abstract or theoretical. The barons who forced the Charter upon King John were not revolutionaries; rather, they acted to 'control the King through the Common Law, baronial assemblies, and alliances with other classes'. The barons acted with the active support of the 'freemen'. In a process of strong assertion followed by compromise, a 'middle way'—a *via media*—was found, which aimed at the most comprehensive consensus possible at the time. That consensus was established in a contract, the Great

191

Charter, which was 'then subject to constant reissues, revisions, infringements, and reassertions'.[2]

Three centuries later, as we have seen, the first Prayer Book of 1549 was
formed by a process remarkably analogous to that which produced the Great
Charter. Cranmer and others built, over a period of a decade or more, not a
consensus but nevertheless a pervasive climate of opinion, that the worship
and belief of the Church in England needed to be changed; and this was not
to be done in the spirit of revolution but rather of revision and amendment.
A 'middle way' was sought between those who were inclined to look to the
late medieval Church for guidance in these matters, and those who were
inclined to look to the continental Reformation for that guidance. This
'middle way' was expressed in a 'contract', the Book of Common Prayer of
1549. The contract was a pragmatic one, eschewing for the most part
matters of doctrinal speculation and controversy in favour of the practical
matter of how the people of England were to worship week by week. It was
understood from the beginning that this contract was 'then subject to
constant reissues, revisions, infringements, and reassertions'. And so it
continues to be until the present day. This continuity is the expression of
the continuing English or Anglican ethos which, although it obviously finds
different expressions in different historical periods and cultural situations,
gives rise in analogous ways to a process of consensus, comprehensiveness
and contract.

PRAGMATISM AND THE LACK OF SPECULATIVE INTEREST

The pragmatism of the English or Anglican ethos has already been noted in
the preceding discussion. While it may be of very limited historical import,
it is certainly appropriate that the only heresy associated traditionally with
Britain is that of the British (or Irish) monk Pelagius (active 410–18) who
argued that the individual, apart from divine grace, makes the initial and
fundamental steps toward salvation. That is a practical, a 'sensible', idea. It
is more significant historically, and quite in keeping with the English ethos,
that English piety and theology has had an earnest Pelagian flavour extending from the Puritanism of the seventeenth century through the Evangelical movements of the eighteenth and nineteenth centuries. It was
probably inevitable that the Salvation Army (1885), with its great stress
on the moral side of Christianity, would arise out of this English ethos. To
be English is 'to do one's duty', as the delightful lyrics of Gilbert and
Sullivan's operettas make clear!

Why this pragmatic orientation arose specifically in England at least as
early as the Great Charter is speculative and probably unanswerable.

What is important for our purposes, however, is that it did arise. It is
embedded in the English constitutional process with its accompanying

juridical system embodied in the 'common law', and it was to give rise to the British philosophical tradition of empiricism and to British leadership in the development of the natural sciences in the eighteenth and nineteenth centuries (see pp. 118–23).

THE STRENGTHS AND LIMITATIONS OF *LEX ORANDI, LEX CREDENDI* WITHIN THE ANGLICAN ETHOS

STRENGTHS

The strengths of the process of *lex orandi, lex credendi* within the Anglican ethos are clearly manifested in the preceding discussion.

First and foremost, this process places a high value upon, and gives great respect to, the traditions which come together to form the Christian faith. More specifically, it is the liturgical expression of these traditions which is primary. This liturgy is, on the one hand, pervasively informed by the symbols, myths and metaphors of Scripture and the traditions; but, on the other hand, Scripture and the traditions are appropriated by the believer within the context of the liturgy as it is prayed in the contemporary situation.

Second, the ongoing appropriation or ordering of the Christian traditions within the historical process can only be accomplished by the body of those persons within whom those traditions live, the church. Third, the ordering of the traditions proceeds by means of the activity of reflection and negotiation which aims at a comprehensive consensus for the ordering of the church and its relation to society. Fourth, the consensus reached at any given point in history is pragmatically formulated in liturgical contract, the Book of Common Prayer, which bodies forth the ordering of the church and its relation to society in a way which is constantly available to all persons. Fifth, because the Book of Common Prayer is couched primarily in terms of the symbols and myths of the various liturgical texts, which by their nature are open to a number of interpretations, the way is left open for the development of a variety of forms of personal piety and of discursive theological systems, as long as those forms and systems do not come into open conflict with the Book of Common Prayer.

Collectively, these strengths result in the following, general characteristics of Anglicanism. First there is a strong sense of tradition, continuity and order. Second, there is a high ecclesiology (see pp. 249–62), because it is the church which holds in trust the Book of Common Prayer upon which order is centred. Third, there is a high anthropology, because it is by means of rational human reflection, deliberation and negotiation that the traditions of the past are brought again and again into a consensus which is adequate to the present. Fourth, because the traditions of the past necessarily are in tension with the need for a present consensus, a self-critical element is present which helps to protect Anglicanism against the idolatry of either past traditions or current reformulations. And fifth, because of its desire for consensus and its high anthropology, Anglicanism leans strongly in the direction of a critical yet positive orientation to human culture, for example, critical historical studies, the natural sciences and the arts (see pp. 351–63).

LIMITATIONS

The limitations of Anglicanism are constituted by the reverse sides of its strengths. Thus, the proven strength of finding order and unity by means of careful respect for the liturgical texts of the Christian tradition carries with it the tendency to expend a disproportionate amount of energy on historical and technical discussions of those texts, to the relative neglect of the contemporary restatement of those traditions which is so essential to the ongoing life of the church. This tendency is countered in part by the positive orientation of Anglicanism toward interaction with its surrounding culture. Nevertheless, *lex orandi* tends to prevail in an unbalanced way over *lex credendi*.[3] In so far as this happens (and there are notable exceptions) there is a betrayal of the Anglican quest for the 'middle way' which strives to achieve balance through the integration of the legitimate claims of both sides of an issue.

Another, closely related set of limitations arises out of Anglicanism's pragmatic desire to reach consensus through negotiation and to embody that consensus in a contract. This desire gives rise to the 'sweet reasonableness' inherent in Anglicanism, which is a legitimate dimension of the gospel of Christ. Its value in promoting order, unity and stability in the church and in society is readily demonstrable. At the same time, however, this pragmatic desire for reasonableness and order is prone to degenerate into a bargaining variety of compromise which loses sight of any vision of unity in favour of 'peace at any price' among the dominating elements of the society. The historical traditions are rehearsed and many points of view are acknowledged, but none is passionately affirmed and an evangelical stance is not assumed. When this spirit prevails it is impossible to sound the clarion call of the prophets, and those who do sound that call are *slowly* (thus preserving the semblance of 'peace') edged out of the Anglican community. The most notable instance of this process took place in relation to John Wesley's Methodist movement during the years from 1739, when Anglican churches were closed to him, to 1784, when the annual conference of Methodist lay preachers was provided with a legal constitution.

ANGLICAN LIMITATIONS, ANGLICAN LEGITIMACY, AND A
WAY FORWARD

The limitations of Anglicanism's pragmatic interest in consensus, as well as its legitimate stress upon the centrality of liturgy and worship, can be placed in a wider perspective through an examination of the philosophy and implicit theology of the French Protestant, Paul Ricoeur (b. 1913). Ricoeur articulates the crucial problem for human discourse in general, and religious discourse in particular, from the eighteenth century until the present day. Technically stated, this problem is: Is the *Cogito* within being, or is it vice versa?[4] In less technical and in explicitly theological language, the problem may be stated thus: Is my life to be found within the reality of God, or is the reality of God derivative from me? This crucial problem is widely recognized, and it has been addressed also by Bernard Lonergan, Karl Rahner, Wolfhart Pannenberg and many others. It is Ricoeur's reflections upon this central problem, however, with their great stress upon the function of symbol and myth in human discourse, which are most pertinent to the concerns of this essay. Consequently, it is to these reflections that I now turn.[5]

What Ricoeur would have us attend to is our lack of awareness of the transcendent order which is absolutely determinative for human life *as such*, that is, for human experiencing, imagining, reflection and action. This transcendental order is referred to variously as the sacred, the holy, Being, God. However named, the sacred addresses us and we respond to it by means of symbols and the narratives or myths which related the symbols to one another. It is this response which constitutes and informs human life in all of its dimensions.

It is easy to miss Ricoeur's point. It is not the case that the sacred is within us and therefore arises as a human construction, a product of human religious consciousness. The sacred is not first of all within us. Rather, we, together with all that we feel and think and do, are within the sacred. The sacred is indeed within every person, but only derivatively as it is mirrored or imaged there from its transcendent source. We are theomorphic; or, traditionally, we are created in the image of God.

What is the character of symbols which permits them to function in this way? Ricoeur writes:

'Symbol gives rise to thought.' This maxim that I find so appealing says two things. The symbol gives: I do not posit the meaning, the symbol gives it; but what it gives is something for thought, something to think about. First the giving, then the positing; the phrase suggests, therefore, both that all has already been said in enigma and yet that it is necessary ever to begin again and rebegin everything in the dimension of thought. It is this articulation of thought left to itself in the realm of symbols and of thought positing and thinking that I would like to intercept and understand.[6]

'Symbol gives rise to thought.' First the giving, then the positing is crucial for the concerns of this essay. *Lex orandi* has the priority, *lex credendi* is essential but logically and ontologically derivative. The dialectical relationship between the two halves is intimate and pervasive. When we first become aware of ourselves as human beings we are already engaged in thinking *about* the symbols. Nevertheless, the order is crucial: first the giving, then the positing. It is this order which situates us individually and corporately within God, and not vice versa. It is this order which is expressive of the intrinsically Anselmic character of Christian faith: faith in search of understanding, understanding in search of an adequate articulation of the faith which undergirds it, which in turn alters what is received. It is within this process that Christian preaching finds its essential and indispensable role; and this process continues throughout the life of the individual and of the Church.

For Anglicans, as for all Christians, this givenness of the sacred is manifested first and most fully in the symbols and mythic narratives which present the life, death and resurrection of Jesus of Nazareth as he is remembered through the activity of the Holy Spirit in the Church. It is these given symbols and narratives which are enacted ritually, prayed, chanted and sung. They constitute the icons of the Christian faith. Meaning appears *there*, just in these symbols as they are assembled in narratives. It is these symbols and narratives which are central and determinative for Christian faith.

Within the staggeringly complex world of symbols, everyone must begin from somewhere. Christians begin from the symbolic life of the ministry, death and resurrection of Jesus as summarized in the Apostles' Creed. This narrative is privileged. Other narratives and devotional practices, such as those associated with the lives of the saints, may be drawn into this privileged symbolic-narrative orbit. And, indeed, certain symbols and myths of other religions may be drawn into this orbit. In such instances, however, that which is received can only be received legitimately insofar as it is congruent with the privileged narrative of the Christ. It is from this given that positing proceeds, that the reflective articulation of faith begins.

The privileged symbols and narratives of the Christ live most fundamentally within Scripture as it is remembered and prayed within the liturgical worship of the Church. The individual's use of Scripture and prayer is dependent upon the more comprehensive experience of the Church. No Christian community or theology ever totally loses sight of the givenness of this dimension of Christian experience, and Anglicanism is most self-

196

conscious and emphatic about it. It is this which provides the experiential and theoretical ground and thus the justification for Anglicanism's insistence upon the primacy of liturgy and the Book of Common Prayer in the life of the church, together with its particular articulation of lex orandi, lex credendi.

If Anglicanism in particular has never completely lost sight of this dimension of its experience, it has too often permitted the centrality of symbol, myth and worship to slip from the centre of its vision as it goes about articulating its theology and its life. When this happens, it is a violation of the intrinsic character of Anglicanism discussed earlier, a violation to which it is prone in part because of its tendency toward compromise, pragmatism and order. The result, as is always the case when an individual or tradition loses its sense of identity, is a diffuseness and lack of creativity which serves itself and others poorly. Thus, while there have been significant Anglican contributions to theology in the twentieth century, particularly in the historical fields (Scripture, patristic and liturgies), nevertheless Anglican theology in general has been marked by this loss of identity and creativity. Anglicanism's contributions to the Liberal theology of the early twentieth century were limited and modest, and its involvement in the mid-century's Neo-orthodox theology was almost non-existent. More recently, Anglicanism's participation in the properly dominant linguistic and hermeneutical concerns of the theology of the last thirty years or so have been restricted to the useful, but very limited, studies of Ian Ramsey and others concerned with the validity of 'God talk'.[7]

The way forward for Anglican theology, then, if it is to be true to the evangelical charge to proclaim the gospel to all the world, is not through some revolutionary new beginning but rather through a reappropriation of its lost vision of the centrality of lex orandi, lex credendi in the life and thought of the Church.

THE SYMBOL GIVES RISE TO THOUGHT: THE REAPPROPRIATION OF LEX ORANDI, LEX CREDENDI IN ANGLICAN THEOLOGY

A climate of opinion has emerged in Anglicanism and beyond affirming the necessity for the Church and for the Christian of an Anselmic movement of faith rooted in a participation in the process of lex orandi, lex credendi as described in the preceding section. The aphorism, the 'tag' if you will, which encapsulates that process is Paul Ricoeur's 'the symbol gives rise to thought'.[8] The aphorism in one sense only restates the Latin tag, but it restates it in a form which by affirmation or implication takes account in the following ways of our having moved through (not around) the great spiritual adventure which has proceeded out of the Enlightenment.

First, 'the symbol gives': we do not create symbols, rather we 'find' them. When we first become aware of ourselves as human beings we discover that we are living and thinking out of a matrix of symbols related to one another in the narrative structure of the myths embedded within our native language. These symbols give us our sense of identity, value, self-worth and order both as a community and as individuals. In brief, the symbols give us our humanity. Thus symbols are manifestations of prevenient grace as they give us to ourselves; and in this sense we find symbols only because they first 'find' us. It is the Christian testimony that that which finds us is the sacred, is God; that the symbols are theophanies; that the privileged symbols and myths of this God are those of Scripture as these are received and lived by the worshipping Church; and that we live within this God whom we reflect or image. It is this situation which undergirds the priority which Anglicans give to prayer over belief, for the symbols around which prayer turns are theophanies.

In one sense this first affirmation pointed to by the phrase 'the symbol gives' only affirms what the Church has said from the beginning. It is now affirmed, however, in a way which recognizes explicitly the vital role of the human subject and language in forming our relationship with God. The recognition of this role has only become possible as a result of the pre-occupation of Western philosophy and psychology with the human subject and with language from the latter part of the eighteenth century to the present. Further, this new way of affirming the priority of prayer is indebted to over a century of study of the history of religions (in which, significantly, Anglicans in their desire for comprehensiveness and consensus have played a prominent part) which has impressed upon us the centrality of symbols and myths in the forming of the consciousness and lives of all peoples. With the recognition of this centrality there comes a thoroughgoing recognition of the pluralistic and historically conditioned character of symbols and myths. There are different symbols and myths both within a particular religious tradition and between different traditions. The symbol gives, and it gives again and again in a historical process which is no more under our control than are the symbols themselves. Therefore, no one symbol or set of symbols, such as that of the Christian faith, can stand in isolation from the others. Nor can the symbols of any one tradition triumphantly assert its supremacy over those of another tradition. Rather, both the symbols within a single tradition and those of different traditions stand in a conversational relationship in which they criticize and complement one another. This is one manifestation of the working of the self-critical principle within the symbolic life. Consequently, while the claim for, and a commitment to, a privileged status for a particular symbolic tradition is both inevitable and essential for those who participate in that tradition, such a claim can only be made on the basis of human testimony and in the full recognition that there will be an ensuing conflict of testimonies which can only be resolved eschatologically. Stephen Sykes wisely points to this in relation to Christianity when he asserts that 'What Christianity entails [is] seen to be essentially contested', and 'Christian identity is, therefore, not a state but a process; a process, moreover, which entails the restlessness of a dialectic, impelled by criticism.'[9]

Second, 'the symbol gives rise *to thought*': if there is to be thought, there must be something to think about. What there is to be thought about are the symbols, the theophanies, which we find and thereby discover ourselves to be found. We are addressed by the symbols, and they demand our response. Our response is thought about the symbols, and this thought initially takes the form of placing the symbols in the narrative structure of ritual and myth, and then proceeds into theological speculation about the significance of these rites and symbols for every area of human activity. It is this process which constitutes religious consciousness. All human thought is rooted in this consciousness, and retains its vitality only in so far as it maintains that rootedness. As Sykes observes more concretely, 'Communal worship [in which the symbols, rites, and myths are continually rehearsed] [. . .] is a theatre in which doctrine, ethics, myth, social embodiment, ritual and inward experience are integrally related.'[10]

All of this is a way of restating the place of *lex credendi* in its relation to *lex orandi*, but again it is restated with a difference. It is now seen that the 'law' of both prayer and belief (thought) is more aptly denominated as 'process' or 'life'. That was implied in the traditional Latin tag, but now it is explicit. It is necessary for this to have become explicit because, again, of the interrelated developments of the modern Western preoccupation with the human subject, with language, and with the emergence of critical historical consciousness. (These developments themselves are rooted in the eschatological and incarnational symbols of biblical and particularly Christian religious consciousness, although that subject cannot be pursued here.) Here all is process as the symbols give rise to thought, which modifies our perception of the practically infinite facets of meaning which inhere in the symbol, which in turn enables the symbol to give rise to new thought. And the process continues. Although it never loses its rootedness in the symbols from which it proceeds, the process is eschatologically oriented toward the new, the future. All claims to finality and completion fall under the rubric of suspicion, and the process continues.

IMPLICATIONS FOR CHURCH, SACRAMENTS AND MINISTRY IN ANGLICANISM

The preceding exploration critically affirms Anglicanism's stress upon worship in general and the sacraments in particular as both a resource and a theatre for theological statement and exploration. The thought to which symbols give rise takes place first and most fundamentally within the context of worship and rite, as individuals standing within a community attempt to respond to and interiorize the presence of the holy which the symbol betokens. What are the implications of this appreciation of *lex orandi, lex credendi* for Church, sacraments and ministry? Limitations of space will permit only the briefest of answers.

CHURCH

On the one hand, the priority of the Church and its discipline of worship over the individual is strongly affirmed. It is the ritually formed Church which is the bestower of the symbols which find us and bestow our humanity upon us. This is often an unpopular message in a society which careers back and forth between uncritical individualism and unthinking conformity to rapidly changing social trends. On the other hand, and for the same reasons, the Church is precluded from laying claim to final and exhaustive (idolatrous) answers to the ends of human life and the means of attaining those ends. The Church does not control, but is created by and is answerable to, the processive unfolding of the symbols, the theophanies of God. Because this is so, theology and the theological community are indispensable to the life of the Church. The symbols and myths do not change, but the doctrines, rituals, canons and so on which proceed from the symbols and myths are continually changing and are always provisional. It is the unending task of theology to examine critically the question of the fidelity of what proceeds from the symbols to the symbols themselves. Anglicanism needs to be less restrictive in its attention to this task than it has been in the past.

SACRAMENTS

On the one hand, the symbols, the theophanies of God, together with the mythic narratives in which they are set, find their most comprehensive and authoritative expression in the Scriptures of the Old and New Testaments. On the other hand, those Scriptures are only transmitted, read and continually reappropriated by the ritually formed community of the Church. Therefore, either the tendency to give a privileged position to sacraments over Scripture (through liturgical preoccupation, ritual preciosity, the de-emphasis or elimination of preaching) or of Scripture over sacraments (through liturgical minimalism, ritual carelessness, the intellectualization of human life) are equally unfaithful to the insights available in the phrase, *lex orandi, lex credendi*—or, 'The symbol gives rise to thought.' Anglicanism has most characteristically succumbed to the former tendency, although recent liturgical scholarship has done much to correct that imbalance. Both tendencies, however, each of which is a deformity, are perennial temptations for modern consciousness.

MINISTRY
Lex orandi, lex credendi yields three fundamental insights which should have a pervasive influence on Christian ministry (see pp. 378–90). First, human life in general and the Christian life in particular is symbolic life; corporately and individually we live in and through symbols, for only through them are we discovered by the fullness, courage and joy of life. Second, symbols are the theophanies of God and presentations to every man and woman of God's prevenient grace. We live in God. Individuals may attempt to reject the symbols, but no one is excluded from the symbols. Finally, the symbolic life, the life of grace, is a processive or eschatological life. Consequently, any final, closed pronouncements as to what constitutes 'truth' and must be believed or as to what constitutes the 'good life' and must be obeyed can only be deemed idolatrous.

BIBLIOGRAPHY
Clarke, W. K. L. (ed.), *Liturgy and Worship: A Companion to the Prayer Books of the Anglican Communion.* SPCK, London, 1932.
Cross, F. L. (ed.), *The Oxford Dictionary of the Christian Church.* OUP 1958, 3rd edn, OUP 1997.
Ricoeur, P., *The Symbolism of Evil.* Beacon Press, Boston, 1967.
Spinks, B., 'Two Seventeenth Century Examples of "Lex credendi lex orandi": The Baptismal and Eucharistic Theologies and Liturgies of Jeremy Taylor and Richard Hooker'. *Studia Liturgica* 21.1 (1991) pp. 165–89.
Stevenson, W. T., 'Is There a Characteristic Anglican Theology?' in *The Future of Anglican Theology.* Edwin Mellen Press, New York and Toronto, 1984.
Sykes, Stephen W., *The Identity of Christianity.* SPCK, London/Fortress Press, Philadelphia, 1984.
Trevelyan, G. M., *History of England.* Longman, Green and Co., London, 1945.
Wainwright, G., *Doxology: The Praise of God in Worship, Doctrine and Life.* OUP, New York, 1980; Epworth Press, London, 1982.

NOTES
1   The origin of the tag *lex orandi, lex credendi* is attributed to a lay monk, Prosper of Aquitaine, from a capitulum annexed to a letter of Pope Celestine I (422–32) between 435 and 442. The phrase originally read *legem credendi lex statuat supplicandi*, 'Let the law of prayer establish the law of belief', and was used to argue (against semipelagianism) that the apostolic mandate to pray for all persons in 1 Timothy 2.1–4 proves that one is obligated to believe that faith is entirely a work of grace. The principle that has been established through the

centuries is that worship and liturgy reflect and express doctrine. Debate has occurred throughout concerning to what extent worship and doctrine are authoritative for each other.
For a more complete discussion, see Wainwright, *Doxology*, pp. 218–50. Wainwright includes development of the principle in the thought of Augustine, Chrysostom, Ambrose, Jerome, Cyprian, Tertullian and Irenaeus. The early history of the principle to the time of Prosper is also sketched by K. Federer, *Liturgie and Glaube: eine theologiegeschichtliche Untersuchung* (Paulus-Verlag, Freiburg in der Schweiz, 1950). *Mediator Dei* (1947; ET, *Encyclical Letter of His Holiness Pius XII on The Sacred Liturgy*, National Catholic Welfare Conference, Washington DC), an encyclical of Pius XII, restates the Roman Catholic position, particularly in paragraphs 49–67 (of the ET). A modern discussion is found in Aidan Kavanagh OSB, *On Liturgical Theology* (Pueblo, New York, 1984); and Robert J. Taft SJ in 'Liturgy as Theology', *Worship* 56 (1982), pp. 113–17.
2 Trevelyan, *History of England*, pp. 170–2.
3 Stevenson, 'Is There a Characteristic Anglican Theology?' pp. 24–5 and *passim*.
4 Ricoeur, *The Symbolism of Evil*, p. 356.
5 The influences upon the philosophy of Paul Ricoeur are extensive and complex. Moreover, he has unified them in a position which is distinctively his own and which defies assigning him to any 'school of thought'. If one has to place him in any one modern theological tradition, it would be that of Neo-orthodoxy with its radical stress upon the primacy of God's address and the dependent quality of our human response to that address. This relationship to Neo-orthodoxy remains unarticulated and only implicit in Ricoeur's writings. The influences upon Ricoeur which are explicit and pervasive include that of the Roman Catholic existentialist philosopher, Gabriel Marcel (d. 1973) which directed Ricoeur toward a concrete ontology and anthropology infused with the themes of freedom, finitude and hope. Methodologically, the greatest influence was provided by the phenomenological writings of Edmund Husserl. Karl Jaspers and Jean Nabert were other important influences. A good introduction to the sources and themes of Ricoeur's philosophy is found in John B. Thompson's 'Introduction' to *Paul Ricoeur: Hermeneutics and the Human Sciences* (CUP, Cambridge, 1981).
6 Paul Ricoeur, *The Conflict of Interpretations* (Northwestern University Press, Evanston, 1974), p. 288.
7 I. T. Ramsey, *Religious Language* (SCM, London, 1957); *Models and Mystery* (OUP, London and New York, 1964).
8 Ricoeur, *Conflict*, pp. 347ff.
9 Sykes, *The Identity of Christianity*, pp. 282, 284.
10 Sykes, *The Identity of Christianity*, p. 267.

7 Councils, Conferences and Synods

FREDERICK H. SHRIVER

In the life of the Church, councils are those representative gatherings which meet for the purpose of finding mutual consent or consensus in Christian belief and practice. In the Anglican tradition, as it has developed from the inheritance of the ancient and medieval Church through the reforms of the sixteenth century to the present, councils have functioned in different ways, with varied authority, purpose and composition. First, there are the 'general' or 'ecumenical' councils which met in the fourth through to the eighth centuries, whose significance has continued to be acknowledged in the Church of England and the other churches of the Anglican Communion.

Second, there are the national, provincial and diocesan councils, more usually called 'synods' or 'conventions', by which the various churches are governed and regulated. In the Church of England this includes the synods of the Provinces of York and Canterbury, known as 'convocations'; and the 'General Synod', which has in recent years, with the addition of lay delegates, taken over much of the historical authority of the two convocations. In the Protestant Episcopal Church in the United States of America the General Convention, which meets every three years, is actually a synod. Each church or province of the Anglican Communion is governed in a similar way, with a synod, composed of clerical, and often lay, delegates, being part of an episcopal polity.

Third, there is the Lambeth Conference of Anglican bishops, which is a kind of council. Although the Lambeth Conference has no legal authority over any of the independent Anglican churches, it does provide an opportunity for discussion of issues facing the Christian churches in general, and the Anglican Communion in particular. And there also exists the Anglican Consultative Council, which is quite different from all of the above, being more of a representative committee, the membership reflecting the international and intercultural nature of the Anglican communion. This chapter will discuss these general topics, and conclude with some remarks concerning conciliarism and its relationship to the Anglican churches and the ecumenical movement of the twentieth century.

THE ECUMENICAL COUNCILS

The first four ecumenical Councils, of Nicaea (AD 325), Constantinople (AD 381), Ephesus (AD 431), and Chalcedon (AD 451), have a special place in Anglican theology, secondary to the Scriptures themselves, but the way in which their authority is acknowledged is complex and very important in its expression of classical Anglican theological method.

In 1559 Parliament, with the assent of Elizabeth I, passed the Act of Supremacy, restoring the sovereign authority of the English Crown over the Church of England (see pp. 8–9, 107–8 and 393–6). In this Act, the 'first four General Councils' were the authority by which heresy was to be defined in the newly reformed church. No 'matter or cause' was to be considered legally as heresy, except:

such as heretofore have been determined, ordered or adjudged to be heresy by the authority of the Canonical Scriptures, or by any other General Council wherein the same was declared heresy by the express and plain words of the said Canonical Scriptures, or such as hereafter shall be ordered, judged or determined to be heresy by the High Court of Parliament of this realm, with the assent of the clergy in their Convocation; any thing in this Act contained to the contrary notwithstanding.[1]

Putting this in positive terms, the dogmatic canons of the first four councils gave, and may still be presumed to give, the Church of England and the other churches of the Anglican Communion the basic doctrine concerning the person of Christ and the relationships of the persons of the Trinity. In common with the Lutheran and Reformed Churches of the sixteenth century, the conciliar theology of the fourth and fifth centuries was considered by the Church of England to be consonant with the doctrine of the holy Scriptures, the absolute ground of Christian doctrine. The relationship between the conciliar theology and the teaching of the Scriptures was further defined in 1563.

In 1563, the thirty-nine *Articles of Religion*, devised by the Convocation as a doctrinal standard for the clergy, clarified the relationship of the decrees of the Councils to the Scriptures (see pp. 90–1). The eighth Article, 'Of the Creeds', made it clear that the Nicene Creed and the Apostles' and Athanasian Creeds (through the latter two were not 'conciliar' creeds) were to be 'received and believed: for they may be proved by most certain warrants of Holy Scripture'. As for councils themselves, Article XXI spells out clearly the authoritative view of 1563, ratified by Parliament in 1571:

General Councils may not be gathered without the commandment and will of Princes. And when they be gathered together (forasmuch as they be an assembly of men, whereof all be not governed with the Spirit and Word of God,) they may err, and sometimes have erred, even in things pertaining unto God. Wherefore things ordained by them as necessary to salvation have neither strength nor authority, unless it may be declared that they be taken out of holy Scripture.

Behind these formulas lie the struggles between the Reformed and Roman Churches in the sixteenth century. The Roman Catholic Council of Trent was coming to an end just as the Articles were being formulated. For the English and continental Protestants, the 'pope's council' was not a free and true general council. But the newly reformed Church of England wanted the world to know that it maintained the traditional Catholic faith of the Church as it existed before the illegitimate additions of extra-scriptural teaching. Also, the Protestants in general wished to affirm the traditional teaching of the Church on the incarnation and the Trinity, because of the radical theologians, like Servetus and Sozzini, who had called those doctrines into question. Moreover, if the doctrine of the ecumenical councils was used to define Christian orthodoxy, then the Roman insistence on later dogmas like transubstantiation, which had brought about the death of so many Protestants in England under Queen Mary, would be shown to be innovations.

But also, in the *Articles of Religion*, the Church of England made it clear that mere 'tradition', i.e. the decrees of councils (as well as of popes), no matter how venerable or true, could not establish beliefs that were 'necessary to salvation'. The Council of Trent had elevated church tradition to a level equal to the Scriptures. The English *Articles of Religion* expressly denied that assertion. The authority of the Church alone could never establish doctrine, but only the Word of God, enshrined and expressed in the Holy Scriptures.

And so, in the beginning of the reform of the Church of England, it was asserted that the ecumenical councils' decrees merely taken by themselves, did not establish the doctrine of the Church of England. The most that could be said is that the Act of Supremacy and the *Articles of Religion* recognized that the dogmatic decrees of the councils—including the 'Nicene' Creed, hallowed also by centuries of use in the liturgy—were definitive, but not absolute. Or to put it another way, the dogmas of the councils had only a derivative authority, because the dogmas truly expressed the teachings of the Scriptures on the vexing issues of the nature of the person of Christ, and the relationships between the persons of the Trinity.

The sixteenth-century attitude has largely been borne out by modern scholarship concerning the councils, the attitudes of the bishops who gathered there, and the way in which the councils' decrees were accepted by the Church. The councils were ecumenical, not because the emperor called the council, or because bishops issued the official statements. Rather, they became ecumenical, because over a period of several centuries the majority of Christians accepted the Niceno-Constantinopolitan Creed, the condemnation of the heresies of Arius, Apollinarius, Nestorius and Eutyches, and other conciliar formulas, such as the 'Tome of Leo' and the Decree of Chalcedon. Most of the bishops at Nicaea, for instance, held a theory of tradition which looked upon it as virtually synonymous with the Scriptures, which might be thought of as 'written' tradition. And for this reason, there was considerable opposition at the Council, and for some decades, to the term *'homoousios'* (of the same substance) which was inserted into the Creed, because it was clearly not biblical. For the Fathers of the Council, and indeed, for the heretics as well, the issue that underlay the

Arian controversy was the proper interpretation of the Church's whole teaching. But that teaching was in no way to be understood as separate from the Scriptures. There had not developed in the conciliar period itself a theory which would have considered the possibility of discrepancy between tradition and Scripture. As S. L. Greenslade put it: 'While the ultimate authority of Scripture was always affirmed, the notion of tradition, though very powerful, was not precise (perhaps by its very nature it cannot be) and the possibility of modifying or correcting tradition by fresh understanding of Scripture was insufficiently considered.'[2]

In the century or so which followed the Elizabethan Settlement it became necessary for Anglican theologians to clarify the meaning of the Church of England's teaching on the authority of the councils. Some Anglican theologians, and the *Book of Homilies* (see pp. 148–50), were ready to acknowledge the authority of the first six; adding to the four cited above, Constantinople (553), and Constantinople (681). But as the *Oxford Dictionary of the Christian Church* succinctly puts it, 'It appears [. . .] that such Councils are ultimately revered in the [Church] of [England] on the ground that their decisions are acceptable rather than vice versa'.[3] Probably the best statement of the Anglican attitude toward the general councils which has prevailed is to be found in the comment on Article XXII of Gilbert Burnet, the Bishop of Salisbury from 1689 to 1715:

> As to the strict notion of a general council, there is great reason to believe that there was never any assembly to which it will be found to agree. And for the four general councils, which this church declares she receives, they are received only because we are persuaded from the scriptures that their decisions were made according to them: that the Son is truly God, of the same substance with the Father. That the Holy Ghost is also truly God. That the divine nature was truly united to the human in Christ; and that in one person. That both natures remained distinct; and that the human nature was not swallowed up of the divine. These truths we find in the scriptures, and therefore we believe them. We reverence those councils for the sake of their doctrine; but do not believe the doctrine for the authority of the councils. There appeared too much of human frailty in some of their other proceedings, to give us such an implicit submission to them, as to believe things only because they so decided them.[4]

In the sixteenth and seventeenth centuries Richard Field and William Laud are typical examples of theologians who would have been in agreement with Burnet. Field was very 'respectful' of the councils and the bishops who sat in them:

when there is a lawful General Council [...] we are so strongly to presume that it is true and right that with unanimous consent is agreed on in such a Council, that we must not so much as profess publicity that we think otherwise, unless we do most certainly know the contrary; yet may we in the secret of our hearts remain in some doubt, carefully seeking by the Scripture and monuments of Antiquity to find out the truth [...] But concerning the General Councils [...] we confess that in respect of the matter about which they were called, so nearly and essentially concerning the life and soul of the Christian Faith, and in respect of the manner and form of their proceeding, and the evidence of the proof brought in them, they are and ever were expressly to be believed by all such as perfectly understand the meaning of their determination.[5]

William Laud (see p. 268), in his 'Conversations with Mr Fisher the Jesuit' pointed out that a council, being representative, has only the authority that belongs to the Church, and nothing more. Agreeing with Augustine, he notes that though a general council may be relied on to have the assistance of the Holy Spirit, that does not mean that general councils are infallible. 'It seems it was no news with St Augustine, that a General Council might err, and therefore [be] inferior to the Scripture.' Or, as he puts it elsewhere, 'the Scripture is absolutely and every way divine; the Church's definition is but *suo modo*, "In a sort or manner", divine. But that which is but in a sort can never be a foundation in a higher degree than that which is absolute and ever such.'[6] In this, Laud was a clear follower of the *Articles of Religion* (as indeed he was obliged to be) and points the way to Burnet.

The rise of modern critical historical study of the Scriptures and Christian doctrine, beginning in the seventeenth century, has required an adjustment in Anglican theology concerning the relationship between tradition (in this instance specifically as concerning the authority of conciliar doctrine) and the Scriptures. It slowly became evident that it could no longer be possible to see this simply in terms of conflict. The decree of Trent concerning tradition and the Scriptures was more controversial in its own day within the Roman Catholic Church than contemporary Protestants would allow, or could understand. Heiko Oberman has distinguished two different attitudes towards tradition in late medieval theology. Oberman calls 'Tradition I' the understanding of tradition as the 'history of obedient interpretation of the Scriptures' within the Church, as represented by the great theologians. This understanding would describe the attitude of Protestant and Anglican theologians of the sixteenth and seventeenth centuries to the relationship of conciliar decrees and scriptural doctrine, and is represented by the quotations from Burnet, Field and Laud above. Oberman's 'Tradition II' is the understanding of tradition as embedded in Scripture but overflowing in extrascriptural apostolic tradition handed down through episcopal succession'.[7] The latter view is what Protestant theologians believed that the Council of Trent's decree entailed. Laud's observation, quoted above, could not be reconciled with such an understanding of tradition. Later Anglican repudiation of the papal decrees on the Immaculate Conception, papal infallibility, and the Assumption in the nineteenth and twentieth centuries would be in keeping with the traditional Anglican distinction.

On the other hand, the Deistic controversy of the eighteenth century, and the hostile environment of the Enlightenment, brought about a much more sympathetic attitude towards tradition within Anglican theology. The Deists and Unitarians showed the orthodox Anglicans that the uninterpreted text of the New Testament could not serve as clear and unmistakable evidence for the doctrines of the Trinity, and the incarnation alone. The Church's *traditional* interpretation, represented by the credal and conciliar *formulae*, as well as a continued recognition of those doctrines by patristic, medieval and post-Reformation Protestant and Roman Catholic theologians alike, brought about the recognition that even Anglicans had to acknowledge *tradition*, albeit according to Oberman's category 'Tradition I.'

In the twentieth century there has been considerable discussion of the place of the councils in the development of a teaching authority in the Church.[8]

The complex way in which their authority came to be understood has led theologians to question to what degree the conciliar theology, particularly its terminology and metaphysical assumptions, must be honoured in order to be loyal to the authority of the Scriptures. Anglican theologians have differed in their opinions concerning this question. Theoretically, the question is how far the Church might go in revising the traditional language by which we speak of the person of Christ and the persons of the Trinity. On the one hand, there are those who would insist that the vocabulary of the conciliar definitions is sacrosanct and unalterable. On the other hand, there are those who believe that the vocabulary is time-bound, and does not express fully either a modern or biblical understanding of God (see pp. 123–7).[9]

SYNODICAL GOVERNMENT

The 'Anglican Communion' may be said to have come into existence with the reformation of the Church of Ireland in the sixteenth and seventeenth centuries. The anomalous Episcopal Church of Scotland was forced into independent existence in 1689, then followed the creation of the Protestant Episcopal Church in the United States of America in 1789 as the result of the American Revolution, and the Anglican Churches in New Zealand, Australia and Canada, and a host of others in the wake of the development of the British Empire and its dissolution. All of these churches, whatever their different relationships to Crown or Parliament, have been governed synodically, even though they also have their individual political characteristics.

It is not possible within the scope of this chapter to discuss the history and development of the varied polities of the Anglican churches. Looking at the global Anglican Communion from the perspective of the late twentieth century, we see the various independent Anglican churches governed by 'councils' which recognize bishops' authority in some form as crucial and distinct, but which include not only representation from the presbyterate, but also from the laity.

This synodical character owes a great deal to the tradition of the Church going back to the second century at least (some would say to the first century, and the 'council' of the church in Jerusalem recorded in Acts 15, c. AD 50) and the common human experience of consulting in a body when important decisions have to be made. But the development of synodical government also reflects the spread of increasingly democratic forms of representative government in the secular governments. If England is in some sense the 'Mother of Parliaments', the Church of England is also a mother of representative government within the Church. The formation of the Episcopal Church in the United States, whose General Convention with a House of Bishops and a House of Deputies, including laymen (and laywomen since 1973), was established in the 1780s, is the first example of the interaction of inherited English secular and ecclesiastical forms producing a new Anglican polity. Since then, the representative character of synodical government in the Anglican churches has been clearly established.

But this representative character affects only individual churches, or independent 'Provinces'. The Anglican Communion, rather like the international fellowships of the other non-Roman Catholic Christian bodies, is not in the Roman Catholic sense, an international 'church'. There is no Anglican authority which stands above the Church of England, the *Nippon Sei Ko Kwai*, or the Church of the Province of West Africa, for instance. There may well be doubts as to whether or not this is a good thing. The missionary movement, British and American imperialism, the dissolution of the British Empire, and serious awareness of the need for independence from assumptions of Anglo-American cultural superiority, brought about the tremendous growth of non-English Anglican churches. An independence of spirit as well as literal independence has ensued. But, naturally enough, the younger churches often look to the mother churches, still richer and more influential in ecumenical dialogue, for guidance. The vestiges of imperial and colonial attitudes are not dead by any means. But just as the nations on the planet have not devised a system of international government, neither has the Anglican Communion been able, or wanted, to create a means by which the different sister churches might unite with some form of central authority. The tensions between a desire for unity and a desire for independence have been evident throughout the Communion, at least since the early decades of the nineteenth century.

THE LAMBETH CONFERENCES

The Anglican tradition's common experience of episcopacy, symbolized by the historical link with the see of Canterbury, as well as a common and complex liturgical tradition, has provided a measure of unity, especially as the Lambeth Conferences have developed. That conference of bishops has demonstrated the usefulness, perhaps even the necessity, of inter-Anglican co-operation , but it has also shown that an overarching authority will not be easy to achieve. If there were to be a greater measure of formal unity within the Anglican Communion it would have to be in some sense conciliar, because of the developments noted above.

The first conference of Anglican bishops met at the Archbishop of Canterbury's London home, Lambeth Palace, in September 1867. It was composed of bishops from England, Ireland, Canada, the United States and various parts of the colonial British Empire. There had been interest expressed in the formation of some kind of international Anglican synod, especially in the United States and Canada, since the 1850s. The actual conference took place because of the action of the triennial Synod of the Province of Canada in requesting Archbishop Longley of Canterbury to summon 'a National Synod of the Bishops of the Anglican Church at home and abroad'.[10] It ended after only four days of meeting without any great accomplishments, but its great achievement was simply to have met.

The second Lambeth Conference, in 1878, was far more significant than the first since it went further in establishing a precedent. The third, in 1888, was summoned by Archbishop Edward White Benson without any petition from abroad. It was in the context of this Conference that the famous 'Lambeth Quadrilateral' emerged (see pp. 249–50). One of the items on the Archbishop's agenda had been the relationship between the Anglican Churches and the other Christian churches. In the General Convention of the Episcopal Church in the United States in Chicago in 1885, a resolution had been passed by the House of Bishops which set out four principles which were to be the basis of discussions on church unity between the Anglican churches and the other churches—the Holy Scriptures, the

Apostles' and Nicene Creeds, the two sacraments of Baptism and the Supper of the Lord, and the historic episcopate 'locally adapted'. This resolution, without any legal or binding force, has come to be regarded by many Anglicans as an important reference point governing the relations with other churches.

It was also at this time that Archbishop Benson enunciated what was to become the generally agreed-upon understanding of this Anglican episcopal conference (the words are taken from his diary):

> I opened the Conference by pointing out that the Conference was in no sense a Synod and not adapted, or competent, or within its powers, if it should attempt to make binding decisions on doctrines or discipline—the unsuitableness to the constitution of our church—and its relation to America—the fact that they had been foreseen and settled by Archbishop Longley and Tait in their addresses,etc.[11]

The subsequent Conferences—among them 1920, with an important appeal for Christian unity, and 1948, which helped heal the terrible disruption brought about by World War II—have reflected the tremendous growth of the Anglican churches outside the Anglo-Saxon world. The range of topics that have been discussed, and that to some degree have been reflected in the printed reports, have developed Anglican self-consciousness in the midst of great cultural diversity. But from the beginning, Christian unity beyond the confines of Anglicanism has also been one of the leading themes. The Lambeth Conferences have become enormous, and consequently there have been serious criticisms concerning their value: for instance their expense, their practical ineffectiveness, the English, or Anglo-Saxon domination in the proceedings, and their limitation to bishops only. But as the practice came into being through a desire for consultation on common problems, there has not yet been created another effective way in which mutual responsibility can be totally exercised.

There were three large international meetings or Congresses of Anglicans, open to laity, held in London in 1908, Minneapolis in 1954 and Toronto in 1963. Today it seems most unlikely that anything quite like them will occur again, but the latter two, in particular, underlined the fact that whatever the importance of the Lambeth Conferences, they could not be understood as being the sole voice of international Anglicanism. The Congresses helped many Anglicans to articulate and understand the variety and unity that were a part of the Communion. With the influence of Archbishop Arthur Michael Ramsey, and Bishop Stephen Bayne, Executive Officer of the Anglican Communion from 1960 to 1967, the Congress in Toronto was a preparation for the work of the Lambeth Conference of 1968. This Conference, reflecting the growing worldwide sense of the problems of the

211

'Third World' and the chasm between the rich and poor nations and churches, established the Anglican Consultative Council. This first met in 1971, and has continued to play an important part in the cohesion of the Anglican Communion. As Bishop John Howe, the Secretary General of the Council from 1971 to 1982, has stated,

> In several respects, the Anglican Consultative Council (ACC) was, and is, unique. It remains the only international Anglican body with a constitution. Also it was authorized by the Communion as a whole [. . .] [It] includes clergy and lay people. Every Anglican Church has members [. . .] The total number is comparatively small, partly to facilitate a frequency of meetings [. . .] The ACC meets every two or three years, and its Standing Committee annually. As far as possible the Council is to meet 'in various parts of the world'.[12]

The Council is still relatively young, and its activities, to the member churches, and individual church members, remain somewhat obscure. It suffers from the same problems that all 'executive bodies' of large institutions endure. But it is, at the very least, like its venerable parent the episcopal conferences of Lambeth, a guarantee that the individual Anglican churches will not be allowed utterly to remain in provincial indifference. And it may well evolve, like the Lambeth Conferences, in ways that will promote the unity of the Communion.

CONCLUSION

The 'conciliar' nature of the Anglican Communion is perhaps one of the least recognized, and yet most characteristic, features of modern Anglicanism. It is a characteristic that is shared with almost all other Christian bodies, and one that has been an important part of the Ecumenical Movement. The hope for a truly general council of Christendom has been in existence with particular poignancy ever since the Great Schism in the papacy in the fourteenth and fifteenth centuries. For the Protestants of the Reformation era, the Council of Trent was decidedly not that hoped-for Council. But, venerating the accomplishment of the first four councils as they did, both Luther and Calvin held up the conciliar ideal as a function of the Church as the *communio sanctorum*—the communion of saints.[13] The Roman Catholic Church experienced a burst of energy and enthusiasm for conciliarism following the Second Vatican Council. The World Council of Churches' Lima Document on Baptism, Eucharist, and Ministry, a 'conciliar' document of a kind, produced in 1972, became one of the most discussed theological pronouncements in the history of the Christian Church. Both of these developments seemed to offer hope for a growing atmosphere conductive to church unity. But as the year 2000 draws near, although Pope John Paul II's gestures toward non-Roman Catholic Christians seem a hopeful sign, the fragmentation and controversy throughout world Christianity, within and between the individual Christian Churches, makes some kind of genuine conciliarism (as well as conciliation!) to be as necessary as it also appears to be unattainable.

Nevertheless, a recognition of the way in which truly ecumenical conciliar principles, which are consonant with one of the most basic of Anglican principles, could work toward Christian communion, must remain a goal. It is necessary for Anglicans to recognize, precisely because of their confrontation with interior controversy, that they are being called to clarify, for themselves and for other Christians, what true conciliarism might become. For Anglicans a modern conciliarism, mirroring the development in Anglican polity, would mean not only retaining the significant role of bishops (often erroneously considered to be the sole distinguishing characteristic of the Anglican Communion), but also representative participation of the other clerical and lay orders in the Church.

If the function of the episcopate in the Church is to call to the individual Churches' attention the fact that the Church is truly a world fellowship—i.e. ecumenical and catholic—then that function is displayed most clearly when the episcopate meets together, in council. The bishops of the church, however, in the developing practice of the independent national or provincial Anglican churches, are not the sole representatives of the *consensus fidelium*, the fellowship of the faithful. The clergy and laity are also part of that representative consensus. If the bishops of the great ecumenical councils of the fourth and fifth centuries saw themselves as truly representative of the faith of the Church as it has been received, and as it was understood by the presbyters and laity, then—in the absence of the imperial authority which called those councils into being—the conciliar nature of the Church must include, in some way, the representatives of the whole Church, and not bishops alone.

The recent statements of the Anglican–Roman Catholic International Commission have dealt with the issue of conciliar authority in the context of the issues of episcopal and papal authority. There, perhaps inevitably, considering that papal infallibility and primacy are the most divisive issues between the Anglican and Roman Churches, councils are assumed to be episcopal councils. Nevertherless, the 1976 Venice Statement on Authority in the Church (I), has acknowledged the place of the clergy and laity along with the bishop in the exercise of the bishops' 'special responsibility for promoting truth and discerning error'. And furthermore that 'the interaction of bishop and people in [the] exercise of [that special responsibility] is a safeguard of Christian life and fidelity'.[14]

The Venice Statement and its 'Elucidation' in 1981 reiterate certain classical Anglican positions, returning to the *Articles of Religion*, and their interpretation by later Anglican theologians. Conciliar decrees are only binding when they 'formulate the central truths of salvation', and when 'faithful to Scripture and consistent with Tradition'. Also, it is pointed out that a balance must be maintained between 'primacy' and 'conciliarity'.[15] The Commission was discussing the immediate issue of the primatial authority of the Bishop of Rome. But the principle could be applied as well to the primacy of any of the bishops within their provincial or diocesan jurisdiction.

The International Commission also clarified the place of the 'reception' by the Church in the authenticity of binding conciliar decrees, by explaining that

Reception does not create nor legitimize the decision: it is the final indication that such a decision has fulfilled the necessary conditions for it to be a true expression of the faith. In this acceptance the whole Church is involved in a continous process of discernment and response. The Commission [. . .] on the one hand rejects the view that a definition has no authority until it is accepted by the whole Church or even derives its authority solely from that acceptance. Equally, the Commission denies that a council is so evidently self-sufficient that its definitions owe nothing to reception.[16]

As has been noted above, the Anglican Communion has no developed positive teaching on conciliar authority, principally because of the recognition of the splintered character of the Catholic Church since the sixteenth century (or perhaps the eleventh). But the whole drift of the history of the Anglican tradition, in the context of the development of parliamentary representation and democratic government, has been to strengthen the impression that the important decisions concerning the Church's faith and life can only be made in the context of a truly representative body. In the latter part of the twentieth century, therefore, Anglicans must articulate a new conciliar theology. On the one hand there is the energizing example of the Second Vatican Council of the Roman Catholic Church under the Pope,[17] on the other is the encouraging example of the conciliar theological consensus developing within the structure of the World Council of Churches.[18] Councils alone have never solved the Church's problems. Their authority is limited and temporary. But they can articulate effectively for their own time authentic Christian witness and belief. Then, like the general councils of the ancient Church, they may be seen to have spoken according to the Holy Spirit. The Christian Church would appear to have found no better way to strive towards unity than through the practice of holding conference in councils.

BIBLIOGRAPHY

Anglican–Roman Catholic International Commission, *The Final Report*. SPCK and Catholic Truth Society, London, 1982.

Board for Mission and Unity, *Towards a Church of England Response to BEM and ARCIC*. Church House Publishing, London, 1985.

Greenslade, S. L., 'The English Reformers and the Councils of the Church', *Oecumenica*, (1967), pp. 95–115.

Hill, C. and Yarnold, E. (eds), *Anglicans and Roman Catholics: The Search for Unity*. SPCK/CTS, London, 1994.

Huizing, Peter and Walf, Knut (eds), *The Ecumenical Council: Its Significance in the Constitution of the Church*. T. & T. Clark, Edinburgh/Seabury Press, New York, 1983.

Margull, Hans (ed.), *The Councils of the Church*. Fortress Press, Philadelphia, 1961, esp. S. Neill, 'The Anglican Communion and the Ecumenical Council', pp. 370–90.

NOTES

1 G. R. Elton, *The Tudor Constitution* (CUP 1965), p. 368.

2 S. L. Greenslade, 'The Authorities Appealed to by the First Four General Councils' in *Councils and the Ecumenical Movement*, WCC Studies No. 5 (WCC, Geneva, 1968), p. 53.

3 *Oxford Dictionary of the Christian Church* (OUP, London, 1957), p. 977.

4 G. Burnet, *An Exposition of the Thirty-Nine Articles* (Oxford 1845), p. 239.

5 R. Field, *Of the Church* (Cambridge 1852), Vol. iv, p.60.

6 W. Laud, *A Relation of the Conference between William Laud [...] and Mr. Fisher the Jesuit* in *Works* (Oxford 1849), Vol. ii, p. 276.

7 Heiko A. Oberman, *Forerunners of the Reformation* (New York, 1966), pp. 54–5 *et passim*.

8 As an example of the difficulty of establishing an *absolute* statement of the authority of a conciliar declaration in Anglican theology, see J. Robert Wright, 'The Authority of Chalcedon for Anglicans' in G. R. Evans (ed.), *Christian Authority: Essays in Honour of Henry Chadwick* (New York and Oxford, 1988), pp. 224–50.

9 The Anglican–Roman Catholic International Commission in their 'Elucidation' of 1981 attempted to deal with this matter, in stating that the 'Scriptures are the uniquely inspired witness to divine revelation', but recognizing that also it is 'impossible' to express the truths of revelation without 'resorting to current language and thought'. The 'Elucidation' uses *'homoousios'* as an example of a word that is 'different from the original text of Scripture without being alien to its meaning'. At the end of this particular section, the Commission calls for a balance between the recognition of the definitive character of the Scriptures and the necessity of drawing 'upon everything in human experience and thought which will give to the content of the revelation its fullest expression and widest application'. Anglican–Roman Catholic International Commission, *The Final Report* (SPCK/CTS, London, 1982), pp. 70–1.

10 J. Howe, *Highways and Hedges: Anglicanism and the Universal Church* (Anglican Consultative Council 1985), p. 62.

11 A. C. Benson, *Life of Edward White Benson* (London 1899), Vol. ii, p. 214, quoted in A. M. G. Stephenson, *Anglicanism and the Lambeth Conferences* (SPCK, London 1978), p. 79.

12 Howe, *Highways and Hedges* pp. 85–6.

13 F. W. Kantzenbach, 'The Call for a Council in the 16th Century—the Protestant View of Councils' in *Councils and the Ecumenical Movement* (WCC, Geneva, 1968), p. 109.

14 Anglican–Roman Catholic International Commission, *The Final Report*, pp. 61-2.

15 *The Final Report* pp. 62, 71–2.

16 *The Final Report* p. 72.

17 Huizing and Walf, *The Ecumenical Council*, esp. essays by Tavard and Alberigo.

18 Günther Gassman, *Documentary History of Faith and Order 1963–1993* (WCC, Geneva, 1993), pp. 203, 209–39.

8 Canon Law

DANIEL B. STEVICK

LAW IN THE CHURCH

In a general sense, every ecclesial body has a law if only because it must have considered, agreed ways of determining and carrying out common purposes. However communitarian, egalitarian, informal and charismatic it may be, every group has structure, leadership and internal rule, even if its self-regulation takes the form of unwritten, largely uncriticized traditions.

Religious movements and groups begin in particular times and places, but as they spread, they become more complex and enclose greater human variety. Gradually they become institutionalized. That is to say, their way of working becomes articulated in social structures, differentiation of functions, and a body of written regulations that govern officers and members. Persons within a group often perceive this process of institutionalization as loss as well as gain, but it is inevitable. An institutional church is implied in the Church's humanity.[1] One might argue that an institutional church is implied in an incarnational faith.

There is no doubt always some tension between Spirit and institution; but a community's maturation need not be thought of as diminishing the role of the Spirit. The free, sovereign Spirit can create order as well as criticize it. Both continuity and innovation, authority as well as the questioning of authority, can be initiatives of the Spirit.

Laws of the state as well as of the Church may at times be unapologeti-

216

cally pragmatic. When it is overtaken by events, the Church, seeking the mind of the Spirit, does what it must, sometimes acting wisely and well. But to follow the criterion of workability or of mere effectiveness can mislead the Church. There may be some things that the Church, living under the cross, is called to do whether or not they yield measurable results. Beyond workability, each faith community's law seeks to express in structures and processes what it sees to be the fundamental nature of the Church. All laws are informed and judged by a body of non-legal material. Church law specifically derives from and is answerable to a theological account of the Church and the faith. However, the deepest nature of the Church is a mystery, 'hidden with Christ in God' (Col. 3.3), which it is always exploring. No forms of institutional life fully bring it to expression. The Church lives by ceaseless self-discovery and self-correction, and all of its laws, procedures and institutions are provisional.

To say that the forms of the Church's life are provisional is not to say that they are unimportant. The Church is itself God-given—the 'pillar and bulwark of the truth' (1 Tim. 3.15). It is, as is often said, 'a part of its own creed'. Some basic institutions seem to belong to the very reality of the Church itself. While forms are not the community, yet through the articulation or formedness of its life, the community is fulfilled. Canon law can assist the Church to be the Church.

Any church is impoverished if it does not have good, stable laws for its own governance. However, if law is necessary, legalism and overlegislation are a burden. A church is ill-governed if its laws do not prescribe with a light touch, speaking principally to things that are essential for unity and mission, trusting the discretion of the baptized people, and keeping the common life free to respond to new conditions when they arise.

LAW IN ANGLICANISM

Having entered these general propositions, we turn to speak more specifically of the ways of law in Anglican experience. The self-governing provinces of the Anglican Communion are united by a loose but identifiable theological, ministerial, sacramental and liturgical tradition. To a great extent, they all cite the same authorities and historical landmarks—from the Prayer Books of 1549 and 1552 to William Temple and Michael Ramsey. This English indebtedness continues even though English Anglicans are now outnumbered by non-English Anglicans, and most of the Provinces of Anglicanism have produced their own leaders of life and thought and have taken somewhat independent directions. When Anglicans anywhere tell their own story, it is, in its opening chapters, an English story.

However, one cannot speak of a common tradition of Anglican canon law as one can speak of an Anglican tradition in theology or liturgy or spirituality. The provinces of Anglicanism can and do take their own way, adapting their institutional life to their social settings. They often act in awareness of one another, but they all have their own histories and cultural backgrounds, their moments of crisis of significant innovation, and they are likely to grow more divergent as the institutional ties with England with which many of them began recede into the past.

In their early generations, most of the churches of the Anglican Communion lived with some of English canon law actually in effect. In some cases, the Church of England was carried abroad to serve the needs of English persons engaged in diplomatic service or trade. In other places colonial populations carried their church with them and replicated its familiar life as much as they could. In still other places, churches grew from the work of English missionary societies, operating with devotion in difficult locations under charters from England and the general oversight of English bishops, building up indigenous Christian congregations. Such law as was in effect in these churches was English church law. In time, some Anglican provinces developed which had no colonial experience.

Through the nineteenth century and into the early twentieth, in England and in the colonial and independent churches, canon law was a pervasive, defining presence; an effectively working church required law and a respect for law. Moreover, church life under law was supported by learned canonists and a tradition of legal scholarship. (Some of the legal scholars were clerics, but some were lay persons who were lawyers and jurists.) The study of church law was worthy of the attention of the first-class minds.

Yet rather rapidly in this century church law has come to be given little attention in Anglican discourse or in the preparation of clergy. The substantial works of history and commentary that were produced in the past have neither been kept up to date nor replaced, and present day canonists are, to a great extent, using a literature several generations old. (The exception is England, where the continued use of ancient charters and the complex matters of property and appointment keep up a demand for persons learned in church law.) Many accounts of Anglicanism say nothing but canon law, and otherwise well-informed Anglicans may hardly be aware of its existence.

Yet 'Laws', as Richard Hooker said, 'are matters of principal consequence.'[2] They touch every church member. They establish structures of common life within which Christians can live with responsibility and joy—or else conditions which hinder life in faith. They bring to present-day life the cumulative wisdom of the past. They seek to adjust fairly the relations between the power centres of a varied and widely spread community engaged under the gospel with its own upbuilding and in witness

218

and service in its society. When laws are doing their work, they can be taken for granted. Occasionally, however, an internal crisis brings the Church's law out of obscurity. Letters in the church press discuss urgently what the law of the Church is and how it should be administered and interpreted. Church lawyers come into prominence; perhaps having to do their work with less background than they wish they had. Some parties contend that the law as it is should be obeyed, others that it should be changed. While some persons think the law should be made more specific, others think it should be left benignly vague. The believability and indeed the future of the community seems to hinge on how it deals with a conflict of authority, doctrine, worship, pastoral discipline or mission. The Church is ill-served when the formal laws by which it coheres as a community are little attended to.

THE TRADITION OF CHURCH LAW

Initially, the institutional life of the Provinces of Anglicanism was modelled on that of the Church of England as much as local conditions permitted. Their tradition and practice of church law traced to English canon law. Canonists in parts of the world far removed from England spoke familiarly of the early councils, of the *Corpus Juris Canonici*, of Lyndwood's *Provinciale*, of the *Canons of 1604*, of Johnson's two volumes of *The Laws and Canons of the Church of England* (1720, republished in 1851), of Sir Robert Phillimore's two even larger volumes of exposition of *The Ecclesiastical Law of the Church of England* (2nd edn, 1895), and of the splendid historical review in the 1947 report *Canon Law in the Church of England*.

Through this British inheritance of laws and comment, the churches of Anglicanism are heirs of an older, Western, Catholic tradition of ecclesiastical law.

This deep history has its origins in the writings of the apostolic generation. The earliest Church was shaped by its traditions concerning Jesus Christ (first in oral form and then in the written Gospels), by the faithfully transmitted kerygma (1 Cor. 15.3–8), the authority of apostles, prophets and teachers (2 Cor. 10—12; 1 Cor. 12.1–11; Eph. 4.11–14; the Pastoral Epistles), the practice of the sacraments (1 Cor. 11.23–6; Rom. 6:3–11), the acknowledged importance of Spirit-led event (Acts 10.34–48), collective deliberation (Acts 15.1–35), some ethical guidelines (Gal. 5.16–26; Eph. 5.21—6:9), and by the place of common custom (1 Cor. 11.16b). Letters gave counsel on such matters as worship (1 Cor. 11—14), marriage (1 Cor. 7.1–24), and distinctions among sins (1 John 5.16–17). These are elements of the common life, present from the beginning, concerning which laws would in time come to be written.

219

From the second century on, church governance was chiefly through bishops' decretals (advisory letters) and regional and (after Nicaea) general councils which gave their determinations in 'canons'. (The word originally meant a stick, a measuring rod or a straightedge. Canons were to guide true church usage.) In the early centuries, express regulation was called forth by differences or questions, and judgements depended heavily on local bishops who followed the customs and precedents they knew. In time, the written laws were gathered, the *Dionysiana* by Dionysius Exiguus, c. 514, being a notable collection. But church law was not ordered in a systematic way until the late Middle Ages—only with Gratian's *Decretum* (mid-twelfth century).

In the centuries of Christendom, the spirituality and the temporality were the same people. Royalty were persons of the Church, and bishops' courts adjudicated some community matters. Throughout the Middle Ages there was often tension between individual innovation and collective authority, between monastic communities and diocesan structures, between Church and Crown, and between central and local judicatories. There were long disputes about property and the power of appointment to office. The important law code, the *Corpus Juris Canonici* (fifteenth century) gathered up the legal texts of the medieval Church. Although there was a large body of written law which centered in papal law, in practice, custom also governed, and church rule depended heavily on cases and on interpretations by courts. Regional differences were common.

The Church in England was fully bound into this medieval system. The greatest medieval English canonist was William Lyndwood (c. 1375–1446) whose *Provinicale* (1430), was a study of the legislation of the Province of Canterbury as related to all canon law. In the last century there was a scholarly effort to claim a measure of independence for English church law, but it was answered by equally competent scholarship.

The sixteenth-century Reformation disrupted old laws and structures and made necessary not only new laws but a new basis for law-making. 'The Submission of the Clergy', an act which passed in both Convocations in 1534, resolved that 'The Bishop of Rome has not in Scripture, any greater jurisdiction in the kingdom of England than any other foreign bishop.'[3] Thus the Church of England removed itself from the jurisdiction of the principal law-making power in the Western Church.

Although medieval canon law continued in effect except where it had been set aside by acts of the Crown, it was awkward to govern by laws which had in part been invalidated by the rejection of papal authority, and under Henry VIII and Edward VI some efforts were made at canonical reform. A monument to this effort is the *Reformatio Legum Ecclesiasticarum*, a large work whose authorization was cut off by the death of Edward VI and which was only published in 1570 under Archbishop Parker.

Under Elizabeth several sets of canons were enacted by Convocation and given royal assent, but it was understood that these laws lapsed with the Queen's death. When James I came to the throne, the need for clearer laws led to the most important piece of church legislation that emerged in the formative decades of the Church of England. The *Canons of 1604* were drawn up largely under Richard Bancroft and were adopted by both Convocations, but not approved by Parliament. This body of 141 canons gathered up changes in church government since the break with Rome. These canons deal with such matters as the authority of the Church and its relation to the Crown, church furnishings and ceremonial, and clerical duties, conduct and dress. The 1604 canons were not a complete code of church law, and prior regulations continued in effect where they had not been superseded. Some of these canons articulated the self-definition of the Church of England, while others in time became quaint and obsolete. These canons have remained a central part of 'the standing orders of the Church of England'.[4]

At this time, Richard Hooker, in his *Of The Laws of Ecclesiastical Polity*, advanced the Church of England's sense of identity. He does not discuss English church law as such, but sets forth a profoundly and subtly argued account of authority and structure in the Church. He stands in the tradition of natural law theorists, seeing law as in the nature of things. Good laws of church or state are a participation in the divine governing of creation. Yet Hooker is also modern, recognizing that laws are human constructions and that sound laws are not everywhere the same and that they change.

Over time, modifications of the 1604 canons were adopted, and many parts of what had been governed by church law and courts came under parliamentary law and civil courts. Since the canon law of England is not codified, its older pre-Reformation components continue in effect except where later legislation has occupied the field. However, when new legislation is adopted, the old law is seldom expressly revoked. Thus the law must be gathered from a variety of canons, acts, charters and decisions of courts, Convocation, Parliament and the Crown. Thus the modern period in English church law is called 'the period of mixed sources'.[5] It is often difficult to establish what the law is as well as to interpret it for present cases. This cumulative and somewhat untidy body of sources can seem unsatisfactory to anyone who looks at it from the vantage of a body of constitutional law produced in the modern period. Indeed, it was found unsatisfactory by many persons in the Church of England.[6] However, this body of church legislation, contained in sources of many kinds from many generations, is a sign

that the law has grown organically from the rich, complex, continuous life of a people.
We shall return to canon law in England. But first we digress.

TRADITION AND MODERNITY

Since the formative legislative events in the Church of England, canon law has had to enter a different environment. Law which had been at home in the world of St Thomas and William Lyndwood and Bishop Gibson had to enter the world of Locke and Montesquieu. Laws and institutions that expressed a static hierarchical social order have had to come to terms with the force of popular sovereignty.

The church settlement that had come about in England in the sixteenth and seventeenth centuries was not developed with the idea that it might be exportable. Yet the slow transition of Anglican institutions into the modern world began outside England.

The ecclesiastical life of Scotland remained independent of England even after the two nations were united under James I (James VI of Scotland). Under the doctrinaire leadership of John Knox and Andrew Melville, Calvinist theology and a Presbyterian church order were established in Scotland. For many generations, the Presbyterians and the churches that continued to follow an episcopal order were in conflict. Under the Stuarts, the Episcopalians flourished; but when, after the Commonwealth and the Restoration, William and Mary were brought to the throne in the late seventeenth century, the Scottish Episcopalians continued loyal to the Stuarts, an allegiance which marginalized and diminished the movement for a century. After the final defeat of the Jacobite cause at the Battle of Culloden in 1746, harsh penal laws were enforced against the Episcopalians, and the church was greatly weakened—a condition in which it remained for a time even after the laws were lifted.

Through these difficult years the continuity of the church was to a great extent provided by a small group of bishops. In 1743 the bishops issued a Code of Canons, an action which moved the church towards constitutional episcopal government. Under these canons, the bishops elected a Primus, who held the office during the pleasure of the other bishops. Presbyters of a diocese elected their bishop, subject to the consent of the Primus and a majority of the other bishops. Synods were comprised of bishops, although deans could attend with voice but no vote. The state of liturgy had become disordered, and the bishops in 1743 commended the use of the Scottish Communion Office, a rite in the richer tradition that traced through the Scottish Prayer book of 1637 to the prayer Book of 1549.

The freedom of the Scottish bishops allowed them to respond to an initiative from America. Samuel Seabury, the bishop-elect of Connecticut, having sought consecration in England for a year without success, came to the Scottish bishops, who having no ties with the state were able to act freely for what they saw as the well-being of the Church. In 1784 at Aberdeen, Seabury was consecrated by three Scottish bishops. He at once entered into a Concordat with them, pledging to seek to have the church of Connecticut follow the Scottish order in its eucharistic liturgy. Through Seabury's influence, the rite of Holy Communion in the Episcopal Church has carried the marks of the Scottish/Nonjuring tradition, as distinct from the tradition of the English Prayer Books.

At the end of the eighteenth century the Scottish Episcopal Church gathered new strength and confidence under the leadership of John Skinner (1786–1816), Bishop of Aberdeen. A revision of canon law in 1811 brought presbyters into the Synod of the church. In a visit to Scotland, John Henry Hobart, Bishop of New York, urged, on the basis of the American experience, that lay persons be involved in the practical administration of the church. His counsel received some favourable response, but it was not until the 1863 revision of the Code of Canons that laymen began to take a significant part in the church's assemblies.

The Episcopal Church in Scotland has continued along lines set by the formative events of the eighteenth and early nineteenth centuries as an episcopal community independent of the British Crown, governed by its own canons, and with a strong liturgical tradition.

At this same time a somewhat similar history was unfolding across the Atlantic. When the colonies on the east coast of the North American continent broke their ties with the British commonwealth, by necessity the authority of English church law was broken as well. Could the ecclesial identity that had been achieved in England since the sixteenth century be carried into the life of another nation? If so, how could loyalty and continuity (not just to the Church of England, but to the Catholic origins which were conveyed through it) combine with a new moment of beginning?

William White of Philadelphia took the initiative to bring the isolated and disorganized former colonial churches together in a series of representative 'conventions'. The newly independent American Church sought to remain loyal to its English heritage, declaring that it was 'far from intending to depart from the Church of England in any essential point of doctrine, discipline or worship; or further than local circumstances require'.[7] In time, the American church secured continuity in doctrine, liturgy, sacraments and ministry with the Church of England—revising the Prayer Book (but not radically), retaining the *Articles of Religion* (but not requiring anyone to subscribe to them), and securing the episcopate (but not easily).[8] However, relatively little continuity was possible in matters of church law and govern-ance. The Crown could not appoint bishops, and patrons and bishops could not select vicars. The charters of the Missionary Societies lapsed. Church property was locally held. Since the old laws were inoperative, a new source of law for the church had to be established.

An early Convention (which included only the congregations of Penn-sylvania) held in 1784, set forth a claim that the newly forming church was self-governing and competent, resolving:

That the Episcopal Church in these states is, and ought to be, in-dependent of all foreign authority, ecclesiastical or civil.

That it hath, and ought to have, in common with all other religious societies, full and exclusive powers to regulate the concerns of its own communion.

That to make canons or laws, there be no other authority than that of a representative body of clergy and laity.[9]

The eighteenth century was a constitution-making age whose thinkers had reflected deeply about political order. They found the legitimization of the state and its laws in common consent. The idea traces, of course, to John Locke, but also to Hooker and Gratian. It was clear to White and those who deliberated with him that if the church is to have laws which it will obey, they must be laws which it has itself enacted for its own self-governance.

When the first complete General Convention met in 1789 it drew up a Constitution of nine articles, which was amplified by a small body of canons. This work has been enlarged and amended in the subsequent two hundred years, but its basic structure still governs the Episcopal Church.

The source of the law of the Episcopal Church would be in the church's plenary synod, a bi-cameral General Convention, consisting of a House of Bishops and a House of Deputies, which brought together clergy and lay deputies from each diocese.

Bishop Seabury of Connecticut, whose consecration in the Scottish succession we have noted, had remained aloof from previous Conventions, fearing that White's plans too much abridged the prerogatives of bishops. But he was brought into the newly forming church in part through the inclusion of a House of Bishops in the church's structure. At first the House of Bishops had weaker powers than did the House of Deputies, but within a short time they were made equal. Legislation can originate in either House; the two must concur for passage.

In most matters, the deputies decide by a simple voice vote. However, on some matters by constitutional requirement and on any matter with the necessary petition, voting is by orders in which the clergy and lay votes are taken separately; and each diocese has a single vote in each order. Thus on matters of importance the church has a tri-cameral legislature.

The representative structure of the General Convention was to be replicated in a convention of each diocese.

It was a matter of deep principle for White that the church's assemblies include lay as well as clergy deputies. (Seabury had been elected by the clergy of Connecticut.) He accepted the judgment that the English Canons of 1604 did not bind the laity because they had not been approved by Parliament, which was meant to express the voice of the laity in the Church of England, and he feared lest a similar situation arise in an American church from whose legislative synods the laity were excluded. He said:

> Without the order of laity permanently making a part of our assemblies, it were much to be apprehended, that the laymen would never be brought to submit to any of our ecclesiastical laws, in such points as might effect the interests or the convenience of any of them, which, it is evident, might happen in many cases: for instance, to mention two of the most important—admission to communion, and exclusion from it. And they would have the principles and the practice of England to plead in their favour.[10]

At first some parts of the church did not share White's conviction, but in time it prevailed.

This principle echoed the article of American political faith that laws derive their just powers from the consent of the governed. Persons are not bound by laws unless, by representation, they have a voice in making and assenting to those laws. This conviction could cite Hooker in its own behalf: 'Laws they are not therefore which public approbation hath not made so.' But consent may be given in representative assemblies where 'our assent is by reason of other agents there on our behalf. And what we do by others, no reason but that it should stand as our deed, no less effectually to bind us than if ourselves had done it in person.'[11] Hooker applies this principle expressly to the laity's voice in church legislation:

> Till it be proved that some special law of Christ hath for ever annexed unto the clergy alone the power to make ecclesiastical laws, we are to hold it a thing most consonant with equity and reason, that no ecclesiastical law be made [...] without consent as well of the laity as of the clergy.[12]

From the beginning it was clear that the Episcopal Church would have bishops but that the bishop's office would be purely spiritual in character and constitutionally limited in powers. After some efforts that miscarried, the episcopate was secured from the English as well as from the Scottish successions. This church's bishops would be elected—recalling that in the early Church bishops were chosen by the clergy and laity of a place from persons known to and trusted by the community. But there was no model for episcopal election. All bishops in the Church of England and in the Roman Church were appointed, either by the Crown or by the Bishop of Rome. It was determined that each diocese would, at its Convention, under the general provisions of the national canons, elect its bishop, assuring the bond between the bishop and the people of a place. However, the choice of a bishop is a matter of national concern, and each bishop takes a place in a college of bishops. So each episcopal election must be approved by the bishops of the Church and by a majority of the dioceses.

It is sometimes observed that choosing bishops by an electoral process results in the choice of compromise candidates, persons who are electable. Certainly the appointive system of the Church of England has brought into episcopal office many forceful, able persons whose election would almost certainly have failed in the Episcopal Church. Moreover, virtually all of the bishops come from parish clergy and tend to model their administration of a diocese on their experience of parish ministry. The great headmaster bishops or scholar bishops of England have had few counterparts in the Episcopal Church. Yet the calibre of persons elected is high; the bonding between bishop and people is close; and there is something to be said for a pastoral conception of episcopal office.

The American form of civil government embodies a principle of 'checks and balances', reflecting its makers' distrust of absolute power—a feature that has been called a 'secular Calvinism'. This principle was carried into the fabric of the Episcopal Church. Very few things can be done by any person or any collective body without the consent or concurrence of some other person or body. Each diocesan bishop must work with an elected Standing Committee. The result is that often things move slowly, for concerted actions must grow from consensus. However, when actions are taken, they tend to be widely understood and supported.

The makers of the US Constitution provided a national polity with a 'separation of powers'. A *legislative* branch makes laws; an *executive* branch puts laws into effect; and a *judicial* branch interprets law and adjudicates cases. Some of the same thinking went into the polity of the Episcopal Church. yet somewhat surprisingly this three-branch form of the nation's Constitution was only partially duplicated in the church's Constitution.

In these formative years, effort concentrated on shaping the Convention and assigning the powers of its two houses. The result was a virtually omnicompetent legislature, but a weak national administration and judicatory.

- At first, the 'presiding bishop' was simply the senior bishop of the church who was also a diocesan bishop and at the same time rector of a large parish. His principal duty for the national Church was to preside at meetings of the House of Bishops. In time, the need for national leadership has led to the enlargement of the role of the Presiding Bishop into a demanding full-time oce and the creation of an Executive Council with sta, budget and programmes.[13]
- However, while this administrative oce has grown, church courts remain largely undeveloped. They are provided for in national and diocesan Constitutions and canons, and judges are named. Yet presentments and trials are infrequent; courts at diocesan, provincial or national levels seldom convene; and when they do, their members must search for a record of such precedents as there may be and struggle even to establish their authority and task. Since the Episcopal Church is separate from the state, its courts are internal tribunals, having only spiritual censures to apply; and in matters such as property and rights, church cases must turn to civil courts. Since church courts are weak, when laws are unclear or ineective, the principal recourse is to return to the legislature and draft and adopt a better law. Thus church law in the Episcopal Church is almost entirely statute law, not case law.

The American churches as they re-formed could incorporate some institutional features that had been improvised during the years when there had been no episcopal supervision. Lacking bishops, archdeacons, endowments, church courts and patrons, the scattered and quite independent colonial congregations had developed local 'vestries' or parish councils which filled some of the functions of patrons, gave substantial initiative to the congregation, and brought lay persons into responsible leadership roles.

The formative events of the American church were in many ways a new start, perhaps seeming close to Locke's primal social contract. However, older ways persisted apart from the church's canons. There has been some question as to what authority pre-1789 English legislation has in the Episcopal Church. Some scholars in the nineteenth and twentieth centuries maintained that English church law and the general law of the West is a part of the law of the Episcopal Church except where it has been set aside by later legislation and that in order to establish what the law of the Episcopal Church is, one must consult the ancient and English canons. However, one must support such a view by citing the continuity of English church law through the colonial experience. But in fact conditions allowed very little such law to take effect in the colonies.[14] No doubt bishops, parsons and congregations do things apart from canons or rubrics, and in doing them they may follow an English or an ancient model. Many English customs have

227

found their way into the life of the Episcopal Church, not, however, as enforceable law.

The Scottish and American experience has been told here at this length, for these churches first demonstrated that Anglicanism could be true to itself while it moved onto a new legal, constitutional foundation. Moreover, this history illustrates many of the issues that come up in other provinces of Anglicanism. While England is the principal source of the Anglican Provinces, it is, in its legal situation, unique, and it can provide only a partial model for the institutional life of churches elsewhere. As the Anglican Communion grew, the Provinces, in assuming independence while remaining loyally Anglican, even though they did not always specifically follow a Scottish or an American pattern, were doing what the Scottish and American experience had shown could be done.

To return to England: beginning in the nineteenth century, a series of steps began to make the Church of England master in its own house to an extent it had not been. Ideas were important; the Oxford Movement criticized the church's subservience to the state and contended for its spiritual independence and authority. From the early eighteenth century until the mid-nineteenth, Convocation had been suppressed, and thus the principal instrument that might have given the church some self-determination and kept its laws up to date did not function. Largely through the effort of Bishop Samuel Wilberforce, Convocation resumed in 1852. However, church measures still required the action of Parliament, and Parliament was unable to give the necessary attention to even important church matters.

In the first half of the twentieth century, action towards effective self-government in the Church of England may be said to begin with the Life and Liberty Movement, led by the energy and conviction of William Temple. As a result of this initiative, in 1919 the Convocations established the Church Assembly as a representative body consisting of a House of Bishops, a House of Clergy and a House of Laity, elected by Diocesan Conferences. The Enabling Act of that same year gave to this Assembly the power to prepare ecclesiastical measures and present them to Parliament for acceptance or rejection. This Act also established a Parochial Church Council in each congregation, giving lay persons a role in local church administration.

These measures partially relieved the Church's position, but dissatisfaction revived when the Proposed Prayer Book of 1928–29 was twice rejected by the House of Commons even though it had been approved by the Church Assembly. A group which was not representative of the church and did not necessarily have its interest at heart was yet in a legal position to control how it might pray—a situation that dismayed many in the church.

At length, in 1969 a General Synod was created which replaced the Church Assembly and assumed most of the powers that had been retained by the Convocations. It too is composed of three houses—bishops, clergy and laity—which must concur for a measure to pass; a two-thirds vote is required for important matters. The act which established General Synod also established in each diocese a Diocesan Synod. While the Church remains by law established, and Parliament must ratify some church measures, the Church of England has now a large measure of participatory self-government.

While these instrumentalities were being created and were finding their roles, attention was given to the body of church law. A Commission which had been appointed in 1939 and was chaired by Cyril Garbett, Archbishop of York, made in 1946 a notable report, *The Canon Law of the Church of England*. After a superb historical review, the work offered a proposed Revised Body of Canons, which stirred discussion. In 1954 a publication considered the canons further; a fresh text was issued in 1959. At length *The Canons of the Church of England* was issued, as adopted by the Convocations in 1964 and 1969, and by the newly created General Synod in 1970. These canons do not form a complete code, but as heretofore in order to find the law of the church one must read the new along with such older church legislation as remains in effect.

Thus events in this century have given the Church of England a representative body to govern its affairs and a revised, flexible and relevant body of church law.

ISSUES OF LAW

We identify several matters of church organization and law which seem to be requiring attention among the Anglican provinces at the turn of the century.

Synodical government is now so widespread as to be a mark of Anglican churches.[15] As the above account will have indicated, the synodical form which had developed by necessity outside England is now well established in England. Bishop Wand, writing at an early stage of the process, remarked that 'the old country has imitated the new'.[16] Representative assemblies bring many of the church's members into responsible roles in its government, treating them as competent adults. A trust has grown in collective deliberation and decision-making.

Yet there remains inevitably some tension between on the one hand a self-governing church which calls itself together in an act of foundation and on the other hand the sense that no church is created in a voluntary act, but is formed within that Catholic community which has been called into being by God's action in Christ and traces by a continuous history from the witness of the apostles. Thus many Anglican Provinces, in their fundamental articles, seek to locate themselves in a larger context, referring to the Scriptures, the early councils, the Catholic tradition, the Church of England or the Anglican Communion. They seek to say to themselves and to others that while they conduct their own affairs without deferring to outside authority, at the same time, they are not self-sufficient, but dependent on historical roots and a wider body of associations.

The churches seek in their laws and structures to express the nature and character of the household of God. However, the church is not understood in exactly the same way throughout Anglicanism, and synodical forms consequently vary. The organization of synods in separate houses (most often into bishops, clergy and laity) draws on the old sense of the 'estates' of the church. But it may be asked: what is the relation between the distinctions based on ordination and the oneness of the *plebs sancta* based on baptism? The ordained ministries, centreing in the episcopate, are clearly a gift of God without which the church could not be fully itself. Yet at the same time, they are from, in and for the church. Although all leadership is given by God, it is grounded in the shared life of grace. To what extent is the church hierarchical by its very nature? To what extent is it a democracy? And to what extent is this alternative, posed in political terms, inadequate to the reality of the church?

It is clear that Anglican synods are not Presbyterian synods, but synods in an episcopally ordered church.[17] (Belated recognition should be given to Richard Baxter, James Ussher and Robert Leighton, three seventeenth-century leaders, who in their different ways had envisioned that church polity might hold together the presbyterian and the episcopal systems.) Throughout Anglicanism, bishops hold a central role in the governmental, teaching, pastoral, sacramental and ministerial life of the church. Although their place in the structure is regarded as essential, their role in relation to other powers of pastoral government is differently expressed. In some provinces a House of Bishops has sole power to propose or determine certain matters such as liturgy or doctrine. In others, the bishops meet and, to a great extent, vote with others. Bishops in some provinces appoint parish clergy, while in other jurisdictions, their power in the matter is advisory at best. In some diocesan synods, by canon or by common understanding, the bishop has a veto power. By custom or by rule, some provinces (or some dioceses within a province) have a tradition of strong bishops, while in others episcopacy is a more constitutionally limited office, taking much of its authority from the pastoral leadership and a deep and genuine habit of respect and deference.

These differences often trace to history. Some provinces from their beginnings had bishops and at least a rudimentary diocesan system. Other provinces had fairly self-sufficient congregations before they had bishops and dioceses, and still others had dioceses before they had a national church. An existing habit of independence or else of strong centralization was built into a church's canonical structure.

Several practical issues of synodical government can be mentioned. When concurrence of the component houses is required for the adoption of a measure, it gives each house veto power. While such division may prevent precipitous decisions, swayed by particular interests, it is perhaps better at slowing action than at expediting it The modes of representation vary; all participating units may be represented equally, or representation may be in proportion to size, with strengths and weaknesses either way. Some churches are concerned that when synodical meetings run over several days, representatives can only be persons who can make a substantial commitment of time—necessarily a select group. Provinces often ask whether or not their general synod is large enough or too large, efficient or clumsy. When provincial boundaries do not coincide with a geographical or political unity, can a Province hold its dioceses in meaningful relations?

Liturgy regularly figures in Anglican canons, but the relation of liturgy to law is complex. Anglican churches, which have no doctrinal confession that is the functional equivalent of the confessions of the Lutheran and the Reformed Churches, have yet everywhere authorized a Prayer Book. The community will cohere, not around a doctrinal manifesto, but around a church-forming, Christian-forming fabric of praise, prayer and sacramental actions. Generally the Prayer Book has been authorized by each church's plenary synod and its use required in every congregation. Disobeying the Prayer Book or its rubrics has been an actionable clerical offence, and the nineteenth century saw several celebrated disputes and trials on matters of ritual.

However, in present-day churches, formed by free association and serving in religiously pluralistic societies, the authority of the Prayer Book lies not so much in its legal authorization as in the fact that it is a very good liturgy which is chosen and loved. Most modern Prayer Books are less prescriptive than older editions were, and they invite officiants and congregations to make choices and to take their worship into their own hands. Some Anglican churches are authorizing alternative rites, including some from other churches. Thus regulation of worship has become much looser than it had been.

One speaks of the Prayer Book and its rubrics as a single, whole document; but clearly not all of its texts and rubrics are of equal importance. Some of the wordings, permissions and prohibitions of the Prayer Book

231

secure the Christian integrity of worship; while others concern matters that are comparatively unimportant. The intention, spirit and proportion of the church's liturgy can be carried out faithfully in a variety of styles and ways. Informed judgement on the part of bishops, priests and people has a proper role in an area of the church's life in which law is clumsy.

In self-governing churches, canon law has a role in putting a liturgy before the Church as well as in enforcing it once it is authorized. While most Prayer Book revisions over the generations had been cautious editings of previous books, when the twentieth-century revisions began, it was obvious that they would be more systematic than any in the past. Each Christian church and each Anglican Province had to address from its own history a new ecumenical liturgical situation and to create a process for meeting it. While a church synod can authorize and own a liturgy, it is not a place in which to draft or edit a liturgy. A group of competent persons has to be given responsibility and trust. Prayer Books since the sixteenth century had given the churches of Anglicanism an advantaged place from which to address the liturgical situation of the mid-twentieth century, and modern revisions have owed much to that tradition. However, when revision commissions set to work, to a great extent they appealed beyond Cranmer and the Prayer Book tradition to the early Church, to which Cranmer himself had appealed, using the best knowledge available to him. The process was a venture of creative fidelity, seeking Cranmer's goals and beginning with the advanced starting place provided by past Anglican liturgies, but often bypassing late medieval models in favour of those from the early centuries.

Taking account of the divergence's in the Prayer Books that emerge from this revision process, concern is often expressed for the continued liturgical unity of the Anglican churches.[18] But liturgy is answerable to its own sources and inner criteria, and church law has limited ability to control the directions it will take. Liturgical scholarship leaped ahead beginning in the late nineteenth century, with Anglicans taking leading roles. In the light of scholarly findings and urgent pastoral needs, the Prayer Books of the tradition, for all of the church's lasting indebtedness to them, seemed locked in a moment of the social and liturgical past. Anglican revisers, as they have worked, have taken their model less from earlier Prayer Books and more from the 'ecumenical shapes' that derive from the simplicity of early models and are influencing the service books of many churches. While laws can hold the Anglican provinces together liturgically only to a limited extent, scholarly findings and pastoral needs seem to be creating a large, ecumenical liturgical consensus which is followed by reason of its own convincing character.

Doctrine is in ferment, and Christians have theological differences, some of them on important issues. Can church law—should it—have a regulative role when doctrinal disputes arise so urgently as to threaten the peace and unity of the Church?

Anglican churches stand in a tradition of theological affirmation and reflection. Yet, generally speaking, it has not been the way of Anglicanism to work from a body of authoritative definition or statement by which other statements can be measured. Rather, its way has been to point to basic sources of doctrine: the Scriptures, the Creeds (whether two or three, and some Anglican churches continue to give some authority to the Thirty-Nine Articles) and the Book of Common Prayer, and to invite its members into the community of theological discourse.[19] It has not set boundaries around what is to be believed, but has pointed its members to central sources which are usually subscribed to by the clergy at the time of their ordination, while the liturgy keeps the Scriptures and the Creeds before the entire community. These sources differ in character and function, and they all require interpretation. They are places in the mind from which theology arises, not points of theological closure. No doubt, some ways of interpreting the Bible and the Creeds, even though well-intended, would subvert these sources and the gospel to which they witness. But the correction for poor interpretation is not laws or trials, but better interpretation. Caution is wise, for many ideas once widely thought subversive have vindicated themselves and are virtually everywhere held or allowed by responsible Christian thinkers. Anglicanism does not attach to any interpretation of the sources the finality that it attaches to the sources themselves.

This centred but open process can seem uncertain and unsatisfactory. Cautious persons often think that doctrine has been given in certain unambiguous past formulations and is not subject to change. Hence they ask church courts to defend this deposit of faith by identifying and rebuking serious deviations from it. However, the role of law in relation to doctrinal discourse is limited. Church law cannot make a theological idea true or untrue. Theology has its own verification. What law can do with reference to the Church's theological discourse is to seek to create a community in which free and responsible theological inquiry can take place—free with respect to forms of theological statement, while at the same time firm in identifying and requiring consent to the essential sources from which theology arises.

The Church's doctrine, deriving from its central message, is not static nor confined to any past formulation. Under the gospel, the Church is oriented to what has been given, but also to what, under the Spirit, is always coming to be. The most recent official and semi-official treatments of doctrine in Anglicanism have described doctrine not as a body of findings or affirmations, but as a process, conducted with reference to authoritative moments in its own past and carrying its own criteria within it. When doctrine is so described it can be seen that is part of the function of church law, serving the living Spirit of Christ in the Church, to keep the community open to the new by affirming and holding in creative tension the various centres of critical thought and pastoral action that create a community of responsible theological discourse.

Canon law figures in the Church's response to current challenges in the areas of *marriage, divorce and remarriage, sexuality* and *the place of women in the Church and in holy orders.* These somewhat different matters will be spoken of here together, for they impact on the process of church law in rather similar ways.

The Church is challenged in these matters because the society in which it lives is challenged. Patterns of marriage, the prevalence of divorce and of remarriage after divorce, attitudes on sexuality, the acceptance of persons of same-sex orientation in the Church and the ministry, and the emergence of women to equal roles in the society and the Church are all in change in virtually all parts of the world. No one can say why they are changing as they are in our time. Why do things that have gone on for centuries suddenly become intolerable? Why do apparently stable, life-supporting institutions at some point seem stifling? No one is making the changes in twentieth-century society happen, and no one can make them stop. The new is not necessarily right against the old nor the old right against the new, but long dormant questions now require urgent attention. The Church is not isolated but is an acting, responding part of a deep, worldwide social, moral stir.

Matters of marriage and family, of sexuality and of the roles of women all are deeply embedded in the social order, indeed in the order of reality and the sense of right and wrong in which one has been formed. They are places of personal self-definition, but also of some insecurity and threatenability. Challenge to existing ways in these areas of experience, when it comes, touches the individual and the collective life deeply. Passions are stirred, and communities can be polarized. Some persons dare, under God, to demand that existing norms, even with all of their accepted sanctions, be changed. Other persons feel that they must, under God, defend those norms just as they have been.

Over the centuries, the Church has formed and supported norms of marriage, sexual conduct and social roles through a tradition of moral theology, doctrine, and often biblical interpretation. Some parts of the standards of the Church, especially those concerning divorce and remarriage, have been taken up in canon law.

Social norms are not universal, but are always specific to a culture, and thus differ at least in some measure from one society or subculture to another. Churches have interacted with the particular moral traditions in which they are set, partly criticizing and partly sanctioning what is done. Thus, although convictions among Christians are strong, they are not uniform. Christians from different cultural groups will look differently at things which are so deeply lodged in the sense of right and wrong that it can sometimes be hard for some of them to credit the good faith of others. The tradition of ethical and pastoral counsel which seems normative to Westerners can be quite disruptive when it encounters without re-examination forms of family life informed by non-Western moral, cultural and social norms. Some Provinces, in their situations, would find it a betrayal of their moral witness to relax their pastoral discipline on marriage, divorce and remarriage. Christians in one cultural situation cannot judge Christians in another. Yet despite their real differences, provinces which are differently situated must accept and understand each other.

When the Church, with its society, is challenged, it begins to sort out long-unexamined ideas. Some prophetic, intuitive persons seem to grasp the issues and anticipate the outcome almost from the start. Others learn and move more deliberately. Others, of course, cling to old certitudes. Some persons can be driven to extreme positions, while others seek to find a middle ground or ways of affirming both sides.

When challenged by new human claims, the Church, like all other participants in the culture-wide discussion, refers to contemporary studies. Whatever is done must use the best information and analyses available and fit in with the reality-sense in which one lives both in church and out of church. But the internal discourse of the Church also refers to its own regulative sources. Its characteristic way is to consult Scripture and tradition deeply. It moves forward and backward at the same time, seeking to avoid trendiness by affirming continuity with its own past. When it approaches the Scriptures freshly, it may find that they have at times been read selectively, unhistorically or through the spectacles of culture and tradition. The Bible may not say about marriage and divorce, or persons of same-sex preference, or the role of women what it has long been taken to say. Sometimes it is important to establish that with respect to a specific question at hand, the Bible says nothing at all. The Church must interpret for its situation sources that were written for a past situation. Going to primal sources with new questions often yields new angles of vision and new findings. Change can be a time of discovery and repossession.

Eventually no new arguments are being generated; parties repeat themselves. Discussion must end and official determination be sought. It often comes down to a single action, perhaps the adoption, the deletion or the amendment of a canon by the Provincial synod. Not all parties are ready to act at the same time. If two houses vote 'aye', while the other votes 'nay', the motion will have to be resubmitted until it passes or else it becomes clear that it cannot pass.

If the Church commits itself to new ways, a process of reception follows. New laws must be supported, as the old laws had been, by new conduct and by new structures of justification. The new ways will take their place in a new sense of what is right and natural—often finding acceptance so quickly and easily that many people wonder why the change had to take so long and be so difficult.

This consolidation of thought, attitudes and actions provides a breathing-space until the next stir of history again requires the Church to respond.

Culture, variability: canon law always takes on some of the form and style of the surrounding culture. Canonical absolutism is out of place. In an imperial society, the Church looked like an empire. Feudal or monarchical societies were in their time reflected in the ordering of church life. In modern Western society, the Church takes on much of the form of a bureaucratic corporation. In a tribal society, the church may well organize its life, its manner of exercising authority, and its ways of internal communication in the style of a tribe. All constructions of society are one-sided and flawed, and the Christian community will often try to moderate or humanize the models it must use.

Through such adaptation a church utilizes the style of corporate life that seems natural to its members. Institutions shape the perceiving self so that the ordered life in which one lives has a feeling of rightness. Persons know how to enter known forms of community, find them supportive, and make them work. Some people in Western society become skilled at making motions, seconding, discussing and adopting them by majority vote, while persons in other societies might find such procedures quite baffling. The basic elements of collective Christian identity—such as Scriptures, creeds, sacraments and orders—do not dictate a form of community life, but are widely adaptable. The matter is important, for now that most Anglicans are non-Western, parts of the multicultural Anglican Communion may well develop ways of organizing the Christian community that are quite unlike the ways of the traditions that have shaped canon law as it has been known—and perhaps not fully comprehensible to persons formed by those traditions.

LAW AND THEOLOGY OF LAW

Law is a theoretical as well as a practical field. Perhaps at least as urgent for Anglicans as the crafting of good canons is the awakening of rigorous, informed discussion about the internal structures and processes of the Church's life. Church law must be more than a body of positive regulations. Laws require for their acceptance and legitimacy the support of a body of discourse about law. 'A community which wants to be taken seriously when it says "The member is answerable to the law" must itself be dealing rigorously with the question "Very well, but what is the law answerable to?" [20] The ordering of the life of the Church is in part a critical intellectual task. In a church which has laws without a body of interpretation of law, laws can seem arbitrary.

Canons are the Church's effort to shape the life of a community which is called into being by that which transcends law. They regulate a life which they do not create. The values and purposes which church laws are to serve are not provided by the laws themselves. The Church should beware of the legal technician who knows the law but is not able to construe law in such a way as to set it within the pre-legal sources from which it arises and the meta-legal ends it is meant to serve.

It was mentioned at the beginning of this essay that since the early decades of the twentieth century the tradition of Anglican scholarship in canon law has waned. In recent years two initiatives and literatures have developed which could give new energy to the field.

RECENT ROMAN CANON LAW STUDIES

Anglican scholarly works in canon law were for a long time indebted to the extensive Roman literature in the field—a tradition representing careful thought and vast learning. However, by the early twentieth century, canon law in the Roman Church had become quite stultified—the business of chancery offices and of ponderous articles dissecting difficult cases. Its theory was tied to scholastic categories. Church law had become the province of specialists, and the tradition grew on itself, having little relation to the deep issues of ecclesiology, ecumenicity and pastoral mission that have occupied the minds of twentieth-century Christians. Imaginative young scholars left church law to the bureaucrats and antiquarians.

To a great extent, the older discussions (among Roman scholars as well as among the Anglican theorists who followed their lead) thought juridically, finding church law rooted in conceptions of divine authority and rule. The foundation of church law was said to lie in the regal authority of Christ which was conferred on the Church and specifically on its hierarchy. So conceived, the aim of church law was, to the extent possible, to bring human life under the firm, benign rule of Christ through which persons are led to salvation. [21] This account of law, in its effort to root ecclesiastical law in divine authority, tended to divinize the Church's canons and to understand the Church's pastoral task in a moralistic way. Laws, it said, come into the Church from above and pass to each member by a process in which the member is largely passive. This descending pattern seems like a legal expression of a *theologia gloriae*.

Then as an unexpected consequence of the Second Vatican Council, canon law in the Roman Church became a vigorous and intellectually challenging field—expressing a new ecclesiology and sensitivity to the human life of the community.[22] Some of the recurrent ideas of this stir of thought are: law is for the sake of freedom; it serves a pastoral, life-imparting function; it, like the Church itself, is for persons; it is to protect the inherent rights of the baptized and curb autocracy; authority is to be exercised locally and collegially. The issues that have been addressed and the concepts that have been developed in this minor renaissance are pertinent to the churches of Anglicanism.

ECUMENICAL STUDIES

Ecumenical and cross-cultural inquiry has considered the Church's institutional life seriously. As long as any church lives in insularity there is little need for it to think critically about the way in which its common life is ordered. But when it engages in dialogue with other churches, which are equally loyal to Jesus Christ, but which bring other histories and self-understandings, it must compare, listen and learn.

Further, when churches together address the world and look outside themselves, they see their inherited forms of community life differently. Western churches drift by habit into ways more suited to denominational self-preservation than to prosecuting a redemptive mission. Such churches can be given a mirror for self-examination by other churches which do not bring the cultural baggage of the West, but are evangelizing communities, living in interface with the great non-Christian world. The churches of the West are facing their own mission field of a secularized society. In most European populations practising Christians are now a minority, and in the US where church membership remains strong, the churches have, to an alarming extent, allowed themselves to be co-opted as chaplaincies to their secularized society. Yet the churches of the West persist in forms of church life which grew from the centuries in which they held an advantaged place in Christendom, and in doing so, they persist in self-delusion.

Inter-church and cross-cultural discussions ask all participants—perhaps none more than Anglicans—to engage in rigorous self-criticism.[23] Are the inherited forms of church life suited to the Church's inherent missionary nature and task? Corporate life gets cluttered. It is better at devising new things than it is at discarding them when they have served their purposes. Yet wholesale economizing, especially when it is driven by ideology, can deprive corporate life of much of its richness and humanity. Old institu-

238

tional forms that seemed to be vestigial may be serving functions that have become unrecognized and unappreciated. We sometimes do not see what something is *for* until we discard it and have to reinvent it. The life of the Church is essentially untidy; there is more to it than we are aware of at any one time.

But the challenge of ecumenicity is even more fundamental. Anglicanism exits from the deep Christian past, and it moves through many deaths and resurrections towards the reunited Church to come—a church that will grow from the present, although it may look significantly different from any church of today. The institutional features of the life of Anglicanism must have the imagination to relativize their present-day church structures in the light not only of the deep Christian past and the ongoing exchange with others, but also in the light of a future which will bring unknown demands and opportunities.

We select a few of the issues that figure in the theoretical and practical agenda for canon law for today and for the future.

THE GOSPEL

The Church is not constituted by law, but by the gift and act of God. It exists for worship, witness and service. Thus the Church's primary account of itself is not juridical, but theological; and theology is an explication of the gospel; and the gospel is a loving, freeing, dignifying act of God for all people, witnessed to in the Scriptures. The Church's members always have access to that gospel, and when the gospel leads them into new, authentic forms of obedience and ministry, canons must test and then follow.

One immediate implication of the general thesis that laws and structures are to serve the gospel is that canonists, while they have their own needed professionalism, must be conversant with theology and its history. They live and think on a frontier where law interacts with theology and with the foundational biblical literature. They are dealing with the institutional side of a spiritual society, and they should be equipped to see the body of proximate things with which they work in relation to the ultimate things of faith. Are matters of church law to be handled by lawyers or by theologians? There are problems either way. Collaboration seems desirable.

CHANGE AND CONFLICT

Change is the human condition and hence the Christian condition. Change in the Church is not just a matter of shifting teachings or liturgical practices. It is measured in personal biographies and in the histories of groups in which change is often perceived at least at first as loss. Emotions are wrenched and patterns of life are disrupted at points where persons had sought stability. When large diversified churches change, they will move slowly, and not all members will move at the same pace. Some persons are convinced that the Church is being called to change, while others see the church they knew and loved passing away, and they feel they must act to preserve it. Serious questions arise for canon law when at length the community decides in a lawful way to make an important change, but some persons refuse to go along with the majority. Passions are so deep and persons are so alienated that dissident groups seem, at times, not to seek reconciliation. Compromise, as they see it, would be capitulation.

Such divisiveness tests church officials and the laws within which they work.[24] How much internal stress can the corporate structures absorb without placing the common good in jeopardy? Can the Church avoid the tyrannies of minorities as well as of majorities? Modern-day churches, as voluntary societies, have only limited powers to compel compliance. What can be done about individuals or groups that will not comply with the lawful actions of the Church? Can room be made, perhaps for a stated period, for a dissident group to remain partially independent, following its own ways? This is a diplomat's way—creating a 'conscience clause', and letting time deal with the matter. But what is patient and considerate for the dissidents can bring alienation or even canonical injustice to persons who are simply being obedient. To take two examples: when some congregations admit all baptized children to communion while others do not, children who have begun to receive communion in one congregation may, for reasons they may find hard to comprehend, be rebuffed at the Lord's Table at another congregation. Somewhat similarly, when many dioceses or national churches admit women to holy orders, while others are allowed to persist in not doing so, a woman who has been lawfully ordered in one jurisdiction may not be recognized as a bishop, priest or deacon throughout the Anglican Communion. Are such anomalies minor and temporary? Or are they signs that the community is threatened? In our time some groups have been led by the dynamics of ideological dissent to actual schism.

Some Provinces have been spared such crises, but in so far as urgent issues of this sort are occasioned by deep, pervasive changes in Church and society, they will continue for many years to test both the Church's legal structures and the persons who must try to make those structures work compassionately and justly.

COMMUNITY

Canon law grows from and in turn shapes the common life; it binds people in a fabric of mutual rights and accountabilities. The dry text of the canons refers to a community of believers dedicated to mutual listening, serving, caring and forgiving. Yet any religious community, however idealistic its beginnings and carefully crafted its laws, will develop flaws. Abrasive features of organized life will emerge, despite good intentions. Groups will confuse their good with the general good. Officials will be perceived as remote and uncaring. The Church's epicentres of authority will come to distrust one another. Power tends to flow towards power, and the weak are left out.

The community to which canon law has reference has a baptismal basis. Its fundamental order is the *laos*, the entire people. Yet church law—traditionally and perhaps inevitably—is heavily occupied with clerical matters, tending to speak of the laity principally in connection with eligibility for church office, marriage and divorce, and access to and exclusion from the sacraments.[25]

It should say more. Baptism is a conferral of worth and dignity, it brings into the life in Christ persons regardless of the place they have occupied in the general society (Gal. 3.27–8). The Church needs to examine the community created by canons, asking such questions such as these: Because of a collective predisposition to see some things and not others, are some persons in the Church 'invisible', i.e., held in a place of diminished regard or second-class rights or access to privilege? Is participation in the acting, decision-making life of the Church, at all levels, open to all persons, according to their gifts and callings? Is information pertinent to church actions freely shared with all members? Are adequate appeals provided for persons who may be aggrieved by the officials and ways of the church? Have dangerous instruments been created by placing absolute power in anyone's hands? Some Roman Catholic writers have proposed a 'Bill of Rights for the Baptized'.[26] Certain institutional irritants can be eased by better laws and more participatory structures. Law is a powerful force which can be used to exclude or include, to diminish or to dignify.

But part of the problem is the spirit in which laws are carried out and structures are made operative. If the gospel which informs law is a freeing, dignifying act of God, church law must be interpreted not in terms of rule, but in terms of support and service (Mark 10.45). The Church exists not for itself, but to participate in Christ's self-giving for the world—a hard principle to envision when the model for laws and their way is so heavily derived from the ways of 'the nations'. Recognizing the fallibility of the Church, the imperfection of the best laws and the lawmakers, canon law must embody a *theologia crucis*. It must check arrogance and embrace a fundamental modesty. Church law should seek to be the servant of the servants of God.

All Anglican Churches seek to work in orderly ways, to follow a law that, albeit given through human agents, is a gift of God. Yet even as they follow law, they must know that it does not make the Church, but rather serves the concrete life of the Church—seeking its inclusiveness, unity and peace, giving it order and fairness in the face of disagreements. And the Church which is served by law serves the gospel.

Thus church law is established in and at the same time relativized by the essential Christian message. It follows that the first task of the Church's leaders and its law-making assemblies is not to represent a position, a party or an ideology, nor to discover the general will and achieve consensus, but to hear the Word of God. Karl Barth, in a lengthy, unexpected, and at times brilliant discussion of 'The Order of the Community', said: 'In great things and small, in all things, true Church law arises from a hearing of the voice of Jesus Christ.'[27]

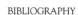

BIBLIOGRAPHY

Berman, Harold J., *The Interaction of Law and Religion*. Abingdon Press, Nashville TN, 1974

The Canon Law of the Church of England, Being the Report of the Archbishop's Commission on Cannon Law, together with Proposals for a Revised Body of Canons. SPCK, London, 1947.

Howe, John, *Anglicanism and the Universal Church: Highways and Hedges 1958–1984*, with '*An Overview 1984–1990*', by Colin Cranston. Anglican Book Centre, Toronto, 1990.

Kemp, Eric W., *Counsel and Consent: Aspects of Church Government*. SPCK, London, 1961.

Mortimer, R. C., *Western Canon Law*. A. & C. Black, London, 1953.

Sachs, William L., *The Transformation of Anglicanism: From State Church to Global Communion*. CUP 1993.

Stevick, Daniel B., *Canon Law: A Handbook*. Seabury Press, New York, 1965.

Sykes, Stephen W. (ed.), *Authority in the Anglican Communion*. Anglican Book Centre, Toronto, 1987.

NOTES

1 'Those who would see a Church so spiritual that no room is left in it for human institutions are depriving the Church of its humanity. Any apology for law is an apology for the humanity of the Church.' Ladislas M. Orsy, 'Law in the Church: Theological Reflections', *The Way* 11 (1971), p. 314.

2 *Laws of Ecclesiastical Polity*, I.x.7.

3 Text in Henry Gee and William Hardy, *Documents Illustrative of English Church History* (Macmillan, London, 1896), Number LVIII.

4 The title of a small book edited by J. V. Bullard (Faith Press, London, 1934), which sought to establish what canon law was actually in force at the time of writing.

5 *The Canon Law of the Church of England* (1947), ch. IV.

6 Writing in the Preface to *Canon Law in the Church of England* (1948), Archbishop Garbett said: At the present time the Church of England, alone among the Churches of the Anglican Communion, lacks a body of Canons which has been revised and supplemented in the light of modern conditions, and which is regarded as authoritative by its members [...] This state of confusion and uncertainty is profoundly humiliating and unsatisfactory, and until it

is remedied it will be difficult to secure order and cohesion in our Church.' Of course, the report in which these words appear was itself a major step towards the remedy of the situation Garbett deplored.

7 From the Preface to the Prayer Book of 1789, which was written by the Rev. Dr William Smith and has been repeated unchanged in the editions of 1892, 1928 and 1979.

8 The best review of the events by which the episcopate was secured for America is Frederick V. Mills, *Bishops by Ballot: An Eighteenth Century Ecclesiastical Revolution* (OUP 1978); Clara O. Loveland, *The Critical Years* (Seabury Press, New York, 1956), remains a good overview of the formative years of the Episcopal Church.

9 William White, *Memoirs of the Protestant Episcopal Church* (Swords, Stanford and Co., New York, 1836), 2nd edn, p. 82f.

10 White, *Memoirs*, p. 88.

11 Hooker, *Laws*, I.x.8.

12 Hooker, *Laws*, VII. vi.8.

13 See Roland Foster, *The Role of the Presiding Bishop* (Forward Movement, Cincinnati, 1982).

14 The leading American scholar in the field some years ago concluded concerning jurisdiction in the colonial church (William W. Manross, *The Fulham Papers of the Lambeth Palace Library* (Clarendon Press, Oxford, 1964), p. xviiif): 'In view of the complete rejection of English canon law in some colonies, the rejection of that large part of it applicable to the laity in all, the existence of a canonically valid jurisdiction only from 1729 to 1748, the very limited effectiveness of that at its strongest, and the absence after 1748 of even a *de facto* authority by which any canon could be enforced or any canonical dispute be adjudicated, the doctrine, upheld by many American canonists, that English canon law extended to the colonies and was inherited by the American Episcopal Church, without reenactment, would seem to be founded on an historical illusion.' On this subject, see the excursus, 'English Canon Law in the Episcopal Church' in Stevick, *Canon Law: A Handbook*, pp. 67–70.

15 The importance of this development was recognized in Henry Lowther Clarke, *Constitutional Church Government: In the Dominions beyond the Seas and In Other Parts of the Anglican Communion* (SPCK, London, 1924. This work of 540 pages by a former Archbishop of Melbourne assembles detailed, accurate information on the forms of polity in all parts of the Anglican Communion as of the time of writing, emphasizing the growth of constitutional church government and citing source documents in full. The work needs to be updated, but the volume of data has grown so much and events move so rapidly that it would be an immense task to bring this work into the twenty-first century at Clarke's level of detail. Quite a lot of current information on constitutional government in the Churches of the Anglican Communion has been summarized in Philip Thomas' article, 'A Family Affair: The Pattern of Constitutional Authority in the Anglican Communion' in Stephen W. Sykes (ed.), *Authority in the Anglican Communion*, p. 120. Thomas speaks of 'black boxes' in the archives of the Anglican Consultative Council that make the needed study possible, even though difficult. Thomas, 'A Family Affair' pp. 121, 142 also gives an appreciative notice and a footnote to an effort in the 1960s to gather up-to-date information on the law and polity of the Anglican churches. Spencer Ervin, a well-informed churchman and lawyer from Philadelphia, Pennsylvania,

assembled many histories and texts of canons and projected a series of small books on 'The Government of the Churches of the Anglican Communion' of which the first, *A Introduction to Anglican Polity* (1964) was completed, along with others on South Africa (1965); the Church of Ireland (1965); and the Scottish Episcopal Church (with Ian B. Cowan, 1966). They were issued by a local publisher. Spencer Ervin had the competence to carry out this task, but alas he died in 1967, the project only just begun. The library of the Diocese of Pennsylvania has, through the kindness of Spencer Ervin Jr, acquired the sources and notes for this projected work, which remain much as they were left more than thirty years ago.

16 J. W. C. Wand (ed.), *The Anglican Communion: A Survey* (OUP 1948), p. 313.

17 There is a running discussion of episcopacy in Anglicanism, occasioned partly by the importance and complexity of the subject, partly by the differences in the ways episcopacy has been understood and practiced in the churches of Anglicanism, and partly by issues that are raised as Anglicans seek to commend episcopacy in ecumenical discussion. The literature is extensive, and the subject is dealt with elsewhere in this volume. A recent symposium which contains some fine essays is J. Robert Wright (ed.), *On Being a Bishop* (Church Hymnal Corporation, New York, 1993).

18 At the Lambeth Conference of 1958 an influential report sorted out features of the Prayer Book that were thought to be of first importance along with some features that were less important and some that might well be changed. This authoritative loyal criticism encouraged the process of revision that was then beginning in earnest. Then in the mid-1960s an inter-Anglican committee addressed what, with specific respect to the Holy Communion, might hold the Anglican liturgical tradition together at a time of liturgical divergence. Its report commended no past or present Prayer Book text, but rather, outlined a sequence of five 'phrases' of eucharistic celebration. (The outline showed the influence of Gregory Dix.) The Holy Communion was described not as a form of words but as a series of actions which might be carried out through a variety of wordings. This report or the thinking behind it was influential.

19 This characteristic way of pointing to sources can be illustrated by the Lambeth Quadrilateral and by the Church of England's Canon A5, 'Of the Doctrine of the Church of England', which says: 'The doctrine of the Church of England is grounded in the Holy Scriptures, and in such teachings of the ancient Fathers and Councils of the Church as are agreeable to the said Scriptures. In particular such doctrine is to be found in the Thirty-nine Articles of Religion, the Book of Common Prayer, and the Ordinal.'

20 Daniel B. Stevick, 'A Theological View of the Place of Law in the Church: An Episcopalian Perspective', *The Jurist* XLII (1982), p.1.

21 To cite one instance among many, E. G. Wood in his small book, *The Regal Power of the Church* (first published in 1888, republished 1948) begins by citing the 'powers which he [Christ] had in his own right as the only begotten of the Father, though granted to him in his human nature as the reward for his obedience'. These powers he commits to the Church, through the apostles. The powers are exercised hierarchically—Wood lays emphasis on Jesus' metaphor of the kingdom, citing Canon Liddon to the effect that Jesus spoke of a kingdom, not a republic. Canon Wood's work is not extreme (in fact it is quite humane and qualified), but it illustrates the scholastic, juridical type of thought

that characterized the field. H. S. Box in his widely used *The Principles of Canon Law* (1949), drew on it extensively.

22 This stir brought forth a remarkable literature, much of it in symposium volumes, which deserves to be better known than it is. Some of the following titles had their origin in the Canon Law Society of America, and several appeared in the *Concilium* series, with contributions by European scholars. They are listed here in order of date of publication. The dates suggest the rush of enthusiasm that in the years immediately after the Council led to this reconceiving of church law. The fact that such monographs and symposia have slowed indicates the caution that in the past few years has overtaken Roman scholars in this field: Teodoro Jimenez-Urresti and Neophytos Edelby (eds), *Pastoral Reform and Reform of Church Government* (Paulist Press, Glen Rock NJ, 1965); James Biechler (ed.), *Law for Liberty: The Role of Law in the Church Today* (Helicon, Baltimore 1967); Neophytos Edelby, Teodoro Jimenez-Urresti and Petrus Huizing (eds), *Renewal and Reform of Canon Law* (Paulist Press, Glen Rock NJ, 1967); James Coriden (ed.) *We the People of God: Towards Constitutional Development within the Church* (Our Sunday Visitor, Huntington IN, 1968); James Coriden (ed.), *The Case for Freedom: Human Rights in the Church* (Corpus Books, Washington DC, 1969); Neophytos Edelby, Teodoro Jimenez-Urresti and Petrus Huizing (eds), *The Future of Canon Law* (Paulist Press, Glen Rock NJ, 1969); Alois Muller (ed.), *Democratization of the Church* (Herder and Herder, New York 1971); Gregory Baum and Andrew Greeley (eds), *The Church as Institution* (Herder and Herder, New York, 1974.)

23 Much of the ecumenical inquiry along these lines can be found in Faith and Order papers. A symposium edited by Nils Eherstrom and Walter Muelder, *Institutionalism and Church Unity* (Association Press, New York 1963), which reports the work of a Study Commission on Institutionalism of the Faith and Order Commission is now rather old, but it remains a basic work in this field. A recent English report, *Working As One Body: The Report of the Archbishop's Commission on the Organization of the Church of England* (Church House Publishing, London, 1995), makes drastic proposals for church organization in the light of the fundamental purposes of the Church. Its authors feel that this Report 'could introduce a new era of openness, optimism and vigour in the Church' (p. xii).

24 See Paul Avis' small, forcefully argued book, *Authority, Leadership and Conflict in the Church* (Mowbray, London, 1992).

25 It may be useful to note that for many centuries councils and canons set forth special, restrictive standards for the sexual behaviour of clergy and religious. However, the Anglican Reformation set such distinctions aside. In most if not all Anglican Provinces, the expectations for Christians in marriage have been and are now the same for clergy and laity.

26 A basic symposium volume is James Coriden (ed.) *The Case for Freedom: Human Rights in the Church* (Corpus Books, Washington DC, 1969), which contains (pp. 33–46) an essay 'The Rights of the Baptized', by the Anglican historian and liturgist, Massey H. Shepherd. See also: Pedro Lombardia, 'The Fundamental Rights of the Faithful' in Edelby, Jimenez-Urresti and Huizing, *The Future of Canon Law*, pp. 81–9; Ladislas Orsy, 'Fundamental Rights in the Church', *The Jurist* XLI (1981), pp. 177–87; and a symposium specifically on the subject, Leonard Swidler and Herbert O'Brien (eds), *A Catholic Bill of Rights* (Sheed and Ward, Kansas City MO, 1988).

27 *Church Dogmatics* (A. & C. Black, Edinburgh, 1956), IV.2, p. 682.

PART FIVE

Church, Sacraments and Ministry

1   Doctrine of the Church

PHILIP H. E. THOMAS

William Reed Huntington is known in Anglican history by a footnote. As
Rector of an influential New York congregation he wrote in 1870 *The
Church Idea*, which first put forward the formula for Christian unity eventually known as the Chicago-Lambeth Quadrilateral. His proposal—that
acceptance of Scripture, Creeds, the sacraments of Baptism and the Eucharist, and the episcopal ordering of ministry should provide the basis for
effective union among the Churches—has stood for nearly a century as a
cornerstone of Anglican ecumenical endeavour.

Huntington's achievement, however, was much closer to the main theme
of Anglican ecclesiology than that incidental footnote might suggest. His
concern for unity was not confined to a defence of denominational norms,
but was placed within the context of the question of what was involved in
being Anglican, and in particular, being Anglican in North America. He
was dismissive of the merely nostalgic appeal of Anglicanism: 'The word
brings up before the eyes of some a flutter of surplices, a vision of village
spires and cathedral towers, a somewhat stiff and stately company of deans,
prebendaries and choristers, and that is all' (p. 124). *The Church Idea* took
the incarnation seriously and saw it as becoming increasingly the perspective of the Church in a changing society.

> If our whole ambition as Anglicans in America be to continue a small
> but eminently respectable body of Christians, and to offer a refuge to
> people of refinement and sensibility, who are shocked by the irreverences
> they are apt to encounter elsewhere; in a word, if we are to be only a
> countercheck and not a force in society, then let us say as much in plain
> terms and frankly renounce any and all claim to Catholicity. We have
> only, in such case, to wrap the robe of our dignity about us, and walk
> quietly along in a seclusion no-one will take much trouble to disturb.
> Thus may we be a Church in name and a sect in deed.

The nature of that charge, brought be it noted some fifty years before
Troeltsch's formative church-sect typology, deserves closer attention. But
Huntington did not restrict himself to criticism. In the ringing tones of
pulpit oratory he continued:

> But if we aim at something nobler than this, if we would have our
> communion become national in very truth—in other words, if we
> would bring the Church of Christ into the closest possible sympathy
> with the throbbing, sorrowing, sinning, repenting, aspiring heart of this
> great people—then let us press our reasonable claims to be the reconciler

of a divided household, not in spirit of arrogance (which ill befits those whose best possessions have come to them by inheritance), but with affectionate earnestness and intelligent zeal (p. 159).

It was in pursuit of that claim that Huntington laid down his version of the Quadrilateral, and in so doing gave an instructive example of the way in which Anglican ecclesiology is pursued.

It is no simple matter to relate Anglican thinking about the doctrine of the Church. Quite apart from well-known internal differences which make it difficult to 'read off' any ecclesiology which would be acceptable to all Anglicans, there is also a notable reluctance on their part to acknowledge any peculiarly Anglican dogma—of the Church or of anything else. Anglicans have received the faith of the Church, it is claimed; and therefore nothing more can or need be said. Whether such a position is tenable is one of the questions that must be explored in this chapter, but one thing to be noted at this stage is the fact that Anglicanism, since its beginnings, has been forged on the anvil of ecclesiological controversy. Part of the case to be presented is that while Anglican ecclesiology cannot offer any consensus on the constitution of the Church, it has been able to maintain its credibility by the way in which Anglican churches have been forced to engage with their own history and with the theological issues raised for them by it. When Huntington addressed the situation faced by the Episcopal Church in his time, and sought to draw out from its inheritance the resources to meet the demands of Christian unity and mission, he was doing something that has been characteristic of the Church of England throughout its history, and that has been carried on by the churches of Anglican Communion ever since. What follows will seek to suggest some of the lines of argument which have given shape to Anglican understanding of the Church, and at the same time attempt to show why most Anglicans do not believe that their lack of a normative ecclesiology is a fatal flaw but is rather the source of a distinctive theological and ecumenical opportunity.

THE DOCTRINE OF THE CHURCH AS RECEIVED BY THE CHURCH OF ENGLAND

The official formularies of the Church of England—the Thirty-Nine Articles, the Book of Common Prayer and Ordinal and the Canons Ecclesiastical are not 'confessional', if by that term it is meant that they provide the foundational dogmas or ideological texts upon which all later Anglican teaching was based (see pp. pp. 131–42, 144–53 and pp. 155–65). What they present are the beliefs which made it possible to change the direction of English Christianity during a decisive period of its development. The sixteenth-century reforms in England may have been occasioned by Henry VIII's marriage problems or by Elizabeth's desire for peace, but such changes were only possible because a set of theological convictions eventually persuaded a majority of Tudor churchmen that the new course set by church and state was a proper one to follow. These convictions were threefold. First there was the belief that the Church of England had a continuous history reaching back to Augustine of Canterbury and beyond. Second, it was held that the life of the Church must be drawn into renewed conformity with the teaching of the Bible, and that this could be done without breaking the continuity of faith and history to which it was heir. Third, while abuses were to be corrected, things of value were to be retained and therefore ceremonies and ideas which were not explicitly contradicted by Scripture were simply left open to the continuing evaluation of the Christian community.

Enough has been said elsewhere about the mixed provenance of the formularies between 1548 and 1662 and the tensions that are reflected by them as a result. There is however no ambiguity about the way in which the Church of England was seen in them to be Reformed yet quite plainly still part of the universal Church. This is evident from the title of the Book of Common Prayer, when it sets forth the 'Rites and Ceremonies of the Church, according to the use of the Church of England'. The compilers of the Prayer Book intended primarily to collect and arrange liturgical resources from the historic Church and make them available for use by the English in their own language. The English liturgy, borrowing as it does from various periods of ecclesiastical history, itself expresses the conviction that the Church is one and the Church of England a part of it. At the heart of their intercessions worshippers were to beseech God to 'inspire continually the universal Church with a spirit of truth, unity and concord', and to pray that 'all they that do confess thy holy name may agree in the truth of thy holy Word, and live in unity and godly love'. At baptism the priest received candidates into 'the congregation of Christ's flock' and declared them to be sacramentally regenerate and 'grafted into Christ's Church' with the expectation that they would become 'lively members of the same'. In the ordination rite the bishop was to lay hands on those being priested with the words, 'Receive the Holy Ghost for the office and work of a priest within the Church of God'. To belong to the Church of England was to be part of Christ's Church, and it was this which gave legitimacy to Anglican liturgy, membership and ministry.

At the same time, the Church of England in the sixteenth century was also represented as being Reformed. Along with the emphasis on continuity, there was an equal stress on the constitutive power of the Word of God in the life of the Church. In the ordination formula the bishop presented the new priest with a Bible (in itself a symbolic change from the earlier practice of offering the sacramental instruments) and prayed that the Church would have grace 'to hear and receive what they shall deliver out of thy most holy Word, or agreeable to the same'. Each congregation, as part of its intercession for the whole state of Christ's Church, prayed for all God's people and 'especially this congregation here present' that 'with meek heart and due reverence, they may hear, and receive thy holy Word'. Catholic tradition was tested and proved against the reading of Scripture.

The same dual conviction concerning Anglican teaching was evident in the Articles (see pp. 144–8). Articles I to VIII reiterate that Anglicans are held to the doctrines of the Church by means of Creed and Bible, while simultaneously acknowledging the Reformers' hermeneutical concerns by clearly defining the theological limits of the biblical canon. At the heart of these opening paragraphs the typical Anglican assertion of the sufficient but not exhaustive authority of Scripture (Article VI) provides the touchstone for all other beliefs (see pp. 90–3). Even the Creeds are received precisely because 'they may be proved by most certain warrant of Holy Scripture' (Article VIII), and altogether eighteen of the Articles allude or refer to the Bible as the source of their authority. So settled was the conviction that the Church of England in the sixteenth and seventeenth centuries was simply the Church of England undergoing an internal process of renovation, that the Canons Ecclesiastical (1604) threatened excommunication to anyone who denied that the English Church was a 'true and apostolical church', or who suggested that its forms of worship 'containeth anything in it that is repugnant to the scriptures'. The apologetic was plainly directed against Roman Catholic critics on the one hand and the more radical spirits of the Reformation on the other, but the positive claim which lay behind it was equally clear: the Church of England was Reformed, but still Catholic.

What understanding of the Church could give rise to that sort of assertion? The answer is spelled out in principle by Article XXXIV. Churches are at least partly the creation of their history and culture. At different times and in different places the life of the Church will be encapsulated in different traditions and ceremonies. 'Particular and national Churches' hold the responsibility for shaping their corporate existence in accordance with the precepts of Scripture but within the context of their own local environment. The universal Church must take on a particular identity.

If the principle underlying the establishment of Reformed Catholicism in England was the concept of the national church, then the procedure depended on the belief, already noted, that many elements of church life were 'in their own nature indifferent' and so could be arranged as matters of convenience rather than conviction. The idea of *adiaphora* or 'things in-

252

different' had been advanced on the continent by Melanchthon and utilized in passing by Calvin (see pp. 264–6). It received a distinctive exposition in an appendix to the 1549 Prayer Book, and this was expanded as part
of the Preface to the Book of Common Prayer in 1662. Abuses and unnecessary burdens, it was explained, had to be abolished; yet in Anglican
liturgy 'the main body and essentials [. . .] have still continued the same'.
Change was not seen as an end in itself and respect for antiquity as well as
good order meant that much that was familiar could still be utilized. No
counsel of perfection could be invoked. The claim for Anglican ceremonial
and worship was simply that it did not 'contain in it anything contrary to
the Word of God, or to sound doctrine, or which a godly man may not with
a good conscience use and submit unto'. What was argued for the Book of
Common Prayer could also be held to apply to the structures and offices of
the Church: its threefold ministry, episcopal ordination, details of vesture
and ritual in worship, along with the continued existence of cathedrals and
universities, the administrative hierarchy of deans, chapters and archdeacons, and, it would appear, much of the old parochial system of pastoral
organization.

With the benefit of hindsight, some commentators have felt able to
discern a distinct national consciousness in the English church almost
from its inception; but the thinking found within the formularies of the
Church of England cannot be described as nationalistic. The English Reformers certainly acted under royal patronage, but the best of them were not
merely opportunist. The sixteenth century saw no independent doctrine of
the Church introduced, but it did see a new confidence on the part of the
Church as 'witness and keeper of Holy Writ' (as Article XX put it) in its
responsibility to judge controversies of faith. Article XIX summed up the
change: it was responsiveness to the word and sacraments that should mark
the Church of Christ, not the form of its outward organization or alle-
giances. When the circumstances of its history demanded that the English
church should mark its autonomy from the Church of Rome at one stage, or
from the radical wing of the Reformation at another, it was not abandoning
its sense of participation in the history of the universal Church any more
than it was denying its broad sympathy with the continental movements for
reform. It was simply choosing to differ over specific interpretations as to
how commitments to the authority of the Bible or tradition were to be
identified and expressed. It is the debates over the range of such interpretations that largely make up the course of Anglican theological history; but
the central belief that makes such discussion possible is that the Church,
while universal in its faith and obligation, also possesses a particular vocation and calling.

THE DOCTRINE OF THE CHURCH AS INTERPRETED
WITHIN THE CHURCH OF ENGLAND

Most Reformed bodies acknowledged the continuing importance of Catholic norms of belief. More than one realized also the utility of allowing that some aspects of the Church's existence were matters of indifference. Where the English Reformers had broken new ground was in retaining intact many of the traditional structures of the Church, and in allowing that certain doctrinal matters could be included among the *adiaphora*. A thoroughgoing biblical critique does impose its own limitation on doctrinal formulae, precisely because the Bible is not doctrinally precise, especially in matters of ecclesiology. The English understanding of biblical authority made it logically necessary to allow that some beliefs were open to dispute, and therefore that a diversity of interpretations had to be allowed in several areas of theological debate. The problem was of course in deciding just when the limits of biblical authorization had been reached, and just what could or could not be considered 'indifferent'.

It was in the terms of that controversy that Richard Hooker compiled *The Laws of Ecclesiastical Polity* (1593–7). Against the Puritan ideal of replicating an exact New Testament model of church organization, Hooker argued that the Church was an organic not a static institution, and that the law of God was such that methods of church government and administration would change according to circumstances. Where the Bible was silent or unclear Hooker claimed that guidance should be taken from four propositions 'such as no man of moderate judgement hath cause to think unjust or unreasonable'. These were: that anything which effectively promotes godliness, has received the approval of antiquity, or has received the support of the Church's own system of government, should prove acceptable; and that conversely, no institution or ordinance which is not expressly commanded by Scripture should be made a matter of necessity for the Church, no matter how useful or profitable it may appear to be.[1]

The biblical radicalism of the first Reformers was arguably better sustained by Hooker and his younger contemporary Richard Field than by their continental counterparts, inasmuch as the former refused to tie the Church of England to particular forms of dogma or discipline, and recognize the eschatological and dialectical nature of truth and purity.[2] They were at one with the Reformers over the central question of the period: 'How can I find a gracious God?' But to the second question, 'Where can I find the true Church?' they gave a more mundane answer. Assurance with regard to the Church was to be found neither in the biblical idealism of the Puritans nor in the conservative traditionalism of the Catholics. The gospel did not come with fail-safe guarantees. The Church always exists under grace, and while truth and purity were not to be taken lightly, their full achievement was still awaited and in the meantime could only be perceived in faith. No form of discipline or safeguards on doctrine could replace that perception.

Hooker's approach to the identity of the Church had its application to church doctrine as well. The question of the visibility of the Church is a case in point. The Reformers inevitably laid emphasis on membership of the invisible Church, an inward thing known only to God, in order to counter the Roman claim that membership of the Church involved participation in the hierarchical structure which centred on the papacy. The Anglican theologians attended to the concept of the Church as the mystical body of Christ or the invisible company of the elect, but never finally at the expense of the reality of the Church in its temporal form. Their language may have been ambiguous at times, but they steadily refused to identify the visible/invisible dichotomy with the notion of truth and falsity in the Church. Hooker was clear that the Church would always contain a mixed membership and that the validity of its life could only be demonstrated by way of costly obedience to the law of God. Neither he nor Field neglected the divine origins of the Church (and that was later reinforced by John Pearson's influential *Exposition of the Creed*, 1659) but concentrated on the concrete, historical existence of the people of God and their role within the body politic. Field, in *Of the Church* (1606–10), responded to the Catholic apologist, Bellarmine, that it was a waste of time his trying to prove to Anglicans that there was and always had been a visible Church, for that fact had never been doubted by them.

Hooker's and Field's attention to the central reality of the Church and their restraint over the question of its circumference presented a theological position more pragmatic, realistic and ecumenical than that of most other second-generation leaders of the reform. One might equally say that they more clearly maintained a grasp on the graciousness of God. Doctrine was not unimportant to the defenders of Anglicanism, but they appreciated that doctrinal precision of itself could never guarantee a full measure of faith, hope or love. At its best, Anglicanism's doctrinal openness recognized that the mystery of God was not to be contained by a formula or by the victory of one biblical principle over another. Just how baptism related to faith, or bread and wine communicated the presence of Christ, or the historic episcopate mediated an apostolic ministry, was never explained in the classical period of Anglican development. Scripture and history keeps such questions alive within the Anglican consciousness and the tradition of continuing debate holds out the hope of increasing clarification of the issues involved. Ideally the Anglican understanding of the Church secures to it the full variety of biblical models and metaphors by which it is described, and attempts to work out the significance of those descriptions in everyday, historical experience.[3]

Grace, however, is not easily lived with, and the demands of ongoing theological articulation are not always welcomed by the Church. Anglicanism is at its least satisfactory when it is able to avoid facing the implications of its own internal tensions. It has often been observed that the Church of England underwent a sea-change between the seventeenth century, when it opposed Puritanism because of its narrowness, and the eighteenth, when it resisted Methodism on account of its enthusiasm. The Puritans may not have been as narrow as is commonly believed and enthusiasm was certainly more complex than it may appear, but it is the change in Anglican self-consciousness that is of importance here. In the first place, as a reaction to the excesses of the Commonwealth and the sufferings of the exiles, episcopal order came to assume a normative importance for Anglicans which it had not held previously. The Church of England became identified with the episcopate. Furthermore the deprivation of the Nonjurors lost to the church a spiritual and devotional legacy which was more important than the actual number of priests and bishops who were involved would suggest. Not only did this diminish the bond of worship which, it was held, still unified different theological emphases within the national church; it also left it firmly established as a guardian of self-interest. The Church of England emerged looking suspiciously like a department of state, ill-equipped to cope intellectually with the spread of Enlightenment thought, or pastorally with the effects of the Industrial Revolution, or theologically with the rise of the Evangelical Revival.

It would be idle to pretend that Anglican restraint in defining doctrine was always the result of a highly principled commitment to comprehensiveness. Equally important was the fact that at critical points of church history no one group was able to dominate for long enough to impose its ideals on the remainder of the Anglican body. The failure of the Church of England during the eighteenth century was most evident in the way it was dominated by the state to such an extent that Newman would have some justification believing that by his day it was the establishment alone which erected the Church of England to unity and individuality. Strip it of this world, he challenged, and it will be a mortal operation, for it will cease to be.[4] Accompanying this virtual Erastianism, partly as a cause and partly an effect, was the loss of any theological sense of the origin and destiny of the Church as such. Such ecclesiology as was advanced—the rights of the episcopate and the necessity of liturgical conformity—was largely used to unchurch and disenfranchise those who in any way dissented from Anglican jurisdiction. Only during the nineteenth century did renewal come, largely through a reassertion of the doctrine of the Church in Anglican thinking.

256

Renewal came from various sources. Churchmen influenced by the Evangelical Revival pressed the need for personal conversion as the key to effective church and social action, although for them this was often expressed in inter-church or voluntary associations of the like-minded, rather than in the mainstream of church life. Leaders like Charles Simeon (1759-1836) (see pp. 181–2), and especially those who learnt from him, ensured that biblical and pastoral preaching found its proper place in parochial ministry. However, they remained relatively unconcerned with proposals for wholesale reform like those advocated by Coleridge or Thomas Arnold in *On the Constitution of Church and State* (1830) and *Principles of Church Reform* (1833) (see pp. 398–400). The liberal or Broad Church voice within Anglican opinion could trace its accents back to the Latitudinarians or the humanist tradition of earlier generations; but the approach of men like Arnold, R. D. Hampden or Richard Whately would only ever appeal to a small if influential minority in the church. At a time when the established church was increasingly marginalized in its influence, theirs was a serious attempt to relocate its position nearer the centre of intellectual and public life in England. The most enduring changes came from the Tractarian or Oxford Movement which in contrast to the liberal group boldly reasserted the divine origins of the church in order to establish its spiritual autonomy from the state. The Tractarians sought to demonstrate its true character by restoring what they believed to be primitive practice in the Church and laying claim to the essential Catholicity of Anglican faith and order.

While the Evangelical emphasis on personal religion and the liberal programme for rationalizing dogma left ecclesiological questions still on the periphery of the church's agenda, the High Churchmen placed them right at the centre. In 1838, W. Palmer's *Treatise on the Church of Christ* had put forward a so-called 'branch theory' of the Church and this was taken up enthusiastically by the Tractarians. It was postulated that there were three authentic scions of Catholic Christianity—the Roman, Eastern and Anglican Churches—which shared common historical and sacramental stock. While not in communion with each other, this common ancestry meant that these three groups of churches alone could claim to be part of the Catholic and apostolic Church. Focusing as it did on a particular idea of apostolic succession, this theory proved too much for some critics (since it left the Reformed tradition within the Church of England exposed to an anomaly), and too little for others (as the departure of Newman and others in favour of the more self-confident claims of the Roman Catholic Communion demonstrated).

The second half of the nineteenth century certainly saw attention directed once again to the doctrine of the Church, but this was accompanied by a hardening of attitudes and an increase in dogmatically held

257

positions. What was even more significant was the failure of the Church of England to find any means of resolving these differences. Falling back on a succession of legal tests ranging from the Gorham Case in 1847 to the Lincoln Judgement of 1890, it proved impossible to use the Articles or the other formularies to define just what were the beliefs of the Anglican Church. Each appellant claimed that his interpretation represented a legitimate line of Anglican theological development. With no means of achieving or even approaching a consensus, the different groupings within the Church of England became increasingly partisan in their attitudes; and the Anglican understanding of the Church took on the varied complexion of apparently contradictory opinion which still typifies Anglicanism in the eyes of some of its critics.

THE DOCTRINE OF THE CHURCH AS AMPLIFIED BY THE ANGLICAN COMMUNION

If the nineteenth century saw a failure to resolve problems of ecclesiology in the Church of England, it also witnessed a dramatic expansion of the context in which they were to be raised. Missionary activity, with commerce and colonization, led to the founding of Anglican churches in many parts of the world. This led to new questions about status and relationship, and in fact gave rise to the situation where it was possible or indeed necessary to talk about 'Anglicanism' as such. The story of the growth of the Anglican Communion and the gathering of the first Lambeth Conferences has been told elsewhere (see pp. 210–12 and pp. 39–43), but these developments had a twofold significance for Anglican ecclesiology. Firstly, they led to a new awareness of the autonomy of the national churches, and secondly, to a consideration of their interdependence.

The freedom of national churches to order their own affairs was of course precisely the right claimed by the Church of England in its most formative period, and by choice or from necessity it was reiterated by the leaders of new churches as they struggled towards their independence. When Huntington challenged Episcopalians in the United States to take their vocation more seriously, he was not only returning to the aspirations of those who had reorganized the church there after the War of Independence, but also the convictions of those who had given the Church of England its particular identity some two centuries earlier. The North American example had in fact proved instructive, as colonial bishops, realizing their own spiritual authority, followed the American example and organized their churches under synodical compacts in order to take responsibility for their own local life and leadership.

At the same time as asserting their independence, the new churches affirmed a strong inclination to maintain connections with the Church of England and to take opportunities for 'brotherly counsel and encouragement' with each other. To this end the first Lambeth Conference met in 1867, and from it stemmed the network of inter-Anglican organization and ideology which gives shape to the Anglican Communion as 'a fellowship of national Churches' today. What sort of shape is it, though? From the beginning the Conferences renounced any legislative powers. The authority of each meeting was limited to the inherent wisdom of its deliberations. Any statement made possessed only the authority of those bishops who put their names to it. The Conference could make recommendations, but it was up to the member churches to judge their worth and take whatever action they deemed appropriate. Each ten-yearly meeting 'focuses the experience and counsels of our communion' explained a statement from the 1920 Conference, 'yet it claims no power of control or command'. A committee of the 1930 Lambeth Conference underlined the conviction concerning Anglican unity: 'There are two prevailing types of ecclesiastical organization: that of a centralized government, and that of regional autonomy within one fellowship.' In common with the Church of the first centuries and with Orthodoxy to this day, it argued, the Anglican Communion was constituted on the second model. It was not always clear, however, just what sort of fellowship Anglican churches shared, nor what gave cohesiveness to their Communion, nor indeed in what way that Communion was Anglican. Various solutions have been proposed. If ideas of a centralized council seemed inappropriate, unity which was based on any statement of peculiarly Anglican beliefs was even less likely to win recognition. The Thirty-Nine Articles, the most likely candidate for such a confessional role, had already faded in Anglican consciousness as a result of their failure to maintain peace during the nineteenth-century controversies in England. To churches intent upon discovering their own indigenous character they seemed remote in the extreme, and in 1968 the Lambeth Conference recommended that churches should formally distance themselves from the Articles, honouring them for their historical significance but discarding any attempt to utilize them as a contemporary confession of faith. For some time it was held, as an alternative source of authority, that the Book of Common Prayer could act both as a bond of union and a principal source of Anglican teaching. The inevitable process of liturgical translation and revision carried out by the national bodies meant that at most, they could only share a common structure of worship. The cultural diversity of the churches of the Communion made the idea of a common liturgical form an impossibility. At a rather different level, the Archbishop of Canterbury, as convenor of the Lambeth Conferences, has played a distinct role in giving cohesion to Anglican unity. His authority like that of the Conferences is moral, given

259

to him by mutual consent and not exercised as of right. As a personal link the office is increasingly valued by the churches, but the Archbishop remains a pivot not a pope, as Randall Davidson put it.[5] The role of the Archbishop, like that of the Conferences, the Anglican Consultative Council and the Primates' Meeting, the Doctrine or Justice and Peace Commissions as they now exist, is a contingent and not a necessary factor in Anglican ecclesiology.

The apparent failure to find in formularies or administrative norms a focus for Anglican identity should neither alarm nor suprise an observer. It brings back into focus, amongst others, William Reed Huntington and his insistence that it was on the basis of faith, sacraments, and a shared ministry that the 'church idea' would be established.

THE DOCTRINE OF THE CHURCH AND THE CREDIBILITY OF ANGLICANISM

Huntington, it will be remembered, was doing two things. He was drawing out of the inheritance of the Church of England theological resources which could unite Christians in North America, and he was doing this in order that the message and reality of the incarnation of Christ might have a formative influence on the emerging life of the new nation. Enough has been said to make it apparent why that work was taken as typical of the way in which the doctrine of the Church is treated within Anglicanism. Anglicans, like the early Church, and like the Orthodox Churches to this day, have refrained from producing a standard, systematic theology of the Church, but that does not mean that they have shown no interest in ecclesiology. All the historic questions about unity, catholicity and holiness have been raised repeatedly in the course of Anglican theological development: numerous ecclesiological models have been put forward from within Anglicanism, but it remains true that Anglican self-consciousness has not been fixated upon any one of them. If it is charged that such indecision robs Anglicanism of the right to serious theological consideration, it must be countered that the Anglican system is not that of a confessional church whose norms and standards are fixed and open to scrutiny, so much as it is that of a confessing church which must demonstrate its credibility by the way it meets successive challenges of faith and history in its ongoing life. Two brief examples must suffice to show the sort of evidence that may count for this purpose.

It must be admitted that quite often talk of Anglicanism's doctrinal comprehensiveness is a mask to cover doctrinal indifference. However, at its best the willingness to hold open various interpretations of the Church makes Anglicanism into what Michael Ramsey has called 'a school of synthesis'. The fact that the Anglican Communion has no complete theological system keeps it aware that the Church awaits its restoration. The fact that the Lambeth Quadrilateral imposes no interpretation on how faith and order are to express the fullness of Christ's salvation is itself a witness to the present incompleteness of the Church, yet it also holds out an anticipation of its achieving eschatological wholeness. If it is true that the gospel of Christ has its Catholic and Protestant principles, that the Bible is concerned with prophetic and with priestly religion, and that the early Church was formed under both institutional and charismatic impulses, then the Anglican attempt to bring together in one fellowship such different understandings of Christian discipleship justifies itself.

Anglicans are painfully aware also that their claim to be a 'bridge church', or the reconcilers of a divided household, has been made to look delusory when tested against the hard realities of ecumenical engagement (see pp. 409–414). It was Michael Ramsey again who emphasized that true Catholicity is not to be found either in the adjustment of confessional differences or in the imposition of particular structures in pursuit of ecumenical agreements. The biblical metaphors of the Church—building, body, vine, ecclesia—all speak of both the givenness of its life under God and also of the way in which it must constantly grow to become perfectly what it is.[6]

A conscious acceptance of the tension between an inheritance from the past and a vision for the future presents a continuing challenge and an opportunity for Anglicanism. The way in which it is able to expound and develop its tradition in the face of its own internal differences—in matters of faith and doctrine, as well as questions of order arising from the ordination of women to the priesthood and episcopate—will determine whether or not they still have anything to offer to the wider Church. If not, then Anglicans will presumably walk quietly into that seclusion which Huntington warned against. If, however, they are able to successfully address the question of their own identity, they may yet be able to model for the Church an important way of maintaining unity of the Spirit in a bond of peace.

It is because the Anglican view of the Church seeks to do justice both to a vision of the Church in its universal dimension and to the reality of the Church in its local manifestations, that it is difficult to envisage a systematic treatment of its teaching. Yet to promote a dogma which resolved the Anglican dilemma at the expense of one or the other aspect of it would be to take from Anglicanism its vocation and its ecumenical and missionary opportunity.

At about the time Huntington was writing in America, E. B. Pusey was called upon to explain to a German correspondent the peculiarities of Anglican ecclesiological scholarship:

You will doubtless have observed that few, if any, of our writings have originated in an abstract love of investigation; our greatest and some immortal works have arisen in some exigencies of the times; the writings of Chillingworth, Hooker, Butler, Bull (and so of the rest) were written not merely to solve problems of importance in themselves, but such as the good of the Church in our country at that time required.[7]

If that is granted, then it must also be acknowledged that while the Anglican view of the Church may be incomplete from a doctrinal point of view, it is not in its spirit or in its teaching unbiblical. Anglican ecclesiology claims more, but no less, than that.

BIBLIOGRAPHY

Avis, P. D. L., *Anglicanism and the Christian Church*. T. & T. Clark, Edinburgh, 1989.

Avis, P. D. L., *Christians in Communion*. Geoffrey Chapman, London, 1990.

Evans, G. R., *Authority in the Church: A Challenge for Anglicans*. Canterbury Press 1990.

Giles, K., *What on Earth is the Church?* SPCK, London, 1995.

Hanson A. T., and Hanson R. P. C., *The Identity of the Church*. SCM, London, 1987.

Kaye, B., *A Church Without Walls: Being Anglican in Australia*. North Blackburn, Dove, 1995.

Nockels, P. B., *The Oxford Movement in Context: Anglican High Churchmanship 1760–1857*. CUP 1994.

Ramsey, A. M., *The Gospel and the Catholic Church*. Longman, London, 1936.

Sykes, S. W., *Authority in the Anglican Communion*. Anglican Book Centre, Toronto, 1978.

Sykes, S. W., *Unashamed Anglicanism*. DLT, London, 1995.

NOTES
1 *The Laws of Ecclesiastical Polity*, V. vi-ix.
2 See Paul Avis, '"The True Church" in Reformation Theology'. *Scottish Journal of Theology*, 30(1977), pp. 319–45.
3 For a Roman Catholic's appreciation of this fact, see Avery Dulles, *Models of the Church* (Gill and Macmillan, Dublin, 1976), p. 10.
4 *Discourses to Mixed Congregations*, XII (1849), pp. 265–6.
5 G. K. A. Bell, *Randall Davidson*, (OUP, 1935), Vol i, p. 444.
6 Michael Ramsey, *Canterbury Pilgrim* (SPCK, London, 1974), p. 110.
7 H. P. Liddon, *Life of Pusey* (1893–7), Vol i, p. 238.

2 The Fundamentals of Christianity

STEPHEN W. SYKES

THE MODERN POSITION

Within Anglicanism there is a long tradition of direct appeal to the 'fundamentals of Christianity', or to 'the fundamental articles of the faith' (the two are not necessarily the same). As we shall see, it is quite mistaken to believe that such an appeal distinguishes the Anglican from other communions. What does seem to be the case, however, is that there are good reasons why the contrast between fundamentals and non-fundamentals found a ready home among Anglicans, and has been in use in various contexts and in various ways to the present day.

Examples of modern use of the distinction are to be found in both the Malta Report and the Final Report of the Anglican–Roman Catholic International Commission,[1] of which Archbishop Henry McAdoo, a distinguished contemporary exponent of this tradition, was Anglican co-chairman.[2] The connection between fundamentals and the comprehensiveness of the Church is made clear in the Report of one section of the 1968 Lambeth Conference: 'Comprehensiveness demands agreement on fundamentals, while tolerating disagreement on matters in which Christians may differ without feeling the necessity of breaking communion.'[3]

A final indication of the importance of the notion of fundamentals and a possible way of construing it is to be found in the formulation and adoption by the 1888 Lambeth Conference of what has become known as the Chicago–Lambeth Quadrilateral. The four elements of this statement (Scripture, the creeds, two sacraments and the episcopate) have received repeated endorsement up to the present, though lately with qualifications and amplification.[4]

As we shall see, there are considerable complexities hidden in the proposal that all Christians do, can or should agree on fundamentals, a proposal which on the surface appears to be self-evident, or at least highly desirable. There is no ready-made precision in the content of the fundamentals, and despite its deployment by some leading Roman Catholic theologians, among them Karl Rahner,[5] it has been regularly dismissed as a Protestant theory, contrary to the unity of the Church as instituted by Christ and unrealizable in practice without an infallible authority to determine its content.[6] The tradition whose history we are to trace is neither redundant nor parochial; nor are all Anglicans agreed about it.

For example, in a sharp and clarifying appendix, 'On the Doctrine of Fundamentals', in his 1838 Treatise on the Church of Christ, the learned Tractarian, William Palmer (of Worcester College, Oxford), wrote:

This term is capable of so many meanings as applied to Christian doctrine, and it actually is, has been, and must continue to be, used in so great a diversity of senses, that it is morally impossible to avoid perplexity while it is employed in controversity. As an ambiguous term, as conveying no one definite notion, it seems unqualified to be of any pratical utility in questions of controversy.[7]

This is a challenge which must be taken seriously.

THE REFORMATION TRADITION

The reason for the Reformed Church of England's interest in 'the fundamentals' is plain enough: it derives from the charge against the Church of Rome that it has departed from the standards of the early Fathers, of the apostles and of Christ, and the corresponding claim that 'we have called home again to the original and first foundation that religion which hath been foully neglected and utterly corrupted' (Bishop Jewel's *Apology of the Church of England*, 1564).[8] The recall to fundamentals is a motif capable of being expressed in a variety of metaphors, of which 'foundation' is only one of the possibilities—but an important one, because it recalls a series of impressive biblical texts. ('If the foundations are destroyed what can the righteous do?', Ps. 11.3; 'Behold I am laying in Zion for a foundation, a stone, a tested stone', Isa. 28.16, cited in 1 Pet. 2.6; the parable of the men who built houses with and without proper foundation, Matt. 7.24–7; Luke 6.47–9; 'No other foundation can any one lay than that which is laid, which is Jesus Christ', 1 Cor. 3.11; 'So then you are [. . .] built upon the foundation of the apostles and prophets, Jesus Christ himself being the chief corner-stone', Eph. 3.20).

At the very start of the Reformation we are introduced to a dispute which has constantly returned to complicate the recall to fundamentals. Erasmus held that it should be possible for Christians to agree upon those few and simple truths which were intimately connected with practical Christian living. Much else, including the complexities of the Reformers' view of the human condition and the terms of salvation, could be left to theological debate. Luther vehemently disagreed with such agnosticism. What he was teaching, he asserted, was simply the plain content of the Scriptures, proclaimed openly to the world and taught to the heart internally by the Holy Spirit.[9] Throughout his voluminous and unsystematic writings there are scattered numerous different ways of summarizing the foundation, the chief article, the head, the heart and so forth of the gospel. For Luther the whole Christian faith hangs together, like a chain, or a ring, or a bell. No one part could be lost, if the whole is to survive.

Erasmus' proposals were ignored by the Council of Trent, but were widely influential in England. So also was another idea, closely related to that of the fundamentals, but with a long and independent history, namely the fact that there were certain matters in relation to which Christians had freedom. These *adiaphora*, or things indifferent, became of great importance to the entire Reformation tradition.[10] Luther, for example, in reply to Henry VIII's *Assertion of the Seven Sacraments* (1521), had argued that whatever went

264

beyond the Scriptures was a matter of indifference and should not be turned into a 'necessary doctrine'.[11] The term *adiaphoron* (plural, *adiaphora*) was frequently used by William Tyndale, and certain doctrines, notably those of purgatory or transubstantiation, became tests of what was necessary and what indifferent. John Frith (c. 1503–33) carefully explained, while awaiting death by burning, that he was convinced that the Christian was free to disagree with the view, held by his episcopal interrogators, that transubstantiation was 'an undoubted article of the faith, necessary to be believed under pain of damnation' ('Articles Wherefore John Frith Died', 1533).[12] Three years later, after issuing his Ten Articles, Henry VIII was instructing his bishops 'in no wise to treat of matters indifferent, which be neither necessary to our salvation [...] nor yet to be in any wise contemned'.[13]

Within England, of course, power was sufficiently centralized for instructions of this kind to be enforced, and one should not underestimate the importance of political pressure for eliminating disagreement. Militating against wider Protestant concord over fundamentals was the fact that the politically separate parts of the movement of reformation accustomed themselves to different solutions of the question. The sixteenth, seventeenth and eighteenth centuries are replete with sincere and devoted persons seeking ecclesiastical agreement between the separate branches of Christendom on the basis of agreements on fundamentals. But the political forces keeping the churches apart were stronger than good intentions. The separate political entities became accustomed to different usages, and resistance to change from outside hardened.

In the early years of the Reformation, however, matters were not so settled. From the Lutheran side, notably Philip Melanchthon (1497–1560) sought to define an area of common ground with Rome.[14] From the Roman Catholic side, solidly in the Erasmian tradition was the remarkable Georg Cassander (1513–66), a Flemish lay scholar who lived latterly in Cologne and devoted himself to the exploration of ground for restoring peace between Roman Catholics and Protestants. In the tireless (and fruitless) work of both there is a discernible emphasis on the cognitive content of Christianity, upon fundamental *articles* of belief as supplying the only secure basis for reconciliation. Thus the Augsburg Confession of 1530, largely the work of Melanchthon, is an article-by-article distillation of Reformation teaching in its most moderate and eirenic form. And Cassander's appeal was to the Creed and the faith of the Church of the first six centuries in agreement with the formula of St Vincent of Lérins (the so-called Vincentian cannon: 'What has been believed everywhere, always and by all'), as supplying the qualifying basis for a Church to be reckoned a true Church.

SEVENTEENTH-CENTURY ANGLICANISM

Stress has been laid on the non-Anglican treatment of fundamental articles in order to place the Anglican reception of this tradition in its proper context. Given Cranmer's knowledge of the Fathers and his comparative liturgical conservatism, Cassander's outline of the basis for reconciliation had obvious apologetic value. A work of the Swiss Reformer, Bullinger (1504–75), the *Decades*, was also highly esteemed in England for its demonstration that the Reformed religion was none other than that professed in the creeds and councils of the primitive Church.

But however much subsequent Anglicans owed to Roman Catholic, Lutheran and Calvinist predecessors, it is important that we observe the possibility of a *de facto* settlement of the question of fundamentals as well as a written theological apologetic. Use can determine what is held to be fundamental, as well as theory. The means by which reformation came about impinge closely on this question; these means include the authorization and imposition of Books of Common Prayer, the successive versions of the *Articles of Religion*, the issuing of authorized homilies and in due course the provision of a Book of Canons (see pp. 6–15, pp. 131–9, and pp. 144–50)—all these were imposed with the authority of King-in-Parliament and the consent of the clergy in Convocation. Although the Thirty-Nine Articles refer to Scripture as the criterion of things necessary to salvation (see pp. 90–3), in none of these instruments of settlement is there a final and authoritative formulation of the fundamentals. That too is significant, as is the eminently reformable and progressive character of the work.

From the last years of the reign of Elizabeth I onwards there developed a considerable apologetic literature to explain and justify the nature of the English Reformation. We have already referred to Bishop Jewel's *Apology*. A little later Richard Hooker himself formulated what he termed 'the essence of Christianity' (in the earliest English use of that phrase known to me) as the God-given unity of the visible Church in the profession of one Lord, one faith and one baptism.[15] The one faith is constituted by those few articles of Christian belief confessed by such early Fathers as Tertullian and Irenaeus. Hooker, who was already embroiled in controversies with moderate Puritans still part of the comprehensive Church of England, is at once drawn into detailed argument about whether one complete form of church polity has been laid out in Scripture, thus forming part of what must be maintained as necessary to salvation. Against such a view, Hooker's position is clear. The articles of the Christian faith and the sacraments of the Church of Christ are absolutely necessary to salvation. The accessories are things which discretion will teach the Church how to decide, and decisions may vary from place to place and time to time without contradicting their God-given basis in natural reason.

In the seventeenth century, the appeal to the undivided Church of the first five centuries commended itself to a number of prominent persons, among them the Dutch jurist and theologian, Hugo Grotius, and the Genovese Calvinist, Isaac Casaubon (1559–1614), who emigrated to England in 1610 and contributed warmly to an apologetic for the Church of England. Georg Calixtus (1586–1656), who met Casaubon in London in 1612, was a German Lutheran likewise impressed with this argument, to which he linked the criterion provided by the Vincentian canon and a certain stress on practical Christian living deriving from Erasmus.

But the 'fundamental articles' tradition lent itself also to the exposition of a strich Lutheran orthodoxy, which it received at the hands of Nicholaus Hunnius (1585–1643). In one of the most penetrating analyses of different kinds of fundamental, Hunnius distinguished between the *substantial* foundation, which is God and Christ, the *organic*, which is the holy Scriptures, and the *dogmatic*, the content of Christian doctrine. The last named is then subdivided between primary articles which all must confess, secondary articles which none must deny, and non-fundamentals which may be ignored or disputed. The point of this treatment is to show that though Lutherans and the Reformed might be agreed about the substantial and the organic fundamentals, there are fundamental differences in primary and secondary articles of doctrine. Here we come face to face with the fact that *per se* appeal to the notion of fundamentals is not, of itself, an ecumenically hopeful procedure. The problems are to be seen in the career of the remarkable Scottish ecumenist, John Durie (1596–1680), whose attempts to achieve European Protestant unity on the basis of agreement on fundamentals were frustrated by a combination of denominational intransigence and political rivalries.

In England the context in which the fundamentals of fundamental articles were principally deployed was that of controversy with Roman Catholic theologians. Bishop Lancelot Andrewes (1555–1626) addressed himself to the attack of the Jesuit Bellarmine on the claim of King James I to be a Catholic. Adopting the theory already advanced by Calixtus, he held that the profession of the creeds and canons of the first four Councils was a sufficient title for the Church of England. His definition of the boundaries of Anglicanism occurs in a sentence later to become famous:

One canon reduced to writing by God himself, two testaments, three creeds, four general councils, five centuries, and the series of Fathers in that period—the centuries that is, before Constantine, and two after, determine the boundary of our faith.[16]

Andrewes was in touch with both Casaubon, to whom he showed his reply to Bellarmine, and somewhat less cordially with Grotius.

Twenty years later William Laud (1573–1645) conducted a famous controversy with a Jesuit theologian, John Fisher (1569–1641), subsequently published as A Relation of the Conference between William Laud and Mr Fisher the Jesuit (1639). Against the proposition advanced by Fisher that all points defined by the Church are fundamental, Laud insists that the term 'fundamental' can only apply to the articles of the Creed. There may be many true deductions from the Creed, of which simple people are unaware, but which it may be necessary for others, more learned, to believe. But nothing is fundamental merely because the Church says it is so, but only because it is of itself. Picking up Andrewes' stress on Scripture and reflecting the earlier work of Protestant controversalists, Laud asserts that the belief that Scripture is the word of God and infallible is a preceding, prime principle of faith to be held along with the Creed. That the Church of England's positive articles are grounded in Scripture, he is content to be judged by the joint and constant belief of the Fathers of the first five centuries (see pp. 110–14):

> To believe the Scripture and the Creeds, to believe these in the sense of the ancient primitive Church, to receive the four great Councils so much magnified by antiquity, to believe all points of doctrine, generally received as fundamental in the Church of Christ, is a faith in which to live and die cannot but give salvation.[17]

Others who wrote in the same sense included Archbishop James Ussher (1581–1656), and later Bishop Jeremy Taylor (1613–67) and Henry Hammond (1605–60).

But did the testimony of the Fathers cohere quite precisely as these apologists claimed? Some held that it did not. A group of scholars in England, known as the Tew Circle, believed that resort to the Fathers only produced confusion, a view which received strong support from the work of the eminent French Protestant patristic scholar, John Daillé, On the Use of the Fathers (French, 1632). The argument of William Chillingworth (1604–44), who was Laud's godson, but who for a period had become a Roman Catholic influenced by the arguments of Fisher, shows a certain withdrawal from the patristic reference. In a controversial writing of 1638, Religion of Protestants a Safe Way to Salvation, he attempts to explain the relation between Scripture and the fundamentals. Once a person is persuaded that Scripture contains all things necessary to salvation (a quotation of Article VI), then it is enough if that person strenuously attempts to find and to believe the true sense of it. There is no final catalogue of all the truths which one must believe, because, on his argument, there is a vital moral component in all believing deriving from human autonomy. Chilling-worth insisted, at the same time, upon the simplicity of the essentials of the faith.[18]

The clarification of an important point, at this time, was the work of another apologist, Edward Stillingfleet (1635–99), replying to the Jesuit account of the controversy between Laud and Fisher. In *A Rational Account of the Grounds of Protestant Religion* (1664) Stillingfleet distinguished between things which are necessary to the salvation of persons as such, in their individual capacities, and things which are necessary to be acknowledged by Christian societies, or as the bonds and conditions of ecclesiastical communion. The discussion of fundamentals had, he held, wavered uncertainly between the two, but they should not be confused. Concentrating upon the latter of the two uses, a later defender of Stillingfleet, William Sherlock (1641–1707), undertook to define 'fundamentals' in the following way:

> A *fundamental doctrine* is such a doctrine as is in strict sense of the *essence* of Christianity, without which the whole building and superstructure must fall; the belief of which is necessary to the very being of Christianity, like the *first principles* of any *art* or *science.*[19]

REDEFINITIONS: THE EIGHTEENTH AND NINETEENTH CENTURIES

If, as suggested earlier, we must be alert to usage as well as to theory, then it must be noted that the seventeenth-century Restoration, which saw the ejection of some 1,760 incumbents from their parishes, set clear bounds to the 'comprehensiveness' of the Church of England. The fact that the Anglican Ordinal insisted that its priests be episcopally ordained must be related to its view of the fundamentals (see pp. 162–3). But how?

One learned, and ecumenically active, contributor to the discussion, Archbishop William Wake (1657–1737), was ambiguous on the point. He had read both Cassander and Grotius and was persuaded that the method of separating out the fundamental articles from the others was, for all its admitted difficulties and dangers, the only feasible way to the restoration of communion, alike with Roman Catholics and within Protestantism.[20] He corresponded extensively on this basis with friendly Roman Catholic theologians in the Sorbonne, but on the quixotic assumption that the Gallican Church would be ready to throw off papal supremacy. The Pope, Wake asserted, had wrongly claimed for himself alone the episcopate 'which Christ bequeathed in part to each several bishop to be held in common'.[21] But Wake had already committed himself enthusiastically to the view, against the Roman Catholic Bossuet's charge of incoherence in Protestantism, that Protestants are already united in whatever is fundamental in the faith (sermon of 1689).[22] Wake stood solidly in the tradition of Hooker, Whitgift and Andrewes in holding that the kind of government of the Church was not a matter affecting the being of the Church, and that although episcopacy is a divine right, it does not follow that a non-episcopal church is no church. He commended the institution of episcopacy to his Reformed and Lutheran friends; he reordained those with Presbyterian orders; but at the same time he wrote that Article XXXVI of the Thirty-Nine Articles 'only asserts the validity of our Book of Ordination, but does not affirm the necessity of the three orders which we retain in our Church' (letter of 1720).[23] Despite extensive correspondence with Swiss theologians notable for their support of the method of defining few fundamentals as a condition of union, the plans came to nothing. Wake found, as others have done since, that far from agreeing on the few Articles in common, many not of his persuasion insisted on laying the greatest emphasis on the points of difference.

A further contribution of major importance to the subject was made by a Cambridge theologian, Daniel Waterland (1683–1740), whose calm and analytic mind illuminated a number of disputes in the eighteenth century and whose works were reprinted constantly into the nineteenth century. In *A Discourse of Fundamentals* (1735), he tackles the question of what should be held to belong essentially to the 'fabric' of Christianity. His solution to the complexities is the work of a systematician. On the premise that Christianity is a covenant, it follows, he argues, that what is essential to Christianity is everything that inheres in the covenant, the two parties, the agreement, the person of the mediator, and the conditions, means and sanctions attaching to the covenant.[24] For the idea of the centrality of covenant, and for numerous features of the argument, Waterland refers to a German Lutheran and disciple of Grotius, Samuel Pufendorf (1632–94).

Following Chillingworth, Waterland asserts that no catologue of fundamental truths is possible. It is adequate to give examples of fundamentals, which must include matters of worship and conduct as well as belief, and a rule for establishing them. If difficulties arise then it is wiser to choose the side of peace and latitude. In the case of doubt the burden of proof lies on those who would assert something to be fundamental.

Waterland acknowledges that other rules have been proposed for deciding upon what is fundamental, and undertakes to support his argument with a brief but radical refutation of alternatives. Notable among those he dismisses are: the definitions of the Church, even of the primitive Churches; the whole of Scripture or even all matters expressly taught in Scripture; the Apostles' Creed (here Waterland acknowledges his disagreement with, amongst others, Calixtus, Chillingworth and Stillingfleet); the mere confession of Jesus as Messiah (with reference to John Locke);[25] and the universal agreement of Christians. His central theological proposal of the notion of covenant as the most comprehensive way in which to determine the terms of church communion leaves open, he believes, the question of the terms of salvation for each individual.

In the second half of the eighteenth century a new set of ideas emerged in European Protestantism to account for the changes in successive historical forms of Christianity. For this way of thinking it became axiomatic that no one historical embodiment of the Christian faith was, or could be, normative for all time, especially no series of propositions. The reasons for this new development were complex, partly the result of investigations into biblical and patristic history which showed internal variety and disagreement, and partly the impact of a new non-cognitive theory of religion, which the Romantic Movement planted indelibly within European Christianity. The result was a need to identify, if possible, an abiding essence behind the changing forms. When Schleiermacher in his epoch-making definition of the 'essence of Christianity' (*Speeches on Religion*, 1799) spoke of Christianity as having an intuited 'principle of coherence', at the same time he denied that it could be constituted by a 'particular quantity of religious matter', a coded way of referring to the 'fundamental articles' tradition.[26]

These European developments coincided with a period in the life of the Anglican Church when the Church of England was at its most self-preoccupied and isolated. The foundation of an independent episcopate overseas occurred through the agency of the Church in Scotland. And welcome though this *de facto* modification of what had hitherto been widely assumed to be fundamental, namely a particular relationship with the sovereign power, might be, it had the effect of intensifying Anglican efforts to explain its own distinctiveness. By the beginning of the nineteenth century, for those groups out of which the Tractarian Movement developed, it was axiomatic that an Anglican defence of its stance as a church must be different from a commonly Protestant one. The altered state of affairs is nicely illustrated in the title of a work by the Irish Bishop of Limerick, John Jebb (1775–1833), *Peculiar Character of the Church of England: as distinguished both from other branches of the Reformation, and from the modern Church of Rome*. It was this work which was given as an example of Anglican apologetic by a young friend of John Henry Newman, Benjamin Harrison, to a Frence abbé whom he had met at a dinner party in Paris in 1834. Jager engaged first with Harrison and then with Newman himself in public controversy over the claim of the Church of England.[27]

The dispute eventually came to centre upon the issue of the fundamental articles. When Newman became involved at the end of the year he had to read himself into the Anglican history we have reviewed, especially the relevant works of Laud, Stillingfleet, Chillingworth and others. In his first intervention, Newman explicitly invokes the idea of fundamentals and continued to justify it throughout the controversy. In his own mind he was merely reproducing the views of Bishop Stillingfleet. But it is now evident, and was evident also to Harrison, that his line of defence amounted to his own theory of fundamentals, a theory which developed into a theory of development, and which eventually helped in his transfer to the Roman Catholic Church.

Jager, who had read some of the *Tracts for the Times*, was evidently astonished to discover that an Anglican was prepared to defend the distinction between fundamentals and non-fundamentals, for him a quintessentially Protestant apologetic. Newman, though his theory of religion was of the mystery lying hid in language, was still keen to insist on the existence of a central immutable core of truth, infallibly taught by the Church. But characteristically he introduced into the discussion a very considerable measure of flexibility and uncertainty about the difference between the core, which he called the apostolic tradition, and exploratory elaborations of it, which he called the prophetic tradition. The theory was indeed his own, and when he wrote it up in full as *Lectures on the Prophetical Office of the Church Viewed Relatively to Romanism an Popular Protestantism* he took pains to emphasize that what he was defending was not Protestantism.[28]

His Tractarian colleagues were more definite. W. H. Froude characteristically told a friend that he nauseated the word fundamental.[29] More seriously, as we have already seen, William Palmer offered to demonstrate the internal inconsistency of the use of the word in the works of Chillingworth, Laud and Waterland. From the last-named person's review of the varieties of opinion Palmer concluded the impossibility of arriving at any adequately agreed rule, and criticized the arbitrariness of thinking that human beings could stand in judgement on divine revelation, a criticism which Karl Barth was to echo a hundred years later.[30] Quoting Keble, Palmer concluded that the only safe way of proceeding was to insist on guarding the whole faith of Christ.

The undoubted advantage of Newman's theory of development was its capacity to absorb the impact of historical relativism. Consistency over time, he argued, required change. Newman's Anglican critics for the most part reverted to earlier static theories. The Church can only be what it has always been, and profess what it always has professed. The works of many of the theologians we have reviewed were reprinted, among them those of Andrewes, Laud, Taylor, Henry Hammond, Herbert Thornlike (1598–1672) and Bishop John Cosin (1594–1672), and were accorded a kind of normative status within Anglicanism (see pp. 177–81). Their defence of fundamental articles preserved a style of theological argument which had ceased to be current in the European context. Although, as we have seen, in its origins it was a tradition shared with a large number of Protestant theologians both Lutheran and Reformed, and a smaller group of Erasmian Roman Catholics, by the nineteenth century it had the appearance of being distinctively Anglican. Both the term 'Anglicanism' and some of the standard definition of its distinctiveness owe much to these developments (see pp. 471–81).

With the challenge of biblical criticism to the doctrine of biblical infallibility, the scriptural basis of the fundamentals became problematic. It was an important development, therefore, when Charles Gore and the *Lux Mundi* school both accepted criticism, and yet continued to defend the truth of all the articles of the Creed. Modern interpretation of the fundamentals tradition is at some pains to argue that the use of reason (as justified by, among others, Hooker and Chillingworth) is part of the method of holding to fundamentals, and that the *Lux Mundi* theologians are the natural heirs of this Anglican tradition.[31] The twentieth century, however, has seen a number of acute controversies relating to doctrines affirmed by the creeds, especially the virgin birth and the (bodily) resurrection of Christ, which raise in an acute form the adequacy of this defence.

MODERN PROBLEMS AND SOLUTIONS

At the beginning of this essay it was remarked that the fundamentals of Christianity are not necessarily to be identified with the fundamental *articles* of Christianity. In the history we have traced, distillation into articles of belief has played a very important part, and is evidently the consequence of an approach to religion which emphasizes its cognitive aspects.[32] A major objection to the 'fundamental articles' tradition is that it is based upon an unbalanced account of what the Christian religion actually is, ignoring or relegating its experiential, ritual or cultural aspect. But there are further difficulties with the appeal to fundamentals *per se* which must also be faced.

First, as Palmer observed, there is no common agreement about what the fundamentals are. Nor is there any agreed rule for determining what they are. Waterland's proposal is ingenious, but in the face of equally plausible competitors it is, *prima facie*, arbitrary.

The charge of arbitrariness raises the question of authority, insistently posed of the 'fundamental article' tradition by apologists for the Roman Catholic Church. Anglican responses which invoke the tradition of the undivided Church, the creeds, or the Vincentian canon bear the aspect of private judgement masquerading as tradition. On close inspection they

273

can be found to furnish either too much or too little.[33] They all suffer alike from what has been called the 'Myth of Christian Beginnings', which were anything but homogeneous.[34]

The recitation of the history of the fundamentals also rarely enough emphasizes the repeated failure of this tradition to solve ecumenical problems. Nor, if Anglicans are honest, does it solve the problems of inner-Anglican ecumenism, the reconciliation of differences over the application of biblical criticism or hermeneutics to matters like the gospel miracles or the patriarchalism of the Scriptures.

Nonetheless, contemporary ecumenism has shown a desire to reinvoke the notion of 'fundamentalism' or a similar term. The official Roman Catholic Response (of 1991) to the Final Report of the Anglican–Roman Catholic Commission (1982) stated that 'there still remain between Anglicans and Catholics important differences regarding essential matters of Catholic doctrine.'[35] A complete ecumenical study devoted itself to the concepts and contents of alleged 'fundamental consensus' and 'fundamental difference'.[36] A successful ecumenical endeavour, involving the British and Irish Anglican Churches and certain Lutheran Churches of the Nordic and Baltic regions, was based on 'a fundamental agreement in faith'.[37]

When terms like the 'fundamentals' or 'the essentials' are being used in such contexts, the parties or persons concerned are offering a judgement between relatively important, and relatively trivial, differences of belief, custom or practice. This distinction enables them to state whether or not the discrepancies are so serious as to be church-dividing. Precisely the same question arises in the minds of those who resisted, or still resist, the ordination of women to the priesthood and episcopate. To change the tradition of male-only ordination implies a judgement that does not belong to the fundamentals of Christianity; to stay (even with serious reservations) in a church which changes its rules implies that the matter is not church-dividing.

Inevitably, when the judgement comes to be made the question arises, what authority this or that organ in the Church has to make such a judgement. In case of Roman Catholicism an explicit answer is returned to that question: the process of ecumenical dialogue 'is followed and encouraged by the Bishops and the Holy See. The Church's teaching authority is responsible for expressing a definitive judgement.'[38] Anglican theology is bound to reflect upon the fact that whenever the decision-making organs of its structures make their judgements on these matters, an implicit claim is made for the legitimacy and propriety of their so doing. The 'fundamentals' do not disclose themselves self-evidently. A church which purports to make these decisions is bound to make explicit its self-understanding in a doctrine of the Church.

BIBLIOGRAPHY
Avis, P., Anglicanism and The Christian Church. T. & T. Clark, Edinburgh, 1989.
Congar, Y., Tradition and Traditions. Burns & Oates, London, 1966. Esp. Excursus B, 'Scripture and the "Truths Necessary for Salvation"', pp. 508–19.
Congar, Y., Diversity and Communion. SCM Press, London, 1984. Esp. ch. 11, 'Agreement on "Fundamental Articles" or on the Positions of the Early Church', pp. 107–25.
Joest, W., 'Fundamentartikel', in Theologische Realenzyklopädie XI. Berlin and New York 1983, pp. 727–32.
Leclerc, J. SJ, Toleration and Reformation, 2 vols, Association Press, New York and London, 1960.
Neill, S. C. and Rouse, R. (eds), A History of the Ecumenical Movement, SPCK, London, 1967. Esp. essays by M. Schmidt, 'Ecumenical Activity on the Continent of Europe in the Seventeenth and Eighteenth Centuries', and N. Sykes, 'Ecumenical Movements in Great Britain in the Seventeenth and Eighteenth Centuries'.
Rowell, G., 'The Confessions of Faith of the Early Church as seen in the Classical Anglican Position': Anglican and Episcopal History 60:3 (September 1991), pp. 305–32.
Valeske, U., Hierarchia Veritatum. Munich 1968. Esp. ch. 3, 'Das Problem der Fundamentalartikel in der Theologiegeschichte der nichtrömischen Kirchen'; and bibliography.
Sykes, S. W., 'Newman, Anglicanism, and the Fundamentals' in I. Kerr and A. G. Hill (eds), Newman after a Hundred Years. Clarendon, Oxford, 1990, pp. 353–74.
Sykes, S. W., Unashamed Anglicanism. DLT, London, 1995.

NOTES
1 Malta Report in A. C. Clark and C. Davey (eds), Anglican/Roman Catholic Dialogue (OUP, London and New York, 1974), pp. 107–15; ARCIC, The Final Report (London 1982), esp. 'Ministry and Ordination', para. 17 (p. 38). The Malta Report is reprinted in The Final Report.

2 See esp. The Spirit of Anglicanism: A Survey of Anglican Theological Method in the Seventeenth Century (ACC, Black, London, 1965); and The Unity of Anglicanism: Catholic and Reformed (Morehouse-Barlow, Wilton, CT, 1983).

3 The Lambeth Conference 1968 (SPCK, London, Seabury Press, New York, 1968), p. 140. It should be made clear that Reports to the Conference carry only the authority of those by whom it was approved, in this case some one-third of the assembled bishops.

4 Bonds of Affection, Proceedings of ACC-6 (ACC, London, 1984), pp. 70–5.

5 Heinrich Fries and Karl Rahner, Unity of the Churches (Philadelphia 1985), pp. 7, 13–23.

6 A. Tanqueray, 'Articles fondamentaux (systéme des)' in Dictionnaire de Théologie Catholique I. iii (Paris 1923), pp. 2025–35, and the encyclical of Pius XI, Mortalium animos (1927), DS 3683, cited by Y. Congar, Diversity and Communion, (SCM, London, 1984), p. 118.

7 E. B. Pusey, Treatise on the Church of Christ I (London 1838), p. 122.

8 Apology of the Church of England (1561), edited by J. E. Booty (University Press of Virginia, Charlottesville, 1974), p. 121.

9 From the Preface to the *Bondage of the Will* (WA 18, p. 603; American edn, 33, p. 5). In J. Dillenberger (ed), *Martin Luther: Selections from his Writings* (New York 1961), p. 170.

10 For an outline of the history of the term see B. J. Verkamp, *The Indifferent Mean: Adiaphorism in the English Reformation to 1554* (Ohio and Wayne State University Presses, Athens, Ohio, Detroit, Mich., 1977), p. 22.

11 Verkamp, *The Indifferent Mean*, p. 96.

12 Verkamp, *The Indifferent Mean*, p. 103.

13 Verkamp, *The Indifferent Mean*, p. 51.

14 On Melanchthon's use of fundamentals see F. Hildebrandt, *Melanchthon: Alien or Ally* (CUP, Cambridge, 1946).

15 Richard Hooker, *Of the Laws of Ecclesiastical Polity*, III. i. 4.

16 L. Andrewes, *Opuscula quaedam Posthuma*, Library of Anglo-Catholic Theology (Oxford 1852), p. 91.

17 *A Relation of the Conference between William Laud and Mr Fisher the Jesuit*, Library of Anglo-Catholic Theology, London 1849), p. 361.

18 See R. L. Orr, *Reason and Authority, The Thought of William Chillingworth* (OUP, 1967), p. 96.

19 William Sherlock, *Vindication of the Defence of Stillingfleet* (London 1682), p. 256.

20 Norman Sykes, *William Wake, Archbishop of Canterbury, 1657–1737*, 2 vols. (CUP, Cambridge, 1957), Vol i, p. 252.

21 Sykes, *Wake*, Vol. i, p. 271.

22 Sykes, *Wake*, Vol. ii, p. 2.

23 Sykes, *Wake*, Vol. ii, p. 19.

24 *The Works of the Rev. Daniel Waterland* (Clarendon Press, Oxford, 1823), p. 95.

25 Locke's reductionist proposals were contained in his *Second Vindication of the Reasonableness of Christianity* (London 1697).

26 F. D. E. Schleiermacher, *On Religion, Speeches to Its Cultured Despisers* (Harper & Row, New York 1958), p. 218. On the history of essence definition, see S. W. Sykes, *The Identity of Christianity* (SPCK, London, 1984), chs 4–8.

27 L. Allen, *John Henry Newman and the Abbé Jager*. OUP, London and New York, 1975.

28 J. H. Newman, *Lectures on the Prophetical Office*. (London 1837); he reissiued this work as a Roman Catholic with a new preface and notes, *The Via Media of the Church of England* (London 1877), Vol. i. See Sykes, *Identity of Christianity*, ch. 5; also 'Newman, Anglicanism and the Fundamentals' in Ker and Hills (eds), *Newman*, pp. 353–74.

29 Cited by J. H. Newman in 'Palmer on Faith and Unity' (a review of Palmer's work on the Church, see n. 7) in *Essays Critical and Historical* (London 1871), p. 174.

30 Barth's discussion of the fundamental articles tradition is to be found in the *Church Dogmatics* I. ii (A. & C. Black, Edinburgh 1956), pp. 863–6.

31 See esp. the argument of P. E. More in 'The Spirit of Anglicanism' in P. E. More and F. L. Cross, *Anglicanism* (London and New York 1935), p. xxxi; also followed by McAdoo (see n. 2).

32 Note esp. G. A. Lindbeck, *The Nature of Doctrine* (SPCK, London/Westminster Press, Philadelphia 1984).

33 See H. B. Swete, *The Holy Catholic Church* (London 1915), p. 241.

34 R. L. Wilkens, *The Myth of Christian Beginnings* (SCM, London 1979).

35 C. Hill and E. Yarnold (eds), *Anglicans and Roman Catholics: The Search for Unity* (SPCK/CTS, London, 1994), p. 157.

36 A. Birmie and H. Meyer, *Grundkonsens—Grunddifferenz* (Frankfurt 1992). This
   work contains a translation into German of this present essay, pp. 132–44.
37 *Together in Mission and Ministry: The Porvoo Common Statement* (1993), p. 16.
38 John Paul II, *Ut Unum Sint* (1995).

3   The Laity
FREDRICA HARRIS THOMPSETT

From time to time in its resolutions and reports, the 1988 Lambeth Conference highlighted 'the ministry of lay people'. The roles lay persons play in
ministry, mission and evangelism were emphasized. The Conference emphatically directed laity:

> [to] take hold of their ministerial responsibility for doing their Christian
> living out in the world. And *only when their Church requires of them* that
> they see their sharing in the life of the streets and shops, of wrestling
> with the land, of feeding, housing and transportation, of business and
> unemployment, *as their Christian vocation of ministry,* will they begin to be
> effective.[1]

This theology concurs with the functional definitions of ministry and mission stated in the Catechism from the American 1979 Book of Common
Prayer. 'The Church carries out its mission through the ministry of all its
members.'[2]

   Over the past three decades, emphasis upon the work of the whole people
of God, most particularly those 99 per cent who are Christian lay persons,
has increased in most denominations. Such assertions evoke the biblical,
Pauline image of the Church as a body built up through the interdependent
activities of its members. Within the contemporary Anglican Communion
there is general theological and familiar rhetorical consensus about encouraging laity to exercise their several and diverse vocations. This vision
of a once and future church that depends heavily upon lay witness, rather
than upon clergy, is not entirely surprising. What is at times controversial,
and certainly consistently problematic, is the challenge of joining reality to
rhetoric, of enfleshing this vision within institutional churches, and of
effectively carrying it out into society at large.

   One source for data on the increased significance accorded to laity is the
scholarly revision of church history. It is no longer enough (if it ever was) to
dwell on scenes of clerical life. Contemporary scholarship demands that
attention be paid to the common folk, to what has been described as
'popular religion'. Critical scholarship has rejected the implicit two-tiered
'producer/consumer' model of supposedly articulate clergy developing

doctrine for presumably inarticulate laity. Historical study of religious life presents more complex paradigms; debate is open as to what factors were and are critical in shaping, nurturing and changing religious beliefs over long periods of time. There is also a new consciousness about those whose experiences and voices have been neglected, whether for reasons of race, class or sex. Those of us who, for example, study the history of women and Christianity bring not only new questions but also new evidence to assess the critical nature of lay witness. The modern ecumenical movement, dating from the World Missionary Conference in Edinburgh in 1910, has also given consistent impetus to studying and extending the global mission of Christian peoples. Following the Second World War, the World Council of Churches pioneered efforts to engage institutional churches in promoting the 'Ministry of the Laity'. The WCC continues to address this agenda as evidenced in the 1982 Faith and Order statement, *Baptism, Eucharist, and Ministry*. One implication of the debates over the ordination of women in Anglican, Catholic and Orthodox Churches has been that church officials, whether pro or con, have come to pay more attention to professional and voluntary opportunities for lay women and lay men. Finally, yet centrally in respect to Anglicanism, it is important to emphasize the role that recent liturgical renewal in several provinces of the Anglican Communion has had in both responding to and shaping new understandings of lay participation both in the Church and in wider society. As a result of these and other factors, there is throughout the Anglican Communion a heightened sensitivity to laity and to new and evolving patterns of the total ministry of all the baptized.

The intent of this chapter is to focus the story of Anglican laity in brief assessments of central topics. This is a compensatory, not comprehensive, perspective designed to point to and deepen understandings of Anglican laity as noted in several other chapters in this volume. Starting with the foundational century of classical Anglicanism, from the Church of England's break with Rome in the sixteenth century, are there distinctive Reformation inheritances for laity today? What principles are called forth when we review understandings of Church, sacraments, mission and ministry from the perspective of the laity? This central aspect in the story of Anglicanism is not a new theme, although several salient characteristics about laity have been eclipsed, underestimated or strategically ignored for long periods of the Church's history. This chapter is intended to encourage the reader's own reflections, to invite further exploration, and to underscore this author's conviction that the ethical character of Christian witness depends upon giving priority to furthering the mission of laity in the world.

LAITY AND THE VISION OF THE ENGLISH REFORMATION

The period of massive religious change that began in the sixteenth century and is collectively called the Reformation was foundational—in both Continental and English contexts and for both Roman Catholic and Protestant formulations—in underscoring the significance of faithful laity in the life of the churches. This period of reform and renewal was one of those historical epochs in which Christians laboured to reclaim the biblical power of the laity and to reform religious life in accord with their understanding of New Testament churches. The Reformation marked a religious movement of considerable strength that was similar to the Evangelical Revival heralded by John Wesley in the eighteenth century, to the awakenings and expansion of religion in nineteenth-century America, to the renewed concern for Christian discipleship among laity in Europe that followed the Second World War, to what has been called the 'Charismatic Movement' that influenced most American denominations by the 1970s, and most recently to the base communities of Latin America. In each of these and in other revival movements, emphasis has been placed on the spiritual equality of clergy and laity.

The Reformation in Europe and in England did succeed in narrowing the distance and breaking down distinctions between clergy and laity. Clergy were permitted, at times encouraged, to marry. Most also gave up late medieval clerical privileges and assumed normal responsibilities of citizenship. Throughout the Renaissance and Reformation, values shifted from elevating the contemplative to advocating the active life. The general Reformation perspective on vocations was that all persons were called. There were differences among vocations, but no spiritual hierarchy. This hallmark of Reformation theology is reflected in a 1985 Church of England study, *All Are Called: Toward a Theology of the Laity*: 'Though we are tainted by our sinfulness, God's woderful grace and love offer us all this common Christian vocation. God leaves everyone free to refuse this call; but the call is there for all without exception.'[3]

There is debate about the impact and benefit of the Reformation on lay people. Recent scholarship has questioned whether most laity were converted to new professions of faith. One historian has suggested that laity 'acquiesced in and accepted' rather than 'promoted and initiated' the Reformation. There were aspects of lay initiative in late medieval life, for example thriving lay confraternities, that disappeared with the Reformation. Historical accounts have underestimated the difficulty of weaning the English populace away from deeply ingrained, habitual, and rich devotional loyalties to late medieval Catholicism. Despite recent revisions of the Reformation's success, the most balanced assessment seems to be that the

279

Reformation did witness in most, if not in all respects, 'a victory of the lay estate over the clerical'.[4] However, it will no longer do for Anglican church historians to describe the Reformation as a 'layman's revolution' or a time of pervasive 'triumph for the laity'.[5]

Historians have also moderated their assessments of the practical extent of lay governance and even royal supremacy. Certainly few bishops from 1540 to 1640 would have agreed that anything like unconditional governing powers had been given to, or won by, laity. Debates over the desirability of real empowerment of laity in church governance continue in the Church of England. They were revived during the 1927–28 fiasco in which the House of Commons rejected a proposed revision of the Prayer Book, the majority vote including a significant number of non-Anglicans, and more recently in deliberations establishing a House of Laity within synodical government.

What then are more accurately modulated assessments of the early Reformation inheritance for laity? What impulses were formative in shaping Anglican expectations of the laity?

A central legacy of the Tudor church was an idealistic social vision of a commonwealth in which the obligation of faithfulness connected all sorts and conditions in their practice of the faith. The Edwardian Homily on Obedience described this vision with inclusive social detail:

> Every degree of people in their vocation, call and office, hath appointed to them their duty and order; some are in high degree, some in low, some kings and princes, some inferiors and subjects, priests and laymen, masters and servants, fathers and children, husbands and wives, rich and poor; and every one have need of other [...] without the which no house, no city, no commonwealth can continue and endure.[6]

The theology of vocations in the English Reformation was not so much a simple imitation of the Lutheran doctrine of a 'priesthood of all believers'. Rather it was an English assertion of encompassing vocations bound together in charity. In this corporate understanding of calling, each person's vocation was set within the social context of the commonwealth. This vision is consistently mirrored in what have been called the 'Great Books' of that time: vernacular Bibles, biblical commentaries (particularly Erasmus's *Paraphrases*), homilies, catechisms, primers, prayer books and other devotional aids.[7]

Tudor Reformers laboured to enflesh the vision of a Christian commonwealth in Tudor England with the assistance of the epoch-making invention of printing. The Reformation, on the Continent and later in England, was the first mass movement to take advantage of the availability of relatively inexpensive printed texts. One author of popular religious tracts asserted that there was 'never so plenty of so good playn bookes prynted, never so good cheap, the Holy Ghost as it were into mennes mouthes offyrnge hys gyftes'.[8] The advent of a print culture, along with the prescripts of Renaissance humanism, triggered a fundamental change toward vernacular education. John Foxe, the zealous reformer and martyrologist, extolled printing as the mightiest weapon against the old religion:

> The Lord began to work for His Church not with sword and target to subdue His exalted adversary, but with printing, writing, and reading [...] so that either the pope must abolish knowledge and printing or printing must at length root him out.[9]

In effect the young printing industry spread the news, shaped the methods, and traced the course of the Reformation.

The medium of print extended and deepened the possibility of a biblically informed faith and the consequent demand for the biblically literate populace. Scripture was the primary authority in the English Reformation. It contained, as stated in the 1563 *Articles of Religion*, 'all things necessary to salvation; so that whatsoever is not read therein, nor may be proved thereby, is not to be required'. The Bible had been part of the medieval world. Biblical images and stories were everywhere, for example in the statues which Thomas Cranmer disparagingly called Catholic 'laymen's books'.[10] What was new was the availability of the Bible (in whole and in part) in printed vernacular translations. Royal and ecclesiastical injunctions dating from the 1530s made it compulsory for English Bibles to be placed in every parish. The Reformers were insistent that the language of revelation was accessible to ordinary citizens. This theme was reiterated in Thomas Cranmer's 1540 preface to the second edition of the Great Bible: 'The apostles and prophets wrote their books so that their special intent and purpose might be understood and perceived of every reader which was nothing but the edification or amendment of the life of them that readeth and heareth it.'[11] The English Reformation literally returned the Bible to the people as the fundamental handbook for Christian living.

Another critical legacy was the Reformation emphasis on religious nurture and education in parishes, households and schools. One of the Reformers' favourite words was 'edification', building up the body of the faithful through learning. Christian humanists had envisaged the reunion of piety and erudition. Erasmus of Rotterdam introduced his translation of the Bible with this optimistic proclamation, 'All can be Christian, all can be devout, and I shall boldly add—all can be theologians.'[12]

Many, though not all, Tudor citizens experienced what has collectively been described as a 'revolution' in educational facilities.[13] By the 1570s overall literacy rates had increased dramatically, though unevenly, across the social strata. There was an increase in the number of petty and grammar

281

schools, as well as a 30 per cent increase in Elizabethans' charitable giving to educational institutions. Publishers' records indicate that printers could rely on a steady demand for printed sermons, Bibles, catechisms, primers, ABCs for adults as well as children, manuals for family and personal devotions, and a seemingly endless demand for religious polemics. Habitual use of the Prayer Book in many English parishes may present an effective index of vernacular religious education, and regular preaching was a centrepiece of religious edification. Efforts to promote religious learning among laity were not in vain. Local studies, like that of the village of Terling in Essex, provide evidence of changing cultural horizons and increased cultural differentiation based upon distinctions in education and religion. One historian has underscored how 'lay involvement in education paralleled the increased laicization of religion'.[14] The overall educational consequences of the Reformation were impressive, indicating 'a heroic effort of religious education by clergy and godly laity alike'.[15]

Hallmarks of the English Reformation for the general populace were an inclusive social vision of the commonwealth, as well as expansive vocational, biblical and educational inheritances. All were fundamental in shaping the ongoing character of Anglicanism. Historians now believe that at least two distinct offshoots of the Reformation were the consolidation of a clerical profession that emphasized the ministry of the 'sacramental Word', and the development of distinct lay religious consciousness exemplified in the confident ability of many (middle and upperclass) laity to contend regularly with clergy in religious debates.[16] By the eve of the English Civil War laity had joined clergy in reliance on the Word, and in increasingly volatile debates over the future of the Church.

LAITY AND THE CHURCH: AN ECCLESIOLOGY FOR THE PEOPLE OF GOD

The theology of the Church has often been problematic in reflecting on the lay movement. One source for dislocation is noted in the 1985 study *All Are Called*: '*The primary location of the laity is in society at large*. It is important that the clergy and lay officials of the Church should understand and respect the truth that most laity are only *secondarily* located in the institutional Church'.[17] Given this fact, it is more accurate and helpful to emphasize that the Church is a corporate body at work in the world, and not primarily or only an institution.

The theology of the nature and purpose of the Church, its ecclesiology, is foundational for comprehending a theology of the laity. Practical theologians from Hendrick Kraemer to Verna Dozier and Bruce Reed have repeatedly urged church officials to pay attention to ecclesiology. The Church

in biblical images and divine example is world-centred. Anglican theologians from Richard Hooker in the sixteenth century to William Temple in
this century have reiterated the theme that the world is properly the
Church's workplace. Hooker referred to the Church as a visible, though
mystical, body marked by mutual fellowship in society. For Temple the
Church, though at times an 'uninspiring spectacle', was the 'means whereby
Christ becomes active and carries out His purpose in the world'.[18] There is
remarkable agreement that the Church's purpose is to serve God in the
world. As Kraemer bluntly insisted, the Church exists primarily 'on behalf of
the world and not on behalf of itself'.[19] Bruce Reed has more pointedly
noted, 'The purpose of the church is to prepare these members so that the
profane world—(the world outside the temple)—can take on the qualities
of the Kingdom.'[20]

Such statements do not resolve the ongoing tensions related to dualistic
separations between the Church and the world, sacred and secular, public
and private. Anglican theologians, however, have contended against artifi-
cial compartmentalization of Church and world. William Temple, for example, laboured throughout his ministry to repudiate two extreme views:
that Christians should have no concern for this passing world, and that
Christians should be totally immersed in the earthly present. He emphasized instead engagement on behalf of Christ:

> We are called as Christians to the service of God here and now; that on
> earth as in heaven His Name is to be hallowed [...] for that Christ
> taught us to pray; for that He has summoned us to work. *Not there but
> here is the sphere of our spiritual concern; not then but now is salvation to be
> won and made manifest.*[21]

Anglican theologians name and retain terms such as 'spiritual' and 'natural',
'sacred' and 'secular' not so much to emphasize the choice of one, but rather
to point truthfully to the tension of living faithfully as Christians in this
world.

The grounding of the Church's mission in the world is essential to
Anglican theology. So too is the emphasis that this is a corporate, not an
individualistic, requirement. The late American theologian Urban Holmes
described the Hebrew concept of the corporate person as informing choices
about how Anglicans move, work and shape their vocations.[22] Social responsiveness was not an option for Anglicans. Decisions focused not on
what one person should do, but on what members of the Church do
together. Holmes recognized that built into this theology of the Church
was the realistic tension of living with loyalty to our particular Church's
mission and remaining open to others. This implies that the Church is
provisional, an earthen vessel, and not in and of itself definitive for

salvation. The Canadian theologian James Wilkes has described how a corporate theology of the Church encourages healthier and more hopeful responsiveness. He argues that only guilt is produced when an individual is exhorted to action in isolation from others and from the social context, and he describes courage as a collective social activity: "Courage continues to live in the covenant which gives us trust in life, allows us to speak the truth, and binds us into relationships of clear and mutual expectation'.[23]

Corporate, socially engaged ecclesiologies which emphasize the dominant role of laity are not always welcomed. One manifestation of this resistance that needs to be named in a chapter on Anglican laity is clericalism. Clericalism may be seen as misplaced resistance to secularism, a process of withdrawal from society into a narrowly defined and often exclusively parochial context. Clericalism is also a progenitor of mutually disabling relationships formed of devaluation of laity and exaggeration of clerical status. The authors of *All Are Called* are frank in their evaluation of the persistence of clericalism among both clergy and laity: 'Clericalism is at bottom a confusion between the status of individuals and a theological understanding of their calling. It has been historically formed and embedded in social life.'[24] They speak too of patronizing attempts to control the laity and consequently confine and restrict the mission of the Church.

Provinces in the Anglican Communion have sought to combat clericalism and open up a wider range of understanding in the Church by urging greater inclusion of laity in church governance. This is not a remedy for clericalism, particularly if it leads to definitions of 'lay ministers' as primarily those who are active within the institutional Church. A clericalist spirit can also continue to thrive in governing bodies, however jointly contrived. Yet from the point of view of ecclesiology, the incorporation of laity into the governing life of churches can provide another opportunity to focus concern for the Church's mission in society at large. The perspective is consistant with the themes of early Anglicanism. Thomas Cranmer referred to the need to include lay participation in the revival of diocesan synods. Thomas Arnold in *Principles of Church Reform* (1833) advocated, as a first step, giving laity a greater share in ordinary church government. Since the 1880s, when Church of England Convocations first agreed upon establishing a House of Laymen, there has been slow but steady progress to the current form of synodical government with its House of Laity. In the United States, the Episcopal Church in its first informal Convention in 1784 declared 'that to make canons there be no other authority than a representative body of the clergy and laity conjointly'.[25] Canadian schemes for governance make lay participation obligatory. The serious inclusion of laity in governance is now standard throughout Anglicanism. This was strongly signalled when the 1968 Lambeth Conference founded a global Anglican Consultative Council

(ACC) with mandated lay representatives as well as clergy from throughout the Communion.

It may seem odd to conclude a discussion on the corporate theology of the Church in the world with references to synodical governments and Lambeth Conferences. Yet starting with an understanding of the Church as a people called into relationship with God and each other, Anglican ecclesiology presents a Church that is grounded in society, provisional, inclusive and responsive. On this foundation, whether from the vantage point of Lambeth, ACC, ecumenical dialogues or inter-religious conversations, Anglicanism provides theological warrants for encouraging the work of the Church in the world.

LAITY AND SACRAMENTS: THE POWER OF COMMON PARTICIPATION

The integrity of a corporate theology of the Church is directly related to the work of the *laos*, a Greek word used in Christian theology to refer to the whole people of God (laity and clergy) assembled for worship. It is not surprising that the modern lay movement has been accompanied, nurtured, and no doubt shaped by liturgical renewal in this century. The development, testing and implementation of the American 1979 Book of Common Prayer, the English *Alternative Service Book 1980*, the Canadian 1985 *Book of Alternative Services*, and the 1989 multicultural and multi-racial *A New Zealand Prayer Book, He Karakia Mihinare o Aotearoa* all reflect the theological and liturgical legitimacy of increased lay participation. The elucidating teaching section in the Canadian book explains this liturgical principle:

> A second difference in the Church of the present day appears in a growing sense among Christians that they constitute a complex and varied community, with many different roles and functions. This vision of the Church, as old as the New Testament, was never entirely lost but was certainly eclipsed during a long period of Christian history. A sharp line ran between the leadership role of the priest and the relative passivity of the laity. Today there is recognition that the Church not only contains but needs many roles and functions in its administration, witness and service as well as in its liturgy.[26]

Moreover, given the intimate relationship in Anglicanism between prayer and belief conveyed in the principle *lex orandi: lex credendi*, these new and alternative service books will continue to ground future generations of Anglicans in liturgical expressions consonant with a theology of the whole people of God at work in an increasingly diverse world.

285

This principle of contemporary liturgical renewal corresponds with, and represents a return to, the liturgical centre of early Anglicanism. The Tudor Prayer Books were designed to encourage accessibility and inclusioh for all; worship was something done by priest and people participating together in *common* prayer. In the scriptural sacraments of baptism and Holy Communion, Cranmer emphasized participation in Christ initially through the regenerating waters of baptism that signify that 'through Christ we are born anew', and through ongoing regular participation of the *laos* in Holy Communion whereby 'we be continually nourished by spiritual food: and that spiritual food is Christ also'.[27] Cranmer was confident about the ability of the people to hear and respond in faith. Thus the people's petition in the Tudor Postcommunion prayer was, 'that we may continue in that holy fellowship, and do all such good works as thou hast prepared for us to walk in'.[28]

Toward the end of the sixteenth century Richard Hooker in his summative work, *Of the Laws of Ecclesiastical Polity*, provided theological exposition of this principle of participation. He believed that our sacramental participation in Christ was shaped by the incarnation, as embodied in 'that mutuall inward hold which Christ hath of us and wee of him', and that the purpose of the incarnation was to alter human nature towards conformity with divine nature.[29] It is important to understand that Hooker was referring not to making humanity godlike, but to the exercise of a mutuality that implies responsibility. Hooker also emphasized the centrality of participation through the theological concept of *metanoia*, a process of ongoing conversion in the hearts of the faithful that gives courage for the amending of life. The result of *metanoia*, turning to Christ, was active charity publicly expressed by the lives of those who received the sacraments in faith. Hooker understood that the central intent of the Holy Communion was changing human lives, not bread and wine.

Throughout the Tudor Prayer Books and in Hooker's theological elucidation, an Anglican theology of humanity was set forth that insisted on true mutuality, the binding relational character of God and the people of God. The contemporary American liturgist Louis Weil has described Anglican liturgy as literally the work of the people. He maintains that worship and prayer are dependent upon the actions of participants, and carry the implication 'that we are all celebrants together'.[30] Contemporary Roman Catholic theologians, building on the work of Edward Schillebeeckx, similarly emphasize the ancient teaching that '"every age concelebrates", young and old alike'.[31]

In the latter half of the nineteenth century, Anglican theologians also underscored empowering involvement of humanity in sacramental participation. The prophet of the Christian Socialist movement, Frederick

Denison Maurice, looked into the heart of the crises engendered by the Industrial Revolution and concluded, not unlike Hooker, that the incarnation was the central theological principle that benefited human nature. The underlying righteousness of humanity was derived from the indwelling Christ: 'Apart from Him, I feel that there dwells in me no good thing; but I am sure that I am not apart from Him, nor are you, nor is any man.' Maurice described the sacraments as expressing unity of God and humanity, *and* of humanity with humanity. Baptism was the sacrament of 'constant union' representing Christ's sacrifice for all people, and the Holy Communion repeatedly presented the powerful drama of God's 'continual presence with His universal family'.[32]

Young Anglo-Catholic theologians who contributed to the essays, *Lux Mundi* (1889), were even more definitive in their expression of the social significance of the sacraments. Francis Paget underlined the pervasiveness of the sacraments in the world: 'Through Sacramental elements and acts Christianity maintains its strong inclusive hold upon the whole of life.' J. R. Illingworth pointed to the incarnational centre of Christianity. 'It is impossible to read history without feeling how profoundly the religion of the Incarnation has been a religion of humanity.' Charles Gore, also in *Lux Mundi*, elucidated how the sacraments through the work of the Holy Spirit in the Church were 'social ceremonies', the means of incorporation into Christian society.[33] Gore built upon this teaching about the social nature of the sacraments in *The Reconstruction of Belief* (1926), in which he argued that the authority of the Church rests on the demonstration of the moral and social witness that is the work of the lay people.

In this century William Temple reiterated in inclusive terms and ecumenical actions the social significance of the sacraments. For Temple, baptism represented a turning away from selfishness, a concept in harmony with *metanoia*. He argued not only for the socially redemptive but also for the socially creative impact of the Eucharist in contemporary society. He suggested that we take bread and wine as symbols of our industrial and commercial life, and offer them as indications of our willingness to continue to serve humanity. For Temple, worship included all of life: sacraments, intercessions, all prayer connected humanity to the world to be won.[34]

These and other Anglican theologians have repeatedly emphasized that the sacraments, indeed the whole of Christian worship, are intended to encourage social responsiveness, whether in the Tudor Commonwealth or the post-industrial world with its multitude of diverse cultures and races. It is this direction that is central in the new liturgies. For example in the baptismal convenant from the Province of New Zealand Prayer Book, candidates promise to 'strive for justice and peace [... and to] accept the cost of following Jesus Christ in my daily life and work'.[35] At baptism and in the Eucharist, liturgical actions are designed to empower the ministry of the people of God in the world.

LAITY AND MINISTRY: THE SPIRIT OF CHRISTIAN MISSION

Contemporary and emerging understandings of laity reflect significant changes in traditional language. The American Prayer Book Catechism defines 'ministry' in a manner that seemingly challenges the historic three-fold ministry:

Q. Who are the ministers of the Church?

A. The ministers of the Church are lay persons, bishops, priests and deacons.[36]

In Christian Churches throughout North America and in denominational and ecumenical statements it is common parlance to refer to 'lay ministry'. This phrase is not only redundant, it is awkward. The work 'lay' can convey second-class status. As Byron Rushing, a legislator and longtime representative to Episcopal General concentions, is fond of asking: Who, if they wanted a second opinion, would go to a 'lay doctor'? Additionally, most laity, despite well-intentioned prodding, are reluctant to call themselves 'ministers'. This is true despite the fact that it is theologically sound to refer to the 'ministry' of the laity, as in the title of a recent book by Patricia Page, *All God's People Are Ministers*. What is at stake is not the task of convincing persons that they are 'ministers'; rather the basic goal is encouraging persons to live authentically as 'Christians' in their daily life. In the global village of the twenty-first century, the exact ordering of ministry will surely not be as critical as the ethical witness of laity in a post-Christian world.

Despite changing use of theological terms, there is a consistent emphasis within Anglicanism upon the laity's responsibility for bearing the Church's mission. However difficult this task continues to be, there is sufficient evidence in Christian history that the work of the laity has *regularly*, not just *episodically*, been that of revival, reform and mission. Roland Allen (1868–1947), a proponent of indigenous mission, wrote of the Church's need to follow the New Testament model of trust in the compulsion of the Spirit, the power of spontaneous expansion.[37] There are abundant examples of this collective impetus in Anglican history: the Evangelical reform societies of the eighteenth century, organizations like the Church Missionary Society founded in 1799 and the interdenominational Student Christian Movement founded in 1892; the tradition of strong lay leadership, primarily

288

that of women (though few held official positions of power), in expanding the foreign and domestic witness of the Episcopal Church in the nineteenth century;[38] and in this century, with the end of colonial identity during the 1950s and 1960s, the vast expansion of indigenous Anglican leadership in Africa.

The increased provision of educational resources has long been an objective of Anglican laity. The Sunday School Movement shaped both religious education and public education in America. It is difficult to underestimate the energy and commitment that this particular nineteenth-century strategy for mission attracted in the American churches. In England, as in North America, and increasingly throughout the Anglican Communion, educational philanthropy has supported the founding of schools, theological colleges and seminaries. Laity have been effective in sponsoring educational work among children, signalled in organizations such as the Boy Scouts and Girl Guides. Laity have also been critical in their advocacy of adult education, represented in the Worker's Educational Association founded in England in 1903 and in the American Settlement House movement. During the 1950s in the United States Christian education again became a central preoccupation in many Episcopal parishes. Within the Anglican Communion, laity have encouraged the vision of an educated Church, rather than only a learned clergy.

The contemporary lay movement has witnessed a vast proliferation of adult educational resources: theological education by extension, diocesan lay training courses and schools, professional theological education degrees designed for laity as well as those seeking ordination, and the provision of training opportunities for lay pastoral care and other specialized aspects of Christian mission. In these programmes, the providers of lay education are often laity. Chief among these today is Education for Ministry (EFM), a four-year programme of part-time study for laity which to date numbers more than 15,000 graduates and which has expanded into twelve other countries. The 1985 English report, *All Are Called*, describes this shift in educational emphasis: 'Adult Christian commitment means an *informed* commitment. It is not a matter of being loyal sheep.'[39] After years of paying lip service to laity in ministry, the institutional Church is beginning to provide serious programmes for the ongoing education of laity. The future integrity of the Church's mission continues to depend on the spontaneous expansion of the Church's mission in society at large. In considering this present challenge, there is no need to tie increasing secularism to a decline in religious commitment. This was not true in the period of the Reformation, and it need not be true in these latter days. Indeed recently there has been an increase in the number of educational resources and guides addressing the everyday ministries with occur outside institutional churches. Once again theologians have focused on the meaning of work.[40] For example, William Diehl in *The Monday Connection* provides stories and tactics for ministry in the workplace; similarly the Canadian Graham Tucker emphasizes the integration of Christian principles and management in *The Faith–Work Connection: A Practical Application of Christian Values in the Marketplace*; and Robert Reber has designed a programme for small group and parish study entitled, *Linking Faith and Daily Life: An Educational Program for Lay People*.[41]

Similarly, there has been a prolific increase in contemporary spiritual resources intended to nurture persons in their everyday life. While 'spirituality' is a term of relatively recent coinage, lay mystics, poets and theological visionaries—from Julian of Norwich to Evelyn Underhill, from Walt Whitman to Annie Dillard, and from Richard Hooker to Dorothee Sölle— have for centuries inspired Christians on spiritual journeys in this world. These and other authors of spiritual 'classics' are alike in their emphasis upon humanity's 'immersion in God' in this world and upon the people of God as corporately engaged and socially responsive.[42] Continuing in this tradition an Episcopal priest, Brian Taylor, has recast Benedictine spirituality—with its balanced alignment of prayer, study and work—as a basis for everyday living; while Caroline Westerhoff has provided everyday stories intended to deepen lifelong understanding of the spiritual force of baptism.[43] These and other authors emphasize an ethical, everyday Christian spirituality which is attentive to faithful living in this world.

One of the selected themes for the 1998 Lambeth Conference is the call 'to be faithful in a plural world'. For such a call to be effective the relationship between the ministries of laity as well as those who Verna Dozier calls 'the institutionally ordained' will need to be re-examined. Clearly, given the vast challenges ahead in the new millennium, there can be no second-class citizens in the household of God. What is the spirit, the substance of Christian witness, that might carry us to the future? Traditional Anglican perspectives on laity will no doubt continue to provide theological sustenance for the various and diverse futures of laity across the Anglican Communion. Thus, for example, the theology of humanity would be socially grounded, enlivened with the incarnational legacy of responsible belonging to God; worship and prayer would be accessible to all regardless of education or social location; educational resources would be expansive, shaped by listening to those with whom we learn; and a spirited ecumenically minded Church in mission would be willing to explore unknown areas with persons of diverse perspectives, faiths and cultures. Through participation in such a Church, Anglican laity would continue to find the holy in the ordinary and to know that truth reveals itself in patterns of human events, in collective testimonies old and new. Together such ordinary people would continue to be called by an extraordinary God.

BIBLIOGRAPHY

All Are Called: Towards a Theology of the Laity. CIO Publishing, London, 1985.

The Calling of the Laity: Verna Dozier's Anthology. Alban Institute, Washington DC, 1988.

Diehl, William E., *The Monday Connection: On Being an Authentic Christian in a Weekday World.* Harper Collins, San Francisco, 1993.

Page, Patricia N., *All God's People Are Ministers: Equipping Church Members for Ministry.* Augsburg Fortress, Minneapolis, 1993.

Sachs, William L., *The Transformation of Anglicansim.* Cambridge University Press, Cambridge, 1993.

Thompsett, Fredrica Harris, *We Are Theologians: Strengthening the People of the Episcopal Church.* Cowley Publications, Cambridge, Massachusetts, 1989.

Westerhoff, Caroline A., *Calling: A Song for the Baptized.* Cowley Publications, Cambridge, Massachusetts, 1994.

NOTES

1 *The Truth Shall Make You Free: The Lambeth Conference 1988,* (The Anglican Consultative Council, 1988), p. 52, see also pp. 49–53, 231–32.

2 *The Book of Common Prayer* (1979), p. 855.

3 *All Are Called: Towards a Theology of the Laity,* p. 3.

4 J. J. Scarisbrick, *The Reformation and the English People* (Basil Blackwell, Oxford, 1984), see pp. 61, 39, 165. See also Christopher Haigh (ed), *The English Reformation Revised* (Cambridge University Press, Cambridge, 1987). For a clear and engaging assessment of late medieval and early Tudor devotional patterns see Eamon Duffy, *The Stripping of the Altars: Traditional Religion in England, 1400–1580* (Yale University Press, New Haven and London, 1992).

5 Stephen Neill, *Anglicanism* (OUP, New York, 1978), 4th edn, p. 35; and Claire Cross, *Church and People, 1450–1600: The Triumph of the Laity in the English Church* (Humanities Press, Atlantic Highlands, New Jersey, 1976), passim.

6 *Certain Sermons or Homilies Appointed to be Read in Churches in the Time of Queen Elizabeth* (SPCK, London, 1851), pp. 109–10.

7 See especially John E. Booty (ed), David Siegenthaler and John N. Wall Jr, *The Godly Kingdom of Tudor England: Great Books of the English Reformation* (Morehouse-Barlow, Wilton CT, 1981).

8 Juan Heinrich Bullinger, *The Godly Boke of Christen Matrimonye* (London 1543), sig. X5.

9 George Townsend (ed), *The Acts and Monuments of John Foxe,* (AMS Press, New York, 1965), Vol. iii, pp. 710–20.

10 Thomas Cranmer, *Works,* Vol. ii, Miscellaneous Writings, ed. John Edmond Cox (CUP, Cambridge, 1846), p. 179; see also Rosalind and Christopher Brooke, *Popular Religion in the Middle Ages* (Thames and Hudson, Leipzig, 1984), p. 130ff.

11 Cranmer, *Works,* Vol. ii, p. 120.

12 From the *Paraclesis* printed in several editions of Erasmus's works including John C. Olin (ed), *Christian Humanism and the Reformation: Selected Writings of*

Erasmus (Harper and Row, New York, 1965), p. 100. For a contemporary interpretation see Thompsett, *We Are Theologians*, pp. 57–86.

13 Lawrence Stone, 'The Educational Revolution in England: 1560–1640', *Past and Present* 28 (1964), pp. 41–80.

14 Richard L. Greaves, *Society and Religion in Elizabethan England* (University of Minnesota Press, Minneapolis, 1981), p. 328; see also Keith Wrightson and David Levine, *Poverty and Piety in an English Village, Terling, 1525–1700* (Academic Press, New York, 1979). On local Prayer Book use see Judith Maltby, ' "By this Book": Parishioners, the Prayer Book and the Established Church' in Kenneth Fincham (ed.), *The Early Stuart Church, 1603–1642* (Macmillan, Basingstoke, 1993), pp. 115-37, 246–69.

15 Diarmaid MacCulloch, *The Later Reformation in England, 1547–1603* (St Martin's Press, New York, 1990), p. 167, also pp. 163–6.

16 Urban T. Holmes III, *The Future Shape of Ministry* (Seabury Press, New York, 1971), pp. 58; Marc L. Schwarz, 'Some Thoughts on the Development of Lay Religious Consciousness in Pre-Civil-War England' in G. J. Cuming and Derek Baker (eds), *Popular Belief and Practice* (CUP, Cambridge, 1972), pp. 171–8; and Rosemary O'Day, *The English Clergy: The Emergence and Consolidation of a Profession, 1558–1640* (Leicester University Press, Leicester, 1979), p. 245.

17 *All Are Called*, p. 67.

18 *Christian Faith and Life*, ed. Roger L. Robert, in *Treasures from the Spiritual Classics* (Morehouse-Barlow, Wilton CT, 1981), pp. 57–8.

19 Hendrick Kraemer, *A Theology of the Laity* (Westminster Press, London, 1958), p. 3; see Verna J. Dozier, *The Authority of the Laity* (Alban Institute, Washington DC, 1982), pp. 39–42.

20 Reed quoted in *The Calling of the Laity*, p. vii.

21 *Fellowship with God* (Macmillan, London, 1930), pp. 207–8, emphasis added.

22 *Ministry and Imagination* (Seabury Press, New York, 1976), p. 19; for similar emphases see also Rowan Williams, *A Ray of Darkness, Sermons and Reflections* (Cowley Publications, Cambridge, Massachusetts, 1995), pp. 164–8.

23 *The Gift of Courage* (Anglican Book Centre, Toronto, 1979), pp. 42–3.

24 *All Are Called*, pp. 7–8. For further history on the 'clerical captivity' of the Church see Anne Rowthorn (Morehouse-Barlow, Wilton, 1986), p. 27–46.

25 Quoted in Neill, *Anglicanism*, p. 285.

26 *Book of Alternative Services*, p. 11.

27 Cranmer, *Works*, Vol. ii, 176.

28 From *The Elizabethan Book of Common Prayer (1559)*, ed. John E. Booty (University Press of Virginia, Charlottesville, 1976), p. 265.

29 Quotations from Hooker are from FE Vol. ii; see sections V.lvi.1 and V.liv.5.

30 Louis Weil, 'Anglican Understanding of the Local Church', *Anglican Theological Review* 64: ii (April 1982), p. 197.

31 Michael G. Lawler and Thomas J. Shanahan, *Church: A Spirited Communion* (Liturgical Press, Minnesota, 1995), p. 79. In 1965 the Second Vatican Council, in *The Decree on the Apostolate of the Laity*, sounded a related note: 'The laity, too, share in the priestly, prophetic, and royal office of Christ and therefore have their own role to play in the mission of the whole People of God'.

32 F. D. Maurice quoted in John E. Booty, 'Christian Spirituality: From Wilberforce to Temple' in *Anglican Spirituality*, ed. William J. Wolf (Morehouse-Barlow, Wilton CT, 1982), pp. 81–5.

33 Charles Gove (ed.), *Lux Mundi: A Series of Studies in the Religion of the Incarnation* (Thomas Whittaker, New York, 1989), pp. 353, 176, 269.
34 William Temple, *The Hope of the New World* (Macmillan, New York, 1943), p. 70; Owen C. Thomas, 'William Temple' in *The Spirit of Anglicanism*, ed. William J. Wolf (Morehouse-Barlow, Wilton CT, 1979), p. 126; and Wolf, *Anglican Spirituality*, p. 87.
35 *A New Zealand Prayer Book* (1989), p. 391.
36 *Book of Common Prayer* (1979), p. 855; the *New Zealand Prayer Book* (1989) adds to this listing 'all the baptised', p. 931.
37 See David Paton and Charles H. Long (eds), *The Compulsion of the Spirit: A Roland Allen Reader* (Eerdmans Publishing, Co., Grand Rapids MI, 1983), for an expansive interpretation of the work of laity; a more limited 'episodic' view of lay engagement is presented in *Doctrine in the Church of England* (SPCK, London, 1938), especially p. 116.
38 See, for example, Mary Sudman Donovan, *A Different Call: Women's Ministries in the Episcopal Church, 1850–1920* (Morehouse-Barlow, Wilton, 1986).
39 *All Are Called*, p. 23.
40 For a review of Anglican reflections on work, see 'Making a Living' in Fredrica Harris Thompsett, *Courageous Incarnation, In Intimacy, Work, Childhood and Aging* (Cowley Publications, Cambridge MA, 1993), pp. 80–125.
41 *The Monday Connection* (Harper Collins, San Francisco, 1991); *The Faith–Work Connection* (Anglican Book Centre, Toronto, 1987); and Robert E. Reber, *Linking Faith & Daily Life, An Educational Program for Lay People* (Alban Institute, Washington DC, 1991). See also Robert Banks, *God the Worker* (Judson Press, Valley Forge, Pennsylvania, 1994).
42 See Dorothee Sölle, *The Strength of the Weak: Toward a Christian Feminist Identity* (Westminster Press, Philadelphia, 1984), p. 102.
43 Brian C. Taylor, *Spirituality for Everyday Living* (The Liturgical Press, Collegeville, MN, 1989); and Caroline A. Westerhoff, *Calling: A Song for the Baptized* (Cambridge MA, 1994).

4   Initiation

DAVID R. HOLETON

The development of the pattern of Christian initiation (baptism, confirmation, first communion) within Anglicanism can only be understood if put in the context of an ongoing tension between theological opinion and popular piety. Until the last few decades popular piety has almost always emerged as victor.

SIXTEENTH-CENTURY REFORM

The medieval baptismal practice and liturgical rites which were inherited by Thomas Cranmer and the English Reformers marked a low point in the long devolution of both baptismal practice and theology. The rises, whose origins lay in the patristic period, had, at the time they were developed, assumed a long period of baptismal preparation (catechumenate) followed by a short, intense final preparation (Lent) culminating in baptism at the Easter Vigil (or Pentecost in case a candidate for some reason was unable to be baptized at the Vigil). The candidates for baptism included both infants and adults, the latter often representing the majority. The various rites which emerged in this process of preparation and baptism (exorcisms, anointings, scrutinies, the giving of the Creed and Lord's Prayer, signing with the cross, chrismation, vesting in a new garment, giving a new light) helped interpret the theologically rich and complex mystery of baptism for those involved—especially if they were adults.

The rites that the Reformers inherited, however, were a pale shadow of their former selves. Rites which had once taken place over an extended period of time, often a number of years, had come to be compressed into a single event. The triumph of Christendom, as well as an exaggerated Augustinian understanding of the fate of those who died unbaptized, had successfully eliminated adults as baptismal candidates (they had all been baptized as infants). Rites that made sense when used with adults thus came to be used on infants generally less than a week old. The communal element of initiation which had been emphasized by restricting the frequency with which baptism took place (except for baptism *in extremis*) disappeared as the Church encouraged the practice of baptism as soon after birth as possible. Finally, the essential unity of Christian initiation (baptism in water, sealing/imposition of hands, reception of communion) had devolved into three rites (baptism, confirmation, first communion) celebrated over an extended period of years. The Reformers recognized some, but not all, of these historical and theological problems as they set about to effect their reforms.

Like the initial efforts of Martin Luther and Huldreich Zwingli, Cranmer's first revision of the baptismal rite (1549) was relatively conservative. The shape of the rite is basically that of the Sarum Manual (*Rituale*), which had the most widespread use in medieval England. It was a rite typical of late medieval baptismal liturgies.

In revising the rite Cranmer maintained some of the Sarum prayers (in English translation) and some of the ceremonial (consignation, exorcism of the devil, chrismation and the presentation of the white baptismal garment); other prayers and ceremonies (the exorcism of salt, the *Ephphatha*, the signing of the hand, the anointing of the breast and the presentation of a lighted candle) were discarded. To this revision Cranmer added texts borrowed from Luther, the *Consultation* of Herman von Wied of Cologne and the Hispanic *Missale Mixtum*.

The resultant rite appears, on first inspection, to be very much in continuity with its late medieval predecessor with only the most obvious of the 'dark and dumb ceremonies', which were anathema to the Reformers, removed. On closer inspection there are definite signs that Cranmer was attempting much more than a cosmetic reform. The first rubric[1] indicates that Cranmer was aware of at least some of the baptismal practice of the patristic Church and that, while he conceded a replication of that period was not possible, some of its insights could well be restored. Baptism was, if possible, to take place only on Sundays and holy days, at a time when the largest number of the community could assemble, and that this public celebration of baptism was to serve as a rememorative event, reminding adults and older children present of their own baptism. Cranmer's choice of text for the chrismation may also indicate his intention to restore the primitive unity of the rite, at least as far as baptism and confirmation are concerned. This point will be discussed later.

The 1549 book provided for a separate rite entitled Confirmation (see pp. 131–6). The model for this rite was not the second post-baptismal anointing of the Roman rite found in the Sarum Manual but instead has its roots in a catechetical rite which emerged from the left wing of the Bohemian Reformation of the previous century. This new rite was not to be administered until the candidate could recite the Creed, the Ten Commandments and the Lord's Prayer as well as answer the questions of the catechism and 'ratify and confess' the questions answered on the child's behalf at baptism by the godparents. The administration of the rite, severely limited to bishops, was to be received by children who have 'come to that age [. . . when] they begin to be in danger to fall into sin'. The effect of confirmation was to give 'strength and defence against all temptations to sin and the assaults of the world, and the devil'.

The last rubric of the rite states: 'And there shall none be admitted to the holy communion: until such time as he be confirmed.' But the last of the introductory rubrics attempts to salve the consciences of those who would not want to delay confirmation for fear that a child might die not having received the Eucharist, which was generally considered necessary for salvation.

And that no man shall think that any detriment shall come to children by deferring of their confirmation: he shall know for truth, that it is certain by God's word, that children being Baptized (if they depart out of this life in their infancy) are undoubtedly saved.

The theological content of the 1549 baptismal rite remained basically that of the medieval West. The primary theological concern is the forgiveness of sin. The first words of the rite set the tone for what is to follow:

Dearly beloved, forasmuch as all men be conceived and born in sin, and that no man born in sin, can enter into the kingdom of God (except he be regenerate, and born anew of water, and the Holy Ghost)...

As in other contemporary Western baptismal rites, other baptismal images (such as baptism as gifting with the Holy Spirit, enlightenment, or sign of participation in the eschatological kingdom) are rare, if not entirely absent. Continuity, rather than change, thus characterizes Cranmer's first revision of the baptismal rite theologically as well as liturgically. Despite Cranmer's expressed preference for infrequent public baptism with as many of the community as possible gathered, private baptism, within a few days of birth, remained the common custom. The provision of a rite for private baptism in a home was a significant concession to popular practice which was not going to be changed easily in spite of the opinions of reforming bishops.

Martin Bucer in his *Censura*[2] is generally approving of Cranmer's initial reforms in the area of initiation and particularly lauds Cranmer's attempts to restore baptism to feast days in the presence of the whole church. Cranmer's new rite of confirmation is also given general approval but with the reservation that the rite not be administered in an automatic or mechanical fashion but that candidates be limited to those who have confirmed the confession of their mouth with a manner of life consistent with it and from whose conduct it can be discerned that they make profession of their own faith and not another's.[3] Bucer also suggested a series of changes and emendations to the 1549 rite. Of particular concern to him were that: (1) baptisms should take place after the sermon at the Eucharist rather than in the context of Matins or Evensong; (2) the initial part of the rite which, following the Sarum/medieval shape, had taken place at the church door, should take place in the body of the church; (3) the baptismal robe and the use of the chrism should be abolished; (4) the baptismal water should not be blessed; (5) nothing should be said to infants, for they understand nothing; and (6) the exorcism is appropriate only for demoniacs and that it should therefore be turned into a prayer for protection.

Cranmer, in his revision of the baptismal rite for the second Prayer Book (1552), takes note of the number of Bucer's suggestions. The entire rite is to take place at the font but remains in the context of Matins or Evensong rather than the Eucharist. The signation, exorcism and godparents' repetition of the Lord's Prayer and Creed were suppressed. The threefold renunciation followed by a threefold profession of faith are each condensed into a single question and answer. The medieval questions and answers: 'What dost thou desire?'—'Baptism', and 'Wilt thou be baptized?'—'I will', are condensed into a single question and answer: 'Wilt thou be baptized in this faith?'—'This is my desire'. The blessing of the font is reduced by a half and effectively ceases to be a blessing. The remaining prayer is to be used at every baptism rather than only monthly as permitted in 1549. The child is named and then, if healthy, immersed (now only once rather than three times) while the baptismal formula is recited. The giving of the baptismal garment (chrisome) and chrismation are omitted and, instead, the priest is instructed to make the sign of the cross on the child's forehead—the place where the second or 'confirmation' anointing had taken place in the med-ieval Sarum rite. The consignation was accompanied by this declaration:

> We receive this child into the congregation of Christ's flock, and do sign *him* with the sign of the cross, in token that hereafter *he* shall not be ashamed to confess the faith of Christ crucified, and manfully to fight under his banner against sin, the world, and the devil, and to continue Christ's faithful soldier and servant unto *his* life's end. Amen.

The revision inserts a bidding that those present give thanks to God that the newly baptized are 'regenerate and grafted into the body of Christ's con-gregation'. The rite concludes with the Lord's Prayer, then another prayer of thanksgiving followed by an exhortation to the godparents in which they are reminded of their duties to their godchild. (Godparents were to see that their godchildren learn the Creed, Lord's Prayer and Ten Commandments in English as well as all other things Christians ought to know; that they be raised virtuously; and that they be brought to the bishop for confirmation.)

The rite of confirmation underwent several important changes in its 1552 revision. The English translation of the Sarum prayer which asked God to send the Holy Spirit on those about to be confirmed is emended so that the candidates are now to be 'strengthened' that the Spirit's 'mainfold gifts of grace might daily increase in them'. The signing with the cross, together with its accompanying prayer and formula, was removed. The bishop is now instructed to lay hands upon each child and to pray:

> Defend, O Lord, this child with thy heavenly grace, that *he* may continue thine for ever, and daily increase in thy Holy Spirit more and more, until *he* come to thy everlasting kingdom. Amen.

The catechetical understanding of confirmation was underlined by an ex-pansion of the rubric concerning admission to communion. Communicants were now required to be able to recite the Catechism as well as the Creed, Lord's Prayer and Ten Commandments to be confirmed.

The rites of initiation as they appeared in 1552 set the basic pattern of initiation with Anglicanism for the next 400 years. While the rites them-selves underwent a number of minor revisions over the next century, their shape and content was but little altered.

The Prayer Book of 1604, in response to Puritan pressure, regulated the conditions under which private baptism could take place and required that emergency baptism be celebrated only by a 'lawful Minister'. The 1662 book regulated the number of godparents, provided a prayer for the sanctification of the baptismal water, and no longer required that communicants be able to recite the Catechism nor that they necessarily be confirmed, but that they 'be confirmed, or be ready and desirous to be confirmed'. The same book also provides a new rite for the 'baptism of such as are of riper years', a response to both the growing controversies with the radical (Anabaptist) reform and the missionary situation of a growing colonial empire.

Thus baptism in infancy, followed by confirmation (usually when children were in their teens), followed by first communion remained—and in many parts of the Anglican Communion remains—the normative pattern for initiation. This pattern, which implicitly assumes a biological model of the sacraments (baptism=birth, confirmation=growth, etc.), solidified both theologically and ritually under external as well as internal attack. Radical Reformers as well as Puritans attacked the rite for its retention of 'popish ceremonial', denouncing with particular vigour the retention of godparents and the consignation.

The seventeenth century saw an extended and singularly acrimonious debate over the question of infant baptism. This debate, which raged with particular ferocity just before and during the Commonwealth, caused Anglican theologians to re-examine the implicit biological model of the sacraments with which they had been working, as well as to question of the propriety of separating first communion from baptism. Jeremy Taylor, later bishop of Down and Conner, was led to remark that a name ought to be invented for those who refuse to give communion to infants that is as disparaging as is 'Anabaptist' for those who refuse to give them baptism.[4] The Restoration saw a quick end to any such radical thought.

The effect of these controversies effectively was to convince Anglicans of the rightness of their own practice. The ceremonial contested by the radical independents and the Puritans was to become entrenched as a touchstone of Anglican orthodoxy, while the theological concessions made to the arguments of Anabaptists were quickly forgotten once the Church of England was re-established with the Restoration of Charles II. Controversy had led only to a rigidity of both ceremonial practice as well as theological position.

The one piece of the pattern of initiation which suffered most over the ensuing centuries was confirmation. Until the strict churchmanship of the early nineteenth century, which grew out of the Evangelical Revival, confirmation was more often ignored than observed. In England this was, in part, the product of the vastness of many dioceses, but also of a serious problem with episcopal non-residency. Overseas it was a question of lack of bishops, there being no Anglican bishop outside the British Isles until 1785. To be confirmed one would have had to make a long and dangerous journey back to the United Kingdom. None of these difficulties, however, ever led to serious consideration being given to delegating the authority to confirm. This is as much a comment on the low view in which confirmation was held as it is on a high view of episcopal authority. Since the early nineteenth century confirmation has been observed with considerable scrupulousness, and has gained a place in Anglican piety unknown during the previous centuries.

THE TRADITIONAL MODEL IN CRISIS

The traditional pattern of initiation worked well as long as Anglicanism continued to exist in a Christendom situation. Its basic assumption, that baptism was as much into a nurturing Christian society as into a nurturing Christian community, remained viable in many parts of the world where Anglicanism existed in strength until after the Second World War. Although there had been a disparity, ever since confirmation had gained its newfound importance, between the numbers who were baptized and the number who later returned for confirmation, the disparity had not been all that great. Both baptism and confirmation were well rooted in popular or folk religion and parents or godparents would usually ensure that the baptized would later attend confirmation class, even though the children had been conspicuously absent from any sort of religious practice during the intervening thirteen years.

By the end of the Second World War this pattern had begun to undergo radical change. Not only was there an increasing disparity between the numbers baptized and the number returning for confirmation, but there was a dramatic fall in the practice rate among those confirmed. Studies indicated that this drop-out was often taking place very shortly after confirmation, and that for many children confirmation had come to serve as graduation not only from any sort of religious education, but also from church itself. The tradition pattern seemed to be falling and became the subject of considerable concern.

THE BEGINNING OF A NEW PATTERN OF INITIATION

The major report on 'The Renewal of Church in Faith' presented at the 1968 Lambeth Conference served to focus the growing concern over the traditional pattern of initiation found in Anglican Prayer Books. In a section of the report devoted to the renewal of the Church and its structures the bishops noted:

> We are concerned at the lack of any form of commissioning for laymen analogous to the ordination of the clergy, and Resolution 25 [see below]is put forward to encourage this need to be met. We commend the following alternatives as possible lines of experiment:
> (a) Admission to Holy Communion and confirmation would be separated. When a baptized child is of appropriate age, he or she would be admitted to Holy Communion after an adequate course of instruction. Confirmation would be deferred to an age when a young man or woman shows adult responsibility and wishes to be commissioned and confirmed for his or her task of being a Christian in society.
> (b) Infant baptism and confirmation would be administered together, followed by an admission to Holy Communion at an early age after appropriate instruction. In due course the bishop would commission the person for service when he or she is capable of making a responsible commitment.
> Experimentation along the first of the alternatives should include careful examination of the bearing of this separation in ecumenical dialogue with (a) those holding to believer's baptism and (b) the Orthodox Churches. In both instances, the intimate relationship of baptism and confirmation with admission to Holy Communion is a matter of major importance.[5]
> Resolution 25. The Conference recommends that each province or regional Church be asked to explore the theology of baptism and confirmation in relation to the need to commission the laity for their task in the world, and to experiment in this regard.[6]

This report, and Resolution 25 in particular, need to be appreciated as seminal in the renewal of initiation practice which has been spreading throughout the Anglican Communion since the 1968 Lambeth Conference.

Many provincial doctrine and liturgical commissions were quick to respond to the bishops' invitation to explore the theology of baptism and confirmation. For many of them the Lambeth statement had come at an important juncture; for they were already engaged in liturgical revision, a process which was to produce the most radical revision of Anglican liturgical texts since the Reformation itself.

The great corpus of liturgical scholarship in the area of Christian initiation which has been produced over the last fifty years, much of it by Anglican scholars, was to bear considerable weight in this theological and liturgical exploration. The historical unity of the rites of initiation were

300

clearly understood in a way that Anglicans (including Cranmer) had not seen in the past. The theological implications of baptism, particularly in relation to eucharistic communion, took on a prominence previously unknown. A number of doctrinal commissions called for the restoration of baptism, confirmation and first communion as a unified rite in which all the baptized who had received the laying on of hands or chrismation would be admitted into the eucharistic fellowship. Typical of this position was that of the Church in Wales which concluded:

> Any separation of [baptism, confirmation and first communion] *either* as successively given at different stages in the initiation rite, *or* as conceivable in isolation from one another, involves grave theological confusion. This is why the disintegrated pattern of Christian Initiation, which the Western Church has inherited, is theologically unsatisfactory. Such separation leads to pseudo-problems that are insoluble theologically, if not in fact meaningless.
>
> In particular, we refer to the impossibility of giving a convincing theology of 'baptism' separated for 'confirmation', or of 'confirmation' separated from 'baptism'. [. . .] Clear thinking, from now onwards, requires that we treat forgiveness of sin, mystical participation in the death and resurrection of the Lord, regeneration and the gift of the Spirit as alternative partial descriptions of a single ontological change of status which carries the privilege of receiving the Holy Communion as an incorporate member of the Body of Christ.[7]

Working on this new paradigm for Christian initiation, liturgical commissions began to produce single, unified, rites of initiation. These new rites encountered serious opposition around the area of episcopal involvement in initiation. While many bishops were able to accept the principles delineated by provincial theological commissions, they were not prepared to accept a pattern of initiation in which they appeared to have little or no ritual part. Few bishops were prepared to accept the argument that they were personally represented at every baptism by the priest whom they had delegated to exercise pastoral ministry in the local community; some were prepared to accepted this delegation if it were to involve the mandatory use of episcopally consecrated chrism. What seemed to lie at the root of the objections was an episcopate that had for too long been forced to define its pastoral ministry in terms of confirmation as well as the understandable and laudable desire to have assurance that there would be some regular moment of pastoral contact with the faithful. A liturgical solution which both respected the conclusions of the theological commissions and took into account the bishops' objections had to be found.

301

A NEW PATTERN EMERGES

A number of the baptismal rites which have appeared during the recent past reflect what may be a growing consensus in the pattern of initiation within Anglicanism. Cranmer's desire to restrict the celebration to Sundays and holy days, at a time when the largest number of the community can be present, is finally coming into its own. New rubrics, often re-inforced by canonical legislation, direct that the service take place during the principal celebration on a Sunday. Some provinces are even more directive and encourage the celebration be limited to five baptismal days during the year (Easter Vigil, Pentecost, All Saints' Day, the Baptism of the Lord and when the bishop visits the parish). Bucer's preference for the Eucharist as the context for initiation is also finally emerging as the norm assumed by most new initiation rites.

Thus the context in which initiation now takes place is quite different from what, despite Cranmer's expressed wish to the contrary, was the liturgical norm. Baptism has finally become a public act of the gathered Church rather than a private act in the midst of a small group of family and friends. Although candidates for baptism would still normally have sponsors (who now should include the parents of infants and young children) the whole congregation is often asked a question of this sort: 'Will you who witness these vows do all in your power to support *these persons* in *their* life in Christ?' The radical shift in liturgical context reflects a post-Christendom Church where the gathered community, rather than society, provides the context in which Christian nurture is to take place. It also reflects a Church in which ministry is no longer seen in solely clerical terms, where various of the community's members are involved in baptismal preparation, and where lay Christians are beginning to demand some sign of commitment to on-going participation in the Christian life from baptismal candidates or their presenting families.

In the new rites themselves there is a clear commitment to the integral unity of initiation itself. There is an increasing unwillingness to make age a distinguishing factor among candidates for baptism. One rite is used for all candidates and all the baptized have equal rights within the community. Baptism is increasingly seen as admission to the Eucharist regardless of age.

The richness of the biblical images which express the mystery of salvation[8] are finding a more copious expression in the new liturgical texts. These are often linked to the recovery of baptismal ceremonies which disappeared in either 1549 or 1552 (the use of chrism, the giving of a baptismal garment and a lighted candle). This again reflects a post-Christendom Church. These once 'dark and dumb ceremonies' now speak clearly not only to the community gathered but also to the baptismal candidates themselves who are, as often as not, adults.

Confirmation, as we shall see below, is emerging once again as a non-initiatory rite of reaffirmation to the covenant made in baptism. It remains an episcopal act, but is taking on a character quite different from that of the past.

A CONSENSUS EMERGES

A significant stage in the renewal of Christian Initiation within Anglicanism was achieved at the Fourth International Anglican Liturgical Consultation (IALC-IV) held at Trinity College, Toronto in August 1991. At this Consultation, sixty-four Anglican liturgical leaders from all parts of the Communion met for five days of lively discussion which issued in the document *Walk in Newness of Life.*[9]

These recommendations took the form of an extended statement covering i) Renewal of the Theology of Initiation; ii) Baptism, Mission and Ministry; iii) Renewal of Baptismal Faith and iv) Rites of Initiation, along with seven 'Principles of Christian Initiation'. This consensus among Anglican liturgists represents an important development in the renewal of Initiation for Anglicans and addresses a number of areas of disagreement. The Principles affirm that:

a) The renewal of baptismal practice is an integral part of mission and evangelism. Liturgical texts must point beyond the life of the church to God's mission in the world.

b) Baptism is for people of all ages, both adults and infants. Baptism is administered after preparation and instruction of the candidates, or where they are unable to answer for themselves, of their parent(s) or guardian(s).

c) Baptism is complete sacramental initiation and leads to participation in the eucharist. Confirmation and other rites of affirmation have a continuing pastoral role in the renewal of faith among the baptized but are in no way to be seen as completion of baptism or as necessary for admission to communion.

d) The catechumenate is a model for preparation and formation for baptism. We recognize that its constituent liturgical rites may vary in different cultural contexts.

e) Whatever language is used in the rest of the baptismal rite, both the profession of faith and the baptismal formula should continue to name God as Father, Son and Holy Spirit.

f) Baptism once received is unrepeatable and any rites of renewal must avoid being misconstrued as rebaptism.

g) The pastoral rite of confirmation may be delegated by the bishop to a presbyter.

IALC-IV also appended the Statement of IALC-I on Children and the Eucharist (Boston, 1985) to the Toronto document. Among other things, the Boston Statement affirmed: that all the baptized (including infants) be admitted to communion; that provincial baptismal rites be reviewed to the end that texts explicitly affirm the communion of the newly baptized; that only one baptismal rite be authorized in each province so that no essential distinction be made between adult or infant candidates; that in the cele- bration of baptism the vivid use of liturgical signs such as the practice of immersion and the copious use of water be encouraged; and that the general communion of all the baptized assume a significant place in all ecumenical dialogues in which Anglicans are engaged.

Walk in Newness of Life is now in the hands of the Provinces. Like the Lambeth Report of 1968, the effects of the document's recommendations are finding themselves reflected in new initiation rites as they appear around the Communion. The restoration of the catechumenate, the communion of all the baptized, the more vivid use of liturgical signs and a renewed sense of relationship between baptism and mission are some of the changes that can be seen in these new rites. IALC-V (Dublin, 1995), which addressed the renewal of the Eucharist, affirmed the inclusion of all the baptized in the Eucharist. In the light of questions raised in some parts of the Communion, it also affirmed that baptism normatively preceeds the Eucharist.[10]

The paradigm for initiation that is slowly emerging in the Anglican world is probably closer to the pattern envisioned by the Reformers than it has ever been. The vision of the public, corporate, act of worship in which the primitive unity of the rite (as the Reformers understood it) was restored was never able to prevail over the traditional forces of popular piety. The direction Christian initiation is taking today is faithful to the vision of the Reformers as well as its natural and logical consequence. It continues as a major item on the Anglican theological and liturgical agenda.

CONFIRMATION

The history and development of confirmation is one of the more compli- cated aspects of the history of Christian initiation. The question is no less complicated within Anglicanism. There are several questions which need some reflection apart from the earlier section of initiation.

CRANMER AND CONFIRMATION

Although Cranmer kept the outline of Western medieval confirmation there was, at the very least, a major shift in the emphasis of what he was doing. There is considerable scholarly debate over Cranmer's intentions. It is immediately evident that there was a shift in emphasis from the administration of the rite itself to the catechizing which preceded it. The extent to which Cranmer saw the new rite as remaining in continuity with the medieval rite of confirmation is much less clear, particularly since he dropped the anointing which, according to medieval theologians, was central to the sacramental nature of confirmation.

Cranmer's intentions are even less certain when put in the light of traditional 'confirmation' elements which he places within the baptismal rite itself. The anointing of the 1549 rite and the consignation of the 1552 rite both are made on the forehead as in medieval confirmation rather than on top or crown of the head as in the medieval rite of baptism. The language Cranmer uses—'the unction of his Holy Spirit' (1549) and the declaration during the consignation (1552) (pp. 297–8)—are typical of language used for confirmation rather than baptism during the Middle Ages. As Cranmer had drawn material from the Hispanic *Missale Mixtum*, where there is but one post-baptismal anointing and no separate rite of confirmation, he cannot have been unaware of a single, unified, rite of initiation.

While there is no clear answer to Cranmer's intentions when he created the rites of baptism and confirmation, it is arguable that he was being bolder than is often thought: the baptismal rite containing what he saw as the essence of medieval 'confirmation' and the confirmation rite as a novelty following in the steps of the Bohemians, Erasmus and Luther.[11] The contemporary political importance of ambiguity rather than clarity makes a final resolution to this question particularly difficult.

VARIOUS INTERPRETATIONS OF CONFIRMATION

While the administration of confirmation within Anglicanism was very lax, and was often neglected altogether during the three centuries after the Reformation, the nineteenth century saw the beginnings of a strict confirmation discipline. With it this discipline brought a sacramental interpretation of confirmation unknown in earlier Anglicanism.

A literal interpretation of the confirmation rubric, which made confirmation a prerequisite to reception of the Eucharist, led to a theology which interpreted confirmation as the second and completing half of the sacrament of initiation. This new theology of confirmation came to have a dominant (but not absolute) influence within the Anglican Communion from about 1890.[12] Alongside this sacramental interpretation of confirmation, the older non-sacramental, catechetical, understanding of confirmation continued to exist.[13]

As long as the question 'What is confirmation?' was never forced, the two theologies were able to coexist without difficulty because the ritual practice was the same: both theologies presumed confirmation before communion. When Lambeth 1968 asked for a re-examination of confirmation theology and the process of liturgical revision began, the question once again became one of considerable debate.

Principles (c) and (g) of IALC-IV (above have important implications for the practice of confirmation within Anglicanism as does the seventh recommendation of IALC-I which asked 'that each province clearly affirm that confirmation is not a rite of admission to communion'. Members of the Toronto Consultation were particularly interested to learn that confirmation had been delegated to archdeacons in Australia during the last century and that it is delegated to presbyters in some African dioceses today.

While patterns and practice are changing at different rates in different parts of the Communion, discussion on the renewal of the practice of confirmation is likely to be ongoing. If there is to be change, however, there is a need for strong episcopal leadership, particularly renewal in the understanding of *episcopé* among the bishops themselves for whom change in confirmation practice is often seen as a challenge to their office.

Confirmation, as celebrated in the new liturgical texts, is clearly emerging as a non-initiatory reaffirmation of the baptismal covenant. Confirmation as a rite of admission to communion is quickly disappearing and instead is becoming an optional rite for those who, having come to a stage of Christian maturity, wish to make a public reaffirmation of their faith in the presence of a bishop. The age at which this is taking place is becoming considerably older than the early teens, the traditional age for confirmation.

BIBLIOGRAPHY
Buchanan, Colin O. (ed.), *Nurturing Children in Communion*. GLS 44, Grove Press, Bramcote, 1985.
Cuming, G. J., *A History of Anglican Liturgy*, 2nd edn. Macmillan, London, 1982.
Fisher, J. D. C., *Christian Initiation: The Reformation Period*. AC, SPCK, London, 1970.
Fisher, J. D. C., *Confirmation: Then and Now*. AC, SPCK, London, 1978.
Hatchett, Marion J., *Commentary on the American Prayer Book*. Seabury Press, New York, 1980.

Holeton, David R., 'Christian Initiation in Some Anglican Provinces', in *SL* 12: ii/iii (1977), pp. 129–50.
Holeton, David R. (ed), *Growing in Newness of Life: Christian Initiation in Anglicanism Today*. Anglican Book Centre, Toronto, 1993.
Jagger, Peter J., *Christian Initiation: 1552–1969*. AC, SPCK, London, 1970.
Meyers, Ruth A. (ed.), *Children at the Table: A Collection of Essays on Children and the Eucharist*. The Church Hymnal Corporation, New York, 1995.
Mitchell, Leonell L., *Baptismal Anointing*. AC, SPCK, London, 1966.

NOTES

1 It appeareth by ancient writers, that the sacrament of baptism in old time was not commonly ministered but at two times in the year, at Easter and Whitsuntide, at which times it was openly ministered in the presence of all the congregation: Which custom (now being grown out of use) although it cannot for many considerations be well restored again, yet it is thought good to follow the same as near as conveniently may be: Wherefore the people are to be admonished, that it is most convenient that Baptism should not be ministered but upon Sundays and other holy days, when the most number of people may come together. As well for the congregation there present may testify the receiving of them, that be newly baptized, into the number of Christ's Church, as also because in the Baptism of Infants, every man present may be put in remembrance of his own profession made to God in his Baptism. For which cause also, it is expedient that Baptism be ministered in the English tongue. Nevertheless (if necessity so require) children ought at all times to be baptized, either at the Church or else at home.

2 E. C. Whitaker, *Martin Bucer and the Book of Common Prayer* (AC, Mayhew-McCrimmon, London, 1974) pp. 82–115.

3 E. C. Whitaker, *Martin Bucer*, p. 114.

4 Jeremy Taylor, *Of the Liberty of Prophesying* (London 1648), pp. 232–3.

5 The Lambeth Conference 1968, *Resolutions and Reports* (SPCK, London, 1968), p. 99.

6 *Resolutions and Reports*, p. 37.

7 The Doctrinal Commision of the Church in Wales, *Christian Initiation* (Church in Wales Publications 1971), pp. 22–3.

8 These have been laid out before the Churches in the opening paragraphs of the Baptism section of the World Council of Churches' document, *Baptism, Eucharist, and Ministry*. The incorporation of a greater number of these biblical images has been a conscious response to the Faith and Order process which culminated in the Lima text.

9 Holeton, *Growing in Newness of Life*, pp. 227–57.

10 Cf. David Holeton, ed., *Renewing The Anglican Eucharist* (Grove Books, Bramcote, 1995).

11 Hatchett, *Commentary on the American Prayer Book*, pp. 260–5 has been the most lucid expositor of this position.

12 This position came to be known as the 'Mason-Dix' line from the work of two of its principal proponents, A. J. Mason, *The Relation of Confirmation to Baptism* (London 1893); and Don Gregory Dix, *The Theology of Confirmation in Relation to Baptism* (Dacre Press, London, 1946).

13 G. W. H. Lampe defends this position in *The Seal of the Spirit*, 2nd edn (SPCK, London, 1967).

5 Holy Communion

WILLIAM R. CROCKETT

The English Reformation was in its beginnings a political rather than a religious reformation. When religious change did eventually come it took first a liturgical rather than a doctrinal form. In 1549 the first edition of the Book of Common Prayer appeared (see pp. 131–6).[1] Its principal author was Archbishop Thomas Cranmer. As far as the eucharistic rite is concerned, it was a half-way measure which followed the traditional Roman Mass quite closely as far as order and structure are concerned.[2] The greatest departure from the doctrine of the older rite is found in the revisions made in the canon of the Mass (Prayer of Consecration or Eucharistic Prayer). The structure of the old canon was followed, but the theological emphasis was placed squarely on the sacrifice of Christ 'once offered' on the cross. All references to the Mass as a sacrifice in any other sense than that of a commemoration of the sacrifice of the cross, a sacrifice of praise and thanksgiving, or the sacrifice of 'ourselves, our souls, and bodies', were carefully excluded. The whole prayer was more clearly oriented around the theme of thanksgiving, in line with the eucharistic prayers of the early Church. The *anamnesis* (*memorial* of Christ's death and resurrection) is restored to a position of central prominence, and an *epiclesis* (invocation) is introduced which invokes both the word and the Holy Spirit on the gifts in view of their reception in communion.

In 1552 the second edition of the Prayer Book appeared. The 1552 eucharistic rite is a much more drastic revision of the old Mass than 1549.[3] Cranmer's 1549 canon had three sections. The first section contained intercessions and commemorations adapted from the Roman canon, the second section contained the thanksgiving for redemption, the epiclesis, and the words of institution, and the third section contained the anamnesis followed by the offering of 'ourselves, our souls, and bodies', and concluded with the doxology. Cranmer moved the first section to a point earlier in the service, immediately after the offertory. The third section became an optional prayer after communion. The epiclesis was removed from the middle section, so that all that remained of the Eucharistic Prayer in 1552 was the thanksgiving for redemption and the words of institution. This was followed immediately by the words for the administration of communion, which now read: 'Take and eat this, in remembrance that Christ died for thee, and feed on him in thy heart by faith, with thanksgiving', and 'Drink this in remembrance that Christ's blood was shed for thee and be thankful'. The reason for these changes is a disputed question.[4]

Anglicanism never developed a doctrine of the Eucharist bearing the distinctive stamp either of a single great Reformer or of common confessional agreement. Rather, within the broad framework of the Anglican Settlement there grew up a spectrum of doctrinal opinion which represented a *via media* between Rome and the continental Reformed Churches. This *via media* was based on a broad appeal to Scripture, the early Church, reason and experience, which became characteristic of the Anglican ethos. Cranmer sought to reorient eucharistic doctrine around the act of communion, rather than around a change in the nature of the elements.[5] In doing this, he broke with the dominant medieval tradition and took up a position more in line with that of St Augustine and the Swiss Reformers. His doctrine can perhaps best be described as a doctrine of the real partaking of the body and blood of Christ in the Eucharist, rather than a doctrine of the real objective presence of Christ in the Eucharist. The sacramental signs are connected with the reality which they signify through their use rather than in an objective manner. Such a standpoint represents an attempt to retain sacramental realism in relation to the faithful believer rather than in relation to the elements:

> And therefore, in the book of the holy communion, we do not pray absolutely that the bread and wine may be made the body and blood of Christ, but that unto us in that holy mystery they may be so; that is to say, that we may so worthily receive the same, that we may be partakers of Christ's body and blood, and that therewith in spirit and in truth we may be spiritually nourished.[6]

During the Elizabethan period, Richard Hooker developed a distinctively Anglican theological method in approaching eucharistic doctrine. Like Cranmer, Hooker's doctrine can be described as a doctrine of the real partaking of the body and blood of Christ in the Eucharist, rather than a doctrine of the real presence of Christ in the Eucharist.[7] This doctrine of the Eucharist, which became characteristic of Anglican theology, is often referred to as 'receptionism'. Hooker does not deny the real presence, but he relates it primarily to the faithful communicant rather than to the elements of bread and wine: 'The real presence of Christ's most blessed body and blood is not [...] to be sought for in the sacrament, but in the worthy receiver of the sacrament.'[8] On the question of the relation of the presence to the elements of bread and wine he adopts a position of deliberate agnosticism:

> Let it therefore be sufficient for me presenting myself at the Lord's table to know what there I receive from him, without searching or inquiring of the manner how Christ performeth his promise; [...] what these

elements are in themselves it skilleth not, it is enough that to me which take them they are the body and blood of Christ.[9]

Hooker's agnosticism regarding the manner of the eucharistic presence reveals the emergence of a distinctively Anglican approach to the issue of authority in matters of faith. It was a cardinal principle of the emerging Anglican tradition that nothing can be proposed as a necessary article of faith which goes beyond the certain testimony of Scripture (see pp. 90–3). Beyond this, agreement with the early Church, consent among the various Christian confessions, and the testimony of reason are further tests which serve either to confirm or deny the truth of a particular doctrine. This led to a distinction in Anglican theology between those doctrines which were regarded as necessary articles of faith, and those matters which could be left in the realm of theological opinion (see pp. 264–9). Hooker is drawing a distinction here between theology and faith. At the level of faith, all that is necessary is that we believe that the body and blood of Christ is really received in the Eucharist by means of the sacramental signs. At the level of theology, it is legitimate to speculate about the manner of the presence, as long as it does not endanger piety.

What then, for Hooker, is the role of the elements in mediating the presence of Christ to the worthy receiver? In addressing this issue, Hooker attempts to steer a middle course between 'Zwinglianism' on the one side and the doctrine of the medieval Church on the other. To explain the relationship between divine grace and the sacraments Hooker, like Aquinas, employs the language of instrumental causality. The sacraments are not causes of grace in an absolute sense. God alone is the author of grace. The sacraments are causes only in a secondary or instrumental sense. God uses them as means of imparting grace. As means of grace, however, the sacraments do not produce their effect automatically, but only conditionally. The sacraments are 'moral instruments', not mechanical or physical instruments.[10] Hooker is employing here what we might today call a 'personalist' rather than a naturalist or mechanical model of sacramental casuality. The operation of the sacraments is analogous to the offering and acceptance of a gift between free moral agents. It is conditional both on God's free offer of grace, and upon the faithful response of the recipient. The offer of grace is unconditional, in the sense that the sacraments depend upon the divine promise. The acceptance of the gift, however, is conditional upon the free and faithful response of the recipient. The sacraments 'really exhibit', but 'they are not really nor do really contain in themselves that grace which with them or by them it pleaseth God to bestow'.[11] The bread and cup are his body and blood, therefore, 'because they are causes instrumental upon the receipt whereof the *participation* of his body and blood ensueth'.[12]

It was characteristic of seventeenth-century Anglican writers to insist on the real presence of Christ in the Eucharist, but to profess agnosticism concerning the manner of the presence in the tradition of Hooker.[13] 'Receptionism' remained the dominant theological position within the Church of England until the Oxford Movement in the early nineteenth century, with varying differences in emphasis. It is important to remember, however, that 'receptionism' is a doctrine of the real presence, but a doctrine of the real presence which relates the presence primarily to the worthy receiver rather than to the elements of bread and wine.

In true Augustinian fashion seventeenth-century Anglican writers distinguish between the *res* of the sacrament, that is, the reality or inward and spiritual grace conveyed by it, and the *sacramentum* or outward and visible sign, by means of which the grace is communicated to the faithful recipient.[14] At the same time, they maintain a 'sacramental union' between the elements and the reality signified by them. The union, however, does not abolish the distinction between the *sacramentum* and the *res*; otherwise the sacrament would cease to be a sacrament, since the nature of a sacrament always consists of two parts, a visible and an invisible, an earthly and a heavenly. While the *sacramentum* and the *res* are joined, therefore, so that the offer of grace is clearly made to all, only the faithful recipient receives the *res* of the sacrament along with the outward signs. The outward signs are received by the mouth and enter into the stomach. The inward grace of the sacrament is only eaten by faith.

The bread and wine become a sacrament by means of their consecration in the Eucharistic Prayer. However, since the purpose of the sacrament is only attained in the act of communion, the consecration is not separated from the 'use' of the elements in communion:

> It is important to remember that by consecration all the Caroline divines seem to have meant the setting apart for the sacred use of communion; this is in sharp contrast to the contemporary Roman view which regarded it as meaning the effecting of an objective change in the substance of the elements.[15]

Hooker had already thought of consecration as the 'hallowing with solemn benediction to use'.[16] This represents a recovery of the patristic notion that consecration is brought about by the recital of the Eucharistic Prayer, rather than the medieval view that consecration is effected by the recital of the words of institution.[17]

While the theme of the presence of Christ in relation to the faithful communicants predominates in seventeenth-century Anglican eucharistic

311

thought, it is not the only eucharistic theme which appears there. With the partial receding of the sixteenth-century polemical context and the renewed study of the Church Fathers, the sacrificial aspect of the Eucharist also begins to appear again in Anglican writings. The Eucharist is described as a 'commemorative' or 'representative' sacrifice, which in no sense adds anything to the saving significance of the cross, and the ecclesial dimension of the eucharistic sacrifice stressed by Augustine comes into view again. In a sermon preached by John Buckeridge at the funeral of Lancelot Andrewes, there is a beautiful text which perfectly expresses this Augustinian emphasis:

> As Christ's cross was His altar where He offered Himself for us, so the Church hath an altar also where it offereth itself [...] not Christ the Head properly but only by commemoration, but Christ the members. For Christ cannot be offered truly and properly no more but once upon the cross [...] This then is the daily sacrifice of the Church in St Augustine's resolute judgement, even the Church itself, the universal body of Christ, not the natural body, whereof the Sacrament is an exemplar and memorial only, as hath been shewed [...] We deny not then the daily sacrifice of the Church, that is, the Church itself, warranted by Scriptures and fathers.[18]

We have described the characteristic Anglican doctrine of the Eucharist as a doctrine of the real partaking of the body and blood of Christ by means of the sacramental signs of bread and wine. This 'receptionist' understanding of the Eucharist is a doctrine of the real presence, but a doctrine of the real presence which relates the presence primarily to the faithful communicants rather than to the elements of bread and wine. What accounts for this distinctive emphasis in Anglican eucharistic doctrine?

During the Middle Ages there developed a gradual separation between the act of consecration and the act of communion, so that the goal of the Eucharist became the production of the real presence rather than the communion of the people. This resulted in a eucharistic piety which focused on the adoration of the host, rather than on the reception of communion.[19] In medieval theology it led to a preoccupation with the question of the manner of Christ's presence in the elements. Anglican theologians from Cranmer onwards were engaged in a project of reorienting eucharistic theology away from its medieval centre and reuniting the act of consecration and the act of communion. For these theologians, the goal of the Eucharist is not the production of the real presence, but the nourishment of Christian believers. The real presence is the presupposition rather than the focus of their thought. The consecration of the elements is not regarded as an end in itself, but is oriented towards the act of communion. Christ is not present in the Eucharist as an object on the altar but as spiritual food and drink to nourish the life of faith. With regard to the manner of the presence, they saw the sacramental presence and communication of the body and blood of Christ as an event in the order of grace. It is this which accounts for their rejection of transubstantiation, which they interpreted as a naturalistic explanation of the eucharistic presence implying a local or physical presence of Christ on the altar. For these Anglican theologians, on the other hand, the presence of Christ in the Eucharist is not an event in the physical world, but a presence-in-grace which is offered to all, but which can only be received by those who receive it with a living faith. The elements play an instrumental role in communicating the presence of Christ to the faithful receiver. This does not occur in a mechanical manner, but only within the freedom of the grace–faith relationship.

In all of this, High Church Anglicans and moderate Anglicans shared a common body of teaching. While the early Anglican High Church tradition can be distinguished from moderate Anglicanism in its sacramental spirituality and its liturgical ideals, it is difficult if not impossible to establish a clear distinction in the sphere of eucharistic theology. We can agree with Richard Buxton that the differences between the two outlooks reflect 'variations of the basic early seventeenth century position',[20] which have more to do with piety than with doctrine.

Two revivals of eucharistic life and thought took place in the latter half of the eighteenth and the early nineteenth centuries. The first of these was the Evangelical Revival of John and Charles Wesley. The second was the Oxford Movement. It is not commonly known today that the Wesleyan Revival was as much a eucharistic revival as it was an Evangelical revival.[21] The genius of the Wesleys, however, lies precisely in the unity which they saw between a sacramental and an Evangelical vision of Christianity. The eucharistic theology of the Wesleys is most clearly expressed in a collection of 166 eucharistic hymns, composed by Charles and John, which combine a rich sacramentalism with joyful Evangelical experience.[22]

The theology of the hymns reflects the eucharistic doctrine of seventeenth-century Anglicanism. The hymns are introduced by an extract from Daniel Brevint's treatise *The Christian Sacrament and Sacrifice*.[23] Brevint is a seventeenth-century Anglican writer. There is nothing in his treatise that cannot be paralleled in other seventeenth-century Anglican writers. What is remarkable about the treatise is its scope and balance, and its recovery of eucharistic themes which had not achieved as clear expression in earlier Anglican tradition.

According to Brevint there are three fundamental aspects to the Eucharist: a past, a present and a future aspect. The Eucharist is, first of all, a memorial of the saving death of Christ. Secondly, it is present grace and nourishment for worthy receivers. Thirdly, it is a pledge which assures our participation in the life of the promised Kingdom of God. Brevint treats the sacrificial aspect of the Eucharist more fully than earlier Anglican writers. He is absolutely clear that the sacrifice of Christ on the cross took place once for all in the past and cannot be repeated, and that it atones completely for sin. The Eucharist, however, can be spoken of as a sacrifice in three senses. It is, first of all, a commemorative sacrifice. Secondly, in line with Augustine, it is a sacrifice of the Church in union with its Head. Thirdly, Christ as the eternal High Priest continually presents before the Father in heaven his completed sacrifice on the cross as the basis of our acceptance before him. In making the memorial of Christ's death in the Eucharist the Church not only commemorates a past action, but Christians on earth are united with Christ in the eternal pleading of his completed sacrifice in heaven. The Wesleys' collection of eucharistic hymns follow the themes in Brevint's treatise very closely, and thus mediate the principal themes of the seventeenth-century Anglican eucharistic tradition to their Evangelical followers.

In the early nineteenth century the Wesleyan Revival was followed by the Oxford Movement.[24] Whereas the Wesleys emphasized the Evangelical heritage of Anglicanism, the Tractarians stressed its Catholic heritage. Central to this Catholic heritage was an emphasis on the sacramental life and on the Eucharist as the centre of Catholic worship. In parishes influenced by the Oxford Movement there gradually developed a recovery of Catholic ceremonial and vestments in the celebration of the Eucharist. In the ritualist phase of the movement pre-Reformation ceremonial was restored or contemporary Roman Catholic practice was introduced, leading to ritual battles with the ecclesiastical authorities. The Oxford Movement has had an influence far beyond the Anglo-Catholic revival itself in bringing about a much greater emphasis throughout the Anglican Communion on the centrality of eucharistic worship.

In their theology of the Eucharist, the Tractarians saw a closer connection between the real presence of Christ in the Eucharist and the elements than did the earlier Anglican tradition. For the Tractarians, there is a strict identity between the earthly body of Christ, his risen body, and his sacramental body. The only difference is in the manner or mode of the presence. While connecting the eucharistic presence of Christ more closely to the elements than did the earlier Anglican theologians, the Tractarians were entirely at one with them in insisting that the manner of the presence is spiritual and not physical or local. It is a presence in the order of grace and not a presence in the order of nature. Christ is present in the Eucharist, however, in a specific way: namely, by means of sacramental signs.

There is nothing here which goes essentially beyond what can be found in the older seventeenth-century Anglican writers, except by way of emphasis.

The Tractarians, however, went decisively beyond the earlier Anglican theology in making a clear distinction between the presence of Christ in relation to the elements and the presence of Christ in relation to the worthy communicants. According to Tractarian teaching, the presence of Christ in relation to the elements is brought about by the act of consecration and is not dependent on their reception in communion. This position was given its clearest theological expression by R. I. Wilberforce.[25] who distinguished not only between the *res* of the sacrament and its *sacramentum* as did the earlier Anglican writers, but also between the *res* and the *virtus* of the sacrament. The *res* of the sacrament is the reality signified by the outward signs: namely, Christ himself. The *virtus* of the sacrament is the blessing, effect, or grace which Christ gives to all who receive the sacrament in faith. The union between the *res* and the *sacramentum* is brought about by the consecration. After the consecration Christ is objectively present in relation to the elements. This union between the *res* and the *sacramentum*, however, is a sacramental union, not the presence of an object in the physical world. Christ is not present in the elements in a physical or natural mode, but in a sacramental mode. The reality or *res* of the sacrament is offered to the communicants by means of the sacramental signs irrespective of their faith, but only those who receive the sacrament by faith receive the *virtus*, or grace of the sacrament. The purpose of distinguishing between the *res* and the *virtus* of the sacrament is to make it clear that Christ is objectively present in relation to the elements by means of their consecration, but present in grace only to those who receive him by faith.

In the twentieth century, the Liturgical Movement and developments in liturgical scholarship have brought about far-reaching changes in the eucharistic life and worship of Anglicanism, and have led in recent decades to extensive liturgical revision throughout the Anglican Communion (see pp. 45–6). The Ecumenical Movement and developments in theology have also profoundly affected the Anglican understanding of the Eucharist.

The Liturgical Movement in the Church of England began as a movement for the more active participation of the people in the liturgy in the context of a commitment to social justice and the mission of the Church in society.[26] The movement was given widespread impetus by the publication of two books by A. G. Hebert, *Liturgy and Society* (1935) and *The Parish Communion* (1937). The proposal for a 'Parish Communion' was to make a sung celebration of the Eucharist with active participation by the people the central act of worship on Sunday morning. This has gained increasing popularity throughout the Anglican Communion in parishes of different churchmanship.

Liturgical scholarship and liturgical revision in Anglicanism began with the work of Archbishop Thomas Cranmer. Cranmer himself revised the

Prayer Book, and various revisions have been undertaken throughout Anglican history.[27] Anglican liturgical scholarship flourished in the seventeenth century.[28] In the late nineteenth and early twentieth centuries this tradition was continued in the work of the great Anglican liturgical scholars, W. H. Frere, F. C. Brightman, and E. C. Ratcliff. The most influential work of Anglican liturgical scholarship in the twentieth century has been *The Shape of the Liturgy* by Dom Gregory Dix (1945).[29] Dix's work had a pivotal influence on all subsequent liturgical revision in the Anglican Communion. His thesis is that the Eucharist is essentially an action which has a fourfold shape, corresponding to the actions of Jesus in 'taking', 'blessing', ('breaking'), and 'giving' the bread and the cup at the Last Supper. These four actions correspond to the Offertory, the Eucharistic Prayer, the Fraction (Breaking of the Bread) and the Communion in the eucharistic liturgy. Dix shows how this fourfold action is exemplified in the structure of the early eucharistic rites, and how it became overlaid and distorted in medieval and Reformation developments. All of the revisions of the eucharistic liturgy which have taken place in the various provinces of the Anglican Communion since the publication of Dix's book show the influence of his emphasis on the shape of the liturgy.

Along with the emphasis on the shape of the rite as a whole, a major concern in the revision of Anglican rites has been to restore the classic structure of the Eucharistic Prayer. Research into the origins and history of the Eucharistic Prayer in the present century has played a major role in Anglican liturgical revision.[30] The tradition of the eucharistic prayer evidently derives from Jewish models, particularly Jewish table prayers of blessing and thanksgiving (*berakoth*), and characteristically the thanksgiving said over the cup at the end of the meal, the *birkat ha-mazon*.[31] Precise derivation, however, cannot be established from the limited evidence. The characteristic structure of early eucharistic prayers is Thanksgiving (for creation and redemption) followed by supplication (which developed into an epiclesis of the Spirit).[32] Recent revisions of the eucharistic rite throughout the Anglican Communion follow this basic structure with variations in wording and theological emphasis and, particularly in the English rites, in the position of the epiclesis.[33]

Ecumenical scholarship and the Ecumenical Movement have also profoundly shaped the Anglican understanding of the Eucharist in the twentieth century. Two examples of this are the Anglican–Roman Catholic *Agreed Statement on Eucharistic Doctrine*,[34] the result of work by the Anglican–Roman Catholic International Commission, and the document *Baptism, Eucharist, and Ministry* of the Faith and Order Commission of the World Council of Churches (see pp. 431–40).[35]

The Anglican–Roman Catholic *Agreed Statement* tackles both the issues of real presence and eucharistic sacrifice. In language which is reminiscent of Hooker, the statement acknowledges the goal of the Eucharist as 'communion with Christ' which 'presupposes his true presence'. With regard to the elements, the real presence of Christ is 'effectively signified by the bread and wine which, in this mystery, become his body and blood'. While this presence 'does not depend on the individual's faith in order to be the Lord's real gift of himself to his Church', it is only through reception by faith that 'a lifegiving encounter results'.

The document uses the notion of the eucharistic memorial as the key to understanding the relationship between Christ's sacrifice and the Eucharist.[36] The Eucharist is seen neither as a repetition of the sacrifice of the cross, nor simply as a mental recollection of an event which took place 2,000 years ago. Rather, the eucharistic memorial is the 'effectual proclamation' in the present of the redemptive reality of events which took place once for all in the past. Through the eucharistic memorial the sacrifice of the cross is made sacramentally present, in order that we may participate in its redemptive reality in the present.[37] The statement ends with the eschatological perspective, highlighting the meaning of the Eucharist as a foretaste of the banquet in the kingdom.

The Anglican–Roman Catholic agreed statement on the Eucharist is only one of a series of ecumenical agreements on the Eucharist which have taken place during the present century. Various bilateral discussions among the Churches have led to similar ecumenical agreements. All of these statements have helped to prepare the way for the document *Baptism, Eucharist, and Ministry* formulated by the Faith and Order Commission of the World Council of Churches at its meeting held in Lima, Peru in 1982 as an expression of theological convergence on baptism, Eucharist, and ministry. Anglicans have played a major role in the theological discussions leading up to the publication of BEM.[38]

BEM treats the Eucharist under five headings: Thanksgiving, Memorial, Invocation of the Spirit, Communion and Anticipation of the Meal in the Kingdom. In contemporary Anglican liturgical revision the thanksgiving character of the Eucharist is reflected in the strong emphasis on the celebration as a communal act of praise and thanksgiving for creation and redemption in contrast to the penitential note characteristic of Cranmer's rites. The central role of the eucharistic memorial for an understanding of the relationship between the sacrifice of Christ and the Eucharist, which is found in the Anglican–Roman Catholic *Agreed Statement*, is also evident in BEM and in recent Anglican revisions of the Eucharistic Prayer. The role of the Holy Spirit in the eucharistic celebration, which has long been emphasized by the Eastern Churches, is now reflected in the restoration of an epiclesis in modern Anglican liturgical rites. Anglicanism has long emphasized the

Eucharist as 'Holy Communion', but as Dix pointed out, most often in an individualistic sense. The new emphasis in twentieth-century Anglicanism is on the Eucharist not only as an act of personal communion, but as a corporate community celebration in which all the participants are built up into communion with Christ and with one another in the Body of Christ.

The emphasis on the Eucharist as an anticipation of the meal in the Kingdom of God has been a neglected aspect in Anglicanism which is beginning to appear in some Anglican revisions, particularly in new eucharistic prayers. The eschatological perspective is one of the earliest eucharistic traditions in the New Testament.[39] This theme became marginalized in later eucharistic tradition as the themes of real presence and sacrifice assumed the centre of the stage, but it is being recovered today.[40] This perspective is clearly linked to the theme of justice. A meal celebrated in prospect of the coming reign of God gives rise to a new social vision, grounded in the promise of the kingdom. Such a vision challenges the *status quo* in society and the prevailing set of economic and social relationships. Sharing in a community meal anticipates a just sharing of all the gifts of creation in justice and love. The Anglican–Roman Catholic *Agreed Statement* and BEM, therefore, both reflect changes which are taking place in the celebration and understanding of the Eucharist within Anglicanism, and offer a challenge to Anglicans to incorporate emphases which have been neglected in our tradition.

The Anglican eucharistic tradition began with liturgical change, and only subsequently developed a tradition of doctrinal and theological reflection on the Eucharist. In the twentieth century liturgical change throughout the Anglican Communion is profoundly transforming Anglican eucharistic life. The revision of Anglican liturgies which has been taking place in the various provinces of the Anglican Communion is shaping the eucharistic consciousness of Anglicans in new ways which require fresh theological reflection. The social and cultural context of Anglicanism has changed dramatically since the nineteenth century. The Anglican Communion no longer reflects English culture, but is a community of indigenous Churches which reflect a plurality of cultural and social contexts.

The international Anglican Liturgical Consultation meeting in Dublin in August 1995 had the Eucharist as its theme. The purpose of the consultation was to develop principles and recommendations to assist the various provinces of the Anglican Communion during the next phase of revision and renewal of eucharistic rites.[41] The consultation emphasized that the Eucharist is the action of the whole community and the variety of roles in the celebration flow from the diverse gifts of ministry given in baptism. The consultation foresees that in the future a common structure rather than common texts will shape Anglican liturgical identity. This common structure includes the following elements: The Gathering of the community, Proclamation and response to the Word of God, Prayers of the People, Thanksgiving over the bread and the cup culminating in Communion, and the Sending out of God's people into the world. 'The fundamental character of the eucharistic prayer' within this wider structure 'is thanksgiving and the whole eucharistic prayer should be seen as consecratory. The elements of memorial and invocation are caught up within the movement of thanksgiving.' The Consultation emphasized that these common structures need to be inculturated employing a variety of symbols, language and ritual characteristic of the cultural traditions of the various provinces of the Anglican Communion.

BIBLIOGRAPHY
Cuming, G. J., *A History of Anglican Liturgy*, 2nd edn. Macmillan, London, 1982.
Crockett, William R., *Eucharist: Symbol of Transformation*. Pueblo Publishing Co., New York, 1989.
Cocksworth, Christopher J., *Evangelical Eucharistic Thought in the Church of England*. CUP 1993.
Stevenson, Kenneth, *Covenant of Grace Renewed: A Vision of the Eucharist in the Seventeenth Century*. DLT, London, 1994.
McAdoo H. R, and Stevenson, K., *The Mystery of the Eucharist in the Anglican Tradition*. The Canterbury Press Norwich 1995.
Holeton, David R. (ed.), *Our Thanks and Praise: The Eucharist in Anglicanism Today*. Anglican Book Centre, Toronto, 1998.
Perham, M., *Lively Sacrifice: The Eucharist in the Church of England Today*. SPCK, London, 1992.
Wainwright, G., *Eucharist and Eschatology*. Epworth Press, London, 1978.

NOTES
1 For the history of Anglican liturgy see especially Cuming, *A History of Anglican Liturgy*.
2 For the text of the rite see Colin Buchanan, *Eucharistic Liturgies of Edward VI* (GLS 34, Grove Books, Bramcote, 1983), pp. 7–20. For commentary see Cuming, *History*, pp. 51–9.
3 Text in Buchanan, *Eucharistic Liturgies of Edward VI*, pp. 21–33. Commentary in Cuming, *History*, pp. 70–74, 77–81.
4 For an interpretation see Colin Buchanan, *What did Cranmer think he was doing?* (GLS 7, Grove Books, Bramcote, 1976).
5 For Cranmer's eucharistic doctrine see Peter Brooks, *Thomas Cranmer's Doctrine of the Eucharist: An Essay in Historical Development* (Seabury Press, New York, 1965); Cyril C. Richardson, 'Cranmer and the Analysis of Eucharistic Doctrine', *JTS* n.s. 16 (1965), pp. 421–37.
6 Thomas Cranmer, *Writings on the Sacrament of the Lord's Supper*, ed. John Edmund Cox, The Parker Society (CUP 1846), p. 79.
7 For Hooker's sources see John E. Booty, 'Hooker's Understanding of the Presence of Christ in the Eucharist' in John E. Booty (ed.), *The Divine Drama in History and Liturgy* (Pickwick Publications, Allison Park PA, 1984), pp. 131–48; for his method see W. Speed Hill (ed.), *Studies in Richard Hooker* (Case

Western Reserve University Press, Cleveland, 1972); for his eucharistic theology see Olivier Loyer, *L'Anglicanisme de Richard Hooker*, 2 vols. (Librairie Honore Champion, Paris, 1979), Vol. i, pp. 475–542.

8 *Laws* V. lxvii. All citations from Hooker are from *Of the Laws of Ecclesiastical Polity* in John Keble (ed.), *The Works of ... Mr Richard Hooker*, 7th rev. edn (Clarendon Press, Oxford, 1888); by book, chapter and section.

9 *Laws* V. lxvii. 12.

10 Cf. *Laws* V. lvii. 4, 5.

11 *Laws* V. lxvii. 6.

12 *Laws* V. lxvii. 5.

13 For seventeenth-century Anglican eucharistic thought see Stevenson, *Covenant of Grace Renewed*.

14 For the Augustinian background of Anglican eucharistic theology see C. W. Dugmore, *The Mass and the English Reformers* (Macmillan, London, 1958), especially ch. 1.

15 Richard F. Buxton, *Eucharist and Institution Narrative: A Study in the The Roman and Anglican Traditions of the Consecration of the Eucharist from the Eighth to the Twentieth Centuries*, AC 58 (Mayhew-McCrimmon, Great Wakering, 1976), p. 131.

16 Buxton, *Eucharist*, p. 131. Cf. Hooker *Laws* V. lxvii. 12.

17 For patristic and medieval views of consecration see John H. McKenna, *Eucharist and Holy Spirit: The Eucharistic Epiclesis in Twentieth Century Theology*, AC 57 (Mayhew-McCrimmon, Great Wakering, 1975), especially ch. 2.

18 Cited in Darwell Stone, *A History of the Doctrine of the Holy Eucharist*, 2 vols. (Longmans, Green, & Co., London, 1909), Vol ii, p. 266f.

19 For the history of this development see Nathan Mitchell, *Cult and Controversy: The Worship of the Eucharist Outside Mass* (Pueblo, New York, 1982).

20 Buxton, *Eucharist*, p. 131.

21 See Paul S. Saunders, 'Wesley's Eucharistic Faith and Practice', *Anglican Theological Review* 48 (1966), pp. 157–74.

22 See J. Ernest Rattenbury, *The Eucharistic Hymns of John and Charles Wesley* (Epworth, London, 1948).

23 See H. R. McAdoo, 'A Theology of The Eucharist: Brevint and The Wesleys', *Theology* 97 (1994), pp. 245–56.

24 For the Tractarians see Alf Hardelin, *The Tractarian Understanding of the Eucharist* (Almquist & Wiksells, Uppsala, 1965).

25 R. I. Wilberforce, *The Doctrine of the Holy Eucharist* (London 1853).

26 See Donald Gray, *Earth and Altar: The Evolution of the Parish Communion in the Church of England to 1945*, AC 68 (Canterbury Press Norwich 1986).

27 See Cheslyn Jones et al. (eds), *The Study of Liturgy* rev. edn. (SPCK, London/ OUP, New York, 1992), pp. 309–24, 328–38.

28 See W. J. Grisbrooke, *Anglican Liturgies of the Seventeenth and Eighteenth Centuries*, AC 40 (SPCK, London, 1958).

29 Gregory Dix, *The Shape of the Liturgy*, with additional notes by Paul V. Marshall (Seabury Press, New York, 1982).

30 For a review of this research see Paul F. Bradshaw, *The Search for the Origins of Christian Worship* (OUP, New York, 1992), pp. 131–60. For the texts of the principal eucharistic prayers in the early and Reformation rites see R. C. D.

Jasper and G. J. Cuming, *Prayers of the Eucharist: Early and Reformed*, 3rd edn, rev. and enlarged (Pueblo Publishing Co., New York, 1987).

31 Jasper and Cuming, *Prayers*, pp. 7–12.

32 See Thomas Talley, 'Eucharist Prayers, Past, Present and Future' in David R. Holeton (ed.), *Revising the Eucharist: Groundwork for the Anglican Communion* (Alcuin/GLS 27, Grove Books, Bramcote, 1994), pp. 6–19.

33 See Colin O. Buchanan (ed.), *Modern Anglican Liturgies 1958–1968* (OUP, London, 1968); *Further Anglican Liturgies 1968–1975* (Grove Books, Bramcote, 1975); *Anglican Eucharistic Liturgy 1975–1985* (Grove Books, Bramcote, 1985); *Latest Anglican Liturgies 1976–1984* (SPCK, London, 1985).

34 Anglican-Roman Catholic International Commission, *The Final Report* (SPCK, London, 1981), pp. 12–16.

35 *Baptism, Eucharist and Ministry*, Faith and Order paper 111 (WCC, Geneva, 1982).

36 See J. M. R. Tillard, 'Roman Catholics and Anglicans: The Eucharist', *One in Christ* 9 (1973), pp. 131–93.

37 For current Anglican views on eucharistic sacrifice see the three Grove booklets, R. P. C. Hanson, *Eucharistic Offering in the Early Church*, Rowan Williams, *Eucharistic Sacrifice—The Roots of a Metaphor*, and Colin Buchanan (ed.), *Essays on Eucharistic Sacrifice in the Early Church* (Grove Books, Bramcote, 1979, 1982, 1984).

38 For the history of the bilateral conversations and the background of BEM see John Reumann, *The Supper of the Lord: The New Testament, Ecumenical Dialogues, and Faith and Order on Eucharist* (Fortress Press, Philadelphia, 1985).

39 See Reuman, pp. 23–6.

40 See Geoffrey Wainwright, *Eucharist and Eschatology* (Epworth Press, London, 1971).

41 For the principles, recommendations and background papers of the consultation, see Holeton, *Our Thanks and Praise*.

6   Ministry and Priesthood

JOHN WEBSTER

MINISTRY AND PRIESTHOOD IN THE ENGLISH REFORMATION

Like its continental counterparts, the English Reformation devoted a great part of its energies to the renewal and restructuring of the pastoral office on the basis of what it took to be a more adequate theology of ministry. '"The eye", that is to say, the preacher of God's Word, "is the light of the body", that is to say, if the curate be godly learned, "then shall all the body be full of light", that is, the Christian congregation shall have the Word of God dwell in them plenteously.'[1] Thomas Becon's allegorical reading of Jesus' teaching says much about the distinctive emphases of the theology of ministry among the English Reformers, notably that the prime function of the ordained minister is to lay Sripture before the congregation. Accordingly, for Reformers like Becon, the provision of a biblically educated clergy was a matter of considerable significance. Anglicanism emerged in a period of generally lax ministerial practice. Studies of the early Tudor period reveal that resident clergy were frequently only casually educated, with university graduates usually non-resident in parishes. The revival of the pastoral ministry thus became a prime concern, not the least because of the need to establish a firm clerical base in the midst of competing confessions of faith.

However, the early Tudor church manifested more than simply lax practice; it also showed the long-term effects of the clericalization of the Western Church in the later medieval period. The separation of priests from laity had many roots—priestly celibacy, the decline of Latin as a popular language, the privatization of the ministry of reconciliation to a transaction between penitent and priest with power to absolve. But unlike movements such as the Lollards in the late fourteenth and earlier fifteenth centuries, the English Reformers did not focus on abuses of priestly prerogative so much as on the renewal of the theology of the ordained ministry. In particular, they sought to displace the cultic and sacrificial emphases of the medieval ordinals then in use (notably the Sarum pontifical). From the Reformed ordinals of 1550 and 1552 and from other documents of the English Reformation, a fairly consistent theology of ministry emerged, which furnished fundamental topics for debate in the century which followed.

Like other Reformed ordinals, the Anglican rites placed weight on the inseparability of ministerial office and the congregation. The point was emphasized partly by the requirement (in the Preface to the 1550 Ordinal) that no one take up office in the Church 'except he were first called, tried, examined, and known to have such qualities as were requisite for the same'; partly by the public interrogation of the candidates by the bishop after the Oath of Supremacy had been administered; partly by the requirement that ordinations should be 'upon a Sunday or holyday, in the face of the church'. In these ways office and the actual exercise of ministerial functions were held closely together.

Equally, however, the significance of the mandate of the wider Church was underscored in the Preface to the 1550 Ordinal by the warning that 'no man by his own private authority might presume to execute' any of the offices of bishop, priest or deacon. And it is clear that the new Anglican ordinals did not envisage ordination as simply delegation of authority by the local congregation. In retaining episcopal ordination (despite queries from some of the Reformers including Cranmer, and later from Hooker, about cases of necessity), Anglicanism sought to retain a ministry 'rightly, orderly and lawfully consecrated and ordered' (Article XXXVI), undertaken by those 'chosen and called to this work by men who have public authority given unto them in (not, note, 'by') the congregation, to call and send ministers into the Lord's vineyard' (Article XXIII).

In terms of content, the ministry of the Word, both in public proclamation and in private exhortation, receives heavy emphasis in the first Anglican ordinals. In the 1550 rite for the priesthood, for example, the bishop, having outlined the work of the priest, addresses the candidates in the Exhortation:

> Seeing that ye cannot, by any other means, compass the doing of so weighty a work, pertaining to the salvation of man, but with doctrine and exhortation, taken out of holy Scripture, and with a life agreeable to the same, ye perceive how studious ye ought to be in reading and learning the holy Scriptures, and in framing the manners, both of yourselves, and of them that specially pertain unto you, according to the rule of the same Scriptures.

In their omission of cultic and sacrificial language, the Edwardine ordinals show themselves to have a theology of ministry quite distinct from that of the pre-Reformation rites. In essence, the Anglican ordinals call into question the notion of a sacrificial priesthood focused on the eucharistic offering, in favour of a pastoral and didactic model of the ministry centring on public proclamation, the orderly administration of the sacraments, and private exhotation. The pre-Reformation Sarum pontifical, drawing on analogies between the Levitical and the Christian priesthood, was rich in sacrificial imagery. Most particularly, that rite included the *porrectio instrumentorum*—the handing over of the chalice and/or paten as symbols of priestly office (an action considered by some medieval theologians to constitute the essential 'matter' of ordination). The action was accompanied by the words 'Receive the power to offer sacrifice to God'. The 1550 Anglican rite, somewhat curiously, retained the action but added the rubric that in addition 'the Bishop shall deliver to every one of them the Bible', and— most significantly—changed the accompanying words to 'Take thou authority to preach the Word of God, and to minister the holy sacraments in the congregation'. The 1552 revision went further by omitting the *porrectio instrumentorum* completely, retaining only the giving of the Bible with the same words as the 1550 rite.

Such moves in the ordinals were consistent with Cranmer's new eucharistic rites, in which the notion of sacrifice was not so much excluded as decisively restructured. 'Sacrifice' has a double function in Cranmer's eucharistic liturgies, referring primarily to the self-offering of Christ on

Calvary, and, in an altogether derivative way, to the self-offering of the people of God in praise and thanksgiving for benefits received. Crucially, however, Cranmer scrupulously separated this self-offering of the Church from any association with the symbols of bread and wine, limiting its occurrence to the post-communion prayer of the people. The Eucharist is thus shaped around the corporate memorial and participation of the redeemed in the benefits of Christ's passion, and not around the sacrificial mediation of the priest, passively observed.

As a consequence, the defining activity of the priest in relation to the congregation shifted considerably. The first part of the 'Homily of the worthy receiving and reverent esteeming of the Body and Blood of Christ' exhorted the believer that Christ 'hath made upon his cross a full and sufficient sacrifice for thee, a perfect cleansing of thy sins; so that thou acknowledgest no other Saviour, Redeemer, Advocate, Intercessor, but Christ only [. . .] thou needest no man's help, no other sacrifice or oblation, no sacrificing priest, no mass, no means established by man's invention.'[2] None of this is a denial of the ordained ministry as a means; rather it is an attempt to clarify in a polemical context how that means relates to its generative source and the events to which it offers public testimony. In effect, the theology of the work of Christ as the High Priest whose work is finished and completely sufficient absorbs much of what previously would have come under the rubric of the theology of ministry. The role of the priest is thus relativized, transformed from what was (however mistakenly) perceived to be mediatory sacrifice to that of ministering (or perhaps better, administering) the saving benefits of Christ's passion through word and sacrament.

In the eucharistic context, then, the mediatory role of the ordained ministry is hedged about with severe restrictions and qualifications designed to avoid any derogation of Christ's uniquely mediatory activity. Something of the same happens to the ministry of reconciliation. The new eucharistic liturgies certainly accord a place to private confession and absolution, and in the *Homilies* and elsewhere in the formularies and Reformation writings they find a restricted role. However, the authoritative commission is conceived to be that of declaring rather than actualizing God's mercy and forgiveness towards the penitent, and the context for the exercise of that ministry is normally the public prayer of the community assembled to hear the Word of God.

THE EMERGENCE OF ANGLICAN THEOLOGY OF MINISTRY

In the theological and institutional development of the English church in the later part of the sixteenth and first half of the seventeenth centuries, it soon became clear that much clarification and consolidation remained to be done.

Cranmer's handling of eucharistic sacrifice in the liturgies did not make an end of discussion of the matter. The retention of sacrificial language is, importantly, not simply to be found amongst those Laudian divines who retained vestiges of Catholic theology and practice, but also amongst others more definitely aligned with Cranmer's eucharistic theology. William Perkins, the most intellectually acute Calvinist theologian of the English church, concedes a sense in which the Eucharist is a sacrifice 'by way of resemblance'.[3] But here he is saying little, if anything, more than Cranmer in affirming that the Eucharist is a 'spiritual' or 'gratulatory' sacrifice as the commemoration and devoted self-offering of the assembly. Sacrifice does not entail the further notion of 'propitiatory', and so does not signify a retraction of the theology of ministry in the formularies. The seventeenth century does, however, see the growth of reflection on the continuing priesthood of the ascended Christ as the ground of the Church's pleading of Christ's sacrifice in the Eucharist. In Tractarian theology, this affirmation was to figure large as a warrant for a particular account of the priestly character of the ordained ministry.

In terms of ministerial order, the early Reformation ideal of an institutionally ordered and hierarchical ministry, biblical, sacramental and pastoral in function, sustained criticism from two directions.

On the one side, Catholic polemic pressed the new theology to furnish an account of the credentials of Anglican orders. The currency of the 'Nag's Head Fable' (a popular legend that Archbishop Parker had been consecrated at the Nag's Head Tavern in Cheapside by an irregular rite) testified to real anxieties on this score. A refutation of the legend published in 1613 by the Anglican apologist Francis Mason takes the form of an imaginary dialogue, and has the Catholic disputant argue:

All that are called of God by the Church derive their authority by lawful succession from Christ and His apostles. If you do so, then let it appear, show us your descent, let us see your pedigree. If you cannot, then whence came you? If you tell us that God hath raised you up in extraordinary manner, you must pardon us if we be slow in believing such things [. . .] In the hatching of the Protestant brood, no ordinary vocation, nor sending extraordinary appeareth; so the ground and foundation being naught, all they which have builded upon it falleth down.[4]

Some strands of Anglican theology of ministry have had, and continue to have, a sore conscience on just this point. The association of apostolicity so closely with 'pedigree' has until recently been a given in Anglican–Roman Catholic polemic on ministerial validity. And Anglicanism has still not quite outgrown the attempts of a number of nineteenth- and twentieth-century writers, including R. C. Moberly and the contributors to K. E. Kirk's *Apostolic Ministry* (1946), to trace a history of descent by which Anglican orders could be certified.

On the other side, the Puritan party in England raised a number of objections to the theology of the Edwardine ordinals over the course of a debate which lasted right until the 1662 Act of Uniformity and indeed beyond, to the end of the seventeenth century. The fear of this group was that the theology of ministry envisaged in the ordinals of the newly con-stituted church was not fully reformed. It went beyond the scriptural norms in its reaffirmation of the threefold order of bishops, priests and deacons, and criticized pre-Reformation models of mediatory cultic priesthood only in a half-hearted way. The continued use of the term 'priest', in view of its absence as a term for a 'special ministry' in the New Testament, became a major point of contention. In reply, Anglican apologists frequently ad-vanced the argument that 'priest' is properly derived not from *sacerdos* but from *presbyter*. Accordingly, it is used, as Hooker suggested, both to signify eldership or leadership in the congregation, and, by way of allusion, to identify 'that which the Gospel hath *proportionable* to ancient sacrifices, namely the Communion of the blessed Body and Blood of Christ, although it have properly no new sacrifice'.[5]

Furthermore, the Puritan party raised a variety of objections to the threefold pattern envisaged in the Ordinal, sometimes to the uncertain status of the diaconate, but most especially to the distinction between bishops and priests, which they claimed to run counter to the New Testa-ment pattern of parity of ministers. The fact that ordination was in practice a prerogative of bishops (even if the practice had no explicit warrant in either the Ordinal or the Articles) became the focus of a long-running dispute. That dispute was only resolved in 1662 by the Act of Uniformity. The Act prescribed *ex animo* consent to the revised Book of Common Prayer and, moreover, insisted that none could lawfully hold benefice in the Church of England 'unless he have formerly been made priest by episcopal ordination'. The effect of the Act far exceeded that of excluding a large number from the public ministry of the restored Anglican Church, in what became recalled in Puritan memory as the 'Great Ejection' of St Bartholo-mew's Day 1662. Most significantly, it pushed to the margins a theology of ministry which could claim at least some basis in the Reformation formul-aries of the Church of England. Many attempts were made in subsequent decades to articulate a theology of ministry sufficiently comprehensive to draw in at least the more moderate of the Puritan party, notably in the work of Richard Baxter. The failure of these schemes was the first of a series of similar abortive attempts to surmount the apparently intractable obstacle of recognizing the competence and validity of the non-episcopally ordained minister. In the present century, the issue emerged in Anglican reluctance to enter into communion with the Church of South India, or in the breakdown of proposals for union with churches which have not retained the threefold order.

'MAGNIFY YOUR OFFICE'

From the end of the seventeenth century until the rise of the Ecumenical Movement in the earlier decades of the present century, the acceptability of Anglican theology of ministry to nonconformism was not a serious issue. Alongside a developing literature setting forth Anglican confidence in its claims to possession of an apostolic ministry, the first half of the eighteenth century witnessed a serious decline in the practice of ministry. As in the pre-Reformation era, a large fraction of incumbents was non-resident, leaving parochial duties to curates. Three separate factors combined to change the theology and practice of ministry between the mid-eighteenth and the mid-nineteenth centuries.

First the Methodist and Evangelical movements in the later eighteenth century did much to call into question the adequacy of established patterns of ministerial practice. In particular, they demonstrated that the deficiency of much post-Restoration theory of ministry in Anglicanism was an over-emphasis on office and a neglect of the function and context of Christian ministry. In effect, the Evangelical Revivalist movements, often tangential to the official ministry of the Church of England and often the targets of some hostility, constituted a charge that the possession of a correctly validated and ordered ministry did not guarantee pastoral effectiveness or responsiveness to the Spirit. Wesley's decision to ordain ministers for the nascent church in America as a matter of necessity not only raised again the seventeenth-century issue of the parity of bishops and priests, but also showed in a vivid way the frustration felt by many with the reluctance of the established order to engage with a changed context for ministry. The issue was to raise itself many times as Anglicanism became a worldwide communion in the era of missionary expansion.

Second, the work of the Ecclesiastical Commission did a great deal in the earlier part of the nineteenth century to revive the ministry of the Church of England by the establishment of more secure administrative and legal structures. And so, for example, the Plurality Acts of 1838 and 1850 did much to reduce the acute problems of non-residence and plurality of benefice, contributing in an indirect way to the revival of ministerial practice.

Third, and most significant, however, for the development of the theology of ministry in the Church of England over the course of the next hundred years was the rediscovery of a vigorous and practical sense of apostolic succession in the early days of the Oxford Movement. Eighteenth-century Anglican apologists had often appeared to use the notion of apostolic succession as a means of insuring the Church of England against serious criticism, whether from within or without its ranks. For Newman and others, however, it served both as a call to clergy to assume ministerial authority and as a means of reviving a practical sense of what Tract XVII called 'the ministerial commission' as 'a trust from Christ for the benefit of his people'. In Newman's hands, apostolic succession was not simply about pedigree; it also constituted a call to responsibility. Certainly in the first of the *Tracts for the Times* Newman wrote with great eagerness of the grace of apostolic orders:

> There are some who rest their divine mission on their own unsupported assertion; others, who rest it upon their popularity; others, upon their success; and others, who rest upon their temporal distinctions. This last case has, perhaps, been too much our own; I fear we have neglected the real ground upon which our authority is built—OUR APOSTOLICAL DESCENT.

But the excited injunction to 'magnify your office' stands alongside that to 'act up to your professions'—to a realization, that is, of the function of the priesthood as affording access to the self-giving God in Christ. Later Tractarians, however, as well as Evangelical critics like Litton, focused more sharply on the question which had engaged Anglican apologists 150 years earlier: 'How is the ministry of the Church of England authorized?'

Two factors made an answer to that question a matter of some urgency. First, critical historical study of the early Church had with some success proposed the theory that the patterns of ministry which were widely supposed to have been inherited intact from the Apostles were more likely to be expedients established in the second century, and could therefore claim no immediate dominical sanction. Advanced in radical dress by German historians of Christianity, or more tentatively by Anglican scholars such as Hatch, Lightfoot or Hort, the theory raised real doubts about the affirmation in the Preface to the Ordinal that 'it is evident unto all men, diligently reading holy scripture, and ancient authors, that from the Apostles' time there hath been these orders of ministers in Christ's Church: Bishops, Priests, and Deacons'. Since the last decades of the nineteenth century, Anglican theology of ministry has not been able to construct the defence of its own validity with the same kind of ease as was possible in periods with a less sophisticated historical sense.

Second, the history of Roman Catholic objections to Anglican orders came to a head with the promulgation in 1896 of the papal bull *Apostolicae*

Curae, which concluded that 'ordinations carried out according to the Anglican rite have been and are absolutely null and utterly void'. The bull evoked substantial controversy in subsequent decades, much of it muddled by hasty accounts of what it had actually claimed about the prerequisites for valid ordination. Although the Second Vatican Council included the Anglican Communion among the separated Churches which 'because of the lack of the sacrament of orders [. . .] have not preserved the genuine and total reality of the Eucharistic mystery',[6] the Council gave fresh impetus to common exploration of the theology of ministry and priesthood. From one perspective, at least, this has set Anglican–Roman Catholic dialogue on the topic in a new context, and done much to set Anglican reflection on ministry along new tracks.

A CONTEMPORARY AGENDA

The history of Anglican reflection on ministry demonstrates that until fairly recently it has been much preoccupied by polemical concerns—the propriety of a sacrificial priesthood, the authorization or 'pedigree' of Anglican orders, the retention of the episcopate. More recently, however, the debates have shifted very considerably, away from the elaboration and defence of competing theologies on generally partisan lines to the establishment of a number of areas where substantial agreement can be reached, both among Anglicans and with members of other Christian traditions.

Because contemporary Anglican theology of ministry has been articulated in a self-consciously ecumenical context, often in the form of reports of inter-church commissions, it has come to share some of the basic common terms of recent discussion. And so, for example, the christological context of ministry, much exposed in recent study, has found its way into Anglican documents: 'The life and self-offering of Christ perfectly express what it is to serve God and man. All Christian ministry [. . .] flows and takes its shape from this source and model';[7] or again, 'Christ is unique: he is our one High Priest. The priesthood of the Church and the priesthood of its ministry are derived from the priesthood of Christ.'[8]

Moreover, widespread dissatisfaction with identifying 'ministry' with 'order', along with a renewed baptismal piety and spirituality in which the Christian enters ministry at baptism rather than ordination, has pushed Anglicanism into statements which define ordained ministry not so much in terms of the possession of special powers, cultic or otherwise, but in terms of the particular functions exercised by the ordained within the ministry of the whole people of God. For this, a variety of terms have come into common use: 'presidency', 'leadership', 'management' of the resources of the people of God and 'enabling' their use, 'focusing' the priestliness of the whole Church. The revised Anglican ordinals generally emphasize that the existence and exercise of ordained ministry cannot be divorced from the corporate ministry of the community. Thus the 1980 Ordinal in the English Alternative Service Book begins the ordination prayer with 'We praise and glorify you, almighty Father, because you have formed throughout the whole world a holy people for your own possession, a royal priesthood, a universal church'; or again, the 1979 Book of Common Prayer of the Episcopal Church of the USA has lay persons involved in the presentation of candidates for ordination to the priesthood. Nevertheless, Anglicanism continues to resist pragmatic accounts of ordination as community delegation. The Anglican–Reformed dialogue report *God's Reign and Our Unity* for example, argues that 'priests' exercise 'their priestly office neither apart from the priesthood of the whole body, nor by derivation from the priesthood of the whole body';[9] and 'Ministry and Ordination' in the ARCIC *Final Report* proposes that ordained ministry 'is not an extension of the common Christian priesthood but belongs to another realm of the gifts of the Spirit'.[10]

One of the primary effects of the rediscovery of the common priesthood of the Church has been a substantial reworking of the notion of 'apostolicity'. Apostolicity has, in effect, been generalized, to cover not simply the existence of certain patterns of ordained ministry but rather the life of the whole Church in faithfulness to the apostolic gospel, in mission, and in service to the world. The apostolicity of the ordained ministry is a function of the apostolicity of the whole body of believers. Moreover, apostolicity has been de-historicized: the apostolic character of the ordained ministry does not, that is, rest in its observable descent from Christ and his apostles so much as in its continuation of the apostolic functions. From the standpoint of most contemporary accounts of primitive Christianity, traditional defences of Anglican ministerial order (including twentieth-century classics such as Moberly's *Ministerial Priesthood* and Ramsey's *The Gospel and the Catholic Church*) have an idealist air. Contemporary Anglicans are unlikely to attempt historical validations of orders, and much more likely to favour instead arguments that are drawn from the character and needs of the Christian community.

The effect of recent work in the theology of ministry has thus been to make traditional demarcations more difficult to sustain. Significantly, the 1973 statement *Ministry and Ordination* by the Anglican–Roman Catholic International Commission explicitly shelves the judgement of *Apostolicae Curae* on Anglican orders. This it does by beginning the dialogue elsewhere — in common affirmations of a broad range of images of ordained ministry in relation to the High Priesthood of Christ and the priesthood of all the faithful. 'Agreement on the nature of ministry is prior to the consideration of the mutual recognition of ministries.'[11]

Significant divergences do, however, remain to be resolved. First, the ordination of women to the priesthood. Like debates concerning the ministry of the laity, those about the ordination of women to the priesthood have done much to alert the Church to the potential distortions introduced into Christianity by uncritical assimilation of institutional patterns derived from elsewhere. The ordination of women to the priesthood is integrally related to a larger contemporary discussion of the ideological character of masculine language and imagery about God and corresponding social arrangements. For some Anglicans, particularly in North America and some parts of the Church of England, restriction of holy order to men is a self-evident contradiction of the gospel of inclusiveness. For other Anglicans, the matter raises debates concerning the defining characteristics of a properly apostolic ministry, and the acceptability of Anglican orders to Rome. The 1979 *Elucidation* of the 1973 statement on ministry attempts to make agreement on 'the origin and nature of the ordained ministry' prior to 'the question of who can or cannot be ordained'.[12] Official Roman Catholic response has not endorsed the distinction, and the practice in some Anglican provinces of ordaining women to the priesthood and, more recently, to the episcopate remains an ecumenical stumbling-block as well as a cause of friction in the Anglican Communion.

Second, the sacrificial nature of the Eucharist and the associated definition of the priestliness of the eucharistic president remain matters of dispute. Like the theology of ministry, the theology of the Eucharist has undergone major reshaping under the impact of renewed biblical and liturgical scholarship, particularly in the development of a dynamic concept of the relation between the eucharistic action of the Church and the sacrifice of Christ. On this account, the eucharistic memorial can be spoken of as a sacrifice 'in the sacramental sense, provided that it is clear that this is not a repetition of the historical sacrifice'.[13] And so,

> Because the eucharist is the memorial of the sacrifice of Christ, the action of the presiding minister in reciting again the words of Christ at the last supper and distributing to the assembly the holy gifts is seen to stand in sacramental relation to what Christ himself did in offering his own sacrifice. So our two traditions commonly use priestly terms in speaking about the ordained ministry.[14]

The effect of this has been to give greater authority to the tradition in Anglicanism which has, from Laud and Andrewes onward, maintained that the eucharistic elements are offered to God by the priest as a commemorative sacrifice. The argument of a Church of England report from the

331

mid-1980s, *The Priesthood of the Ordained Ministry*, places great weight on this tradition, and can show with some success that it has remained a consistent presence in Anglicanism from the Caroline period, however shaky its presence in the sixteenth-century formularies of the Church of England.

Third, the threefold order stands in need of clarification, both theoretical and practical. The threefold order enjoys quasi-axiomatic authority in most Anglican institutional practice and liturgical provision, having often been identified as a prime instrument of the Church's unity, catholicity and apostolicity. This authority has been reinforced by the tendency of twentieth-century ecumenical theology to accord considerable weight to the pattern of bishops, presbyters and deacons. It remains unclear, however, exactly what the threefold order consists in: though Anglicans are generally committed to three orders of ministry, the content of the orders is a matter of debate. The relation of bishops to priests (for example, in respect of the ministry of confirmation), or of deacons to priests, are matters of renewed debate. Anglican practice is generally a development of the Western medieval pattern of regional episcopate, vestigial diaconate, and prebyterate as the basic local order of ministry; but the pattern is not beyond question. Furthermore, the threefold order and the centrality of the prebyteral office with which it is often associated, are for some Anglicans a hindrance to the recognition of ministries which have traditionally fallen outside the normative structure (such as men and women of prayer, teachers, or evangelists). Anglicanism lacks a means of affirming such ministries as permanent and genuinely apostolic, and so often finds that its categories of office are insufficiently flexible to embrace its ministerial practice. Sorting through the practical and theological issues involves not only a reassessment of the nature of the presbyterate but also a more probing inquiry into the relation of office and ministry.

BIBLIOGRAPHY

Bradshaw, P. F., *The Anglican Ordinal: Its History and Development from the Reformation to the Present Day.* SPCK, London, 1971.

Church of England Board for Mission and Unity, *The Priesthood of the Ordained Ministry.* CHP, London, 1986.

Echlin, E. P., *The Story of Anglican Ministry.* St Paul's, Slough, 1974.

Hanson, A. T., *The Pioneer Ministry.* SCM Press, London, 1964.

Holmes, U. T., *The Future Shape of Ministry.* New York, 1981.

Hughes, J. J., *Absolutely Null and Utterly Void.* London, 1968.

McDonald, D. R., *Towards a Theology of Priesthood.* New York, 1982.

Moberly, R. C., *Ministerial Priesthood,* new edn. SPCK, London, 1969.

Ramsey, A. M., *The Gospel and the Catholic Church.* Longman, London, 1936, 1955; SPCK, London, 1990.

Sykes, N. *Old Priest and New Presbyter.* CUP, 1956.

NOTES
1 Thomas Becon, *Works* (Cambridge 1844), Vol. ii, p. 421.
2 *Homilies* (London 1908), p. 477.
3 William Perkins, *A Reformed Catholike* (Cambridge 1598), p. 204.
4 Francis Mason, 'Of the Consecration of the Bishops in the Church of England' in P. E. More and F. L. Cross (eds), *Anglicanism* (SPCK, London, 1935), pp. 379f.
5 Richard Hooker, *Of the Laws of Ecclesiastical Polity*, V. lxxiii. 2.
6 W. M. Abbott (ed.), *The Documents of Vatican II* (Geoffrey Chapman, London, 1966), p. 364.
7 ARCIC, *Final Report* (SPCK, London, 1982), p. 30.
8 Board for Mission and Unity, *The Priesthood of the Ordained Ministry*, p. 97.
9 Anglican–Reformed International Commission, 1971–1984, *God's Reign and Our Unity* (SPCK, London/St Andrew's Press, Edinburgh, 1984), p. 79.
10 ARCIC, *Final Report*, p. 36.
11 ARCIC, *Final Report*, p. 38.
12 ARCIC, *Final Report*, p. 44.
13 ARCIC, *Final Report*, p. 20.
14 ARCIC, *Final Report*, p. 35.

7   Episcopacy

RICHARD A. NORRIS, JR.

Bishops—and with them the distinction of office between bishops and presbyters—were simply a given of the English reform. Henry VIII, though he separated the church in England from papal jurisdiction and brought it under the exclusive supervision of the Crown, altered none of its other constitutional or pastoral structures. In the days of Edward VI, accordingly, when the party that sought fundamental doctrinal, liturgical and pastoral reform achieved ascendancy, its programme was carried out by royal authority acting through the inherited legal structures of the church, and its leaders were bishops. As a consequence, English Reformers saw no reason to think that there was any inherent opposition between episcopacy and the cause of reformation, however much they might object to the prelatical shape assumed by the episcopal office in medieval Europe, and whatever degree of merit they might discern in the type of church order that prevailed in Reformed Churches in Switzerland or Germany. The Edwardian ordinal regarded it as 'evident [. . .] that from the Apostles' time there have been these Orders of Ministers in Christ's church; bishops, Priests, and Deacons', and insisted that it was God, by the Holy Spirit, who had 'appointed divers Orders of Ministers' in the Church. The Elizabethan Settlement of 1559 maintained these principles and the practice which they implied. Scrupulous care was taken, in the arrangements made for the

333

consecration of Matthew Parker as Archbishop of Canterbury, to assure that the traditional conditions for the ordination of a bishop were met.

Nevertheless it was not in episcopacy the the English Reformers saw the distinctive mark of their system of church government. What set the English church apart was precisely the principle and the fact of royal, as opposed to papal, supremacy. The English Reformation was seen to be the work of the 'godly prince', whose supremacy in ecclesiastical as well as civil causes, in the ordering of the spiritual as well as the temporal affairs of the kingdom, the Reformers justified by appeal to the models provided by such Old Testament figures as David and Solomon. Episcopacy could indeed be— and was—supported by reference to the practice of Christian antiquity and to unvarying tradition 'from the Apostles' time', and such an appeal was entirely consistent with the general stance of a church that sought to restore, as Jewel put it, the faith of 'the apostles and old catholic fathers'. But the ordering of the church was the work of the prince. It was royal authority that maintained the primitive pattern of ecclesiastical government and ministry in England. Monarch and bishop stood or fell together, as James I asserted, and Charles I and his archbishop demonstrated.

For this reason among others, the earlier English Reformers were occu-pied less with justifying the institution of bishops or offering theoretical accounts of its place in the life of the Church than with indicating what they understood the business of bishops to be. Bishops were ministers of the Crown for the *spiritual* government of the nation. In a reformed church, this meant that bishops were to see to it that 'the pure Word of God is preached, and the Sacraments be duly ministered according to Christ's ordinance' (Article XIX); for the defining mark of a true church was fidelity to Scripture in preaching, teaching and sacramental observance. The bishop, then, was not to be a feudal magnate or a court official, but a pastor in the proper sense, governing the people by the gospel word of grace and of judgement as one 'to whom is committed the office to instruct the people', as Jewel insisted.[1]

Unfortunately, neither custom, nor circumstance nor royal policy co-operated with the Elizabethan reformers in their desire to achieve this ideal of a ministry devoted, in all its orders, to preaching and teaching the gospel. Bishops in particular remained distant figures, garbed in the habiliments of prelacy. Inevitably, then, that party within the English church which was most attached to reformation on the Swiss and German model became increasingly dissatisfied with what its members regarded as hesitant and half-hearted measures of reform. It called for the creation of the truly scriptural church in England, and, to that end, for the institution of the Calvinist 'discipline'—i.e., for a presbyterian type of church government. Under the leadership of Thomas Cartwright and

Walter Travers, this 'Puritan' party therefore attacked not merely the bishops themselves and the policies they represented, but the very institution of episcopacy; and it was in the ensuing controversy—which in one form or another lasted for a good deal more than a century—that Anglican understandings of the episcopal office, its status and its function were formed.

THE OFFICE OF A BISHOP

One prominent and central issue in this controversy concerned the Puritan contention 'that between a Presbyter and a Bishop the Word of God alloweth not any inequality or difference to be made'.[2] This doctrine of the parity of ministers (i.e., of pastors: deacons and suchlike were not under consideration) was reinforced by appeal to Jerome's oft-cited *Epistle to Evagrius*, as well as to a scholastic tradition dating to Peter Lombard, which held that bishops are superior to presbyters not in power of order, but only in jurisdiction. Since neither Jerome (whose principal animus was directed against deacons) nor the scholastics in question actually sought to abolish the distinction between presbyters and bishops, some Anglican authors—especially those concerned to reconcile the episcopal and presbyterian forms of church order—were content to follow a view that made the distinction one of office of dignity rather than strictly of order. The majority, however, took a sterner line. They discerned even in the New Testament clear adumbrations of imparity. The Lord himself, according to Luke, sent both the Twelve and the Seventy,[3] and with differing commissions, thus laying the basis for the later distinction of bishops and presbyters; and the office conceded by the Apostle to Timothy and Titus clearly set them over ordinary elders. This evidence, moreover, was confirmed by the universal practice of the primitive Church. Hence Bishop Carleton of Chichester could object strenuously, at the Synod of Dort, to the introduction into the Belgic Confession of 'a strange conceit of the parity of ministers'.

If the episcopate is a distinct order, however, and not merely a job assignment, in what does its characteristic office consist? Following, in substance, the view stated by Bishop Thomas Bilson in his treatise of 1593, *The Perpetual Government of Christ's Church*, Richard Hooker explained:

A Bishop is a Minister of God, unto whom with permanent continuance, there is given not onely power of administring the Word and Sacraments, which power other presbyters have; but also a further power to ordain Ecclesiastical persons, and a power of Cheifty in Government

335

over Presbyters as well as Lay men, a power to be by way of jurisdiction a Pastor even to Pastors themselves.[4]

For Hooker, then, the difference between bishop and presbyter could be expressed in terms of the derivation of authority. A presbyter is a full minister of Word and Sacrament, but his 'authority to do these things is derived from the Bishops which doth ordein him thereunto, so that even in those things which are common unto both, yet the power of the one, is as it were certain light borrowed from the others lamp'.[5] On this view, which sees the distinctive marks of the episcopal office in 'latitude of the power of order' and 'in that kind of power which belongeth unto jurisdiction',[6] there is a distinction, but no separation, to be made between these two powers: the bishop's jurisdictional or supervisory authority is derived from the power of ordination. In this general account of the bishop's office Hooker is almost uniformly followed by his successors. John Cosin (Bishop of Durham, 1660–72), for example, in a sermon preached in 1626 when he was Archdeacon of York, sees the authority of the episcopate to consist in the power of the keys: 'the key of order to send as Christ sent, and the key of jurisdiction to govern as he governed'.[7]

This account of the episcopal office was not intended either to minimize the role of the bishop as minister of Word and Sacrament or to disallow a collegial relation of bishop and presbyters in the diocese. The difference of order that Anglican apologists insisted on was always a difference between the bishop and 'other presbyters'; and they would have agreed with Archbishop Whitgift of Canterbury (d. 1604) when he observed that 'touching the ministry' of word and sacrament 'there is an equality of all ministers of God's word [. . .]; for [. . .] the word preached, or the sacraments ministered, is as effectual in one [. . .] as it is in another'.[8] Furthermore, when they spoke of the power of jurisdiction or government, what they had in mind was not, as a modern might think, the business of organizational adminstration, but primarily the administration of discipline under the Word of God—a "spiritual' function; and in this work the bishop had other presbyters as (subordinate) colleagues and counsellors. Hooker, following Jerome, sees 'no cause why the Bishop should disdain to consult with them, and in weighty affairs of the Church to use their advice', and indeed thinks that 'Churches Cathedral', where the bishop is associated in his work with dean and chapter, 'are as glasses wherein the face and very countenance of Apostolical antiquity remaineth even as yet to be seen'.[9] The collegial relation between bishop and presbyters in the work of the diocese was a foundation stone of Archbishop Ussher's scheme for the reconciliation of episcopal and presbyterian church orders—though of course his proposals came to nothing, and practical adoption of his ideas had to await the day of synodical forms of diocesan government, which first appeared in Anglican churches outside of England.

APOSTOLICITY, DIVINE RIGHT, AND SUCCESSION

In the face of both Roman Catholic and Puritan or Nonconformist criticism—not to mention what John Cosin called the 'voluntary and transcendent impiety' that brought about the abolition of episcopacy under the Parliamentary and Cromwellian regimes—Anglican writers of the late sixteenth and seventeenth centuries addressed themselves repeatedly to questions about the relation of the episcopal to the apostolic office, about the 'divine right' (jus divinum) of the episcopal office, and about the importance of succession in office and continuity in ordination.

There were, needless to say, significant tracts of common ground shared by the participants in these discussions. Basic to the whole Anglican view of episcopacy was the principle that 'the office of publick preaching, or ministering the Sacraments in the congregation' was not one which any individual could assume or lay claim to in his own right. As an office in the church and for the church, it could belong only to 'those [...] which be chosen and called to this work by men who have publick authority given unto them in the Congregation, to call and send ministers'. Framed—no doubt deliberately—in the most general terms, these words of Article XXIII make no mention of bishops; they nevertheless enunciate the principle that a necessary condition of valid ministry is its derivation through the church considered as an ordered body. The ordering that the English church judged normal and appropriate was then specified in the Ordinal and its Preface, which made it clear that in practice the expression 'men who have publick authority' refers to bishops. Further, the reason given to justify this ordering of the church under bishops—that it has marked the Church 'from the Apostles' time'—adds another dimension of meaning to the practice demanded by the Ordinal. To insist upon ordination by bishops who have themselves been ordained in traditional fashion by other bishops is a way of testifying that licit reception of authority—as distinct from mere appropriation or seizure of it—presupposes both continuity in office and orderly transmission of office. The habitual Anglican appeal to continuity and antiquity, however, suggests further that, at the level of order, it is the bishop in whom the unity of the church in one place and time with the church in other places and times is, as a matter of fact, represented and effected.

Ordination must be performed by those who have received authority to

337

exercise *episcopé* in the Body, and to admit others to share in that ministry. This acknowledgment by the Body of the authority of the ordaining member means that his own ordination to the ministry of *episcopé* must be recognized and accepted. From this arises the principle of continuity by succession, which appears to be indispensable, at least from a human point of view.[10]

A second point on which there was general agreement among Anglican thinkers was the conviction that the office of a bishop in the church represents a partial continuation of the office of an apostle. John Pearson, Bishop of Chester (1673–86), explains in a neat rhetorical turn that 'an apostle is an extraordinary bishop', while 'a bishop is an ordinary apostle'.[11] No doubt by these words he intended to convey more or less what Andrewes had alleged in his statement that 'overseers' carry on 'the chief part of the apostolic function, the oversight of the church; and power of commanding, correcting, and ordaining'.[12] Hooker, as might be expected, had been more circumspect in his handling of this matter. He acknowledges that in their capacity as chosen eye-witnesses, directly commissioned by Christ as founders of the Church, the apostles had, and could have had, no successors. He further argues that in so far as the apostles were ministers of word and sacrament, their office is continued in that of the presbyter. He thinks, however, that a function of oversight was intrinsic to the apostolic office, and that this function was continued in the Church's bishops. 'For to succeed them is after them to have that Episcopal kind of power which was first given to them.'[13]

To say, however, that the episcopal office continues one or more distinctive functions of the apostolic office is to record a matter of fact, not of right. Yet the Puritans, by asserting that some form of presbyterian church order was prescribed by the Scriptures themselves, were appealing beyond the data of traditional practice to raise, in essence, the question what type of church order could claim divine institution. In reply, the defenders of episcopacy stated a position which was indeed calculated to claim a divine right for the office of bishop, but which at the same time rested that claim on an appeal to the continuous practice of the Church—to tradition.

The elements of this position can be found in the writings of Archbishop Whitgift. In correspondence with Theodore Beeza at Geneva, Whitgift was straightforward in his assertion that episcopacy is *de jure divino*. On the other hand, he denied that any form of church government is fully or explicitly prescribed by Scripture—a denial connected, in his mind, with the distinction between matters 'necessary unto the salvation of the Church' and matters of 'government'.[14] For him it was conceivable in abstract principle that the Church should be without episcopacy, even though the institution of bishops is 'apostolical and divine'. No doubt he would have agreed with Robert Sanderson, Bishop of Lincoln (1660–63), who recognized two senses of the expression *jus divinum*: one in which it implies a positive precept, and a second in which it refers to something of apostolic institution and practice.

The most thorough exponent of this position was Richard Hooker. In Book III of his *Ecclesiastical Polity*, Hooker concurs with Whitgift in disputing the Puritan view that 'no form of Church Polity is [. . .] lawful, or of God, unless God be so the author of it that it be also set down in Scripture'.[15] He also distinguishes 'matters of faith, and in general matters necessary unto Salvation', which must be 'expressly contained in the word of God', from matters of 'government'[16] or 'external regiment'.[17] On the other hand, he does not deny that some forms of church order are more clearly consonant with Scripture than others, and asserts that 'there have ever been and ever ought to be [. . .] at leastwise two sorts of ecclesiastical persons, the one subordinate unto the other; as to the Apostles in the beginning, and to the Bishops always since, we find plainly both in Scripture and in all ecclesiastical records, other ministers of the word and sacraments have been.'[18] There is, then, an analogy between apostles and bishops, between the church government seen in the New Testament and that seen in the later history of the Church. But is episcopacy of apostolic institution and in that sense *de jure divino*?

This question Hooker addresses only in Book VII, where, notoriously, he seems to be of two minds. On the one hand, he sets out a theory of the origins of episcopacy which is not unlike that suggested by J. B. Lightfoot in the nineteenth century. That is, he sees the bishop as emerging, so to speak, from the body of presbyter-bishops in a local church in response to the need for a single focus of authority in the community, and thus assuming, within a limited jurisdiction, the power of oversight which the apostles had exercised without such limitation. As to the question whether it was the apostles who were directly responsible for this development—whether episcopacy is of apostolic instituion—Hooker is uncertain. He explains the view that his argument presupposes: 'that after the apostles were deceased, churches did agree amongst themselves [. . .] to make one presbyter in each city chief over the rest'.[19] But he also announces in the same breath that he is less persuaded than formerly of this view, and is more inclined to believe that 'the apostles themselves left bishops invested with power above other pastors'. Nevertheless Hooker declines to rest his case on this proposition—and, one suspects, not merely because of scholarly caution, but also because in argument with the Puritans he is above all concerned to deny that everything that is of God is contained in Scripture or belongs to the first Christian generation. He is confident that the apostles had *some* hand in the emergence of episcopacy. But 'whether the apostles alone did conclude of such a regiment, or else they together with the whole church judging it a fit and needful policy did agree to receive it for a custom' is, for him, a question of little moment, since episcopacy 'had either divine appointment beforehand, or divine approbation afterwards, and is in that respect to be acknowledged the ordinance of God [...]'.

Hooker's position—which amounts to a claim that 'divine right' can be ascribed simply on the basis of the universal practice of the Church—was not generally echoed among writers of the following generation, who were convinced of the apostolic institution of episcopacy. Lancelot Andrewes, for example, held that 'the apostles ordained overseers to have a general care over the churches instead of themselves';[20] and seventeenth-century discovery of the genuine works of Ignatius of Antioch, which seemed to show monepiscopacy as established in the immediate post-apostolic Church, encouraged this view. John Pearson—himself the most learned among the students of Ignatius—summarized the common view: 'As the Father sent Christ, so Christ [sent] the Apostles, and the Apostles, their successors.' Hence 'By this apostolic action of handing-on [*traditio*], the entire power of ordination is resident in bishops'.[21]

Nevertheless Hooker had his followers. John Cosin, for example, had no hesitation in asserting that episcopal authority was *jure divino*, but for all that affirmed that it stemmed from 'Apostolical practice and the perpetual custom and canons of the Church' rather than from 'any absolute precept that either Christ or His Apostles gave about it'.[22] Edward Stillingfleet (Bishop of Worcester, 1689–99) in effect recorded his conversion to Hooker's view when he repudiated his youthful belief that 'the Form of Church Government was left at Liberty by any Law of Christ', and affirmed that 'there is as great Reason to believe, the Apostolical Succession to be of Divine Institution, as the Canon of Scripture, or the Observation of the Lord's Day'.[23] It is Stillingfleet's line, moreover, that is repeated in the report of the Committee on the Unity of the Church at the Lambeth Conference of 1930:

> The Episcopate occupies a position which is, in point of historical development, analogous to that of the Canon of Scripture and the Creeds [...]. If the Episcopate [...] was the result of a [...] process of adaptation and growth in the organism of the Church, that would be no evidence that it lacked divine authority, but rather that the life of the Spirit within the Church had found it to be the most appropriate organ for the functions it discharged.[24]

'BEING,' 'WELL-BEING,' OR ...?

There are, then, certain principles which, in the controversies of the late sixteenth and seventeenth centuries, became the common property of Anglicanism. In the office of bishop the apostolic function of oversight, which includes and indeed derives from the power of ordination, is continued. Further, the institution of episcopacy, whether by reason of apostolic institution or by reason of the universal practice of the Church, is normative for the government of the Church. Finally, regular episcopal succession in office—which requires succession through the laying on of hands of other bishops—not only guarantees the legitimacy of the Church's ministry but establishes the local church's unity, communion and continuity with the universal Church.

From early on, however, acceptance of these principles brought the English church—and later its daughter churches—face to face with the issue of what they implied for the relation of the church thus ordered to other churches, and in particular to churches whose ministries were not episcopally ordained. In this connection, there are three successive phases to be considered in the development of Anglican thought and practice.

First there is the question of the attitude and practice of the English Church prior to 1662. There can be no doubt that the defence of episcopacy in that period was conducted on the assumption that foreign Reformed Churches ordered on the presbyterian model were genuine churches—churches in which the word was truly preached and the sacraments rightly ministered, and hence churches in which a real ministry existed. Furthermore, the principle on which this affirmation was made can be detected in the very terms in which episcopacy was asserted: it was a matter of 'government' or 'external regiment' not of faith, and hence, even if divinely instituted, not 'necessary to salvation'. On the other hand, this attitude was not extended to embrace presbyterian (or other) groups within the English nation. The reason for this apparent inconsistency becomes evident when one notes that the legitimacy of non-episcopal orders in foreign churches was conceded on the precise ground of 'necessity', that is, on the ground that such churches had in practice been compelled to make a choice—between reformation according to scriptural norms of doctrine and practice on the one hand, and, on the other, retention of episcopacy. The Anglican divines of the seventeenth century, with few exceptions, regarded episcopacy as normative and presbyteral ordination as anomalous; but they also realized just how fortunate the English nation had been in its possession of 'godly' princes, whose policies had made a choice between correct faith and proper order unnecessary. Hence they commanded episcopal ordering of the church at home

341

(for domestic dissenters could make no claim of 'necessity') and commended it abroad, acknowledging their fellowship with Reformed Churches overseas.

Second, account must be taken of the changed situation after the restoration of Charles II. The Act of Uniformity of 1662 formally excluded clergy who had not been episcopally ordained from pastoral office in the English church. This action was primarily directed against domestic dissenters and expressed the animus of Anglicans against those who had cooperated with the outlawing of episcopacy and of the Book of Common Prayer in the days of Parliamentary rule. There is little evidence that the Act of Uniformity marked a fundamental change of attitude towards Refromed Churches outside of England. These were still regarded as true churches, whose ministries, though irregular and anomalous, were real and effective. Nevertheless it affected the English church's practical policy with regard to clergy who had been presbyterally ordained to the ministry of foreign churches. Prior to 1662—though with visible qualms and on rare occasion—English bishops had apparently permitted foreign clergy to hold pastoral charges without episcopal ordination. Such gestures were no longer possible.

Third, the dawning of the eighteenth century, following on the unhappy reign of James II and the 'Glorious Revolution' of 1689, brought significant change both in the circumstances of the English church and in the attitude of stiff or 'High Church' Anglicans towards questions of church order. For one thing, this was the Age of Reason, when the very suggestion that human actions and institutions might authoritatively mediate a divine reality was received with indifference or contempt. Moreover, the position of the church in English society had really, if subtly, changed. No longer could it count upon the 'godly prince' to maintain its traditions and identity. In their very different ways, both James II and William III had made that clear. Further, it could no longer truly claim to be a national church—the 'spirituality' of England. Instead it was the established church of a nation that tolerated nonconformity. Its life was openly subjected to the secular, civil authority of Parliament; and its bishops, whose votes in the House of Lords had become necessary to the continuance in office of any government, were becoming political figures, whose attention to pastoral duties, even given the best intentions, had to be severely limited.

In this situation—especially when its paradoxes and problems were brought into sharp focus by the deprivation of bishops who had refused the oath of allegiance to William III and Mary II—it is not surprising that 'High Church' clergy, to whom all these developments were distasteful, should begin to envisage the episcopal ordering of the church not simply as a divinely approved or appointed 'external regiment', but as a divine gift that marks out the sphere of covenanted grace; or that they should seek in the apostolic office of the bishop a basis for the church's authority and identity that was independent of Parliament. John Pearson himself had been sure that there can be no power of absolution or authority to consecrate the elements in the Lord's Supper on the part of one who has not been episcopally ordained. William Beveridge (Bishop of St Asaph, 1704–8), who came to prominence in the church during the crises attendant on the reign of James II and its aftermath, saw the succession of bishops, in traditional fashion, as perpetuating 'the Apostolical office'; yet for him the primary importance of this succession lay in its character as a sign and seal of the fact that 'Christ himself' is 'continually present at such imposition of hands; thereby transferring the same Spirit, which He had first breathed into His Apostles, upon others successively after them'. The 'Apostolical office' of the episcopate marks out the church itself as 'truly Apostolical' and is thus a guarantee of its identity as Christ's Church; but it does this because in fact it is a mediating sign of the sanctifying presence of the Spirit in the Church.[25]

On this basis it was open to the Nonjuror William Law, in his attack on the Erastian views of the Bishop of Bangor, to insist that 'Administering of a Sacrament is an Action we have no Right to perform, considered either as Men, Gentlemen, or Scholars, or Members of Civil Society', and to argue on this ground the necessity of an 'Uninterrupted Succession of Authorised Persons from Christ'; for 'If there be no Uninterrupted Succession, then there are no Authorised Ministers from Christ; if no such Ministers, then no Christian Sacraments; if no Christian Sacraments, then no Christian Covenant, whereof the Sacraments are the Stated and Visible Seals.'[26] The Church's constitution is independent of that of civil society; and only by maintaining that constitution—ordination by persons standing in succession to the Apostles—can the Church retain its identity. As one Bishop of Norwich argued in 1791: 'Without this rule we are open to imposture, and can be sure of nothing; we cannot be sure that our ministry is effective, or that our sacraments are realities.'[27]

Here, then, there has taken place a significant shift of emphasis. Originally episcopacy had been defended as the normative, divinely ordained or approved ordering of the Church; but the one absolutely indispensable mark of a church was taken to be its continuance in apostolic and scriptural teaching. Now, however, episcopacy has come to count as a factor that grounds the identity of the Church; for the Church is constituted not only by the hearing and receiving of a message, but also by the historically established order that marks it out as the convenanted sphere of God's continuous working through the Spirit—and hence as an ordered society historically independent, and indeed transcendent, of civil society. Episcopacy is therefore an institution which counts as part of the definition of

'Church'. And of course it is this 'High Church' tradition which was not only reasserted by the Tractarian Movement and its posterity, but encouraged by the thought of F. D. Maurice, who saw in 'the episcopal institution', as he put it, 'one of the appointed and indispensable signs of a spiritual and universal society'.[28]

In this shift of perspective and emphasis there lie the roots of the modern debate—stimulated in part by the rise of the Ecumenical Movement—between those who see 'the historic episcopate' as belonging to the very definition of the Church (its *esse*, as the phrase goes), and those who see it as a matter of the 'well-being' (*bene esse*), or perhaps the 'full being' (*plene esse*), of the Church. The debate has by no means ended; but the 'high' or, as it has been called, 'exclusivist' view has had a permanent influence on Anglican understandings of the importance of church order. This is attested clearly enough by the so-called 'Chicago–Lambeth Quadrilateral', in which Catholic order takes its place alongside norms of teaching and of sacramental practice as a factor essential to 'the visible unity of the Church'. This influence, however, has not meant a general commitment to the view that where there have been no bishops—or no 'Essential Ministry', to use the phrase of K. E. Kirk—there has been no Church. Rather it seems to have led to the conclusion that the divisions of the Church produce an anomalous situation in which the Body is manifested only in defective form. The Lambeth Conference of 1948 suggested that it is, for Anglicans, impossible either 'to declare the sacraments of non-episcopal bodies null and void', or 'to treat non-episcopal ministries as identical in status and authority with the episcopal ministry'.[29] This marks a return, in effect, to the practice of seventeenth-century Anglicanism with regard to its relations with 'foreign' churches, but not a return to the view that questions of order are questions of indifference to the being or identity of the Church.

PROBLEMS

This survey of the themes and issues that have dominated Anglican discussion of episcopacy indicates that from the days of Whitgift and Hooker apologetic and polemical concerns have stood at the centre of attention. In consequence, little energy has been devoted to examination of the actual workings of episcopacy, or to the sort of theological reflection on ordained ministry generally, and episcopal ministry specifically, that might support critical understanding of the role of bishops in the Church. Such understanding, however, has become the more necessary since the custom of ordaining women not only as presbyters but as bishops has been inaugurated in three of the churches of the Anglican Communion, and some church members have not only fathers but also mothers in God. This practice, moreover—which in some quarters seems entirely natural but is experi-enced, in others, as radically irregular and controversial—bears, at least in principle, the promise of focusing debate and discussion on the actual functions of episcopacy *within* the Church. For too long Anglicans have, in ecumenical settings, made claims for episcopacy that their own practice does not justify. On the other hand, there are positive lessons to be learned from that practice itself, in all its variety of cultural setting and style; and these too have been neglected. On the subject of episcopacy, then, there is an extensive list of agenda that are long overdue for systematic consideration.

To begin with, the debate concerning the ordination of women, not only to the diaconate or presbyterate but to the episcopate, requires reflection on a great deal more than the narrow questions of whether women are in principle 'qualified' for ordination or in what such 'qualification' might consist. Those questions are in process of becoming something less than the liveliest of issues, given the reality not so much of women's ordination as of women's active and fruitful ministry in the roles of presbyter, bishop and deacon. More important are the questions raised by this reality itself. For example—at a strict theological level—the curious practice of permitting the ordination of women to one or two orders of the ordained ministry but not to the 'highest' intimates an issue which Anglicans, even in ecumenical dialogue, have seldom weighed: that of how seriously they take the *unity* of the Christian ministry. Is it better to speak of a 'threefold ministry' or to speak of three distinct and separate *ministries*, as the practice referred to seems to suggest? Further, in as far as the ordination of women opens up issues of gender (and not just of sex), the presence of women in the body of the ordained will inevitably raise questions about another range of ne-glected problems—those that concern the character and quality of minis-terial authority and the mode of its exercise in the Church. These are not new problems, to be sure, nor are they simply a product of feminist thought; but the feminist contribution to debates about the meaning of ordination has co-operated with other circumstances to lend them a new prominence.

Thus there is the related matter of the teaching office of the bishop. The English Reformers saw the bishop primarily in two roles: a role of govern-ment or oversight that stemmed from the power of ordination; and a teaching-role as guardian and exponent of the Church's common faith. Almost all Anglican apologetic and polemic has been concerned with the former of these matters; yet in the classical ordinals, three of the eight questions asked of a bishop-elect at his consecration stressed the bishop's office of teaching and preaching, which was to be directed not merely to the clergy but to all the people. Behind this stress on teaching there lay, no doubt, the Reformers' vision of the bishop as pastor in the proper sense—as the principal minister of word and sacrament in his *paroikia.* Yet it is not this vision of episcopacy that Anglicans have normally stressed in their own practice; and certainly it is not the vision they have ordinarily conveyed in their earnest efforts to commend episcopacy in ecumenical dialogue, where all too often the bishop ends up being envisaged more as regional administrator than as local pastor. The question therefore arises whether the Reformers' ideal is in fact justified, theologically and historically; and if it is, the further—and more controversial—question arises of the conditions under which the bishop's role as a source of teaching and of nurture for the Church in which he or she functions as 'shepherd' can be actualized. Serious attention to this matter, in its practical as well as its theoretical dimensions, would have direct, and perhaps even disturbing, relevance to discussions of the mission or function of the Church.

Another matter that calls for attention is the issue of bishops' collegial relationship both to fellow presbyters within their individual jurisdictions and to fellow bishops within a province or national church. Episcopacy in the Anglican tradition has not infrequently been tainted by prelacy or inordinate individualism, or both; and these defects, it might be argued, stem at least in part from structures and attitudes that isolate bishops from those relationships of fellowship and communion whose maintenance is the very *raison d'être* of the episcopal office. The issue here is not merely one of polity and administration (though no doubt it is that). It is an issue, as feminists might say, about whether the bishop is over the Church or a focal person within the Church; and for that reason it also concerns the bishop's role as teacher of the Church and the nature and setting of the bishop's pastoral activity. There is need, therefore, for exploration—theological and practical—of the relation between the bishop's role as one who speaks to the Church and his role as one who speaks for the Church and with it.

Finally—and more generally—Anglicans need to be critically aware of the cultural and social models that shape, and to some extent distort, their perception of the episcopal office. On any account of the matter a bishop is an 'authority figure'. The question what an authority figure is and does, however, depends to a considerable degree on perceptions and expectations that are shaped by the common practice of a given society. It is easy, in modern Western societies, for the bishop's authority to be modelled on that of the expert manager who 'gets results', or on that of the political representative who is elected to forward the views and interests of a particular constituency. In other times and places, other such models offer, or have offered, themselves: that of the civil magistrate, for example, or the feudal lord, or the tribal leader. In every case, however, the issue must be raised of the extent to which the model in question runs the risk, *in its own time and place,* of distorting the nature of pastoral authority in the Church; and this issue in turn can only be addressed on the basis of a theological grasp of the nature and source of authority in the Church.

BIBLIOGRAPHY

Episcopal Ministry: The Report of the Archbishops' Group in the Episcopate. CHP, London, 1990.
Jenkins, C., and MacKenzie, K. (eds), *Episcopacy Ancient and Modern.* SPCK, London, 1930.
Kirk, K. E. (ed.), *The Apostolic Ministry. Essays on the History and Doctrine of Episcopacy.* Hodder & Stoughton, London, 1946.
Mason, A. J., *The Church of England and Episcopacy.* Cambridge 1914.
Moore, P. (ed.), *Bishops—But What Kind?* SPCK, London, 1982.
Sykes, N., *Old Priest and New Presbyter.* CUP, 1956.
Today's Church and Today's World with a Special Focus on the Ministry of Bishops. (The Lambeth Conference 1978 Preparatory Articles.) CIO Publishing, London, 1977.

NOTES
1 John Jewel, *An Apologia of the Church of England* in T. H. L. Parker (ed.), *English Reformers*, Library of Christian Classics 26 (SCM Press, London, 1966), p. 21.
2 Richard Hooker, *Of the Laws of Ecclesiastical Polity* VIII.x.1.
3 Luke 9.1–3 and 10.1–12.
4 Hooker, *Laws*, VII.ii.3.
5 Hooker, *Laws*, VII.vi.3.
6 Hooker, *Laws*, VII.vi.1.
7 John Cosin, *Works* (Oxford 1843–55), Vol. I, p. 88.
8 John Whitgift, *Works*, ed. J. Ayre (Cambridge 1851), Vol. II, p. 290.
9 Hooker, *Laws*, VII.vii.1.
10 *The Lambeth Conference 1958*, p. 288.
11 John Pearson, *Minor Theological Works*, ed. E. Churton (Oxford 1844), Vol. I, p. 284.
12 Lancelot Andrewes, *Works* (Oxford 1854, reprinted New York 1967), Vol. VI, p. 355.
13 Hooker, *Laws*, VII.iv.1–4.
14 John Whitgift, *Works*, Vol. I, p. 184.
15 Hooker, *Laws*, III.ii.1.
16 Hooker, *Laws*, III.ii.2.
17 Hooker, *Laws*, III.ii.4.
18 Hooker, *Laws*, III.xi.20.
19 Hooker, *Laws*, VII.xi.8.
20 Andrewes, *Works*, Vol. VI, p. 355.
21 John Pearson, *Minor Theological Works* (Oxford 1842–55), Vol. II, pp. 73, 75.
22 John Cosin, *Works* (Oxford 1855), Vol. IV, p. 402.
23 Edward Stillingfleet, *Fifty Sermons* (London 1710), pp. 357, 374.
24 *The Lambeth Conferences, 1867–1948* (SPCK, London, 1948), p. 218.
25 William Beveridge, *Works* (Oxford 1842–8), Vol. I, p. 11.
26 William Law, *Works* (London 1762, reprinted 1892), Vol. I, pp. 8–9.

27 Quoted by A. J. Mason, *The Church of England and Episcopacy* (Cambridge 1914), p. 410.
28 F. D. Maurice, *The Kingdom of Christ*, ed. A. R. Vidler (SCM Press, London, 1958), Vol. II, p. 106.
29 *The Lambeth Conferences, 1867–1948*, Part II, p. 50.

PART SIX

Anglicanism in Practice

1   Anglican Spirituality

A. M. ALLCHIN

I

In 1869 Matthew Arnold began the preface to his book *Culture and Anarchy* with an appeal to the SPCK to republish Bishop Thomas Wilson's *Maxims of Piety and Christianity*. It was a book which in Arnold's judgement was even more valuable than the Bishop's better-known collection of prayers, *Sacra Privata;* 'a sample of the very best perhaps, which our nation and race can do by the way of religious writing'.[1] If Wilson was little known in 1869, at the end of a period of forty years which had seen an immense activity of republishing classical works of Anglican theology and spirituality from the sixteenth to the eighteenth centuries, it is certain that he is much less known today. As we shall see, the whole field of Anglican spirituality is one where a great deal of exploration remains to be done, and where many of the basic texts are simply inaccessible.

What was it that had caught the attention of the nineteenth-century poet and literary critic in the works of the eighteenth-century Bishop of Sodor and Man? Why should he refer so insistently to a book of private thoughts on religious questions at the start of a work which has as its subtitle, *An Essay in Political and Social Criticism?* Wilson, he tells us, drew his admiration because of the way in which he combines spiritual, intellectual and human qualities which are too often separated from one another. He joins 'ardour and unction' with

> downright honesty and plain good sense. With ardour and unction re-
> ligion as we all know, may still be fanatical, with honesty and good sense
> it may still be prosaic [. . .] Bishop Wilson's excellence lies in a balance of
> the four qualities, and in a fullness and perfection of them [. . .] His
> unction is so perfect and in such happy balance with his good sense, that
> it becomes tenderness and fervent charity. His good sense is so perfect,
> and in such happy alliance with his unction that it becomes moderation
> and insight.[2]

Here is a picture of a character, rounded and complete, in which different elements, personal and social, active and meditative, human and divine are harmoniously blended and at one.

As we read on in Arnold's essay, we find, of course, other elements in Wilson's life and writing which had won Arnold's admiration. In the first place the bishop seemed to him to embody a combination of what he called the Hebraic and Hellenic aspects of our Western tradition: the earnest striving after righteousness is there, but there is also the contemplation of the heavenly beauty, the recognition of God's glory at work in all things. Then, he provided a much-needed corrective to the unbridled individualism of the nineteenth century. He reminds us that we are members one of another.

> Individual perfection [Arnold writes] is impossible so long as the rest of mankind are not perfected along with us [. . .] And to this effect Bishop Wilson has striking words, 'It is not, says he, so much our neighbour's interest as our own that we love him.' And again, he says, 'Our salvation does in some measure depend upon that of others.[3]

The inner life of the Christian is evidently in no way divorced from his social and political relations with his fellow men and women. But it was above all Wilson's living testimony to the importance of the inward life of prayer, reflection and meditation, which Arnold valued, constituting as it did a rebuke to the nineteenth century's obsession with organization and machinery, machinery often seen as an end in itself, 'most absurdly disproportioned to the end which this machinery, if it is to do any good at all, is to serve'.[4]

Against this whole tendency—which, we may note, sounds remarkably twentieth-century—Arnold set his own idea of culture, 'a study of perfection, a perfection which consists in becoming something rather than having something, in an inward condition of the mind and spirit, not in an outward set of circumstances'.[5] This ideal is clearly formulated in Arnold's words and not in Wilson's. It has been purposely cut off from the dogmatic bases on which, in the bishop's scheme of things, it firmly rests. Yet it is clearly not unrelated to the older ideal of Christian holiness, with perfection as its aim, an aim which involves being and becoming rather than possessing, and which makes much of the often neglected potential of the human heart and mind for development and growth. In our twentieth century many have felt a need for a recovery of the contemplative dimension of human life. Arnold does not use that word, but he seems in the nineteenth century to envisage a similar need and similar operation.

II

We have started from this point not only because, as we shall find, Matthew Arnold was remarkably perceptive in his discernment of some of the salient features of the Anglican spiritual tradition, but also because the very fact of such a tribute to a venerable churchman from a distinctly agnostic poet and literary critic is a sign of the close links which have existed between poetry and faith, literature and religion in the last four centuries of the Anglican tradition. In part, of course, these links have their origin in the Bible itself and in the central place which it has taken in the prayer and devotion of all the Reformation traditions. In England the period of translation which had begun with William Tyndale culminated in the splendour of the Authorized (or King James) Version (1611), which remained for three centuries un-rivalled amongst English-speaking Christians.

Within Anglicanism the influence of the Bible was channelled and reinforced by the influence of a second book, scarcely less important in the formulation of Anglican tradition: the Book of Common Prayer. It was the genius of Cranmer to bring together into a single volume many different things: the texts necessary for the Sunday Eucharist, the texts for the daily office, the services for ordination, the occasional offices which accompany the believer from birth to burial. Thus there was, in the hands of any churchman who could read, a book which linked private with public prayer, which showed the Bible as a text to be used in worship, and which embraced the whole range of human life, personal as well as social. It represented a balanced and inclusive vision of Christian prayer and wor-ship. It is a work which has had great influence on those who use it, often unconsciously, occasionally consciously, as for instance with W. E. Gladstone who as a young man on holiday in Naples in 1832 found himself reading the Prayer Book with new eyes.

> It presented to me Christianity under an aspect in which I had not yet known it; its ministry of symbols, its channels of grace, its unending line of teachers joining from the Head; a sublime construction, based throughout upon historic fact, uplifting the idea of the community in which we live, and of the access which it enjoys through the new and living way to the presence of the Most High.[6]

Here in the Book of Common Prayer was a vision of the Church as a corporate reality at once of time and eternity, the context in which the individual finds his or her way to God, presented in pages of memorable prose, straightforward yet solemn.

This relationship between literature and faith implicit in the liturgy becomes explicit in the tradition of Anglican poetry and prose. In the series of distinctly theological poets, from John Donne, George Herbert or Henry Vaughan in the seventeenth century to T. S. Eliot, W. H. Auden and R. S. Thomas in our own day. It can be seen in the very quality of prose-writing to be found in this tradition, whether in theology, in preaching or in prayer and mediations. One might think of Hooker, Andrewes and Taylor or Traherne in the seventeenth century, of William Law in the eighteenth, of Coleridge and John Henry Newman in the nine-teenth, of C. S. Lewis and Austin Farrer in our own day. This is a tradition which by its form as well as by its content seems to speak of a particular perception of the link between grace and nature, faith and culture, divine and human, which has been characteristic of Anglican spirituality as a whole, and has had its influence more widely in the intellectual history of the English-speaking world.

In our own century this relationship is found at its most fascinating in the life and work of T. S. Eliot. If Arnold in 1867 was anxious to record a sense of indebtedness to Thomas Wilson, how much greater was the debt which Eliot revealed to another and more distinguished bishop, in the little book which he published in 1927 called *For Lancelot Andrewes*. Arnold, at times, seems to be using his quotations from Wilson as pegs to hang his own ideas on. Eliot in his essay on Andrewes makes it clear that he is writing of a man to whom he feels he owes something of his life and sanity. This, after all, was the book in which Eliot announced his adherence to the Catholic faith. He has no use for Arnold's dream of 'culture' as an autonomous reality, which can take the place of religion. For him spirituality needs to be grounded in belief, prayer needs the support of dogma. And it is the peculiar fusion of faith and prayer, of theology and experience, of feeling and thinking which for him gives to Andrewes his power and authority. In Andrewes' sermons he finds a dogmatic-ecstatic quality which enables them to convey the truths which they expound, and as it were to embody them.

To persons whose minds are habituated to feed on the vague jargon of our time, when we have a vocabulary for everything and exact ideas about nothing [...] when the language of theology itself [...] tends to become a language of tergiversation—Andrewes may seem pedantic and verbal. It is only when we have saturated ourselves in his prose, followed the movement of his thought, that we find his examination of words terminating in an ecstasy of assent. Andrewes takes a word and derives a world from it, squeezing and squeezing the word until it yields a full juice of meaning which we should never have supposed any word to possess.[7]

The many-faceted words of the Bible recover their full weight of meaning. So by a way which looks pedantic, but which in fact demands a great concentration, and is itself the product of a long discipline of prayer and study and meditation, Andrewes is able to enter into his subject and expand it from within. He can speak with the authority of one who has assimilated the things which he is speaking about. He does this by way of two unifications: first the unification of his own faculties, thinking, feeling and willing, into a single movement of assent and adoration, then the unification of himself with the subject which he is considering.

When Andrewes begins his sermon, from beginning to end you are aware that he is wholly in his subject, unaware of anything else, that his emotion grows as he penetrates more deeply into his subject, that he is finally 'alone with the Alone', with the mystery which he is seeking to grasp more and more firmly [...] Andrewes' emotion is purely contemplative; it is not personal, it is wholly evoked by the object of contemplation to which it is adequate; his emotion is wholly contained and explained by its object.[8]

Here we have an expression of the indebtedness of one of the greatest poets of our century to the man who for him had come to stand for the tradition into which he entered. Eliot and Andrewes can tell us something both of theology and mysticism. I use the words together because only together will they do justice to the nature of Andrewes' teaching and his devotion, to that vision of faith which is enshrined in the Preces Privatae no less than in the sermons. The word 'mysticism', in all its variations, always implies unity or union between God and humankind, between the eternal and the temporal. But for Andrewes this unity is not the unity of identity, which is at the centre of the Eastern religions, it is the unity of co-inherence and communion of which the whole Christian tradition speaks. As Nicholas Lossky writes in his recent masterly study of the preaching of Lancelot Andrewes—a work with the significant sub-title, The Origins of the Mystical Theology of the Church of England:

> The ultimate objective of the spiritual life being union with God, we can say that the theology of Lancelot Andrewes is a mystical theology, on condition of making some precision in the meaning of this term. It is not a case of an exceptional experience reserved for some, in some way outside the traditional paths of theology. On the contrary it is a question of the interiorisation of the revealed Christian mystery, to which Andrewes summons all the baptized. This theology is mystical in the sense that it is not an abstract reflection, but a way of living the mystery in the deepening of faith through prayer and the renunciation of ones own will [...] For Andrewes it is entirely evident that this is only possible in fidelity to the data of revelation, that is to say in the biblical and patristic tradition, i.e. in the catholicity of the Church.[9]

If Matthew Arnold in his praise of Thomas Wilson has drawn our attention to the Anglican desire for moderation and wholeness, to the longing for a just balance between the things of this world and the things of the world to come, Eliot in his assessment of Andrewes has made us recognize a deeply mystical element, present in the teaching of the seventeenth-century bishop, but never wholly absent from Anglican spirituality since. This is a dimension of Anglican devotion which has often been overlooked. Some of the standard works on the subject have nothing to say on it. But if one looks deeply into writings of Charles Wesley or William Law in the eighteenth century, and E. B. Pusey, R. M. Benson or B. F. Westcott in the nineteenth, it is difficult not to recognize its presence. In our own century it may be seen in writers as different as Evelyn Underhill, Charles Williams and Michael Ramsey. It was indeed not altogether absent from Thomas Wilson himself, for all his good sense and downright honesty. Among his maxims we find 'The end of Christianity is to perfect the human nature by participation of the divine.'[10]

In the last ten or fifteen years it has become common to recognize the influence of the fourteenth-century mystics in the development of English Christianity. Perhaps it is time for us to recognize a constant vein of mystical religion in our inheritance, not only in great but relatively isolated figures like George Fox and William Blake, but in many whose lives lay much nearer to the centre of the mainstream of religious life, who like Andrewes had an intense concern for the unity and catholicity of the Church. To do this would involve a considerable alteration in our picture of ourselves and who we are.

III

We have looked at the work of two eminent poets and critics whose writings are studied wherever English language and literature are studied. We have seen their evaluation of two Anglican bishops whose works are very little known, even in Anglican centres of theological learning. We have come across one of the salient facts about the Anglican tradition of spirituality. In this century it has been much more intensively studied in departments of English literature than in departments of theology. This has been the case not only in Britain and the United States of America, but also in countries as widely separated as Canada, Australia and Japan. Indeed two of the fundamental studies for an understanding of the theological bases of Anglican spirituality have been written in the English departments of universities in France. To one of these we have already referred, Nicholas Lossky, *Lancelot Andrewes, The Preacher, The Origins of the Mystical Theology of the Church of England* (Oxford 1991). To the other we shall shortly turn: Oliver Loyer, *L'Anglicanisme de Richard Hooker* (Lille/Paris 1979).

But first we must ask what it is that attracts students of English literature and civilization to the study of Anglican spirituality and theology, as it manifests itself in the work of the seventeenth-century poets, but not only there. There is evidently something in this tradition which has the effect of linking prayer and devotion with theological reflection and learning. There is something here which seems to activate and transform the human imagination. These are often learned writers steeped not only in the knowledge of the Bible, but also of the Christian tradition both in its patristic and scholastic phases. We may remark in passing that this capacity of the Anglican tradition to give rise to works of great artistic distinction, is evident also in the field of music. From the Reformation until today, there has been a constant tradition of liturgical music, centred in the English cathedrals, and spreading far beyond them. The creativity of this tradition is seen in the fact that it continued to flourish during those periods of the eighteenth and nineteenth century when the composition of secular music seemed almost dead in England. What is the root of this persistent capacity to stimulate the creation of works of art directly linked to the prayer of the Church?

There are of course many factors involved in such a cultural phenomenon, but at their heart we can surely see the primary influence of the greatest of Anglican theologians since the Reformation, Richard Hooker. In one sense Hooker is a humanist. He defends the rights of human reason, of civil laws, of the historic experience of nations, of the traditions of the churches against the criticisms of a form of Calvinism which was already tending to exalt God at the expense of man, to insist one-sidedly on the supremacy of revelation over reason. He is, as Loyer puts it, in his penetrating and detailed study of his thought, a thinker for whom the categories of conjunction and participation are vital at many different levels.

So the disjunctions which in the course of sixteenth-century controversy had become sharpened and hardened, between Scripture and tradition, between grace and nature, between the inward and the outward elements in prayer and worship, and finally between faith and religion, are consistently rejected by Hooker. Always he seeks to unite the two. Hence his high estimate of what we should call culture, his positive evaluation of human wisdom. These things are indeed the works of man, but they are the works of man inspired and sustained by God. For, in the end, Hooker's humanism is a very particular form of humanism—a theocentric humanism. As C. S. Lewis remarks, 'Few model universes are more filled—one might say, more drenched—with Deity than his . "All things that are of God", (and only sin is not) "have God in them and he them in himself likewise", yet "their substance and his wholly differeth" God is unspeakably transcendent; but also unspeakably immanent.'[11]

We must notice too how large a part of the *Laws of Ecclesiastical Polity* is devoted to the defence of the Church's tradition of prayer and worship. In this defence, Hooker is always tracing back particular points of controversy—about sacred times and sacred places for instance—to the theological principles which lie behind them. In his defence of the Book of Common Prayer, a whole understanding of human nature is implicit; it is a nature which is social as well as personal, which needs to express itself outwardly as

357

well as inwardly. The deep roots of prayer for Hooker are to be found in the very nature of humankind; we are creatures whose end is God himself, made with a longing to go beyond ourselves into God. Loyer argues that, in Book V, Hooker links the elements of preaching and doctrine in worship with the elements of prayer and sacrament, uniting them into a single movement of divine initiative and human response.

> The great texts on the divine participation and presence, that is to say on the reciprocal relations of God and man complete naturally those which define the relations between doctrine and prayer. The internal logic which prolongs the mystery of the Word and of Prayer in the mystery of the Eucharist becomes clearly evident to the reader. The progress of thought makes the eucharistic sacrament the completion of the liturgical celebration, the theology of the incarnation, and the fulfillment of the theology of the Word and Prayer.[12]

So God's taking our nature in the incarnation of the Son, his imparting of that nature through the preaching of the word and the celebration of the sacraments which make us members of Christ, has as its consequence our humanity's return to God, the return for which our whole being longs. From Hooker's treatment of these closely related themes there grew in the seventeenth century a richly varied meditation on the eucharistic nature of Christian prayer and worship, to which writers as different as Cosin and Brevint, Taylor and Thorndike contributed.[13]

Hooker insists that it is the whole man who is caught up into this activity of worship, not heart alone, nor mind and will alone, but all together in a movement in which the body and the senses have their part. This is the point of his celebrated passage in praise of music, which is more than simply an example of his style at its most eloquent and elaborate. As so often happens in his writing, Platonist and Aristotelian motifs are fused in the same paragraph, which celebrates the place of music not only in worship but in all human life.

> More than the other arts, it has this faculty to integrate contemplative reason and sensory perception; it is harmony and proportion, it speaks to the highest part of the soul, evoking the divine perfection; but first of all it speaks to man's inferior faculties and makes use of their power.[14]

It touches the heights of the spirit by touching the senses and emotions. So there is in music an analogy with the sacraments, which also stoop to our bodily nature in order to arrive at the inmost secrets of our spiritual being.

All this, it may be complained, is a tradition which is excessively élitist; a tradition of learned poets, of aristocratic devotion, of cathedral music. That there is some element of truth in such an allegation it is impossible to deny.

But it is certainly nothing like the whole truth. For this tradition of faith and prayer affirms that God is to be found in all creatures. There is in it an awareness of the sacramental quality of all things, both in the sense that the sacrament of Holy Communion has universal application, and in the sense that the whole world is intended to be the vehicle of God's presence to us. No one in the seventeenth century develops this theme with greater brilliance than Thomas Traherne, the Rector of Credenhill, a writer whose theological seriousness has been too little recognized.

In the eighteenth century a verse from Charles Wesley's 'Hymns on the Lord's Supper' gives striking evidence of the conviction that the Eucharist has a universal significance.[15]

Return and with thy people sit
  Lord of the sacramental feast,
And satiate us with heavenly meat
  And make the *world* thy happy guest.

Christ's presence in the midst of his people is to result in the calling together of the nations into the feast of the Kingdom. This conviction takes new form in the nineteenth century, in the preaching of F. D. Maurice and his successors in the Christian Socialist movement. For them, the sacrament is the sign and symbol of all human sharing.

But perhaps still more important in Anglican tradition is the conviction that all things may become sacraments to us, meeting-places between God and man. In the seventeenth century, George Herbert writes,

All may of thee partake
  Nothing can be so mean
That with this tincture 'For thy sake'
  Will not grow bright and clean.[16]

So the most menial daily tasks may become divine. Two centuries later, the same thought is expressed by John Keble in an even more familiar verse:

The trivial round, the common task
  Will furnish all we ought to ask,
Room to deny ourselves, a road
  To bring us daily nearer God.[17]

In a paradoxical way, John Keble, in Newman's judgement the true and primary author of the Oxford Movement, testifies to this sense of God's presence in all things and in all people at the very moment when he might seem to be most enmeshed in the old, literary culture of the Anglican tradition. Keble had been Professor of Poetry at Oxford, and according to the established custom he delivered his lectures in Latin, and in Latin they were published in 1844. Not till 1911 did an English translation appear. But these lectures were dedicated to one of the greatest, if not the greatest of the English romantic poets, William Wordsworth. The terms in which this dedication is phrased demand our careful attention in the context of this study.

To William Wordsworth / True philosopher and inspired poet / Who by the special gift and calling of Almighty God / Whether he sang of man or of nature / Failed not to lift up man's heart to holy things / Nor ever ceased to champion the cause / Of the poor and simple / And so in perilous times was raised up / To be a chief minister / Not only of sweetest poetry / But also of high and sacred truth [...] [18]

Here the Christian priest pays tribute to the Christian poet, and recognizes how closely their callings are interwoven. Here, in particular, he celebrates the poet's gift to lift our hearts and minds to the things of eternity through the things of time, and acknowledges his calling to champion the cause of the poor and simple. The Oxford Movement began in a very academic milieu. It was a movement of the mind and spirit. But it soon had the effect of driving men and women out into the slums of nineteenth-century England and out onto the frontier of the new West in the United States, in service of their fellow human beings, because it was clearly seen, as Thomas Wilson had taught, that the salvation of each one is bound up with the salvation of all and that 'our life is with our brother'. So as Louis Bouyer commented in his study of Newman:

The most powerful, and also the most respectable attraction of the new movement was to put forward and multiply examples of a Christianity which was at one and the same time eager for holiness and creative of it. It was the demands which this religion made, not simply in the abstract, but immediately and in practice which gained for it such enthusiastic and effective support. [19]

All human faculties, affective as well as intellectual, active as well as contemplative were involved in this movement.

IV

In this essay we have considered some of the salient features of the Anglican spiritual tradition over the last four centuries, in particular its search for wholeness and balance, its desire at once to spread itself outwards in a concern for all human life, and at the same time to turn inwards to explore the heights and depths of the mystery of God's presence at the heart of human life. We have seen how close have been the links between spirituality and literature, not only in the century between 1590 and 1690, but in a variety of ways ever since. Throughout the centuries there has been the practice both of the inner life of prayer and meditation, and of the outward life of liturgy and service in the world, which had been reflected in manuals of devotion, commentaries on Scripture and the Prayer Book, collections of sermons and meditations, works of poetry and prose alike. In our own day too, particularly in the last thirty years, there has been a new flowering of this tradition of reflective spirituality and spiritual theology, which we can see in writers as diverse as Alan Ecclestone, W. H. Vanstone, Monica Furlong, Kenneth Leech and Rowan Williams. Much, of course, has not been said here. Whole schools of spiritual writing, the Cambridge Platonists of the seventeenth century, the Evangelicals and Methodists of the eighteenth, and the later development of Anglo-Catholicism in the nineteenth have been passed over in silence. The central place of Coleridge in the literary and religious history of the nineteenth century has only been hinted at.

We have however begun to glimpse the fact that Anglicans are heirs to a tradition of which at the present they are often almost unaware. There is here a need for a recovery of memory, which will allow for a recovery of identity. We need to make an act of *anamnesis* of the presence and power of God not only in the lives of men and woman in the Old and New Testament periods, but in the subsequent history of the Church. Voices speak to us from our own past with words we should be able to hear today. We have thought of the influence of Lancelot Andrewes in the development of T. S. Eliot's religious faith. It is no less a striking fact that it was some lines of George Herbert which marked a decisive point in the spiritual journey of Simone Weil. Such texts need to be made available for others.

We have spoken here of bishops whose names are now scarcely known. Let us conclude with another of them, Edward Reynolds, who was Bishop of Norwich from 1660 to 1676. Perhaps because during the Commonwealth period he conformed to the presbyterian arrangements then in force, perhaps for other reasons, he has been almost wholly neglected. All Anglicans owe him a debt of gratitude for two of the best-loved prayers of the 1662 Prayer Book, the General Thanksgiving and the Prayer for All Sorts and Conditions of Men—prayers which have been adapted in the new liturgical formularies. Sixty years ago, P. E. More and F. L. Cross included four extracts from his writings in their anthology, *Anglicanism*. From them one could grasp something of the beauty of his style, the depth of his insight, the extent of his learning and the clarity of his mind. These qualities become more evident when we begin to read him at length, whether in his sermons or in his more formal treatises, as for instance on *The Passions and Faculties of the Soul of Man*.

361

The work of such a man who can speak of the mercy of God in the sacraments as he does, is not of mere historical interest.

It were almost a contradiction in anything save God's mercy, to be so deep that no thought can fathom it, and yet so obvious that each eye may see it [. . .] so humble is his mercy, that since we can not raise our understandings to the comprehension of divine mysteries, he will bring down and submit those mysteries to the apprehension of our senses.[20]

He is one who speaks of the beauty of God revealed alike in his work of creation and redemption in terms such as these:

The sum and total of all God's works are the world and the church; the world is called *kosmos* for the beauty and comeliness of it; in which everything was very good when the Lord took a view of it. But the Lord has chosen his church upon which to bestow more abundant glory [. . .] In the world we have the foot-prints of his greatness; but in the Church we have the image of his holiness.[21]

Above all, he is one who can speak of God's love as that living centre around which all other human loves can find their meaning and direction:

The master-wheel or first mover in all the regular motions of this passion is the love of God, grounded on the right knowledge of him; whereby the soul being ravished with the apprehension of his infinite goodness is earnestly drawn and 'called out', as it were, to desire a union and participation of his glory and presence; yielding up itself unto him (for by love a man giveth himself to the thing he loves), and conforming all its actions and affections to his will [. . .] And therefore the wise man, speaking of the love and fear of God, tells us, that it is *totum hominis*, the whole of man [. . .] to love any creature either without God, or above God, is *cupiditas*, lust, which is the 'formale' of every sin, whereby we turn from God to other things, but to love the creatures under God, in their right order—and for God, to their right end (for he made all things for himself) this is *caritas*, true and regular love.[22]

In affirming the possibility of humankind to love and know God, the capacity of the human person for union and participation in the divine glory and presence, and in affirming that this possibility is the only true and ultimate fulfillment of the deepest longing of the human heart and mind, the Anglican spiritual tradition is asserting nothing that is not universally Christian. But in the insistence that all things created can be loved in and for God, a point which Reynolds makes in many different contexts, there is perhaps an emphasis which is peculiar to this particular way of prayer and faith, a longing to gather together the fullness of the created order in all its diversity, into the unity of the Kingdom.

And it is the wonder of love (as St Chrysostom speaketh) to collect and knit together in one things separated from each other. Wherein stands the mystery of the communion of the church on earth, both with itself, and in all the dispersed members of it, and with Christ the head, and with that other part of it which triumpheth in heaven.[23]

BIBLIOGRAPHY

Allchin, A. M., 'Holiness in the Anglican Tradition', in M. Chavchavadze (ed.), *Man's Concern with Holiness*, Hodder and Stoughton, London, 1970, pp. 37–58.
Bouyer, L., *Orthodox Spirituality and Protestant and Anglican Spirituality*. Burns and Oates, Tunbridge Wells, 1966.
Lossky, N., *Lancelot Andrewes, The Preacher (1558–1626); The Origins of the Mystical Theology of the Church of England*. OUP 1991.
Loyer, O., *L'Anglicanisme de Richard Hooker*. Université de Lille 1979.
McAdoo, H. R., *Anglican Heritage: Theology and Spirituality*. Canterbury Press 1991.
Martz, L. L., *The Poetry of Mediation· A Study in English Religious Literature of the Seventeenth Century*. Yale University Press, New Haven CT, 1954.
Moorman, J. R. H. *The Anglican Spiritual Tradition*. DLT, London, 1983.
Prickett, S., *Romanticism and Religion: The Tradition of Coleridge and Wordsworth in the Victorian Church*. CUP 1976.
Stevenson, K. *Covenant of Grace Renewed: A Vision of the Eucharist in the Seventeenth Century*. DLT, London, 1994.
Stranks, C. J., *Anglican Devotion: Studies in the Spiritual Life of the Church of England between the Reformation and the Oxford Movement*. SCM, London, 1961.
Thornton, M., *English Spirituality: An Outline of Ascetical Theology according to the English Pastoral Tradition*. SPCK, London, 1963.

NOTES

1 Matthew Arnold, *Culture and Anarchy: An Essay in Political and Social Criticism*, ed. J. Dover Wilson (Cambridge 1932), p. 4.
2 Arnold, *Culture and Anarchy*, p. 5.
3 Arnold, *Culture and Anarchy*, p. 192.
4 Arnold, *Culture and Anarchy*, p. 50.
5 Arnold, *Culture and Anarchy*, p. 48.
6 John Morley, *The Life of William Edwart Gladstone* (1903), Vol. i, pp. 87–8.
7 T. S. Eliot, *For Lancelot Andrewes* (Faber and Faber, 1927), p. 16.
8 Eliot, *For Lancelot Andrewes*, p. 17f.
9 Lossky, *Lancelot Andrewes, The Preacher*, pp. 335–6.
10 Thomas Wilson, *Maxims of Piety and Christianity*, ed. F. Relton (1898), p. 27.
11 C. S. Lewis, *English Literature in the Sixteenth Century excluding Drama* (OUP 1954), pp. 459–60.
12 Loyer, *L'Anglicanisme de Richard Hooker*, Vol. i. p. 447.
13 Stevenson, *Covenant of Grace Renewed*, passim.
14 Loyer, *L'Anglicanisme de Richard Hooker*, p. 474.

15 J. E. Rattenbury, *The Eucharistic Hymns of John and Charles Wesley* (Epworth, London, 1948), p. 249.
16 *Hymns Ancient and Modern, New Standard Edition* (Norwich 1983), No. 240.
17 *Hymns Ancient and Modern, New Standard*, No. 2.
18 Quoted in Stephen Prickett, *Romanticism and Religion, The Tradition of Coleridge and Wordsworth in the Victorian Church* (CUP 1976), p. 109.
19 Louis Bouyer, *Newman* (Burns and Oats, London, 1951), p. 223.
20 P. E. More and F. L. Cross (eds), *Anglicanism* (Milwaukee 1935, reprinted London 1962), p. 410.
21 More and Cross, *Anglicanism*, p. 771.
22 Edward Reynolds, *The Whole Works* (1826), Vol. vi. pp. 61–2.
23 Reynolds, *The Whole Works*, p. 73.

2   Anglican Morality

PAUL ELMEN

To ask what kind of moral theory and what kind of moral acts are distinctly Anglican is to invite a dubious answer. There is a cluster of possible replies, each heavily dependent on the type of churchmanship of the respondent, on his theological presuppositions, and also on the prejudices buried in the period in which he speaks. There is no uniform Anglican morality in theory, much less in practice. But it is also true that moralism has been a traditional preoccupation of Anglicans, and in each century Anglicans have made a contribution towards understanding the unending ambiguities of translating the love of God into some sort of appropriate specific decision or concrete action. Some of those contributions bear recounting, if only, as Hooker said in his *Laws of Ecclesiastical Polity*, 'that posterity may know we have not loosely through silence permitted things to pass away as in a dream'.[1]

I

A few common threads may be detected. The goal of *via media* is the effort to establish an identity which is both Catholic and Reformed, yet in a special sense neither. In moral theology this called for a middle ground between authority and liberty. Paul Elmer More said, in the anthology *Anglicanism*, that the effort might be seen as political, resisting the claims of both Rome and Geneva; or it may have been, as John Donne admitted, a convenient way of avoiding difficulties. But a more adequate account would be the one More settled for, that the aim of *via media* was 'to introduce into religion, and to base upon "the light of reason", that love of balance, restraint, moderation, measure, which from sources beyond our reckoning appear to be innate in the English temper'.[2] The hallmark of Anglican morality has been the *aurea mediocritas*, the Golden Mean, the measure of nothing too much.

Another major theme, present in Anglican moral treatises from the beginning, is the insistence on the priority of *praxis* over *theoria*. According to Paul Elmer More, 'If we are looking for a single term to denote the ultimate law of Anglicanism, I do not see that we can do better than adopt a title which offers itself as peculiarly descriptive [. . .]; I refer to the title "pragmatism".'[3]

The preference for pragmatic application rather than speculative insight is not of course an Anglican innovation. It appears with varying emphases in all the world's religions. Monotheism did not appear under the world scene as a metaphysical theory, but was from the beginning a way of life. It was the central idea that animated the prophets and the later Talmudic sages. John reported that Jesus knew well that divine knowledge was possible only after the test of action: 'If any man will do his will he shall know the doctrine, whether it be of God, or whether I speak of myself' (John 7.17). British temperament was especially hospitable to such biblical ideals, and some empiricists went so far as to claim that all knowledge came from experience. The motto scientists chose for the Royal Society was *Nullius in Verba* (cf. Horace, *Epistles* 1.1.14).

Pragmatic priority became a characteristic of British cultural history, and Anglican morality may be understood as its expression in religious form (see pp. 191–3). In the fourteenth century, William Langland's *Piers Plowman* pointed to the power of goodness resident in every human being, enabling him to do what he needed to do in order to be saved; in Langland's view even ploughing a field had spiritual significance. The theological unity of the feudal-monarchial world characteristic of the Middle Ages was never completely dissipated in England by the advent of bourgeois democracy and the industrial age. Churchmen thought that making a moral protest against the injustice of secular society was not irrelevant to Christian theology, but instead was derived directly from it. Reinhold Niebuhr concluded this:

> From Gerald Winstanley, the leader of the Diggers in the seventeenth century, through Keir Hardie, Robert Smillie, Arthur Henderson, George Lansbury, Stafford Cripps, and Acland in the past decades, British Christianity, whether sectarian or state church, has generated prophets of religio-social criticism.

Niebuhr offered a plausible guess: 'It may be that the unbroken character of the Christian ethos in Britain is also the cause of the unbroken socio-political history since 1688.'[4] What Niebuhr describes is the distinctive Church-world relationship of what Ernst Troelsch called the *church-type*, in comparison with the *sect-type*. In the former the organizational structure

365

of the Church is formally related to the political power of the society, and so is 'established', and seeming to be, in the eyes of Free-Church people. 'worldly'.

Theology which expressed itself not as concept but as deed was a favourite seventeenth-century Anglican theme. Illustrations can be chosen almost at random. The comment of John Smith, one of the Cambridge Platonists, may serve as typical. Christ, he said, did not spell out canons, articles of belief, and codes of conduct. The reason is that he was 'not so careful to stock and enrich the World with Opinions and Notions, as with true Piety, and a Godlike patterns of purity, as the best way to thrive in all spiritual understandings. His main scope was to promote an Holy Life.'[5] George Herbert's 'The Elixir' is perhaps the best-known poetical example of the Caroline translation of theory into praxis:

Teach me, my God and King,
In all things thee to see,
And what I do in any thing,
To do it as for thee [. . .]

A servant with this clause
Makes drudgerie divine;
Who sweeps a room, as for thy laws,
Makes that and th' action fine.

Jeremy Taylor's *The Rule and Exercise of Holy Living* (1650 may be considered the paradigmatic Anglican theological statement for the Christian morality of the period. It may be that the period of the interregnum, which turned the Church of England into a conclave and made formal priestly guidance impossible was the immediate occasion of Taylor's book. There was widespread Anglican scorn for Puritan theology, which could express itself as regicide. But this very occaasionalism is one of the aspects of the continuing Anglican reference of theological reflection to life structures. *Holy Living* carried on the tradition prominent since the English Reformation, and stressed by Colet, Erasmus and More: that morality should be in the foreground of the Church's attention, while dogma was kept in the shade.

The insistence that practice determine the soundness of doctrine carried with it certain risks. For example, Jeremy Taylor was hostile to the doctrine of original sin, not because it was theologically unsound, but because it could be used to justify evil living. Such Pelagianism may have cost him a bishopric in England. The Caroline ethicists were hostile to the Roman Catholic doctrine of deathbed repentance, in our time illustrated in Evelyn Waugh's novel *Brideshead Revisited*. The Carolines would have said that Sebastian's reliance on a last-minute forgiveness leaned too heavily on the example of the thief on the cross. It wiped out the sinner's need for a reformed life, and so represented imperfect contrition. Taylor was sure that immorality was proof of heresy: 'Because faith is not only a precept of doctrine but of manners and holy life, whatsoever is either opposite to an article of Creed, or teaches ill life, that's heresy.'[6]

Critics have not been wanting, even among Anglicans, who claim that this preference for morality over doctrine had disastrous consequences, leading, as Bellarmine claimed, to 'nipping at the name of Christ.' The charge has been that the teaching of such radical immanence led to the Deism of the eighteenth century, and to the secularism of the twentieth. But the benefits of this dominant morality were also visible. Casuistry became most important, and the necessity of a good life, especially of sound social conduct, had the effect of vivifying the gospel. When dogma had a diminished role, tolerance became more common. In any case, Anglicanism developed its distinctive moral style, a kind of sober ecstasy, a way in which rational men and women could lead a 'godly, righteous, and sober life' (Book of Common Prayer). The recognition of the Incarnation, the point where the Word became enfleshed, required a union between asceticism and morality, turning the model from a juristic to a pastoral form, and serving to enliven both sermons and the spread of lay vocations.

Of course the recommendation that Christians should live their faith rather than simply to profess it called immediately for a supplementary guide. Missing from this formula was elucidation on what constituted a Christian life, and some form of criteria for evaluating whether or not that goal was achieved. What after all was the distinctive character of a holy deed? After Plato, how could any particularity adequately reflect the holy will of God? From such questions the Middle Ages developed the science of moral theology, deductive, rational, Aristotelian-Thomistic. As H. R. McAdoo has pointed out in his primary account, *The Structure of Caroline Moral Theology* (1949), Caroline moral theory was both derivative and innovative in regard to Roman Catholic antecedents. Thomas Aquinas suited exactly an essential Anglican need, that of recognizing the presence of divine grace without at the same time denying the efficacy of created nature and natural laws. In Aquinas' wide embrace the order of creation bedded happily with the order of redemption. The formal cause was man, a rational animal, finding himself a part of the cosmic order which had been laid down by God, and expected to take his appropriate place in the march toward fulfillment and perfection. The literary world reflected the basic anthropology. The Shakespearean plays turn on the assumption of a cosmic order which could be denied, but only at the cost of chaos and death. If one challenged that intimate connection, as Ulysses said in *The Tragedy of Troilus and Cressida,*

Strength should be lord of imbecility,
And the rude son should strike his father dead.[7]

The mysterious stay against chaos called Order was not thought to be a human contrivance, but a divine plan. Despite minor differences, detected by any close study in the moral theory of Richard Hooker, Jeremy Taylor, Robert Sanderson and Joseph Hall, it was a major theme of the seventeenth century. The question of one's exact status in the Order remained unanswered. In the absence of any announced hierarchy, and without a developed casuistry supported by authoritative ecclesiastical rewards and punishments, the way in which *synderisis* (cosmic order) related to *syneidesis* (application to concrete cases) remained uncertain, and Anglicans were forced to rely on the conscience as the instrument of moral decisions. Three important Anglican works dealt with the problem: Sanderson's *De Obligatione Conscientiae* and Taylor's *Ductor Dubitantium* (both published in 1660); and Kenneth Kirk's *Conscience and Its Problems* (1927).

The Caroline period was not only productive in casuistry and in metaethical reflection, but also in a fruitful penetration of political structures by the clergy. Richard Bancroft, an early Bishop of London, licensed books, watched ports for seditious literature, and led a mission which negotiated a treaty with the Dutch. William Juxon, a later Bishop of London, had the care of the nation's treasury as part of his charge. William Laud was Archbishop of Canterbury, but he was also Chancellor of the University of Oxford and a member of the Privy Council, High Commission and Star Chamber. The line which separated sacred from secular activity was indistinct.

The eighteenth century was very concerned with the role that reason should play in determining Christian theology and life-style. Anglicans since Richard Hooker had challenged a naive bibliolatry, and had insisted that divine truth was accessible to man not only by revelation, but, as Aquinas had said, by the very nature of law. This law could be grasped by natural reason. Bishop Joseph Butler (1692–1752) played a leading role in demonstrating that moral obligation is an essential feature of the rational universe. But he was not a Deist, and had no confidence in the use of reason which was unrelated to divine law. In sermons preached at the Rolls Chapel in Salisbury between 1718 and 1726, and in a crucial essay, 'On the Nature of Virtue' appended to his *Analogy of Religion* (1736), he argued that rules of nature and supernature, body and spirit, self-love and benevolence, were not opposed polarities but were supplementary to each other. Something primal and self-evident in human nature, which was created by God, provided the grounds on which the morality of an action must be judged. 'Man', he said 'hath the rule of right within; what is wanting is only that he honestly attend to it.'[8]

The seventeenth and eighteenth centuries made notable strides in the direction of a reasonable faith, but some people judged Anglicanism to be too earthbound, a victim of its own formal theory. It could not match sectarians in the areas of doctrinal conviction, emotional warmth and personal salvation. The Church, some thought, needed to recapture its ancient authority, and if the world were again to be shaken by what William Wilberforce called 'vital Christianity', it would surely not be by appeals to common sense. Two forms of the revisionary mood in the nineteenth century were the Evangelical Revival and the Oxford Movement.

II

The sustained supernaturalism of Evangelicalism, its concern for inward feeling and personal holiness and its goal of individual salvation in the next life, seemed to promise few resources for healing the social illnesses of the new century, or even recognizing that they existed. There was suffering in the cities following the Industrial Revolution, and neither casuistry nor conversion promised social reform. Fortunately, the Anglican concern for life structures, surviving from an earlier methodology, remained strong, even in sectarian circles. *The Christian Observer*, the Evangelical trade journal, and the Cambridge Evangelicals were very clear that conversion indeed meant love, but love informed with knowledge, and knowledge translated into deed. The theology led to a renewed social concern, exactly as it had done to the fourteenth-century *Devotio moderna*, the Brothers of the Common Life. Very like too, the Jewish Hasidim, founded as a reaction to the excessive rationalism of the Torah, and emerging in the eighteenth century as a transfiguration of common activities. Thomas Scott's *Commentary on the Bible* (1792), which served as a primary reference text for the Clapham Sect, is proof enough that early Evangelicalism did not neglect social duties. From these foes of the Enlightenment emerged in brilliant succession the beginnings of public education and the attacks on the slave trade. Regardless of their concern for a personal ethic of holiness rather than for communal obligations of love, it was the Evangelicals who reformed prisons, supported factory laws and started charities aimed at cushioning blows suffered by the victims of the new urban slums.

The Oxford Movement had its own seriousness, but it was in the beginning more concerned with the authority of the Church and the recovery of ritual. There was at first little understanding that the function of liturgy is to send people into the world to practice love. Keble praised Hooker's 'practical

369

good sense' when he observed that 'the poor should be good at fasting. Since their perpetual fasts are necessary, [they] may with better contentment endure the hunger, which virtue causes others to choose.'[9] But the second-generation Tractarians were a different breed, interested in ritual, but only because it reinforced charity. Father A. H. Mackonochie of St Albans, Holborn, went together with an East Londoner, Charles Lowder, to Keble's funeral in 1866. R. W. Church, the historian, wrote to another first-generation Tractarian, John Copeland, that the younger crowd seemed like good fellows, but looked at him darkly.

Running parallel with the Tractarians' plea for the authority of the church, new voices challenged Establishment shibboleths and began asking embarrassing questions about the relationship of the Church to property and wealth. Actually closer to Cardinal Manning than to the early Tractarians, the Christian Socialists were a new breed of pragmatists. J. M. Ludlow had experienced personally the cruel suffering of the poor in the early nineteenth century, and he was sure that society needed to be remade rather than rehabilitated. His companion, F. D. Maurice, was rather less radical than Ludlow, but he too chose the same unstable elements from the Anglican past, and called for social reform based on Christian principles. He founded Producers' Co-operatives and the Working Men's College.

According to M. B. Reckitt, 'Maurice's capacity to be what he was and to lead as he did arose from no special interest or knowledge of social questions, but from a profound grasp of the answers which God in Christ had already given.'[10] Other stalwarts, such as Charles Kingsley and E. Vansittart Neale, followed Maurice's lead, defining each in his own way a renewed Christianity which could be called muscular. Various kinds of churchmanship were engaged in this renewal. The Anglo-Catholic Charles Gore thought it obvious that social justice was not an adventitious addition to the gospel, but was its essential element. In his report to the Church Congress in 1896, he said that the principal of the Incarnation was denied unless the Christian spirit could be allowed to concern itself with everything that interests and touches human life. He thought that *Catholicism* should be defined as the religious term for *brotherhood*.

The way had been cleared for the Conference on Politics, Economy, and Citizenship (COPEC) which met in Birmingham in 1924. It had been sponsored by a vigorous ecumenical group called the Collegium, and its chairman was William Temple, the Archbishop of York. Fifteen hundred delegates, many from foreign countries, met to give formal attention to the claim of Jesus Christ that he was the Way, the Truth and the Life. COPEC asserted the social relevance of the gospel, and brought cultural, economic and political problems under Christian scrutiny. It had lasting influence, though perhaps its more important contribution was to the new ecumenical movement.

Two decades later, at the beginning of World War II, the time seemed ripe for the recovery of the COPEC vision. According to William Temple, 'Few of the younger generation have heard of C.O.P.E.C.; fewer still know what was said there. They do not know of the great tradition of Christian social teaching associated with the names of Ludlow, Maurice, Kingsley, Westcott, Gore, Scott Holland.'[11] The intention at Malvern was also to pay more attention to the theological reference of ethical decisions, the divine intentions as visible in the natural order. 'Our concern,' said Temple, 'was to find a Christian remedy for specific evils rather than to examine the whole order of existing society in the light of the intrinsically right relation of the various functions of society—financial, productive, distributive, cultural, spiritual—to one another.'[12] All were to be addressed with one purpose—they way in which God's kingdom might best be served.

The difficulty at Malvern did not arise out of the contention that political questions are primarily theological, but rather with the question of which political formula would best serve the coming kingdom. All agreed on the goal of a more just order in society, but the fundamental means of establishing such an order was questionable. At Malvern there were conservatives such as T. S. Eliot, ardent socialists such as Sidney Dark, editor of the *Church Times,* and common ownership advocates such as Sir Richard Acland. The latter invented a new word: 'The private ownability of the major resources of our country is indeed the stumbling block which is making it harder for us to advance towards the Kingdom of God on earth.'[13]

Temple was able to get all the delegates to approve the *Malvern Manifesto* which came out of the conference, though there were some abstentions, and some, like T. S. Eliot and Alec Vidler, repudiated it later. Temple used what he called his 'parlour trick', which was really the use of 'middle axioms' first used by J. H. Oldham in 1937. Oldham had defined them as compromises 'between purely general statements of the ethical demands of the gospel and the decisions that have to be made in concrete situations [. . .] They are not binding for all time, but are provisional definitions [. . .]'[14] Temple changed Acland's private ownership 'is indeed the stumbling block' to 'may be such a stumbling block'. He had found the uneasy middle ground between the concrete decision which would offend some well-meaning Christians, and Thomas Aquinas' primary natural law: that good must be sought for and evil avoided. After Malvern the Church could still retreat into its normal enclave, wasting its energy on such topics as the wording of the Prayer Book, or the sex of its priesthood; but after Malvern, it could not do so gracefully. It could forget the deep Anglican tradition of a firm biblical faith which expressed itself in historical concern. And Temple's conclusion after Malvern seems more than ever decisive:

> The Church must announce Christian principals and point out where the existing social order at any time is in conflict with them. It must then pass on to Christian citizens, acting in their civic capacity, the task of reshaping the existing order in closer conformity to the principles.[15]

In the United States, Christian Socialism had no such charismatic leader as William Temple, and it confronted a more resolute opposition. But here also there were brave priests willing to pay the price for challenging an entrenched capitalism. In the late nineteenth century, at New York City's Grace Church, Henry Codman Potter set out to serve as many as possible of his parishioners' needs, whether they be physical, social, intellectual or, more familiarly, spiritual. There were others: George C. Hodges at Calvary Church, Pittsburgh (later Dean of Episcopal Theological School), Philo W. Sprague, William D. P. Bliss, Frederic Dan Huntington, Henry S. Nash, William Scarlett, and several others whose names are recorded in the Book of Life. Reinhold Niebuhr said that his interest in the relevance of theology to industrial injustice was given its early impetus by the teaching and example of the Bishop of Michigan, Charles D. Williams. Nevertheless the main impetus of the Social Gospel movement in America came from such non-Episcopalians as Washington Gladden and Walter Rauschenbusch.

The social movement in the Church has of course been subject to criticism by persons profiting from established privilege, but also from some who used more sophisticated epistemological grounds. D. N. Munby called attention to the socialists' lack of detailed consideration for concrete reality, which he called 'unrepentant Platonism'. Perhaps the religious mind has always been tempted to supply a priori resolutions to complex socioeconomic questions. 'The Christian prophetic witness has failed,' according to Munby, 'because it has been misinformed, cocksure, and too ready to assume that theological correctitude was a sufficient substitute for theoretical knowledge.'[16] The clue may be the Church's penchant for do-goodism, a reliance on a supposed omnipotence of mind not challenged by actual conditions of everyday life. When someone said to Charles Kingsley that there were no such things as water babies, he replied, 'How do you know that? Have you been there to see? And if you have been there to see, and had seen none, that would not prove that there were none.'[17]

During the 1960s a new development in Anglican moral thought caught the attention of the Western world: situation ethics. Some of its initial advocates were Anglicans. It was a modernized version of the Caroline insistence on holy living, though it claimed more ancient roots, a recovery of biblical patterns. Like the recommendation of love, the new morality was methodological rather than substantive, and thus incorporated by design a vagueness of outline which proved costly. Taking a cue from philosophical Existentialists, the situationists claimed that the tradition of Christian morality through most of Christian history had been gravely distorted by an unwarranted legalism. Each situation was said to be unique, and the agent had for reference only one unchangeable law, the law of love.

Through critics and also supporters of the new method sometimes spoke of themselves as innovative and even radical, the movement relied heavily on such traditional Anglican themes as holy living and the *via media*. 'The thing to note', said Joseph Fletcher, 'is that situation ethics is in the middle, between moral law and ethical extemporism.'[18] Though the point was missed by some outraged conservatives, the new method was intended to turn away from both authoritative legalism on the one hand, and antinomian freedom on the other, so preserving the tried wisdom of 'nothing too much'.

In England the new ethicsts were led by a bishop, John A. T. Robinson, a New Testament scholar who seemed most at home in the *Sitz im Leben* of the contemporary world. His popular *Honest to God* (1963) was determined not to conceal from God the truth about modernity. Ironically this implied an abandonment of a 'supernaturalist' way of thinking. In the new Reformation for which the Bishop played the Anglican Luther, doctrine was not to play the role which it played in the sixteenth century, but was rather to yield the dominating role to practice. The reason given is that times have changed, and most 'doctrinal questions today, in contrast with the previous Reformation, present themselves in the first instance as moral questions'.[19] Behind the drive for social relevance was the concern for the intelligibility of the gospel to the modern world.

Another strong British voice supporting the new Reformation in the 1960s came from Douglas Rhymes. Like Robinson, he was an eager immanentist. For him, prayer, which might seem at first to involve speaking to a God who is 'out there', turns out to be nothing of the sort. Prayer is really 'the inChristness which lights up all our actions in daily living from within'. Rhymes plays the Anglican Brother Lawrence, conversing with God, not on his knees, but absorbed in kitchen work, amidst the clatter of pots and pans. 'If you say to me, "But this is not prayer, this is Christian living," I shall reply, "There is no difference." What makes it prayer is that it is Christian living *consciously thought out and consciously motivated for Christ's sake.*'[20]

In the United States a professor at Episcopal Divinity School, Joseph Fletcher, was the early prophet of situation ethics. He thought of himself as in truth traditional, and was surprised at the hostility which greeted the new method. Was it not obviously biblical? St Paul had 'replaced the precepts of Torah with the living principle of *agape*—*agape* being good will at work in partnership with reason'.[21] There was of course no capitulation to traditional dogma. 'I believe', he wrote, 'that the only sin of which we can meaningfully speak is personal sin, not original sin.' And again, 'I see no viability in any objective theory of the atonement.'[22] Similar views about the Church's 'excess baggage' of inapplicable doctrine were expressed in the turbulent 1960s by other situationalists such as Norman Pittenger and James Pike.

Situation or contextual ethics did not have a long life of prominence in Anglican history, but there can be little question that it has left lasting marks. Mainline Anglicanism responded gladly to the reminder that one does not accept something as true simply because some authority has declared it to be so. Ideals must be tested in the crucible of living. Valuable insights were offered on the New Testament theme of Christian freedom under the tutelage only of love. But there were also some elements which would give pause even to Anglicans who were not always tutiorists. There was in the method a tendency towards autonomy, a message little needed in an undisciplined modern world. And there seemed also something smug about paying only polite attention to the moral guidelines of the past, and no attention at all to deontological factors, nor to the effect of future consequences as a cost for such radical freedom. If one were to identify a flaw, it probably would be an error precisely opposite to that which spelled the doom of Christian Socialism. The socialists were armed with an admirable ideal, but they took little cognizance of the texture of the concrete world in which their fragile ideal would be invited to live. The Existentialists seemed exquisitely aware of life structures, but were cavalier about the doctrinal principles which they proposed to enflesh in society.

III

In the coming century, moral clarity and firmness could play a more decisive role in the puzzling business of attempting Christian living in a secular age. But if they do so, they will seek out and cherish their classical strength, and seek out and try to eliminate the strain of weakness which has crippled the enterprise in the past. Its strength has certainly been its tradition of confronting the historical present rather than enunciating dogmatic formulas from the past. Its weakness has probably been its failure to establish the historical Christian code which limits the freedom of initiating a decision regarding the historic present. Both strength and weakness point to the need of turning from Christian Ethics, with its utilitarian stress on ideal possibilities, and embracing instead Moral Theology, which stresses the concrete decision of the present moment, but also tries to bring into corre-lation Christian principle and specific problem. Our hope seems to lie in just such a traditional contemporaneity.

It might be said that casuistry has fallen into disrepute, though not with the fervour of Pascal's strictures against Jesuitry. It has been called overly subtle, disingenuous, or even intellectually dishonest, threatening the role of divine grace. The standard criticism of Catholic moral theology is that it has caused a disastrous separation of ascetics and spirituality. But it has kept alive the need of relating *theoria* to *praxis*, and has proved hospitable to the present fashion of practical theology. Casuistry must be recognized as a dangerous and yet promising instrument for achieving Christian living, not only serving as guide for the private conscience but also for establishing larger social strategies.

In any case, Moral Theology has been the classical Anglican posture regarding Christian conduct. The Caroline moralists, led by Joseph Hall, Jeremy Taylor and Herbert Sanderson, specialized in case studies, perhaps reacting to the legal prohibition against clerical direction. But the British mind has always had a bias toward empiricism, as the American mind has leaned toward pragmatism. The formal plea for Anglican casuistry begins with James Skinner, *Synopsis of Mind and Ascetical Theology* (1870). F. D. Maurice revived the old title of his course at Cambridge, 'Casuistry and Moral Theology'. It was the subtitle of his book on *The Concience: Lectures on Casuistry* (third edition, 1883). Maurice was especially interested in a concrete application for Christian piety, but he was vague about the Chris-tian principles which were being applied. The leading Oxford Anglican casuist was the Bishop of Oxford, Kenneth E. Kirk. He called one of his important books, *Conscience and its Problems: An Introduction to Casuistry* (1927). The normally judicious bishop was so eager a casuist that he found himself arguing that, under certain circumstances, a wife who had been unfaithful to her husband would be justified in saying nothing about it (p. 210). It might be that her short-tempered husband, hearing of her infidelity, could murder her lover, and it might also be that the Bishop of Oxford had forgotten what Holy Scripture says about adul-tery.

What is called for is a new, more defensible casuistry. The Christian rule, the *synderesis*, demands the ablest professional study. Identifying authorities calls for a highly sophisticated orchestration: Holy Scripture, tradition, canon and secular law, natural law, the magisterium of the Church. Identify-ing the rule calls for fastidious reflection and study. This is not of course simply a mental exercise. *Conscientia*, the application of the rule, calls for a competent study of the situation in which the rules are to be applied, the weight of the support and opposition, and techniques of changing social power structure. It is at this point that lay specialists can be of invaluable aid to the professionally religious, who presumably would be more adept at identifying the relevant rule.

An example of a refined casuistry might demonstrate its superiority as a moral method to the guidance of a single virtue, such as love. An established biblical rule could be taken from the Decalogue: 'Thou shalt not kill' (Exod. 20.13). *Kill* is a verb with a wide reference, ranging from beheading a chicken to murdering an enemy. Understanding what the rule means requires study of its original intent as well as its reception by a reader today. It would help if a paradigmatic example could be agreed on. A drive-by shooting into a schoolyard filled with children would seem to have the elements intended to be prohibited by Holy Scripture. The so-called 'hard cases' might be brought under judgement by measuring each case with the standard of the paradigmatic example. Similarity with the model example would merit its rejection by the Christian conscience. Such a scrutiny would throw light on such 'hard cases' as abortion, capital punishment, euthanasia, war, or suicide.

It has often been observed that we are living in a new, secular society, in which the ultimate question no longer is how God's will may be satisfied. Though not dead, God has become obscure, allowing Rilke to cry, *'O du verlorener Gott! du unendliche Spur!* (O thou lost God! Thou infinite trace!)' We need to renew the search which Anglicans began two centuries ago, the search for the truth of ultimate being which includes the fullness of experience and the well-being of the whole created universe. The area of concern should include international crises such as war, as well as domestic crises such as poverty. There should be a free debate between churchgoing conservatives and the group which Harvey Cox called 'the New Breed'.[23] There should be room for the old breed, which confronted our various crisis with a social service motif, and the new breed, which would give prior place to political motifs seeking structural change.

Of course the Church which refuses to be passive, but busies itself by actually being the instrument by which the Word of God penetrates and transforms existence, runs a risk of losing itself in the world and becoming simply an agency of social reform.[24] But the alternate risk is more frightening: a Church which is comfortable with its role as a cultic enclave, self-righteous and anachronistic, an archaic, dogmatic company, rightly ignored by the world. The remedy for such oblivion is surely that commonplace transcendence which was seen by Anglicans from the beginning, and is now widely recognized. We must learn anew to take seriously and then to act upon the claims of our Lord over the total existence of his creatures astride our whirling planet.

BIBLIOGRAPHY
Elmen, P. (ed.), *The Anglican Moral Choice*. Morehouse-Barlow, Wilton CT, 1983.
Browning, D., *The Moral Content of Pastoral Care*. Westminster Press, Philadelphia, 1976.
Kirk, K., *Conscience and its Problems. An Introduction to Casuistry*. Longmans, Green and Co., London, 1927.
McAdoo, F. R., *The Structure of Caroline Moral Theology*. Longmans, Green and Co., London, 1949.
O'Donovan, O. M. T., *Resurrection and Moral Order: An Outline for Evangelical Ethics*. Inter-Varsity Press, Leicester, 1986.
Reckitt, M. B., *Maurice to Temple. A Century of the Social Movement in the Church of England*. Faber and Faber, London, 1947.
Sedgwick, T. F., *Sacramental Ethics: Paschal Identity and the Christian Life*. Fortress Press, Philadelphia, 1987.
Temple, W., *Christianity and Social Order*. Penguin Books, Harmondsworth, 1942.

NOTES
1 *The Works of* ... *Mr Richard Hooker*, ed. John Keble (OUP 1845), Vol. i, p. 125.
2 Paul Elmer More and Frank Leslie Cross (eds), *Anglicanism* (SPCK, London, 1962 [1935]), p. xxii.
3 More and Cross, *Anglicanism*, p. xxxii.
4 O. B. Robertson (ed.), *Love and Justice* Westminster Press, Philadelphia, 1977), p. 84.
5 'The True Way or Method of Attaining to Divine Knowledge', *Select Discourses* (London 1660), p. 9.
6 *The Liberty of Prophesying* in *The Whole Works of the Rt Rev. Jeremy Taylor*, ed. Charles P. Eden (London 1853), Vol. v, p. 409.
7 W. Shakespeare, *Troilus and Cressida*, I, iii, 114–15.
8 Joseph Butler, *Sermons* (Robert Carter & Bros., New York, 1858), p. 48.
9 Hooker, *Works*, V, ii, lxxii.
10 Reckitt, *Maurice Temple*, p. 19.
11 William Temple, *Malvern, 1941* (Longmans, Green & Co., London, 1941), p. 224.
12 Temple, *Malvern*, p. 220.
13 Temple, *Malvern*, p. 161.
14 W. A. Visser t'Hooft and J. H. Oldham, *The Church and Its Function in Society* (Willett, Clarke, Chicago, 1937), pp. 193ff.
15 William Temple, *Christianity and Social Order* (Penguin, Harmondsworth, 1942), p. 35.
16 D. L. Munby, 'The Importance of Technical Competence' in D. M. Paton (ed.), *Essays in Anglican Self-Criticism* (SCM, London, 1958), p. 49.
17 Charles Kingsley, *The Water Babies*, ed. J. H. Stickney (Boston 1916), p. 63.
18 Joseph Fletcher, *Situation Ethics. The New Morality* (Westminster Press, Philadelphia, 1966), p. 26. I have been helped in my discussion of the New Morality by Edwin G. Wappler, 'Four Anglican Situationists and their Tradition', unpublished Ph D dissertation, Duke University, 1972.
19 J. A. T. Robinson, *The New Reformation* (Westminster Press, Philadelphia, 1965), p. 38.
20 Douglas Rhymes, *Prayer in the Secular City* (Lutterworth Press 1967), pp. 48–9.
21 Fletcher, *Situation Ethics*, p. 69.
22 Joseph Fletcher and Thomas Wassmer, *Hello Lovers! An Introduction to Situation Ethics* (Corpus Books, Washington, 1970), pp. 108, 125.

23 Harvey G. Cox, 'The "New Breed" in American Churches: Sources of Social Action in American Religion' in W. G. McLoughlin and R. N. Bellah (eds), *Religion in America* (Beacon Press, Boston, 1968), pp. 368–83.
24 See Langdon Gilkey, *How the Church Can Minister to the World Without Losing Itself* (Harper & Row, New York, 1964).

3 Anglican Pastoral Tradition

O. C. EDWARDS JR

INTRODUCTION

In pastoral tradition, as in most matters, the way to discover what is distinctively Anglican is to study the Book of Common Prayer. In the present case the most relevant document in the Ordinal (see pp. 155–62). Thus the Exhortation for the ordering of Priests (1662) we read:

> We exhort you, in the name of our Lord Jesus Christ, that you have in remembrance, into how high a Dignity and to how weighty an Officer and Charge you are called: that is to say, to be Messengers, Watchmen, and Stewards of the Lord; to teach, and to premonish, to feed and provide for the Lord's family; to seek for Christ's sheep that are dispersed abroad, and for his children who are in the midst of this naughty world, that they may be saved through Christ for ever.

This duty is further specified in the next paragraph:

> See that ye never cease your labour, your care, and diligence, until ye have done all that lieth in you, according to your bounden duty, to bring all such as are or shall be committed to your charge, unto that agreement in the faith and knowledge of God, and to that ripeness and perfectness of age in Christ, that there be no place left among you, either for error in religion, or for viciousness of life.

The means for performing this ministry are 'doctrine and exhortation taken out of the holy Scriptures' and 'a life agreeable to the same'. The ordination formula itself describes 'the Office and Work of a Priest in the Church of God' as being that of 'a faithful Dispenser of the Word of God, and of his holy Sacraments'. Not all of the pastoral duties of parochial clergy are mentioned in the rite for ordaining priests, however. Some are in the form for making deacons. The duties of the diaconate, though, are not lost when the deacon becomes a priest because the priest continues to be a deacon. Thus it takes two rites to list all of the pastoral duties of parochial clergy.

It appertainth to the Office of a Deacon, in the Church where he shall be appointed to serve, to assist the Priest in Divine Service, especially when he ministereth the holy Communion, and to help him in the distribution thereof; and to read holy Scriptures and Homilies in the Church; and to instruct the youth in the Catechism; in the absence of the Priest to baptize infants; and to preach, if he be admitted thereto by the Bishop. And furthermore, it is his Office, where provision is so made, to search for the sick, poor, and impotent people of the Parish, to intimate their estates, names, and places where they dwell, unto the Curate, that by his exhortation they must be relieved by the alms of the parishioners, or others.

There are many ways in which the duties of clergy listed in the ordinals can be specified in more detail. In another context I have tried to enumerate the duties of contemporary clergy of the American Episcopal Church. They included: officiating at liturgy, preaching, evangelization and missionary activity, catechesis and Christian education, parochial administration, spiritual direction, Christian social action, moral guidance, the incorporation of new members into the parochial community, theological explanation, leadership in stewardship, spiritual renewal in the parish, enablement of the ministry of the laity, ministry to the sick and bereaved and to families in crisis, pastoral counselling, denominational duties, ecumenical involvements, and community activities.[1] A more compact list, however has been drawn up by Anthony Russell in *The Clerical Profession:* leader of public worship (Sunday worship), leader of public worship (surplice duties), preacher, celebrant of the sacraments, pastor, catechist, clerk, officer of law and order, almoner, teacher, officer of health and politician.[2] While Russell is more concerned with the sociological description of the duties of a profession than with a theological listing of the responsibilities of clergy, his categories offer a convenient way to analyse the activities that have made up the Anglican tradition of pastoral care.

VARIABLES WITHIN THE TRADITION

Before an analysis of the Anglican pastoral tradition can be undertaken, there are certain variables that need to be noted. The first of these is to recognize that the ministry of clergy in the Church of England has always been that of the representatives of an established Church. This has not always been true of the work of clerics in other national branches of the worldwide Anglican Communion. In the Episcopal Church in the USA, for instance, parish clergy function in many ways as chaplains to the people who have voluntarily associated themselves with the local community which practices the Christian faith as this Communion has received it. Their conception of their responsibility is very different from that which Church of England priests have for certainly the spiritual and to an extent the physical welfare of all who live within the bounds of their parishes. And, of course, Anglican clergy in some parts of the world exercise their ministry in cultures far more radically pluralistic than even that of the United States. In Nigeria, for instance, the spectrum of Christian Churches includes the indigenous churches, making it far more variegate than American Christianity. But Christendom also exists there in a marked pluralism of religions which includes an Islamic community which is still probably larger than the Christian one, and devotee of African traditional religion with various degrees of commitment. This means that the whole style of ministry exercised in the classic pattern of Anglican ministry has been greatly adapted to cultures with a wide diversity of religious situations.

A second factor which must be taken into consideration when attempting to understand the differences between the way that pastoral care was administered in the Church of England until recently and the way that it is administered in other Anglican Churches is the system of patronage. At the time of the Reformation the parishes of the English Church had provisions to supply income to their clergy. Very often the right to decide which priests would be appointed to a parish and receive that income was in the hands of a religious order. Thus when the monasteries were dissolved and the Crown transferred their assets to favoured persons, this right of presentation (as it was called) was one of the assets transferred. Thus lay people such as the local squire received the right of naming who would serve in those parishes. Other parishes were in, or came into, the presentation of the Crown or the local bishop.

Presentation, however, was to the benefice or 'living', which is to say, to the right to receive the income rather than to the duty to perform the services of a priest. This meant that both conceptually and practically the compensation became separated from the work. Two results of this distinction between receipt of pay and performance of duties were absenteeism and pluralism. The person presented to a benefice would often hire a curate to do his work for him and thus feel free to live outside the parish. And it was as easy to live outside several parishes as it was to live away from one, so some clergy came to be preferred to several livings, to receive the income of all of them, and to serve in none of them. The extent of these practices and their effect on the life of the Church of England has been discussed at length elsewhere and need not be considered here. It is enough to remember that a significant factor in the way that the Anglican tradition of pastoral care developed was influenced by this less-than-ideal system for the deployment and payment of clergy.[3]

It should be noted here that the present essay is more concerned with ideals than with practice, with how the pastoral duties of Anglican clergy have been conceived than how they have been discharged. Yet such a discussion must take place in a context of awareness that the ideals have seldom been totally realized and that the mere statement of a standard does not mean that it has always been executed punctiliously.

This observation is relevant to the third factor that should be remembered in distinguishing between the English and other manifestations of the Anglican pastoral tradition: the historico-sociological development discussed in the work by Anthony Russell already cited. His study is an 'attempt to show that the clergyman's roles, as it is currently structured, resulted from processes of change in English society in the late eighteenth and nineteenth century, and in particular, that of professionalization' p. 305). This is to say that in the nineteenth century, clergy took the professions that were emerging at the time as their 'model and reference group'. Prior to that, the role of the clergy was that of 'an occupational appendage of gentry status' (p. 6). While his argument as presented is reductionistic in seeing exclusively social reasons for the evolution of the Anglican pastoral tradition and in failing to note that theological, spiritual and benevolent motives were also involved, Russell does perform a service in reminding us that such social factors are always involved in the life of the Church and that it never has any existence that is exclusively religious. But the social factors which shaped the development of the English pastoral tradition are different from those which shaped the development of other branches of the Anglican Communion.

One other aspect of the historical context in which the Anglican pastoral tradition developed must be noticed before we begin an examination of the individual elements of that tradition. This aspect has influenced the other countries into which Anglicanism has spread as well as England. It is the shift from a predominantly rural setting for parochial ministry to an urban setting for much of it that occurred in the nineteenth century. Such a change of the social conditions under which ministry was practiced required adjustments of the tradition of pastoral care to fit the new situation.

The final contextual aspect which must be borne in mind is the internationalization of that pastoral tradition as the Communion has spread around the world. Attention has been called to this element incidentally in the discussion of the first variable, establishment, but more changes were involved in the transplanting of Anglicanism into other lands than just that of moving from establishment to disestablishment. The issue becomes one of discovering what, to change the metaphor, was lost or at least altered in the translation.

THE ESSENTIAL CHARACTERISTIC

With all of that out of the way, it is now possible to identify what is really most distinctive about the Anglican pastoral tradition. It is that its ministry is given its form by the Book of Common Prayer (see pp. 131–42). As Roger Lloyd said:

> The common property of all Churches of the Anglican Communion is the Book of Common Prayer; and that more than anything else binds them together. It is therefore in the Prayer Book that we find the heart of Anglicanism laid bare, and the Prayer Book is the manual of the art of ministering as Anglicans have understood it down the ages and practise it today.[4]

By that is meant far more than that the Prayer Book furnishes us with the forms of our corporate worship, although this 'praying from a book' is one of the most distinctive things about the worship of Anglicans. The point instead is that beyond supplying our liturgy, the Prayer Book makes provision for the total life of the Church and therefore furnishes the shape of ministry in all of its aspects. After presenting the basic regular liturgy of Morning and Evening Prayer, the Litany and the Holy Communion, the 1662 English book, for instance, moves into cradle-to-grave care of Christians at all of the 'wonder moments' of life: baptism at birth, catechesis for the young, confirmation for those ready to take on adult responsibility, matrimony for those who will start families of their own, visitation for those who are ill, and burial for the dead. These rites are followed by the Thanksgiving for women after childbirth (out of order and as an afterthought), the Commination against sinners, the Psalms, a form of prayer to be used at sea, the Ordinal by which persons are provided to engage in ordained ministry, a form for celebrating the anniversary of the sovereign's accession, and the Articles which state the Church's position on issues of theological controversy.

Against this list must be placed the list of forms of pastoral care borrowed from Russell: leader of public worship (Sunday worship), leader of public worship (surplice duties), preacher, celebrant of sacraments, pastor, catechist, clerk, officer of law and order, almoner, teacher, officer of health and politician. There can be no doubt that the first six of these duties are expected by the Prayer Book. Some of the remaining six are almost as easy to account for. Duties as a clerk grow out of the necessity to record baptisms, weddings and burials, for instance. The mandate for the almoner could come from the form for making deacons if the duty were not already so explicit in the New Testament as to be a basic Christian activity. The sympathy shown for the sick in the provision for spiritual care is naturally expressed in their physical care as well; then, too, the Lord's example is ready at hand. One of the reasons that Evangelical clergy, at any rate, kept schools was to teach poor children how to read the Bible; thus this teaching could be considered an extension of catechesis.[5] The Accession Service, accompanied (until Queen Victoria intervened) by the inclusion in the calendar of commemorations for King Charles the Martyr, Charles II's birth and accession, and the 'Papist's Conspiracy', shows some involvement of the Church with the civil government and thus with law and order. Only the activity of the politician seems not to have a degree of authorization from the Prayer Book table of contents, although many clergy today feel that their ordination vows to care for the suffering impel them into political activity. The total vision of pastoral care in the Anglican Communion is thus shaped by the Book of Common Prayer.

There is probably no other communion that has its life so shaped by one book. Of course many Evangelical groups claim to be based on the Bible in this thoroughgoing way, but the Bible is so large and diverse that all Churches claim to be based on it and none can document its claims in an exclusive way. Among the non-liturgical Churches and even some liturgical ones the amount of space needed to print forms of worship can be small enough for the end-matter of hymnals to be adequate. Roman Catholics, on the other hand, need a number of books for their liturgical materials. And for Anglicans the Prayer Book comprehends much more than the rites of corporate worship; it shapes every aspect of our life as a Christian community. The situation was caught very well by C. S. Lewis when he quoted form *Tristram Shandy* in order to specify what his own faith added to *Mere Christianity;* 'About [my own beliefs], as I said before, there is no secret. To quote Uncle Toby: "They are written in the Common Prayer Book."'[6]

MINISTRY IN THE PRAYER BOOK WORLD VIEW

The Ordinal, as quoted in the opening paragraph of this essay, implies an understanding of the universe and the place of human beings in it. God created the world so that human beings can enter into relationship with him and enjoy the blessings that he has prepared for them both here and hereafter. The purpose of human life is to enter that relationship; the only real good consists in doing so and the final evil consists in failing to do so. Clergy exist in order to assist people in entering and remaining within that relationship. Thus they are of vital importance to the whole human enterprise. It is this which makes their office and charge 'weighty'. As messengers they are to inform men and women of this state of affairs, of what God has prepared for them through Christ. They are watchmen to protect those who have heard and accepted this message. And they are stewards to care for that which belongs to God. They must teach, premonish, feed and provide for their flocks. Implied in this are two assumptions: (1) that clergy have responsibility for the people of their cures both individually and corporately, and (2) that their task is by no means easy nor its results assured. The world is 'naughty', but eternal salvation is at stake.

Thus the duty of clergy is to bring the people for whom they are responsible to mature Christian faith so that no place is left in the entire community 'either for error in religion or for viciousness of life'. The technique for discharging this ministry has not changed since the time of Chaucer's Poor Parson:

> Christes lore and his apostles twelve
> He taughte, but first he folwed it himselve.

Or, as the Ordinal puts it: 'doctrine and exhortation taken out of the holy Scriptures' and 'a life agreeable to the same'.

This world-view is presupposed by the Prayer Book as a whole. Its understanding of the purpose of human life, for instance, comes out in the Catechism's specification of what is prayed for in the Lord's Prayer:

> I desire my Lord God our heavenly Father, who is the giver of all goodness, to send his grace unto me, and to all people; that we may worship him, serve him, and obey him, as we ought to do. And I pray unto God that he will send us all things that be needful both for our souls and bodies; and that he will be merciful unto us, and forgive us our sins; and that it will please him to save and defend us in all dangers ghostly and bodily; and that he will keep us from all sin and wickedness, and from our ghostly enemy, and from everlasting death. And this I trust he will do of his mercy and goodness, through our Lord Jesus Christ. And therefore I say, Amen, So be it.

Clergy are those appointed by the Church and enabled by God to be channels by which all those prayers are granted. That is the Prayer Book view of ministry.

Some of the implications of that view have been spelled out in the essay of Roger Lloyd to which attention has already been called. He finds 'five principles drawn from the Book of Common Prayer which govern the whole range of an Anglican ministry and give to it its particular colour among the several ministries of the Church Universal':

> 1. The refusal to accept any barrier between what is done in church and the life lived outside it.

384

2. As its very title, Book of *Common* Prayer, suggests, it is strongly and radically communal.

3. [. . .] It envisions the whole congregation as the unit of pastoral and evangelistic work of the parish.

4. At the same time the prayer Book is very personal in the sense that it rates the responsibility of the worshipper very high.

5. [. . .] The pastoral responsibility of priest and people is unlimited. They have a charge before God for every soul in the parish, not merely those who worship in the parish church.[7]

The essentials of this view have been maintained in the revisions the Prayer Book has recently undergone, although what Marion Hatchett has said of the ordinal of the American book of 1979 is essentially true for the English *Alternative Service Book* of 1980: 'The old form emphasized the teaching, preaching, and pastoral roles. The revised form incorporates emphasis upon the liturgical and sacramental roles of the priest, and the role of the priest in the councils of the church.'[8] He also points out that the exhortation of the older forms was essentially a translation of Bucer's treatise *De ordinatione legitima* and that it views the laity as 'a passive and helpless body'. The latter interpretation is obviously one with which Lloyd would have disagreed, at least as far as the understanding of ministry in the Prayer Book as a whole is concerned. In any case, it can still be maintained that the Anglican under-standing of the nature of ministry comes from the Book of Common Prayer and the shape of that ministry is given by the entire Prayer Book.

Another point to be made about this Prayer Book understanding of ministry is that it contains no assumption that anything new was being established at the time of the Reformation, as the preface to the Ordinal indicates. This sense of continuity was so strong that when the American Episcopal Church drew up a Course of Ecclesiastical Studies in 1804 to be pursued by those who were 'reading for orders', along with Gilbert Burnet's *Discourse of the Pastoral Care* and Thomas Wilson's *Parochialia* was included St John Chrysostom's *Christian Priesthood* as a textbook in pastoral care.[9] How widely this sense was shared may be seen by the fact Wilson said in his cover letter for his handbook that his clergy already had two excellent books on the subject of pastoral care, Gregory the Great's *Pastoral Care* and George Herbert's *Country Parson*.

Finally, it can be seen that in this Anglican world view taken from the Prayer Book the understanding of the purpose of pastoral care is that the priest should be involved in the nourishing of a community of the faithful in which individuals in the community as a whole can grow in holiness and enjoy the salvation Christ made available here and hereafter. That is to say, the object of Anglican pastoral ministry is the sanctification of the people of God. Thus it is very appropriate that this chapter on pastoral care should appear in the section of this book devoted to Sanctification.

THE COMPONENTS OF PASTORAL CARE

In the short space that remains brief notice will be given to each of the areas of pastoral care listed by Russell.

LEADER OF PUBLIC WORSHIP (SUNDAY DUTIES)
This is obviously the most characteristic work of the priest. Isaac Walton has made the world familiar with the practice of George Herbert in the public recitation of the daily offices in a way that 'brought most of his Parishioners, and many Gentlemen in the Neighbourhood, constantly to make a part of his congregation twice a day' and so affected workers in the field that they 'would let their Plow rest when Mr. *Herberts Saint-Bell* rung to Prayers, that they might also offer their devotion to God with him'.[10] Not all clergy have been able to maintain so high a standard, but, as Russell has shown, even during the worst part of the eighteenth century Sunday duty was usually performed, even if it was done by curates who came to be called 'gallopers' from their practice of living in a market town and hurrying around to conduct services in several surrounding churches every Sunday.[11]

Most churches expected Morning Prayer, Litany, Antecommunion, and sermon in the morning and Evening Prayer with or without a sermon in the afternoon. As indicated in the quotation from Hatchett above, the tendency to place more emphasis on the sacraments since the Oxford Movement has caused the Eucharist to become the most common Sunday service. In 1887 the Lower House of Convocation in the province of Canterbury drew up an extension of the Catechism which, although never approved by the Upper House, appeared in the Second Office of Instruction in the American Prayer Book of 1928. In it the people say: 'My bounden duty is to follow Christ, to worship God every Sunday in his Church; and to work and pray and give for the spread of his kingdom.' With the duty of attending Sunday worship so important for laity, it is small wonder that leading Sunday worship should be so prominent among the duties of the clergy.

LEADER OF PUBLIC WORSHIP (SURPLICE DUTIES)
By this category Russell referred to *rites de passage* conducted by clergy, such as Churching of Women, Marriages and Burials (p. 76). Baptism is not included in this category because he treats it under 'Celebrant of the Sacraments', and preparation for confirmation is discussed as one of the priest's duties as a catechist. This involves a certain amount of question-

begging about the number of sacraments, but in any such analysis arbitrary lines have to be drawn. Surplice duties, then, are the actions for which some American clergy are accustomed to say that they receive 'stole fees'. Russell tells us that even resident clergy in the eighteenth century liked to crowd as many of these as possible in between the morning and afternoon services on Sunday. These services are related to the 'cradle-to-grave care of Christians at all of the "wonder moments" of life' referred to above. Thus they reflect the creational, incarnational, sacramental view of life that is so characteristic of Anglicanism and its view of ministry.

PREACHER
The Prayer Book world-view described above involves a very prepositional understanding of knowledge, including theological knowledge. It assumes that there are 'truths' that one must know, believe, and act on—truths that are revealed in the Bible—in order to have a fulfilled life both here and hereafter. Preaching is regarded as one of the most effective ways of communicating these truths and thus has usually been regarded as a duty closely linked and on a par with conducting public worship. Thus George Herbert was able to say; 'The Country Parson preacheth constantly, the pulpit is his joy and throne' (The Country Parson, ch. vii). In twelve pages of his Discourse Of the Pastoral Care (ch. ix), Gilbert Burnet is able to offer advice about preaching from which many clergy today could still profit, even though he so much admired the sermons of Archbishop Tillotson in whom Archbishop Briloth finds concentrated the moralism that he considers the bane of Anglican preaching.[12] By the time that John Henry Blunt produced his Directorium Pastorale in 1864, however, the partisan spirit that grew out of the Evangelical and Catholic awakenings had begun to be reflected in attitudes toward preaching. Thus the author of the Eighty-Ninth Tract could be quoted as saying: 'We would not be thought entirely to depreciate preaching as a means of doing good. It may be necessary in a weak and languishing state; but it is an instrument which Scripture, to say the least, has never recommended.' And an Evangelical spokesman can be cited to the opposite effect.[13] Even though John Henry Newman is generally conceded to have been one of the greatest preachers that the Church of England has produced, it must be admitted that clergy in general have placed less emphasis on their preaching duty since the Oxford Movement. May this soon change!

CELEBRANT OF THE SACRAMENTS
Enough has probably seen said about this role in the discussion of the leadership of public worship with the exception that the impression could have been left that infrequent celebrations before the middle of the

387

nineteenth century indicated a low esteem of the sacraments. To see how misleading such an impression is, one need only to look at what Herbert says about the Eucharist:

> The Country Parson being to administer the Sacraments, is at a stand with himself, how or what behaviour to assume for so holy things. Especially at Communion times he is in a great confusion, as being not only to receive God, but to break and administer Him. Neither finds any issue in this, but to throw himself down at the throne of grace, saying, Lord, thou knowest what thou didst when thou appointedst it to be done thus; therefore do thou fulfill what thou didst appoint : for thou art not only the feast, but the way to it. (ch. xxii)[14]

CATECHIST

The propositional view of religious knowledge mentioned above has led to great emphasis on teaching the Catechism (see pp. 165–75). In this as so many things, Herbert set a high example, both requiring all his parishioners to be present for catechesis and taking great effort to see that words were not only memorized but also understood (chap. xxi). Even he did not go so far as Richard Baxter, whose *The Reformed Pastor* was written after he had left the Church of England but in an effort to secure ecumenical co-operation in a programme of examining every family in the parish on its knowledge of the Christian faith by a system of hourly appointments.[15] The sad state from which confirmation began to emerge under the Catholic revival and the improvement of transportation has been well reported by Peter C. Hammond in *The Parson and the Victorian Church*.[16]

PASTOR

One of the ways in which the difference between Anglican attitudes toward pastoral care and that of Protestants can be seen is the way that historians of the subject have limited pastoral care to ministry to individuals, especially in times of crisis. For John T. McNeill, pastoral care is 'the sustaining and curative treatment of persons in those matters that reach beyond the requirements of animal life'.[17] For Clebsch and Jackle it is 'helping acts, done by representative Christian persons, directed toward the healing, sustaining, guiding, and reconciling of troubled persons whose troubles arise in the context of ultimate meanings and concerns.'[18] In his history of pastoral care in America, E. Brooks Hollifield confines his attention to the 'private interchange (of clergy) with parishioners seeking counsel'.[19] This is to say that all of the clerical duties treated above would not have been regarded as pastoral care by the definitions used by these histories.

While Anglicanism thus has a far wider understanding of what pastoral care is, this sort of concern for the spiritual, psychological and physical welfare of individuals has never been lacking in our tradition. It has usually been discussed in the textbooks under the rubric of 'Visitation'. Such visitation was often with the express purposes of ascertaining the spiritual health of the family visited and exhorting its members to higher achievements.

A continuing aspect of this in every period since the Reformation has been a concern with the sort of spiritual direction that has been so much in vogue generally in recent years. The concern for sanctification has never been absent. A special aspect of this concern has been the practice of private confession. Explicit provision for it has been made in every Prayer Book and while, from time to time, there have been Anglicans who have opposed its use, the permission of the Church for it has always been clear. There has been argument over whether the absolution pronounced was precatory, declaratory or authoritative, and theologians have differed over whether the provision was for ordinary or exceptional use, but the possibility of private confession was always there.[20] Indeed, McNeill says: 'No other great communion has given greater attention to the cure of souls, either in theory or in practice' (p. 246).

In the United States especially, the rise of modern psychology has permitted a reduction of pastoral care to pastoral counselling, as is indicated in the subtitle to Hollifield's history of American pastoral care: 'from salvation to self-realization'. So characteristic of American culture has this psychologism become that Philip Rieff has suggested that psychology has replaced theology as America's 'unitary system of common belief'.[21] At times it has been hard to distinguish between pastoral counselling and psychotherapy, and the competence of many clergy to do such counselling has been a cause of concern. This is not to deny the immense contribution of psychological insight to pastoral care. In any case, Episcopal clergy have not been so inclined as some others to this reductionist approach to pastoral care.[22]

CLERK, OFFICER OF LAW AND ORDER, ALMONER, TEACHER, OFFICER OF HEALTH AND POLITICIAN

Russell astutely distinguished between the 'charter' elements of the clerical role that were authorized by the Ordinal and the ancillary elements that had accrued to the role in traditional society (p. 38). Most of the elements listed in the title for this paragraph are not charter elements and can bear omission from this discussion.[23] Only two points need to be made here. The first is to recall what has been said above about the work of an almoner is a charter element of the duties of a deacon and is intrinsic to any concept of Christian ministry, lay or ordained. The second is to point out how clergy have continued to organize schools wherever the Anglican Communion has spread. Often in Third World countries church schools are the best available. Also the popularity of parochial schools in the American Episcopal Church suggest that teaching may be more than a traditional accretion to Anglican ministry: it may belong to the nature of the work.

CONCLUSION

Clebsch and Jaekle have said:

> Among the helping professions upon which modern society so heavily relies—medicine, social work, teaching, law, psychiatry, and so forth—the ministry or priesthood is the least specialized, though by no means the least helpful. It is not too much to say that the parish parson [...] is the last remaining genus of the general-practitioner-at-helping-people. (p. xv)

They say this from their limited perspective of restricting pastoral care to ministry to individuals in crisis. When one considers how much more inclusive the understanding of pastoral care is that the Anglican tradition has maintained, one can realize what a glorious calling it envisions. While the ways in which this ministry will be exercised in the future are beyond our present knowledge,[24] we see what an impoverishment of the Church it would be for this tradition of pastoral care in its basic shape to vanish. Its contribution to the sanctification of the people of God would be sorely missed.

BIBLIOGRAPHY
Allan, P., *The Fire and the Clay: The priest in today's church*. SPCK, London, 1993.
Addison, W., *The English Country Parson*. J. M. Dent 1947.
Anon., *The Clergyman's Instructor or a Collection of Tracts on the Ministerial Duties*, 6th edn. OUP 1855.
Clebsch, W. A., and Jackle, C. R., *Pastoral Care in Historical Perspective*. Harper & Row, New York, 1964.
Edwards, O. C. Jr, 'Preaching and Pastoral Care' in J. E. Griffis (ed.), *Anglican Theology and Pastoral Care*. Morehouse-Barlow, 1985.
Hammond, P. C., *The Parson and the Victorian Church*. Hodder & Soughton, Wilton CT, London, 1977.
Herbert, George, *The Country Parson (1652), The Temple*, ed. John N. Wall Jr. Paulist Press, 1981.
Lloyd, R., *The Book of Common Prayer and Pastoral Ministry*. SPCK 1949; and *The Anglican Digest* Transfiguration, Michaelmas, and Advent 1984 and Lent 1985.
McNeill, J. T., *A History of the Cure of Souls*. Harper & Row, New York, 1951.
Melinsky, H., *The Shape of the Ministry*. Canterbury Press, Norwich 1992.
Ramses, M., *The Christian Priest Today*. SPCK, London, 1985.
Russell, A., *The Clerical Profession*. SPCK, London, 1980.

NOTES

1 O. C. Edwards, 'Preaching and Pastoral Care,' pp. 133–58.

2 Russell, *The Clerical Profession.*

3 Russell, *The Clerical Profession*, pp. 28–41. Cf. Rosemary O'Day, *The English Clergy: The Emergence and Consolidation of a Profession 1558–1642* (Leicester University Press 1979); and Hammond, *The Parson and the Victorian Parish.* Roughly half of Gilbert Burnet's *A Discourse of the Pastoral Care* (1692) is directed against the evils of this system.

4 Roger Lloyd, 'The Book of Common Prayer and Pastoral Ministry', *The Anglican Digest* (Transfiguration 1984), p. 25.

5 Russell, *The Clerical Profession* p. 188.

6 C. S. Lewis, *Mere Christianity* (Macmillan, London 1943, 1945, 1953; edn cited is that of Macmillan Paperbacks of 1960), p. 8

7 Lloyd, 'The Book of Common Prayer', *The Anglican Digest* (Michaelmas 1984), pp. 20–23. This article, written in 1949, is remarkably prophetic in its view of what today would be called 'mutual' or 'total' ministry.

8 Marion J. Hatchett, *Commentary on the American Prayer Book* (Seabury, New York, 1980), p. 521.

9 Powell Mills Dawley, *The Story of the General Theological Seminary* (Oxford 1969), p. 22.

10 Izaac Walton, *Life of George Herbert* (1670; reprinted Oxford 1973), p. 302.

11 Russell, *The Clerical Profession*, pp. 54, 55. Some clergy did resort to stratagems to make this conducting of services unnecessary as William Addison shows in the chapter on 'Sporting Parsons' and elsewhere in his delightful book on *The English Country Parson* (J. M. Dent 1947).

12 Yngve Brilioth, *A Brief History of Preaching* (Fortress, Philadelphia, 1965), p. 179.

13 John Henry Blunt, *Directorium Pastorale: Principles and Practice of Pastoral Work in the Church of England* (London 1864), p. 99.

14 Cf. Jeremy Taylor, *Rules and Advices to the Clergy of Down and Connor* (1661; edition used that published in *The Clergyman's Instructor, or A Collection of Tracts on Ministerial Duties* (Oxford 1855), xxix.

15 Edition used was that of Hugh Martin (John Knox, Atlanta GA, 1956).

16 Peter Hammond, *The Parson*, pp. 169–75.

17 McNeill, *A History of the Cure of Souls*, p. vii.

18 Clebsch and Jaekle, *Pastoral Care in a Historical Perspective*, p. 4.

19 E. Brooks Hollifield, *A History of Pastoral Care in America: From Salvation to Self-Realization* (Abingdon, Nashville TN, 1983), p. 12.

20 For an excellent concise summary of the history of private confession in Anglicanism see McNeill, *A History of the Cure of Souls*, pp. 218–46.

21 Philip Rieff, *The Triumph of the Therapeutic: Uses of Faith after Freud* (Harper & Row, New York, 1966).

22 For an extensive consideration of this whole issue, see my article, 'Preaching and Pastoral Care'.

23 Something of the range of possible duties of clergy can be ascertained by looking at the Table of Contents in John Ellerton (ed.), *A Manual of Parochial Work for the Use of Younger Clergy,* (SPCK, London, 1892).

24 For an interesting but by no means exhaustive consideration of the possibilities, see Russell, *The Clerical Profession*, pp. 289–306.

4 Church–State Relations

PETER HINCHLIFF

It has never been easy to relate the ideals of the Christian life to political structures. There are, perhaps, two reasons in particular why this is the case.[1] In the first place, moral principles which may seem clear and obvious in relation to the private life of individuals can be complex and difficult to apply to the corporate life of a society. Secondly, since politics is about the exercise of power, the considerations which govern political action are often directly opposed to those qualities which the New Testament regards as the marks of the Christian life—gentleness, humility, patience and love.

Moreover, in the nineteen centuries since the New Testament was written, there have been significant changes in both the position of Christians in relation to government and in at least the theoretical structure of those governments under which most Christians live. Romans 13.1–3 and 1 Peter 2.13, urging simple obedience to government as a 'given', were written at a time when no Christian participated in the exercise of power or had any say in how government was constituted or in what policies it chose to pursue. But by the fourth century, Christians had begun to be both makers of policy and exercisers of power. For such people, simple obedience to a government of which they were an important constituent was no longer a sufficient moral principle. In more modern times, in democracies where Christians are voters sharing in the creation of government and yet at the same time subjects of those governments, the position is even more confusing. When one has a responsibility (however indirect) for the very existence of government, one cannot simply take refuge in the belief that God has put it there and that one's moral duty is exhausted by obedience.

Shifts in the nature of government have been particularly important in the history of the religious establishment in England—from which, in a sense, all Anglican thinking about Church and state has begun. The Church of England is often said to be a part of the British constitution. But Britain has no written constitution: what is called 'the British constitution' is simply a name for the way in which British government happens to work at any given time. Some of it is enshrined in statute. Some of it is merely convention. None of it is entrenched or protected in any special way.

Moreover, the English religious establishment of the sixteenth century was built upon the relationship between Church and state that had already existed in the Middle Ages. Some aspects of that relationship—tithes, endowments, educational institutions—continued virtually unchanged. Others were modified or adapted, in varying degrees, to take account of the new situation. Others again were drastically altered by law to express a particular theory of the relationship between Church and state. Therefore the establishment was not a single relationship, neatly embodied in a fundamental constitutional document, but a complex of relationships often regulated by nothing more definite than tradition and custom.

The theory of the establishment under Henry VIII was, however, clear and simple. It is set out in the preamble to the Act in Restraint of Appeals (1533) which saw the realm as consisting of two parts, a temporalty—secular and lay persons—and a spirituality—ecclesiastical and clerical persons. At the head of each of these two parts, and uniting them, was the Crown. The Act was not about the Church of England as 'the nation at prayer'; that would hardly have been a point worth making in the sixteenth century. It asserted the king's control over a single administrative structure of government and abolished the independent jurisdiction of the medieval Church. For all that the Act seems to describe a symmetry of temporalty and spirituality , it was an Act of *Parliament* and therefore contrary to its own theory. The imbalance was made even more clear by Henry's forcing the clergy to submit publicly to his authority. That submission, too, was embodied in an Act of Parliament which forbade the clergy to meet in convocation or to enact canons without royal approval. What the legislature of the spirituality might do, in other words, was limited by the legislature of the temporalty.

The Henrician establishment did not assume that a new Church was being created. Henry himself was theologically conservative, though his system could probably not have been put into effect without the assistance of the many who desired reform for theological and religious reasons. But no one really thought in terms of introducing a new Church: the Church was being reformed. For the most part it continued to use the old forms of service and to act administratively as it had always done. Even when, in the reign of Henry's young son Edward VI, an English Prayer Book was introduced and a more Protestant theological stance adopted, a great deal remained unaltered.

The settlement of religion achieved by Elizabeth I strove for a balance which would bring as many people as possible within the English Church. For Elizabeth inherited a sharply polarized situation. Her predecessor and half-sister, Mary Tudor, had restored the jurisdiction of the papacy in England and had driven Protestants into exile. Elizabeth was, therefore, faced with papalists in power and returning exiles anxious to obtain control. She was no more willing than any other ruler of her time to tolerate a variety of religious denominations within her kingdom. The only alternative was a Church which would encompass as wide a range of opinion as possible.

At the same time, her solution was more radical than her father's. It was founded upon two Acts of Parliament which date from very early in her reign. The Supremacy Act revived a string of statutes from the reign of Henry VIII and Edward VI, forbidding appeals and the payment of taxes to Rome; and re-enacting the submission of the clergy, the method of appointing bishops, and the Crown's jurisdiction over the Church. And it also imposed upon all who held office in Church or state an oath recognizing the supremacy. While Elizabeth took the title of supreme governor, rather than revive Henry's title of supreme head of the Church, this was a change in name rather than in fact. There was no diminution of the powers that her father had claimed. Moreover, by incorporating some of the legislation of Edward VI's reign, the Act authorized a more Protestant theological position than Henry had ever been willing to tolerate. Even more important, a schedule of provisos annexed to the Act defined heresy as what could be proved to be contrary to Scripture or the decisions of the first four general councils of the early Church or had been declared to be heresy by Act of Parliament with the assent of convocation. It was a new and radical departure for Parliament to claim the right to determine what constituted heresy. (see pp. 6–15 and pp. 203–8).

The other Act which brought in the Settlement was the Act of Uniformity legalizing a new Prayer Book. It was substantially the second Prayer Book of Edward's reign, but softened and modified at many points so as to make it less obviously Protestant.

It would seem that Elizabeth had not originally intended to move so quickly in the matter of the Prayer Book, but the House of Commons contained a substantial number of members sympathetic to the viewpoint of the returning Protestant exiles. They attempted to turn the Act of Supremacy into an Act of uniformity also, by annexing Edward's Prayer Book to it. Since this would have alienated the more conservative, the Queen was virtually forced to devise her own alternative. Convocation had no hand in framing the Prayer Book, and it was authorized simply by Act of Parliament.

The new Settlement did not prevent continuing unrest and division. The Puritan party continued to resist it throughout Elizabeth's reign and radical opinion began to oppose the very principals of royal supremacy and a national Church. From 1566 onwards, having been defeated in convocation on the matter of the use of vestments, dissidents worked through Parliament, introducing into the Commons a whole series of bills which would have radically altered the Settlement. Elizabeth opposed them by arguing that it was intolerable for Parliament to intervene herself and the convocations, a device which—however inconsistent with her earlier actions—did something to restore the theoretical equality of the partnership between Church and state.

Puritans continued to demand further reform, and had to be kept under tight control. Recusants—Roman Catholics who refused to accept the Settlement—remained outside it and were persecuted for doing so. But there remained only one legally recognized Church in England and, as a new generation grew up, the established Church came to be regarded no longer as a compromise but as a thing in itself.

Towards the very end of Elizabeth's reign, Richard Hooker embodied this new view of the Church of England in his famous *Laws of Ecclesiastical Polity* which maintained that the Church and the state were two inseparable aspects of the one commonwealth. He argued, against the Puritans, that it was 'a gross error to think that regal power ought to serve for the good of the body, and not of the soul; for men's temporal peace and not for the eternal safety; as if God had ordained kings for no other end and purpose but only to fat men like hogs [...]'.[2] But he was not merely concerned to defend on pragmatic grounds what happened to be there. He may, indeed, have intended to transform as much as to defend the Settlement. He stood for a genuinely Christian society where the monarch's authority, limited by law and custom, would reflect the spirituality of the people as a whole. It is really from Hooker that the idea derives that the Church of England should be the nation at prayer (see pp. 254–7).

Puritans became less and less willing, however, to remain quiescent in the latter part of Elizabeth's reign and in that of her successor, James I. In the Civil War with Charles I, the parliamentary party embraced the Puritan cause and by 1643 had begun to make the Church of England presbyterian. It is, again, important to realize that Parliament did not think of itself as substituting a Presbyterian denomination for an Anglican one. It was, rather, taking the reform of the national Church further than before. It abolished episcopacy in 1643 and in the same year created the Westminster Assembly.

This body was set up to advise Parliament on a new form of government for the Church. Its clerical members had, of course, been ordained and licensed in the Church of England but were Puritan by conviction. The few convinced episcopalians who had been nominated to it boycotted the meetings. There was a vigorous and vociferous minority of Independents, who believed that each local congregation had the right to determine its own affairs, its own doctrine and ministry. But the majority was committed to Calvinist doctrine and to a presbyterian pattern of church government.

Before Parliament and the Assembly could really contrive to make England prestyterian, however, differences developed between the House of Commons and its army. Eventually the triumph of the army under Cromwell led to the victory of Independency over presbyterianism. The Puritans were divided and were used to exercising private judgement in matters of religion. It was too late to insist that the essence of a presbyterian polity was a strict system of discipline designed to maintain uniformity in doctrine and polity.

Cromwell's Commonwealth is a period of particular importance in the history of relations between Church and state. All real power was in the hands of the army, but it did not wish to govern directly. The constitution-making which went on at intervals throughout the Commonwealth was a series of attempts to achieve an effective but compliant parliamentary government, none of which succeeded. Similarly the religious Settlement of the Protectorate was an attempt to establish Independency, itself almost a contradiction in terms. Independency stood for the sovereignty of the local congregation.

Toleration under the Commonwealth was far from complete. Episcopalians and papists were never tolerated—though a blind eye was sometimes turned on their activities. Unitarians and some of the more radical sectarians were also, from time to time, excluded. But the basic design of Cromwell's Settlement was to take the unfinished presbyterian pattern of the Westminster Assembly and to broaden it. A commission selected ministers, whose views were generally Independent, Presbyterian or Baptist and who became part of the new establishment. Another commission weeded out of the Church those unsuitable clergymen who survived from Charles I's time. But in addition to the comprehensive and variegated establishment that resulted, considerable toleration was allowed to others, so that a wide range of denominations flourished for the first time and acquired an organization and a form.

The effect of this policy was to ensure that there existed in England a variety of Christian denominations, too large and too firmly rooted to be eradicated again when the monarchy was restored. The return of Charles II in 1661 was expected to produce a new Settlement of the Church on Elizabethan lines and, indeed, a new Act of Uniformity and a new Prayer Book in 1662 were the outcome of that expectation. Once again there was a body of returning exiles, but this time they were High Churchmen and monarchists who wanted an 'Anglican' and episcopal establishment headed by the king. The presbyterian Puritans within the Commonwealth establishment hoped that any new Settlement would include themselves but not the more radical secaries or Independents. The king himself, by the Declaration of Breda issued before his return, had promised 'liberty to tender consciences'. He made a further declaration after his return, which appeared to promise a Settlement acceptable to presbyterians, and at the so-called Savoy Conference an attempt was made to devise such a compromise. It failed and the new Settlement was, in fact, imposed by a Parliament which was full of enthusiasm for the restoration of the old order. But it was equally determined to prevent ultimate control of the Church from passing out of lay hands. Nevertheless the convocations revised the Prayer Book and episcopacy was made an essential part of the Church of England. The so-called Clarendon Code imposed limitations on those who were not members of the established Church. Holders of municipal office were required to receive the sacrament in the Church of England by the Corporation Act. An act of 1664 made attendance at services other than those of the Church illegal. The Five Mile Act made it an offence for dissenting clergymen to come within that distance of any town or city. But nonconformity did not disappear. For the first time in English history there were large denominations outside the established Church, which could not be destroyed however much they might be made subject to a variety of penalties.

The king, perhaps because of his sympathies with Roman Catholicism, continued to try and make things easier for those who would not conform. In 1663 he issued a Declaration of Indulgence which would have relieved dissenters from some of their disabilities. Opposition in Parliament rendered the attempt fruitless. In 1668 he again attempted to bring Presbyterians into Settlement and again Parliament refused to agree. In 1670 he tried once more to use the royal prerogative to dispense with some of Parliament's laws. The Church of England would have been protected in its privileges but all penal religious laws against those who did not conform were to be suspended. Parliament refused to recognize the king's Declaration of Indulgence and in 1673 passed the Test Act, which required all office-holders under the Crown to take the oath of supremacy, forswear transubstantiation and receive the sacrament in the Church of England.

Perhaps the most radical changes in the establishment took place in the eighteenth and nineteenth centuries because the unwritten constitution of England was itself changing drastically in the period. Constitutional monarchy, parliamentary government and cabinet responsibility all began to develop. Through the Crown continued for a time to have some freedom in their choice, ministers gradually became primarily responsible to Parliament. A cabinet had also begun to emerge, though it was a long time before collective cabinet responsibility was established. Even when Victoria became Queen, the political control of the House of Commons over the government had not yet excluded the Crown entirely. But real power was passing into the hands of the Commons and an embryonic party system began to take shape. Those who could control the majority of seats in the Commons were those entitled to govern. The royal prerogative came to be exercised less by the sovereign acting on his or her own responsibility: it became an accepted convention that the Crown must act on the advice of its ministers.

At the beginning of the nineteenth century the establishment was taken for granted. It was regarded as the symbol of England's character as a

Christian country. Politicians no less than churchmen regularly described the Church as 'part of the constitution'. That seems to imply a clearly defined, solid structure, enshrined in the nation's legal system, whose place and function could be easily understood. Yet in 1888, when Edward King, Bishop of Lincoln, was accused of illegal ritualist practices, the Archbishop of Canterbury had to revive a court which had only functioned once since the Reformation, which really owed its existence to the fact that in the Middle Ages the archbishops had also been papal legates, and which was of doubtful legality.[3] No one new whether it really existed. No one knew whether one could appeal from its decision to the Privy Council—the final court in ecclesiastical causes—because no one knew what its authority was.

It was apparent, then, by the end of the century that the establishment was a confused and incomprehensible thing. What had happened was that the constitution had changed, partly because of legislation such as that which gave political rights to Roman Catholics or repealed the Test and Corporation Acts in 1828 and 1829, and partly because of changes in the conventions of government. Yet the significance of the changes had not really been perceived. Moreover, the Church of England was no longer the Church of the nation. It was one Christian body among many. It had certain privileges, but it was also tied to an uncertain and fluid legal system which was changing all the time.

Not surprisingly there was much opposition to the establishment. This came, initially, not only from dissenters who claimed that, in matters such as tithe, church rate and education, the privileges of the establishment were unjust; it also came from those who thought that the whole idea of a religious establishment was archaic and inefficient. *The Extraordinary Black Book* of 1831, for instance, argued that the ecclesiastical revenues of England and Ireland were greater than those of the rest of Europe put together, and were so inefficiently used that the ministry for which they paid catered for only about one-third of the population. The answer to charges of inefficiency was largely provided by Charles James Blomfield, Bishop of London 1828–56, and the Ecclesiastical Commission.[4] The Commission limited the size and incomes of cathedral chapters, evened out episcopal revenues and made provision for the creation of additional bishoprics. It also established a central fund from which the stipends of poorer clergy could be argumented. It thus created the first element of central administrative machinery in the Church of England.

It is not surprising, either, that the nineteenth century was also a period of much discussion of the theory of establishment. The Oxford Movement, because of its clear understanding of the nature of the Church, influenced much of this thinking. It is sometimes pointed out that Tractarians appeared at first to be defenders of the *status quo* and only became critical of the state connection subsequently. In fact, as is clearly shown by John Keble's famous 'National Apostasy' sermon of 1833, it was an ideal relationship with the state which they were concerned to defend. Indeed much Tractarian writing was concerned with attempting to identify the 'ideal Church'.

Other significant works on the idea of establishment from the period are Samuel Taylor Coleridge's *The Constitution of Church and State* of 1820, Thomas Arnold's *Principles of Church Reform* of 1833 and W. E. Gladstone's *The State in its Relations with the Church* of 1838.

Coleridge's position is important because he recognized that religion and politics each had its own proper concern, different from that of the other. These concerns he called 'ideas', necessary regulative conceptions, which may never have been fully actualized in historical event. The state is concerned with citizenship : the Church with nothing less than the promotion of the harmonious development of those qualities and faculties which characterize humanity. But the 'church' in Coleridge's writing was neither the transcendent theological concept of the ideal Church nor the actual Church of England. It was the sum of all the nation's spiritual resources, including art, science, literature and scholarship. Though his thought influenced the ideas of many, including Newman, it did not, therefore, have much direct bearing upon the development of the actual establishment.

Thomas Arnold's *Principles of Church Reform* was much more concerned with practicalities. His fundamental premise was that it is impossible to demonstrate, beyond all question, the truth of the theological propositions. Doctrinal disagreement was therefore inevitable. From this he drew the conclusion that the national Church should be as inclusive as possible, not based on dogmatic formularies nor uniformity of practice. Such a Church, he believed, would once more be an established Church which was truly national.

Gladstone's book, written while he was still a relatively young man, a junior politician and a Tory, was very much a defence of the establishment more or less in the form in which it existed. Where his work differed from the conventional defence of establishment was that it did not ask why it might be proper for the Church to accept the state connection. Instead it asked why it was proper for a state to establish a Church. There were two aspects to his answer to that question. On the one hand he insisted that politics and government must have a moral dimension, that there were things that the state must do because they were right, irrespective of whether they were expedient. Therefore it was important that the state should proclaim—by establishing a Church—that it accepted particular beliefs. Secondly, and as a necessary consequence of this, he believed that the state had a duty to defend the *true* Church.

This theory became increasingly difficult for Gladstone to maintain. By 1840, when he wrote a second work on the topic, *Church Principles Considered in their Results*, he had begun to insist far more firmly upon the divine authority of the Church. But as a Liberal, dependent, in part, on the electoral support of Free Churchmen, it was politically difficult to insist that the Church of England was the only true Church; and when he found himself responsible for the government of Ireland, where hardly any of the people were Anglican and where it was almost impossible to justify the establishment of an Anglican Church, it became morally difficult. Moreover, as England became more and more secular, Tractarian ideas of what constituted the truth became more difficult to maintain in society and uphold by law.

Some of the difficulties and anomalies of establishment were revealed most clearly in the colonies. Since the Elizabethan Act of Supremacy asserted the Crown's jurisdiction over all ecclesiastical persons and causes in all its territories, the establishment was automatically extended to the colonial empire at it came into existence. This was something different from the idea that the state should subsidize religion, for subsidies were often given to all denominations in a colony, including Roman Catholics. Indeed, as a dispute over clergy reserves in Canada showed, financial support from government was sometimes an alternative to establishment.[5]

Establishment existed in the colonies as part of the prerogative power of the English Crown. It was a personal nexus between the supreme governor of the English Church and his or her Anglican subjects. This is shown by the fact that the Church of Scotland was not similarly assumed to be established in British colonies: the Scottish religious Settlement did not recognize any ecclesiastical authority vested in the sovereign. Further evidence that establishment was as much concerned with persons as with territory is that in some colonies there could be more than one established Church. In the Cape Colony, which was captured from the Dutch during the Napoleonic wars, the Dutch Reformed Church was guaranteed all the privileges it had formerly possessed without this in any way affecting the assumption that the Church of England was 'by law established' in the colony.

By an Order in Council of the reign of Charles I, the Bishop of London had exercised episcopal jurisdiction in the colonies, but this could obviously not be very effective. Bishops were consecrated for India and various colonies and, indeed, after some difficulties, for America also. Bishops in British territory needed letters patent from the Crown to make their consecration lawful, just as English bishops did, and it was assumed that their legal status was exactly that of bishops in the Church of England. But when colonial bishops reached their dioceses and needed to issue regulations, adapt English customs to local conditions or put diocesan finances on a proper footing, they found that some kind of synodical body was desirable. Several colonial bishops tried to summon such bodies, but Henry VIII's Act for the submission of the clergy had specifically forbidden the holding of any synod without royal permission. And it would have been absurd for the Crown to create ecclesiastical legislatures exercising an authority independent of the local civil power.

The alternative might have been to persuade the British Parliament to pass an Act permitting the Church in the colonies to hold synods. In 1853 the Archbishop of Canterbury actually introduced a bill into the Lords which would have allowed this, but it was rejected by the Commons. Indeed, some of the colonial bishops were uneasy about the proposal because it seemed to them that it would have subjected the Church too firmly to the state. It proved, in fact, extremely difficult to transfer the delicate concept of establishment to the colonies. And if English colonists saw nothing incongruous in the existence of a 'Church of English' in Africa, North America, Asia or Australasia, not all colonies were colonies of settlement. Much British territory overseas was ruled rather than settled by the English. In black Africa it must have seemed odd to be required to subscribe to articles of religion which included the proposition that 'the Bishop of Rome hath no jurisdiction in this realm of England'. Yet the anomaly was not thought disturbing.

The 'Eton College' judgement of 1857 first raised doubts about the existence of the establishment in those colonies where the Crown, by creating an independent colonial legislature, had limited its own prerogative powers. By this time some parts of the Church overseas had already begun to experiment with synodical government and there followed a period in which even those overseas dioceses which had no reasons of their own for desiring it were virtually compelled to devise a form of organization and discipline for themselves. The first Lambeth Conference drew up a prototype constitution, which was one of three models upon which the emerging Anglican provinces based their own forms of government. The others were the Archbishop's draft bill of 1853 and the constitution of the American Church.

The question of establishment had come to a crisis in a series of legal cases related to the Church in Southern Africa[6] and arising directly or indirectly from an attempt to prosecute Bishop Colenso for heresy on account of his critical approach to the Old Testament. He was tried before a court set up by the Bishop of Cape Town who claimed the jurisdiction of a Metropolitan. Colenso was found guilty, excommunicated and removed from office.

But the Bishop of Cape Town, Robert Gray, had already run into problems over summoning a synod and, like other colonial bishops, had been given conflicting advice by the law officers of the Crown. Bishops in Canada and New Zealand had, however, been told by these same officers that there was no legal bar to their holding synods if they wished. Gray had therefore summoned a synod in Cape Town in 1856. One of his clergymen refused to attend, and the judicial committee of the Privy Council held that the Bishop and his synod could only exercise authority over those who voluntarily accepted it. It also held that the letters patent issued to the Bishop were invalid because the Cape had acquired its own legislature. The Bishop had no authority over the recalcitrant clergyman.

By the time this judgement was delivered, Gray had tried Colenso for heresy. He believed that his authority in this matter was unassailable because Colenso had taken an oath of canonical obedience to him, thus apparently voluntarily accepting his jurisdiction. But the judicial committee held that, because the letters patent were invalid, Colenso ought not to have taken the oath at all. It was also held that although neither bishop possessed valid letters patent, both had been created ecclesiastical persons by the Crown and only the Crown could unmake them.

Colenso then sued the Colonial Bishoprick's Fund for the payment of his stripend, which the Fund had been withholding since this excommunication. The master of the Rolls, Lord Romilly, heard the case and declared that ecclesiastical persons, created by the Crown, were corporations capable of holding property in the name of the Church of England and that, in that sense, the Church of England as by law established could exist in the colonies in spite of all the privy Council judgements since the Eton College case.

The South African Church, smarting under the tangle created by the courts, adopted a constitution which rejected the jurisdiction of the Privy Council. But in 1882 there was a further case from South Africa in which it was held that any Church which did not recognize that jurisdiction could not be the same as the Church of England.

Nevertheless it was clear that most parts of the Anglican Communion could not be legally established Churches and they adopted constitutions which based their corporate life upon a voluntary compact rather than upon establishment. The Church in the United States was not, in case, established—nor was the Episcopal Church in Scotland. All these Anglican provinces were in a relationship with the state exactly like that of the Free Churches in England. The secular courts—if appealed to—would regard their disciplinary procedures as being analogous to those of, for instance, the Jockey Club.

The number of such provinces has grown continually. The Church of Ireland was disestablished in 1871 and the Church in Wales in 1920. Since World War II the vast majority of the overseas territories ruled by the British

Crown have become independent. There is now no part of the Anglican Communion outside England where the Church is certainly established.

Even in England itself the establishment continued to be modified. In 1903 a Representative Church Council was brought into being as part of a process, initiated a decade earlier, to reform the convocations and give laymen some part in their proceedings. In 1917 William Temple launched the Life and Liberty Movement to press for some degree of ecclesiastical autonomy, and in 1919 an enabling Act was passed by Parliament which created the Church Assembly. It had become plain that Parliament simply had not the time to give to ecclesiastical business. But the cumbersome character of this new machinery was very clearly revealed by the revision of the Prayer Book in the 1920s. Each stage in the lengthy business had to be considered by both convocations and the Church Assembly, and it was still subject to parliamentary approval. The proposed book, having been approved by the convocations and the Assembly, was sent to Parliament in 1927. It was passed by the Lords but rejected by the Commons. It was revised again in certain respects by the ecclesiastical legislatures and again rejected, provoking from the bishops of the province of Canterbury what amounted to a declaration that they would treat the revised Prayer Book as though it had been authorized.

Disestablishment was for a time a hotly debated issue; and the relationship between Church and state has, in one way or another, been under discussion during most of this century. There have been three commissions to report on possible modifications of it. The General Synod of the Church of England, with a substructure of diocesan and deanery synods, replaced the Church Assembly in 1969. The system of canon law has been revised, the Alternative Services Book authorized and a new method of appointing bishops put into effect. The Synod has established a right to autonomy in matters of doctrine and worship. But it is, in the last resort, a creation of Parliament; and there have been several occasions since it came into existence when it has seemed that there might be confrontation between the two bodies. Crises have been evaded rather than resolved, and there has been no final trial of strength like the controversy over the 1928 Prayer Book (see pp. 45–6).

In the 1990s, however, because of the divorce of the Prince and Princess of Wales and the Prince's expressed wish to be 'defender of faith' rather than 'Defender of the Faith', there has been a growing tendency to doubt whether the establishment can continue in its present form. Both the Labour Party and the Liberal Democrats are committed to a reform of the House of Lords and it seems unlikely that bishops of the Church of England could continue to sit in it, as of right, if that were to be done. But an attempt in 1994 to persuade the General Synod to take a modest first step in removing the appointment of bishops from the crown failed to receive the necessary majority. It seems likely that disestablishment will continue to come by means of a gradual process initiated by the Crown or by Parliament or by other secular developments rather than because the Church of England has requested it.

Historically, establishment has tended to make the Church, at least in some respects, the servant of the state. It might be thought, then, that the Anglican tradition would have been one which was conservative politically and disinclined to challenge the government. This has not, however, been the universal pattern. In some parts of the Anglican Communion, as in South Africa or Uganda, there has been outright condemnation of the policies and actions of governments. And even in England itself in recent years the Church has been prepared to criticize the political party in power. In part this is, no doubt, a consequence pf a growing awareness of the points made at the very beginning of this chapter about the nature of power and about the new patterns of relationship between government and Christian citizens. But it may also be that living with a tradition of establishment has given Anglicans a sense that religion is something which belongs in the public domain. A long history of being involved with government has meant that the Church has been consulted about a variety of issues in which political action is to be taken. It has become accustomed to expressing a view on such matters. It has had to realize that political actions have a theological, religious and moral dimension.

BIBLIOGRAPHY

Bogdanor, V., *The Monarchy and the Constitution*. OUP 1995.
Buchanan, Colin, *Cut the Connection: Disestablishment and the Church of England*. DLT, London, 1994.
Butler, Perry, *Gladstone: Church, State and Tractarianism*. OUP 1982.
Clarke, W. K. Lowther, *Constitutional Church Government in the Dominions Beyond the Seas and in other parts of the Anglican Communion*. SPCK, London, 1924.
Coulson, John, *Newman and the Common Tradition: A Study in the Language of Church and Society*. OUP 1970.
Dibdin, L., *Establishment in England*. Macmillan, London, 1932.
Elton, G. R., *The Tudor Constitution*. CUP 1960.
Figgis, J. N., *Churches in the Modern State*. Longmans Green 1913.
Hinchliff, Peter, *The One-Sided Reciprocity: A Study of the Modification of the Establishment*. DLT, London, 1966.
Jackson, M. J. and Rogers, J. (eds), *Thomas Arnold: Principles of Church Reform*. SPCK, London, 1962.
Jordan, W. K., *The Development of Religious Toleration in England*, 4 vols. George Allen & Unwin 1932.
Kemp, E. W., *Counsel and Consent : Aspects of the Government of the Church as Exemplified in the History of the English Provincial Synods*. SPCK, London, 1961.
MacCulloch, D., *Thomas Cranmer: A life*. New Haven and Yale, 1996.

McGrade, A. S., 'Introduction to Book VIII, *Of The Laws of Ecclesiastical Polity*', in W. Speed Hill (ed.), *The Folger Library Edition of the Works of Richard Hooker*, Vol. 6. Harvard University Press 1988.

Moses, J., *A Broad and Living Way: Church and State a Continuing Establishment*. Canterbury Press, Norwich, 1995.

Moyser, George (ed.), *Church and Politics Today: The Role of the Church of England in Contemporary Politics*. T. & T. Clark, Edinburgh, 1985.

Nicholls, David, *Church and State in Britain since 1820*. Routledge Kegan Paul, London, 1967.

O'Donovan, O. M. T., *The Desire of the Nations: Rediscovering the Roots of Political Theology*. CUP, 1996.

Rhodes, P. E., *Law and Modernization in the Church of England*, 3 vols. University of Notre Dame Press, South Beud IN, 1990.

Thompson, K. A., *Bureaucracy and Church Reform*. OUP 1970.

Warren, M. A. C. *The Functions of a National Church*. Epworth Press 1964.

NOTES

1 For an extended discussion of the problems see P. Hinchliff, *Holiness and Politics* (DLT, London, 1982).

2 *Of the Laws of Ecclesiastical Polity* VIII. iii. 2. (Book VIII was published in 1651.)

3 For an account of the trial see A. C. Benson, *Life of Edward White Benson*, 2 vols. (Macmillan 1899, 1900), Vol. ii, pp. 319ff.

4 For an account of the commission see G. F. A. Best, *Temporal Pillars* (CUP 1964).

5 P. Burroughs, 'Lord Howick and Colonial Church Establishment', *Journal of Ecclesiastical History* XXV (1974), pp. 381-405.

6 P. Hinchliff, *The Anglican Church in South Africa* (DLT, London, 1963), pp. 48–53, 87–103, 111–29.

5 Sociology of Anglicanism

W. S. F. PICKERING,

revised by PETER BRIERLEY and GRACE DAVIE

QUESTIONS OF IDENTITY AND ORGANIZATION

The Anglican Communion, or Anglicanism viewed as a global phenomenon, is not, as the name implies, a unified Church or even a number of Churches controlled by an authoritative body. It is made up of a loose federation of Churches which are in communion with the see of Canterbury. The constituent Churches acknowledge the fact that they have emerged from the Church of England, and the Christian doctrines and practices they exemplify approximate closely to those of that Church.[1]

The Anglican Communion as a social entity may be said to have come into existence in 1867 when C. T. Longley, Archbishop of Canterbury, called together Anglican bishops throughout the world. This gathering, the first of what were to be called Lambeth Conferences, was initially requested by bishops of Canada. Subsequent conferences have continued

405

to be held approximately once every decade. They have been called by the Archbishop of Canterbury, who is very much the figurehead—the *primus inter pares* —and who has a bestowed status which makes him the point of union of the Anglican Communion. In 1968 machinery was set in motion to create an Anglican Consultative Council which would act as a more permanent advisory body.

The Lambeth Conferences are an official recognition of the growth of various branches of the Anglican Church throughout the world. Such conferences, however, have always been consultative. They do not legislate, make binding decisions, or exert power in the name of a universal Anglican Church. Strictly speaking there is no such body as the Anglican Church, unless the name is taken to mean, as it usually is, the Church of England and nothing more. Different Anglican Churches exist in various parts of the world. They are autonomous and are not subject to direct controls from other Churches, even the Church of England.

Quite apart from its relative smallness in following, the social organization of the Anglican Communion is far removed from that of the Roman Catholic Church, which is an international, autonomous Church with a centralized legislative base in Rome, and where power is ultimately exercised by one man, the pope.

The Anglican Communion has spread around the world through the agency of several factors. Initially, the Church of England extended itself beyond the British Isles to other parts of the globe through immigrants who, as members of the Church, settled in such places as North America, the West Indies, Australia and so on. Outposts continued to grow as fresh waves of immigrants came from the mother country (see pp. 39–41). The second agency has been in the form of missionary societies, once again originating in England, which have been active in converting non-Christians within the boundaries of the fast-expanding British Empire, particularly in the nineteenth century (see pp. 484–9). The most obvious examples are India, Africa and parts of the Far East. The work of missionaries from the Church of England was in some cases supplemented by that of missionary societies formed in immigrant Churches. For example, the Church in Japan, the Nippon Sei Ko Kwai, was founded through missionaries from Anglican Churches in the United States and Canada, as well as the Church of England. Today, among the Churches of the Anglican Communion, that in England remains by far the most missionary-inclined, as one in six of those working in missions abroad are from it. Another factor in the growth of various Churches has been the natural increase of families who are members of them. Again, growth has come through conversions without any missionary agency, sometimes through mixed marriages involving Christians of other denominations, as well as those of other religions. It is said of the Episcopal Church in the United States that half its members are transfers from other Churches and from none.

Either through problems arising from geographical distance or theological conviction (it is not clear which), the immigrant Churches during the nineteenth century, at a time when growth was most marked, were in some cases accorded a high degree of independence. In this respect, Anglicanism has veered towards a Protestant rather than a Roman Catholic ideal in supporting the concept of national Churches. Various Anglican Churches have been able to forge their own independence and develop particular paths of expression, while at the same time holding on to the overall doctrine and ethos of the Church of England. This has allowed for the possibility of indigenization, but at the same time let it be noted that many Churches did not in fact utilize such possibilities. Some of them developed a fixation on all things English and therefore tended to follow slavishly the ethos of the Church of England and the English nation (see p. 450). For example, the Anglican Church in Canada always prided itself on its ties with England; its original name, the Church of England in Canada, was not changed until as late as 1958, and that in the face of six years of opposition. In Australia similar changes were adopted even later, and the Church of England in Australia became known as the Anglican Church of Australia only in 1981. In Ontario the Church rejected the state interference which the Church of England experienced, but wanted to retain all else; it created its own synod in 1851. In New Zealand synodical government came in 1857. The dominance of the Raj meant that bonds with England were particularly close in India, not least in the concept of the Indian Ecclesiastical Establishment, which ministered only to the British population. The Church in India was particularly slow in appointing Indian bishops and in establishing synodical government. The latter came in 1930.

What happened in the United States really set the pattern for the possibility of indigenization and freedom from British control. As a result of the War of Independence (1733–76), it became politically expedient for those American citizens who were of the Anglican faith to form a group totally cut off from the Church of England. Further, it would seem that the church authorities in England were of the opinion that there was no theological reason why the affairs of Anglicans in the United States should be controlled directly by the archbishop of Canterbury and the British Parliament. Once the Anglican Church in the United States had obtained autonomy, a way was open for other Anglican Churches to follow suit. At least, there was no reason why they should not. Immigrants, as they developed new colonies, found themselves for religious purposes directly within the province of the Church of England. Only as a result of time and historical circumstances did they gradually sever their links with the mother Church.

Freedom given to member Churches has in certain instances meant that they have left the Anglican Communion altogether. This happened to the Anglican Church of India, Pakistan and Ceylon, when as a champion of church unity, the Church became at various stages part of the Church of South India (1947) and the Church of North India (1970). These might be called sanctioned losses, and mean that care has to be used in comparing statistics for certain years. A different case is where Anglicans have formed themselves into schismatic denominations or sects. There are two kinds. In those involving whites, it is estimated that over the past century or so 200,000 Anglicans have formed themselves into 16 schismatic bodies. Larger have been defections amongst non-whites, particularly in Africa, but also Asia, where, according to Barrett, 3.9 million members have created and become members of 850 schismatic groups.[2] Of course the Anglican Communion has also been weakened by transfers of individuals and small groups to other denominations, as well as a withdrawal into 'no religion' (see below).

Thus, the Anglican Communion as an autonomous federation of Churches has no authoritative power to determine doctrine, ritual and policy which is in any way binding on its members. Each Church is responsible to itself and governs itself in its own particular way according to a great variety of constitutions. The only factor which binds the Churches together is loyalty to a heritage which is bound up with the Church of England.

All Anglican Churches have accepted a Catholic concept of church order, namely, one based on the historic episcopacy (see pp. 333–47). The claim of apostolic succession means that the Church of England traces its ecclesiastical formation back to the early Church. Episcopalianism defined this way is what theologically marks off Anglican Churches from others, and such a characteristic makes Anglicanism unique amongst Reformed Churches.

DEMOGRAPHIC AND OTHER CONSIDERATIONS

It is difficult to give precise and at the same time meaningful statistics about any large religious group. In the case of worldwide Anglicanism the problems are compounded by the fact that in some countries, not least in England, the gathering of statistics, until relatively recently, has not been seen to be a worthwhile occupation. On the other hand, some Churches, such as the Anglican Church of Canada, have taken the task more seriously. Another problem is the more common enough one of creating statistical categories for membership, practice and belief which have generally accepted significance. The pioneering work of David B. Barrett, with limited

Table 1. Anglican Communion. Global figures of affiliated membership for 1995 according to region[4]

Region	Total affiliated (millions)	Members (% affiliated)	Adult members (millions)
Africa	18.1	16.4	5.1
Europe	25.6	61.9	1.8
South America	0.2	1.7	0.1
North America	3.7	9.3	2.4
Oceania	5.1	10.1	1.0
Asia	0.6	0.4	0.2
Total	54.5	100.0	10.6

help from certain dioceses and Provinces is among the most reliable in providing a statistical picture of the Anglican Communion.

According to Barrett there were, in 1980, 49.8 million baptized Anglicans. The absolute number has been increasing since 1900 when it was 30.6 million and in 1970 it was 47.6 million, but as a proportion of the world's population it has been declining from 1.8 per cent in 1900 to 1.3 per cent in 1970 and 1.1 per cent in 1980.[3] If one employs a somewhat vaguer category of professing membership, which includes those not known to the Churches, the number rises to just under 60 million in 1970, which represents 1.7 per cent of the world's population.

In 1990 the number of adult members was 10.6 million. Thus globally on any reckoning Anglicans constitute a tiny religious body. To be sure, over 160 countries have Anglican Churches; but one country, England has 40 per cent of the total Anglican membership, depending on the category of membership selected. In every other country Anglicans form a minority and are outnumbered by other Christians. In ten Churches or other bodies, Anglicans are less than 1 per cent of the total population. About two-thirds of the churches are located in the Third World; the total number of churches is just under 30.[5]

Each year new dioceses are created throughout the world. The emergence of more dioceses might well reflect an increasing membership but, on the other hand, more dioceses might be created by a growing, practical policy of making smaller units of episcopal administration.

Although the communion as a worldwide organization continues to grow in absolute numbers, its position now seems less convincing than it was in the 1920s and 1930s, when the British Empire was at its zenith in the awake of the enormous expansion in the nineteenth century. Since the breakup of that empire the authoritative claims of Anglicanism have considerably weakened. Indeed many of the tensions in the contemporary Anglican Communion seem analogous to those in the British Commonwealth.

In the face of secularization in Western industrial society, those countries where Anglican membership is declining are Britain, the United States, Canada, Australia and New Zealand. Membership is now growing mainly in African countries and in Papua New Guinea. In projected figures, baptized members in Africa have grown from 6.8 million in 1970 to 18.1 million in 1995, and so their percentage of total membership in that period has risen from 15 per cent to 34 per cent.[6]

England is experiencing the greatest falling away, but the general sentiment remains strong for the Church and polls have indicated that a very large proportion of the population thinks the Church of England is 'a good thing'. There is no strong desire to change its establishment status. When it comes to practice, it is a different matter. On an average Sunday less than 3 per cent of the adult population attend an Anglican Church in England, and the level does not rise much more at Easter. It is probably not too strong to say that the enfeeblement of the mother Church has caused distress and even a lack of self-confidence among her daughters who have always had such a high regard for her. Similar enfeeblement, however, can be found in other parts of the world. For example, a survey in the diocese of Toronto showed that three-quarters of the Anglican population were inactive, although such people gave high value to their 'dormant' membership. It should also be noted that 90 per cent claimed to have British roots.

Characteristics relating to social class vary enormously between the various Churches within the Anglican Communion and most likely between the parish churches of any one country or province. In some areas such as India, Central Africa and South Africa, the majority has been derived from the economically disadvantaged classes—outcasts and poor black Africans. In South Africa, the Church has been particularly influential among those who have suffered under the apartheid system, mixed-race as well as black Africans. Bishop Trevor Huddleston and Alan Paton have been leaders of those who have been oppressed. And Archbishop Desmond Tutu has become foremost among black leaders seeking the alleviation of the sufferers of white domination. In India, Anglo-Indians have been a group much influenced by the Anglican Church.

By contrast, one might point to the United States, where the Episcopal Church has a following which, on a per capita basis, makes it very much the Church of the wealthy and the status-seeking.

In England, the Church has relatively few members who might be designated working-class. At the same time it is not strongly supported by the upper-middle classes and nobility. Its main strength is derived from the upper-working classes, the lower-middle classes and professional groups, which are proportionally more in the churches than in society at large.

The age-structure of Anglican congregations inevitably varies from province to province and from parish church to parish church. As Barrett demonstrates, Churches in the Third World have a much younger age-structure than those Churches set in predominantly white countries.[7] Kenya in particular is a young Church. Nevertheless, in Australia and North America congregations are relatively younger than in the United Kingdom. In part it is due to the younger age-structure of the societies in which the congregations are set. But it is frequently the case that even in the 'newer' countries, the age-groupings in Churches are more weighted towards the elderly than they are in society. The Church of England has lamentably failed to influence the young. The exception perhaps is in the Evangelical wing of the Church, which in recent times has gained considerable strength particularly amongst young adults. Further, in England and in many places elsewhere, there is a predominance of females over males: the ratio of females to males is often in the order of 2 to 1.

UNIQUENESS: A COMBINATION OF TRADITIONS

The Anglican Communion cannot be understood ecclesiastically and socially apart from a thorough comprehension of the Church of England, its mother. Various Churches within the Communion thoroughly reflect the Church of England in many matters and yet in others significantly differ from it. What is important is to come to terms with and to appreciate the body which has given rise to the worldwide Communion. One must always start with the Church of England, because its reflection in other Churches has to be grasped before divergencies can be appreciated.

To the outsider who has some acquaintance with the development of Christianity, the Anglican Communion appears to be an extraordinary mixture of Christian traditions, something akin to what the French would call a *mélange*. Such a characteristic, which is sometimes proudly identified with comprehensiveness,[8] embraces some aspects of the two major Western traditions of Christianity from the sixteenth century onwards—Roman Catholicism and Protestantism. Both (and, within Protestantism, Calvinism in particular) have coherent theological systems. Not so Anglicanism. It has turned out to be an amalgam of the two systems, plus later liberalizing elements, which seems difficult to accept by those not brought up as Anglicans, or those who do not appreciate a *via media* position. Such a stand aims to obtain the best of both worlds—a biblically-based faith, expressed in the early creeds, which also allows for some degree of personal interpretation, as well as the use of Catholic forms of worship and church

ler. Today, many Anglicans do not see themselves as being just Protes-
. Rather, they want to be understood as Catholic and Reformed. They
o see Christendom itself as compromising four major groups—Roman
lic, Eastern Orthodox, Protestant and Anglican. That the last of these
ries is an amalgam of the first and third does not create in their own
mbiguities which others brought up in either one of them might see.
nt of self-congratulation rests on the establishment of a logically
eligious system but on a vague pragmatism. The Church holds
many who want to be neither Protestant nor Catholic: their
herefore tends to be negative rather than positive. 'It's what we
ner than what we are.'
lifficult to comprehend in Anglicanism is the existence of
parties all claiming to be loyal to its principals. Such parties
of England, for example, are very removed from each other
ions of loyalty. Revivals in the eighteenth and nineteenth
......uries—the Evangelical Revival and High Church movements—eventually became accepted as legitimate or semi-legitimate components of the
Church (see pp. 33–9). It may well be that comprehensiveness, that is, the
ability to absorb extremes and at the same time be the milieu for debate
without giving rise to disunity, is the overriding virtue of Anglicanism. It is
in a special position of acting as a bridge between Protestantism and Roman
Catholicism. But it can be argued that virtue has arisen out of necessity.
Why necessity? Because the Church of England as an autonomous body
had no power to exclude members of movements which were initially held
to be undesirable. It had no alternative but to accommodate Liberals, Evangelicals and Anglo-Catholics. All these groups—and others—have made
great contributions to the theological, pastoral and spiritual life of the Church.

The internal tensions brought about by the presence of these parties
within Anglicanism, which first arose in England, may not be as fierce in
other parts of the Communion as they have been, and to a large extent still
are, in England. There are many reasons for this. In certain Churches or
provinces, dioceses and parishes of contrasting churchmanship are often
well separated geographically compared with England, where parishes of
radically different churchmanship are often contiguous and therefore
people are well aware of such differences. Another reason is that church
parties, in establishing their own missionary societies—for example, Bible
Churchmen's Missionary Society (now Crosslinks) or the United Society for
the Propagation of the Gospel—were able to agree that each society would
operate in territories which were generally widely separated from each other.
In this way they did not act as local rivals. Such an agreement seemed
sensible, in the light of the enormous task which evangelism in the nineteenth century faced. Religious orders which undertook work overseas, such

as the Society of St John the Evangelist and the Community of the Resurrection, also accepted this gentleman's agreement. Thus converts to Anglicanism and their successors, growing up under the aegis of different societies, were in numberless cases unaware of the existence of a different type of churchmanship to that of their own. A contrast for the ordinary churchgoers only became apparent when they moved from place to place, or when they came to England.

So the issue of churchmanship in particular Churches has varied according to regions. Many Anglican Churches, such as the Anglican Church of Canada, have never experienced extremes of churchmanship which have occurred in England. Sometimes a more balanced position has emerged due to the presence of Low Church influences (not necessarily Evangelical), rather than the fact that in Canada and Australia Anglo-Catholics of a more extreme kind were never able to make extensive gains. In Canada such extremes never developed, because parish ministers were partly answerable to a parochial, lay governing body. In some Churches, such as that of the United States, historical reasons have made certain dioceses uniformly Anglo-Catholic and others not so. Areas such as South America and the Middle East, because of the initial missionary influence, have been generally recognized as Evangelical or Low Church spheres of influence. On the other hand, the West Indies, Papua, Korea, Japan and Ghana are predominantly Anglo-Catholic (or High Church) because of corresponding missionary activity. In South Africa, Anglo-Catholic congregations are found amongst the Africans and Coloureds.

The Church of England did not undergo the radical changes which churches on the Continent experienced in the sixteenth and seventeenth centuries. It reserved episcopacy as the linchpin of church order, but English bishops were placed in such a position that they governed their flocks and clergy in quite a different way from their predecessors of the Middle Ages. In the Church of England, the absence of a workable canon law and the tenure of parish priests (freehold) which still exists today, has meant two things.[9]

First, a remarkable combination of two components which has facilitated the establishment of extreme parties—the combination of an ideological position, which came early in the history of the Church, namely that of avoiding extremes, and which later turned into the notion of comprehensiveness; and the tenure of clergy who could be removed from the livings only on very limited counts. This association was particularly effective from the nineteenth century onwards in the emergence of a fast-accelerating religious pluralism.

The other implication relates to the role of bishops. As they become less involved in the affairs of state and more concerned with their dioceses they found their powers of administration were seriously limited. They were responsible for their sees yet they could not move their clergy from parish to parish either to try to stem a growing secularization, or to remove a priest on account of his religious extremism or pastoral incompetence. By contrast, bishops in countries outside England found they could function in a much more authoritarian manner and more like bishops 'of old'. For example, they could exert some control over clergy who were without the protection of tenure. Further, bishops often had the authority of synod behind them and could employ, but at the same time be subject to, an effective canon law.

Anglicanism, as a worldwide religious phenomenon, displays one severe limitation, which another contributor has called 'the Anglo-Saxon captivity' (see p. 450). With English the foremost international language, a danger exists that church leaders, with access to jet travel, falsely imagine that the Anglican Communion is representative of cultures around the world. It is true that fourteen Churches and similar bodies have titles which are non-English. Everywhere the vernacular is employed for services of worship and for preaching, and the proceedings of the 1978 Lambeth Conference required simultaneous translation into French, Japanese and Spanish. None the less some 90 per cent of Anglicans live in countries of which the official language is English, nearly two-thirds of them in Western Europe.[10] And this limited internationalism is compounded by the fact that, despite later encouragement to indigenization, nearly all the Churches have adopted ecclesiastical terms unique to the Church of England, or at least rarely found in other Churches. Amongst these are archdeacon, rural deanery, church warden, rector (vicar, however, is not so common), suffragan bishop, House of Bishops (after the Houses of Parliament), together with organizations such as the Girls' Friendly Society, the Mothers' Union, the Guild of the Servants of the Sanctuary. The way clergy dress, or used to dress, has been taken from the English patterns.

THE FUTURE

The genius of Anglicanism is frequently said to lie in its blending of Christian traditions—its comprehensiveness. It can be seen as a living witness to the parable of the wheat and the tares. Great variety is allowed in the matter of belief and practice. Divergent elements grow side by side, and the final judgement rests in the hands of Someone transcending the human predicament. The Anglican Communion can also be said to reflect the divergencies and conflicts that existed within the primitive Church. Anglican Churches remain spiritual homes for the devout and committed; shelters for doubters and the perplexed; debating chambers for the unbelieving, the arrogant and the suspicious. Expressed in more institutional terms, Anglicanism claims to preserve the old, the traditional, the Catholic.

Its inevitable appeal is to history: it stakes everything on what has happened in the past—a past that goes to the beginning of Christianity. Yet at the same time it is prepared to change and to reform itself. Liturgies of today have developed extensively from those of Cranmer (see pp. 45–6 and 139–42); most Churches have synodical government and there is a greater involvement of lay people in every area of its life.

One major event of the 1990s in English Anglicanism was the ordination of women. In 1987 legislation allowed women to be ordained as deacons rather than deaconesses as they were previously. Then in 1992 came the historic vote, by the slenderest of margins, which paved the way for the ordination of women as priests. The first such ordinations took place in 1994. By the following year, 783 of the 10,459 stipendiary clergy were woman, 7.5 per cent or one priest in every 13.

Others, however, disapproved of such action and left the Church. Over 300 clergy resigned on the issue taking perhaps 15,000 lay people with them. About half of these priests submitted to the Roman Catholic Church, nine put themselves under the jurisdiction of His Holiness Patriarch Ignatius IV of Antioch to form the British Anthiochian Orthodox Deanery, some left the priesthood altogether, and about 1,000 joined differing alternative Anglican denominations. The largest of these is the Anglican Catholic Church which began in 1992 and five years later had 27 congregations numbering 650 people in all.

Yet its strength harbours its weakness. The flabbiness that many see in Anglicanism is a sufficient reason for some to forsake it and embrace another denomination. It has been the case in the past: it is true also today. In some instances Anglicans of a High Church persuasion have left to join the Church of Rome or the Orthodox Church; the exit or partial exit of certain Evangelicals, on the other hand, has been into non-denominational New Churches. Joining another Church is not the only solution to being free of the alleged flabbiness of Anglicanism. Continuing Churches can be established, and certainly that has been the case in the United States and Canada where there are the Anglican Catholic Church; the American Episcopal Church; the United Episcopal Church; the Anglican Rite Jurisdiction of the Americas; and the Anglican Catholic Church of Canada. The membership of all these groups together is estimated in the order of 50–60,000. Such groups maintain links with various Anglo-Catholic bodies in Anglican Churches around the world. These continuing Churches by their very limited size and mentality indeed become sects. And if the larger Churches of the Anglican Communion are seriously weakened by the exodus of groups dissatisfied with present doctrine and practice, such Churches would in fact become sects, or if they already possess sectarian qualities, these would become more accentuated.

Is Anglicanism, as a unique component of Christianity, destined to survive? The question invites two kinds of response. The first is to ask whether the doctrines, practices and ethos of Anglicanism, despite local variations, will continue in the face of church reform, liturgical change, charismatic enthusiasm, the influences of ecumenism, and a desire on the part of many young Christians to blur—even to the point of extinction—differences between denominations. Indeed, one might ask how far does the Anglican in the pew want to keep the distinctive characteristics of Anglicanism? This issue needs to be researched and cannot be explored here. The second response focuses on the existence of the Anglican Communion as a concrete social expression of Anglicanism. Will this survive? It is impossible to predict, and in any case sociologists in general hold that futurology is not part of their trade. None the less the question of the Anglican Communion in the years ahead is more pressing now than heretofore.

In one sense it would seem that the future of the Anglican Communion is assured. As has been shown, its overall growth continues and expansion in one part of the world offsets losses in another. The general state of Anglicanism will depend on how it can cope with a rising secularization, strongly evident in the West, but emerging in all societies influenced by it. Growing affluence is so often the enemy of religious belief and practice. Some would doubt whether the comprehensiveness, and what has been called the flabbiness, of Anglicanism can stem the tide of universal secularizing processes.

Another factor relates directly to internal tension and dissatisfaction, with what appears to be the ever-widening parameters of diversity within which unity is extended. Are there no clear limits beyond which tolerance is exhausted? Among sociologists there is no consensus that only one component, be it belief, practice or culture, is the *sine qua non* of the unity of a social entity such as a Church. Unity itself is not a unitary concept, but open to variability and diversity. Something more decisive than 'live and let live' is required when issues of the gospel and the Church are at stake. Yet any attempt to create new formulae to draw sharper boundaries of membership goes against the grain of an important strand of historic Anglicanism. Herein lies its dilemma.

1998 APPENDIX

STATISTICAL UPDATE
Peter Brierley

Some of the statistics W. S. F. Pickering cites in his chapter come predominantly from the publications edited and produced by David Barrett. Dr Barrett has continued to update his massive *World Christian Encyclopedia*, published in 1982 with annual Tables in the January issue of the *Inter-*

national Bulletin of Missionary Research, as he works towards his three-volume revision of the *Encyclopedia* to be published in 1999, again by Oxford University Press.

However, another volume was published in 1997 which came from the database of Patrick Johnstone, called the *World Churches Handbook,*[11] *or WCH*. This also gives an overview of world Christianity. It puts the 1995 percentage of the world's population which are Christian at 28 per cent, a lower percentage than that given by Dr Barrett. It is lower for three reasons—the *WCH* omits the 'marginal Protestants' (Jehovah's Witnesses, Mormons, etc.) which Dr Barrett includes, it takes a lower view of the number of Russian Orthodox Christians, and did not assume that the number of charismatic Christians continued to increase in the 1990s as fast as they had in the 1980s.

There is a further important difference between these two sources of world Christian statistics. Dr Barrett's figures show that the percentage of the world's population which are Christian is increasing, whereas the *World Churches Handbook* projects a slight decline, to 27 per cent by 2010.

Dr Pickering quotes Dr Barrett's figure of 49.8 million baptized Anglicans in 1980, a figure slightly lower than the 50.3 million given in the *WCH.*[12] By 1990 the *WCH* figure of Anglicans worldwide was 53.0 million. As a percentage of the world's population these figures are: 1980—1.1%; and 1990—1.0%.

This gradual drop in the percentage of the world who are Anglican reflects two elements. First, the world population generally is growing faster than the number of Christians (Anglican or not)—thus between 1995 and 2000 an estimated 53,000 people become Christian every day around the world, but the world's population increased by the 240,000 every day. Christians are thus 22 per cent of the daily increase, but were 27 per cent in the period 1985–90 for example.

Second, the Anglican church is not increasing as fast as other denominations. Thus between 1980 and 2010 Anglicans are projected to increase by just over 9 million worldwide, a percentage increase accross these 30 years of 18 per cent, or an annual increase of 0.54 per cent.

Anglicans are losing out partly because the world is becoming less Christian, but mostly because other types of Christianity are more popular. The three groups expanding fastest are the indigenous (located mostly in Africa), the Pentecostal churches and other Churches, which include the many smaller, and sometimes charismatic, denominations, like the Church of the Nazarene, Christian Brethren, Seventh-day Adventist Churches, Evangelical Free Churches, Salvation Army, Churches of Christ, Disciples of Christ, Congregational Churches, missionary churches, etc.

417

These three denominations are characterized by smaller congregations (240 on average in 1995 against 660 for Anglican churches), much less formality, but perhaps a greater authoritarian structure at the local congregational level.

The growth of these denominations must however, be put in perspective. In 1995 they cumulatively accounted for 18 per cent of the world's Christianity, against Anglican's 3 per cent.

The situation in 1960 was rather different. Anglicans were the fourth largest denominational group then, whereas by 1995 they had become seventh.

In the 1990s the Anglican Communion worldwide is growing at the rate of about 900 people per day, just under 2 per cent of the total growth of Christianity.

The Anglican community grew less between 1880 and 1990 than it did in earlier decades, or is projected to do so afterwards. The figures for Christendom grew greatest in that same decade, showing basically that the competition between denominations was very intense in the 1980s. The fastest growth went to the non-institutional Churches. In other words, the growth of especially the charismatic Churches in the 1980s meant that some who might have otherwise joined the Anglican Church joined those of other denominations instead. How much have the Anglican churches worldwide learned from this, and adjusted their culture to meet the demands of new people who might join in the 1990s?

The growth of the Anglican Church in the latter part of the twentieth century, and projected into the twenty-first, is almost entirely because of the huge expansion in the African continent.

Anglicanism is losing out in North America where the Pentecostals are strong (third largest denomination, in South America where the Pentecostals are also strong (second largest denomination), and in Asia where the smaller non-institutional other churches are strong (second largest). This suggests that in these continents non-institutional Christianity is especially attractive, though Anglicanism might still have a unique contribution to make!

Anglicans have also grown quite quickly in South America and Asia, but the numbers are relatively small. Anglicans have grown in Oceania, slowly but with sizable numbers. Anglicans have decreased in both North America and Europe, although at a much slower pace in Europe than in North America.

Since Dr Pickering wrote his chapter several editions of the UK *Christian Handbook*[13] have appeared. These give statistics on Anglican missionary societies. Of those with people serving overseas, the Church Mission Society is the largest with 287 members in 1997, followed by the United

Society for the Propagation of the Gospel with 163, and Crosslinks, formerly the Bible Churchman's Missionary Society, with 105. Three others had between 50 and 100: the South American Missionary Society with 75, the Intercontinental Church society with 71 and Missions to seamen with 54. In total Anglican societies working overseas had 906 members in 1997, compared with half as many again in 1980.

Anglican missionaries served mostly in Tanzania in 1997 (75 from all Societies), followed by Uganda with 73, and Israel with 34.

The Anglican Church is seeking to face the problems it faces as an institutional Chuch, and is willing to face opposition from some quarters while it pursues change. The recent ordination of women in the Church of England is an example. The unwillingness to allow agenda items to be fixed for the Lambeth Conference which did not involve worldwide support is another. Leadership is tackling the authority issues, and making wlecome additions and changes to the liturgy. The Anglican Communion is looking at the worldwide issues of debt and poverty. It is willing in many places to integrate ethically. All this does not guarantee 'success'—what is success in theological terms ?—but is does show a Church willing to grapple with the problems of the Third Millennium.

SOME SOCIOLOGICAL REFLECTIONS
Grace Davie

Since the first edition of this book, the ordination of women has become a reality in most, if not quite all, of the Provinces of the Anglican Communion, not least in the Church of England itself. Such a move (or series of moves) has brought great joy to many both inside and outside the church: those, and they constitute a large majority, who feel that Anglicanism has been entirely justified in its positive response to changes in Western society. Sociologically the shift is interesting, for this is clearly a case in which the Church has reacted to economic and social transformation. Had not the position of women in the modern West evolved so dramatically in the post-war period, it is unlikely that the Churches—and among them Anglicanism—would have initiated discussion in this area. It was society that set the agenda, not the Church.

Precisely this point, however, has led a certain number within the Church to reject the ordination of women. The Church should look to its own tradition with respect to faith and order, not to the shifts of modern society, and where necessary the latter should be resisted rather than duplicated. A second set of objections question the right of the Anglican Church to initiate a change of this nature independently of the Catholic and Orthodox communities, particularly in view of long-term ecumenical aims. As a result, different views, in the form of different integrities, are tenaciously

419

held, at times jeopardizing—seriously—the fundamental basis of Anglicanism, correctly defined by W. S. F. Pickering as incorporating those Churches which are in communion with the see of Canterbury. Some of these churches are barely in communion with each other, never mind with Canterbury—a situation that can only be exacerbated by the consecration of increasing numbers of women as bishops in some provinces of the Anglican Communion.

The future is hard to predict. A change of such magnitude was unlikely to come about without considerable and sustained opposition. Whether or not such opposition will prove enduring beyond a generation or two (the natural unit of time in measuring religious change) remains to be seen. Schism is unlikely given the reduced size of the opposition to the ordination of women, but splinter groups are quite possible. Since each of these impoverishes the Church as a whole, their cumulative effect may be damaging. No more so, however, than on previous occasions, for there are always some who reject current policy-making in the Church, particularly a Church as broad as Anglicanism in its aspirations. The ordination of women should not be seen in isolation in this respect.

A second shift in the context of Anglicanism takes a rather different form. It concerns the changing nature of the modern world in terms of its political alignments. The following example is particularly pertinent for the nature of Anglicanism. In 1945 Europe had come close to self-destruction for the second time in a century. The idea of European unity was barely conceivable as individual nations struggled to rebuild the fabric of their devastated societies. Surprisingly quickly, however, the seeds of the European Community began to germinate in the form of Coal and Steel Agreements which embodied the principle that the weapons of war should themselves be under supranational, if not always international, control. Since then (the mid-1950s) Europe has moved inexorably, if not very steadily, towards a greater common identity.

The religious factor within this identity is of considerable significance, not least in terms of the somewhat ambivalent attitudes in Britain to what is going on. In England, particularly, a state Church which owes its origins to a 'break from Rome'—which included an explicit political as well as theological rejection of any kind of external authority over national affairs—is unlikely to be the most effective encourager of European ideals. It is at least plausible that the Catholic or Reformed minorities will take the lead; both, unlike Anglicanism, belong to the major spiritual traditions of continental Europe.

The nature of the Anglican Communion, itself the fruit of a long and extensive colonial history, exacerbates this situation. The Church of England did indeed turn its back on Rome some 400 years ago. One consequence of this situation was the expansion of Anglicanism in a different direction as missionaries followed the flag, and both interacted with a multiplicity of commercial motives. What emerged in due course was the Anglican Communion as we know it, an important international grouping even at the end of the twentieth century, but one which is anything but European in its emphases. How the Communion is to move forward within a rapidly changing world remains an open question. At its most negative, the Mother Church of the Anglican Communion could become a spiritual arm of English (if not British) isolationism from Europe. More positively, the Church of England is in a position to offer its European partners a whole set of international linkages. This potential is particularly attractive to those who wish to avoid the idea of a 'fortress Europe'. All the churches of Europe offer an important contribution in this respect, but it is a role in which the Anglican Communion can share with proven competence and particular enthusiasm.

A final point concerns once again the shifting nature of the modern world and, more particularly, the complex relationship between religion and modernity at the turn of millennium. Or to put this in a different way, sociological thinking has become increasingly sceptical of the secularization thesis, seen more and more as a one-sided view of what is going on. The crucial point to grasp in understanding this scepticism is to appreciate that the secularization thesis itself developed within a European framework. For certain stages in Europe's religious development, moreover, there is a convincing fit between the argument and the data. As Europe's economic and political life developed, it was evident that religion diminished in public significance; religious aspirations continued to exist, but were increasingly relegated to the private sphere.

Bit by bit, however, the thesis rather than the data began to dominate the agenda. The 'fit' became axiomatic, theoretically necessary rather than empirically founded. So much so that Europe's religious life was considered a prototype of global religiosity; what Europe did today everyone else would do tomorrow. Secularization was a necessary part of modernization and as the world modernized, it would automatically secularize. But if this was the case, how was it possible to accommodate the very different situation found in the United States within the same theoretical framework? The answer lay in trying to understand American exceptionalism; i.e., in accepting that America was different and in elucidating the specificities within American society which could account for the successful cohabitation of vibrant religiosity and developed modernity. So far, so good; the secularization thesis remains intact even if deviations from the norm can be found in the modern world.

Not everyone, however, has continued down this path. Peter Berger and

David Martin,[14] for example, have suggested that the argument be reversed. Exceptionalism undoubtedly exists, but it is Europe rather than the United States which is exceptional. Not only, following Berger, is the non-Western world as 'furiously religious as ever',[15] the United States itself continues by all conventional criteria to be an intensely religious country. So what happens to the argument about relativism breeding secularity? In the US it simply has not happened. What has emerged in its place has been a healthy and competitive market of religious institutions, some of which appear to be thriving more vigorously than others. Paradoxically, it is the more conservative religious groups which attract the greater numbers of religious adherents as the twentieth century draws to a close. It is, it seems, those who resist compromise most successfully that flourish in cultures of increasing uncertainty.

Where, though, does this leave the question of Anglicanism? In its European forms it is, indeed, likely to encounter the corrosive effects of the decline in religious practice, even if a certain level of cultural belief maintains itself. The same will also be true of the English-speaking dominions— Canada, Australia and New Zealand—all of which have adopted European patterns, but to a lesser extent. Elsewhere, however (and not least in the United States), Anglicanism's most likely competitors will be diverse forms of conservative religion rather than indifference or pervasive secularity.

Americans, for example, are not ceasing to be religious; they are, rather, shifting their allegiance to more conservative forms of religious organization. Episcopalians, like other forms of liberal Protestantism, suffer as a result. Beyond the English-speaking world, the alternatives may well be other faith communities rather than different versions of Christianity, themselves subject to similar sorts of pressures in their relationships with modernity. In short, conservative rather than liberal forms of religion flourish in the modern world. This, on the eve of the millennium, is the global context in which Anglicanism must find a place if it is to sustain itself into the twenty-first century; it has changed significantly since the first edition of this appeared.

BIBLIOGRAPHY

Barrett, D. B., 'The Anglican World in Figures', in Lambeth Conference. Preparatory Information Statistics: Documentation: Addresses: Maps. CIO, London, 1978.

Barrett, D. B., World Christian Encyclopedia. OUP, Oxford and New York, 1982.

Barrett, D. B., 'Annual Statistical on Global Mission: 1986', International Bulletin of Missionary Research (January 1986), pp. 22–3.

The Church of England Year Book. CIO, London, annual.

Inter-Anglican Theological and Doctrinal Commission (IATDC), For the Sake of the Kingdom. Anglican Consultative Council, London, 1986.

Mehl, R., The Sociology of Protestantism (ET) SCM, London, 1970.

Pickering, W. S. F. 'Protestantism and Power: Some Sociological Observations', *Social Compass* 32: ii/iii, (1985), pp. 163–74.

Sykes, Stephen W., *The Integrity of Anglicanism*. A. R. Mowbray, Oxford, 1978.

Sykes, Stephen W. and others, *Four Documents on Authority in the Anglican Communion*. Anglican Consultative Council, London, 1981.

Wand, J. W. C. (ed), *The Anglican Communion: A Survey*. OUP, Oxford, 1948.

NOTES

1 The present list of Churches' Provinces and Councils is found in *The Church of England Yearbook* (CIO, London, 1986). See also D. B. Barrett, 'The Anglican World in Figures', in *Lambeth Conference. Preparatory Information. Statistics: Documentation: Addresses: Maps* (London, 1978).

2 Barrett, 'The Anglican World'.

3 Barrett, ' The Anglican World'.

4 Brierley, Peter, ed., *The World Churches Handbook* (jointly by the Lausanne Committee on World Evangelization and Christian Research, London, 1997).

5 Barrett, 'The Anglican World'.

6 Brierley, *The World Churches Handbook*.

7 Barrett, 'The Anglican World'.

8 S. W. Sykes, *The Integrity of Anglicanism* (Mowbrays, Oxford, 1978), contains an analysis of the notion of comprehensiveness.

9 W. S. F. Pickering, 'Protestantism and Power: Some Sociological Observations', *Social Compass* 32.ii/iii (1985).

10 Barrett, 'The Anglican World'.

11 Brierley, *The World Churches Handbook*.

12 The WCH in fact gives a figure of 48.9 million, but revised figures for Canada have been included throughout the 1998 Appendix, which makes the figure as given.

13 P. Brierley and H. Wraight, eds., *UK Christian Handbook 1998/99* (jointly by Christian Research and Paternoster Publishing, London, 1997). The 1998/99 edition is supplemented by the volume, *UKCH: Religious Trends 1* (1998/99).

14 P. Berger, *A Far Glory: The Quest for Faith in an Age of Credulity* (Doubleday, New York, 1992); and D. Martin, 'The secularization issue: prospect and retrospect', *British Journal of Sociology* 42 (3) (1991).

15 Berger, *A Far Glory*.

PART SEVEN

Prospects

1 The Ecumenical Future

MARY TANNER

Anyone reviewing the history of Christianity in the twentieth century will be struck by the fact that this has been the century of ecumenism. Although there have been few signs of success in terms of the coming together of denominations, with such notable exceptions as the Church of South India, the Church of North India and the Church of Pakistan, yet the advances in mutual understanding and the commitment to join action in life have been dramatic. The years that have seen such changes in the relation of the churches to one another have also witnessed great changes in the Anglican Communion and in Anglican self-understanding. These have been in part affected by Anglican involvement in the Ecumenical Movement. The eve of the Twelfth Lambeth Conference is an appropriate time to ask, where are we and where are we going as Anglicans in the ecumenical future? In what follows, some of the developments that have brought us to the ecumenical present will be charted. Only then will an assessment of Anglicans and the ecumenical future be attempted.

THE DEVELOPMENT OF THE ECUMENICAL MOVEMENT

In writing about the Ecumenical Movement at the turn of the century Stephen Neill emphasizes the commitment of individuals and of like-minded groups rather than the commitment of churches.[1] Certainly groups like the YMCA (founded in 1844), the Evangelical Alliance (1846) and the Student Christian Federation (1880) provided opportunities for young Christians to form deep and lasting friendships and to develop a shared vision of unity. It was, however, the meetings of the missionary societies in 1888 and 1900 and finally the Edinburgh Conference in 1910 that gave birth to the modern Ecumenical Movement. The participants at Edinburgh saw clearly that the scandalous divisions were a grave hindrance to the mission of the Church: mission and unity belong together. It was, more than anyone else an Anglican, Bishop Charles Brent of the Episcopal Church of the USA, who discerned at Edinburgh that unity would only be brought about on the basis of agreement of faith. He determined to bring together bishops, church leaders and theologians to begin the task of studying the reasons for the divisions of the Church. After many setbacks, not least the ravages of the First World War, the theological arm of the Ecumenical Movement was set up and the First World Faith and Order Conference met in Lausanne in 1927. Here Orthodox, Anglicans and Protestants began to face divisive questions and set an agenda of work, a

427

part of which matured sixty years later in the agreed statement, *Baptism, Eucharist and Ministry*.[2] The theologians at Lausanne agreed with Bishop Brent's concern that there would never be any true unity without communion in faith and the acceptance of a common doctrine of the ministry. The four points of the Lambeth Quadrilateral—covering the normative authority of Scripture, the witness of the primitive creeds, the sacraments of baptism and Holy Communion and the ministry—which had formed the basis of the Anglican 'Appeal to all Christian People' in 1920, were acknowledged as having had a formative effect upon the agenda set by Lausanne.

Two years prior to Lausanne another ecumenical group had gathered to consider problems of war and peace, race, education, capital and labour, and the social order facing the churches; and so the second arm of the Ecumenical Movement, Life and Work, was born. A decade later the two movements that were eventually to merge to form the World Council of Churches met: Faith and Order under the chairmanship of Bishop William Temple, and Life and Work under Bishop George Bell. These conferences raised questions that continue to engage the Ecumenical Movement: the relation of Scripture and tradition; the nature of the sacraments; apostolic succession and a sacramental episcopate; the nature of the Church. Underlying many of the debates was a tension between a Western intellectual approach and logic, and an Eastern sacramental approach. However, the experience of daily shared worship had a profound influence upon the movement, and the decision by the Archbishops of York and Canterbury to extend eucharistic hospitality was both a foretaste of the unity that lay ahead and a bitter reminder of the pain of continuing divisions.

The merging of Faith and Order and Life and Work, together with Christian Aid, had to wait another war-torn decade. The First Assembly of the World Council of Churches met in Amsterdam in 1948. Another Anglican, Archbishop Geoffrey Fisher, was in the chair when the formal decision to set up the Council was approved by representatives from over a hundred churches, Orthodox, Anglican and Protestant. Although Anglicans played a major part in the history leading up to the formation of the Council, their voice was not always uncritical. Bishop Charles Headlam prophetically warned of the inevitable tension between the interests of Faith and Order and Life and Work, and the danger of political involvement of the Council foreshadowed in the capitalist–communist confrontation at Amsterdam. He asked, too, whether the setting up of a council pointed to a goal of church unity which was a federal model and not that to which he was himself passionately committed, a truly united Catholic Church. The First Assembly of the Council in 1948 marked a turning point in the Ecumenical Movement. At Amsterdam the churches, as churches, committed themselves to a common search for unity. Anglicans had played a leading role in setting up and giving direction to the movement.

It is not possible to do more than indicate some key developments in the World Council of Churches and its agenda from Amsterdam to the Sixth Assembly in Vancouver in 1983. First, the Council has become much more representative: over 400 churches were represented at Vancouver. The growing number of Orthodox churches have significantly affected the Council's work and its spirituality. Following on from Vatican II, the Roman Catholic attitude has changed from one of hostility to partnership. Official observers from the Roman Catholic Church play an important part in Assemblies, and even more significant, the Roman Catholic Church is a full member of the Faith and Order Commission, and so is a fully participant in the theological reflection of the Council. It is not only the ecumenical representation that has changed the face of the Council. What began as a white, Western, largely male gathering of church leaders now embraces women and men, clergy and laity from every part of the world, representing many cultures.

Secondly, as the community of the Council has widened, the members have added new concerns to the agenda. The pragmatic agenda that was once the concern of the Life and Work movement has sometimes seemed to be in opposition to the cerebral, academic work of the Faith and Order Movement. This tension has been felt equally within the Faith and Order Commission itself. However, the Commission has struggled in its own programmes on racism, the handicapped, women and men and, more recently, the work on ecclesiology and ethics, to show that the two agendas are interrelated. The search for agreement in faith, seen so clearly by Bishops Brent and Headlam as necessary for the visible unity of the Church, may not be surrendered; but the unity of the Church is not a matter of cerebral agreement or ecclesiastical joinery but is about a life of unity expressed in a community which is itself constantly being renewed in its own life. The early movement saw that unity and mission belong together; developments in the 1970s highlighted unity and renewal. The Faith and Order Commission still struggles to articulate the theological undergirding of unity and renewal in its current programme on 'The Unity of the Church and the Renewal of the Human Community'. This is vital for the effect on its own agenda and for the foundation of the work of the entire Council.

A third development has come in the style and method of work. An attempt is made to ground the work of the Council in the lives of Christians in the member churches. Not only are agendas prepared for in various parts of the world but statements and reports are 'received' by member churches and local congregations. The multilateral work is no longer tightly in the control of a few towering ecumenical giants, but is shared by an ever wider community. This change is still in its infancy but it is testimony to a developing ecclesiological understanding of the Church as the whole people of God, a community of interpretation, of faith and of life.

A fourth contribution lies in the developing and deepening vision of the goal of unity which has emerged in successive Assembly statements. An important contribution to this developing goal has been made by Faith and Order's work on sacraments and ministry, in its present work on a common confession of the apostolic faith, and on structures of decision-making and teaching authoritatively.

A final development is the way all of this is carried by a growing life of shared worship. The gradual discovery of the richness of the different spiritualities bore fruit at the Vancouver Assembly, where it was recognized that it is possible to preserve a rich variety of spirituality in a visibly united Church. Moreover, the Lima Liturgy presided over at Vancouver by the Archbishop of Canterbury, assisted by a Lutheran woman minister and a presbyter from the Church of South India, marked a significant moment in eucharistic sharing and was a foretaste of a shared sacramental life.

While the twentieth century has seen the development of the multilateral search for the visible unity of the Church, relations have developed between two or more partners. One of the earliest bilateral conversations between Anglicans and Roman Catholics, the Malines Conversations, began in 1921. The aim was to see whether, and on what conditions, Anglicans could be reunited with the Church of Rome, 'united, not absorbed'. The talks were closed by Pope Pius XI in 1928. The Bonn agreement of 1931 established a relationship of intercommunion between Anglicans and Old Catholics. A similar concordat was reached between some Anglican provinces and the Philippine Independent Church. To these can be added the close ties of intercommunion between the Lutheran Church of Sweden and the Church of Finland and the Church of England.

It has, however, been on the sub-continent of India that the greatest advance has been made. The Church of South India, founded in 1947, joined for the first time episcopal and non-episcopal churches in an episcopally ordered church. The union brought together Anglican, Methodist and Reformed traditions in an independent regional church. Now, some thirty-five years after its inauguration, there remains a lack of clarity about the precise nature of the relationship with the Anglican Communion. The General Synod of the Church of England in 1985 refused to declare itself in full communion with the Church of South India, partly because there are still a few non-espicopally ordained presbyters in the church and partly because the notion of full communion has developed since 1947 and is now seen by many to involve sharing together in universal structures of decision-making and teaching authoritatively. Whatever the verdict of the Church of England, the Church of South India has been important for its example in uniting episcopal and non-episcopal ministries; for developing an autonomous regional church rooted in the local culture which can hold together differing denominational traditions; and for struggling latterly to understand what organs can best link the regional to the universal manifestations of the Church. The Church of South India also provided an example which was followed by the Church of North India and the Church of Pakistan in 1970. The success of union schemes involving Anglicans on the sub-continent of India has not, however, been matched in other parts of the world. In England, the failure of the Anglican–Methodist scheme and later the Covenant Proposals have their counterparts in failures in South Africa, Tanzania, New Zealand, the States and elsewhere.

A more hopeful sign, however, can be seen in the area of theological conversations. Bilateral dialogues at the international level proliferated as a result of the commitment of the Roman Catholic Church to unity following Vatican II. The texts of four bilateral dialogues are before the Anglican Communion for official response in the mid-1980s. The Anglican–Lutheran, Anglican–Orthodox, Anglican–Reformed and Anglican–Roman Catholic dialogues, while pursuing agendas relating to the specific cause of division between the partners, show remarkable convergences in understanding, particularly on the sacramental agenda of baptism, Eucharist and ministry. They have learnt to take into account each other's work as well as to build upon the convergences of understanding reached in the multilateral text, *Baptism, Eucharist and Ministry.* Some dialogues go further towards reaching consensus than others. The Anglican-Roman Catholic dialogue claims 'substantial agreement' for its work on Eucharist and ministry and remarkable convergence in its understanding of authority and primacy.[3]

The Anglican–Reformed dialogue, more than any other, has held together the search for the unity of the Church within the perspective of mission and the eschatological fulfillment; and within this broad perspective it has sought creatively to understand those areas of faith and order which continue to keep the churches apart.[4] The Anglican–Orthodox dialogue has deepened the understanding of the inner reality of the Church.[5] The almost simultaneous publication of these texts helps to show that they are not rival ecumenisms but each belong within the one search for the visible unity of the Church which must be grounded in agreement in faith.

The picture of the Ecumenical Movement involving Anglicans would be incomplete without reference to the essential growing together of Christians at the local level. Regional councils of churches and local councils have encouraged the denominations to get to know one another, to reconcile memories of past divisions and hatred and, on the basis of the Lund

431

Principle, to do only on their own what cannot yet be done together.[6] The Week of Prayer for Christian Unity, established in 1946, has helped to ground the movement in prayer. In some parts of the world, in New Zealand in England and in Wales, Anglicans share with others in Local Ecumenical Projects, sharing buildings, worship and life, and with an increasing degree of shared ministry. In the United States of America Anglicans and Lutherans have entered into an agreement of 'interim eucharistic sharing' which acknowledges a degree of agreement in faith and a commitment to shared life. The theological convergences of the international dialogues, particularly the *Lima Text*, provide 'a charter' which gives a doctrinal basis for advances in shared life. Closer relationships at the local level are, in some places of the world, now involving Roman Catholics. Local covenants between Anglicans, Roman Catholics and the Free Churches in England, for example, provide a formal commitment to the sharing of life and witness. Another hopeful sign is an increase in sharing at the level of episcopal oversight, providing opportunities for joint witness to the world. And the facing and overcoming of divisions by individuals in 'mixed marriages' is an important sign of the ecumenical advance.

Against all of these advances in the way Christians relate to those of other denominations there remain the places of bitter divisions and polarization. The division between Roman Catholics and Protestants in Northern Ireland is an example and even in England, where so much can be recorded in ecumenical advance, the voices of a few raised in angry protest at the work of the Anglican–Roman Catholic International Commission testify to the need for greater determination in overcoming the entrenched positions and commitment to outmoded categories which go back to the Reformation.

THE ECUMENICAL FUTURE

The ecumenical scene in the mid-1980s is thus a complex one. It is difficult to hold together the multilateral and bilateral conversations, the regional schemes for unity and the many local initiatives which make up the one Ecumenical Movement. Against such a complex background it is appropriate to ask: what are the directions for the Ecumenical Movement? Is it possible to detect emerging a vision of unity to which Anglicans, together with others, can commit themselves, and what are the next steps that might be taken towards such an end?

The World Council of Churches is concerned to call all churches to the goal of visible unity. The Uppsala Assembly (1968) described this goal as 'conciliar fellowship'. This refers not only to outward structures which hold Christians who are united in each place together, but is a quality to be displayed by the Church in each given situation. That quality has its model—more than that, its source—in the life of the Triune God and in the self-giving love of the incarnate Christ. The Nairobi Assembly (1975) recognized at least three basic marks of 'conciliar fellowship': consensus in the apostolic faith; mutual recognition of baptism, Eucharist and ministry; and conciliar gatherings for common deliberations and decision-making. In spite of the fact that the Nairobi Statement made quite clear that 'conciliar fellowship' does not describe any present reality, certainly not the World Council itself, and the repeated attempts by Faith and Order theologians to show that 'conciliar fellowship' is not an alternative to organic union, the concept has yet to gain widespread reception. More recently the Vancouver Assembly (1983) underlined the three 'marks' of the Church, while re-emphasizing that the Church is called to be a prophetic community through which and by which the transformation of the world can take place.[7] It can only be such a sign as long as it is itself being renewed in its own life.

The emerging goal in the multilateral dialogue is being further developed by the work of the Faith and Order Commission. The Lima Text has deepened the understanding of the second 'mark', the Church's sacramental life: the latest programme, 'Towards a Common Expression of the Apostolic Faith Today', has made a start on what a shared confession of the apostolic faith in word and in the life might be when the faith is authentically expressed in different cultural contexts; preliminary work has begun on common structures of decision-making and teaching authoritatively. In developing these basic 'marks' or characteristics of the Church, the work of the multilateral dialogue will sharpen the picture of a Church, living in unity, confessing a common faith, sharing in the Eucharist, served by a single ministry and held together by structures of decision-making. Anglicans will have a contribution to make this reflection from their own experience, as well as insights to receive from the wider community.

The vision emerging from the bilateral dialogues in the coming years will need to be considered against the work of the multilateral forum. It is the Anglican–Reformed dialogue that resembles most closely the vision of the World Council. This dialogue holds together the universal aspect of the Church with the manifestation of unity at the local level. The aim is for reconciled local communities, each of which is recognizable as 'church': that is, 'communities which exhibit in each place the fullness of ministerial order, eucharistic fellowship, pastoral care, and missionary commitment and which, through mutual communion and co-operation, bear witness on the regional, national and even international levels'.[8] While providing the most impressive overall ecclesiological vision set within the context of mission and the eschatological purpose of God, there are many points at which Anglicans may wish to deepen the convergence with the Reformed: the understanding of the Eucharist and sacrifice, the relation of personal, collegial and communal aspects of ministry, the exercise of personal oversight and a universal personal focus of unity and continuity.

Relations between Anglicans and Lutherans have been especially close. It is therefore of great interest to reflect in the 1980s on how this relationship might develop in the light of the results of the bilateral dialogue. The expressed aim has been to move towards 'full communion'. 'Full communion' is taken to imply that members may receive the sacraments of the other; bishops of one Church may take part in the consecration of bishops of the other; when invited, an ordained minister may exercise liturgical functions in a congregation of the other body and that there would be regular organs of consultation.[9] The emphasis is upon 'interdependent while remaining autonomous', upon 'reconciled diversity' which takes into account the legitimacy of confessional differences and the need to preserve them.[10] Whether this points in the direction of a goal compatible with 'conciliar fellowship' remains to be assessed in the next stage of the dialogue as Anglicans move forward with Lutherans within the wider context of the ecumenical fellowship. But, at first sight, the emphasis upon 'interdependent while remaining autonomous' would seem to imply something less than the vision of organic union expressed by, for example, Bishop Charles Headlam when the World Council was set up in the 1940s.

The Anglican–Orthodox dialogue in 1977 expressed the goal of unity as 'the union of all Christians in one Church'.[11] This, however, has to be seen in the context of the statement that 'Anglicans [. . .] see our divisions as within the Church [. . .] Orthodox believe that the Orthodox Church is the one Church of Christ which, as his body, is not and cannot be divided'.[12] Here we are back at the ecclesiological difference that has reverberated throughout unity discussions since Lausanne. The resolution of this fundamental difference lies in the future. It may be, as one Orthodox theologian recently suggested, that in receiving the convergences of the sacramental agenda of the *Lima Text*, some implications will be realized for the reconciling of apparently conflicting ecclesiologies.[13] Whether or not this is a possible way forward in future, Anglicans, in dialogue with the Orthodox, will continue to develop an understanding of the inner reality of the Church grounded in the life of the holy and undivided Trinity.

The most developed dialogue, that between Anglicans and Roman Catholics (ARCIC), began with the intention of working towards 'full visible unity', 'full organic unity of our two communions'.[14] The concept of the Church which underlies this dialogue is that of *koinonia*, communion: the Eucharist is the effectual sign of *koinonia*, *episkope* its servant, and primacy its focus. *Koinonia* is both the goal and the way. One of the most welcome things to emerge from this dialogue is what unity and proper

434

diversity might mean in a united Church. Unity must be focused in persons and in structures, transcending the local. A Church that has a universal primate who is never divorced from the wider collegiality of bishops, a servant figure, should be able to tolerate and sustain more, not less, diversity. In this dialogue, as in the dialogue with Lutherans, there appears some ambiguity. The quotation of Pope Paul VI's assurance that there will be no seeking to lessen the legitimate prestige and patrimony of piety and usage proper to the Anglican Church, while being a comfort to some who fear being 'swallowed up' by a larger body might be thought to hint at an Anglican right or jurisdiction within a reunited Church which would basically retain it own liturgy and canon law. This might seem to some a different perspective from one which holds together local and regional churches shaped more by the variety of their local history, cultural context and immediate missionary task than by old denominational loyalties. The future work of ARCIC II will be important in clarifying the notion of *koinonia*, the goal to which the two communions are committing themselves.

Bishop Lesslie Newbigin has written: 'A sincere intention to seek unity is incompatible with an intention to remain permanently uncommitted to any particular form of unity.'[15] Future work in both the multilateral and bilateral conversations will need to develop the remarkable convergences emerging in the sacramental agenda. But perhaps the most significant contribution of the next years will be to develop, using the convergences already achieved, a vision of a united Church. The goal can only be provisional, for new things are perceived as the Ecumenical Movement progresses, but the articulation of a vision would provide the Ecumenical Movement with a new impetus, and without a desire and a longing for unity the movement will achieve nothing. A vision would also help to set local initiatives and schemes in a wider context, thus ensuring a proper relation between the local and universal aspects of the Church.

In the future work of developing the vision of unity, Anglicans may have some special contributions to make from their own emerging self-understanding. The century that has seen the rise of the Ecumenical Movement has also seen dramatic changes within the Anglican Communion and, perhaps most significant of all in the last few years, a discovery of what it is that holds the Anglican Communion together. It is no accident that in the reports of the last three Lambeth Conferences attempts to deepen the understanding of Anglican identity are to be found in section reports on unity and renewal. It is often in dialogue with others that self-perception is sharpened. The ecumenical debates on apostolic succession, for example, have helped to free Anglicans from a narrow view of tactile succession and to concentrate rather on faithfulness to the apostolic teaching and mission symbolized in the succession of bishops. The four principles of the Lambeth Quadrilateral, embodied in the 1920 'Appeal to All Christian People', are acknowledged to have played a formative part in the development of the early ecumenical agenda. Now, Anglicans have come to recognize that these principles express not only the gifts of God which hold their own communion together, but that they also point towards that which God is calling the whole Church in unity more fully to become. The Quadrilateral thus describes both 'that vision which God has given, and that to which he calls'.[16] In dialogue with others, Anglicans will come to understand how to embody these principles more fully in word and life.

There are further aspects that might be offered by the Anglican Communion to the Ecumenical Movement. The Communion is held together by a theological method in which Scripture, tradition and reason are characteristically interrelated and also by a characteristic piety. The latter is no longer narrowly understood as worship according to the Book of Common Prayer. The 1978 Lambeth Conference emphasized the central position which the ordered worship of the Church occupies in the distinctive basis of the Anglican Communion. This worship 'patterns and limits the diversity which has characterised Anglicans from the first'.[17] The new forms of liturgy in almost every Province resemble each other in main outline and witness to the unity, not uniformity, of the Communion. This may point to that legitimate diversity which will be a proper mark of the universal Church. In a speech to the General Synod of the Church of England in 1985, the Archbishop of Canterbury brought the four principles of the Quadrilateral together with the shared piety of Anglican worship as he described what holds Anglicans together. The Quadrilateral is not a kind of ecclesiastical check-list:

> It is rather a description of the common life of the body of Christ. We share the Gospel of God when the Creeds are recited. We share the life of the crucified and risen Christ when Baptism and Eucharist are celebrated [...] Having this common life is what communion means. It is deeper than denominational and confessional constitutions. It is about the participation of human beings in God and each other.[18]

The identity of Anglicanism lies in communion in faith, maintained and built up in sacramental living and ministered to by an ordered ministry. A further aspect is developing as the Communion moves away from perceiving itself as the Church of England on a world scale to a fellowship of twenty-five autonomous Provinces drawing together the world's races, cultures and social conditions. 'Bonds of affection' in terms of persons and structures are emerging to maintain and nurture the internal unity of the Communion. The collegiality of bishops has been focused since 1886 in Lambeth Conferences; in 1954 the Anglican Consultative Council was set up, bringing together clergy and laity from every Province and thus providing for inter-Anglican solidarity; and more recently a meeting of Primates has been formed as well as an Inter-Anglican Doctrinal Commission. These various structures of consultation provide an arena for listening to the concerns of the various parts of the world and carrying those concerns back to different regions. They provide also an arena for helping the Provinces to take common decisions. The Archbishop of Canterbury has emerged as the senior bishop of the Communion, 'the eldest brother in a family' with a role 'to nurture the churches and not to rule them'. This development means that universal primacy, of which the Anglican–Roman Catholic dialogue speaks, is already, in a sense, a part of Anglican experience.

These 'bonds of affection' in terms of both structures and persons may be one contribution Anglicans have to make to an ecumenical vision of the unity of the Church in which local and regional manifestations of the Church are held together and embodied at the world level. However, as these structures have emerged, so also have new and difficult questions: is it possible to ensure in a communion of such diversity that all the voices are heard and a genuine community of interpretation brought into being; what is the proper place and role of the episcopal voice in the oversight of any communion; where and how can the laity take their proper place in decision-making and teaching authoritatively; how can the voice of women be heard in the structures of a Church in which oversight still remains with men; what are those areas of faith and order which may properly be decided upon by autonomous provinces, and what must wait for the emergence of a common mind of the whole Communion, or indeed, of a truly ecumenical council; and what place is to be afforded to the process of receiving the decisions of councils by the local churches? In the past this last question was often focused in debates over eucharistic sharing and whether one province might proceed contrary to the mind of other parts of the Communion.[19] Currently, the question of unity and legitimate diversity has been focused in the matter of the ordination of women to the priesthood and of the consecration of women to the episcopate. The matter is one not simply of order, but what is believed about the nature and being of God, of women and men created in God's image and the nature of the Church. It affects the internal unity of the Anglican Communion. Can the communion between Anglicans remain unimpaired where priests from one province are not recognized by another province? How Anglicans proceed with this has implications for their own internal unity: it also has implications for the whole Ecumenical Movement, as those churches who do already ordain women look for an affirmation of their decision. Clearly the Anglican Communion is being tested by this issue.

It is perhaps, paradoxically, in the development, during the last years of this century, of an understanding of what holds the Anglican Communion together, that Anglicans will make their most significant contribution to the Ecumenical Movement. It could be that, in expanding the Lambeth Quadrilateral to embrace the 'bonds of affection' that hold the Communion together, Anglicans would in turn develop the understanding of that third 'mark' of the Church which the Vancouver Assembly determined as necessary for the visible unity of the Church.

So far, emphasis has been placed upon the contributions Anglicans may make to the Ecumenical Movement in the future. The Ecumenical Movement calls equally for changes to be made in the lives of single denominations now. The World Council of Churches has invited those churches which recognize the 'faith of the Church through the ages' in the *Lima Text* to consider what changes in their own lives are appropriate on the basis of such agreement in faith, and what changes are appropriate in their relations with one another. By making changes in their own life on the basis of an affirmation of the theological convergence's in the theological dialogues, Anglicans would signify a serious recommitment to the Ecumenical Movement. The *Lima Text* challenges Anglicans, for example, to review an apparently indiscriminate baptismal policy; to look at their exercise of episcopacy with the existence of unwieldy dioceses and the anomaly of suffragan bishops; to discover ways of reconstituting the third order of ministry; and to reconcile seemingly opposing understandings of the priesthood of the ordained ministry that exist amongst Anglo-Catholic and Evangelical Anglicans. Lying behind a number of issues is the challenge to Anglicans to reaffirm a theological method based upon a proper relation of Scripture, tradition and reason which understands the place of a dynamic tradition and is not tempted to elevate Anglican formularies to rigid confessional statements (see pp. 464–75). By working at these issues in their own lives Anglicans would show that they are concerned with more than mere assent in word to ecumenical agreements, and that they are prepared for costly change in their own life for the sake of the unity of the Church.

In relations with others there are steps that can be taken in the immediate future. An interim eucharistic sharing agreement has already been made in the USA between Episcopalians and Lutherans on the basis of their bilateral dialogue. A similar agreement might be the next appropriate step between Anglicans and Lutherans in other parts of the world. The Church of England is currently considering new ecumenical canons to make closer relations legal with other denominations on the basis of the theological convergences expressed in the ecumenical texts. Now may well be the time to consider a greater degree of sharing of oversight at local and regional levels, the establishment of more officially recognized ecumenical projects and local covenants, and a greater determination to live according to the Lund Principle of never doing alone what can already be done together.

Finally, Anglican–Roman Catholic relations will need special consideration after the official response is given by both churches to the *Final Report* in 1988. Both churches have been asked to consider in advance what are the next 'concrete steps' that might be taken on the basis of the substantial agreements and convergence of the texts. Should these advances be affirmed, then two particular issues will need to be faced: the degree of eucharistic sharing that is appropriate on the basis of such agreement, and the possibility of the Roman Catholic Church recognizing future Anglican ordinations. The letter of Cardinal Johannes Willebrands to the Co-Chairmen of ARCIC II in July 1985 holds out promise for future progress in this second area.[20]

It is not easy to do justice in such as short essay to the rise of the Ecumenical Movement and to Anglican involvement in that movement. It is a complex movement involving relations between many partners at many different levels: between members of a single family, between churches at local, regional and international levels, sometimes bilateral relations, sometimes multilateral. The agenda covers theological dialogue as well as the facing together of the common problems of the contemporary world and the discovery of ways of worshipping together. Anglicans have, undoubtedly, played a significant and often leading part from the beginning of the movement. The criticism heard so often—that Anglican involvement has been full of promise but short on achievement—is not easy to assess. The undoubted failure, all too obvious in the 1980s, to bring about more united churches like South India and North India has in many instances been the result of Anglican withdrawal from negotiations at a damagingly late stage in the process. It may prove in the long run to be a temporary and short-lived failure. It may prove to have been an attempt to safeguard and bring about that real and costly agreement in faith necessary for the confident acceptance of one another. We have to recognize one another as sharing one faith in word and life if we are credibly to celebrate that common faith, hope and love together in the face of a broken and divided world. If such a charitable verdict is right, Anglicans will need to recommit themselves with even more determination and devotion to the Ecumenical Movement in the future. The search for the visible unity of the Church, grounded in the life of the Holy Trinity, focused in a common confession of the apostolic faith in word and life, in shared sacraments and ministry and in bonds of affection, is not an optional extra but an essential part of our Christian obedience. It is our fidelity to the prayer of Jesus that those who follow him might be one.

In the search for the visible unity of the Church, commitment to the development of Anglican self-understanding and identity ought not to be set against the advance of the Ecumenical Movement. The heightened awareness of being a part of a worldwide Anglican Communion, with all the gifts and riches of cultural diversity that offers, ought itself to be marvellous preparation for being part of a truly universal Church. Anglicans need to preserve a balance by being open to receive the riches safe-guarded in other traditions as well as preserving those things in their own life which can be contributed to the whole, but always ready to surrender that which is outdated for the sake of richer and better gifts that god desires to give to his Church. There will always be diversity in the Church, but what part denominational traditions will have to play in the rich diversity held together in unity in the Church of the future is a question still to be answered. At least some Anglicans are ready to believe that 'Anglicanism is not a confession: and is not primarily interested in Anglicanism'[21] (see pp. 249–62).

Even this agenda of ecumenism looks narrow when set against what some were bold enough to call 'the wider ecumenism' of the 1980s, namely the relations between Christians and those of other faiths. What we have learned about the principles of dialogue amongst Christians, about listening attentively to others and only then responding, about searching together, believing that each has something to communicate and that no one person, no single system is the depository of the whole truth, are equally important in this dialogue. The wider framework of inter-faith dialogue is a necessary and proper context for the Christian search for the visible unity of the Churches. As Christians together engage in dialogue with those of other faiths, they will be led to perceive new things in the gospel they share and are commanded to share with the world. It is those who, in ecumenism and inter-faith dialogue, show the characteristics of openness to others as well as a commitment to safeguard the 'jealousies' of their own tradition as they see it, who will be able to overcome the blind and rigid fundamentalism that threatens everywhere the contemporary world.

FROM 1988 TO 1995—ECUMENICAL WINTER OR ECUMENICAL SPRING?

The 1988 Lambeth Conference, like each conference before it, had ecumenism high on its agenda.[22] It gave encouragement to local develop-ments: co-operating parishes in New Zealand, Shared Ministries in

Canada and Local Ecumenical Partnerships in England. It also encouraged Anglicans to fuller commitment to councils of churches and to playing their part in regional unity schemes like the Consultation on Church Unity in the United States of America and the Welsh Covenanting Proposal. On the basis of responses from the provinces the bishops welcomed *Baptism, Eucharist, and Ministry*, the text of the multilateral conversation, noting its importance for supporting relationships with other churches and urging a continuing reception in life of its insights. Again, on the basis of provincial responses, the Lambeth bishops gave a positive response to the *Final Report* of ARCIC, recognizing that the work on Eucharist and ministry is 'consonant in substance with the faith of Anglicans', providing a firm basis for the next steps towards the reconciliation of our churches. ARCIC's work on authority was seen as a foundation for the direction and agenda of the continuing work on authority. Resolutions encouraging continuing dialogues with the Orthodox, the Oriental Orthodox, the Lutherans and the Reformed were passed as well as resolutions asking for new dialogues with the Old Catholics, the Methodists and the Baptists. All of this highlighted the continuing commitment of the Lambeth bishops to all-round ecumenism and all level ecumenism.

One other matter at the Conference was closely related to the question of unity—Anglican unity and the unity Anglicans seek with other Christians—namely the question of the consecration of women to the episcope. The bishops resolved, by a large majority, that each province should respect the decision of others on the matter of the consecration of women to the episcopate without that respect 'necessarily indicating acceptance of the principles involved' and maintaining the highest degree of communion possible. This demonstrated Anglican commitment to living in unity with diversity while a matter touching the ministry of the universal Church was put to a process of open reception, among Anglicans and among the wider Christian community. This decision was to have its effect on ecumenical partners. Those churches which ordained women welcomed the decision while both the Roman Catholic and Orthodox Churches saw it as an obstacle to visible unity.

In the period following the Lambeth Conference the ecumenical euphoria of the 1970s diminished. The long awaited Roman Catholic official response to the *Final Report* of ARCIC, while welcoming much in the text, did not agree with the Lambeth bishops that the texts on the Eucharist and ministry were 'consonant in substance with the faith of the Roman Catholic Church'. Further assurance was sought on a number of matters. In time this request led ARCIC II to produce it *Clarifications* which, while satisfactory to the Vatican, were seen by some Anglicans to cast doubt on the original consensus which they had in 1988 recognized in the text.[23]

441

The process of text, request for clarifications and *Clarifications* has given rise to a major debate about ecumenical method in formulating agreed statements in fresh language, and about the respective response/reception process of churches which have different structures of decision-making. The processes which the churches have gone through in the last thirty years are new ones and it is not surprising that, without any existing guidelines, confusion will occur.

Nevertheless, in spite of setbacks, relations between Anglicans and Roman Catholics in many parts of the world remain close. The work of the theological dialogue continues and the publication of an important ecclesiological text, *Church as Communion*, has been followed by *Life in Christ, Morals, Communion and the Church* which acknowledges that living in unity entails a common moral stance.[24] Behind this text, as so many ecumenical texts, lies the question of authority. How in a united Church would decisions be made, whether in the area of faith, order or morals? What is the role of the magisterium and what place have the whole people of God in discerning and receiving the mind of Christ for the Church? The work of ARCIC II in this area will be an important contribution to Lambeth 1998.

The most significant progress since Lambeth 1988 has come in the Area of Anglican–Lutheran relations. Encouraged by the Lambeth bishops to look for progress in the regions, the United States of America, building on the 1988 Agreement on Interim Eucharistic Hospitality, has now proposed a *Concordat of Agreement* which would bring the two churches into what the text calls 'full communion'.[25] The Concordat provides for the reconciliation of ministries in which all future consecrations of bishops will be jointly carried out by Anglican and Lutheran bishops. Thus Lutherans will take on the sign of the historic episcopal succession. At the same time Anglicans will suspend for a period the requirement of the ordinal for episcopal ordination, signifying that they recognize the authenticity of Lutheran ministers who have not been ordained by bishops in the historic succession. The new relationship of full communion will mean that the two churches will live more closely together while each will maintain its own structures and organization.

While this progress has been made in the United States of America, the European region has also made notable progress. The Meissen Agreement of 1991 brought the Church of England into close fellowship with the Evangelical Church of Germany, which embraces Lutheran, Reformed and United Churches.[26] The agreement commits these churches to share as much of their life and mission as possible in a Europe seeking to find its own unity. *The Meissen Common Statement* is based upon an agreement on the goal of visible unity, a high degree of agreement in faith and an honesty

442

about where differences remain, in particular in the area of the episcopate, apostolicity and succession. The *Porvoo Common Statement* between the Anglican churches of Britain and Ireland and the Nordic and Baltic Lutheran Churches is based upon a similar agreement on the goal of unity and explicit agreement in faith.[27] However, it reaches full agreement on the question of apostolicity and succession and brings the churches into visible unity with a common faith, common sacramental life, a single reconciled ministry in the historic succession and sets up bonds of conciliar life. All of this is for the strengthening of a common mission in the European context.

These three agreements in the United States of America and Europe between Anglicans, Lutherans and Reformed are significant moves forward in the ecumenical movement of the twentieth century. There are also close relationships between Anglicans and Lutherans in other countries— Canada, Tanzania and Australia. The official agreements rely heavily upon the bilateral and multilateral texts produced in the 1970s and early 1980s. They ensure that those texts do not remain on library shelves but that the fruits of theological dialogue form the basis of changed relationships in life. The *Concordat of Agreement* in the United States of America, the Meissen and Porvoo Agreements in Europe take their place with the number of United/Uniting Churches, including the Churches of North India, South India and Pakistan. Anglicans continue to be party to union conversations, for example in the United States of America in the COCU proposals, and in the discussions in South Africa.

In line with Anglican commitment to all-round ecumenism the important dialogue with the Eastern Orthodox Church has continued since Lambeth 1988, working on the subject of ecclesiology. The dialogues with the Oriental Orthodox and with the Reformed have been maintained by international committees and a new and important international dialogue with the Methodists has produced its Report, *Sharing in the Apostolic Communion*.

With so much ecumenical discussion, it is difficult to talk about an ecumenical winter. The dialogue is matched in some parts of the world by a closer relationship in worship and in acts of witness and mission at local level. In other places it has to be admitted that Christians have hardly begun to come out of their isolationisms and to get to know one another, nor do they see any need for closer unity. One of the most taxing questions on the ecumenical agenda remains, what sort of unity are we seeking?

The agreements between Anglicans and Lutherans in the United States of America and in Europe at first sight seem to favour different models of unity. The former, at least for the foreseeable future, sees the continuation of recognizable denominations in which Lutherans will continue to witness as Lutherans to the doctrine and critical function of justification by faith through grace. On the other hand Anglicans in the Porvoo Agreement favour a model of unity which points to a single life and witness, to a life of full visible unity.

The question of the goal of visible unity was once again on the agenda of the Assembly of the World Council of Churches.[28] The Sixth Assembly in Canberra in 1991 formally adopted the Canberra Statement, *The Church as koinonia: gift and calling.*

The theme of *koinonia,* variously translated as communion, fellowship, participation, is understood as fundamental to the life of the Church. The life of the Church is grounded in communion in the life of God the Holy Trinity. Christians are called to make visible this gift of divine unity in a visible common life of faith, sacraments, ministry and conciliar life for the sake of service and mission in the world. The Canberra Statement is clear that visible unity does not mean uniformity but a rich diversity. 'Diversities which are rooted in theological traditions, various cultural ethnic or historical contexts are integral to the nature of communion.' However, one of the sharpest challenges at the Assembly was to say whether there are any limits to diversity. A very clear, but reticent statement emerged: 'Diversity is illegitimate when, for instance, it makes impossible the common confession of Jesus Christ as God and Saviour, the same yesterday, today and forever; salvation and the final destiny of humanity as proclaimed in the Holy Scripture and preached by the apostolic community.' The question of limits to diversity is one of the most urgent questions on the ecumenical agenda.

The Canberra Statement makes reference to the place of the struggles for justice, peace and the care of creation as a mark of the unity of the Church. Here, as in the work ARCIC, can be seen a new emphasis in understanding the unity of the Church in terms of ethical community. The old division between the work of Faith and Order and the work of Life and Work is being bridged. The World Council of Churches in the period following the Canberra Assembly has worked to show how struggles for justice, peace and the care of creation can be seen to be *'koinonia-* generating'. The work has emphasized that the unity of the Church must reflect the unity of a moral community. It may be that this relating of the vision of church unity to the Church's vocation to witness and service will help to show what sort of unity is required for what sort of mission.

The Fifth World Conference on Faith and Order, the first world conference for thirty years, in response to its own question: 'Where are we? Where are we going in the ecumenical movement at the end of the ecumenical century?'[29] replied, 'Towards *koinonia* in faith, life and witness.' The Conference title was itself a statement that the ecumenical movement is still on the move—and that its goal is a communion in faith, sacramental life and witness. The Conference was clear: 'There is no turning back, either

444

from the goal of visible unity or from the single, ecumenical movement that unites concern for the unity of the Church and concern for engagement in struggles of the world.'

The 1998 Lambeth Conference will take place on the eve of the millennium. What lead will the Lambeth bishops give to Anglicans to continue their ecumenical vocation? What vision of unity will the Lambeth bishops inspire and what renewal will they call for in Anglican life so that Anglicans themselves become more unitable with?

BIBLIOGRAPHY

Bell, G., *Documents on Christian Unity 1920–57*, 4 vols. OUP 1924–58.
Boegner, M., *The Long Road to Unity*. Collins, London, 1970.
Crow, P., *Christian Unity: Matrix for Mission*. Friendship Press, London/New York, 1982.
Davies, R., *The Church in Our Times*. Epworth Press 1979.
Fey, H., *A History of the Ecumenical Movement Vol ii, The Ecumenical Advance, 1948–1968*. SPCK, London, 1970.
Goodall, N., *The Ecumenical Movement*, 2nd edn. OUP 1964.
Neill, S., *The Church and Christian Union*. OUP 1968.
Neill, S., Rouse, R. (eds), *A History of the Ecumenical Movement*, Vol i, *1517–1954*. SPCK, London 1970.
Radner, E., and Reno, R. R. (eds), *Inhabiting Unity: Theological Perspectives on the Proposed Lutheran–Episcopal Concordant*. Eerdmans, Grand Rapids, 1995.
Runciman, S. et al., *Anglican Initiatives in Christian Unity*. SPCK, London 1967.
Till, B., *The Churches Search for Unity*. Penguin Books, Harmondsworth, 1972.

NOTES
1 S. Neill, *The Church and Christian Union*.
2 *Baptism, Eucharist, and Ministry* (*The Lima Text*), Faith and Order Paper 111 (WCC Geneva, 1982).
3 *The Final Report of the Anglican–Roman Catholic International Commission*, (CTS/SPCK, London, 1982).
4 *God's Reign and Our Unity*, The Report of the Anglican–Reformed International Commission (SPCK, London, 1984).
5 *Anglican–Orthodox Dialogue*, The Dublin Agreed Statement, (SPCK, London, 1984).
6 'Should not our Churches ask themselves whether they are showing sufficient eagerness to enter into conversation with other Churches and whether they should not act together in all matters except those in which deep differences of conviction compel them to act separately?' *The Report of the Third World Conference on Faith and Order* (Lund 1952), p. 34.
7 *Gathered for Life*, Report of the Vancouver Assembly (WCC, Geneva, 1983), Section 2.
8 *God's Reign and Our Unity*, para. 110.
9 *Anglican–Lutheran Dialogue*, The Report of the European Commission (SPCK, London, 1983), para. 62.
10 *Anglican–Lutheran Relations*, Report of the Anglican–Lutheran Joint Working Group (ACC 1983), para. 25.

11 *Anglican–Orthodox Dialogue*, The Moscow Agreed Statement, (SPCK, London 1977).
12 *Anglican–Orthodox Dialogue*, The Dublin Agreed Statement, (SPCK, London 1984).
13 N. Nissiotis, *A Credible Reception of Baptism, Eucharist and Ministry* (Conference of European Churches, Geneva, 1986).
14 A. Clark, and C. Davey, *Anglican–Roman Catholic Dialogue* (OUP 1974). The Common Declaration by Pope Paul VI and the Archbishop of Canterbury, pp. 1–3.
15 L. Newbigin, *All in Each Place* (WCC, Geneva, 1981).
16 *The Report of the Lambeth Conference 1968* (CIO, London, 1968).
17 *The Report of the Lambeth Conference 1978* (CIO, London, 1978).
18 *Report of Proceedings*, General Synod November Group of Sessions, 1985, Vol. xvi. no. 3, pp. 10355–42.
19 S. Neill, *The Church and Christian Union*, p. 203.
20 Correspondence between Cardinal Johannes Willebrands and the Co-Chairmen of ARCIC II, in *Women Priests: Obstacle to Unity?* (CTS, London, 1986).
21 D. Paton, *Anglicans and Unity* (Mowbray, Oxford, 1962).
22 *The Truth Shall Make You Free*, The Lambeth Conference 1988 (Anglican Consultative Council, 1988).
23 *Clarifications on Eucharist and Ministry* (ACC and Pontifical Council for Christian Unity, 1994).
24 *Church as Communion*, An Agreed Statement by the Second Anglican–Roman Catholic International Commission, ARCIC II (Church House Publishing and Catholic Truth Society, London, 1990). *Life in Christ, Morals, Communion and the Church* (Church House Publishing and Catholic Truth Society, London, 1994).
25 *A Concordat of Agreement* (Forward Movement Publications, London, 1991).
26 *The Meissen Common Statement* (Council for Christian Unity, Church of England, 1992).
27 *The Porvoo Common Statement* (Church House Publishing, London, 1993).
28 *Signs of the Spirit*, Official Report of the Seventh Assembly (WCC Publications, Geneva, 1991).
29 *On the Way to Fuller Koinonia*, Faith and Order Paper No. 166 (WCC Publications, Geneva, 1994).

2 Non-Anglo-Saxon Anglicanism

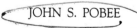

JOHN S. POBEE

The world Christian scene features a category called the world Communions, i.e., families of denominations. And so, autocephalous Orthodox Churches constitute one communion with the Ecumenical Patriarch as the President and spiritual head. On another side of spectrum stands the World Alliance of Reformed Churches, a family which nevertheless has no spiritual head. There is also the Lutheran World Federation which also does not have a spiritual head. In between the Orthodox 'communion' and the

446

Reformed style of communion stands the Anglican Communion, a world-wide family of churches whose spiritual home is the See of St Augustine of Canterbury and which, therefore, sees the Archbishop of Canterbury as its focus of identification.

The very designation Anglican indicates that the Communion has its origin in the English expression or minting of Christian Church, the 'one holy Catholic and Apostolic Church', and at the same time, belonging to Reformation tradition. That Communion has defined itself as a church committed to the Chicago–Lambeth Quadrilateral, i.e., Scriptures, creeds, sacraments (especially baptism and Eucharist) and historic episcopate. And as the Latin American Anglican theologian, Jaci Maraschin, has put it,[1] 'Anglicanism was a liturgical revolution.' As such, Thomas Cranmer's Book of Common Prayer is very much part of Anglicanism's identity and integrity. It seems to me, therefore, the area of worship is one of the crucial areas for testing the continuities and discontinuities of Anglicanism as a Communion.

One more thing about the origins of the Anglican tradition. The English King Henry VIII (1509–47) in 1534 proclaimed the Act of Supremacy by which the church was called *Anglicana Ecclesia*, the English Church. By that Act Anglicanism became the church of the people, *Volkskirche*. As that *Volkskirche* has grown out of and beyond England to many other lands, that identity as *Volkskirche* is certainly up for review. For in a place like the Gambia where the entire Christian population is about 2 per cent in a predominantly Muslim country, the letter and spirit of a *Volkskirche* are non-starters, though it is also true that Anglicanism in many places has had the temptation to behave as if it were the established church of the nation. Outside the United Kingdom, the spirit of *Volkskirche* is neither desirable nor viable.

Consistent with the beginnings of the Anglican tradition, it was at least until the beginning of this century very much an English thing. The centres of Anglicanism were the British Isles (especially England), Australia, New Zealand, Canada and USA, i.e., the Anglo-Saxon world with their overseas missions. Their numbers have been falling even in these Anglo-Saxon areas. Such Anglican churches as were in the non-Anglo-Saxon world were by and large missionary churches. In this century, however, a great change has happened to world Christianity whereby its centre of gravity has shifted from the North to the South, where Christianity is still growing by geometric progression.[2] This is very much reflected in the Anglican Communion.

The Anglican provinces of the Communion outside the Anglo-Saxon world are:

Africa: Provinces of Burundi, Central Africa, Indian Ocean, Kenya, Nigeria, Rwanda, Southern Africa, Sudan, Tanzania, Uganda, West Africa, Zaire (twelve Provinces);

Asia:	Sri Lanka, Korea, Myanmar, Philippines, East Asia, Japan (six Provinces);
Caribbean:	West Indies (one Province);
Latin America:	Brazil, Southern Cone of America (two Provinces);
Middle East:	Jerusalem and Middle East (one Province);
Oceania:	Melanesia, Papua New Guinea (two Provinces).

To these we may add the United Churches of South India, North India, Pakistan and Bangladesh which are in full communion, and the Extra-Provincial areas of the Lusitanian Church of Portugal and the Spanish Reformed Episcopal Church. Of the thirty-seven Provinces of the Communion, at least twenty-five are non-Anglo-Saxon, to which will be added the United Churches in full communion as well as the extra-provincial church.

This spread of the non-Anglo-Saxon Anglicanism portrays an Anglican Communion which has moved beyond the Anglo-Saxon moorings to embrace other cultures. This church which began English is today entering French, Spanish, Portuguese and numerous Asian and African contexts and cultures. On the agenda of the Anglican Communion, then, is the significance and implication of this new pluralism for Anglican identity, especially its original English ethos. But the pluralism has another story to it: the new fact that the overwhelming percentage of professing Christians live in the Southern continents. Walls writes: 'theology that matters will be theology where Christians are, and it looks as if the bulk of Christians are going to be in Africa, and Latin America and certain parts of Asia.'[3] These are the big and growing churches. How does that demographic fact show in the structures of the Communion and impact of Anglicanism in these new times? Will Anglicanism's theology remain the same? And in which directions will it have to change?

Even individual provinces reflect this pluralism of peoples, languages and cultures. Of the inauguration of the 37th Anglican Province of South East Asia, the Anglican World bears this testimony under the title 'One Province, Many Peoples':

> The new diocese brings together four very different dioceses and many more centres. The Diocese of Kuching is composed of two countries, Sarawak and Brunei Darussalam. The Diocese of Singapore unites Anglican churches in Indonesia, Thailand, Vietnam, Laos, Cambodia and Singapore. The Diocese of West Malaysia and Sabah also brings together different peoples, languages and cultures.[4]

The pluralism is not only at the world level but is also evident and characteristic even at the provincial, if not national level. If I may dare use language used in other circumstances, the Anglican Communion is no longer the English at prayer but a rainbow of God.

One more detail of potentially enormous significance. Hitherto, the churches of the south have been coterminous with the poorer part of the family. Some of these dioceses now are located in the rich 'Tiger' countries.

> In the East, Asia, Japan and the 'seven dragons' (Thailand, Malaysia, Indonesia, Hong Kong, Singapore, Taiwan and South Korea) are experiencing the world's highest growth rates [...] In a class by itself stands Japan. Its miraculous economic success sends chills down the spine of even the mighty United States which experiences a very unfavourable balance of trade with Japan [...].[5]

If the churches of the East benefit from this development on the national economic front, then some of these churches will have a capacity which can have implications for the life and spirituality of the Communion. Thus Canon John L. Peterson, incumbent Secretary General of the Anglican Communion, writes:

> The Anglican Communion looks forward to the strong support this new province (South East Asia) can give fellow Anglicans world-wide, especially in crisis situations. The South Asia resources are bountiful and could be enormous help to less fortunate areas of the Communion where a strong Christian witness is needed. I welcome their new united presence in the family with open arms.[6]

This new situation of the emergence of the non-Anglo-Saxon Anglicanism, both because of the demographic shift of the centre of gravity of Anglicanism and because of the economic clout of some of the countries involved has far-reaching consequences for the Communion. And for precisely that reason as well as for the temptation to abuse power, the Communion needs to face the question of what spirituality must undergird its life together. If I may recall the Russian Orthodox theologian Nicolai Berdyaev's famous statement, the question of bread for myself is a material question, but the question of bread for my neighbour, indeed for everyone, is a spiritual and religious matter. Should one's material clout determine one's standing in the Communion? For the same reason, I also would press for the Communion to try to hold together images of communion, body and family as integrally involved one with another, and to work out on the ground what the combination of this triad looks like.

THE ANGLO-SAXON CAPTIVITY OF *ECCLESIA ANGLICANA*

In the article published in the 1988 edition of this book, I made heavy weather of this captivity. The indices of the Anglo-Saxon captivity include the dogged use of the Book of Common Prayer with all its marks of English culture, the use of *Hymns Ancient and Modern* and the *English Hymnal* despite the foreigness of their rhythm and idiom, the quasi-Establishment mentality and the retention of church structures which reflect alien (English) culture and social organization. These structures are proving more problematic in Africa and the Caribbean, for example, than could have been imagined.

Mission agencies, which were related to the Anglican Church but not its official instruments, e.g. the Society for the Propagation of the Gospel, The Church Missionary Society, The Universities Mission to Central Africa etc., did a mighty work in initiating missions to the non-Anglo-Saxon world. But they have also been criticized by Africans for paternalism, at the very least. Today churches in the non-Anglo-Saxon world are taking responsibility for their own missionary vocation, to be missionaries to themselves, even if they still welcome foreign workers. In this respect the creation of African's genius, the catechist, is the unsung hero of African Christianity.

As to the Anglo-Saxon captivity, some of it has been brought on the non-Anglo-Saxon churches by those churches themselves, sometimes for seemingly good and respectable reasons, at other times by careless thinking. On the seemingly respectable side is the question of fidelity to tradition. In what does faithfulness to tradition consist? Does it mean non-Anglo-Saxon churches doggedly following the tradition minted in and shaped by the Anglo-Saxon provinces? Does it make sense for Africans to call their bishop 'My Lord bishop'? Does the parish organization make sense in the African situation where the demarcation of the country and town is not as in Britain?

Besides, that captivity made for inefficiency. The English cultural baggage becomes an albatross around the necks of the non-Anglo-Saxon churches, making them irrelevant promontories in politically independent African or Asian landscapes. Hence in Ghana the Anglican tradition was called *aban mu asor*, literally 'the religion in the Castle', and therefore closest to the seat of the colonial administration. It was a foreign bishop, John Orfew Aglionby who addressed this inefficiency of the North Atlantic captivity, when on 14 January 1925 he told a diocesan conference in Accra: 'As long as people believed—as they did—that they were the Government Church supported by Government funds, it is no wonder that they were content to fold their hands and open their mouths to see what would drop into them.'[7] Non-Anglo-Saxon Anglicans taking owner-ship of the 'project' of being church is on the agenda.

THE MOVEMENT OF AFRO-ANGLICANISM

There are today signs of strenuous efforts to grow out of the Anglo-Saxon captivity. First is the rise of the Afro-Anglicanism movement. Its first meeting took place in Barbados in the West Indies, in 1985, on the theme 'Afro-Anglicanism: Present Issues, Future Tasks'. The second, held in Cape Town, South Africa, was on the theme 'Afro-Anglicanism: Iden-tity, Integrity and Impact in the Decade of Evangelism'. Before the Twelfth Lambeth Conference, through the office of Black Ministries of the Episcopal Church USA, it sponsored a consultation of Afro-Anglican bishops who 'expressed, from their unique perspectives, concerns about the direction of the church'.[8] George Carey, incumbent Archbishop of Canterbury, in a message to the Cape Town Conference, also stated:

> This Conference is a significant sign of that development (i.e. 'the wonderful diversity we enjoy and also the underlying spirit of mutual love which binds us together'). The growing interest of the African tradition within the Communion is one of the most remarkable and exciting signs of the past thirty years. That you have gathered together from so many parts of the world at this time to celebrate our common roots, and I hope, to challenge one another and us all with your discus-sions and your resolutions, is very encouraging.[9]

We may here add that at these conferences representation from other non-Anglo-Saxon Anglicans as well as Anglos have been selectively invited to participate. At the Cape Town consultation, Bishop Goodridge, of the province of the West Indies, identified the contours of the search for Afro-Anglicanism as including sensitivity to the historical legacy, which is more what we create with it than it is preserving the past, the nature of liturgy, respect for cultural diversity, missionary sensitivity, searching for theological maturity and evangelical accountability.[10]

ANGLICAN ENCOUNTER IN THE SOUTH

The second development is the Anglican Encounter in the South. There was an earlier meeting in Kenya in 1995 and a second one took place in February 1997. This also is attempting to get dialogue going between the Anglican provinces of the South, so that the non-Anglos can struggle together to define our common heritage and place and role in the Communion.

THE SEARCH FOR LOCAL LITURGIES

The third is the search for local liturgies that are faithful to the spirit of Anglican worship, but also sensitive to the mood and ethos of the locale. In November 1996 there was an All African meeting on the search for renewing worship in Africa, to find ways of reaching liturgy and worship at the wavelength of the people, employing the idiom, rhythm and symbols, song and music of non-Anglos. In my view this is perhaps the most important aspect for in culturing Anglicanism in the non-Anglo context, because the majority of non-Anglos are not literate in the English language and idiom, and also because ritual is one of the cornerstones of religion. What this says is that the viability of non-Anglo-Saxon Anglicanism will in part depend on worship which has the capacity to renew particular people, and not on sticking doggedly to Cranmer's Prayer Book or whatever.

CATHOLICITY AS A GUIDE IN THE SEARCH FOR ANGLICAN IDENTITY

There are three guideposts for the construct. The first criterion is that the construct should be Catholic, which is defined in the language of the Chicago–Lambeth Quadrilateral as Scripture, creeds, sacraments and ministry. But these need interpretation, where we endeavour to have the original intent of the elements of the Quadrilateral in dialogue with the various contextual situations of the Communion. Declaration 20 of the 1930 Constitution of the Church of India, Burma and Ceylon stated it well: 'As the Church of England, receiving Catholic Christianity from the individual Church, has given characteristically English interpretation to it, the Church of this province aspires to give characteristically national interpretation of that common faith and life.'

However, the following comment on Catholicity drafted by the All African Consultation on Ecumenical Theological Education held in August 1995, can, I believe be adopted by Africans and other non-Anglo-Saxon Anglicans:

> Catholicity means, *inter alia*, expressing a common humanity with all people and cultures as well as belonging to the church universal. Catholicity also means that the search for unity in ecumenical formation does not mean uniformity but a respect for and encouragement of the enriching differences of culture, tradition and experience.[11]

In other words, it is not enough for the non-Anglos to repeat the Catholicity of the Church; more important is it for them to give it content and shape and rediscover the meaning and significance of it for their context.

PROTESTANTISM AS GUIDE

Second, it has to be Protestant. Anglicanism was part of the Reformation movement, seeking a return to faith built on and nurtured by the Scriptures which were believed to be a life-giving message capable of engaging people for salvation. But the Anglican, while faithful to the Anglican principle of 'probable reason', cannot adopt a literalistic approach to the Scriptures; the serious Anglican is committed to critical engagement with the biblical text and situation. Yet more, non-Anglo-Saxon Anglicans need to develop their hermeneutic for reading the Scriptures so that the word of God can truly be experienced as the gospel of hope. In this task I dare to dream that the search for a hermeneutic for our non-Anglo-Saxon regions must be done ecumenically. I suggest mission and ecumenism must be the general perspective for engaging with the Bible in our regions. In this regard the religious and tribal pluralism of our regions demand the ecumenical perspective and methodology. Critical scholarship is not enough: relevance to the context is more important. Above all, the Scripture must be engaged with in the vernacular. In Africa the religious and spiritual epistemology and ontology as well as the communitarian epistemology and ontology must be engaged with and fostered and critiqued by any engagement with Scripture.

EPISCOPAL GOVERNANCE AS GUIDE

Third, the construct must be episcopal. Anglicanism is committed to episcopacy as the focus of identification of the local church and in the fellowship and harmony of the family of God.

However, the Catholic emphasis on episcopacy needs to be liberated from the Anglo-Saxon trappings. The concept and practice of episcopacy have been assimilated to the Anglo-Saxon cultures. There is therefore, a need to examine theologically, sociologically, empirically and practically in a non-Anglo-Saxon context, what it means to exercise *episcope*. The structures that relate to *episcope* must be seen in terms of wholeness of ministries which bring wholeness to the people of God, as to humanity.

VIA MEDIA AS A STYLE

In insisting on the traditional Anglican norms of Catholicity, Protestantism and episcopacy, I have also insisted on the necessity for the particular interpretation by the non-Anglo-Saxon churches. That is what the Anglican characteristic of commitment to the *via media* demands. The

453

contours of that standard include (a) spiritual freedom ministered by the refusal to lay down rigid lines; (b) the willingness to accept each other across the board; and (c) order and propriety which are not too obtrusive. In theory at any rate, this means that there is room for a relative degree of diversity in holy chaos and the recognition of each member of the church. Diversity does not necessarily compromise essential Anglicanism. The *via media* commits Anglicans to excluding limited interpretation and to seeing the Communion as a family in which there is free association, discussion and mutual esteem among all. It should also be the key to the liberation of the younger churches from their Anglo-Saxon captivity. It means the freedom to devise theology and worship consonant with a non-Anglo-Saxon ethos and usage.

ECUMENICAL COMMITMENT

The vocation of the Anglican Communion is not primarily to make many people Anglicans. Looking at the Anglican Communion in terms of the Christian faith itself, one may desire to say there is no special virtue in being an Anglican. To be an Anglican is only a half-way house to the kingdom of God. Besides, to revel in denominationalism is to undermine the credibility of the Church as God's agent of reconciliation of all things to God in Christ. In our Africa, for example, plagued by divisions of tribes, races and sexes, denominationalism only exacerbates the problem of creating the human family of God. Besides, ecumenism is a gospel imperative. Thus, for reasons of theology and historical circumstances, the ecumenical task is an urgent one.

Unfortunately, the non-Anglo-Saxon churches have learnt their European lessons all too well, so that they are not exactly on the way to structural reconciliation. In Ghana, for example, whereas Anglicans initially made a tremendous input in the Church Union negotiations, it was also the Anglicans of the then diocese of Accra who pulled out of the negotiations in 1973–4. Part of the problem was the arrogance of the denomination. But it was also the fear of falling out of communion with the mother church. The present writer was one of the Anglican delegation to the Church Union negotiations. One Archdeacon said to him: 'Are you Canterbury, to even negotiate about and even dare to think of a Union scheme?' For him, if Canterbury does not move, African Anglicans dare not move. It thus behoves the older parts of the Anglican Communion to take seriously their ecumenical vocation. I am encouraged by the memory that some of the giants of the ecumenical movement in this century have been Anglicans—Archbishops William Temple, Michael Ramsey, Geoffrey Fisher etc. I learn from their commitment to the modern ecumenical movement that such commitment is not inconsistent with commitment to Anglicanism as such but sees Anglicanism as a provisional stance. Besides, the model of the via media logically leads to ecumenism, a diversity in unity.

MISSIONARY COMMITMENT

Ecumenical commitment is inextricably linked with mission. In this Decade of Evangelism when mission has come into its own, we need to say that the goal of the mission imperative is not so much to create a denomination as to invite all peoples into the one household of God. There is much rejoicing that Christianity is growing by geometric progression in the nations of the South. But what Tom Tuma wrote in 1977 is still valid. He wrote:

Although the church in Africa is growing steadily, this growth has been both encouraged and facilitated more by the prevailing situation than by a developed and systematic policy of discipling which the church does not have the machinery to sustain. It may well be advisable to start developing a systematic policy of discipling before Islam, which is gradually increasing its influence in Africa, becomes a major threat to the churches there.[12]

There is more work to be done in fulfilling the missionary vocation of the Church in the non-Anglo-Saxon world. And precisely because it is undertaken in very pluralist contexts, it is important for ecumenism to be the perspective for mission.

The elements of the contemporary ecumenical task include the unity of the Church, mission and the common struggle for the common human dignity of all peoples. Konrad Raiser, General Secretary of the World Council of Churches, states that ecumenical task as follows:

The ecumenical movement is a movement of Christians from all churches searching for the places where the 'light of the presence of God shines forth and transforms our dark world'. They are to reflect the light that has shone upon them. In a dark place even a small, flickering light is a source of hope [...] For me the ecumenical movement is essen-tially people discovering one another in trust and committing themselves to each other in that trust. That is a very rare thing in our world.

THE SEARCH TOGETHER FOR A NEW MODEL OF COMMUNION

A COMMUNION

We define ourselves as a communion. But the demographic spread of the Communion means that the old model of being a communion minted when there was an Anglo-Saxon predominance is no longer adequate. How do we deepen the sense of communion between our different parts so that each part may see in the other an authentic expression of the 'one, holy, Catholic and apostolic Church', each part joining in the one proclamation of Jesus the Christ and Lord, co-operating in mission and human service, and sharing in the sacraments? We, therefore need to have a new model for being together in a communion.

In this regard I have two suggestions. First, I submit that following regular sociological principles, a community must have a focus of identification who represents the unity, solidarity, permanence, continuity and perfection of the community. I am persuaded that it will make most sense to have our focus of identification in Canterbury where it all began. In a presentation to the Cape Town meeting of ACC in 1933 I suggested, 'The See of St Augustine can [...] become the symbol of unity, solidarity, continuity, and our striving for perfection. In any event a communion like the Anglican Communion is better served by a focus of identification, like a *primus inter pares*.'[13] At the inauguration of the Province of South East Asia, the Archbishop of Canterbury said to the incoming Primate of that province: 'Bishop Tay, I give you this Primatial Cross as a sign of the Ministry we share with our Lord Jesus Christ. May his love be your inspiration, His suffering your example, and His humility your authority as chief shepherd of His church in this place.'[14] Each Primate is a focus of identification in the Province and its face to the wider society. The model is shared ministry.

Earlier on, I proposed that the Communion should see the images of communion, body of Christ and family as the uppermost elements in constructing our model of communion. The word 'Communion' in its biblical usage has the primary and predominant sense of participation.[15] There is communion where each party participates and sees itself as having a stake in the business of the community; none is an outsider and an onlooker even though there may be different roles and functions. For that reason I wish also to emphasize mutuality as a mark of the Communion. The Akan of Ghana have a saying that 'the left hand washes the right hand and the right the left hand'. Such is the mutuality that should exist between the Anglo-Saxon part of the Communion and the non-Anglo-Saxon part. The task is to search for the practical expression of this participation and mutuality.

A BODY

The other imagery is that of the body. The body is, of course, one of the images of the Church. But I dare here to use it of the Anglican Communion. It captures the diversity in unity, the different gifts that must be brought into the common well-being of the Communion. But above all, the image speaks of the common destiny of the Communion, so that when one part suffers the other parts suffer. That is why Archbishop Desmond Tutu, in a bitter and dangerous struggle with apartheid ideology in the Republic of South Africa, became such a powerful symbol for rallying the Communion on the side of Christian witness against apartheid. Archbishop Robert Runcie articulated it when in his Christmas message for the 1985 he said: 'We are learning in the Communion that when one member suffers, we all suffer. And we are trying to express our common sympathy in ways which we build up the common good.' We need to explore further what applying the image of 'body' to the Anglican Communion would look like on the ground.

A FAMILY

I am an African, a people who define themselves by an extended family and not so much the nuclear family. Elsewhere I describe this epistemology as *cognatus sum, ergo sum*, i.e., I am related to others, therefore I am. The people in the Communion, the 'all sorts and conditions' of people in the Communion, together with the common allegiance to Christ and being in communion with the See of Canterbury, makes me go for the language of the communion as a family, an extended family. The only thing to add is that in the African context this family consists of the living, the dead (or the 'living dead' as Africans see them) and those yet to be born. We contemporary non-Anglo-Saxon Anglicans belong with all Anglicans that have gone before us, with Thomas Cranmer, with William Temple, with Michael Ramsey, with J. Luwum, martyr of Uganda, with Philip Quaque the first African Anglican priest from the Gold Coast (eighteenth century), with Bernard Maseki—we all belong to one family. And in this living together we belong to a yet wider family, the whole household of faith.

One last point. One of the things characterizing biblical faith is the commitment to the transcendent and to eschatology. We non-Anglo-Saxon Anglicans belong to a family which has a sense of the transience of our present existence and are straining towards the transcendent and the eschatological realization of God's kingdom in the whole of God's creation, and in particular, our respective non-Anglo-Saxon situations. We are a people living on eschatological tiptoe, waiting for the realization of God's ultimate purposes. Our pain and our suffering reinforce our living in eschatological expectation, straining for the consummation of God's purposes.

BIBLIOGRAPHY

Barrett, D. B., *The World Christian Encyclopedia. A Comparative Survey of Churches and Religions in the Modern World AD 1900 to 2000.* OUP 1982.

Dadson, J. K., 'The Church of the Province of West Africa'. *Anglican Theological Review* LXXVII: 4 (Feb. 1995), pp. 537–42.

Goodridge, Sehon S., 'The Integrity of Anglicanism. Myth or Mission'. *Anglican Theological Review* LXXVII: 4 (February 1995), pp. 471–49.

Kater, John (ed.), *We Are Anglicans. Essays in Latin American Anglicanism.* Episcopal Church of Panama, Panama, 1989.

Lee Shiu Keung, *The Cross and the Lotus.* The Christian Study Centre of China Religion and Culture, Hong Kong, 1971.

Okorocha, Cyril C., 'African Social History and the Christian Mission in Africa: Implications and Challenges for Afro-Anglicanism'. *Anglican Theological Review* LXXVIII: 4 (Fall 1995, pp. 480–96.

Pobee, John S. 'Mission, Paternalism and Peter Pan Syndrome', in Turner, P. and Sugeno, F. (eds), *Crossroads Are for Meeting. Essays on the Mission and Common Life of the Church in Global Society.* SPCK, London/Swanee/Tennessee, 1987, pp. 91–108.

Pobee, John S. 'Afro-Anglicanism. Quo Vadimus?' *Anglican Theological Review* LXXVII: 4 (Fall 1995), pp. 502–20.

Pobee, John S., 'Afro-Anglicanism: Meaning and Movement'. *The Journal of Religious Thought* 440:1 (1987), pp. 35–54.

Taber, Charles (ed.), *The Church in Africa.* William Carey Library, South Pasadena, 1977.

Tuma, Tom and Phans Mutubuwa (eds), *A Century of Christianity in Uganda 1877–1977.* Church of Uganda, Uganda, 1978.

NOTES

1 Jaci Maraschin, 'Liturgy and the Latin American Anglicanism' in John Kater Jr, *We Are Anglicans. Essays in Latin American Anglicanism.* Episcopal Church of Panama, 1989, p. 31.

2 Andrew F. Walls, 'Towards Understanding Africa's Place in Christian History' in J. S. Pobee (ed.), *Religion in a Pluralistic Society.* E. J. Brill, Leiden, 1976, pp. 180–9; D. B. Barrett, 'AD 2000: 350 Million Christians in Africa' in *International Review of Mission 50* (1970), pp. 39–54.

3 Walls, 'Towards Understanding', p. 183.

4 *Anglican World* (Pentecost 1996), p. 8.

5 John S. Pobee, *Worship of the Free Market and the Death of the Poor* (Life and Peace Institute, Uppsala, 1994), p. 10.

6 *Anglican World* (Pentecost 1996), p. 8.

7 *Golden Shore* 1: vii (January 1926), pp. 177–8.

8 Harold T. Lewis in *Anglican Theological Review* LXXVII: 4 (Fall 1995), p. 444.

9 'Message from the Archbishop of Canterbury to the Second International Conference on Afro-Anglicanism', *Anglican Theological Review* LXXVII: 4 (1995), pp. 448–9.

10 Sehon Goodridge, 'The Integrity of Anglicanism: Myth or Mission?', *Anglican Theological Review* LXXVII: 4 (1995), pp. 471–9.

11 'Renewal Out of Africa', *Ministerial Formation* 71 (October 1995), p. 6.

12 Tom Tuma, 'Directions on Church Growth' in *Today's Church and Today's World* (CIO, London, 1977), p. 99.
13 Laura McGeary and James Rosenthal, *A Transforming Vision* (Church House Publishing, London, 1993), p. 121.
14 *Anglican World* (Pentecost 1996), p. 8.
15 J. Y. Cambell, 'Koinonia and its Cognates in the New Testament' in *Three New Testament Studies* (E. J. Brill, Leiden, 1965), pp. 3–28.

3 What is 'Anglicanism'?

PAUL AVIS

What is Anglicanism? Anglicanism may be said to consist of the faith, practice and spirit (or the doctrine, order and worship) of the churches of the Anglican Communion. But a merely phenomenological formula is inadequate to the demands of a rigorous, critical ecclesiology. We need to apply a hermeneutic of suspicion to this bland, descriptive definition and to ask: Is the faith, practice and spirit of the churches of the Anglican Communion merely a product of the accidents of history, a legitimization, for reasons of expediency, of the way things have happened to turn out? And is the faith, practice and spirit of Anglicanism therefore destined to be dissolved into its constituent elements by equally contingent and irrational historical forces in the future? Or is Anglicanism possibly the embodiment of some genuine ecclesiological truth or principle with some degree of abiding relevance and with something of value to offer to the whole Church? To sharpen the question further: is Anglicanism merely the decadent legacy of unprincipled Anglo-Saxon imperialism, or is it able to take its stand on, and find its justification in, the essence of Christianity, the Christian gospel?

The ambiguity of posing the dilemma of Anglican ecclesiology in this way is brought out in William Temple's remark that nowhere was the Reformation accomplished with so little assertion of abstract principles as in England. We might agree with Temple that, from the point of view of a church committed to a developmental view of Christian truth (though this of course is not how the Reformers would have seen it) and to respect for the claims of individual conscience (this certainly was acknowledged up to a point by the Reformers), it is a matter for profound thankfulness that the English Reformation, at least under Henry and Elizabeth, was primarily a political rather than a theological movement and consequently tied the Church of England to dogmatic definitions less than it did churches

459

elsewhere.[1] However, it remains the case that the political, social and cultural context can only provide the occasion for a church and contribute to the shaping of its outward form. It cannot provide the definition of a church or its *raison d'être*.

THE TERMS 'ANGLICAN' AND 'ANGLICANISM'

Like the terms 'Catholic' and 'Protestant', the terms 'Anglican' and 'Anglicanism' present what the theological polemic of the past used to call 'a nose of wax'—something that could be shaped arbitrarily to suit one's requirements. Certainly the concept of Anglicanism offers a field day for tendentious interpretations and definitions. It is not controversial, however, that these terms derive etymologically from the Latin *Anglicanus* = English. *Ecclesia Anglorum* ('the church of the English') goes back to Gregory the Great who used it in his letters to Augustine of Canterbury early in the seventh century. *Ecclesia Angliae* ('the Church of England') is found in Anselm at the end of the eleventh century and the first decade of the twelfth. The expression *ecclesia Anglicana* was commonly used from the middle of the twelfth century, for example in the Becket correspondence and in John of Salisbury, and was translated 'Church of England'. *Anglicana ecclesia* occurs in Magna Carta (1215) in the statement: *Quod Anglicana ecclesia libera sit* ('that the English church shall be free').[2]

The expression 'Church of England' at this time had no nationalistic or even necessarily patriotic connotations. It simply referred to a geographical entity (sometimes including Wales), the provinces of the western Church situated in England (cf. *Anglicana provincia*). Similarly, *Ecclesia Gallicana* carried no Gallican ideological overtones for the Church in France. Furthermore, *ecclesia Anglicana* looked to the papacy for protection from royal control and sought the freedom from royal interference that would enable it to render obedience to the pope. Magna Carta, contrary to the interpretation beloved of later Anglican Protestants, was recognizing the liberty of the English Church from royal interference, not liberty from papal control.[3]

At the Reformation, the precedent of Magna Carta was invoked and reinterpreted (in fact reversed) to emphasize the claim of the reformed English church to independence from foreign (i.e. papal) jurisdiction. In times past, as 'divers sundry old authentic histories and chronicles' testified, the English church had enjoyed a primitive freedom and independence lately curtailed by the usurpation's of the Bishop of Rome. Thus the act of 1534 confirming the royal supremacy spoke of the sovereign (Henry VIII) as 'the only supreme head in earth of the Church of England called *Anglicana Ecclesia*'.[4] John Jewel, Bishop of Salisbury, entitled his defence of the English Reformation *Apologia Ecclesia Anglicanae.* In Richard Hooker, who conducted his argument in the vernacular from the outset, this became 'the Church of England'.

The term 'Anglican' first appears in the mid-seventeenth century, but in the eighteenth and nineteenth centuries it began to shed its national connotations and to refer more specifically to a distinct theological position. Thus Burke refers to 'Catholics, Anglicans or Calvinists', Macaulay to Anglican doctrine and discipline, and Gladstone to Anglican orders. The ground was prepared by this development for the adoption of the title 'Anglican' for the colonial churches which looked both pastorally and canonically to Canterbury. But ultimately a term was at hand to describe the family of churches of the emerging Anglican Communion even when they had become legally emancipated from the mother church in England.

The French form *anglicanisme* occurs, presumably by analogy with *gallicanisme*, in Lamennais in 1817. 'Anglicanism' was employed by Newman, who by this time had little sympathy with the national aspects of English religion, in 1838. The extreme wing of the Tractarians condemned moderate High Churchmen as 'mere Anglicans'. For them 'Anglican' was a pejorative term. The first Lambeth Conference was referring to the 'Anglican Communion' in 1867 (the term having first appeared in 1851).[5]

However, Anglicanism as an ecclesiological concept is a preoccupation of a later generation, when national ties had been much weakened, pluralism of religious expression was becoming acute, and the social and political aspects of religious belief and practice were beginning to grip the attention of theologians. The situation was then ripe for the common faith and life of the diverse churches of the Anglican Communion to be evaluated as an ideology (the term is not necessary pejorative here), by analogy with Catholicism, capitalism, Marxism and so on.

The present concern with Anglican identity and integrity stems from the application to Christianity generally and Anglicanism in particular of theological analysis informed by the methods of ideological criticism which have been applied to such conceptual and social structures as the Enlightenment and Marxism. The inevitably corrosive effects of this critique are being felt throughout the Christian Church and in all departments of Christian theology, not merely in ecclesiology. If we wished to avoid these unpleasant effects, the study of Anglicanism would have to be uncoupled from the theological discipline of ecclesiology where rigorous theological scrutiny is the order of the day. Anglicanism would then be completely free to develop unhampered by any objective theological assessment or criticism! Free rein would then be given to individuals and groups to operate in pursuit of their ends by direct political manipulation, untrammelled by theological principles which attempt to ground the existence of the Church in the person and destiny of Jesus Christ. Then we would witness the naked pursuit of self-interest, power and prestige, and the blatant gratification of unreconstructed psychological fantasies. This would indeed be flagrantly ideological in the pejorative sense and the answer to our initial question, whether Anglicanism merely expresses and protects the interests of specific groups, or whether it can claim also to be the embodiment of genuine theological principle, would be abundantly clear. Although criticism is sometimes hard to take, I doubt whether most Anglicans, in this case, would wish their church to escape the searching scrutiny of a critical ecclesiology.

ANGLICAN APOLOGETIC

The claims that Anglicans over the centuries have made for their church have not been articulated, needless to say, in a timeless realm of abstract truths but in response to the challenge or threat of the moment—over against Rome, or the Puritans, or modern science, or ecumenism, or the feminist movement, or the chronic pluralism of the modern world. In responding to these challenges or threats, Anglicans have singled out various aspects of the Anglican synthesis that have seemed to be relevant.

In the sixteenth and seventeenth centuries Anglicans defended their continuity with the pre-Reformation Church, rebutted charges of schism, and refuted the claims of the papacy. Thus they emphasized the catholicity of the Church of England, as a church that lacked no essential part of catholic faith and order. At the same time however, they had to contend with the threat from the extreme Protestants, or Puritans, who maintained that reform had not gone far enough and that the Church of England was no true church. In response to this internal challenge, such apologists as Whitgift and Hooker upheld the fully reformed character of the Church of England as worthy to stand beside the best reformed churches in Christendom.

In these battles the weapons of controversy were those of biblical and historical scholarship—and in the case of Hooker, at least, a grasp of the first principles of law. (This is not to say that Anglican scholarship was never deployed tendentiously or the evidence never distorted.) The Church of England took its stand on the new humanist learning of the Renaissance and the accumulation of erudition in the seventeenth century. The appeal to sound learning was, therefore, already a significant factor in Anglican apologetic. Furthermore, this appeal was imbued with a certain philosophical and ethical spirit, marked by moderation in argument, caution in the claims that were made, pragmatism and a grasp of what was possible, philosophical probalilism, and a sense of the limits of human speculation. In the hands of Hooker, Locke and Butler, arguments characterized by these

462

modest but by no means ubiquitous qualities, were not merely ineffectual literary gestures, as we might be inclined to suppose, but devastating cumulative arguments that successfully defended the Anglican position against its enemies both within and without.

In the second half of the nineteenth century Anglican thought began to grapple—not without trauma—with developments in the modern worldview: biblical criticism, evolutionary theory and immanental philosophy. The appeal to sound learning entered a new phase with the symposium *Lux Mundi*, edited by Charles Gore, in 1889. The aim of the contributors, Oxford Anglo-Catholic clerics, was ' "to succour a distressed faith" by endeavoring to bring the Christian creed into its right relation to the modern growth of knowledge, scientific, historical and critical, and to modern problems of politics and ethics'.[6]

In the twentieth century Anglican apologetic began to respond to the vision of the emerging ecumenical movement and the claim began to be heard that the combination of catholic, reformed and scholarly factors in Anglicanism qualified it to serve as a paradigm of Christian unity. The Anglo-Catholic document *Catholicity* (1947) suggested that Anglicanism's success in holding together living principles that in other traditions had been torn asunder opened the way for 'the Church of England [sic] to be a school of synthesis over a wider field than any other church in Christendom'. Anglicanism, it was claimed, had maintained a special witness to the Christian tradition in its fullness: 'The history of Anglican theology shows that it possesses a power of construction which has made for synthesis rather than for division.'[7]

The claim that Anglicanism possesses a unique gift for fostering synthesis between Christian traditions cannot go unchallenged. This is not generally supported by the internal experience of Anglican churches. The domestic traditions of churchmanship, the so-called ecclesiastical parties—High, Low and Broad, as they once were; now Catholic, Evangelical and Liberal—seem to have largely gone their own way, taking care to reinforce their prejudices all along the line through party patronage of livings, partisan theological colleges and tame newspapers and journals. There are signs that this polarization is moderating, but until recently internal ecumenism has been minimal. Compromise may have occurred but not synthesis.

How is synthesis achieved? Synthesis may be achieved explicitly through theological work: research, dialogue and reconstruction. Or it may be effected tacitly through the emergence of new symbols in leadership, worship, spirituality and mission that bridge divisions and help to heal old conflicts. As far as the symbolic life of the Church is concerned, we are largely at the mercy of the framers of liturgy and the extent of their awareness of the dynamic nature of symbolism as an integral living tradition with a life of its own that can indeed be fostered, shaped, renewed and even reborn, but not contrived. Greater respect for hallowed symbols, and the fostering of true creativity, will help to bring about synthesis and integration (though not without conflict) at the tacit level of the symbolic life of a religious community. Meanwhile, however, there is much that we can do to enhance theological enquiry and awareness. Theologies that are ideologically dubious and critically incoherent may be discredited—even if not completely banished from the scene—by criticism and education. In this way theological obstacles to the realization of at least one aspect of the Anglican vocation—the openness to new knowledge—may be demolished.

Finally, the feminist movement—as momentous a revolution as the Reformation or the Enlightenment—presents the latest challenge to Anglican integrity. Once again it is secular knowledge—in this case the contributions of psychology, sociology and human biology—that compel us to reassess our assumptions as to gender identity that underlie virtually every aspect of Christian doctrine, including the doctrine of God, Christology and ecclesiology. By engaging with relevant non-theological disciplines, theology may be brought into line with what we know about the human world. But once again we have to admit that we do not have the same control over the subliminal archetypal projections and images that pervade our perception of the realm of gender identity. It is these unacknowledged, unreconstructed psychological inhibitions that often present the most intractable obstacles to the progress of Anglican thought in dialogue with contemporary knowledge and insight. Inadequate explicit theologies, which are often so implausible that their true status as the rationalization and legitimization of psycho-social factors is concealed from no one, are easier to deal with. The questions raised by the feminist movement constitute the latest challenge to Anglicanism's appeal to sound learning, its method of drawing on all the resources of truth and understanding, its intellectual catholicity.

ANGLICAN SELF-DEFINITION

One approach to the question of the essence of Anglicanism is to look at various formulations of Anglican self-definition through the centuries, bearing in mind the particular circumstances in which they were made and the audiences to which they were addressed. Anglican exercises in self-definition fall broadly into two categories: those that focus on the material ingredients of the Anglican synthesis—Scripture, tradition, reason and so on—and those that claim a distinctive method, ethos or praxis for the Anglican way. Those in the first category hark back to the formation of Anglicanism in the sixteenth and seventeenth centuries. Between the English Reformation and the Oxford Movement there was a

464

consensus as to the identity of Anglicanism as a reformed church confessing with all the Reformers the supreme authority of Scripture, justification by faith, the legitimate role of the laity (embodied in the sovereign and parliament) in the government of the church, and a particular national and regional identity. Those in the second category of Anglican self-definition—the appeal to an elusive ethos—belong to the period since the Oxford movement, for the radical Tractarians successfully challenged this consensus by asserting the authority of tradition ('The Church to teach, the Bible to prove'), compromising the forensic doctrine of justification by faith with the notion of justification by infused sacramental grace, clericalizing the government of the church and repudiating the partnership between church and a now partly secularized state. The Church of England, according to the Tractarians, derived its claims, its authority and its integrity from its apostolic foundation through the historic episcopal succession rather than from the dynamic event of the preaching of the gospel (Luther) or the sanction of the state (Erastian Protestants).[8]

The established consensus which, with whatever variations of emphasis and reservations on the part of individuals, upheld the broadly Protestant character of the Church of England, and to which all parties of churchmanship subscribed, was effectively shattered. The Protestant elements in Anglicanism, detached however from the high ecclesiology of the High Church tradition and from the liberality of the Latitudinarian or Broad Church tradition, became the special preserve of Evangelicals. Appeal could now be made, where Anglican self-definition was concerned, only to a consensus that remained elusive, a matter of ethos and approach, tacit rather than explicit, an unwritten understanding between members of a common fellowship.[9]

To define distinctiveness of Anglicanism in this way is certainly to make a virtue of necessity. The notion of a tacit consensus residing in a common ethos is a *post factum* accommodation to the demise of doctrinal accord within the church. To say that, however, is not by any means to reject the concept of a tacit consensus subsisting in the realm of praxis, but simply to make it abundantly clear that what we are talking about is not a supposed timeless essence of Anglicanism, but a conceptual construction, a pragmatic adjustment to the facts of history.

THE ANGLICAN SYNTHESIS

Now let me bring forward some witnesses to Anglican self-definition—first as to the threefold composition of the Anglican synthesis. King James I (but not for his unsavory personal reputation) may speak for Jacobean Anglicanism. 'I am such a catholic Christian,' James declared in 1609, 'as believeth the three creeds, that of the apostles, that of the Council of Nice, and that of Athanasius [. . .] And I believe them in that sense as the ancient fathers and councils that made them did understand them [. . .] I reverence and admit the four first general councils as catholic and orthodox [. . .] As for the scriptures, no man doubteth I will believe them.'[10] James mentions the Scriptures last, not as the least important, but because their paramount authority can be taken for granted. The Thirty-Nine Articles had already affirmed: 'Holy scripture containeth all things necessary to salvation' (Article VI). Implicit in the Articles is the notion of primary and secondary truths, things necessary to salvation and things indifferent—or, to use the terminology of the Second Vatican Council, a hierarchy of truths. The creeds themselves are acknowledged to derive their authority from the fact that 'they may be proved by most certain warrants of holy scripture' (Article VIII). The same asymmetry between Scripture and tradition is exhibited in the Church of England's canon law: 'The doctrine of the Church of England is grounded in the holy scriptures and in such teachings of the ancient fathers and councils of the Church as are agreeable to the said scriptures' (Canon A5). This combination of Scripture and tradition, with Scripture in the dominant position, constitutes Anglicanism's reformed Catholicism.

When in the nineteenth century it became necessary to stretch the fabric of the Anglican synthesis to accommodate the findings of biblical scholarship, scientific discoveries and immanental world-views, this reformed catholicism became transmuted into 'liberal catholicism'—and of this development Charles Gore (1853–1932) was the outstanding exponent. Not that Gore intended in any way to play down the scriptural component in Anglican theological method. 'The character of the Anglican church', he wrote, 'has been from the first that of combining steadfast adherence to the structure and chief formulas of the Church catholic with the "return to scripture" which was the central religious motive of the Reformation.' Anglicanism, therefore, according to Gore, bears witness to a scriptural catholicism, 'a catholicism in which scripture is enthroned in the highest place of controlling authority in the church'. But the revival of learning at the Renaissance had introduced a third participant in the Anglican synthesis, the appeal to scholarship:

It is the glory of the Anglican Church that at the Reformation she repudiated neither the ancient structure of catholicism, nor the new and freer movement. Upon the ancient structure—the creeds, the canon, the hierarchy, the sacraments—she retained her hold while she opened her arms to the new learning, the new appeal to scripture, the freedom of historical criticism and the duty of private judgement.

466

At the beginning of his public career, in 1889, Gore affirmed not only the reformed but also the liberal character of Anglican catholicism: 'a catholicism [. . .] which is scriptural and represents the whole of scripture; which is rational and can court the light of all genuine enquiry; which is free to deal with the new problems and wants of a new time'. At the height of his influence, as Bishop of Oxford in 1914, Gore reiterated this position. Anglicanism has stood since the Reformation for a 'liberal or scriptural catholicism' in which Scripture constitutes 'the sole final testing ground of dogmatic requirement'. The characteristically self-assured and autocratic way in which Gore attempted to freeze this synthesis in order to prevent further development—in particular to inhibit intercommunion with non-episcopalians, critical positions that went beyond those of *Lux Mundi* (1889), and unauthorized liturgical innovation—is not our concern here. But in his threefold appeal to catholic, Protestant and scholarly components, Gore is representative of classical Anglican self-definition.[11]

This conception of the Anglican synthesis was endorsed in a report submitted to the Lambeth Conference of 1930 which declared (the statement was drafted by William Temple):

> Our special characteristic and, as we believe, our peculiar contribution to the universal Church, arises from the fact that, owing to historic circumstances, we have been enabled to combine in our one fellowship the traditional faith and order of the catholic Church with that immediacy of approach to God through Christ to which the evangelical churches especially bear witness, and freedom of intellectual enquiry, whereby the correlation of the Christian revelation and advancing knowledge is constantly effected.

Anglican apologists have sung the same song until recently. In 1965 Archbishop Michael Ramsey, writing for a Roman Catholic audience, played down the liberal ingredient in the Anglican synthesis but stressed its reformed catholicity. 'Our church has two aspects,' Ramsey explained:

> On the one hand we claim to be a church possessing catholic tradition and continuity from the ancient Church, and our catholic tradition and continuity includes the belief in the real presence of Christ in the blessed sacrament; the order of episcopacy and priesthood, including the power of priestly absolution. We possess various institutions belonging to catholic Christendom like monastic orders for men and women.

Nevertheless, Archbishop Ramsey went on:

> Our Anglican tradition has another aspect as well. We are a church which has been through the Reformation, and values many experiences

467

derived from the Reformation, for instance the open Bible: great importance is attached to the authority of the holy scriptures, and to personal conviction and conversion through the work of the Holy Spirit.[12]

Let me add a few words of assessment at this point. To describe Anglicanism as a synthesis of catholic, protestant and liberal elements is correct, but it does not get us very far. It is not sufficient to bring out the distinctive character of Anglicanism. Bilateral dialogue with the churches of the Reformation has made Anglicans more aware of the extent to which these churches also appeal to the undivided Church and to the classical doctrines of patristic Christianity. Neither are the Reformation churches short of sound learning or spiritual liberty. Furthermore, the process of reform within the Roman Catholic Church, initiated by the Second Vatican Council, while it by no means completely neutralizes Anglican objections to Roman Catholic claims, goes some way towards muting the traditional anti-Roman stance of Anglican apologetic. The common ground achieved in the area of doctrine by the Anglican–Roman Catholic International Commission (ARCIC), while not beyond criticism and lacking the full endorsement of the Vatican, nevertheless mitigates further the aspect of Anglican apologetic that has served traditionally to distinguish Anglican identity from Rome.

All shades of Anglican churchmanship can be found subscribing to the view that the Anglican faith is both catholic and reformed at the same time hospitable to intellectual enquiry. But the conclusions that they draw from this commitment are rather different. To some this threefold appeal will mean ordaining women; to others, not on any account doing so. To some it will follow that there is no theological obstacle to intercommunion with, say, Lutherans; to others, no such conclusion follows. To some it will entail adopting a tolerant attitude to doctrinal radicals within the Church; to others, this would be a betrayal. This paradoxical situation might well lead us to ask whether the distinctiveness of Anglicanism lies not in the ingredients—which are not unique to Anglicanism—but in the nature of the mixture.

THE ESSENCE OF ANGLICANISM

Is Anglicanism then ultimately an ethos, a method of approach, an attitude of mind? If the 'static' view of the Anglican synthesis that we have been considering so far represents an attempt at a *via media*, a balancing act between various factors based on compromise and mutual concessions, the more mystical view of the Anglican synthesis sees it as an attempt to reconcile opposites and to transcend conflicts. If the first stands for 'the love of balance, restraint, moderation, measure' (P. E. More), the second invokes vision, passion and risk. The first is conservative in tendency, the second progressive. The former defensive, the latter innovatory.

As Michael Ramsey has written, Anglican theology is not a system or a confession, but 'a method, a use and a direction'. Though appeal is made to the gospel, the Catholic Church and sound learning, these do not run side by side, as it were, but are fused creatively, reacting upon one another, modifying one another and generating new combinations. Ramsey's *The Gospel and the Catholic Church* is a notable attempt to achieve this. Both Ramsey and Vidler found such an approach in the thought of F. D. Maurice with his insistence on digging beneath competing systems to discover the living principles which they at the same time systematized and distorted. It was inconceivable to Maurice that those principles, born of encounter with 'the divine order', could be ultimately incompatible. Thus Vidler too insists that what is distinctive of Anglicanism is not a theological system but a vocation:

Anglican theology is true to its genius when it is seeking to reconcile opposed systems, rejecting them as exclusive systems, but showing that the principle for which each stands has its place within the total orbit of Christian truth, and in the long run is secure only within that orbit or[. . .] when it is held in tension with other apparently opposed, but really complementary principles.[13]

In his indispensable study of seventeenth-century Anglicanism, H. R. McAdoo has claimed to detect this reconciling method at work. Drawing attention to the 'polarity or quality of living tension' which he regards as 'an overall characteristic of Anglican theological method', McAdoo holds up the Caroline divines (together with the 'Holy Party' who produced *Lux Mundi*) as its most authentic exponents. Of this approach, from Hooker onwards, he writes:

Beneath the surface was the feeling for the *via media* which was not in its essence compromise or an intellectual expedient but a quality of thinking, an approach in which elements usually regarded as mutually exclusive were seen to be in fact complementary. These things were held in a living tension, not in order to walk the tightrope of compromise, but because they were seen to be mutually illuminating and to fertilize each other.

Scripture and tradition, revelation and human reason, 'credal orthodoxy and liberty in non-essentials, the appeal to antiquity and the welcome to new knowledge, the historic continuity of the Church and the freedom of national churches'—all were held together to form the distinctive spirit of Anglican theology. The question of whether this is not a rather idealized picture of what was going on in Anglican internecine strife and theological polemic in the seventeenth century does not detract from the attractiveness of McAdoo's thesis.[14]

Something similar was advocated at the 1930 Lambeth Conference. The conference committee set out, without specifying doctrines, the 'ideals for which the Church of England [sic] has always stood'. These ideals are not unique: 'they are the ideals of the Church of Christ. Prominent among them are an open Bible, a pastoral priesthood, a common worship, a standard of conduct consistent with that worship and a fearless love of truth.'[15] Here it is the qualifiers that are significant.

The Bible is open: available, unchained, not subject to control, monitoring and binding interpretation by ecclesiastical authority. The pre-eminent place accorded to Holy Scripture in the Anglican formularies is no mere lip service, but is matched by the freedom enjoyed by Anglican laity since the Reformation to read and to study the Bible in the vernacular and to arrive at their own convictions and to express them (within certain political constraints in the sixteenth and seventeenth centuries).

The Anglican priesthood is a pastoral one: neither a sacerdotal caste serving to restrict the spiritual privileges of the laity, the people of God, nor a didactic, scribal, rabbinic, judicatory order that lays down the law as to belief and practice and is entrusted with the duty of policing its enforcement. It is a priesthood—it has authoritative, sacramental and even mediatory functions (provided that these are understood as embodying the priestly character of the people of God who are baptized into Christ's priestly office)—but a priesthood that involves all the gentleness, the attention to human needs, the listening ear, and the solidarity in our human condition of the true pastor.

Worship is common: that is to say, not performed by a vicarious priesthood on behalf of a liturgically unqualified laity, but shared by the whole priestly body of the Church whose comprehending participation (to use a phrase of Stephen Sykes) is vital. Moreover, under the parochial system, it is the common prayer of a given community, that already exists for other, secular purposes, not of a self-selecting élite. The nature of Anglican common worship constantly militates against all sectarian tendencies.

Finally, Anglicanism's love of the truth is fearless. The scholarly pursuit of truth and the conscientious witness to it are safeguarded in Anglicanism. I am aware of the irony of citing this particular note of the essence of Anglicanism in the light of Stephen Sykes' criticisms of Anglican comprehensiveness as being marked, not by a fearless love of the truth, but by a deliberate fudging of theological issues that appeals to an unrestricted comprehensiveness as a let out for lazy minds trying to prop up a decadent church. However, I think it is defensible to claim that Anglicanism has put a special value on scholarly integrity and has permitted a breadth of theological opinion to flourish within its borders.

The Anglican ideal is certainly a noble one, though one that remains to be fully attained. It appears to focus on a particular view of the role of authority in the sphere of religion. It appeals to Scripture, tradition and reason, but does so in the acknowledged context of our modern pluralistic situation. As a result, these three sources or criteria are combined in a dynamic way in order to serve as mutual qualifiers, checks and balances, not merely to restrict and relativize each other but also to generate innovative thinking in dialogue with the Church's cultural and ideological context. The result is a muted— some would say emasculated— notion of authority, but it is one that is eminently suited to our condition.

The question of the distinctiveness of Anglicanism is a legitimate and necessary one, but it must never become our prime concern. The problem of identity is one that troubles both individuals and institutions, including churches, but to become obsessed by it would be neurotic. Identity is not an end in itself, but it is a corollary of integrity. While Stephen Sykes has argued that there is no integrity without identity, I would prefer to put the equation the other way round. A distinctive identity does not necessarily guarantee integrity. While identity can be contrived by all sorts of dubious means, including the manipulation of people's perceptions by the public relations industry, there is no short cut to integrity. Pursue integrity and identity will take care of itself. Anglicanism exists. Its political, social and cultural parameters, with all their compromises, are given. We should not fret about them. The vocation of Anglicanism must be to proclaim the gospel of Christ within those parameters appealing, as is its wont, to all valid sources of information and insight, and to spend itself in the service of Christ for the redemption of humanity. As Michael Ramsey wrote more than half a century ago:

> While the Anglican Church is vindicated by its place in history, with a strikingly balanced witness to gospel and Church and sound learning, its greater vindication lies in its pointing through its own history to something of which it is a fragment. Its credentials are its incompleteness, with the tension and travail in its soul. It is clumsy and untidy, it baffles neatness and logic. For it is sent not to commend itself as 'the best type of Christianity', but by its very brokenness to point to the universal Church wherein all have died.[16]

THE VOCATION OF ANGLICANISM

Anglicanism aspires to be a catholic faith with its roots in Christian antiquity and in continuity of faith and order, worship and witness, from the apostles. The Reformers appealed to the antiquity of the British Church, an autonomous church that long antedated the mission of St Augustine of Canterbury in 597. The claim was made (for example, by Archbishop Parker under Elizabeth) that the English episcopate derived from the visit of Joseph of Arimathea. Jewel insisted that the Church of England had departed, not from the Catholic Church, but from the errors of Rome. Whitgift pointed out that the Church of England was 'reformed' not 'transformed' because 'we retain whatsoever we find to be good, refuse or reform that which is evil'.[17] In a later generation, Charles Gore believed that Anglicanism could offer 'catholicism without Rome' and Garbett affirmed: 'Uncompromisingly the Church of England is the catholic Church in this land, set free from subjection to the Church of Rome.'[18]

The catholicity of Anglicanism rests on its continuity of worship, employing ancient forms purged of medieval accretions, and of pastoral care in the parishes and parish churches whose origins, in Britain, go back to time immemorial. Anglican Catholicity rests also on the retention of the threefold order of bishops, priests and deacons in the historic succession. Above all, the catholic character of Anglicanism is revealed in its adherence to the Scriptures, the creeds and the councils of the undivided Church (canonically, the first four), which give the Church its christological and trinitarian dogmas. The catholicity of Anglican faith is further evinced by the fact that it acknowledges the authority of the Church (and of a particular church) to adjudicate in disputed matters of faith. In appealing to the authority of the Church gathered in council, Anglicanism shows itself to belong to the conciliar, as opposed to the monarchical tradition of Catholicism.

Anglicanism aspires to be a reformed faith. The essentially reformed character of Anglicanism is evidenced above all in the place that it gives to Holy Scripture as the norm by which all other sources of Christian truth are evaluated. It was by the touchstone of Scripture that the Reformers rejected aspects of medieval Catholicism: the universal jurisdictiction of the pope, the sacerdotal office of the priesthood, the propitiatory sacrifice of the Mass, withholding the cup from the laity, transubstantiation which overthrows the nature of a sacrament, the liturgy in a foreign tongue, compulsory clerical celibacy, mandatory sacramental confession, purgatory and the treasury of merits, the cultus and mediatory role of the saints, the downgrading of the lay vocation compared with the religious life. Correspondingly, it was on the authority of Scripture, as they read it, that the Reformers upheld the role of the magistrate, the godly prince of the Old

472

Testament, as supreme governor in spiritual as well as temporal affairs. They appealed to Scripture (incontrovertibly) for their forensic doctrine of justification—by faith alone without merit accruing to good works—and insisted on this doctrine, furthermore, as the criterion of a standing or falling church (as Luther put it).

Anglicanism aspires to be a rational faith. Its tradition of offering hospitality to scholarly enquiry pre-dates the Reformation and many a scholar persecuted by stricter regimes has found sanctuary in the Church of England. Anglicanism can sustain criticism of its claims and beliefs as few churches can. It is amazingly tolerant of the clash of opinion within its ranks. Provided outward forms are observed—and these are not to be despised as a mere charade: they are actually the symbolic expression of the Church's most fundamental convictions—it is satisfied. A principle of spiritual liberty gradually emerged from the power struggles of Anglican history. Anglicanism is irrevocably committed to liberty of prophesying. If, as Karl Popper insists, rationality consists in openness to rational criticism, Anglicanism may fairly claim to be a rational faith.

Bishop Wand claimed: 'On the evidence of friend and critic alike, the three most obvious features of Anglicanism are tolerance, restraint and learning.'[19] Though I would be happier if he had said faith, hope and charity, Wand's trinity is not to be sniffed at. Garbett called the Church of England 'the most liberal-minded church in the world', adding: 'Perhaps we may say it is the most charitable of all churches.' That sounds better, for the greatest of Christian virtues is charity.

The tolerance and restraint that gave scope to sound learning were not the products of an enlightened ideal of individual liberty and of the supremacy of conscience. It would be anachronistic to look for that in the sixteenth century. They were an expression of the cold compromises of Tudor statecraft (in Hensley Henson's memorable phrase). But this policy looked like moderation. It had the appearance of tempering the excesses of ecclesiastical authority and could be reinterpreted into a principle of spiritual liberty. It was for reasons of political expediency that Elizabeth declined to make windows into men's hearts and minds, but that policy eventually came to acquire theological legitmation as the expression of a principle of religious reticence. Thus the reality of political manipulation could become transposed into the rhetoric of spiritual liberty. And why not? As Vico and Freud have taught us, some of our highest aspirations have their historical or evolutionary origins in somewhat unedifying earthly and fleshly needs.

As Henson pointed out against Creighton's rather rosy reading of the role of sound learning in the English Reformation, what emerged from this process by the end of the seventeenth century was not merely an appeal to sound learning in general, but an acceptance of the function of criticism

473

in particular—'a frank acceptance of sound learning as competent to revise the current tradition, both by interpreting afresh the sacred text, and by certifying through independent research the true verdict of Christian antiquity.'[20] The claims of learning implied the right of criticism which in turn rested on a principle of spiritual liberty.

For all its lack of definition, its pragmatism, muddle and inconsistency, its hospitality to lost causes and unreconstructed prejudice, its apathy and inertia, Anglicanism nevertheless offers a home and an environment congenial to the fearless pursuit of truth without let or hindrance by an ideologically motivated ecclesiastical authority whose aim is not to seek 'the truth as it is in Jesus' but to defend the structures that give some individuals power over the souls of others. As Hensley Henson put it:

> The doctrinal incoherence of the Church of England, though it is unquestionably perplexing, practically embarrassing and not infrequently actually scandalous, has its roots in something far more respectable than an indolent acquiescence in undiscipline or a reprehensible indifference to truth. It reflects the reluctance of considering and responsible English churchmen to thrust the rough hand of authority into the sphere of religious opinion. Not an indifference to truth but a juster perception of the conditions under which truth must be sought and defended, leads them to shrink from discouraging individual efforts to discover a solution of the problem which now confronts, in various measures of urgency, every section of the Christian Church, namely how to reconcile the theological tradition expressed in creeds and immutable in theory, sacrosanct by time, and the ever-growing knowledge of mankind. [21]

Anglicanism is committed historically to a distinctive approach to the question of authority. Its sources of authority, dispersed as they are through many channels, are both mutually restricting and mutually illuminating. In the modern intellectual situation this is beneficial since it inhibits the rash enunciation of dogma, the over-confident articulation of absolutes and the heavy-handed exercise of ecclesiastical authority. Though all these might bring a temporary sense of satisfaction to all those of us who are frustrated by the dilemmas of contemporary Christianity, they are likely to prove, as they have in our sister churches, a millstone around our necks. The vocation of Anglicanism, then, is to create the climate of spiritual liberty in which individuals may bear witness to the truth as they see it, submitting themselves to the criticism of their peers without fear of ecclesiastical censorship. However, the indispensable condition of this liberty is continued participation in the worshipping life of the Church and profession of the fundamental baptismal faith (and in the case of the clergy, canonical obedience to the bishop). This discipline helps to curb rampant individualism and ensures that the individual thinker remains embedded in the tradition that has nurtured them. I would certainly wish to add that any celebration of the spiritual liberty of an Anglican must go hand in hand with a stronger and more respectful attention to the Anglican theological heritage so that we learn to work more explicitly with the resources that have made us what we are, and do not indulge the fantasy that we can sit light to them or despise them.

On this interpretation, the distinctive identity of Anglicanism is located in the sphere of theological method and the understanding of authority that informs it, rather than in terms of liturgy, spirituality or polity. But let it not be thought that this theological identity of Anglicanism is intended in an élitist sense, as though only 'professional' theologians could receive the full benefit of being an Anglican. Every thinking Christian, lay or ordained, is engaged continuously in doing theology, reflecting on the things of God, whether in the liturgy and private prayer, Bible study and reading, or in taking part in the governance of the Church at parochial or synodical level or in dealing with the mundane necessities of life or engaging in its more creative enjoyments. Every decision we take and every priority we make exemplifies, for good or ill, Anglican theological method. In Anglicanism we do not have these things dictated to us: we are involved in the making of them. As Anglicans we are intellectually privileged. Our theological tradition is a noble one. Our theological resources, if not munificent, are at least ample. If at the present time we deserve to be chastised for a nerveless failure to grapple with Christian truth rigorously and systematically, that indicates a departure from our tradition, a decline, and one that we must try to remedy.

BIBLIOGRAPHY

Avis, P. D. L., *Anglicanism and the Christian Church: Theological Resources in Historical Perspective.* T. & T. Clark, Edinburgh/Augsburg/Fortress, Minneapolis, 1989.

Avis, P. D. L., *Authority, Leadership and Conflict in the Church.* Mowbray, London, Trinity Press International, New York, 1992.

Avis, P. D. L., 'Keeping Faith with Anglicanism', R. Hannaford (ed.), *The Future of Anglicanism.* Gracewing, Leominster, 1996, pp. 1–17.

Avis, P. D. L., 'The Distinctiveness of Anglicanism', C. J. Podmore (ed.), *Community–Unity–Communion.* CHP, London, 1998.

Hannaford, R. (ed.), *The Future of Anglicanism.* Gracewing, Leominster, 1996.

McAdoo, H. R., *The Spirit of Anglicanism.* A. & C. Black, London, 1965.

More, P. E. and Cross, F. L. (eds), *Anglicanism: The Thought and Practice of the Church of England, Illustrated from the Religious Literature of the Seventeenth Century.* SPCK, London, 1935.

Neill, S., *Anglicanism.* Mowbray, London, 1977.

Sachs, W. L., *The Transformation of Anglicanism: From State Church to Global Communion.* Cambridge University Press 1993.

Sykes, S. W., *The Integrity of Anglicanism.* Mowbray, London and Oxford, 1978.

475

Sykes, S. W., *Unashamed Anglicanism*. DLT, London, 1995.
Van der Pol, W. H., *Anglicanism in Ecumenical Perspective*. Duquesne University Press 1965.
Vogel, A. (ed.), *Theology in Anglicanism*. Morehouse Barlow, Wilton, 1984.
Warren, A. (ed.), *A Church for the Nation? Essays on the Future of Anglicanism*. Gracewing, Leominster, 1992.
White, S. R., *Authority and Anglicanism*. SCM, London, 1996.

NOTES

1 F. A. Iremonger, *William Temple* (OUP 1948), p. 487.
2 Z. N. Brooke, *The English Church and the Papacy* (CUP 1931), pp. 10–20. See also pp. 477–81.
3 Brooke, *The English Church and The Papacy*, p. 20.
4 G. R. Elton, (ed.), *The Tudor Constitution* (CUP 1972), p. 355.
5 A. R. Vidler, *Essays in Liberality* (SCM, London, 1957), p. 157n. A. M. G. Stephenson, *Anglicanism and the Lambeth Conferences* (SPCK, London, 1978). pp. 7f.
6 C. Gore (ed), *Lux Mundi*, 10th edn. (Murray, London, 1904), preface.
7 *Catholicity: A Study in the Conflict of Christian Traditions in the West, being a report presented to His Grace the Archbishop of Canterbury*, (Dacre, London, 1947), p. 49.
8 See further, Avis, *Anglicanism and the Christian Church*, pt 3.
9 Cf. J. McManners, 'The Individual in the Church of England' in Doctrine Commission of the Church of England, *Believing in the Church* (SPCK, London, 1981), esp. pp. 222ff.
10 More and Cross, *Anglicanism*, p. 3.
11 C. Gore, *Dissertations on Subjects Connected with the Incarnation*, 2nd edn. (Murray, London, 1896), p. 196; *Catholicism and Roman Catholicism* (Mowbray, London, 1923), p. 48; *Orders and Unity* (Mowbray, London, 1909), pp. 198ff; *The Mission of the Church* (Murray, London,) pp. 36f; *The Basis of Anglican Fellowship in Faith and Organization* (Mowbray, London, 1914), pp. 4f; J. Carpenter, *Gore: A Study in Liberal Catholicism* (Faith Press, London 1960), pp. 42ff.
12 M. Fouyas, *Orthodoxy, Roman Catholicism and Anglicanism* (OUP 1972), pp. 86f.
13 Vidler, *Essays in Liberality*, pp. 166f.
14 McAdoo, *The Spirit of Anglicanism*, pp. 321f.
15 P. H. E. Thomas, 'The Lambeth Conferences and the Development of Anglican Ecclesiology 1867–1978', PhD diss., Dept of Theology, University of Durham, 1982, p. 82.
16 A. M. Ramsey, *The Gospel and the Catholic Church* (Longmans, London, 1936), p. 220.
17 Parker Society, *The Works of the English Reformers* (Cambridge 1840): Whitgift, Vol. I. p. 3; Jewel Vol. III, p. 79.
18 C. Garbett, *The Claims of the Church of England* (Hodder and Stoughton, London, 1947), p. 28.
19 J. W. C. Wand, *Anglicanism in History and Today* (Weidenfeld and Nicolson, London, 1961), pp. 241, 28.
20 H. H. Henson, *The Church of England* (CUP, 1939, p. 59).
21 Henson, *The Church of England*, p. 108.

4   Anglicanism, *Ecclesia Anglicana*, and Anglican: An Essay on Terminology

J. ROBERT WRIGHT

At what historical point can and should the study of Anglicanism begin? One logical answer would be to begin at the earliest point at which something called 'Anglicanism' is acknowledged to exist in recorded thought. Admitting that oral usage frequently antedates to some extent the written word, and holding to conservative principles of editing, the *Oxford English Dictionary* in 1933 recorded the earliest written occurrence of the term 'Anglicanism' as being in 1846 by Charles Kingsley,[1] and in its 1972 supplement moved this point back to John Henry Newman in 1838.[2] So in one real sense, the sense in which contemporaries would have acknowledged the existence of the term, the study of 'Anglicanism' can only begin with the nineteenth century. Yet most people today believe the term must represent a meaning that is broader and deeper than this. After all, the term 'Anglican Communion' would soon originate, on both sides of the Atlantic, first in 1851;[3] and certainly by this time the adjective 'Anglican' had come to mean not simply 'English' or 'pertaining to the Church of England', but also, ecclesiastically and more broadly, 'historically descended from the Church of England'.[4]

An early projection of Anglicanism back in time was recorded by Newman himself in his *Apologia* (1864): 'Anglicanism claimed to hold that the Church of England was nothing else than a continuation in this country [. . .] of that one Church of which in old times Athanasius and Augustine were members.'[5] And so also modern Anglican writers characteristically reverse their chronological perspective for the concept 'Anglicanism', even if they can not do this for the factual use of the word itself. Professor John Macquarrie, one of the most eminent of modern Anglican theologians, writes (1970), 'Anglicanism has never considered itself to be a sect or denomination originating in the sixteenth century. It continues without a break the *Ecclesia Anglicana* founded by St Augustine thirteen centuries and more ago, though nowadays that branch of the Church has spread far beyond the borders of England.'[6] And Bishop H. R. McAdoo, a leading exponent of what is thought by many to be a, or the, characteristic Anglican method in theology, states (1965):

Anglicanism is not a theological system and there is no writer whose work is an essential part of it either in respect of content or with regard to the form of its self-expression [. . .]. The absence of an official theology in Anglicanism is something deliberate which belongs to its essential nature, for it has always regarded the teaching and practice of the undivided Church of the first five centuries as a criterion.[7]

At first such a disclaimer of 'an official theology' seems in conflict with the OED definition of Anglicanism itself, 'Adherence to the doctrine and discipline of the reformed Church of England (and other churches in communion therewith) as the genuine representative of the Catholic Church';[8] but in fact the OED definition is consistent with what is now widely claimed. Macquarrie, for example, continues:

> It is often claimed that Anglicanism has no special doctrines of its own and simply follows the universal teaching of the Church. When one considers the nature of the English Reformation, one sees that there is strong support for the claim. In England there was no single dominant figure, such as Luther or Calvin, who might impress upon the Church his own theological idiosyncrasies. The conscious aim of the English Reformation was to return, so far as possible, to the Catholic Christianity of the undivided Church of the first five centuries.[9]

And the late Bishop Stephen Neill, in his best-selling paperback *Anglicanism* (1958) even asserted, 'There are no special Anglican doctrines, there is no particular Anglican theology [...]. In the strict sense of the term there is, therefore, no Anglican faith.'[10] At the more official level, there is the Report to the Lambeth Conference of 1930 on 'The Anglican Communion', commended in Resolution 48 of the Conference itself, which at first seems to suggest that there is something essentially new and distinct about Anglican doctrine, but then defines it in essentially the same way as Macquarrie, McAdoo and Neill:

> We desire emphatically to point out that the term 'Anglican' is no longer used in the sense it originally bore. The phrase 'Ecclesia Anglicana' in Magna Carta had a purely local connotation. Now its sense is ecclesiastical and doctrinal, and the Anglican Communion includes not merely those who are racially connected with England, but many others whose faith has been grounded in the doctrines and ideals for which the Church of England has always stood.
> What are these doctrines? We hold the Catholic faith in its entirety: that is to say, the truth of Christ, contained in Holy Scripture; stated in the Apostles' and Nicene Creeds; expressed in the Sacraments of the Gospel and the rites of the Primitive Church as set forth in the Book of Common Prayer with its various local adaptations; and safeguarded by the historic threefold Order of the Ministry.[11]

The Report on 'The Anglican Communion' for 1948 Lambeth repeated the same theme: 'The English Reformers were not trying to make a new Church. It continued to be the Church of England, the Ecclesia Anglicana, as Magna Carta described it in 1215. For this reason, the Anglican Communion is not a sect. It is a true part of the Church Catholic.'[12]

And so we come to a preliminary conclusion, that the study of Anglicanism must begin much earlier than the first occurrence of the term in 1838 or thereabouts; but now the question is, how much earlier? Let us ask, with Richard Hooker, but in a different context today, 'where our Church did lurk, in what cave of the earth it slept for so many hundreds of years before the birth of Martin Luther?' (Ecclesiastical Polity III.i.10). It must be observed that the continuity being asserted by Macquarrie and McAdoo, as well as by the Lambeth Reports of 1930 and 1948, projects an understanding of Anglicanism in essentials that extends not only prior to the nineteenth century but prior to the Reformation as well, back at least to the foundation of the see of Canterbury in the sixth century, even back to the patristic period historically[13] and to the New Testament doctrinally. Of course recent years have seen the discovery of much archaeological evidence from Britain in the patristic period, such as the Silchester basilica, the Lullingstone villa, the Hinton-St Mary mosaic, the Shepton Mallett cross, the Walesby and Icklingham lead baptismal tanks, the Water Newton and Mildenhall silver treasures, the 'Pater Noster' word-squares, and other things, all of which indicate the widespread historical origins of British Christianity in the second, third, and fourth centuries.[14] But can we agree, in common with the authorities cited above, that the Anglicanism of today stands in essential continuity even with the Church of this early period? Or was there perhaps some essential change, most probably at the English Reformation, some new doctrine or emphasis that all Anglican authorities then and now would regard as essential, that allows a modern interpreter to trace his or her concept of 'Anglicanism' back beyond 1838 to the sixteenth century but not earlier? Is it really true, as some might assert, that the de facto distinctiveness of Anglicanism only began in the sixteenth century? More specifically, did a 'Church of England' replace a 'Church in England' at the time of the Reformation?

One important view is that of Professor A. G. Dickens, a historian of distinction, who in 1964 wrote:

The common medieval term Ecclesia Anglicana never meant 'Church of England' in the post-Reformation sense of an independent national Church claiming parity with that of Rome. Whatever its material reservations, the medieval English church acknowledged the spiritual overlordship and jurisdiction of the Papacy. It administered in its courts a

body of law based upon papal decrees and upon the canons of international church councils. Only on its fringes, for example on matters
concerning titles and testamentary jurisidiction, had this law been modified by English national custom.[15]

Professor Dickens' view has not gone uncriticized,[16] but perhaps the sharpest contrast can be seen, from an official English/Anglican position, in the
volume *Ecclesiastical Law* from Halsbury's *Laws of England* as edited for the
Church Assembly (1957):

> In law the Church of England [...] is that branch of the Holy Catholic
> and Apostolic Church which was founded in England when the English
> were gradually converted to Christianity between the years 597 and 686
> [...]. The accepted legal doctrine is that the Church of England is a
> continuous body from its earliest establishment in Saxon times [...].
> When the statutes to exclude papal jurisdiction were passed in the
> reign of Henry VIII, the Church of England was regarded as an existing
> church and there was no intention to vary from the congregation of
> Christ's Church, but the papal authority in England was regarded as a
> usurpation.[17]

In the contrast of those views one hears echoes of the late nineteenth-
century Stubbs–Maitland controversy over the place of papal canon law in
late medieval England. This classical debate can not be rehearsed in these
few pages, but from some modern studies[18] related to it certain further
observations can be made that bear upon the question of how early to
begin the study of Anglicanism today. First there is the fact, now clearly
established, that the common medieval phrase *ecclesia Anglicana* (meaning
literally 'English church' as in the phrase '*quod Anglicana ecclesia libera sit*' of
the Magna Carta of 1215) was normally translated 'Church *of* England' by
Englishmen of the later Middle Ages: in Latin '*ecclesia de regno Angliae*' from
1290, in French '*eglise Dengleterre*' from 1341, and in English 'chirche of
Engelond' from the later fourteenth century.[19] Second, the phrase *ecclesia
Anglicana* was given definitional equivalents, confirming the same point, by
Pope Alexander III in 1173 ('the archbishops, bishop, and other prelates
and all the clergy and people constituted in England')[20] and by Archbishop
Hubert Walter in 1195 ('that portion of the Western Church which the
Most High has planted in England').[21] Third, *ecclesia Anglicana* was also
understood, by about this time, to include Wales as well as England.[22]
Fourth, that there were other Churches elsewhere roughly corresponding
to the *ecclesia Anglicana* was acknowledged by (among many others) Archbishop Henry Chichele in 1434, who spoke of it as formerly 'excelling other
churches'.[23] Fifth is the fact that the phrase *ecclesia Anglicana* came into

common use around the middle of the twelfth century[24] (not, as has at times been erroneously supposed, in 1215 with Magna Carta), when it replaced synonymously such earlier phrases as *ecclesia Angliae* ('Church of England'), as in the letters of St Anselm,[25] and *ecclesia Anglorum* ('Church of the English'), as in the early twelfth-century *Historia Novorum* of Eadmer or earlier in the *Ecclesiastical History* of the Venerable Bede.[26] Sixth, the Latin adjective *Anglicanus* obviously meant 'English' in medieval usage, stemming ultimately from the noun 'Angle-land' which is first recorded in the late ninth century; for the Church it had a geographical reference and did not carry with it any doctrinal limitation or particularity. Returning finally to the *Oxford English Dictionary*, we find that the earliest sense given for the adjective 'Anglican', which translates the Latin *Anglicanus*, is exactly the same: 'of or peculiar to the English ecclesiastically', and even its second sense is defined as merely 'of the reformed Church of England, and other churches in communion therewith'.[27] No particular doctrinal definition is attached to it, but its geographical reference is also compatible with the multi-cultural and multi-racial diversity of membership that comprises the Anglican Communion today.

Just as the term 'Anglicanism' cannot be found in common usage before the nineteenth century, so the terms 'Anglican' and even 'Church of England' in their various translations can be shown to have a continuous and consistent non-doctrinal use that stretches from the modern era well back into the Middle Ages. Where, then, should the study of 'Anglicanism' begin? Certainly not in 1838. If the term is to be used descriptively, and not narrowly or prescriptively, it must finally go back conceptually/doctrinally to the New Testament and historically/geographically to the martyrdom of St Alban in the 'patristic' period of 'Anglican' church history.[28] It was Queen Elizabeth herself who said that she and her people followed 'no novel and strange religions, but that very religion which is ordained by Christ, sanctioned by the primitive and Catholic Church and approved by the consentient mind and voice of the most early Fathers'.[29]

NOTES
1 *The Oxford English Dictionary* (1933), Vol. i, p. 327.
2 OED, Vol. i, p. 89. No change in the OED's second edition (1989), Vol. i, p. 464. The term *anglicanisme* occurs in the French language, in a non-ecclesiastical sense, as early as 1801: *Dictionnaire historique de la Langue Française*, ed. Alain Rey (Paris 1992), Vol. i, p. 75; *Trésor de la Langue Française*, ed. Paul Imbs (Paris 1974), Vol. iii, p. 19; *Nouveau Dictionnaire etymologique et historique*, ed. Albert Dauzat, Jean DuBois, and Henri Mitterand (Paris 1964), p. 34; and *Grand Larousse de la Langue Française* (Paris 1971), Vol. i, p. 174.
3 R. S. Bosher, *The American Church and the Formation of the Anglican Communion 1823–1853* (Evanston, Illinois, 1962), pp. 12, 13, 21; A. M. G. Stephenson, *The*

First Lambeth Conference 1867 (SPCK, London, 1967), pp. 55–6; A. M. G. Stephenson, *Anglicanism and the Lambeth Conferences* (SPCK, London, 1978), pp. 5–8.

4 Borden W. Painter, 'Bishop Walter H. Gray and the Anglican Congress of 1954', *Historical Magazine of the Protestant Episcopal Church* xlix: 2 (June 1980), p. 158.

5 *OED*, 2nd edn (1989), Vol. i, p. 464.

6 John Macquarrie, 'What Still Separates Us from the Catholic Church? An Anglican Reply', *Concilium* 54, *Post-Ecumenical Christianity*, ed. Hans Küng, pp. 45–46.

7 H. R. McAdoo, *The Spirit of Anglicanism* (Charles Scribner's Sons, New York, 1965), p. v. For this author's interpretation of 'the' Anglican method, cf. e.g. p. 49: 'the authentic note of Anglicanism which consistently rejected the idea that it had any specific doctrines of its own in that it demanded subscription to no confession other than the creeds, its aim being one of interpretation by means of a theological method which combined the use of Scripture, antiquity and reason'.

8 *OED*.

9 Macquarrie, 'What Still Separates Us?'

10 Stephen Neill, *Anglicanism*, 3rd edn (Penguin Books, Baltimore, 1965), pp. 417–18.

11 *The Lambeth Conference 1930* (SPCK, London, n.d.), pp. 54, 154.

12 *The Lambeth Conference 1948* (SPCK, London, 1948), part ii, p. 83. The claim that Anglicanism has no special doctrines of its own has been effectively demolished by Stephen Sykes ('Anglicanism and the Anglican Doctrine of the Church', pp. 156–77 of *Quadrilateral at One Hundred*, ed. J. Robert Wright (Forward Movement, Cincinnati and Mowbray, London 1988), also published in Supplementary Series No. 10 of *Anglican Theological Review* (March 1988)), but it is noteworthy that he does not locate the historical origins of Anglicanism's special doctrines in the sixteenth century.

13 An attempt to illustrate this continuity in representative sources has been published uniformly with this volume: G. R. Evans and J. Robert Wright (eds), *The Anglican Tradition: A Handbook of Sources* (SPCK, London, 1991).

14 For a recent survey see Charles Thomas, *Christianity in Roman Britain to AD 500* (University of California Press, Berkeley and Los Angeles, 1981).

15 A. G. Dickens, *The English Reformation* (Batsford, London, 1964), pp. 86f.

16 Denys Hay, 'The Church of England in the Later Middle Ages', *History*, liii: 177 (February 1968), p. 35.

17 Church House Bookshop, London, 1957, pp. 33, 34, and note(s).

18 Hay, 'The Church of England'; J. W. Gray, 'Canon Law in England: Some Reflections on the Stubbs–Maitland Controversy'; *Studies in Church History*, Vol. iii (1966), pp. 48–68; Charles Donahue Jr, 'Roman Canon Law in the Medieval English Church: Stubbs vs. Maitland Re-examined after 75 Years in the Light of Some Records from the Church Courts', *Michigan Law Review*, lxxii: 4 (March 1974), pp. 647–716.

19 Hay, 'The Church of England', p. 48. This usage is even continued in the Act of Supremacy, 1534: 'the Church of England, called *Anglicana Ecclesia*'. The earliest printed English translation of the Magna Carta, by George Ferrers in 1534, also translated *Anglicana Ecclesia* as 'church of England': Faith Thompson, *Magna Carta: Its Role in the Making of the English Constitution 1300–1629* (University of Minnesota Press, Minneapolis, 1948), pp. 151, 147.

20 Z. N. Brooke, *The English Church & the Papacy from the Conquest in the Reign of John* (CUP 1931), pp. 11, 20: 'archiepiscopis episcopis et [. . .] aliis ecclesiarum praclatis et universo clero et populo per Angliam constitutis.'
21 Booke, *The English Church*, p. 13: 'hanc occidentalis ecclesiae portionem quam in Anglia plantavit Altissimus.'
22 C. R. Cheney, *Pope Innocent III and England* (Anton Hiersemann, Stuttgart, 1976), p. 168, n. 179.
23 Hay, 'The Church of England' p. 48.
24 Charles Duggan, 'From the Conquest to the Death of John' in *The English Church and the Papacy in the Middle Ages*, ed. C. H. Lawrence (Burns & Oates, London, 1965), pp. 107–8.
25 Brooke, *The English Church*, p. 5.
26 Martin Brett, *The English Church under Henry I* (OUP 1975), p. 13. The examples cited from Bede are found at bk. i, ch. 27, 29, and bk. iii, ch. 29. Whereas Bede had used the Latin genitive plural for the Churches of the English and of the French, reserving the adjectival form for the Roman Church alone (*Roman ecclesia*, as in bk. i, ch. 27), later usages would commonly write of an *ecclesia Scoticana, Hibernicana*, and, of course, *Gallicana*.
27 OED, which dates the earliest uses of the English adjective 'Anglican' to 1635 and 1660. Further see Borden W. Painter, 'Anglican Terminology in Recent Tudor and Stuart Historiography', *Anglican and Episcopal History* Ivi: 3 (Sept. 1987), pp. 237–49.
28 For a stimulating and provocative theological critique of this entire subject, see S. W. Sykes, *The Integrity of Anglicanism* (Mowbray, London and Oxford, 1978).
29 J. M. Rigg (ed.), *Calendar of State Papers, relating to English Affairs, Preserved Principally at Rome* (1916), pp. 154–5.

5   Anglicans and Mission

T. E. YATES

Anglicans have made a considerable contribution to the mission of the Church universal. Unlike the Roman Catholic Church, there is no body of theory to which the enquirer may turn for an understanding of the Church's mind. Since Vatican II, the study of such formative documents as the Dogmatic Constitution of the Church (*Lumen Gentium*), the Decree on the Missionary Activity of the Church (*Ad Gentes*) and the Declaration on the relationship of the Church to the non-Christian Religions (*Nostra Aetate*) have offered a rounded Roman Catholic perspective on the Church's missionary activity. By contrast, the Anglican contribution has to be pursued by study of its practice and the writings of individuals, with occasional references in official documents. Certain characteristic emphases can be discerned. First, there has been a stress on indigenization in terms of planting the Church and of drawing out an indigenous ministry. As early as 1765 Philip Quaque, an ordained African, ministered on the West Coast

483

of Africa for fifty years. He was an isolated instance but was to be followed by the Indian Abdul Masih (ordained in 1825), the Canadian Indian Henry Budd (1850) and by the freed slave and first African bishop, Samuel Crowther (consecrated in 1864). Secondly, there has been a strong emphasis on learning, whether it be to equip converts or the incipient ministry. Codrington College, Barbados, founded as a school in 1745 and reconstituted as a theological college in 1830; Bishop's College, Calcutta, founded in 1820; Fourah Bay College in Sierra Leone, founded in 1827, of which Samuel Crowther was one of the first pupils; St John's College, Auckland, towards which SPG paid £5,000 on its foundation in 1847, were among many notable institutions which have been a mark of Anglican mission. With this dual emphasis there has been an accompanying stress on the translation of the Bible and the Anglican liturgy into the vernacular languages. Along with much heroism in the field, which has included martyr bishops like J. C. Patteson in Melanesia in 1872 or the boy martyrs of Uganda in 1884, there have been profound missionary thinkers and writers. The world Church is indebted to certain great Anglicans in this field. It suffices to mention, among the many, thinkers and missionary strategists such as Henry Venn, Roland Allen and Max Warren, with scholars like Bishop Stephen Neill and Bishop Kenneth Cragg.

BEGINNINGS: THE EIGHTEENTH CENTURY

The Book of Common Prayer of 1662 recognized the responsibility of Anglicans for the non-Christians among whom they lived. The office for the 'Baptism of such as are of riper years' 'may be always useful for the baptising of Natives of our plantations and others converted to the faith'. Nevertheless, the seventeenth century, which saw the formation by Rome of the Sacred Congregation for the Propagation of the Faith (Propaganda) in 1622 and such remarkable missionaries as the Roman Catholic Robert de Nobili (1577–1656) among Indian Brahmins and the Presbyterian John Eliot (1604–90) among the Iroquois Indians of North America, had no Anglican equivalent. Thomas Bray (1656–1730), Rector of Sheldon in Warwickshire, whose activities have been noticed in an earlier essay (see p. 40) was responsible by the end of the seventeenth century for the oldest Anglican missionary society, the SPCK (Society for Promoting Christian Knowledge, founded 1698) and for the foundation of the SPG (Society for the Propagation of the Gospel, 1701) at the beginning of the eighteenth century. By Royal Charter of William III, the SPG was to supply the 'want of learned and orthodox ministers' in the plantations, colonies and 'factories beyond the seas'. It was this limitation which meant that it was SPCK, rather than SPG, which supported the Danish mission at Tranquebar in India and employed German missionaries, some in Lutheran orders, in territories not administered by the Crown of England. Nevertheless, SPG accepted dual responsibility from the beginning, both to 'settle the State of Religion as well as may be for our *own People* [. . .] and then to proceed in the best methods they can towards the *conversion* of the *Natives*'.[1] As well therefore as providing chaplains to the colonies of North America (among whom was numbered John Wesley in Georgia in 1736), SPG began work among the Mohawk Indians in Albany, north of New York, in 1704, four of whom were presented to Queen Anne in London. The Queen gave them a set of silver communion plate for 'her Indian Chappell of the Mohawks'.Work was also begun among the negro population of New York. One eighteenth-century plantation owner, Christopher Codrington, Governor of Barbados, was moved to leave his estate, with its negro slaves, to SPG in 1710. From this gift Codrington School developed in 1745 and, later, Codrington College, where many Anglican clergy have been nurtured. Finally, the plight of slaves prompted one of SPG's chaplains, Thomas Thompson, to visit the West Coast of Africa. Through his initiative three African boys were taken to be educated in England. From them the first non-European Anglican priest, Philip Quaque, was ordained in 1765.

The work of SPG received a crushing blow through the American War of Independence. After the surrender of English forces in 1781 the SPG mission came to an end; but not before the society had recorded eighty years of service to the American church, during which 300 clergy had been supported, of whom 100 died while working in the American church.

THE ERA OF VOLUNTARY SOCIETIES: THE NINETEENTH CENTURY

Where SPG was a chartered society, owing much to the individual initiative of Thomas Bray but also limited by its royal patronage and charter, its sister society, the CMS (Church Missionary Society) was a voluntary association with no such limitations. The end of the eighteenth century had seen the rise of various missionary societies. Among them the inter-denominational London Missionary Society (founded 1795) provided both a model and a catalyst for Evangelical Anglicans. Members of the Eclectics Society, a clerical and lay discussion group, were sensitive to criticisms of lack of churchmanship to which involvement in societies like LMS and the inter-denominational British and Foreign Bible Society laid them open. This, as well as a genuine concern for the 'heathen', led Charles Simeon to ask, at a meeting in 1796: 'With what propriety and in what mode can a mission be established to the Heathen from the Established Church?' The foundation of the 'Society for Missions to Africa and the East' followed in

485

1799 and became the Church Missionary Society (today, Church Mission Society). From the same circle and again inspired by the LMS, the 'London Society for promoting Christianity among the Jews', which today is known as the Church's Ministry among Jewish people, developed in 1809. The Colonial and Continental Church Society, now the Inter-continental Church Society, was also Anglican Evangelical in its origins.

There is some truth in the comment that, where SPG became the *Church* missionary society, CMS was the society for the propagation of the gospel. By this is meant that, whereas SPG had been at pains to emphasize that those supported by the society were agents of the church (a policy which led in the nineteenth century to all candidatess being required to sit the Archbishops' Board Examination) the CMS showed historically a greater independence. Again, where SPG laid great emphasiss on church planting, CMS stressed above all individual conversion.[2] Yet such judgements must be severely qualified. The founders of SPCK and SPG were in touch with the springs of Pietism in men like A. H. Francke of Halle and with the Pietist emphasis on conversion which he represented; and no one believed more firmly in church planting than Henry Venn, the CMS secretary of the mid-nineteenth century. Some of the founder members of CMS were also members of SPG. One, Josiah Pratt, a CMS secretary, went so far as to commend SPG to the public for funding in an anonymous pamphlet of 1819. Flanked by SPG and LMS, however, the response of John Venn as a founder of CMS was typical of the Anglican Evangelicals: 'the Church principle but not the High Church principle'. The ordering of relationships between CMS and the developing Anglican episcopate overseas was to be one dominant theme of its history.

William Wilberforce professed as deep a concern for India as for the abolition of the slave trade. Both provided a missionary dynamic in the early nineteenth century. In the case of India, the East India Company's operations were, like SPG's, governed by Royal Charter. Wilberforce pressed long and hard for ecclesiastical provisions to be included in the charter, hoping to open India to missionaries. Other colonial models, such as the Danes at Tranquebar and the Dutch in their East Indies possessions, suggested official encouragement for missionaries when the charter was renewable in 1793. He had to be content with EIC chaplaincies, accepted by various godly men often influenced by Charles Simeon's ministry in Cambridge, of whom the brightest star of the galaxy was Henry Martyn (1781–1812) on account of his academic brilliance, piety and dedication, cut short by an early death. In 1813, the new charter secured the appointment of a Bishop of Calcutta in T. F. Middleton and Wilberforce's so-called 'Pious Clause' to facilitate missionary work passed after sustained and strenuous resistance.

This was one sign among many in the century that it was not always to the advantage of the missionary movement to be closely related to organs of influence, whether traders or colonial administrators. The new bishop held that his Letters Patent from the crown did not permit him to exercise any powers in relation to native Indians, and he was embarrassed by the presence of missionaries. His successor, Reginald Heber, felt less inhibited. He decided to ordain Henry Martyn's convert, Abdul Masih, in 1825. If this was a sign of an early Anglican determination to indigenize the ministry, Daniel Wilson's episcopate (1832–58) was to demonstrate the continuing tension between the established church structure of government by bishops and the voluntary missionary society. It was a tension known to the Roman Catholic communion as one experienced between the religious orders, with their capacity to initiate and develop in mission, and the central machinery of government in Rome. Eventually a concordat was hammered out between the bishop, a friend of CMS but determined to uphold order, and the committee in London in 1839.

Both CMS and SPG developed extensive missionary work in the Indian sub-continent during the century. They were joined by such bodies as the Cambridge Mission to Delhi (1877) and the Church of England Zenana Missionary Society (1880) who, in time, were to merge with SPG and CMS respectively.

The slave trade gave rise directly to the first CMS mission in Africa. Zachary Macaulay, father of the historian, had founded the Sierra Leone Company in 1791. It was to be a colony for liberated slaves, many of them re-captives of the British naval squadron, landed after rescue from the ships of slavers. The CMS mission there gave rise to the dream of men like T. F. Buxton that Africa could be civilized and transformed by the combined effect of commerce and Christianity. In his *African Slave Trade and its Remedy* (1839) Buxton wrote: 'Let missionaries and schoolmasters, the plough and the spade, go together [...] civilisation will advance [...] and Christianity [...] as the proximate cause of this happy change.'[3] One of the early re-captives was Samual Adjai Crowther. After schooling at Fourah Bay College he was ordained in 1834. He and others entertained another 'pleasing dream': the various tribes-people landed at Sierra Leone should become missionaries to their own tribes. He himself became a CMS missionary to the Yoruba in modern Nigeria in 1843.

After the loss of the American colonies the government were faced with finding an area for the transportation of convicts. They decided on Botany Bay. William Wilberforce's ubiquitous philanthropy found a chaplain, Richard Johnson, willing to sail to Australia in 1786. Both SPG and SPCK helped with his payment and equipment. He was joined later by Samuel Marsden, whose eyes turned to New Zealand as a mission field.

Marsden persuaded CMS to launch a mission, which was to be first civilizing and then missionary. Among Anglican missions, perhaps only the mission to the Arctic, where some 80 per cent of Esquimaux (Inuit) became Anglican Christians, is more remarkable than the early Maori missions. Here a cannibalistic and warlike people showed itself highly responsive to the Christian message and capable of spreading it rapidly and spontaneously in the 1830s and 1840s. Once again, relationships between Selwyn, a heroic pioneer bishop, and CMS were not easy. Like Daniel Wilson, he maintained his rights as bishop and, in his case, tried to extend them further in regard to the placing of missionaries. His ideas on church government, synodical and free of the apparatus of legal establishment, also alarmed traditionalists in Salisbury Square, headquarters of the CMS.

Henry Venn, the controlling mind at Salisbury Square, must be regarded as the leading Anglican missionary strategist of the century. He was the son of one of the founders of CMS and became honorary secretary from 1841–72. He coincided with his great SPG counterpart, Edward Hawkins (SPG secretary 1843–64), with whom he kept in close contact. Venn did his best to relate CMS, as a voluntary society to the episcopate at home and the developing overseas episcopate, which grew in his time from nine to over fifty. Venn's real claim to greatness lay in his vision for, and implementation of, indigenous churches. He developed his ideas in a series of papers written for CMS. First, indigenous churches should be developed 'from the bottom upwards' rather than created by organizational fiat from above. Small groups of 'native Christians' would coalesce into native pastorates, which would become 'self-supporting, self-governing and self-extending'. The role of the mission was to be the scaffolding, to be removed in due course, so leading to the '*euthanasia* of the mission'. The indigenous church could then be left to itself; and the missionaries, often European exotics, would move on to the 'regions beyond'. As the native pastorates developed, they would group into a diocese. The 'crown' of this indigenous church edifice would be the native bishop.

Underlying Venn's thinking was a sharp distinction between the evangelist, whose function was to preach the gospel in the 'regions beyond', and the pastor, whose role was to build up the 'settled Church'. When, however, Venn first realized his vision in Sierra Leone in 1861 the European bishop remained, partly on account of the presence of Europeans in the colony. When he persuaded Samuel Crowther to become a bishop, Crowther became, in fact, not the bishop of a settled church, the 'crown' of Venn's plan, but an evangelist in episcopal orders as Bishop on the Niger. It was in part due to failure to follow through Venn's own logic that, sadly, a great Christian pioneer, translator and pastor became, not so much the sign that Africans were ready for leadership (as Venn had intended), as a 'symbol of

488

the supposed failure of African leadership'.[4] Even so, it was a sign of Venn's vision that an African bishop should have been envisaged in 1864, sixty years after CMS entered West Africa. It was another example of the Anglican desire for an indigenous church and ministry.

By its jubilee in 1849, CMS had sent out 350 missionaries to India, East and West Africa, New Zealand, Canada and China. SPG had entered the fields of the West Indies (1712), West Africa (1752), Canada (1759), Australia (1793), India (1818), South Africa (1820), New Zealand (1841) and Borneo (1847).

FROM THE INDIAN MUTINY TO THE END OF THE CENTURY

In Anglican missionary history the year 1857 is a turning point. It was the year of the Indian Mutiny, after which the government replaced the East India Company as the controlling power. For Africa there were to be special developments after David Livingstone's addresses at the ancient universities of Oxford and Cambridge in that year. In his speech at the Senate House in Cambridge he had said: 'I beg to direct your attention to Africa. I know that in a few years I shall be cut off in that country which is now open. Do not let it be shut again! I go back to Africa to try to make an open path for commerce and Christianity. Do you carry on the work which I have begun. I leave it with you!' A strange result of Livingstone's eloquence was that a Scottish Presbyterian, who had been in the employment of the LMS but had exchanged the life of a missionary for that of an explorer, was instrumental in founding a great Anglo-Catholic mission in 1858. Originally the title had been the 'Oxford and Cambridge Mission to Central Africa'. The advent of Durham and Dublin universities changed this to the 'Universities' Mission to Central Africa'. UMCA had anything but an auspicious beginning. C. F. Mackenzie, consecrated in 1867 as 'bishop to the mission and the tribes dwelling in the neighbourhood of Lake Nyassa and the River Shire' personified the dream of certain Tractarians that the bishop should be the pioneer evangelist and missionary leader. Mackenzie soon died of malaria but his successors, Bishops William Tozer and Edward Steere, consolidated the work of UMCA. Tozer moved the mission's base to Zanzibar, and Steere had the satisfaction of building Christ Church Cathedral with his own hands on the site of the Arab slave market. A later bishop, John Hine, expressed the aim of UMCA as 'the building up of a Native Church [...] the Church of the people of the land, irrespective of European influence, adapting itself to the special circumstances of the race and country in which it exists'.[5]

The South American Missionary Society was founded in 1844 by

Captain Allen Gardiner, a retired naval officer like another great pioneer of the Maori mission, Henry Williams. It was not until after his tragic death by starvation in Tierra del Fuego in 1851 that the mission really developed. During the century the mission entered Paraguay (1888) and Chile (1895) and after 1900 Argentina (1911) and Peru (1974). Again there has been an emphasis on developing an indigenous ministry. The first Mapuche Indian was ordained in 1937 and a group of seven Mataco Indians in 1966. The society has now developed branches in other parts of the Anglican Communion, for example in the Church of the Province of South Africa and the Episcopal Church of the United States. It goes today by the name SAMS International. A feature of the Anglican Communion is that missionary societies, founded within the Church of England, have established themselves in sister churches overseas, as, for example, Australian and New Zealand CMS, each independent missionary bodies.

Space forbids a full account of Anglican missions in the second half of the nineteenth century in all their exuberant vitality. The opening of the Far East to missionary activity, however, deserves special notice. First, it was an example of the doubtful advantages to the Christian mission of Western gun-boat diplomacy and commercial pressure. China was pressed by Britain, first, into a treaty to open certain 'treaty ports' to trade in 1842 and then in 1858 to permit access to the interior. One result of the treaties was the import of opium as part of British policy in China. Japan, a parallel case of isolation, was forced by American pressure to open her ports in 1854. Second, both these fields were reminders that Anglican mission was no longer the preserve of the English-based societies. American and Canadian Anglicans were a growing force to be reckoned with. In China, W. J. Boone, a missionary of the American Episcopal Church, established a mission of his church in Shanghai in 1840 and was consecrated bishop in China in 1844. This was to raise questions of ecclesiastical jurisdiction among English Anglicans with the CMS. Boone was joined later by one of the greatest of all Anglican missionaries, linguists and translators in the Jewish convert S. I. J. Scherewschewsky in 1859, who was consecrated bishop in 1877. Despite nearly total paralysis of body after 1881 he added to his mandarin translations of the Bible and the Book of Common Prayer further renderings of both into another Chinese form, 'easy *Wenli*'.

Japan was a field in which Americans of the Episcopal Church and later Canadians of the Anglican Church of Canada served with missionaries of both the SPG and the CMS. Each had oversight in different geographical areas. Channing Moore Williams, one of the early American missionaries, became Bishop of China and Japan in 1866 and was resident in Osaka and Tokyo from 1869. The arrival of Edward Bickersteth, who had served with the Cambridge Mission to Delhi noted above, as bishop in 1886 led to his vision of an indigenous Japanese Anglican church, *Nippon Sei Ko Kwai*, being realized in 1887, in which all the various Anglican components were represented. At least one notable Anglican institution, St Paul's School, Tokyo (founded 1874), now Rikkyo University, was and is an example of the Anglican approach to mission through educational institutions. Bishop Williams was its founder. An equally notable medical institution, St Luke's Hospital, Tokyo (founded 1900) was established by another American, also from Richmond, Virginia, in Dr Rudolf Teusler. It was a Virginian missionary and bishop, Henry St George Tucker, Bishop of Kyoto, who was to encourage self-government in NSKK in the early twentieth century. Although the Anglican body remained very small by reference to the whole population of Japan (some 50,000 only today), cultural penetration was achieved through these and other educational and medical foundations.

THE TWENTIETH CENTURY: FROM MISSIONS TO MISSION

Although there had been earlier international missionary conferences in Liverpool (1860), London (1888) and New York (1900), the World Missionary Conference at Edinburgh in 1910 was of special significance. For the Anglicans this was symbolized by the presence of the Archbishop of Canterbury, Randall Davidson. In common with the leaders of SPG, he had hesitated to attend a conference which might not be fully representative of all views. In fact, a very broad selection of Anglican opinion was represented. Bishop Charles Gore, Father H. H. Kelly of the Society of the Sacred Mission (now charged with training candidates for the Anglican mission in Korea), Bishop Montgomery, the secretary of SPG, Temple Gairdner, CMS missionary and Arabic scholar, who was to write a widely read account of the conference, and, as a young man and steward, William Temple. Among the leaders of the 'younger Churches' was V. S. Azariah, later Anglican Bishop of Dornakal in India. Davidson, in his address to the conference, underlined that for him, as a representative figure in the Anglican Church, 'the place of missions in the life of the church must be the central place'. Azariah gave voice to the new relationship needed between the national leaders and the expatriate missionaries: 'Through all ages to come the Indian church will rise up in gratitude to attest the heroism and self-denying labours of the missionary body. You have given your goods to feed the poor. You have given your bodies to be burned. We ask for *love*. Give us FRIENDS.'[6]

Another prophetic voice raised against received missionary practice was that of Roland Allen (1868–1947), SPG missionary in China and writer. In 1912 Allen published *Missionary Methods: St Paul's or Ours?* He asked whether the aim was to plant churches or to perpetuate missions. In contrast to St Paul, Western missionaries had failed to give the local church the full spiritual authority needed for its healthy development. Allen was equally suspicious of missions and large 'national' churches. Both stifled the development of God's gifts to the local body. He called for a greater trust in the Holy Spirit, over against imposed orthodoxies and external administration by societies or national churches. His charge that missionaries made converts over-dependent on themselves recalls the Sierra Leonean convert's comment on the death of the great missionary, W. A. B. Johnson: 'We looked more to Mr Johnson than to Jesus.'[7] To Allen, this was the ultimate indictment, a fault from which St Paul was free because he moved on, devolving leadership on local elders.

It is not possible here to do more than notice the profound questions raised to all non-Christian peoples by the World War of 1914–18, which led to the disillusionment of many with the so-called Christian nations. Between the wars, the Bible Churchmen's Missionary Society was added to the societies in England, after alarm among certain CMS supporters at what was regarded as a drift into liberalism by its leadership. The split came in 1922. BCMS (Crosslinks today) has worked in Burma, China, Iran, India, the Arctic, Canada, East Africa and Morocco. It has also been a notable example of the Anglican tendency to wish to revive ancient Christian bodies rather than proselytize or divide. This was true of CMS in South India among the Syrian Malabar Church in the 1820s and 1830s. It was now true of BCMS in Ethiopia with the ancient Coptic Church. Alfred Buxton of BCMS visited Ethiopia in 1931 and judged that 'it would be sound policy to stimulate and help this ancient church [...] to carry out [...] her own proper share in the work of evangelisation'.[8] This policy was followed. In East Africa, spiritual revival brought fresh, invigorating renewal to church life. The *balokole* or 'saved ones' spread this influence throughout East Africa and beyond during the 1930s. The Ruanda mission, of which Dr J. E. Church was a prominent member, remained in association with CMS but was known for supporters as CMS Ruanda.

When Archbishop William Temple was enthroned in Canterbury Cathedral in 1942 he referred to the 'great new fact of our era', a reference to the existence of the Church of Christ in every major ethnic group in the world. It was a fitting tribute to the missionary movement. It also pointed to the new future, expressed at the Lambeth Conference of 1958 as 'mission to the whole world (with) no frontiers between "Home" and "Foreign"'.[9] In 1963 at the Anglican Congress in Toronto, Archbishop Michael Ramsey went further: 'We must plan our mission together and use our resources in the service of a single task. The word "missionary" will mean not colonialism of any kind but going to one another to help one another. Let African and Asian missionaries come to England to help convert the post-Christian

492

heathenism in our country and convert our English church to a closer following of Christ.'[10]

An aspect of this 'one world' was the growth of awareness of the other great religious traditions and the confidence of Islam, Hinduism and Buddhism often associated with nationalist aspirations after 1950. Later, in addition to this, there was a growing presence of people of other races and religious traditions among the 'sending' nations. A pioneering study in the realm of inter-faith relations was made by the Anglican scholar and profound student of Islam, Bishop Kenneth Cragg, in his *Call of the Minaret* (1956). This book impressed the secretary of CMS, Max Warren, very deeply. He himself edited the 'Christian Presence' series of studies by Anglican scholars of the great religious traditions, where he espoused Cragg's way of dialogue in his general preface as the proper approach to those of other faiths: the first need is to 'take off our shoes [...] else we may find ourselves treading on other men's dreams [...] to ask what is the authentic religious content in the experience of the Muslim, the Hindu, the Buddhist or whatever he may be [...] to be "present" with them'.[11] It was a decade when the Roman Catholic Church was to see dialogue as a means for Catholics to 'preserve and promote the spiritual and moral goods found among these men' (*Nostra Aetate*). In an England confronted by a World Festival of Islam in 1976, Bishop David Brown, like Cragg an Arabic scholar and student of Islam, produced a widely received monograph, *A New Threshold* (1976), which sought to guide those perplexed by manifestations of the Muslim presence in a traditionally Christian context. The missionary societies responded by setting up the BCMS/CMS Other Faiths Theological Project, with Bishop Stephen Neill as its first chairman in 1979. A series of Lambeth Inter Faith lectures also pointed to the importance of this issue.[12]

A new organ of consultation for the whole Anglican Communion, the Anglican Consultative Council, met at Limuru, Kenya in 1971, with the Archbishop of Canterbury as President and representatives from all Anglican provinces. This meeting too commended dialogue, emphasizing that it 'will not be simply another form of evangelism' but 'each [...] will lay himself open, not only to his partner but to the Spirit of God'.[13] Successive meetings of the ACC at Dublin (1973), Trinidad (1976), Ontario (1979), Newcastle on Tyne (1981) and Badagry (1984) have set up 'Partners-in-Mission' consultations, have carried mission on their agendas but have emphasized the changed nature of mission in the twentieth century. In the words of the Dublin report 'there is but one mission in all the world [...] the responsibility for mission in any place belongs *primarily* to the Church in that place'.[14] As Bishop Stephen Neill wrote in 1964: 'The age of missions is at an end; the age of mission has begun.'[15]

493

ISSUES FOR THE FUTURE

This essay has been concerned with the history of the great Anglican missionary societies. Throughout their history there have been calls for their integration into the church in, perhaps, a board of mission. Bishop Samuel Wilberforce was a nineteenth-century advocate of this policy, and he has had a number of twentieth-century followers. The creation of the Partnership for World Mission in 1978 with a secretariat in London has been an attempt to hold together the strengths of the voluntary society with the need for a representative body which is recognized as, for example, corporately representing the societies to overseas member churches, who may prefer to deal with such a body than with individual societies. In the words of the Partners in Mission consultation in England of 1981, 'voluntary societies should be integrated with the structures of the church but without losing their identity and flexibility' because 'voluntary societies encourage enthusiasm and personal engagement at parish level. We must not lose this.'[16] Some unification has been noticed above as between CMS and CEZMS and between SPG, CMD and now UMCA. Since 1965 SPG and UMCA have merged to become USPG. In 1986, CMS, USPG and PWM were housed in the same building in London.

The issue of the voluntary society and the structures of the Church remains and now has an international dimension, not only in the case of SAMS noticed above, but now also with the Church's Ministry to Jewish people. As a result of the Partners in Mission consultation set up by the ACC, the General Secretary of the Board of Mission of the Episcopal Church has invited the society to form CMJ/USA in 1982, based in Fairfax, Virginia. It remains to be seen how far those parts of the Anglican Communion which have been used to handling mission through central boards like the Episcopal Church of the United States, in common with a British church like the (presbyterian) Church of Scotland, will relate to new initiatives by the societies. The societies themselves may develop a function and role as organs of response to the mission needs of the whole Anglican Communion, holding the whole church to its missionary vocation in word and deed by promoting the interchange of personnel, funding and ideas. An example which may provide a model was a programme for renewal mounted by the diocese of Hokkaido, with East African church leaders as missioners, funded by the CMS from London. The use of a near-universal language as a means of communication in English is no negligible factor at the disposal of Anglicans in mission. Since 1989 the churches of Eastern Europe have welcomed support from Anglicans. Anglican (CMS) mission partners have been invited to work with Russian Orthodox in St Petersburg and

Moscow and to assist the Rumanian Orthodox Church in medical, pastoral and youth work.

Two further issues may be considered in conclusion. First, it is likely that mission will remain on the agenda of the Anglican Communion in a world which, as the Vatican II document *Ad Gentes* pointed out, two billion remain unevangelized. Here the original insight of the BCP with which this essay began remains valid: missionary responsibility is present in the persons of those who are unattached or ignorant or unconvinced among whom Anglicans live. This is but another way of saying that the Church is missionary in its being: that, in Emil Brunner's words, 'the Church lives by mission as a fire lives by burning'. Second, the Anglican Church, with the Church Universal, faces a sharp change of perspective. Much of the liveliest Anglican life exists in Africa south of the Sahara, in Asia and in Latin America. These voices will claim a hearing increasingly in Anglican consultations and may act as a healthy corrective to the Anglicanism of the comparatively settled, wealthy and arid north, arid in the view of many of these communities because of what is perceived as an over-intellectualized theological tradition and a weakened spirituality. As Archbishop Michael Ramsey suggested at Toronto, it may be that the vitality of the younger churches in the Anglican communion is needed to renew the older churches in their mission. The creation in 1990 of ten new 'missionary dioceses' by the Anglican Church of Nigeria and of its own Church of Nigeria Missionary Society in 1997, parallel initiatives by Asian Anglicans, for example from Sabah and Singapore, towards their Asian neighbours, alongside the formation of a Standing Commission on Mission for the Anglican Communion (MISSIO) in 1994, may be signs that the archbishop's words were prescient of a fresh impulse among Anglicans towards mission as the new millennium opens.

BIBLIOGRAPHY
Dewey, M., *The Messengers*. London, 1975.
Gibbs, M. E., *The Anglican Church in India 1600–1700*. Delhi, 1972.
Hewitt, G. H. G., *The Problems of Success. London*, Vol. i 1972; Vol. ii 1977.
Jacob, W. M., *The Making of the Anglican Church Worldwide*. SPCK, London, 1997.
McLeod Campbell, J., *Christian History in the Making*. London, 1946.
Murray, J., *Proclaim the Good News*. London, 1985.
Nazir-Ali, M., *From Everywhere to Everywhere*. Collins, London, 1990.
Neill, S. C., *A History of Christian Missions*. London, 1964.
Stock, E., *The History of the Church Missionary Society*. 3 Vols., London 1899; Vol. iv, London 1916.
Thompson, H. P., *Into All Lands*. London, 1951.
Warren, M. A. C., *The Missionary Movement from Britain in Modern History*. SCM, London, 1965.
Yates, T. E., *Christian Mission in the Twentieth Century*. London, 1994.

NOTES

1 SPG First Annual Sermon quoted in Thompson, *Into All Lands*, pp. 20–21.
2 This is still the case. See the remarks of the then President of CMS, Dame Diana Reader Harris, in 'What we hold dear', USPG/CMS Consultation 8–10 February 1973: 'We have great unanimity over the centrality of conversion in Christian experience.'
3 T. F. Buxton, *The African Slave Trade and its Remedy* (1839), pp. 282, 511.
4 B. G. M. Sundkler, *The Christian Ministry in Africa* (SCM, London, 1960), pp. 46–7.
5 M. Anderson-Morshead, *History of the Universities' Mission to Central Africa* (1955–62) Vol. i, p. 220.
6 *Edinburgh World Missionary Conference Report* (1910), Vol. ix, pp. 150, 315.
7 Stock, *History of the Church Missionary Society*, vol. i, p. 118.
8 S. F. Russell, *Full Fifty Years* (1972), p. 45.
9 *Lambeth Conference Report* (1958), resolution 58.
10 *Anglican Congress, Toronto Report* (1963), p. 16.
11 Editor's preface for series by M. A. C. Warren as found in P. Schneider, *Sweeter than Honey: Christian Presence and Judaism* (SCM, London, 1966), p. 12.
12 For an acute Anglican mind grappling with these issues from a context of religious pluralism see Bidhop Lakshman Wickremesinghe, then Bishop of Kurunugala in Sri Lanka, in *Crucible* (Oct–Dec 1979), the Second Lambeth Inter-faith Lecture.
13 ACC Limuru Report, *The Time is Now* (ACC, 1971), p. 44.
14 ACC Dublin Report (ACC, 1973), p. 53.
15 Neill, *History of Christian Missions*, p. 522.
16 Report, *To a Rebellious House?* (CIO, 1981), p. 33.

GLOSSARY

ACC: the Anglican Consultative Council, established after the 1968 Lambeth Conference. Its membership drawn from each province of the Anglican Communion and inclusive of bishops, priests, deacons and lay people, the Council provides a continuity of consultation and guidance on policy. The permanent secretariat is based in London, and meetings are held in different parts of the world at two to three year intervals.

Act in Restraint of Appeals (1533): asserted that England was an empire to whose supreme head and king all in the realm, both temporal and spiritual, owed obedience. By removing England from the authority of Rome and restricting the power of the English Church to spiritual matters this Act enabled the annulment of Henry VIII's marriage to Catherine of Aragon and made possible his marriage to Anne Boleyn.

Acts of Supremacy: the Act of 1534 summed up the claims of Henry VIII to be supreme head of the Church of England, and claimed for the king both spiritual and temporal jurisdiction over the realm. It made England an ecclesiastically sovereign state, though it did little more than ratify what had already been accomplished. The Act of 1559 was part of the Elizabethan Settlement, and used the term 'supreme governor' in reaffirming the Crown's spiritual authority in England—a terminology which placated some opponents (See also Royal Supremacy).

Acts of Uniformity: the first Act of Uniformity (1549) commanded the use of English in all services except in universities and in private, and made use of the First Book of Common Prayer compulsory in English churches, subject to increasingly severe penalties. The second Act (1552) enforced the use of the revised Prayer Book, and increased the strictures of the first Act. Both were repealed by Mary Tudor in 1553. The Act of Uniformity (1559) enforced the Elizabethan Settlement, repealed the Roman practices of Mary Tudor, established regulations for church discipline, and contained seeds of future controversy with the Puritans. The Act of 1662 followed the Restoration (qv) of Charles II, and was the first of a number of restrictive measures known as the Clarendon Code (qv). It commanded the use of the 1662 Prayer Book and demanded that all ministers publicly assent to it and, if not ordained, be ordained. As a result of this Act the Great Ejection (in which 2,000 Presbyterian, Baptist and Independent ministers left the Church), and an irretrievable division between Anglicans and Puritans, marked the beginning of English non-conformity.

Andrewes, Lancelot (1555–1626): Bishop of Winchester, a notable scholar and apologist for Anglicanism, and an outstanding preacher. He was involved as a translator in the 1611 Authorized Version of the Bible. His sermons and posthumous *Preces Privatae* have attracted much modern interest, chiefly due to the championship of T. S. Eliot (See also Caroline Divines).

Anglican Communion, the: the fellowship of Churches in communion with the see of Canterbury, sharing a common theology and liturgical tradition with the mother Church; focused since 1867 in the Lambeth Conferences (See Lambeth Conferences), the Anglican Consultative Council (See ACC), and the meetings of the Primates of the Communion (See Primate Meeting).

Anglicana Ecclesia: the term describing the Church of England in the 1534 Act of Supremacy.

Anglo-Catholicism: a dogmatic and sacramental position within Anglicanism emphasizing the continuity of links with the early Church, displaying an affinity with medieval Christianity, and rejecting the label 'Protestant'. Its immediate forebear was the Oxford Movement (qv), of which it was a late phase.

Archbishop of Canterbury: Augustine's first church in Britain (597) was at Canterbury, which therefore became the centre of the English Church. By the fourteenth century the Archbishop of Canterbury had the rank of Primate of All England, to which today is added his accepted role as leader and head of the Anglican Communion (qv).

ARCIC: the Anglican–Roman Catholic International Commission. The first Commission was set up in 1970 following the Archbishop of Canterbury's visit to Pope Paul VI, and the second in 1983. One of several post-Vatican II ecumenical initiatives, its conclusions have envisaged a future reunion of the two Churches, subject to much further discussion.

Articles: the Thirty-nine Articles reached their present form in 1571, and were preceded by the Ten Articles (1536), the Bishops' Book (1543), and the Forty-Two Articles (1553). They form a statement of the doctrinal position of the Church of England with respect to various theological issues of the sixteenth century and have been variously interpreted and used in the Anglican Communion since.

Bangorian Controversy (1717): the crisis precipitated by a sermon preached by Bishop Hoadly of Bangor before George I. The Lower House of Convocation accused Hoadly of erroneous teaching on the nature of the Church and the work of the Holy Spirit, and appealed to the Upper House to censure him. The conflicts which existed between the upper and lower clergy were thereby aggravated, and the consequent war of words led to the King's proroguing of Convocation. It was not to meet again for 135 years.

Bell, George Kennedy Allen (1883–1958): Bishop of Chichester 1929–58 and elected honorary president of the WCC in 1954, Bell was a significant figure in the Ecumenical Movement. He was chaplain to the Archbishop of Canterbury 1914–24, and while at Lambeth was involved in several early ecumenical initiatives; later he was influential in Life and Work 1937–48.

Book of Common Prayer: see Prayer Book

Broad Church: an imprecise term sometimes used to denote the loose 'party' of the Cambridge Platonists and Latitudinarians in the seventeenth century. Used in the nineteenth century of those who objected to what they saw as the dogmatic rigidity of Evangelicals (qv) and Anglo-Catholics (qv). They affirmed that God has given reason to human beings for the verification of revelation, and sought for a larger freedom for the interpretation of revelation in contemporary culture. The contributors to *Essays and Reviews* (qv) can be regarded as Broad Churchmen.

Butler, Joseph (1692–1752): Bishop, apologist and moral philosopher. Butler's major work was the *Analogy of Religion* (1736), which was a major weapon against Deism and a book of enduring influence. Against the Deists' argument from design, Butler argued that nature and revelation are both characterized by order and also by difficulties. The former he attributed to a divine Creator, the latter to human finiteness. He emphasized the weight of probability in evidences.

Cambridge Platonists: rejecting the doctrine of total depravity taught by the Calvinistic Puritans, the Platonists (who were based on Emmanuel College, Cambridge) held that human reason was an inner light and that good and evil, and an awareness of the infinite, were ineradicably part of human nature.

Canons: The *Book of Canons* (1604–6) adopted by James I was a manual of church law, essentially preserving the Elizabethan Settlement and making few concessions to Puritanism. It remained little changed until 1939, with the establishment of a canon law commission. Since then canon law has been continuously revised, such revision now being in the hands of a commission of the General Synod of the Church of England. Each Province of the Anglican Communion (qv) has its own canon laws, all related to but all different from the canon law of the Church of England.

Caroline Divines: the name given to a group of theologians, many of them bishops, of the seventeenth century, represented by Lancelot Andrewes (qv) and William Laud (qv), opposed to extreme Calvinism and Latitudinarianism (qv).

Catechism: instruction by question-and-answer. Used extensively by the Reformers, both because of its significance for the young and its suitability for teaching the poorly educated. Major catechisms were Luther's *Small Catechism* (1529), the Heidelberg Catechism (1563), the catechism before confirmation in the Prayer Book (added 1604) and the Westminster *Larger Catechism* (1658).

Chicago–Lambeth Quadrilateral: see Lambeth Quadrilateral.

Clarendon Code: a series of restrictive statutes passed by the Cavalier Parliament 1661–5. The intention was to strip those not conforming to the Church of England of all spiritual and secular leadership (See also Acts of Uniformity; Five Mile Act).

Commonwealth: following the execution of Charles I and the abolition of the House of Lords, England was declared a 'Commonwealth or Free State'. Government was by a Council of State and the drastically purged Rump Parliament. The Commonwealth saw the abolition of episcopacy and the Prayer Book, and the Church of England was proscribed.

Comprehension: the character of the English Church prior to the reign of Charles I, whereby a refusal to narrow doctrinal boundaries ensured that many not entirely happy with the Anglican Church nevertheless felt able to remain within it. 'Comprehensive' is a term often used today to indicate the element of inclusiveness thought to be integral to the definition of Anglicanism.

Convocation: regional gatherings of clergy in Canterbury and York, predating Parliament. The bishops formed the Upper House, the rest of the clergy the Lower. Conflicts between the two led to the suspension of Convocation for 135 years (See Bangorian Controversy). In 1920 the Church Assembly was created as a parallel body, and in 1969 functions of both were combined in the creation of the General Synod. Convocation still exists, though with greatly reduced powers.

Cranmer, Thomas (1489–1556): Archbishop of Canterbury 1533–55, Cranmer was the architect of English liturgy. He produced the vernacular liturgy of 1544, and in 1549 his first Book of Common Prayer. Other writings included *The True and Catholic Doctrine of the Lord's Supper* and a revision of canon law. Having joined the cause of Lady Jane Grey at the death-bed wish of Edward VI, he was condemned to death with the accession of Mary in 1553, though he was not executed until 1556.

Ecclesiastical Commission: Elizabeth I's chief instrument of governship of the Church, authorized by the 1559 Settlement.

Edward VI (1537–53): while still in his minority, Edward succeeded his father, Henry VIII (qv) on the throne, and under the guidance of a Protestant-minded protector, forwarded the Reformation in England. The English Bible returned to authorized use, Prayer Books (qv) in English were provided, Articles of Religion (qv) were devised, and these and other instruments of reform were enforced through Articles and Injunctions of Visitation.

Elizabeth I (1533–1603): Elizabeth's reign was marked by increased toleration and adroitness. The Elizabethan Settlement (1559) displayed both qualities, and was opposed by Roman Catholics and Puritans. The Settlement established the monarch as 'supreme governor' of the Church, and sought for religious uniformity through the enforced use of the 1552 Book of Common Prayer, conservatively revised. The Settlement was further defined during the Queen's reign in process of the conflict emerging between its defenders and those who were opposed to it.

Erastianism: the doctrine, named after the Swiss theologian Thomas Erastus (1524–83), that the state has the right to intrude upon the affairs of the Church and overrule decisions. In a limited sense the Church of England is an Erastian Church. The doctrine was opposed by Gore (qv) and others.

***Essays and Reviews* (1860)**: a collection of seven essays, radical and sometimes sceptical in nature, demanding an openness from the Church to the findings of modern criticism. It provoked a bitter controversy, which confirmed that liberal theology had a significant following.

Establishment: technically, the instituting of a Church system by law; in wider use, the term embraces the identification of Church and state and the supremacy of the sovereign as spiritual head of the Church—both concepts affirmed by the English Reformation (See also Act of Supremacy; Royal Supremacy).

Evangelical: a term derived from the German 'evangelisch', used by Luther to signify the character of the Christian Church as renewed by the gospel. It achieved greater prominence in English religious usage after the Evangelical Revival (qv). Anglicans who identify themselves as Evangelicals are generally characterized by commitment to the mission of the Church, often inclusive of social action, by stress on the atoning work of Christ and the necessity for conversion, and by use of the Scriptures as alone normative for faith and life. They are sometimes referred to as 'Low Church', in contrast to High Church (qv), for their comparative lack of concern for ceremonial and tradition, and for their ready association with Evangelicals of other Churches.

Evangelical Revival: often called the 'Wesleyan' Revival because of the crucial role of John Wesley (1703–91). The movement in England which began with the field-preaching of Wesley and George Whitefield (1714–70) was closely related both to the Moravian movement on the continent of Europe and the First Great Awakening in New England. Hymns were a feature of the Revival, and Charles Wesley (1707–88) was one of the most gifted of all English hymn-writers. The Evangelical Revival, with its emphasis on the value and worth of the individual, was responsible for extensive social reform and education.

Field, Richard (1561–1616): a close friend of Richard Hooker, Field was one of the outstanding theologians of his day. His major work, *Of the Church* (1606), was an affirmation of the Church of England against Rome. He maintained that Anglicanism was a continuation of old (pre-Trent) Catholic conciliar tradition and that modern Catholicism was echoing the errors of Donatism in its claim to exclusive purity.

Five Mile Act (1655): one of the rigorous measures of the Clarendon Code against those not assenting to the beliefs and practices of the Church of England, the Act made it an offence for Non-conformist ministers or teachers to approach within five miles of any city, town or borough.

Glorious Revolution, the: the revolution of 1688 which deposed James II and inaugurated the reign of William and Mary. Its cause was the widespread belief that James intended to implement a thorough-going Catholic state (as indicated by e.g. his preferment of Catholics to high office), and the fact that the birth of the Prince of Wales indicated that a Catholic dynasty was now secured. Early legislation of William and Mary dismantled much of the Clarendon Code.

Gore, Charles (1853–1932): Anglo-Catholic bishop who exerted a liberalizing influence on the Oxford Movement (See *Lux Mundi*). Gore was associated with the Christian Socialist movement, the Community of the Resurrection, and the Worker's Educational Association. A gifted scholar, he wrote numerous books and had a wide ministry and influence. He was an opponent of Erastianism (qv).

Henry VIII (1491–1547): although the head of the Reformed Church of England, Henry's sympathies remained Catholic. The dissolution of the monasteries was arguably an economic rather than a spiritual act, and the breach with Rome was inextricably implicated with his need for a male heir (See also Act of Supremacy; Royal Supremacy).

High Church: Laudianism; also more generally, any emphasis on ritual, order, and pre-Reformation church practice within the Protestant Churches (See also Laud).

Hooker, Richard (c. 1554–1600): preacher and minister, but more notably scholar and theologian. A landmark both in the history of English prose and also that of the English Church, Hooker's *Laws of Ecclesiastical Polity* (1593 and 1597) is a masterly defence of reason and order in ecclesiastical practice, which became a profoundly influential defence of Anglicanism and a strong argument against the Puritan case.

Huntington, William Reed (1838–90): American Episcopalian priest who in 1870 framed the four principles which were adopted in 1886 as the Chicago Quadrilateral and in 1888 as the Lambeth Quadrilateral (qv).

Glossary

Inter-Anglican Theological and Doctrinal Commission: this commission was established in 1980 on the recommendation of the first meeting of the Anglican Consultative Council.

Jewel, John (1522–71): Bishop of Salisbury 1560–71. Jewel was deeply influenced by, and involved with, continental Reformers. A refugee in Mary's reign, shortly after his return to England he wrote *Apologia Pro Ecclesia Anglicana* (1562), a major defence and justification of the English Reformation. He supported the Elizabethan Settlement and opposed the Puritans.

Keble, John (1792–1866): hymnwriter and author of *The Christian Year* (1827). Keble's Oxford Assize Sermon of 1833 against Erastianism (qv) was held by Newman to be the beginning of the Oxford Movement (qv), of which, with Pusey, he was a prominent leader.

'King-in-Parliament': the concept that the king ruled surrounded by his subjects, present either in person or by representation. Henry VIII's laws gave the Crown powers which extended over canon law and the church courts. Nevertheless there was a tacit assumption that the king and the law were not the same thing; a tension which by the reign of James I had become a major constitutional issue.

Lambeth Conference: the first Lambeth Conference met in 1867, at the suggestion of C. T. Longley, the Archbishop of Canterbury, and was attended by 67 bishops. Longley's proposal was that an informal gathering of bishops should meet at his invitation to discuss Anglican problems. The Conferences have continued approximately every ten years, attended by most Anglican bishops. Issues discussed include theological, domestic, church unity and social issues. The statements of the Lambeth Conferences are not binding on member Churches, being only expressions of the bishops' opinion, though they are of great influence.

Lambeth Quadrilateral: the 'Chicago–Lambeth Articles': four Articles adopted by the American Episcopal Church in Chicago in 1886 and by the 1888 Lambeth Conference. They cover Scripture, the creeds, the two sacraments and the historic episcopate, and attempt to establish common ground in discussions on church unity. The Articles have been influential in the Ecumenical Movement.

Latitudinarians: seventeenth-century divines, often very influential, who appealed to reason as well as to Scripture and the Church. Many had been students of the Cambridge Platonists. Their faith in reason led many to become interested in science, and some became members of the Royal Society. They emphasized moderation, morality and a distrust of extremes such as Puritanism and Deism.

Laud, William (1573–1645): Archbishop of Canterbury 1633–45. Laud was an opponent of Puritanism and a champion of order and external uniformity, pre-Reformation liturgy, and episcopacy. He initiated a campaign to reintroduce ritual, ornament and genuflection into the churches, and his influence extended into all sectors of English life. Out of the Laudian programme emerged the High Church party, which emphasized Arminianism over Calvinism and shared Laud's views on worship and church life. Laud, who had become identified with the despotism of Charles I, was executed for treason in 1645 during the Civil War.

Liberal Catholicism: a term coined by Charles Gore to describe the synthesis of incarnational theology and evolutionary thought of the authors of *Lux Mundi*. He

502

maintained that its combination of Catholic doctrine, critical method and social concern was the authentic Anglican vocation. Later liberal Catholicism was more experiential and critical, and is represented by *Essays Catholic and Critical*, ed. E. G. Selwyn (1926). To be distinguished from the eclectic and theosophical Liberal Catholic Church, founded 1918.

Locke, John (1632–1704): a father of deism, Locke argued that the mind is a *tabula rasa*, and knowledge is the result of ideas derived from sense-experience and awareness of self. For Locke, faith was the result of proof. He opposed Enthusiasm, and in *The Reasonableness of Christianity* (1695) he demonstrates a very high view of reason—a view which had considerable influence on subsequent theology. He discarded most dogma, was an advocate of toleration, and accepted that high moral and ethical imperatives must follow from his rationalism.

Lux Mundi: a Series of Studies in the Religion of the Incarnation (1889): collection of essays from a position of liberal Catholicism (qv) edited by Charles Gore, critiquing the Anglo-Catholic movement and arguing for a more socially aware and contemporary Catholicism in the Church of England. It was an attempt to unite Tractarian theology with critical scholarship and sound learning.

Maurice, F. D. (1805–72): a leading Anglican theologian and founder member, with Charles Kingsley and J. M. F. Ludlow, of the Christian Socialist movement. A prolific and influential writer, his works included: *The Kingdom of Christ* (1838), his major work in which he addressed the issue of unity between Christians in the light of the incarnate Christ; and *Theological Essays* (1853), which contained unorthodox and controversial views on eternal punishment.

Modernism: in general, used of theological developments showing accommodation to scientific, historical and philosophical argument. In Roman Catholicism of the early twentieth century, a heterogeneous movement represented by A. Loisy, F. von Hügel and G. H. Tyrrell; they were sceptical of dogma and endorsed higher criticism. Anglican Modernism was roughly contemporary, influenced by continental liberal Protestantism, was the heir to the Broad Church movement and focused, in the 1920s, in the Modern Churchmen's Union. Unorthodox and radical views expressed by the Modernists provoked controversy.

Newman, J. H. (1801–90): of Evangelical upbringing, Newman became in 1828 vicar of St Mary's, Oxford. He was an early Tractarian (qv), but moved from advocacy of the *via media* to a controversial Catholic interpretation of the Thirty-nine Articles in Tract XC (qv). In 1843 he resigned his living and in 1845 converted to Roman Catholicism. He published *Apologia Pro Vita Sua* in 1864, *Grammar of Assent* (an apologetic work) in 1870, and became a cardinal in 1879.

Non-conformist: a term originating after the Restoration to describe those not conforming to the doctrine and practice of the Church of England.

Non-jurors: those of the Church of England who did not take the Oath of Allegiance to William and Mary (See Glorious Revolution). Also, from 1714, used of those who did not swear allegiance to George I.

Oxford Movement: a nineteenth-century movement within the Church of England against Erastianism (qv) and liberalism, deriving from the High Church party. Generally regarded as dating from Keble's 1833 sermon (See Keble), it soon acquired the name 'Tractarianism' (qv). When its anti-Reformation leanings were perceived it aroused hostility. From 1840, part of the movement shifted towards Rome under the leadership of Newman (qv; See also Tract XC). In 1845 Newman converted to Rome, and the movement lost its Oxford base and acquired the label 'Anglo-Catholic' (qv). The Oxford Movement emphasized High Church practices and the traditions of Old Catholicism.

Prayer Book: the 1549 Book of Common Prayer followed the 1544 English liturgy and the 1548 *Order of Communion*. A new, vernacular liturgy, Cranmer's Prayer Book was a replacement for its Latin equivalents, based substantially on the old Sarum rites but significantly Protestant—a characteristic strengthened in the 1552 Prayer Book, produced in response to demands from English and continental Reformers. The 1552 book was abolished by Queen Mary, was restored in 1559 by Queen Elizabeth with few but significant changes, resisted appeals for change from e.g. Puritans, was again lightly revised in 1604, and was abolished in 1645. The Prayer Book as enforced by the 1662 Act of Uniformity was essentially unchanged, though with some additions and many minor revisions. Other Prayer Books appeared as the Anglican Communion expanded, including the 1789 book of the Episcopal Church in the United States.

In England in 1927 there was a revision in response to developments that had begun in the late nineteenth century, to include e.g. reservation of the sacrament. This was perceived by Parliament as an attempt to shift the doctrinal emphases of the Church of England, and rejected. Although revised Prayer Books have been introduced in various Provinces, no further revisions to the 1662 Prayer Book have been authorized in England, and it remains the official service book, the work produced in 1980 being strictly therefore an *Alternative Service Book*.

Primates Meeting: a group composed of the presiding or senior bishops of the autonomous Provinces of the Anglican Communion. Given a more prominent status at the 1978 Lambeth Conference, it has met on a regular basis since 1979 and constitutes one of several recent moves to strengthen communication and consultation within the Anglican Communion.

Puritan: originally a movement within the English Church, Puritanism in the reign of Elizabeth argued for a more complete reformation than was achieved under Henry VIII. The first Puritans in the accepted sense were Marian exiles, returning to England intent on purifying the Church on the basis of the supremacy of Scripture, the right of individual access to the Bible and the importance of teaching it to the people, and a Calvinistic perspective drawn from continental Reformed Churches. The Puritans were disappointed with the Elizabethan Settlement and their demands to James I met with only limited response. By 1640 they were the dominant force behind Parliament in the Civil Wars, but by the time of Cromwell were divided among themselves. Puritanism, which began within the Church, was forced outside it by the Clarendon Code, and thereafter the Puritan ideal of a total reformation of Church and state withered.

'Puritanism', in both learned and popular forms, was often misused as a term, a practice which began in Elizabeth's reign. Modern usage is a reminder that historic Puritanism was identified by a distinct lifestyle and discipline.

Queen Anne's Bounty: a fund established by Queen Anne in 1704 to redistribute clerical taxes in a more equitable system of clerical incomes.

Recusant: a Roman Catholic who refused to accept the Elizabethan Settlement, specifically the provisions of the 1559 Act of Uniformity (qv). Increasingly harsh penalties against recusants culminated in the years after 1688. The Catholic Emancipation Act (1829) finally removed most of the penalties.

Restoration: the return of Charles II to the English throne in 1660 and the restoration of the Stuart dynasty. It meant the re-establishment of the Church of England (See Savoy Conference).

Royal Supremacy: in contradistinction to papal supremacy, describes the process whereby Henry VIII progressively, and conspicuously in legislation of 1529–34, removed from the pope jurisdiction, prerogatives and revenues previously his due from England. The process culminated in the Act of Supremacy (1534) (qv), which gave Henry supreme headship of the English Church.

Savoy Conference (1661): a conference comprising twelve bishops and twelve Puritan divines, convened after the Restoration (qv) to resolve disagreements over the nature of the restored Church. The Puritans argued strongly for satisfaction of grievances extending back to the Elizabethan Settlement, but the result was only minor revision of the Prayer Book and numerous Puritan secessions following the 1662 Act of Uniformity (qv).

Simeon, Charles (1759–1836): leading Evangelical, influential in Cambridge, a noted preacher and involved in many Evangelical enterprises. Founded the Simeon Trust to promote Evangelicalism in the parishes.

Supreme Governor: see Acts of Supremacy

Synod: in general church usage, a council of senior clergy to discuss doctrine, policy etc. In England such assemblies have had various titles (See Convocation). The needs of Scottish Episcopalians after the 1690 establishment of the (Presbyterian) Church of Scotland led to the first example of constitutional and synodical government known in the history of Anglicanism. The first post-revolutionary American General Convention was held in 1785 in Philadelphia, and contained both clerical and lay members. From the mid-nineteenth century the term 'synod' was regularly used for gatherings of bishops, clergy and lay persons to govern the corporate life of an Anglican Church outside England, by common consent.

Temple, William (1881–1944): Archbishop of York 1929–42, Archbishop of Canterbury 1942–44, and chairman of the Archbishops' Commission on Christian Doctrine (1922–37). A leader in the Ecumenical Movement, he presided at the inaugural meeting of the British Council of Churches, and was instrumental in the founding of the World Council of Churches. He was a distinguished theologian and apologist who espoused, notably in *Nature, Man and God* (1934), a metaphysical philosophy in which Christ is the highest realization of the world process.

Test Act (1673): passed by Parliament in opposition to Charles II's 1672 Declaration of Indulgence, the Test Act required all office-holders under the Crown to, in effect, publicly and legally embrace membership of the Church of England. The Act made many enemies for the Church, and committed Dissenters to active opposition.

Tractarianism: the period of the Oxford Movement that saw the publication of the *Tracts for the Times*. Written by e.g. J. H. Newman, E. B. Pusey, R. H. Froude, R. W. Church and J. B. Mozley, the Tracts, which were widely distributed, expounded the credal statement, 'I believe in one holy, Catholic and Apostolic Church.' Tract I, by Newman, urged the reclamation of the doctrine of apostolic succession. In all, 90 Tracts were issued.

Tract XC (1841, J. H. Newman): Tract in which Newman argued that the Thirty-Nine Articles did not, as had been wrongly supposed, condemn many Roman Catholic practices. Its hostile reception indicated to Newman that Anglicanism's claims to be a *via media* (qv) were not tenable.

Tyndale, William (*c.* 1494–1536): English Reformer, popularly known as 'the English Luther'. Tyndale's vernacular English Bible was printed on the continent in difficult and fugitive circumstances. Opposed by Thomas More and other English churchmen, Tyndale was given help by expatriate English sympathizers. When it appeared in England, Tyndale's New Testament was publicly burned in London.

Author of several theological works as well as a prolific translator, Tyndale is a significant literary figure besides a seminal contributor to the English Reformation. He was executed at Vilvorde, near Brussels, in 1536.

Via Media: 'the middle way', a designation for the stance of Anglicanism between Roman Catholicism and one form or another of Protestantism. The significance of the term is ambiguous, since on occasions extreme or radical Protestantism (Anabaptism) is taken as one pole, in which case Anglicanism shares the 'middle way' with e.g. Lutheranism; on other occasions the designation is intended to contrast Anglicanism with more central forms of Protestantism, e.g. Puritanism (qv), Presbyterianism, and what J. H. Newman called 'popular Protestantism'.

Whitgift, John (*c.* 1530–1604): Archbishop of Canterbury 1583–1604, Whitgift was staunchly aligned with the Anglicanism of Queen Elizabeth and instituted numerous measures against Puritans, including the publishers of the *Marprelate Tracts*. His Calvinist revision of the Thirty-Nine Articles (the Lambeth Articles) was rejected by Elizabeth.

Wilberforce, William (1759–1833): Anglican Evangelical (qv) at the core of the Clapham Sect, Wilberforce was a social reformer most notably committed to the abolition of the slave trade, which took place in 1807 as a result of his and his associates' work. His *Practical View of the Prevailing Religious System* ... (1797) was an Evangelical challenge to nominal Christianity, and was highly influential; he and the Clapham Sect were also active in evangelizing the upper classes.

Index

à Lasco, John 12
Absenteeism 380
Acland, Richard 371
Acts of Parliament: for communion in two
kinds 11–12; Act in Restraint of
Appeals (1533) 393; Act for the
Submission of the Clergy (1534) 220;
Act of Supremacy (1534) 447, 460;
Six Articles Act (1539) 13; Act of
Uniformity (1549) 12; Second Act of
Uniformity (1552) 137; Act of
Supremacy (1559) 16–17, 203–4,
205, 394; Act of Uniformity (1559)
108, 149, 394; requiring clerical
subscription to Articles (1571) 13;
Act of Uniformity (1662) 326, 342;
Corporation Act 397; Five Mile Act
397; Test Act (1673) 397; Toleration
Act (1689) 21; allowing consecration
of foreign bishops (1786) 40; Church
Building Act (1818) 36; Plurality
Acts (1838, 1850) 327; Public
Worship Regulation Act (1874) 45
Adam, Thomas 33
Adiaphora 180, 252–4, 264–5
Africa 30, 40, 450–2, 483–96 passim
Aglionby, John Orfew, Bp 450
All African Consultation on Ecumenical
Theological Education 452
Allen, Roland 288, 491–2
Altars 12
Alternative Service Book 1980 46, 174
American Church see Protestant Episcopal
Church of the USA
Andrewes, Lancelot, Bp 178–80, 338, 340,
354–5; definition of Anglicanism
267–8; popularized by T. S. Eliot
354–5; discussed by N. Lossky 355
Anglicana ecclesia see Ecclesia anglicana
Anglican Catholic Church 415
Anglican Centre (Rome) 49
Anglican Communion, nature of 30ff.,
67–8; origin and growth 40–1, 208–
10, 461
Anglican Congresses see Congresses of
Anglicans
Anglican Consultative Council 49, 203,
212, 284–5, 456
Anglican Encounter in the South 451
Anglican–Lutheran relations 434
Anglican–Methodist schemes for unity
(1969, 1972) 48
Anglican–Orthodox relations 47, 434
Anglican–Reformed dialogue 431
Anglican–Roman Catholic International
Commission (ARCIC) 48, 55, 213–
14, 274, 434–5, 468; Agreed Statement
on Eucharistic Doctrine 316–8, 431;
and ordained ministry 330, 431;
(ARCIC II) 441–2
Anglicanism: nature 459–76; etymology
460–1, 477–83
Anglo-Catholicism 45; see also Lux Mundi
Anne, Queen 21, 27
Anti-Subscription Movement 38
Apocrypha 93, 107
Apostolic succession 18, 27, 30, 114, 257,
328, 337–40, 408
Apostolicity 330, 337–40
Archbishop of Canterbury, international
role of 50, 259–60, 406
Archbishops' Commission on Christian
Doctrine 44
ARCIC see Anglican–Roman Catholic
International Commission
Arianism 107, 205–6
Arminianism 24
Arnold, Matthew 351–2, 354–5
Arnold, Thomas 38, 284, 399
Articles of Religion 144–8, 150–3; Forty-
two (1553) 7, 13; Thirty-nine
(1563–71) 9, 13, 22, 24, 69–71, 87,
93, 106, 110, 111, 204–5, 259;
prefatory declaration 19–20, 146;

Articles of Religion (*cont.*)
replaced by presbyterian system 20;
clerical subscription to 38, 151–2;
significance within Anglicanism 65,
105; structure 94
'Associated Parishes' (USA) 46
Association for the Promotion of the
Unity of Christendom 47
Atonement 94 n. 10
Augsburg Confession (1530) 73–4, 145,
265
Augustine of Hippo 102, 103, 110–1,
167–8
Australia, Anglican Church of (formerly
the Church of England in Australia)
41, 407
Australian Prayer Book (1978) 174
Authority 471; of the Bible 11, 101–2,
252; of the Church 96–7, 107, 113–
14, 205, 213–14; of church councils
206, 472; of tradition 104, 465; of the
Prayer Book 231, 259; of bishops
337–8; in a united Church 442
Authorized Version of the Bible (1611) 9–
10, 18, 353

Bacon, Francis 8
Bancroft, Richard, Abp 10, 368
Bangorian Controversy 32
Baptism 66–7, 134, 295–7 *see also*
Initiation
Baptism, Eucharist and Ministry (Lima
Statement, 1982) 212–13, 432
Barrett, David B. 408–11, 416–17
Barth, Karl 242, 272
Baxter, Richard 110, 140, 326, 388
Bayne, Stephen, Bp 49, 211
Becon, Thomas 149, 321–2
Bell, G. K. A., Bp 47, 428
Benson, Edward White, Abp 173, 210,
211
Berridge, John 33–4
Beveridge, William, Bp 343
Bible 87–100; authority 11, 101–2; canon
93–6, 101; inspiration 88–90, 273;

sufficiency 90; primacy 91–3; and
tradition 96–7, 101; influence 353;
open to laity 470 *see also* Canon *and
names of individual translations*
Bible Churchmen's Missionary Society
492
Bibles ordered to be placed in every
church 44, 148, 281; given to new
priests 252, 323
Biblical theology 44
Bickersteth, Edward, Bp 490
Bilson, Thomas 335
Bishops *see* Episcopacy
Bishops' Book (*The Institution of a
Christian Man*, 1537) 144
Blackburne, Archdeacon 38
Blomfield, Charles James, Bp 40, 398
Boleyn, Anne 6
Bonn Agreement (1931) 48, 430
Bonner, Edmund, Bp 149
Book of Common Prayer 131–44;
importance in Anglican tradition
58–9, 67–8, 231, 353, 447; source for
other traditions 79; and ordained
ministry 382–6
(1549) 7, 11, 60, 105, 131–6, 170, 189,
192, 295–6, 308
(1552) 7, 136–8, 296–7,308
(1559) 8, 12, 138–9, 394
(1604) 9, 139, 298
Scottish (1637) 139
(1662) 23, 139–40
American (1789) 62, 140–1
Irish (1877) 141
nineteenth-century revision 141
twentieth-century revision 31, 60–2,
65–6, 141–2, 172– 3, 403
proposed (1928) 46, 66, 165, 228
American (1928) 386
ECUSA (1979) 66, 190, 277
New Zealand (1989) 287–8
Book of Homilies (1547, 1559, 1571) 107,
144, 148–50
Boone, W. J., Bp 490
Bouyer, Louis 360

Bramhall, John, Abp 112, 151
Bray, Thomas 22, 40, 484
Breda, Declaration of 396
Brent, Charles Henry, Bp 47, 185, 427
Brevint, Daniel 313
British Antiochian Orthodox Deanery 415
British Critic 36
Broad Church 38, 257
Brooks, Phillips, Bp 185
Brown, David, Bp 493
Bucer, Martin 106, 135, 155, 296, 385
Buckeridge, John 312
Bull, George 113
Bullinger, Heinrich 266
Burgon, Dean 87
Burial rite 135, 138
Burnet, Gilbert, Bp 151, 206, 387
Butler, Joseph, Bp 120, 368–9; *Analogy* (1736) 25, 33
Buxton, Thomas Fowell 487

Calixtus, Georg 267
Calvin, John: on justification 74–5; on sacraments 79; on sanctification 77
Calvinism in Anglican Evangelicals 34
Calvinist 'discipline' urged by Puritan Reformers 335
Cambridge Camden Society 45
Cambridge Mission to Delhi 487
Cambridge Platonists 24–5, 109
Canada, Anglican Church in (formerly the Church of England in Canada) 41, 42, 407
Canon law 9, 17, 216–46, 413–14, 480
Canon of Scripture 93–6, 101
Canons 9
Cape Colony 400
Capitalism 371–2
Carey, George, Abp 451
Caribbean Islands, early Anglican congregations 22
Carleton, Bp 335
Caroline Divines 24
Carrington, Philip, Abp 185

Cartwright, Thomas 110, 334–5
Casaubon, Isaac 267–8
Cassander, Georg 265–6
Casuistry 375–6
Catechisms 13, 165–76, 388
Catechists 450
Catherine of Aragon 6
Catholicity (1947) 463
Charles I, King 19–20, 146, 334
Charles II, King 20–23
Chicago–Lambeth Quadrilateral *see* Lambeth Quadrilateral
Chillingworth, William 268–9
China 490
Christian Socialist Movement 359, 370–2
Christian Observer (1802–) 35
Christology 94
Church, R. W. 179, 182
Church Assembly 228–9, 403
Church Congress *(York, 1866)* 41
Church Congress *(1896)* 370
Church Missionary Society 35, 41, 485–6, 488
Church–State Relations 392–405
Church's Ministry to the Jews 494
Clapham Sect 34, 369
Clarendon, Earl of 21; Code 397
Clark, Samuel 38
Clarke, Henry Lowther 229 n. 15
Clayton, Bp 38
Clergy 379–81; *see also* Ministry; Ordinal
Clericalism 284
Codrington School/College 485
Colenso, J. W., Bp 41, 401–2
Coleridge, S. T. 38–9, 121, 125–6, 399
Colet, John 4
Collects 63–5, 88, 90, 133
Colonial Bishoprics Fund 40
Colquhoun, Frank 173
Commission for the Revision of the Catechism 172
Commonwealth (Cromwell's) 396
Communion tables 12, 23
Comprehension 25, 31, 38, 240, 260–1, 263, 269, 411, 413, 414

Conference on Politics, Economy, and
Citizenship (*Birmingham, 1924*)
370–2
Confession 389
Confirmation 134–5, 138, 170, 295,
298–9, 304–6
Congresses of Anglicans 211; (*Toronto,*
1963) 492–3
Conscience 103, 368, 375
Consecration, of elements in Eucharist 12
Continuing Churches 415
Convocations 203; intended as adjuncts to
Parliament 15; meetings ended
(1717) 26, 32; revived (1852) 41–2,
228; House of Laymen added 284
COPEC 370–2
Copleston, Edward 38
Cosin, John, Bp 140, 336, 337, 340
Councils of the Church 202–16;
Chalcedon (451) 108; Clovecho
(747) 168; Constance 108; Jerusalem
(c. 50) 209; Nicaea (325) 107, 108;
Nicaea (787) 112, 205; Trent (1545–
63) 8, 108, 110, 204, 205, 207
Counselling 389
Court of High Commission 26
Cragg, Kenneth, Bp 493
Cranmer, Thomas, Abp 7, 10, 11, 13, 47,
105, 189; Easter anthems 57–8; view
of ministry 105; attitude to papacy
109; prayer of consecration 94; and
the Articles 145; and the *Book of*
Homilies 148; and ordinal 159;
eucharistic theology 170, 323–4;
ecclesiology 286; revision of
baptismal rite 294–7; confirmation
rite 296, 305 *see also* Collects
Creeds 13, 68, 204
Cromwell, Thomas 6, 16–17
Crowther, Samuel Adjai, Bp 40, 484, 487,
489
Cupitt, Don 44–5
Cyril of Jerusalem 107

Daubeny, Charles, Archdeacon 36

Davidson, Randall, Abp 491
Deacons 161–2
Declarations of Indulgence (1663, 1687,
1688) 21 n. 27, 397
'Defender of the Faith' 6
Deism 25, 32–3, 208
Demography 408–11
Dickens, A. G. 479–80
Diehl, William 290
Directory of Public Worship 20
Disestablishment 402, 403–4
Dissolution of the monasteries 7, 17
Divine right of bishops 337
Dix, Gregory 46, 316
Doctrine: and canon law 233–6; and
liturgy 59–69; *see also* Ecclesiology
Donne, John 177
Dort, Synod of (1618) 24
DuBose, William Porcher 184
Durham Book 140
Durie, John 267

East India Company 22, 39
Easter anthems 57–8
Eastern Churches Association 47
Eastertide 57–8
Ecclesia anglicana 7, 450, 460–1, 477–83
Ecclesiastical Commission 17, 26, 398
Ecclesiological Society 45
Ecclesiology 249–62, 282–5, 457–8
Eclectics Society 485
Ecumenical Councils 107, 203–8
Ecumenical Movement 31, 46–9, 55, 104,
212–13, 267, 427–46, 454–5; and
canon law 238–9, 261, 274, 278, 316;
in seventeenth century 388
ECUSA *see* Protestant Episcopal Church
of the USA
Education 281–2, 289, 383, 389–90, 484
Education for Ministry 289
Edward VI, King 7, 148
Egbert, Abp 168
Eliot, T. S. 179, 187, 354–5
Elizabeth I, Queen 8–9, 10, 15, 106
Elizabethan Settlement (1559) 16, 333–4

Elland, Society 34
Episcopacy 333–47; place of bishops in
    Parliament 26, 32; differing
    interpretations of 42; essential to
    Anglicanism 56, 111–12, 453; in New
    Testament 97; and ordinals 159–61;
    restoration 163; Wake's view of
    269–70; and initiation 301, 306;
    claimed origin of English episcopate
    472
Episcopal appointments 17; consecration
    of overseas bishops 40
Erasmus, Desiderius 4, 5, 263
Essays and Reviews (1860) 39, 122, 123
Essays Catholic and Critical (1926) 43
Establishment 21, 40, 379–80, 392–405
Ethics 92–3 *see also* Morality; Situation
    ethics
Eton College case (1857) 40, 401
Eucharist 12, 23, 106, 308–21, 358, 359;
    frequency of celebration 24, 45; a
    community act 58, 105; theology of
    94; and baptism 67; rites 133–4, 136,
    137–8, 140, 142; and Evangelical
    revival 313–14; and priestly office
    331, 388
Evangelical Revival 30, 33–5
Experience 123–4
Extraordinary Black Book (1831) 398

Faith: common to the Church 58; and
    liturgy 68, 77–8; nature 90–1
Faith and Order Movement/Commission
    316–8, 428–9, 433; Lima Statement
    212–13, 432
Farrer, Austin 124
Fathers of the Church 101, 268
Feathers Tavern Petition 38, 151
Field, Richard 110, 112, 206–7, 255
Fisher, Geoffrey, Abp 47, 48, 428
Fisher, John, Bp 7
Fletcher, John 33
Fletcher, Joseph 373–4
Foundations (1913) 123
Foxe, John 281

Freehold of benefices 413–14
Frith, John 265
Froude, Richard Hurrell 36–7
Froude, W. H. 272
Fundamentals 262–77

Garbett, Cyril, Abp 229, 472
General Synod 203, 229, 403
Gardiner, Allen 490
Geneva Bible (1560) 9, 10
George I, King 21, 26
George II, King 21
Gibson, Edmund, Bp 32
Gladstone, W. E. 353, 399–400
Goodridge, Sehon, Bp 451
Gore, Charles, Bp 43, 183, 273, 287, 370,
    466–7, 472
Gospel: in Anglicanism 55–83; nature
    90–1
Grant, Archdeacon 41
Gray, Abp 41
Gray, Robert, Bp 401–2
Great Awakening 33
Great Bible 7, 281
Great Tew 24, 268
Gregory the Great, Pope 108
Grimshaw, William 33
Grindal, Edmund, Abp 14
Grotius, Hugo 267–8

Halifax, Viscount 48
Hall, Joseph, Bp 180
Hammond, Henry 112
Hampton Court Conference 9, 139
Hanson, R. P. C. 88 n. 3
Hare, Julius 38
Harpsfield, John 149
Harris, Howell 33
Harrison, Benjamin 271
Hawkins, Edward 488
Headlam, A. C., Bp 47
Headlam, Charles, Bp 428
Heber, Reginald, Bp 487
Hebert, A. G. 44, 46, 315
Heidelberg Catechism (1563) 169

Henry VIII, King 4; *Assertio Septem Sacramentorum* 5–6; divorce 6; *King's Booke* (1543) 13; and royal supremacy 16; and *adiaphora* 265
Henson, Hensley 93, 473–4
Herbert, George 166–7, 171–2, 361, 366, 385, 386
Heresy 204, 367, 394, 401–2
High Church movement 35–7
Hine, John 489
Hisley's Primer (1539) 170
Hoadly, Benjamin, Bp 32
Hobart, John Henry, Bp 36, 223
Holiness 352
Holmes, Urban 283
Holy Communion *see* Eucharist
Hook, W. F. 37
Hooker, Richard 11, 13, 14, 15, 16, 25, 177–8, 179, 180–1, 188, 221, 225, 357–8; on reason 115–18; on the Roman Catholic Church 110; on the sacraments 72–3, 78–9, 88, 309–11; ecclesiology 254–5, 283, 286; definition of the essence of Christianity 266–7; and episcopacy 335–6, 338–40; on church and state 395
Horne, George 35
Horsley, Samuel 35–6
Hort, F. J. A. 43, 183
Hoskyns, E. C. 44
Howe, John, Bp 212
Humanism 3–4, 101
Huntington, William Reed 42, 249–50, 258, 260
Hymn books 46

Ignatius of Antioch 112
Illingworth, J. R. 123, 287
Incarnation 78, 88, 94
Incarnational theology *see* Liberal Catholicism
India 22, 40, 408, 486–7; *see also* South India, Church of; North India, Church of

Infant baptism 298
Inglis, Charles 40
Initiation 293–307
Injunctions, Elizabethan 16
Inter-Anglican Theological and Doctrinal Commission 50, 80
International Anglican Liturgical Consultation:
(1st, Boston, 1985) 304, 306
(4th, Toronto, 1991) 303–4, 306
(5th, Dublin, 1995) 304, 318–9
Ireland, Church of 22, 46, 208, 402

James I, King 9–10, 19, 49, 465–6
James II, King 21
Japan 490
Jebb, John, Bp 271
Jenkins, David, Bp 44, 126
Jesus Christ: and word of God 87–8
Jewel, John, Bp 13, 110, 150, 264, 472
Johnson, Richard 487
Johnson, Samuel 184
Johnstone, Patrick 417
Jones, William 35
Jowett, Benjamin 39, 116
Justification by faith 13, 34, 69–77
Juxon, William 368

Käsemann, Ernst 95
Kavanagh, Aidan 68
Keble, John 36, 113, 122, 182, 359–60, 399
King, Edward, Bp 45, 398
'King-in-Parliament' 5, 15
King James Bible *see* Authorized Version
King's Book (*A Necessary Doctrine and Erudition for any Christian Man*, 1543) 144, 148, 170
Kingsley, Charles 370, 372
Kirk, Kenneth E., Bp 375
Kraemer, Hendrik 282–3

Laity 277–93; inclusion in synodical government 40
Lambeth conferences 30, 210–12

(1867) 40, 42, 405–6
(1888) 42
(1920) 47
(1930) 49, 152, 259, 340, 467, 470, 478
(1948) 479
(1958) 49, 141, 492
(1968) 49, 152, 211–12, 263, 299–300, 306
(1978) 50, 436
(1998) 277, 440–1
Lambeth Quadrilateral 42, 47, 95, 210–11, 249–50, 263, 428, 436
Langland, William 365
Latimer, Hugh, Bp 149
Latitudinarianism 25–7, 37–9
Laud, William, Abp 20, 23, 151, 206–7, 268, 368
Law, William 33, 113, 343
Lee, F. G. 47
Leighton, Robert, Abp 184
Leo X, Pope 5–6
Leo XIII, Pope 164
Levant Company 39
Lewis, Bp 42
Lewis, C. S. 357
Lex Orandi—Lex Credendi 187–202, 285
Liberal Catholicism 43, 44, 466–7
Liberal theology 37–9, 257
Liddon, H. P. 43
Life and Liberty 228, 403
Life and Work 428–9
Lightfoot, J. B., Bp 43, 183, 339
Lima Statement 55, 80, 432, 434, 438
Liturgical developments 31
Liturgical Movement 46, 60–1, 315
Liturgy: and faith 58; significance in Anglicanism 58–9; and doctrine 59–69; and canon law 231–3; local liturgies 452
Livingstone, David 489
Lloyd, Roger 382, 384–5
Local ecumenical projects 48, 432
Locke, John 37–8, 39, 113, 115–20
Lollardy 3–4
London Missionary Society 485

Longley, Charles, Abp 42, 405
Lossky, Nicholas 355
Loyer, Oliver 356–8
Ludlow, J. M. 370
Lund Principle 431–2
Luther, Martin 5, 169, 264–5
Lux Mundi (1889) 43, 122–3, 126, 273, 287, 463
Lyndwood, William 220

McAdoo, Henry, Abp 263, 367, 469, 477–8
Mackenzie, C. F. 41, 489
Mackinnon, D. M. 124
Macquarrie, John 124, 126, 477, 478
Magna Carta 191–2
Major, H. D. A. 43
Malines Conversations 48, 430
Malvern Manifesto 371
Manning, Henry Edward 37
Marashin, Jaci 447
Marriage of clergy 7
Marriage rites 135
Marsden, Samuel 487–8
Marsh, Herbert, Bp 151
Marshall's Primer (1534) 168
Martyn, Henry 486
Mary I, Queen 8
Mary II, Queen 21
Mason, Francis 325
Maurice, F. D. 38–9, 182, 286–7, 344, 359, 370, 375, 469
Mede, Joseph 109
Meissen Agreement (1991) 49, 442
Middleton, T. F., Bp 486–7
Millenary Petition 139
Ministry 321–33, 379–80; threefold 18, 105–6, 159–62, 270, 326, 328, 332, 345
Mission 41, 288–91, 455, 483–96
Missionary societies 406, 412–13, 485–96
Moberly, R. C. 126, 326
Modern Churchmen's Union 43
Moore, Aubrey 123
Morality 364–78

More, Hannah 185–6
More, Henry 109–10
More, Paul Elmer 364–5
More, Thomas 4, 5, 6, 7
Mountain, Jacob 40
Munby, D. N. 372
Music 357, 358
Mysticism 355–6
Myth 125

Nag's Head Fable 163–4, 325
National Society 36
Neale, E. Vansittart 370
Neale, J. M. 45
Neill, Stephen, Bp 478, 493
New Zealand, Church of 41, 407
Newbigin, Lesslie, Bp 435
Newman, John Henry 36–7, 114, 151, 182, 271–2, 328
Nicene Creed 68
Niebuhr, Reinhold 365
'Nobody's Friends' (club) 35
Noetics 38
Nonjurors 21, 22, 23, 256
Norris, H. H. 36
North India, Church of 48, 431
Nowell, Dean 13, 170

Oakeley, F. 36
Oberman, Heiko 207–8
Oldham, Ashton, Bp 171
Oldham, J. H. 371
Order 368
Ordinal 90, 105, 135–6, 138, 155–65, 322–3, 378–9
Ordination: episcopal 18, 27; requirements for 156–7
Ordination of women *see* Women
Overall, John 170
Owen, John 103
Oxford Movement 30, 35–7, 47, 121–2, 257, 314, 328, 369–70, 398–9

Paget, Francis 287
Pakistan, Church of 48, 431
Paley, William 38, 119

Palmer, William 37, 257, 263, 272
Pan-Anglican Congresses 49
Papacy, jurisdiction in England 6
Papias of Hierapolis 101
Parish and People 46
Parish Communion 46, 315
Parker, Matthew, Abp, 145, 150, 163–4, 334, 472
Partnership for World Mission 494
Pastoral theology 378–91
Patronage 17
Pattison, Mark 119, 120–1
Pearson, John, Bp 112, 147, 255, 338, 340, 343
Pelagius 192
Perkins, William 11, 13, 325
Pietism 33
Pius V, Pope 9, 106
Pluralism: of Bible 87; of Church 79–81, 119; of society 21, 27; of benefices 380; religious 413
Politics 92–3 *see also* Social concern of the Church
Porvoo Common Statement 443
Pragmatism 365
Pratt, Josiah 486
Prayer 59, 60; *see also* Liturgy
Preaching 12, 14, 32, 34, 337, 387
Priesthood 470 *see also* Ministry; Women
Primates' Meeting 50
Printing 5, 280–1
Privy Council 7, 17, 41, 402
Prophecy 89
Protestant Episcopal Church of the USA 46, 223–8; proposed Book of Common Prayer (1977) 174; Prayer Book (1979) 66; General Convention 203, 209, 284
Puritans 9, 12, 13, 16, 17, 23, 106, 111, 139, 163, 395; and ordinals 326; and episcopacy 335
Pusey, Edward Bouverie 36–7, 182; *Eirenicons* 47; and Anglican ecclesiology 261–2

Quaque, Philip 483–4, 485
Queen Anne's Bounty 27

Radical theology 44
Raiser, Konrad 455
Ramsey, A. M., Abp 48, 211, 261, 467–8, 469, 471, 492–3
Ray, John 178
Reason 103–4, 115–28, 368–9, 473
Reber, Robert 290
Receptionism 309–13
Reed, Bruce 282–3
Reformation, the: English and continental 3–26 *passim*
Reformed Churches 341–2
Reformed theology, origins of 5
Religious Tract Society 35
Representative Church Council 403
Reservation of the sacrament 46
Restoration 21
Reynolds, Edward, Bp 361–3
Rhymes, Douglas 373
Ricoeur, Paul 195–6
Rikkyo University 491
Ritual, significance of 60
Ritualism 45–6
Robinson, J. A. T., Bp 44, 373
Rogers, Thomas 147
Rowland, Daniel 33
Royal Commissions on Ritual 45
Royal supremacy 15–18, 108, 334, 393–4, 460
Runcie, Robert, Abp 457
Rushing, Byron 288
Russell, Anthony 379, 381

Sacraments 71–3, 88, 157, 285–8, 387–8; sacramental worship 77–9; *see also* Baptism; Eucharist
Salvation 69–77
SAMS International 490
Sancroft, William, Abp 21
Sanctification 69–71, 74–5, 77
Sanderson, Robert, Bp 339
Sarum pontifical 323

Savoy Conference 396
Scherewschewsky, S. I. J., Bp 490
Schleiermacher, Friedrich 8, 271
Science and religion 122
Scotland, Episcopal Church of 22, 40, 208, 222–3
Scotland, Reformed Church of 22
Scott, Thomas 369
Scottish Communion Office 222
Scripture *see* Bible
Scudder, Vida 186
'Sea of Faith' network 45
Seabury, Samuel, Bp 40, 223, 224, 225
Secularization 421–2
Selwyn, G. A., Bp 41, 488
Shaftesbury, Earl of 35
Shakespeare, William 367–8
Sherlock, William 269
Sierra Leone 41
Sikes, Thomas 36
Simeon, Charles 35, 181–2, 257, 485
Simeon Trustees 35
Situation ethics 372–4
Skinner, James 375
Skinner, John 223
Smith, John (Cambridge Platonist) 366
Social concern of the Church 283–5, 368–70
Social Gospel movement 372
Society for the Promotion of Christian Knowledge 22, 39–40, 484–5, 487
Society for the Propagation of the Gospel 22, 39–40, 484–6, 487, 488
Sociology 405–23
South Africa, Church of the Province of 41
South American Missionary Society 489–90
South India, Church of 48, 430–1; ordinal 165
Southern Africa, Church in 400–2
Spirituality 351–64
Spong, John, Bp 44
Statistics 408–11, 416–19
Steere, Edward, Bp 489

Stevens, William 35
Stillingfleet, Benjamin, Bp 117
Stillingworth, Edward 269, 340
Sunday School Movement 289
Supremacy *see* Royal supremacy
Symbols 197–9, 201, 463–4
Synodical government 40, 203, 208–10, 222, 229–31, 401–2, 407
Synthesis 463–8

Taylor, Brian 290
Taylor, Jeremy, Bp 113, 116, 127, 180–1, 298, 366–7
Teaching *see* Catechisms; Education
Temple, William, Abp 31, 44, 47, 123–4, 183–4; ecclesiology 283; sacramental theology 287; chairs COPEC 370–2; Faith and Order 428 *see also* Life and Liberty
Tenure of benefices 413–14
Tertullian 78
Teusler, Rudolf 491
Tew Circle 24, 268
Theological colleges 484
Theology practice in liturgy 68
Thirlwall, Connop 38
Thompson, Thomas 485
Thorndike, Herbert 112
Thornton, Lionel 44
Tillotson, John, Abp 32
Tindal, Matthew 33
Tolerance 473 *see also* Comprehension
Tozer, William, Bp 489
Tractarianism 36, 45, 94, 113, 122, 257, 272, 314–5, 325, 328, 398–9, 465
Tradition 96–7, 101–4, 205–8, 450, 465
Traherne, Thomas 359
Travers, Walter 335
Trent, Council of 75–6
Troeltsche, Ernst 365–6
Tucker, Graham 290
Tucker, Henry St George, Bp 491
Tuma, Tom 455
Tutu, Desmond, Abp 457
Tyndale, William 5, 265

Underhill, Evelyn 186
Unitarianism 21
United States 407 *see also* Protestant Episcopal Church of the USA
Universities' Mission to Central Africa 41, 489
Ussher, James, Abp 111–12, 151, 336–7

Van Buren, Paul 44
Van Mildert, William 36
Venn, Henry 486, 488
Venn, John 486
Vernacular, in Bible and Prayer Book 11; in liturgy 11–12
Vestments 12
Via media 70, 76, 176, 191–2, 309, 364–5, 453–4, 468
Vidler, Alec 469
Vincentian canon 265
Visitation of the sick 135, 138
Vocations 280

Wake, William, Abp 47, 269–70
Wales, Church in 22, 402
Walker, Samuel 33
Warburton, William, Bp 119
Ward, W. G. 36
Warren, M. A. C. 493
Waterland, Daniel 33, 270–1, 273
Watson, Archdeacon 36
Watson, Joshua 36
Weil, Louis 286
Weil, Simone 361
Wesley, John 33–4, 313–14
West Indies, Province of 41
Westcott, B. F., Bp 43, 183
Westerhoff, Caroline 290
Westminster Assembly 395
Westminster Confession of Faith (1643) 20, 108
Whately, Richard, Abp 38
White, William 223, 225
Whitefield, George 33
Whitgift, John, Abp 17, 110, 336, 338
Wilberforce, Robert Isaac 182, 315

Wilberforce, Samuel, Bp 228, 494
Wilberforce, William 34–5, 486, 487
Wiles, Maurice 124
Wilkes, James 284
William III, King 21
Williams, Channing Moore, Bp 490
Williams, Henry 490
Wilson, Daniel, Bp 487
Wilson, Thomas, Bp 351–2
Wolsey, Thomas 4, 6
Women, ordination of 48, 50, 331, 344–5, 415, 419–20, 437–8; consecration to episcopate 441
Woodforde, James 32
World Conference on Faith and Order: (*Lausanne, 1927*) 47; (*Edinburgh, 1937*) 47
World Council of Churches 47, 428–9; Assemblies: (*1st, Amsterdam, 1948*) 428

(*3rd, Uppsala, 1968*) 432
(*4th, Nairobi, 1975*) 433
(*5th, Vancouver, 1983*) 433
(*6th, Canberra, 1991*) 444
see also Faith and Order; Life and Work
World Faith and Order Conference (*1st, Lausanne, 1927*) 427; (*5th*) 444
World Missionary Conference (*Edinburgh, 1910*) 47, 427, 491
Worship 187–202, 470; in sixteenth-century England 10–12; during Commonwealth 20–21; after Restoration 23; eighteenth century to the present 45–6; relationship to faith 59–60; see also Liturgy
Wyclif, John 4

Zenana Missionary Society 487

The Society for Promoting Christian Knowledge (SPCK) has as its purpose three main tasks:

- Communicating the Christian faith in its rich diversity
- Helping people to understand the Christian faith and to develop their personal faith
- Equipping Christians for mission and ministry

SPCK Worldwide serves the Church through Christian literature and communication projects in over 100 countries. Special schemes also provide books for those training for ministry in many parts of the developing world. SPCK Worldwide's ministry involves Churches of many traditions. This worldwide service depends upon the generosity of others and all gifts are spent wholly on ministry programmes, without deductions.

SPCK Bookshops support the life of the Christian community by making available a full range of Christian literature and other resources, and by providing support to bookstalls and book agents throughout the UK. SPCK Bookshops' mail order department meets the needs of overseas customers and those unable to have access to local bookshops.

SPCK Publishing produces Christian books and resources, covering a wide range of inspirational, pastoral, practical and academic subjects. Authors are drawn from many different Christian traditions, and publications aim to meet the needs of a wide variety of readers in the UK and throughout the world.

The Society does not necessarily endorse the individual views contained in its publications, but hopes they stimulate readers to think about and further develop their Christian faith.

For further information about the Society, please write to:

SPCK, Holy Trinity Church, Marylebone Road,
London NW1 4DU, United Kingdom.
Telephone: 0171 387 5282